CHURCH HISTORY

A Complete History Of The Catholic Church To The Present Day

For High School, College, and Adult Reading

by

Rev. John Laux, M.A.

INSTRUCTOR OF RELIGION, CATHOLIC HIGH SCHOOL, AND PROFESSOR OF
PSYCHOLOGY, VILLA MADONNA COLLEGE, COVINGTON, KY.

WITH ILLUSTRATIONS AND MAPS

*"Another parable he proposed unto them, say-
ing: The kingdom of heaven is like to a grain
of mustard seed, which a man took and sowed
in his field. Which is the least indeed of all seeds;
but when it is grown up, it is greater than all
herbs, and becometh a tree, so that the birds of
the air come, and dwell in the branches thereof."*
—Matthew 13:31-32

TAN BOOKS AND PUBLISHERS, INC.
Rockford, Illinois 61105

Nihil Obstat: ARTHUR J. SCANLAN, S.T.D.
                  Censor Librorum

Imprimatur: ✠ PATRICK CARDINAL HAYES
                  Archbishop of New York
                  New York
                  May 20, 1930

ISBN: 0-89555-349-X

Library of Congress Catalog Card No.: 88-51074

Printed and bound in the United States of America.

TAN BOOKS AND PUBLISHERS, INC.
P.O. Box 424
Rockford, Illinois 61105

1989

AUTHOR'S PREFACE

In addition to providing a textbook for students, the author has also endeavored to present to the general reader, especially the Catholic layman, a concise, clear history of the Catholic Church.

Although there are several Church histories in English, some are too elementary to be satisfying to the adult lay reader, while others are too technical or voluminous. More especially, they do not present sufficient matter on the history of the Church in our own country, and they all lack the illustrative material which is so helpful and even necessary to the full understanding of the persons, events, and places read about. It is hoped that the copious illustrations and maps appearing in this volume will make it still more interesting to the reader, while the numerous excerpts from the writings of the Fathers, Doctors, documents of the Councils of the Church and of the Popes, etc., will make for better acquaintance with these interesting phases of Church History.

May these pages, with the blessing of God, have some share in inspiring our Catholic people with a deeper appreciation of our Holy Church, whose history is the most glorious monument of her greatness and her power.

The author desires to thank the Rev. Michael Leick, of Villa Madonna College, Covington, Ky., for his many valuable suggestions and for the time and trouble involved in reading the proof sheets.

For permission to cite a number of passages, verbatim or in condensed form, from copyrighted works, the author is under obligation to the following: Henry Holt and Company, publishers of Professor Richard Newhall's *The Crusades*; Charles Scribner's Sons, publishers of *The Ante-Nicene Fathers* and Thatcher and McNeal's *Source Book for Medieval History*; G. P. Putnam's Sons, publishers of Canon Barry's *The Papal Monarchy*; B. Herder Book Co., publishers of Southwell's *Triumphs Over Death*, the English translations of Pastor's *History of the Popes* and Janssen's *History of the German People* and of Addis and Arnold's *Catholic Dictionary*; Mr. Arthur Preuss, editor and publisher of the *Fortnightly Review*; The Macmillan Company, publishers of Bryce's *Holy Roman Empire*; the America Press, publishers of the Quarterly Magazine *Thought*; and the Queen's Work Press, publishers of *Growth of the Churches in the United States: a Chart* by Leo A. Doyle, S.J.

JOHN J. LAUX

COVINGTON, KY.
Feast of Sts. Peter and Paul
June 29, 1930

INTRODUCTION

The pupil whose formal education ceases with his graduation from a Catholic High School has in the past found no place he could read the magnificent epic foreshadowed in the prophetic text "Going, therefore, teach ye all nations" (Matt. xxviii, 18). This little volume is intended to supply the deficiency.

What is hardest in the task of the high school teacher in religion is to show how the human element in the Church is continually thwarting the divine, and how at the same time Divine Providence is daily making use of this human element in helping the Church achieve her destiny. At no time has the tendency to pass by in silence the claims of the Church to a special deference as God's mouthpiece been more blatant than at present. Hence the weight of the old scholastic argument "*Ab esse ad posse valet illatio*," the historical argument. As a review of the practical results of the Church's activity in the world, results both to the world and to the Church, such a compendium of Church History is an indispensable companion volume to a student of the Church's teaching mission. In the eyes of the unfriendly, the *apparent* failure of the Church in achieving the purposes of her dogmatic and sacramental armory, presents the most promising angle of attack and confutation, and hence, the educated Catholic layman must have a correct understanding of the fundamental position of both sides of the controversial problem and a knowledge of the sources of more specialized polemical weapons in meeting these attacks.

Incidentally Church History thus puts the pupil in contact, during his most impressionable years, with the annals of the greatest humanizing agency the world has ever seen, and serves as a correlation point for the more secular intellectual treasures the race is bequeathing the student during his initiation into mental maturity and breadth of outlook. As a supplement to the more formal study of his religion, and its dealings with the individual soul, or as a basic text in Church History, this volume should assist in emphasizing the social values of the Church, values that become more important as society becomes more complex.

The treatment of the subjects is possibly novel but hardly radical. The author has kept in mind very definitely the class of reader for whom the book is intended. While introductory, it is far from a bare outline, and should prove adapted peculiarly well to its objective, the Catholic student high school body of America. As indicated, it would seem to achieve its purpose best as supplementary study in the formal religion classes. Of particular value in this connection are the readings from the original sources appended to each chapter. They give a contemporary flavor to the narrative and acquaint the student with the works of the great Christian writers. This approach is strengthened by the brief but adequate and vivid biographies interspersed in the text. Another feature of classroom value is the series of summaries of the so-called "turning points in the history of the Church." The entire book, therefore, keeps in view not only the needs of the high school pupil, but does it with the help of modern pedagogy, so that we have here a text that should find its way soon into the hearts of both teachers and pupils.

REV. FRANCIS J. BREDESTEGE

CINCINNATI, OHIO
June 24, 1929

CONTENTS

CONTENTS

PAGE

SECTION III

The Church in Modern Times from the Protestant Revolt to the Present Day, A.D. 1517-1933

FIRST PERIOD: FROM THE PROTESTANT REVOLT TO THE FRENCH REVOLUTION, A.D. 1517-1789

List of Maps

St. Boniface, the Apostle to the Germans, felling the "sacred" oak tree dedicated to the god Thor at Geismar. A vast crowd of pagans watched intently, expecting some dire misfortune to overwhelm St. Boniface. But when the oak tree fell to the ground and the saintly Bishop remained unharmed, the pagans with one accord praised the God of the Christians and asked to be received among His followers. St. Boniface baptized them, and out of the wood of the tree he built a little oratory dedicated to St. Peter. (See page 221).

The Ancient Church to the Beginning of the Pontificate of Gregory the Great, A.D. 590

FIRST PERIOD

From the Founding of the Church to the Edict of Milan, A.D. 313

CHAPTER I

PREPARATION OF THE WORLD FOR CHRISTIANITY

1. The "Fullness of Time"

The Church appeared in the world with our Lord and Savior Jesus Christ. "When the fullness of time was come," writes St. Paul, "God sent His Son, born of a woman, born under the Law, that He might redeem them who were under the Law, that we might receive the adoption of sons" (Gal. 4, 4-6). The "fullness of time" presupposes a period of development during which mankind was prepared for the coming of the Redeemer. For the Kingdom of God did not appear unheralded in the world. God had promised a Redeemer immediately after the fall of our first parents, but His coming was delayed for thousands of years. Man had to learn by experience the evil and misery of sin and the necessity of a Divine Liberator.

In order that the hope in a future Redeemer might not vanish entirely from the earth during this long period of waiting, God chose Abraham and made a special covenant with him that the Messias should be born of his posterity. He also set aside Abraham and his descendants, the Israelites, from all other nations and from time to time revealed Himself to them in a wonderful manner. He raised up prophets among them, who by their teaching and preaching, by their threats and admonitions, again and again converted the people from idol worship, and by their prophecies kept alive the hope in the Redeemer to come.

But when Christ, the promised Redeemer, appeared, the Jews had ceased to be an independent nation. They were a part of the vast empire of Rome. The existence of such a world-empire as that of Rome, and the fact that the Jewish nation was incorporated with it, was of the greatest significance for the spread of the Gospel of Christ and the development of His Church.

2. The Roman Empire

After several hundred years of almost constant warfare the Romans had succeeded in bringing under their sway all the lands that bordered on the Mediterranean Sea. When Augustus put an end to the Roman Republic by proclaiming himself emperor, his realm was bounded on the north by the British Channel, the Lower and Middle Rhine, the Danube and the Black Sea; on the west by the Atlantic Ocean; on the south by the Sahara Desert and the Ethiopian Mountains, and on the east by the Arabian Desert and the kingdom of Parthia. Britain was soon to be added to this gigantic domain, as well as parts of southern Germany and the lands north of the Lower Danube.

The dependence of all these nations and races upon Rome was not merely nominal. Most of them were governed directly by Rome as provinces; the rest were subject to the Roman authority as allies. The governors of the provinces had to send reports on their districts at regular intervals to the emperor and his counselors; taxes were levied with inexorable severity; garrisons were stationed along the frontiers, and war vessels stood in readiness on the lakes and rivers to repel any attempts at invasion. The old barriers between the different lands had been broken down. Owing to excellent roads, abundance of ships, and the prevalence of peace and orderliness, travel was easy and usual throughout the Roman world. Men might pass on business or pleasure from the Rhine to Carthage, from the Euphrates to the Atlantic, without fear of interference. The language difficulty had also to a great extent been overcome. Since the days of Alexander the Great, Greek was the common language of the East, and Latin was becoming the universal speech of the West. Numerous flourishing cities in the East and the West had become the centers of a common civilization which had resulted from the union of Greek and Latin culture There were no serious obstacles, therefore, for the spread of common ideas and beliefs. The Mediterranean world was ready. humanly speaking. to receive a common religion.

3. *The Religion of the Empire*

Outside of Palestine the vast majority of the inhabitants of the Empire were *pagans.* Originally pagan worship had been connected with the government of the various cities and countries. As long as these big and little states had remained separate and independent, their religious rites had been faithfully kept up by the public officials. But when they became part of the Roman Empire their official worship of the gods gradually fell into decay. There was no common religion for the Empire as a whole. The Imperial Government required, it is true, the *worship of the genius of Rome and of the Emperor as gods,* and their temples were the meeting-places of the provincial councils, their feasts and games the great popular reunions; but this worship became in time hardly more than the expression of the political allegiance to Rome and her laws. Many, especially the common people, remained attached to their ancient gods and temples; others selected whatever gods or goddesses pleased their fancy or happened to be fashionable in their neighborhood; others, again, who had a leaning towards the occult and the mysterious, joined one or other of the numerous secret cults (e.g., of Baal and Astarte, of Isis and Serapis, of Cybele, and of Mithra) that had found their way from Syria, Persia and Egypt into all the centers of civilization. The finer natures among the learned and the wealthy, disgusted with the popular superstitions and the immorality which accompanied them, sought rest for their souls in the stern doctrines of the Stoics.

Pagan worship, no matter what form it took, did not make for morality; quite the reverse. Gods to whom were attributed good and bad qualities; who, at their best, were so little superior to men; who were often at feud with one another; who were patrons of theft, lying, and every disgraceful crime; whose worship in many cases consisted of nothing less than public immorality—such gods could not prove an inspiration to elevate the moral tone of those who believed in them. Is there any wonder that Roman society, from the lowest to the highest, was rotten to the core, that sin and unnatural vices prevailed on all sides? (Cf. Rom. 1, 18-32.)

But sin and vice, lust and cruelty are not natural to man, and therefore cannot satisfy his heart. "Men may be weak, and men may sin, but there is something in human nature that rebels and chafes against a perpetual round of vice and that hopes for higher things." Never before in the world's history had man become so fully conscious of his needs and of his helplessness. The longing for a Divine Liberator from sin and suffering and despair grew more and more intense. Virgil's writings bear witness to this longing. He speaks of the "sighing" of the Sibyls, the priestesses of Apollo, for a Savior, and of their prophecy that when He comes He shall dispel all darkness from the minds and hearts of men.

4. The Jews in the Empire

Alone of all the nations of antiquity, the Jews had preserved the knowledge and worship of the one, true God. In the course of their long and checkered history they had come in contact with all the great empires of the world, with Egypt and Babylon, Assyria and Persia, Macedonia and Rome. Since the eighth century B.C. they were no longer confined to the narrow limits of their barren homeland. Through the Assyrian and Babylonian captivities, as well as through their own native genius for trade and commerce, tens of thousands of Jews had been scattered throughout the world. These exiles by choice or compulsion were known as the "Jews of the Dispersion." They had their strongest foothold in Egypt, especially in the great city of Alexandria. They enjoyed the reputation of being industrious and peace-loving citizens. Their religion was tolerated by the civil authorities, and their national customs were regarded with respect. Most of them had adopted the Greek language and read their Sacred Books in a Greek translation (called the Septuagint). They held their religious services in the synagogues, one or more of which were to be found in every large city of the Empire. At the seasons of the great national festivals, thousands of them journeyed to Jerusalem to offer the prescribed sacrifices in the Temple.

Unlike their co-religionists in Palestine, the Jews of the Dispersion mingled freely with their pagan neighbors. In this way many Greeks and Romans became acquainted with the Jewish religion and its Sacred Writings. The great antiquity of this religion, its pure concept of the Supreme Being and its sublime moral code made a deep impression on them and induced not a few to adopt it as their own. But only those who promised to obey the whole Law of Moses and submitted to the rite of Circumcision were regarded as Jews; the rest were known as the "God-fearing." Many of these *proselytes* eagerly embraced Christianity when it was preached to them by the Apostles. They formed, as it were, the bridge by which the Gospel passed from Judaism to the Gentile world.

In Palestine, since the days of the Machabees, the Jews were divided into two great parties, distinguished from each other both in politics and religion. The *Pharisees* were rigorists in religion and extreme nationalists in politics. They not only insisted on the strict observance of the letter of the Law, but were also most zealous defenders of the traditions and usages that had grown up around the Law and made its observance an intolerable burden. They were bitterly opposed to all foreign influence in the affairs of Palestine. The *Sadducees*, to whom most of the Jewish nobility and the priesthood belonged, were the liberals and freethinkers of their day. They acknowledged the Law of Moses, but rejected tradition and attributed no value whatever to rites and ceremonies. They denied personal immortality, the resurrection of the body, and the existence of good and bad angels. Politically they favored peace and co-operation with Rome.

When the "scepter had passed from Juda," and the Promised Land had become a Roman province (63 B.C.) the thoughts and hopes of the people centered on the Messias, the Christ, whose coming their prophets had foretold. But they did not look for a Redeemer who would be merely a religious reformer; they expected a national hero, a victorious King, another David, who would restore the independence of their country and "make their enemies His footstool."

Thus, we see that the poor benighted pagans of the far-flung Roman realm, with all their crude superstitions, their mad novelties in religion, their lust and their cruelty, were better prepared to welcome the Savior of the world than the self-righteous Pharisees, the sneering Sadducees, and the multitudes who followed these blind leaders to destruction. "He came unto His own, and His own received Him not."

The Emperor Gaius Caligula Insists on Being a God

During the reign of Gaius Caligula (37-41 A.D.), one of the worst emperors of Rome, the people of Alexandria burned down several Jewish synagogues and set up images of the Emperor in the rest. The Jews protested vigorously against such an outrage, and there was civil strife and bloodshed in the city until each side sent an embassy to wait upon the Emperor. The Jewish embassy was headed by the learned philosopher *Philo*, who has left a description of the interview, which J. B. Bury has summarized as follows:

"Gaius was at this time engaged in transforming the house and gardens of the Lamias into a royal residence, and the rival embassies from Alexandria were summoned thither. They found him hurrying about from room to room, surrounded by architects and workmen, to whom he was giving directions, and they were compelled to follow in his train. Stopping to address the Jews, he asked:

" 'Are you the god-haters who deny my divinity, which all the world acknowledges?'

"The Alexandrian envoys hastened to put in their word.

" 'Lord and Master,' they said, 'these Jews alone have refused to sacrifice for your safety.'

" 'Nay, Lord Gaius,' said the Jews, 'it is a slander. We sacrificed for you, not once, but thrice; first when you assumed the empire, then when you recovered from your sickness, and again for your success against the Germans.'

" 'Yes,' observed Gaius, 'you sacrificed *for* me, not *to* me.'

"Thereupon he hurried to another room, the Jews trembling, and their rivals jeering, as in a play. The next remark he addressed to them was, 'Pray, why do ye not eat pork?' Finally he dismissed them with the observation, 'Men who deem me no god are, after all, more unlucky than guilty.' "

—J. B. Bury, *Student's Roman Empire*, p. 228.

Review Questions and Hints for Further Study

1. What is meant by a "covenant"?
2. What is the difference between a *Hebrew*, a *Jew* and an *Israelite?* Look up these words in the dictionary.
3. Give four reasons why travel was easy and usual in the Roman Empire.
4. Can you name some great roads that connected different parts of the Empire with Rome?
5. Show from the sad state of morality in the Roman Empire that Religion and morality are intimately connected.
6. Comment on the following statement: "The Jews of the Dispersion formed the bridge by which Christianity passed from Judaism to the Gentile world."
7. Do you know why we speak of the "stern doctrines of the Stoics"? Consult the *Cath. Encyclopedia*, art. *Stoics*.
8. Why was Christ rejected by the vast majority of the Jews?

CHAPTER II

THE FOUNDING OF THE CHURCH

Jesus Christ, the Redeemer of the World and Founder of the Church.—"In the fifteenth year of the reign of Tiberius Caesar" the Redeemer of the world leaves the seclusion of Nazareth and begins His public ministry as a teacher in Israel, "mighty in word and work." First to the people of Galilee, and then to all the inhabitants of Palestine, He announces the glad tidings of salvation and confirms His preaching with many signs and wonders. Out of His disciples He chooses twelve men, whom He carefully prepares to be His Apostles, the bearers of His message to all mankind. Henceforth they are His inseparable companions, the witnesses of His miracles and of His Resurrection. He invests them with the powers which He Himself had received, and appoints Simon Peter to be their head and leader.

The vast majority of the Jewish people, above all the Pharisees and the Sadducees, dissatisfied with the ideal of a purely spiritual kingdom which Jesus preached, refuse to accept Him as the promised Messias, condemn Him to death as a blasphemer, and deliver Him up to the Romans to be crucified (April 3, 30 A.D.). But even His death bears witness to His divine mission. Miraculous events accompany it. The veil of the Temple is rent in twain from top to bottom, as a sign that the Old Covenant which God had made with the Jews is ended, and that a new one is beginning, to which all mankind is called. On the third day He Himself, as He had foretold, arises again from the dead and, after tarrying forty days with His followers on earth, returns to Him who had sent Him.

Since His Ascension into Heaven, Christ dwells no longer visibly amongst His own. But He lives on as the Redeemer of the world in His Church, the Kingdom of God on earth. He founded the Church when, a year before His death, He said to Simon, the Son of Jonas: "Thou art Peter, and upon this rock I

7

will build My Church, and the gates of Hell shall not prevail against it" (Matt. 16, 18). After His Resurrection He confirmed Peter as the visible Supreme Head of this Church when He said to him: "Feed My lambs, feed My sheep" (John 21, 17).

First Christian Community in Jerusalem.—The founding of the Church was completed on Pentecost Day, when the Holy Ghost descended upon the disciples who were assembled in Jerusalem together with Mary, the Mother of Jesus. Immediately the Apostles, who had hitherto been weak men, earthly-minded, and distrustful of themselves, became bold and determined. Filled

Perugino

JESUS GIVES THE KEYS TO ST. PETER

with "power from on high," they issued from the Upper Room and faced the great crowd that had gathered in the city from all parts of the world for the festival. Peter, their spokesman, declared: "Jesus of Nazareth, whom God approved by wonders and signs, whom you have crucified and slain by the hands of wicked men,—this Jesus hath God raised again, whereof all we are witnesses; therefore let all the house of Israel know most certainly that God hath made both Lord and Christ this same Jesus whom you have crucified" (Cf. Acts 2, 22 ff.).

Deeply moved by the words of the Apostle, three thousand men and women asked to be baptized. In a few days their number grew to five thousand. Most of these remained in Jerusalem and formed with the Apostles and disciples of the Lord the first Christian Community; the rest returned to their homes after the festival days were over and became the first missionaries of the Church. *The Feast of Pentecost was thus, in the real sense of the word, the Birthday of the Church.*

The faithful in Jerusalem were "one heart and one soul." At first they continued to attend the services in the Temple with their neighbors and, following the example of our Lord, also went to the synagogues. But they had their own meetings, too, usually on the first day of the week, where they could worship God according to their belief in Christ. Besides this, they met frequently, if not daily, in private for the "breaking of bread," that is, for the celebration of the Holy Eucharist, which was usually preceded by the *Agape*, or *Love-Feast*.

Their genuine love for one another and the great number of poor people in the community gave rise to a species of *Communism*. "They had all things in common. For as many as were owners of lands or houses sold them and brought the price of the things they sold and laid it down before the feet of the Apostles, and distribution was made to everyone according as he had need" (Cf. Acts 4). But this community of goods was absolutely voluntary, as we know from the story of Ananias and Saphira (Acts 5).

First Persecution.—As the number of the believers increased, the Pharisees and the priests took alarm. They summoned Peter and John before the Great Council and forbade them, under pain of the severest punishment, to preach in the name of Jesus. But the Apostles replied boldly that they were bound to obey God rather than man (Acts 4, 19). Not long afterwards they were arrested a second time and would no doubt have been put to death if a Pharisee named Gamaliel, "a doctor of the law, respected by all the people," had not intervened in their behalf. "If this counsel or this work be of men," he said, "it will come to nought; but if it be of God, you cannot overthrow it." The fanatical Pharisees were for the time satisfied with this judgment, and the Apostles were dismissed, but not before they had been ignominiously scourged. Rejoicing that they had been accounted worthy to suffer reproach for the name of Jesus, Peter and John continued to teach and preach as before, in the Temple and from house to house.

St. Stephen, the Proto-Martyr.—The Church in Jerusalem was composed of Palestinian Jews and Greek-speaking Jews of the Dispersion (known as Hellenists). Amongst the latter there were very many poor people who had come to the city as pilgrims and remained there. These were especially in need of succor from the common fund. Some of them, however, seem to have been neglected, and they accused the "Hebrews" of favoring their own countrymen. To put an end to their murmurings, the Apostles selected seven "Hellenists," who enjoyed the respect of all, imposed their hands upon them, and set them over the daily ministrations towards the needy members of the community. They were known as the Seven Deacons (from the Greek word *diakonein*, to minister), or servitors.

Stephen, one of the Seven, was a man of exceptional gifts. He was "full of faith and the Holy Ghost"; and as his spiritual power

Fra Angelico

PREACHING AND TRIAL OF ST. STEPHEN

manifested itself in mighty deeds and words, he became a marked man in Jerusalem. Being himself a Jew of Greek culture, he naturally tried to win over his fellow Hellenists. A public disputation took place between them in a synagogue which was frequented chiefly by Jews from North Africa and Asia. In eloquent language Stephen vindicated the claim of Jesus to be the promised Messias. But they treated his words as "blasphemies against Moses and against God." Pharisaic zealots seized him and brought him before the Sanhedrin on the charge of speaking against the Temple and the Law. Stephen defended himself with fire and dignity. He upbraided them for their obstinacy, and accused them of being the betrayers and murderers of the Messias; in conclusion he cried out: "I see the heavens opened, and the Son of Man standing on the right hand of God."

The infuriated listeners, without even going through the formality of condemning him to death, dragged him out of the city and stoned him. With a prayer for his executioners, the first martyr of Christ went to his eternal reward.

The death of Stephen was the signal for a violent persecution of the followers of Jesus. The faithful were dispersed through Judea and Samaria, and even as far as Syria and the island of Cyprus. The Apostles alone remained in Jerusalem.

The Conversion of Saul.—During this persecution a young Pharisee had distinguished himself by his fanatical zeal. He had confronted Stephen in the synagogue, had borne testimony against him before the Sanhedrin, and had assented whole-heartedly to his death. At the place of execution he had stood guard over the garments of those who stoned him. This was *Saul*, who was also called *Paul*, of the tribe of Benjamin, a native and Roman citizen of Tarsus, in Cilicia. When he had finished his education in his native city, he went up to Jerusalem, where he eagerly applied himself to the study of the Scriptures in the school of Gamaliel.

Saul was by trade a tentmaker, but his ambition was to become a Doctor of the Law. It was because he believed that Stephen and the other followers of the Nazarene were enemies of the Law and bent on its destruction that he became their most implacable foe. He sought them out in the synagogues and in their homes; and when they fled to other cities, he obtained letters from the High-Priest, empowering him to arrest them and bring them bound to Jerusalem.

All the world knows the story of his conversion. As he neared Damascus on one of his missions of persecution, Jesus Himself appeared to him in His risen and glorified Humanity. He arrived at Damascus, the eyes of his body closed to the light of day, but the eyes of his soul opened to the light of truth. After three days of prayer and fasting, he recovered his sight and received Baptism For three years he preached at Damascus and other cities of Syria and Arabia. Then he paid his first visit to Jerusalem since his conversion, for the purpose of making the personal acquaintance of Peter, and remained with him fifteen days. When his Jewish opponents planned to do away with him, he left the city and spent the next ten or eleven years in different parts of Syria and Cilicia. We shall meet him again at Antioch.

A Jewish Testimony to Christ

In his well-known work *The Jewish Antiquities* Flavius Josephus, the Jewish historian and commander (b. 37; d. about 95 A.D.) gives the following account of Christ. (The sentences in brackets are regarded by some critics as Christian interpolations) :

"At this time appeared Jesus, a wise man, [if it be right to call him a man, for he worked miracles]. He was the teacher of men who received the truth with joy, and he drew after him many Jews and many Greeks. He was the Christ. On the denunciation of the first men of our nation, Pilate condemned him to the cross; but those who loved him from the beginning did not cease to love him. [For he appeared to them risen on the third day, as the divine prophets had foretold concerning him, as also a thousand other marvels about him.] The sect which receives from him the name of Christians exists even to this day."

XVIII, 3, 2.

Hints for Study

1. Acquaint yourself thoroughly with the life and teaching of Christ as recorded in the Four Gospels. You might read a life of Christ; a very good one is Fouard's *The Christ, the Son of God.*
2. Read the *Acts of the Apostles* Chs. 1-8 and Ch. 9, and the parallel passages in the *Epistles of St. Paul.*
3. How does the Communism practiced in the early Church in Jerusalem differ from the Communism preached by certain social reformers in our day?
4. Look up the article *Agape* in the *Catholic Encyclopedia.*
5. Why is Pentecost called the *Birthday of the Church?*
6. Is the Deaconship a Sacrament?
7. What is the meaning of the words *Synagogue, Sanhedrin, Hellenist, Proto-martyr, Eucharist?*
8. Read Part III, Chs. I-III, of God, Christianity, and the Church (*A Course in Religion for High Schools,* Part IV).

CHAPTER III

THE CHURCH INVADES THE PAGAN WORLD

The First Convert from Paganism.—The persecution of the Church in Jerusalem resulted in the spread of the doctrine which it was intended to arrest. The dispersion of the disciples scattered the good seed to the four winds of heaven. Philip, one of the Seven Deacons, preached with marked success in Samaria, Simon Magus being one of his converts. He also received the first Gentile into the Church.

A "God-fearing" pagan, the chamberlain and treasurer of Queen Candace of Ethiopia, had made a pilgrimage to Jerusalem and was returning home by way of Gaza. Philip met him as he was reading a passage from the Prophet Isaias (53, 7) which puzzled him greatly. Philip explained it to him, showing how every word had been fulfilled in Jesus of Nazareth; and shortly afterwards, when they came to a pool of water by the roadside, he baptized him.

Philip's success in Samaria brought the Apostles out of their seclusion in Jerusalem. Peter and John made a journey of inspection through the district, laying hands on those who had been baptized, in order that they might receive the Holy Ghost.

Philip continued his preaching in the ancient country of the Philistines and as far north as Caesarea, and with such success that before long there was no place of importance along the sea coast without a Christian community. Peter went down from Jerusalem to visit these communities, and for a time made his headquarters at Joppe.

The First Roman Convert.—There was in Caesarea a centurion of the Roman army, named Cornelius. He was a just man and God-fearing. One day an Angel appeared to him, saying that his prayers and good deeds had been agreeable to God, and that he was to send for one Simon Peter who was then living at

Joppe, in the house of a tanner by the seaside. Cornelius obeyed and despatched three men to the Apostle. Peter hesitated whether to go, but was persuaded by a vision and the warning not to call anything unclean that God had cleansed. He accordingly accompanied the messengers to Caesarea, where he baptized Cornelius and his whole family.

The importance of this incident cannot be exaggerated. Up to this time Christianity had been practically a *national religion,* a Christian synagogue, into which no one could enter without being a member either by birth or by adoption of the people of Israel. And now for the first time an Apostle, at God's express command, had received into the Church a Gentile, who had not passed through the synagogue, who had not been circumcised, nor sworn to obey the Law of Moses. The Church, from this day, ceased to be a Jewish community; henceforth "it will be an *international society* where shall meet as brothers, without distinction of rite or race, the Jew and the Gentile, the master and the slave, the poor and the rich. In vain does Israel promise herself the first place in the kingdom of God. Israel can disappear without causing a vacuum; her mission is ended and her place henceforth will be taken by a spiritual Israel made up of all the faithful" (Kurth, *The Church at the Turning Points of History,* p. 37).

The news of the baptism in Caesarea stirred up no little excitement among the members of the Church in Jerusalem. Peter silenced all opposition, for the moment at least, by declaring in a public speech that he had acted only on the order of the Lord Himself.

The "Christians" of Antioch.—Under the pressure of persecution the disciples had been scattered as far north as Phoenicia and Syria. Some of these settled down at Antioch, the metropolis of the East, which had a population at that time of more than five hundred thousand souls. Thanks to their perfect command of the Greek language, the missionaries succeeded in bringing a large number of pagans into the Church. Barnabas, a native of Cyprus, was sent by the Apostles from Jerusalem to supervise the activities of this mixed and rapidly growing community. Feeling himself unable to cope alone with the new conditions which had arisen, he sought out his friend Saul in Tarsus and brought him back to Antioch. For a whole year the two remained in the city, organizing the Church and instructing numerous converts.

It was at Antioch that the followers of Jesus were for the first time called *Christians.* The pagans gave them the name in order to distinguish them from the Jews. Heretofore they had been known to their enemies as Galileans or Nazarenes; in their own circles they called themselves *brothers, saints, believers,* or *disciples of the Lord.*

The First Martyr-Apostle.—The storm of persecution had gradually subsided. During the reign of the Emperor Gaius Caligula the High-Priest and the Great Council had other matters to attend to. Caligula insisted on being worshiped as a god by his subjects. When the Jews protested, he ordered the governor of Syria to set up his statue in the Temple of Jerusalem. On the intervention of Herod Agrippa the order was countermanded. Great was the joy of the Jews when this same Herod Agrippa, the grandson of Herod the Great, was appointed by the Emperor Claudius king of the Jews (41-44). His zeal, private and public, for Judaism is praised by the Jewish writers of the time, and we have a typical example of it in the persecution which he started against the hated followers of Jesus. Looking about for a victim among the Apostles who should be sacrificed to the animosity of the Jews, it was on James the Elder, the brother of John, that the blow fell first. About the feast of the Passover, 44 A.D., James was seized by his order and condemned to be killed with the sword. A tradition preserved by Clement of Alexandria tells how the accuser of the Apostle, "beholding his confession and moved thereby, confessed that he too was a Christian. So they were both led away to execution together; and on the road the accuser asked James for forgiveness. Gazing on him for a little while, he said, 'Peace be with thee,' and kissed him, and then both were beheaded together."

Seeing that the execution of James pleased the Jews, Agrippa laid hands on Peter also and imprisoned him, intending to put him to death after the Passover. But the whole Church prayed to God for him, and he was miraculously delivered from prison by an angel. He retired to the house of Mary, the mother of Mark, and then went to "another place." Agrippa died soon afterwards at Caesarea, "eaten up by worms," and the Church was at peace once more.

How a Persecutor of the Christians Died

"Herod Agrippa was exhibiting shows at Caesarea in honor of Claudius. On the second day of the shows he put on a garment made wholly of silver, of wonderful contexture, and came into the theater early in the morning. There the silver, lit up by the beating of the sun's first rays upon it, shone forth marvelously, and by its flashing cast a fear and terror upon those who gazed at him. And straightway his flatterers cried out, one from one place, and another from another, not for his good, addressing him as a god; and they added, 'Deal kindly with us; if hitherto we have revered thee as man, yet henceforth we confess thee superior to mortal nature.' The king rebuked them not, nor rejected their impious flattery—A great pain arose in his belly, from the outset most violent. Looking, therefore, upon his friends, he said, 'I, your god, am now bidden depart this life, for so Providence confutes the lying words even now spoken of me; and I, who was by you called immortal, am now hurried away to death.'"

—Josephus, *Jewish Antiquities*, *XIX*, 8. Cf. Acts 12, 20-24.

Hints for Study

1. Read the *Acts of the Apostles* Chs. 8-13.
2. What is meant by a "God-fearing" Gentile?
3. Why was the baptism of Cornelius and his family a "turning point" in the history of the Church?
4. What do the Gospels tell us about James the Elder? Why do you think Herod Agrippa selected St. James the Elder as his first victim?
5. Do you know anything about the shrine of St. James at Compostella, Spain? (See *Cath. Encyclopedia.*)
6. Antioch has been called the "second Mother Church of Christendom"; why? Which is the "first Mother Church"?

CHAPTER IV

THE MARCH ON ROME

1. *St. Paul's First Missionary Journey*

Saul and Barnabas in Cyprus and Asia Minor.—During the long period of peace which followed the death of Herod Agrippa (43-64) the first systematic efforts were made to conquer the Roman Empire spiritually for Christ. The leaders in this gigantic enterprise were Saul and Barnabas. Antioch was their headquarters; the Island of Cyprus and Southwestern Asia Minor, their first field of operations.

About the spring of the year 46, Saul and Barnabas, with Mark as their assistant, set sail for Cyprus. At Paphos, the chief town of the island, they met with their first important success. The Roman proconsul, Sergius Paulus, after an interview with the missionaries, openly embraced the Christian faith. From this time on, Saul calls himself exclusively by his Roman surname *Paul*, under which we revere him as the great *Apostle of the Gentiles.*

From Paphos the Apostles crossed over to the mainland and made their first stop at Perge in Pamphylia. Here Paul decided to push inland, straight for the Taurus range and the high table-land 3600 feet above sea-level. Mark recoiled from such a perilous and arduous journey, and returned to Antioch. It was in the late summer or autumn of the year, when Paul and Barnabas arrived in South Galatia. They made Pisidian Antioch, Iconium, Lystra, and Derbe successively their headquarters. Everywhere their preaching was received with enthusiasm by the Gentiles and with hostility by the Jews.

Missionary Methods.—Paul still earned his bread by the labor of his hands, plying his trade as a tentmaker wherever opportunity offered. Whenever he came into a town or village, he sought out the Jews dwelling there. On the Sabbath Day he visited the synagogue. After the reading of the Scriptures he would rise up and

17

address the assembly, which usually consisted of Jews, proselytes, and God-fearing Gentiles, preaching to them Jesus, the promised Messias. Few Jews, but many of the God-fearing, were converted. This resulted in many places in dissension and schism and even bloodshed. The unconverted Jews became Paul's bitterest enemies. They dogged his steps from city to city and aroused the people against him. Gradually Paul turned away from his countrymen and devoted his attention almost exclusively to the Gentiles. "To you," he said to the Jews in Pisidian Antioch, "it behooved us first to speak the word of God; but because you reject it, and judge yourselves unworthy of eternal life, behold we turn to the Gentiles."

Wherever Paul founded a Christian community, he placed a body of presbyters (elders) at its head, he himself retaining the overseership (episcopal authority) over all. There was as yet no clear-cut distinction made between priests (presbyters) and bishops; that came only after the death of the Apostles. In some places we hear of deaconesses, that is, virgins or widows whose duty it was to instruct the women, to assist at their baptism, to visit them in their homes, and to minister to the needs of the sick and afflicted.

Hailed as a God—then Stoned.—At Lystra Paul healed a poor cripple who had listened intently to his preaching and in his heart believed in Christ. When the multitude saw what Paul had done, they thought the gods had come down to them, as they had come of old—so the story went—in this very land to Philemon and Baucis. They called Barnabas, Jupiter, and Paul, Mercury, because he was the chief speaker; and oxen and garlands were brought, and all things prepared in order to offer sacrifice to them. But when the Apostles rent their garments in grief and declared that they were mere mortals, the enthusiasm of the fickle crowd quickly turned into hatred. At the instigation of some Jews who had come from Pisidia and Iconium, they stoned Paul and dragged him outside the city, believing him to be dead. But he soon recovered, and on the following day set out with Barnabas for Antioch, where they reported to the brethren "all that God had done with them, and how He had opened the door of faith unto the Gentiles."

The Council of Jerusalem.—When the Jewish Christians of Jerusalem learned of the great influx of Gentiles into the Church

Raphael

St. Paul Hailed As a God at Lystra

through the activity of Paul and Barnabas, they thought the time was come to make a supreme effort to save Judaism. Zealots hurried to Antioch and began to teach the Gentile converts that there was no salvation for them unless to their Baptism they added circumcision and the observance of the Law of Moses. They also sent missionaries to Galatia to preach to the same effect. Paul and Barnabas took up the gage, and as the Judaizers claimed that they had the support of the Church in Jerusalem, it was decided to have the issue settled in Jerusalem itself.

As soon as Paul and Barnabas arrived in Jerusalem, a council of the Apostles and the Elders was convoked to discuss the mooted question. Peter, who spoke first, agreed with Paul that the Gentile Christians were to be free from the ritual and ceremonial obligations of the Law. "Why," he asked, "put a yoke upon the necks of the disciples which neither our fathers nor we have been able to bear?" James sided with Peter; but in order to conciliate the extreme Judaizers and to facilitate intercourse between the Gentile Christians and their brethren educated in the Law, he proposed that the converts from paganism be required to abstain from food sacrificed to the gods, from blood, from things strangled, and from fornication. The whole assembly approved the decision, which was then put in the form of a decree and sent by special messengers to the "brethren of the Gentiles" at Antioch and in Syria and Cilicia.

The question which had threatened to disrupt the unity of the Church was settled for all time; but the wounds which had been inflicted did not heal at once. Some of the Judaizers were not satisfied with the decision of the Council. Clinging obstinately to their national prejudices, they continued their opposition to the teaching and practice of the Church and to the evangelization of the Gentiles. After the fall of Jerusalem they degenerated into an insignificant sect known in history as the Ebionites.

The Apostolic Decree issued by the Council of Jerusalem bears the clearest testimony to the fact that there was from the beginning in the Church of Christ a teaching authority whose duty it is to decide, with the assistance of the Holy Ghost, all questions pertaining to faith and morals: *"It hath seemed good to the Holy Ghost and to us,"* the Decree reads, "to lay no further burden upon you than these necessary things" (Acts 15, 28).

2. St. Paul's Second Great Mission Tour

New Helpers.—Not long after the Council of Jerusalem Paul proposed to Barnabas a visitation of the churches they had founded. Barnabas insisted on taking Mark along again. To this Paul objected on the ground that he had proved unreliable on their first Mission tour. The feeling caused by this difference in regard to Mark's fitness was sufficient for Paul and Barnabas to follow separate courses. Barnabas went to Cyprus and Paul towards Asia Minor, and we never read again of them laboring together, though Paul continues to refer to his old companion in the kindliest terms.

Paul found a colleague in *Silas* (Silvanus), a leading man in the Church of Jerusalem, and like himself a Roman citizen. They set out from Antioch probably in the summer of the year 50 A.D. Their way lay through the lands which Paul had evangelized on his first missionary journey. At Lystra he found a helper to replace Mark in a young man named *Timothy*, the son of a Jewish mother and a Greek father, who was to become "his true son in the faith," the sharer of trials and triumphs, and of his undying glory.

Paul traversed Galatia, intending to preach the Gospel in Bithynia. But God had reserved this field to other laborers, and he was told by the "Spirit of Jesus" to change his course. Directing his steps westwards through Mysia, he reached the coast of the Aegean Sea at Alexandria in Troas. It was here, it seems, that *Luke* joined the missionaries. He became one of the most faithful helpers of Paul, who calls him his "beloved physician." For many years a witness of his master's deeds and sufferings, he was fitted, as no one else, to become his biographer. We are indebted to him for two of the most important books of the New Testament: the Third Gospel and the Acts of the Apostles.

Paul Enters Europe.—From Troas the way was open to Paul to preach in the great centers of Greek culture, Ephesus and Miletus, or to return to Antioch by the sea route. God revealed to him what course to pursue. A man of Macedonia appeared to him in a vision and besought him, saying, "Come over into Macedonia and help us." The vision was at once accepted as a command from Heaven; the help wanted by the Macedonians was no doubt the preaching of the Gospel.

The party set sail from Troas, landed at Neapolis, and journeyed on foot to Philippi, the chief city of Macedonia. At Philippi numerous conversions rewarded the preaching of Paul and Silas, and gained them the honor of being scourged, chained and imprisoned. During the following night an earthquake shook the prison to its foundation; the doors burst open, and the bands of the prisoners were loosed. The jailer, a witness of the miracle, was converted, washed the wounds of the Apostles with his own hands, and prepared a meal for them in his house. The next day the magistrates set Paul and Silas free, and when they learned that the men whom they had scourged were Roman citizens, they begged them almost on their knees to leave the city.

Paul passed on rapidly to the great seaport Thessalonica, where he converted a few Jews and a large number of pagans and God-fearing Greeks. The Jews stirred up the rabble against him, and he withdrew by night with Silas to Berea, in the hope of returning when the excitement had subsided. But Jewish intriguers from Thessalonica aroused a tumult against him, and he was forced to flee alone, first to the coast, and then by sea to Athens.

The Gospel of Jesus and the "Wisdom" of the Greeks.— From Athens Paul sent word to Silas and Timothy to join him.

While waiting for their arrival, he spoke to the Jews in the synagogue and to the Greeks in the Agora (market place), and disputed with the Epicurean and Stoic philosophers in the schools. His invariable theme was Jesus and the Resurrection. At last some philosophers, curious to know more details about the new religion and its founder, brought him before the Areopagus, the Great Council of the city. Here Paul was face to face with the learning and the wisdom that made Athens famous throughout the world. "Ye men of Athens," he began, "I perceive that of all men you are the most attached to the worship of the gods. Passing through your city I saw your temples and your statues. On an altar I read the inscription: *To the unknown God.* Now this God, whom you worship without knowing Him, I preach to you."

Raphael

St. Paul Preaching at Athens

All listened attentively to this masterly exordium; but when he spoke of the Judgment and the resurrection of the dead, the raillery of some and the impatience of the others obliged him to close his discourse abruptly. He had failed to make the Gospel of Christ palatable to these professors of "Greek wisdom." Still, he had not spoken altogether in vain; a few men embraced the new faith, among them Dionysius the Areopagite, who later became the first bishop of Athens, and a woman named Damaris.

Eighteen Months in Corinth.—Without waiting for the arrival of Silas and Timothy, Paul moved on to Corinth. This ancient city, destroyed by the Romans in 146 B.C., had been rebuilt by Julius Caesar, settled with Roman colonists, and made the residence of the Roman governor of Achaea. Its situation on the isthmus of Corinth made it one of the great commercial centers of the Empire. It was also the center of the worship of Aphrodite, which accounts in great measure for the licentiousness and wanton luxury of its inhabitants. It was "in fear and in much trembling," Paul tells us, that he began his ministry among the Corinthians. But his dauntless faith in the "moral majesty" of the Gospel of the Cross, which he preached in all simplicity, vanquished every obstacle.

Immediately on his arrival he gained two fresh fellow-workers, who played an important part in his future ministry, *Aquila*, a Jew of Pontus, and his wife *Priscilla.* They had but lately come from Italy, the Emperor Claudius having by a special edict banished all Jews from Rome. Probably they were already Christians, and as they too were tent-makers, Paul shared their house and their work for eighteen months. The spiritual harvest which he reaped was so great that Corinth soon took its place beside Jerusalem and Antioch among the Churches of the Empire. An attempt of the Jews to drive him out of the city was frustrated by the Proconsul L. Junius Gallio, a brother of the famous Stoic philosopher Seneca.

The Epistles of St. Paul.—It was in Corinth, perhaps in the winter of 51-52, that Paul wrote his first missionary letter: the first *Epistle to the Thessalonians.* Silas and Timothy had rejoined him, and the news they brought from Thessalonica occasioned the epistle. It was soon followed by a second letter to the same Church.

All the epistles of St. Paul are written more or less on the same plan. They contain a doctrinal and a moral section, with an introduction and a conclusion. St. Paul usually dictated his epistles to a secretary; only the greetings at the end were written with his own hand as a proof of their genuineness. The Epistles to the Galatians and to Philemon he seems to have written himself. All the epistles were written on special occasions and to meet

special needs, but every one reflects the keen mind and noble character of the Apostle and gives a deep insight into the sublime
mysteries of the Faith. They are indeed, as some one has said,
"the life-blood of a noble spirit," poured forth to nourish its
spiritual offspring. Some of them are of such power that St.
Jerome, when reading them, thought he heard thunder rather than
words. On account of their doctrinal depth and certain peculiarities of style and diction, they are not always easy to understand,
and the warning of St. Peter is as timely to-day as it was in the
first century: "There are in the epistles of our most dear brother
Paul certain things hard to be understood, which the unlearned
and unstable wrest, as they do also the other scriptures, to their
own destruction" (2 Pet. 3, 16). The Acts of the Apostles contains a marvelous record of St. Paul's achievements, but if we
wish to know the Apostle of the Gentiles intimately, we must study
his epistles. No man of pagan or Christian antiquity stands so
vividly before us as St. Paul in the mirror of his writings.

When the Church in Corinth had been firmly established, Paul,
accompanied by Aquila and Priscilla, returned to Antioch by way
of Ephesus, Caesarea and Jerusalem.

3. Third Missionary Journey. A Dramatic Chapter in the Life of St. Paul

Two Years in Ephesus.—After a brief sojourn in Antioch,
Paul proceeded on his third missionary journey, the center of
which he had already chosen in Ephesus. Aquila and Priscilla
had preceded him and were preparing the ground. Mainly through
their efforts the learned and eloquent Alexandrine Jew *Apollos* was
won over to the faith and trained in the apostolate. Paul first
visited the Churches in Galatia and Phrygia, and must have
reached Ephesus before the winter of 53 A.D.

As was his custom, he began his preaching in the synagogue;
but the growing hostility of the Jews caused him to transfer his
headquarters to the "School of Tyrannus," a public lecture-room
which any one could hire. Perhaps in no other city did he exert
such a far-reaching influence. This was due not only to his personality and his persuasive eloquence, but also to the miracles
which accompanied his preaching. During his two years' ministry

ın Ephesus the whole province of Asia, we are told, was made
acquainted with the Gospel of Christ.

The Corinthian Troubles.—At Ephesus disturbing news
reached Paul from Corinth. Moral laxity had crept into the
community during his absence and, what was worse, a spirit of
faction was manifest which threatened the unity of faith and practice to which Paul always attached such great importance. He
sent Timothy to Corinth to study the situation, and he himself
wrote a long letter to the Corinthians exhorting them in the most
moving terms to be loyal to his teaching and above all to practice
charity. Timothy's report was so unfavorable that he thought
it advisable to pay a personal visit to Corinth. He had to excommunicate an obstinate member of the Church for a very grave
offense,—a measure which did not meet with the approval of all.
On his return to Ephesus he sent *Titus,* a Greek of great prudence
and tact, who had but recently joined him, with another letter
to the Corinthians, with the understanding to meet him in Troas.
Circumstances, however, forced Paul to leave Ephesus earlier than
had been arranged with Titus.

The Tumult of the Silversmiths.—The number of the faithful increased so rapidly that the manufacturers and vendors of
idols became alarmed. One of them, the silversmith Demetrius,
whose specialty was the manufacture of miniature models of the
great Temple of Diana, called his fellow-craftsmen together and in
an inflammatory speech excited them to rise up against the enemies
of Diana and her worship. The tumult spread, and before long
the whole city was full of confusion. The magistrates quelled the
outbreak, but Paul thought it prudent to absent himself from
Ephesus for a time.

He passed over into Macedonia, where he met Titus, and wrote
another letter to the Corinthians. Then he went on to Corinth in
order to judge for himself what effect his letter had produced.
Here he wrote his great Epistle to the Romans. For many years
his thoughts had turned to the capital of the Empire, but as Christianity had already been established there, he put off his visit
from year to year. Now, however, he was fully determined to see
Rome, even if only for a short time on his way to preach the
Gospel in Spain, and his letter was to prepare the way for him.

Paul's presence in Corinth restored peace and harmony to the
distracted community, and after a stay of three months he went

by way of Philippi, Troas, Miletus, and Tyre to Jerusalem in order
to deliver in person the large sum of money which he had collected
from his converts for the relief of the poor.

Vinctus Christi—The Prisoner of Christ.—He was received
with open arms by the brethren, but when he was falsely accused
of having taken the Greek Christian Trophimus with him into the
Temple, the Jews caused a riot, determined to stone him to death.
He was rescued by the Roman tribune Claudius Lysias. To prevent further attempts against his life, Lysias sent him in chains to
Caesarea, where the Jews were free to bring forward their accusations against him before the tribunal of Felix, the procurator of
Judea. Anxious to humor the Jews, Felix kept Paul a prisoner for
two years, hoping at the same time that Paul or his friends would
purchase his freedom with a handsome bribe.

4. Paul Enters Rome—in Chains

The Appeal to Caesar.—Portius Festus, who succeeded Felix
about the year 60, was inclined to deliver Paul into the hands of
the Jews. Paul boldly replied: "If I have injured the Jews, or
have committed anything worthy of death, I refuse not to die;
but if none of those things are true whereof they accuse me, no
man may deliver me to them: I appeal to Caesar." Festus answered: "Hast thou appealed to Caesar? To Caesar shalt thou
go."

Before leaving for Rome Paul had an opportunity to plead his
cause before King Agrippa II and his sister Bernice. The effect
of his eloquent address was such that the king cried out: "In a
little thou persuadest me to become a Christian." "I would to
God," Paul replied, "that both in little and in much, not only thou,
but also all that hear me this day, should become such as I also
am, except these bands."

This beautiful answer won over the whole assembly to Paul.
"This man hath done nothing worthy of death or of bands," was
the general verdict. And Agrippa remarked to Festus: "This
man might have been set at liberty, if he had not appealed to
Caesar."

The Shipwreck.—Early in the autumn of the year 60 Paul
sailed for Rome with the centurion Julius and a detachment of
soldiers as his escort. Timothy, Luke and Aristarchus of Thes-

salonica had managed to secure passage on the same ship. Julius treated his prisoner courteously and permitted him to remain in the company of his friends. Near the island of Crete a terrific storm overtook them and for a fortnight played havoc with the ship. It was wrecked at last on the coast of Malta, but all on board were saved. During this crisis Paul's nobility of character and his sublime courage and trust in God won him the admiration and gratitude of his fellow-passengers.

After a delay of three months the voyage was resumed. At last Italy is reached, and Paul is met by detachments of Roman Christians, who came as far as Forum Appii and Tres Tabernae to welcome him.

Paul's captivity lasted two years. It was of the milder kind known as *custodia militaris*. He lived in a private house in the vicinity of the Praetorian camp. He was free to receive and to pay visits. A soldier, however, guarded him night and day, and when he went abroad, his right arm was chained to the left arm of the soldier. Thus, though a prisoner and in chains, he continued his apostolate, "preaching the kingdom of God, and teaching the things which concern the Lord Jesus to all that came to him." A passage in the *Epistle to the Philippians*, which he wrote at this time, tells us with what marvelous fruits the preaching of the "prisoner of Christ" was blessed: "Now, brethren, I desire that you should know that the things which have happened to me have fallen out rather to the furtherance of the Gospel; so that my bonds are made manifest, in Christ, in the whole Praetorian camp, and in all other places; and many of the brethren in the Lord, growing confident by my bands, are much more bold to speak the word of God without fear."

St. Clement of Rome on the Spirit of Faction at Corinth

That the spirit of faction, which caused so much trouble to St. Paul, was a chronic habit of the Corinthians, may be seen from the words of St. Clement of Rome written to the Church at Corinth about 98 A.D.:

"Take into your hands the Epistle of the blessed Apostle Paul. What did he first write to you, at the outset of the Gospel-preaching? Of a truth he wrote to you in the Spirit concerning himself and Cephas (Peter) and Apollo, because even at that time you made factions. But that former faction involved less guilt for you. For then you were separated into parties over Apostles well approved, and a man to whom they had borne witness. But now reflect who they are that have perverted you, and have diminished the august name of your world-renowned fraternity. It is a shameful thing, an exceeding shameful thing, dearly beloved, and one altogether misbecoming the conversation that is in Christ, to hear that the established and ancient church of the Corinthians is in a state of revolt against the Elders by reason of one or two persons."

—Ep. ad Corinthios, XLVII.

Hints for Study

1. Read the Acts of the Apostles, Chs. 13-28, and the parallel passages in the Epistles of St. Paul.
2. In order to form some idea of St. Paul's power of feeling and inspiring friendship of the noblest order, read the Epistles to the *Philippians* and to *Philemon.*
3. Mention and locate the cities of the Empire in which St. Paul spread the Gospel.
4. Mention the most prominent of the companions of St. Paul. Were they Jews or Gentiles?
5. Give two reasons for the great importance of the Council of Jerusalem.
6. Can you name all the Epistles of St. Paul? Why are many of them hard to understand?
7. Why was St. Luke especially fitted to be the biographer of St. Paul?
8. Why did the Jews hate and persecute St. Paul?
9. For an account of the Epistles of St. Paul and selections from each see Laux, *Introduction to the Bible,* pp. 253-291.

CHAPTER V

THE ROMAN CHURCH

The First Roman Christians.—"The Church of Rome bursts upon us in the Epistle to the Romans as one whose 'faith is proclaimed throughout the world'; yet of the first sowing of that faith we know little or nothing" (Lattey, Introduction to the *Epistle to the Romans*, p. xiii). The Gospel had reached Rome very early. There was constant intercourse between Rome and the East. Whatever happened in Syria or Palestine quickly found an echo in the Capital. Soldiers of the Italian cohort may have been converted at Caesarea by the Deacon Philip or by St. Peter, like the centurion Cornelius, and on their return to Rome spread the knowledge of the new religion; or, what is more likely, the first Roman Christians may have been Roman Jews converted on Pentecost Day while on a pilgrimage to Jerusalem. We are expressly told in the *Acts* that there were "strangers of Rome" present at St. Peter's first sermon. But whoever may have been the founders of the Roman Church, it seems certain that they held no official position in the Church at large.

When St. Paul wrote to the Romans, the Roman Church was well organized and possessed several house-churches. Who was responsible for this work of organization? Tradition answers that it was St. Peter. In the *Acts* (12, 17) we read that Peter "went to another place." Was this Rome? If it was, then St. Peter arrived there in 44 or 45 A.D. He left the city again after a short activity, for we find him presiding at the Council of Jerusalem, which took place no later than 49 A.D. He was not in Rome when St. Paul wrote his epistle to the Romans from Corinth in 57 A.D. But he was there again after St. Paul's first captivity, for his first Epistle is dated from "Babylon," which can only be Rome.

The members of the Church in Rome were mainly Gentiles,

with a minority of Jews and proselytes. As in every other city where Christianity took root, serious dissensions arose between the synagogue and the Church. The Jews even resorted to acts of violence, and the police had to interfere. To get rid of the turbulent Jews, the Emperor Claudius issued a decree banishing both parties from Rome. Before long both returned, and the Roman Church grew so rapidly and showed such signs of living faith that it soon became known throughout the Empire. We have already seen what St. Paul's presence in Rome meant for the Christian community, and how the faith spread through his preaching.

St. Paul's Last Mission Tour.—The hope of an early release from his captivity, which Paul expressed in his letters to the Philippians and to Philemon, was fulfilled. He was acquitted before the tribunal of Nero and, it seems, immediately carried out his intention of visiting Spain. From there, as we can gather from the First Epistle to Timothy and from the Epistle to Titus, he journeyed eastward. He spent some time in Ephesus and left Timothy there. In Crete he founded a Christian community and placed it in charge of Titus. He was in Miletus and in Troas. The rest of his movements are veiled in darkness. . . .

Burning of Rome under Nero and the Persecution of the Christians.—On the 18th of July, 64 A.D. some storehouses near the Circus Maximus caught fire. The flames rushed on with inconceivable rapidity and fastened upon the whole center of Rome. For ten days the conflagration raged. Ten of the fourteen districts of the city were destroyed. The rumor spread that Nero himself had caused the fire. It was reported that "at the very time Rome was in flames, he sang the destruction of Troy in his private theater, likening the present disaster to the ancient catastrophe." In order to divert the masses from what they believed to be the true origin of the fire, Nero, perhaps at the suggestion of the Jews, charged it to the Christians. A few of these were at once arrested and a false confession of guilt forced from them by torture. Through them the names of other Christians were learned, and then a huge multitude were seized. When they were brought to trial, it was impossible to convict them of incendiarism; so the accusation of being "enemies of the human race," of practicing magic, and of perpetrating the most abominable crimes was lodged against them, and they were delivered over to the most excruciating tortures and death. Many were covered with skins and tossed to hungry dogs to be devoured; others were crucified or burned to death in the gardens of Nero. There were women, too, amongst the martyrs. Like Dirce in the Greek myth, they were tossed and gored by wild bulls in the arena or, like the daughters of Danaos, were given as prizes to the victors in the gladiatorial contests and then murdered in cold blood.

The Martyrdom of St. Peter and St. Paul.—According to a very credible tradition, Paul was in the East when the persecution against the Christians broke out in Rome. He met St. Peter in Corinth, and they traveled together to Rome. Here they were seized and thrown into prison. From this prison Paul wrote to

Michelangelo

THE CRUCIFIXION OF ST. PETER

his "beloved son" Timothy, giving him some account of his sufferings and urging him to come to him as speedily as possible. He was ill treated, he says, "even unto fetters as an evil doer." He is not certain as yet of his approaching death. But he sees his blood "already poured out in sacrifice," and the time of his departure at hand. "I have fought the good fight, I have finished my course, I have kept the faith. Henceforth there is laid up for me the crown of justice which the Lord, the just Judge, will render to me in that day; and not only to me, but to them also that love His coming" (2 Tim. 4, 6-8).

Perhaps there is nothing so sublime in all the writings of Paul as these words of the aged athlete, whose faith is stronger than ever, who knows no weariness, who leaves the stadium because the race has been won.

St. Peter was martyred in the Circus of Nero. A constant Roman tradition asserts that he died on the cross, like his Divine Master. His mangled remains were buried nearby, and over his grave the first Christian Emperor, Constantine the Great, erected the first Church of St. Peter. St. Paul, being a Roman citizen, was beheaded on the Ostian Way. The magnificent basilica of "St. Paul Outside the Walls" marks the place of his martyrdom.

INTERIOR OF ST. PAUL'S BASILICA, ROME

In after ages the tombs of the Princes of the Apostles were the goal of numberless pilgrims from every Christian land. It was the vision of the Martyr-Apostles that inspired the Christian poet to pen the beautiful lines sung by the Church on their festival day:

O Roma felix, quae duorum Principum
Es consecrata glorioso sanguine!
Horum cruore purpurata ceteras
Excellis orbis una pulchritudine.

O happy Rome! who in thy martyr-princes' blood,
A twofold stream, art washed and doubly sanctified.
All earthly beauty thou outshinest far
Empurpled by their outpoured life-blood's glorious tide.

To all appearances the persecution of the Christians was confined to the city of Rome; but here it lasted till the death of Nero.
The impression which it made on the Roman world was deep and
lasting: henceforth the Christian name was outlawed; to bear it
was to be branded as a criminal, and therefore worthy of death.
The life and death struggle between Christianity and pagan Rome
had begun; it was not decided for nearly three hundred years.

Nero Persecutes the Christians

The historian *Tacitus*, who was a boy in Rome when the persecution took place, gives the following description of the outrages,
tortures, and deaths to which the Christians were subjected by the
infamous Nero:

"In order to stifle the rumor that he had himself set Rome on fire, Nero
falsely charged with the guilt and punished with the most fearful tortures
the persons commonly called Christians, who were hated for their wicked
practices. *Christus*, the founder of that name, was put to death as a
criminal by Pontius Pilate, procurator of Judea, in the reign of Tiberius;
but the pernicious superstition, repressed for a time, broke out again, not
only through Judea, where the mischief originated, but through the city
of Rome also, whither all things horrible and disgraceful flow from all
quarters as to a common receptacle and where they are encouraged. Accordingly, first those were seized who confessed; next on their information, a
vast multitude were convicted, not so much on the charge of burning the
city, as of hating the human race.

"In their very deaths they were made the subjects of sport: for they
were covered with the hides of wild beasts, and worried to death by dogs,
or nailed to crosses, or set fire to, and when the day waned, burned to serve
for the evening lights. Nero offered his own gardens for the spectacle, and
exhibited a Circensian game, indiscriminately mingling with the common
people in the dress of a charioteer, or else standing in his chariot. For this
cause a feeling of compassion arose towards the sufferers, though guilty and

deserving of exemplary capital punishment, because they seemed not to be cut off for the public good, but were victims of the ferocity of one man."
—Tacitus, *Annals*, XV, 44.

Hints for Study

1. Consult the *Cath. Encyclopedia* (Art. Peter) or the *Encyclopedia Britannica* (Art. Peter) for further proofs that St. Peter labored and died in Rome.
2. The novel *Quo Vadis?* by Sienkiewicz, contains a vivid picture of the burning of Rome and the persecution of the Christians.
3. Two other historical novels dealing with the Neronian age are well worth reading: Spillmann, S. J., *Lucius Flavus*, and Keon, *Dion and the Sibyls*.
4. A life of St. Paul which will appeal to our Catholic youth is Fink, *Paul, Hero and Saint* (Paulist Press, N. Y.).

CHAPTER VI

ST. JAMES, ST. JOHN, AND THE OTHER APOSTLES. THE DESTRUCTION OF JERUSALEM AND THE FINAL DISPERSION OF THE JEWS

St. James the Less (i.e. the Younger).—James, who by reason of his kinship with Christ is called the Brother of the Lord, was appointed by his fellow-Apostles the first Bishop of Jerusalem. St. Paul numbers him, with Peter and John, among the "pillars" of the Church. He was called the "Just" by his countrymen, on account of the severity of his life and his strict adherence to the Law of Moses. It was James, as we have seen, who at the Council of Jerusalem made the proposal not to exempt the converts from paganism altogether from the observance of the Law. Between the years 50 and 62 he wrote an Epistle to the Jewish Christians dwelling in Palestine and the adjacent countries, which contains the famous counsel for the sick, "to summon the priests of the Church" to pray over them, and to anoint them with oil in the name of the Lord.

According to one account James was hurled from the pinnacle of the Temple and then clubbed to death. Josephus reports that he was stoned to death by order of the High Priest Ananus (Annas), during the time that intervened between the death of Festus and the arrival of Albinus, the new procurator of Judea (A.D. 62-63). The Jews no doubt had insisted on wreaking vengeance on some one, after St. Paul had escaped their fury by his appeal to Caesar.

St. John, the Beloved Disciple.—John probably remained in Jerusalem till the death of the Mother of Jesus, who had been entrusted to his care by his crucified Master. Later on, we find him at Ephesus, guiding the destinies of the Churches of Asia Minor. According to his own words in the Apocalypse (1, 19), he was banished to the Island of Patmos, probably by the Emperor Domitian. After his release he returned to Ephesus, where he wrote his Gospel and died in extreme old age (about the year 100).

35

The Other Apostles.—We know little or nothing about the fate of the other Apostles. According to Origen and Eusebius, St. Thomas labored in Parthia, St. Andrew in Scythia, and St. Bartholomew journeyed as far as India. St. Matthew first preached to the Jews, for whom he wrote his Gospel in their own language;

Murillo

THE CRUCIFIXION OF ST. ANDREW

later he labored amongst various nations. St. Jude, the brother of James, is the author of the Epistle that bears his name; it was written before 63, probably in Palestine, and addressed to Jewish converts. Tradition is silent about the other Apostles, Philip, Simon, and Matthias. The Evangelist Mark, the companion of St. Peter in Rome, is credited with the founding of the Church of Alexandria in Egypt. After the death of St. Paul, Luke the Evangelist preached the Gospel in different parts of Achaea and finally suffered martyrdom in Thebes.

The Destruction of Jerusalem.—Whilst Nero was acting the clown and the tyrant in Rome, events of great moment occurred in Palestine. The Jews were in the throes of a revolt against Rome. A revolutionary party had existed for a long time, but it was divided into rival factions which were constantly fighting each other. The exactions of the Procurator Gessius Florus caused them to lay aside their private quarrels and to unite against the common foe. They called themselves the *Zealots* and the new Machabees. There were many outbreaks in Jerusalem and in other parts of Judea. At last Roman blood was shed. Florus marched against Jerusalem and was badly beaten by the Zealots.

Open war henceforth existed. Vespasian, Rome's greatest general, soon appeared in Palestine with 60,000 legionaries. The war was carried on with the utmost ferocity. The inhabitants of the conquered towns were massacred in cold blood or divided as slaves amongst the soldiery. After three years of almost constant fighting the whole country was subdued with the exception of Jerusalem. Vespasian was preparing to lay siege to the city when he was proclaimed emperor. He hurried to Rome, leaving his son Titus to carry on the war.

The siege of Jerusalem began in the spring of the year 70, shortly before the feast of Easter. Nearly a million men, women and children were in the city when it was invested. The Zealots, Simon bar Gioras and John of Gischala at their head, were determined to conquer or to die. Their blind fanaticism brought about the greatest disaster in history. At first the besieged offered vigorous resistance, and even gained some advantage over the besiegers. But, before long, famine, pestilence and dissension played such havoc in the ranks of the Jews that their efforts grew feebler from day to day, and on August the 10th the city was taken by storm. The whole city and the Temple were burned to the ground. All who were taken with weapons in their hands were put to the sword. The survivors, 97,000 in number, were sold into slavery.

"No city ever suffered such miseries," says Josephus, "but neither did any age from the beginning of the world ever breed a generation more fruitful in wickedness than this was."

"The capture of Jerusalem by Titus is one of the most memorable events in the history of mankind. It caused the expulsion of an entire race from its home. The Roman valor, skill, and persistence were never more conspicuously displayed. No more desperate resistance was ever opposed to the eagle-emblemed mistress of the world. There is no event of ancient history the details of which are more minutely known. The circumstances in all their appalling features are given to us by the eye-witness, Josephus, so that we know them as vividly as we do the events of the career of Grant" (Hosmer, *Story of the Jews,* quoted in *The Great Events by Famous Historians,* Vol. III, p. 151).

The Christians, mindful of the prediction of Jesus, had fled across the Jordan to Pella when the war broke out. The bond that had still, though loosely, connected Christianity with Judaism was forever severed.

The Final Dispersion of the Jews.—About fifty years after the fall of Jerusalem the Jews rose once more against their oppressors. The revolt was quickly suppressed by the Emperor Trajan. When his successor Hadrian arrived at Jerusalem in 130 on his tour of the Empire, he resolved that the Holy City of the Jews should be rebuilt as a Roman colony and its name changed to Aelia Capitolina. A temple of Jupiter was erected on the site of the Temple of Solomon, and a shrine of Venus was planted on the very spot hallowed by the crucifixion of Christ.

By these and other measures the spark of revolt was once more kindled. A fitting leader appeared in the person of Simon bar Cochba. The conflict which ensued lasted from 132 to 135, and every excess of cruelty was committed on both sides. It was not until their leader fell in battle amid thousands of his followers that the Jewish forces were defeated. Nearly half a million people were killed in this war. The survivors were dispersed to every quarter of the known world—and remain so to this day.

St. John and the Robber

"When the Apostle John returned to Ephesus from the isle of Patmos, he was often invited to the adjacent territories to appoint bishops, to set in order whole Churches, or to ordain such as were marked out by the Spirit. Having come to one of the cities not far off, and seeing a youth powerful in body, comely in appearance, and full of ardor, he said to the Bishop:

" 'This young man I commit to you in all earnestness, in the presence of the Church, and with Christ as witness.'

"The Bishop accepted the charge and promised all, and John set out for Ephesus. And the Bishop taking home the youth committed to him, reared, kept, cherished, and finally baptized him. After this he relaxed his stricter care and guardianship, under the idea that the seal of the Lord which he had set on him was a complete protection to him. But on his obtaining premature freedom, some youths of his age, idle, dissolute, and adepts in evil courses, corrupted him. First they enticed him by many costly entertainments; then afterwards by night issuing forth for highway robbery, they took him along with them. Then they dared to execute together something greater. And he by degrees got accustomed; and having entirely despaired of salvation in God, he no longer meditated what was insignificant, but having perpetrated some great exploit, now that he was once lost, made up his mind to a like fate with the rest. Taking them and forming a band of robbers, he was the prompt captain of the bandits, the fiercest, the bloodiest, the cruelest.

"Time passed and, some necessity having arisen, they send again for John. He, when he had settled the other matters on account of which he came, said to the Bishop:

"'Come now, O Bishop, restore to us the deposits which I and the Savior committed to thee in the face of the Church over which you preside.'

"The Bishop was at first confounded, not knowing what John meant; but when the Apostle said 'I demand the young man and the soul of your brother,' the old man, groaning deeply and bursting into tears, said:

"'He is dead.'

"'How did he die?'

"'He is dead to God. For he turned wicked and abandoned, and is at last a robber; and now he has taken possession of the mountain in front of the church, along with a band like him.'

"Rending his clothes and striking his head with great lamentation, the Apostle said:

"'It was a fine guard of a brother's soul I left! But let a horse be brought me, and let some one be my guide on the way.'

"He rode away, just as he was, straight from the church. On coming to the place, he was arrested by the robbers' outpost; neither fleeing nor entreating, but crying, 'It was for this I came. Lead me to your captain.'

"The captain was meanwhile waiting, armed to the teeth. But when he recognized John as he advanced, he turned, ashamed, to flight. John followed with all his might, forgetting his age, crying:

"'Why, my son, dost thou flee from me, thy father, unarmed, old? Son, pity me. Fear not; thou hast still hope of life. I will give account to Christ for thee. If need be, I will willingly endure thy death, as the Lord did our death for us. For thee I will surrender my life. Stand, believe; Christ hath sent me.'

"And he, when he heard, first stood, looking down; then threw down his arms, trembled, and wept bitterly. And, on the old man approaching, he embraced him, speaking for himself with lamentations as he could, and baptized a second time with tears. John, pledging and assuring him that he would find forgiveness from the Savior, led him back to the church."

—Clement of Alexandria, *On the Salvation of the Rich Man*, XLII.

(Scribner's *Ante-Nicene Fathers*, Vol. II, p. 603f.)

Hints for Study

1. Refer to your New Testament for the prophecy of our Lord concerning the destruction of Jerusalem and the Temple.
2. Read the articles on the Apostles in the *Cath. Encyclopedia*; also the article on *Josephus*.
3. Make out a list of the Apostles and Evangelists; when are their feasts celebrated? Are their feasts of a higher class than those of other saints? Name some famous Churches dedicated to them.

CHAPTER VII

THE RAPID SPREAD OF THE CHRISTIAN RELIGION DURING THE FIRST THREE CENTURIES

The Mustard Seed Becomes a Tree.—Before the death of the last Apostle the Christian Religion was firmly established in most of the provinces of the Roman Empire. In the course of the second and third centuries it spread beyond the limits of the Empire to every part of the known world.

In the year 112 Pliny the Younger, writing to the Emperor Trajan, who had named him governor of Bithynia. in northern Asia Minor, expressed his alarm at the vast number of Christians in his province. "The contagion of the Christian superstition," he says, "is no longer confined to the towns; it has invaded the villages and the country, and has seized upon people of every age, rank and sex. Our temples are almost entirely abandoned. and the ceremonies in honor of our gods utterly neglected."

Forty years later St. Justin writes: "There is no race of men, whether of barbarians or of Greeks, or bearing any other name, either because they live in wagons without fixed habitations, or in tents leading a pastoral life, among whom prayers and thanksgivings are not offered to the Father and maker of the universe through the name of the crucified Jesus."

At the end of the second century Tertullian tells the magistrates of the Empire: "We are but of yesterday and we fill your towns, your islands, even your camps and your palaces, the senate and the forum; we have left you only your temples." On another occasion he speaks of the immense revenue which might be collected, if each Christian were allowed to purchase the free exercise of his religion for a sum of money.

By the year 250 the position of Christianity was so impregnable that the systematic persecutions which began at this time could not hinder its final victory. At the beginning of the fourth century about half the people of Asia Minor, Greece and Egypt had been converted, and there were flourishing Churches in Persia, Armenia, Arabia, Abyssinia, Syria, Italy, Northern Africa, Spain, Gaul, and Britain. It has been estimated that at this time there were nearly four million Christians in the Roman Empire alone. Thus the prophecy of Jesus had been literally fulfilled: the grain of mustard seed had become a tree, which had begun to cover the earth.

Causes of the Rapid Diffusion of Christianity.—The primary cause of the rapid spread of the Christian Religion was the *divine assistance* which had been promised by Christ: "Behold I am with you all days even to the consummation of the world." He had also given them His power to work miracles, and the Acts of the Apostles and the writings of the Fathers attest that numerous miracles accompanied the preaching of the Gospel. But since this power was given, as St. Paul explains, not for the sake of the believers, but for the sake of the unbelievers, when the Church had been firmly established, miracles became less frequent, though in no age of the world have they completely ceased.

Another most important influence for the spread of Christianity was the *zeal of its converts,* the great majority of whom regarded themselves as missionaries and did what they could to extend the new Faith. They were ready, too, to lay down their lives for their Faith, and the fact that vast numbers of both sexes did so made a lasting impression on their fellow-citizens, and forced them to inquire into the truth of a doctrine for which such sacrifices were made. St. Justin states that, in embracing Christianity, he was in no small degree influenced by observing that the Christians encountered torture and death without fear.

Moreover, Christianity did not appeal to one class or race of people, but to all mankind; nor did it regard itself as one among many religions, but as *the one, true revealed religion,* to which the whole world must be converted. The driving force of such an uncompromising attitude—the attitude of absolute truth—can be readily imagined. The conviction of the truth of a cause can alone inspire enthusiasm in its upholders.

We have already referred to the preparation of the world for Christianity. The state of society in the second and third centuries was especially favorable for its rapid diffusion. "It was a time of moral reformation, when men were awaking to the need of better and purer living. To all who felt this need Christianity offered the highest moral ideals. It was a time of great religious interest, when old cults were being revived and new ones were finding acceptance on all sides. Christianity, with its one God, and its promise of Redemption and a blessed immortality based upon Divine Revelation, met as no other faith did the awakening religious needs. It was a time also of great social unrest. With its principle of Christian brotherhood, its emphasis upon the equality of all believers in the sight of God, and its preaching of a new social order, it appealed strongly to multitudes, particularly of the poorer classes."

Christianity not only offered eternal happiness to its followers and promised to make up for the injustice and misery of this life in a perfect world hereafter, it did more than all the other agencies combined to make the present life more endurable by its unbounded charity in the relief of suffering and poverty. The fulfilling of the precept of charity, so frequently inculcated by Christ and His Apostles, was undoubtedly one of the most beautiful features of the life of the early Church, and did perhaps more than anything else to make the Christian life attractive. "See how these Christians love one another," was a common saying among the pagans.

Lastly, the *feeling of unity* which bound Christians everywhere together, and which found expression in a strong organization, did much for the spread of the Church; it was, in fact, the condition of its permanence. "One Lord, one faith, one baptism, one God and Father of all," was the motto of the Christians. They looked upon themselves as forming one great body under the command of Christ, their Supreme Leader. They prided themselves on being soldiers of Christ, and called all idolaters *pagans,* that is, countrymen or rustics, a term applied by the Roman soldiers to all who did not belong to the regular army. Strict discipline was enforced; unworthy members were thrust out (excommunicated), and re-admitted only after a long period of severe penance. The individual communities formed the units of the great Christian army. Each unit had at its head a bishop, or overseer, who was assisted in the performance of his duties by priests and deacons. A close bond of union existed between the larger communities and the smaller ones of a province or a district. Rome was the center of ecclesiastical life for Italy and all the

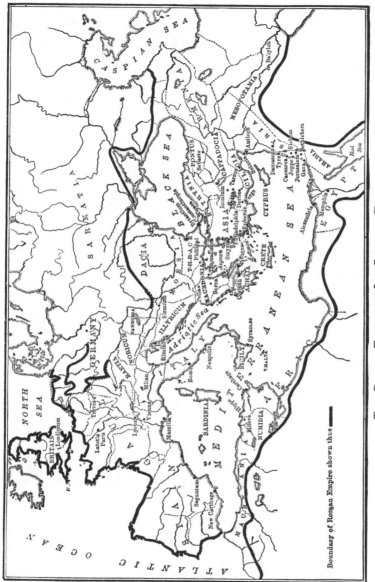

The Roman Empire at Its Greatest Extent

Boundary of Roman Empire shown thus ▬▬▬

BRONZE STATUE OF ST. PETER IN ST. PETER'S, ROME

West, Antioch for Syria, Caesarea for Palestine, Alexandria for Egypt, Ephesus for Asia Minor, Carthage for Northwest Africa. Since the end of the second century the bishops of the various provinces met frequently in councils (synods) to discuss important matters touching the spiritual welfare of their subjects.

But the strongest bond of union was the fact that all the Christian communities, even those founded by the Apostles, recognized the Roman Church as the Head-Church of Christendom. and the Bishop of the Roman Church as the successor of St. Peter and the heir of his Primacy. Union with the Roman See was always regarded as a fundamental requisite of Unity, Apostolicity, Catholicity, and Holiness, the distinctive marks of the true Church of Christ. "With this Church of Rome," writes St. Irenaeus at the end of the second century, "on account of her superior headship, it is necessary that every other church should be in communion." Questions of faith, or even of universal discipline such as the date of Easter, were always referred to the Bishop of Rome, and his decisions were accepted throughout Christendom. St. Ignatius of Antioch was but voicing the sentiments of all Christians when he spoke of the Roman Church as "presiding over the assemblage of Charity," i.e., the Church of Christ.

Obstacles to the Spread of Christianity.—If many circumstances favored the growth of Christianity, there were obstacles and difficulties to be overcome which, humanly speaking, were utterly insurmountable. The period of its growth is the *heroic age* of the Church, the age of martyrs—the age during which the profession of Christianity was an heroic venture. We cannot understand the true character of Christianity unless we bear in mind that, for three hundred years, to be a Christian meant a summons to martyrdom. "If they have persecuted Me, they will also persecute you," the Divine Master had said. We have seen how these words were fulfilled immediately after His own death on the Cross. We have also seen how the Roman Empire, in the person of Nero, took up the work begun by the Jews. *Christiani non sint*—"Let the Christians be exterminated!" This was, according to Tertullian, the laconic edict that ushered in the Neronian slaughter of the followers of Christ, and it remained the rallying-cry of paganism until the last pagan emperor himself bowed before the standard of the Cross.

Why the Christians Were Persecuted.—But why did Rome, which was otherwise so tolerant of all kinds of religions, even the most degrading, rave with such fury against Christianity? The reasons are not far to seek.

The Christians were at once the objects of hatred and contempt. Because they were intolerant of all other religions, because they either denied outright the existence of heathen deities or regarded them as evil spirits whose worship was the greatest sacrilege and treason to the true God—they were called narrow-minded bigots; because they held that it was sinful to make images of the pagan gods or to offer sacrifices to them, every artist and image-maker, every butcher who sold the meat of animals offered to the gods, and every priest of the gods who shared in the profits of their worship, was the sworn enemy of the Christians; because the Christians held their meetings in secret, and oftentimes at night or early in the morning to avoid interference, they were accused of immoral practices; because distorted reports of the Eucharistic rite reached the pagan world, the Christians were charged with killing children, eating their flesh and drinking their blood; because by their prayers they often healed the sick and drove out devils, they were looked at askance as sorcerers and magicians; because they refused to pray to the false gods and to be present at the official sacrifices to them, they were blamed for all the ills that befell the world. "If the Tiber cometh up to the walls, if the Nile cometh not up to the fields, if there be any earthquake, if any famine, if any pestilence, 'The Christians to the lions' is forthwith the word" (Tertullian).

The Roman Government persecuted the Christians not merely in order to humor the populace, but from reasons of State. The Roman and the Christian conceptions of the State were diametrically opposed. The Romans believed in the absolute authority of the State and in its right to pass laws on any subject it chose, even in matters of faith. The Christians were an organized body of men of every nation who obeyed the laws of the State as long as they did not conflict with the laws of God. When they did, they refused to obey them and followed their consciences. Evidently there was not room in the world for two such organizations.

The Empire and the Emperor—these were the highest ideals of the Roman; he lived and died for them. For the Christian, not Rome, nor the Emperor of Rome, but God was the supreme

Reality, and he refused to pay divine honors to the Emperor, living or dead, as the law commanded. In the eyes of the law he was an enemy of the State, and guilty of high treason against the head of the State. But Rome was also the world, the human race; and the Christian, therefore, by implication, an "enemy of the human race," who could not be tolerated.

Thus, we see that the Romans had only to invoke the existing laws—the laws against high treason, magical practices, secret assemblies, and the introduction of new cults—in order to proceed against the Christians with the rack, the gibbet, and the sword.

It is usual to speak of the ten great persecutions of the Church: the persecution of Nero (64-68), of Domitian (95-96), of Trajan (106-117), of Marcus Aurelius (161-180), of Septimius Severus (202-211), of Maximin the Thracian (235-238), of Decius (249-251), of Valerian (257-260), of Aurelian (274-275), of Diocletian and Galerius (303-311). Of these the most violent were the persecutions carried on by Nero, Trajan, Septimius Severus, Decius, Diocletian and Galerius.

What a Pagan Thought of the Christians

The *Octavius* of the Roman lawyer *Marcus Minucius Felix* is a veritable gem of early Christian literature. It is a dialogue on Christianity between the pagan Caecilius Natalis and the Christian Octavius Januarius, the friend and fellow-student of the author. In the course of the dialogue Caecilius gives the following description of the Christians, which sums up all the accusations brought against them by the pagans:

"The Christians are men of a desperate, lawless, reckless faction, who collect together out of the lowest rabble the thoughtless portion, and credulous women seduced by the weakness of their sex, and form a mob of impure conspirators, whose bond of union is nocturnal assemblies and solemn fastings and unnatural food. A tribe lurking and light-hating, dumb for the public, talkative in corners, they despise our temples as if graves, spit at our gods, deride our religious forms; pitiable themselves, they pity, forsooth, our priests; half-naked themselves, they despise our honors and purple; monstrous folly and incredible impudence! Day after day their abandoned morals wind their serpentine course; over the whole world are those most hideous rites of an impious association growing into shape. They recognize each other by marks and signs, and love each other almost before they recognize each other; promiscuous lust is their religion. Thus does their vain and mad superstition glory in crimes.

Why their mighty effort to hide and shroud whatever it is they worship, since things honest ever like the open day, and crimes are secret? Why have they no altars, no temples, no images known to us, never speak in public, never assemble freely, were it not that what they worship and suppress is subject either of punishment or of shame?"

(Transl. by Cardinal Newman.)

Early Christianity Seen from Within

About the year 150 Diognetus, a learned Greek, expressed a desire to know what Christianity really means—"What is this new race of men who are neither pagans nor Jews? What is this new interest that has entered into men's lives now and not before?" In the *Letter to Diognetus* the answer to the query is given. We do not know who the author of this letter was, but he was a man of no ordinary power, and the letter itself is "one of the noblest and most impressive of early Christian Apologies." In a passage of great eloquence he shows that Christians have no obvious peculiarities that mark them off as a separate race, and that devotion to Christ, the Son of God, is the vivifying principle of their association:

"Christians differ not from other men in country, speech, or customs. They do not live in cities of their own, or speak in any peculiar dialect, or adopt any strange modes of living. They inhabit their native countries, but as sojourners; they take their part in all burdens, as if citizens, and in all sufferings, as if they were strangers. In foreign countries they recognize home, and in every home they see a foreign country. They marry like other men, but do not disown their children. They obey the established laws, but they go beyond them in the tenor of their lives. They love all men, and are persecuted by all; they are not known, and they are condemned: they are poor, and make many rich; they are dishonored, yet in dishonor they are glorified; they are slandered, and they are cleared: they are called names, and they bless. By the Jews they are assailed as aliens, by the Greeks they are persecuted, nor can they who hate them say why.

"Christians are in the world as the soul in the body. The soul pervades the limbs of the body, and the Christians the cities of the world. The flesh hates the soul, and wars against it, though suffering no wrong from it; and the world hates Christians. The soul loves the flesh that hates it, and Christians love their enemies. Their tradition is not an earthly invention, nor is it a mortal thought which they so carefully guard, nor a dispensation of human mysteries which is committed to their charge; but God Himself, the omnipotent and invisible Creator, has from heaven established among men His Truth and His Word, and has deeply fixed the same in their hearts; not, as might be expected, sending an angel or a subordinate messenger to teach them, but the very Maker of the Universe Himself. Him God sent to man, not to inflict terror, but in clemency and gentleness, as a King sending a King who was His Son; He sent Him as God to men, to save them. He hated not, nor rejected us, nor remembered our guilt, but showed Himself long-suffering, and, in His own words, bore our sins. He gave His own Son as a ransom for us, the just for the unjust. For what other thing, except His righteousness, could cover our guilt? In whom was it possible for us, lawless sinners, to find justification, save in the Son of God alone? Sending, then, a Savior, who is able to save those who of themselves are incapable of salvation, He has willed that we should regard Him as our Guardian, Father, Teacher, Counsellor, Physician; our Mind, Light, Honor, Glory, Strength, and Life."

(Transl. by Cardinal Newman, *Grammar of Assent*, p. 466 ff.)

Hints for Study

1. If the Church had not been hated and persecuted, would she be the true Church of Christ?
2. Can the rapid diffusion of Christianity be explained by natural reasons alone? (This question is treated by Cardinal Newman, *Grammar of Assent*, pp. 451-456).
3. Why were there so many bishops in the early Church?
4. Name and locate the great Ecclesiastical Centers of the first three centuries. Which of them are still of importance?

CHAPTER VIII

THE AGE OF THE MARTYRS

"Afflict us, torment us, crucify us,—in proportion as we are mowed down, we increase; the blood of Christians is a seed."— Tertullian, *Apolog.* 50.

St. Francis Xavier, his biographers tell us, had such a reverence for the letters of his spiritual father St. Ignatius that he used to read them on his knees. We, who are the "children of the Martyrs," should regard with equal reverence the records of their deeds and sufferings. Was not their life-blood the seed of the Church? "I have often sat before the *Acts of the Martyrs* with tears in my eyes," writes Adam Moehler, the eminent historian, "sympathizing with them in their sufferings, marveling at their deeds, moved to the depths of my soul by their heroism. If we can ever be so ungrateful as to forget the Martyrs, we deserve to be forgotten by Christ the Savior."

1. *The Persecutions from Nero to Decius*

After the death of Nero the Christians were not molested again until the last years of the reign of Domitian (95-96). Domitian was the first of the Roman Emperors to call himself officially *Dominus et Deus*, "Lord and God," and it was but natural that he should proceed against those who refused to pay him divine honors. He put his own cousin, the senator and consul Titus Flavius Clemens, to death for "atheism," and banished his wife Flavia Domitilla to the rocky island of Pandataria. Another victim of his cruelty was the Consul Acilius Glabrio. St. John the Evangelist was banished to the Island of Patmos, and a number of Christians of Pergamum and other Churches of Asia Minor were beheaded.

St. Ignatius of Antioch.—Under the mild rule of the aged Nerva (96-98) the Christians enjoyed peace; but a new persecu-

48

tion broke out under his successor, Trajan (98-117). Simeon, who had succeeded St. James in the See of Jerusalem, was one of the first victims. Being a Jew and not a Roman citizen, he was condemned to die on the cross. In the year 107 (or 110) *Ignatius of Antioch*, a disciple of the Apostles, was cast to the lions in the amphitheater at Rome.

After the Apostles themselves, there is no more famous name connected with the early Church than that of Ignatius; yet about his career we know almost nothing. The little we do know is

ST. IGNATIUS OF ANTIOCH

gathered from the Seven Epistles which he wrote after he had been sentenced to death and was being sent in charge of a band of soldiers to Rome "to fight the beasts in the Arena." It seems that he had been converted from paganism late in life. He bore the beautiful surname of Theophorus, that is, "God-clad" or "bearing God." It is impossible to say when he became bishop of Antioch. He was the successor of St. Evodius, but we do not know when Evodius died. But if the Epistles tell us little of his life, they give us an excellent picture of the man himself, of his heroic soul, of his hatred of heresy and schism, of his solicitude for the unity of the Church, and of his ardent desire for martyrdom.

Ignatius is the first to use the term "Catholic Church," and for him the Catholic Church without the episcopacy is unthinkable: "Wherever the bishop is, there let the people be, as where Jesus is, there is the Catholic Church." And in another place: "Respect the bishop as a type of God, and the presbyters as the council of God and the college of the Apostles. Apart from these there is not even the name of a Church."

One of the chief dangers to the Church at this time came from the Docetists, who denied the reality of the humanity of Christ and ascribed to Him a phantom body. Hence Ignatius lays the greatest stress on the fact that Christ "was *truly* born and ate and drank, was *truly* persecuted under Pontius Pilate." The bodily Resurrection of Christ is beyond dispute:

"For I know and believe that He was in the flesh after the Resurrection: and when He came to Peter and his company, He said, 'Lay hold and handle Me, and see that I am not a bodiless spirit,' and straightway they touched Him and believed, being joined to His flesh and blood. Therefore also they despised death, nay, were found superior to it; and after His Resurrection He ate and drank with them, as one in the flesh, though spiritually He was united with the Father. . . . The Docetists abstain from the Eucharist, because they allow not that It is the flesh of our Savior, which flesh suffered for our sins, and which the Father of His goodness raised up."

The following words show that he was an intense admirer of St. Paul: "You are sharers in the mysteries with Paul, the holy, the martyred, the ever-blessed Paul, in whose footsteps may I be treading when I come to meet God."

Heroism speaks out of every line of his epistle to the Romans. He is afraid that something may prevent his attaining the crown of martyrdom which he is determined to gain. He writes:

"I look forward with joy to the wild animals held in readiness for me, and I pray that they may attack me; I will coax them to devour me, so that they may not, as happened in some cases, shrink from seizing me. . . . I bid all men know that of my own free will I die for God, unless ye should hinder me. . . . Let me be given to the wild beasts, for through them I can attain unto God. I am God's wheat, and I am ground by the wild beasts that I may be found the pure bread of Christ. Entice the wild beasts that they may become my sepulcher . . . ; come fire and cross and grapplings with wild beasts, wrenching of bones, hacking of limbs, crushings of my whole body; only be it mine to attain unto Jesus Christ. . . . I am God's wheat, and I am ground by the teeth of wild beasts, that I may be found Christ's pure bread."

The Martyrs of Bithynia.—St. Clement, the third successor of St. Peter in Rome, and many other Christians suffered death during the reign of Trajan, but no details of their martyrdom have come down to us. We are better informed concerning the sufferings of the Christians in Asia Minor, thanks to the correspondence between Pliny the Younger, governor of Bithynia, A.D. 112, and the Emperor, which has been preserved. After his arrival in Bithynia Pliny had put a number of Christians to death, but when more and more, among them old men, women, and children, were brought before his tribunal, he became alarmed at the prospect of sacrificing so many lives, and wrote to Trajan for advice.

Pliny to Trajan

"It is my custom, Sire, to refer to you in all cases where I am in doubt, for who can better clear up difficulties and inform me? I have never been present at any legal examination of the Christians, and I do not know, therefore, what are the usual penalties passed upon them, or the limits of those penalties, or how searching an inquiry should be made. I have hesitated a great deal in considering whether any distinction should be drawn according to the ages of the accused; whether the weak should be punished as severely as the robust, or whether the man who has once been a Christian gained anything by recanting? Again, whether the *name* of being a Christian, even though otherwise innocent of crime, should be punished, or only the crimes that gather around it?

"In the meantime, this is the plan which I have adopted in the case of those Christians who have been brought before me. I ask them whether they are Christians; if they say 'Yes,' then I repeat the question the second time, and also a third—warning them of the death-penalty involved; and if they persist, I order them to be executed. For I do not doubt that—be their admitted crime what it may—their pertinacity and inflexible obstinacy surely ought to be punished.

"There were others who showed similar mad folly, whom I reserved to be sent to Rome, as they were Roman citizens. Later, as is commonly the case, the mere fact of my trying such cases led to a multiplying of accusations, and a variety of cases were brought before me. An anonymous pamphlet was issued, containing a number of names of alleged Christians. Those who denied that they were or had been Christians and called upon the gods with the usual formula, reciting the words after me, and those who offered incense and wine before your image—which I had ordered to be brought forward for this purpose, along with the regular statues of the gods,—all such I considered acquitted,—especially as they cursed the name of Christ, which it is said a real Christian cannot be induced to do.

"Still others there were, whose names were supplied by an informer. These first said they were Christians, then denied it, insisting they had been, but were so no longer, some of them having recanted many years ago, and more than one full twenty years back. These all worshiped your image and the statues of the gods, and cursed the name of Christ.

"But they declared their guilt or error was simply this: on a fixed day they used to meet before dawn and sing hymns to Christ, as though he were a god. So far from binding themselves by oath to commit any crime, they swore to keep from theft, robbery, adultery, breach of faith, and not to deny any trust money deposited with them when called upon to deliver it. This ceremony over, they used to depart and meet again to take food—but it was of no special character, and entirely harmless. They had ceased from this practice after the edict I issued, by which, in accord with your orders, I forbade all secret societies.

"I then thought it the more needful to get at the facts behind their statements. Therefore I placed two slave-women, called deaconesses, under torture, but I found only a debased superstition carried to great lengths, so I postponed my examination, and immediately consulted you. This seems a matter worthy of your prompt consideration, especially as so many people are endangered. Many of all ages and both sexes are put in peril of their lives by their accusers; and the process will go on, for the contagion of this superstition has spread not merely through the towns, but into the villages and farms. Still I think it can be halted and things set right. Beyond any doubt, the temples, which were almost deserted, are beginning to be thronged with worshipers; the sacred rites, which long have lapsed, are now being renewed, and the food for the sacrificial victims is again finding a sale, though up to recently it had almost no market. So one can safely infer how vast numbers could be reclaimed, if only there were a chance given for repentance."

Trajan to Pliny

"You have adopted the right course, my dear Pliny, in examining the cases of those cited before you as Christians; for no hard and fast rule can be laid down covering such a wide question. The Christians are not to be hunted out. If brought before you, and the offense is proved, they are to be punished, but with this reservation—if any one denies he is a Christian, and makes it clear that he is not by offering prayer to our gods, then he is to be pardoned on his recantation, no matter how suspicious his past. As for anonymous pamphlets, they are to be discarded absolutely, whatever crime they may charge, for they are not only a precedent of a very bad type, but they do not accord with the spirit of our age."

From Trajan's answer it is clear that the profession of Christianity was regarded as a crime punishable with death. The principle laid down by Nero: *Christiani non sint* (Let the Christians be exterminated), is upheld. Any one can lodge an accusation against a Christian, and the accused has only the choice between

A GROUP OF CHRISTIANS AWAITING MARTYRDOM

apostasy and death. Pliny's question, whether women and children
and old men should be spared, is passed over in silence, which
meant that they were to be treated like the rest.

Hadrian's Rescript.—The animosity of the populace against
the Christians increased from day to day, especially in the cities
of the province of Asia, where Christians were very numerous, and
where the cult of the Emperors was far more intense than in Rome
itself. When the governors did not show sufficient alacrity in
proceeding against the Christians, the rabble took the law in their
own hands. Tumults were raised in which the homes of Christians
were stormed and the inmates torn to pieces. At the public festivals the cry would suddenly be heard: "Death to the Christians!"
and before the magistrates could interfere, some Christian youth
or maiden had been tossed to the lions. Crowds would assemble
before the tribunals of the governors and clamor for the punishment of the despisers of the gods.

How many Christians fell victims to the fury of the pagan mob,
we have no means of telling. One governor, at least, had the
courage to put a stop to mob violence. This was Serenus Granianus, Proconsul of the Province of Asia. He thought it unjust
not only that Christians should be sacrificed to the clamors of

the mob, but that they should be punished at all simply for being Christians. He wrote to this effect to the Emperor Hadrian, A.D. 123 (or 124). Hadrian directed his answer to Granianus' successor, Minucius Fundanus. Two eminent Christians, the Athenian philosopher Aristides, and Quadratus, a veteran missionary and disciple of the Apostles, had about this time addressed *Apologies* (pleas for the Christians) to the Emperor, and perhaps these noble and fearless writings were responsible for the very favorable tone of the imperial Rescript.

Hadrian to Minucius Fundanus

"I received a letter from the illustrious Serenus Granianus, your predecessor. It is an affair well worthy of your consideration to put a stop to vexatious suits, and to give no handle to informers to carry on the trade of malice. If, then, the people under your government have anything to say against Christians, and will prove it in public, so that Christians may answer for themselves in open court, it is your duty to hear them in a judicial way only, and not to be overborne by the petitions and tumultuary clamors of the people; for it is your place, and not the mob's, to judge of the merits of the cause. If, therefore, the informer shall make it appear that Christians have done anything contrary to the law, punish them according to the quality of the crime; so verily on the other hand, if you find it to be a malicious charge only, take care to condemn and punish as the malice deserves."

St. Polycarp, the Friend of St. John.—Antoninus Pius was even more favorable to the Christians than Hadrian. Still, his reign will ever be memorable for the martyrdom of St. Polycarp, the aged bishop of Smyrna. For nearly thirty years Polycarp had been a disciple and companion of the Apostle St. John. St. Irenaeus, who was a pupil of Polycarp, gives a graphic account of their familiar intercourse. He writes:

"I remember the events of that time more clearly than those of recent occurrence. The lessons of childhood grow with the growth of the soul, and become one with it. And so I can describe the very place in which the blessed Polycarp used to sit as he discoursed, and his goings out and his comings in, and his manner of life, and his personal appearance, and the discourses which he made to the people, and how he would describe his intercourse with John and the rest who had seen the Lord, and how he would relate their words. And whatsoever things he had heard from them about the Lord, and about His miracles, and about His teaching, Polycarp, as having received them from eyewitnesses of the life of the Word, would relate all in keeping with the Scriptures. . . ."

The martyrdom of St. Polycarp is described in a letter addressed by the Church of Smyrna to the Church of Philomelium, a city of the neighboring province of Phrygia. It is the first authentic account of a martyrdom that has been preserved.

In the year 156 a cruel persecution of the Christians broke out at Smyrna, in which both the pagan and Jewish inhabitants took part. Their hostility was especially directed against Polycarp,

ST. POLYCARP

because he was the head of the hated sect. After several Christians had been tortured and thrown to the lions, the multitude clamored for the death of the Bishop. Yielding to the urgent entreaties of those around him, Polycarp quitted the city; but he was pursued and brought back. The proconsul, who had reluctantly allowed him to be arrested, was anxious to save him.

When he was led forward, a great tumult arose among those that heard he was taken. At length, as he advanced, the proconsul asked him whether he was Polycarp, and when he answered that he was, he urged him to deny Christ, saying, "Have a regard for your age," and adding similar expressions such as were usual for them to employ.

"Swear," he said, "by the genius of Caesar. Repent. Say, 'Away with those that deny the gods.'"

But Polycarp, with a countenance grave and serious, and contemplating the whole multitude that were collected in the stadium, beckoned with his hand to them, and with a sigh looked up to heaven and said, "Away with those that deny God."

The governor continued to urge him, saying: "Swear, and I will dismiss you. Curse Christ."

"Curse Christ!" Polycarp replied. "Eighty-and-six years have I served Him and He never did me wrong; and how can I now blaspheme my King who has saved me?"

The governor continued to urge him, and in vain threatened him with the wild beasts. At length a herald was ordered to proclaim in the midst of the stadium that "Polycarp confesses he is a Christian." Thereupon the multitude cried out, "This is that teacher of Asia, the father of the Christians, the destroyer of our gods," and demanded that he should be burned alive; and the governor gave sentence accordingly.

According to the horrid custom of the times the executioners were about to fasten his hands to the stake by spikes, when he begged that he might be merely bound, saying that He who gave him strength to bear the flames would also give him strength to remain unmoved on the pyre. This last request was granted; and, being bound to the stake, he uttered this beautiful prayer:

"Lord, God Almighty, Father of Thy well-beloved and blessed Son Jesus Christ, through whom we have received the knowledge of Thee, God of angels and powers and all creation, and of all the family of the just that stand before Thy face, I bless Thee that Thou hast thought me worthy of the present day and hour, to have a share with Thy Martyrs in the chalice of the Passion of Christ unto the resurrection of eternal life, both of the soul and the body, in the incorruptible felicity of the Holy Spirit. May I be received among these in Thy sight this day as a rich and acceptable sacrifice, as Thou, the faithful and true God, hast prepared, hast revealed, and fulfilled. Wherefore, on this account and for all things, I praise Thee, I bless Thee, I glorify Thee through the eternal High Priest Jesus Christ, Thy well-beloved Son, through whom glory be to Thee with Him in the Holy Ghost, both now and evermore, Amen."

The flames did not immediately seize upon him; so one of the executioners plunged a sword into his body, and so ended his sufferings. A centurion then placed the body in the midst of the fire and burned it, "as was the custom of the Gentiles.

"But we, taking up his bones, valued more than precious stones, more tried than gold, deposited them in a suitable place. There also, as far as we can, we will celebrate the natal day of his martyrdom in joy and gladness, both in commemoration of those who finished their contest before, and to prepare those that shall finish hereafter."

There is something wonderfully touching, remarks a modern historian, in this reference to the "natal day of his martyrdom." Those who wrote it thought that the day on which Polycarp was pierced by the sword was not the day of his death, but the birthday of a new and happier life (H. Cox, in *The Great Events by Famous Historians*, Vol. III, p. 232 ff.).

St. Justin, the Martyr-Philosopher.—Marcus Aurelius (161-180), the "philosopher on the throne," was undoubtedly the noblest of pagan rulers. The little book of *Meditations* which was found after his death in a fold of his toga, is one of the classics of philosophical literature. And yet Marcus Aurelius must be reckoned amongst the persecutors of the Christians. As a Stoic philosopher he despised the Christian Religion, because it was a religion of suffering and self-abasement. In his *Meditations* he attributes the Christians' fearlessness in the face of death to "mere obstinacy." He was ignorant of the source whence these nameless heroes drew a strength superior to his own. This contempt for the Christians is also manifest in his decree "against new and unknown religions." He does not even deign to mention the Christian Religion by name, although the decree was directed against them in the first place:

"Whoever introduces new sects or religions whose true nature is unknown, and thereby excites the people, he shall be banished if he be of noble birth, and killed by the sword if he be of mean extraction."

This decree was the signal for a violent persecution of the Christians throughout the Empire—in Rome itself, in Asia Minor, Africa, and Gaul. One of the first victims was the famous Apologist *St. Justin*.

Justin was born early in the second century at Sichem in Palestine of Roman parents. In his youth he studied all the current systems of philosophy, but found no rest for his soul. An aged

Christian, whom he met accidentally in a lonely place, advised him to study the Christian writings and to pray for light, and he would come to the knowledge of Christ and of true wisdom. After his conversion Justin wandered about arguing with Jews and

St. Justin

Gentiles for the truth of the new faith. He finally settled in Rome and opened a school of Christian philosophy. In his *Dialogue with Trypho* he defends the truth of the Christian Religion against the Jews, and his two *Apologies* addressed to the Emperor Antoninus Pius, the Senate, and the Roman people, are amongst the most precious documents of the early Church.

In the reign of Marcus Aurelius, but in what year is not known, Justin and six other Christians, among them a woman, were accused before Rusticus, the prefect of Rome, of refusing to sacrifice to the gods. We still have the record of their trial written down by an eye-witness. It concludes as follows:

> *The Prefect* (to Justin): "Hearken, you who are called learned and think that you know the truth: if you are scourged and beheaded, do you believe that you will ascend into heaven?"
>
> *Justin:* "I hope that if I endure these things I shall have this privilege, for I know that to all who have thus lived there abides the divine favor until the consummation of the world."

The Prefect: "Do you suppose that you will ascend into heaven to receive such a recompense?"

Justin: "I do not suppose it, but I am fully persuaded of it."

The Prefect: "But let us come to the matter in hand, which must be speedily settled. Let all of you sacrifice to the gods."

Justin: "No one who is in his right senses will pass from piety to impiety."

The Prefect: "If you do not obey, you will be punished unmercifully."

Justin: "It is our heart's desire to be martyred for our Lord Jesus Christ and then to be happy forever."

Thus also said the other Christians, "Do what you will, for we are Christians and do not sacrifice to idols."

Thereupon the Prefect pronounced sentence, saying, "Let those who have refused to sacrifice to the gods and to obey the command of the Emperor be scourged and led away to suffer decapitation according to the law."

The holy martyrs having glorified God and having gone forth to the accustomed place, were beheaded, and perfected their testimony in the confession of the Savior. And some of the faithful, having secretly removed their bodies, laid them in a suitable place.

The Martyrs of Lyons.—Passing from Rome to Gaul we witness at Lyons the memorable scenes that marked the baptism of blood and fire with which the infant Church of that city was baptized.

On the 8th of August, A.D. 177, and the following days a solemn public festival was to be celebrated at Lyons. Towards the end of July, whilst the preparations were in progress, the populace began to vent its long-pent-up fury against the Christians. They were driven from the Forum, the Baths, and all the public buildings. Whenever one of them appeared in the streets, he was greeted with shouts of derision, with blows, kicks, and showers of stones and other missiles. The magistrates, making common cause with the rabble, cast a number of the Christians into prison.

The governor of the province was absent during these first scenes of violence. On his return, the Christians were dragged before his tribunal. He asked each but one question, "Art thou a Christian?" and if they confessed, they were tortured most inhumanly and then led off to death. A few, ill-prepared and frightened by the dreadful torments inflicted on their companions, denied their faith, to the great sorrow of the rest; but they afterwards repented and most of them wiped out the disgrace of their apostasy by a glorious death. Six of the martyrs were devoured by wild beasts in the amphitheater, eighteen died of their sufferings in prison, twenty-four suffered death in various forms. *St. Pothinus,* the bishop of the city, a man of more than ninety years, was so brutally maltreated by the officers of the law and the mob that he died of the effects after an imprisonment of two days. *St. Blandina,* a slave-girl, was so weak and tender by nature that her companions feared not a little for her constancy. But from morning till evening she endured every kind of torment. "Her executioners, wearied out, were forced to acknowledge themselves vanquished, and marveled that tortures, each one of which would have seemed sufficient to cause death, should not be able to quell her courage. The words, 'I am a Christian' ever gave her fresh strength. She was at last thrown before a wild bull, who tossed her with his horns, gored her, and trampled her to death." The bodies of the martyrs were cast before the dogs, and the few bones that remained were burned, and the ashes scattered upon the waters of the Rhone. . . .

All these details, and others equally melancholy, are preserved in a letter addressed by "the servants of Christ, dwelling in Vienne and Lyons in Gaul, to the brethren in Asia and Phrygia."

St. Irenaeus.—St. Pothinus was succeeded as bishop of Lyons by St. Irenaeus, who has been justly styled the "most learned, most prudent, and most illustrious of the early heads of the Church in Gaul." Originally from Smyrna, in Asia Minor, where he was a disciple of St. Polycarp, he had migrated to Gaul, shortly after the Church had been established in that country, and settled down in the city of Lyons. He employed the twenty-five years of his episcopacy (177-202) in propagating the faith and defending by his numerous writings the doctrines of the Church against the heresies which had already infested the Church in the East, and which were beginning to penetrate also into the West. His chief work, written about 180, is "The Refutation and Overthrow of Gnosticism," usually called *"Against the Heresies."* It is of inestimable value for the history of the early Church and her teaching. Another work of his, *"The Proof of the Apostolic Teaching,"* was discovered only recently in an Armenian translation. It contains a clear statement of the fundamental truths of Christianity. It is the oldest Catechism in existence, and shows that Irenaeus was able not only to expound and defend Christianity as a learned theologian, but also to preach it to the simple layman.—According to a later tradition, St. Irenaeus crowned his labors for Christ

St. Irenaeus

St. Cyprian

Origen

Tertullian

and His Church by martyrdom in the year 202, during the persecution of Septimius Severus.

The *Gnostics* (so called because of their pretended higher knowledge of divine things—Gr. *gnosis*), whom St. Irenaeus refutes in his great work, held that there was one Supreme Spirit, who was incomprehensible and so entirely removed from the world that He had no care of it. Out of this Supreme Spirit there emanated a graduated series of divine powers or existences, called *aeons*; each was a personification of some particular attribute of the Supreme Godhead, and all of them, together with the Godhead, made up the *Pleroma* or fullness of the Godhead. On the other hand there exists matter, which is also eternal and in itself evil. The world in which we actually see evil in existence was created by one of the aeons from this evil matter.—It is evident that, according to the Gnostics, evil comes to us, not by our own choice, but by the essential constitution of our nature. There is no *moral* evil properly so called; but evil does exist; it is *matter,* which defiles by its very contact. The Gnostics divided all men into three classes: the *spiritual,* the *animal,* and the *material,* according as the heavenly or the material element prevailed in them. All religious perfection consisted in the assimilation of the "knowledge" proffered by the Gnostics (Bonnar in *Atonement,* p. 202 f.).

The Martyrs of Scilla.—The concluding scene of the persecution under Marcus Aurelius takes us to North Africa. On the 17th of July, A.D. 180, seven men and five women from Scilla, a town in Numidia, were tried and executed at Carthage by the Proconsul Vigellius Saturninus. The *Acts* of their martyrdom are at once the earliest historical document of the African Church and the earliest specimen of Christian Latin. "The document is in brief legal form, beginning with the date and the names of the accused, and giving the actual dialogue between them and their judge. It closes with the proclamation by the herald of the names of the offenders and the penalty. *Speratus* is the principal spokesman of the Christians. He claims for himself and his companions that they have lived a quiet and moral life, paying their dues and doing no wrong to their neighbors. But when called upon to swear by the genius of the emperor, he replies: "I recognize not the empire of this world; but rather do I serve that God whom no man hath seen, nor with these eyes can see." Here he uses the language of Tim. 1, 6, 16; and it is interesting also to note that in reply to the question, "What are the things in your satchel?" he says, "Books and letters of Paul, a just man." The martyrs are offered a delay of thirty days to reconsider their decision, but this they all alike refuse. "And so they all together," says the Christian editor of the *Acts,* "were crowned with martyrdom; and they reign with the Father and the Son and the Holy Ghost, for ever and ever. Amen." (J. A. Robinson in *Encyclop. Britannica*). Later a basilica in their honor was built at Carthage where their *Acts* were publicly read at the annual commemoration of their martyrdom.

We have good reasons to believe that *St. Caecilia,* a noble Roman lady, suffered martyrdom under Marcus Aurelius; the controversy, however, has not been settled, and probably never will be. She was condemned to be suffocated in her bathroom, but remaining unharmed by the hot vapors, she was killed with the sword. She is represented in Christian art with an organ-like instrument. Her claim to musical accomplishments, and her consequent elevation to the rank of patroness of sacred music, rests on a passage in her legendary Acts describing her wedding-day: "Whilst the instruments (*organa*) played, the Virgin Caecilia sang thus in her heart: 'Let my heart and my body be undefiled, that I may not be confounded'" (Ps. 118, 80). In literature she is commemorated by Chaucer in the "Seconde Nonnes Tale" and by Dryden in his beautiful "Ode in Honor of St. Caecilia's Day," set to music by Handel.

Marcus Aurelius died on the 17th day of March, 180 A.D., far from Rome, while engaged in a long and desperate war with Germanic tribes on the banks of the Danube. The persecution of the Christians ceased almost immediately upon the accession of his son Commodus, and was not renewed till Septimius Severus issued a decree (A.D. 202) against the Jews and the Christians, prohibiting both Circumcision and Baptism—a very effective means, if successful, of stamping out both Judaism and Christianity. Dire times followed for the Christians, especially in Egypt and Africa.

St. Leonidas, the Father of Origen.—At Alexandria in Egypt, Leonidas, the father of the great Origen, was thrown into prison, tortured, and beheaded. Whilst his father was languishing in prison, young Origen's desire for a martyr's death became so uncontrollable that his mother could scarcely hinder him by her tears and prayers from delivering himself up to the heathen judge. She was even forced to hide his clothes to prevent him from leaving the house. Origen thereupon wrote a letter to his father, in which he extolled the glory of martyrdom and begged him not to forfeit the martyr's crown through love of his wife and children. We shall meet this heroic youth again.

Tertullian, Apologist and Heretic.—During the closing years of the second century Africa was once more the scene of a violent persecution. Multitudes of Christians were cast into prison, torn with iron hooks, devoured by wild beasts, beheaded, burned at the stake, or crucified. *Tertullian,* who was a witness of these horrors, wrote one book after another either to defend the Christians against their persecutors or to encourage them in their trials. His full name was Quintus Septimius Florens Tertullianus. He was born about 160 A.D. at Carthage, where his father was serving as a centurion of the proconsul of Africa. After an excellent training in Greek and Latin literature, he became a lawyer and practiced his profession in Rome for many years. After his conversion to Christianity (about 193 A.D.) he settled in Carthage. St. Jerome says that he was advanced to the priesthood, but this is hardly probable; to all appearances Tertullian lived and died as a layman. Tertullian was easily the most original and the most prolific of all the early Latin writers. He has been justly called the "Father of Ecclesiastical Latin." His chief work is the *Apologeticus,* a defense of the Christians addressed to the governors of Proconsular Africa in 197. It disposes in masterly fashion of the charges brought against the Christians for secret crimes and public offenses, and proves the absolute superiority of Christianity over all other religions and philosophical systems.

Unfortunately, about the year 203 Tertullian fell under the influence of the Montanists and in 213 went over to them altogether; and henceforth he employed his great talents in defending and propagating the tenets of that sect of fanatic rigorists. Some of his favorite contentions after he had become a Montanist were that the Church could not absolve persons guilty of very grave offenses, such as apostasy and adultery; that Christians were not at liberty to avoid persecution by flight or to purchase their safety with money; that second marriage was adultery; that amusements of all kinds were sinful, and that the power to rule in the Church depended on spiritual endowments and not on the Sacrament of Holy Orders.

The Martyrdom of St. Perpetua and Her Companions.— On the 7th of March, 203, Perpetua, Felicitas, and their companions suffered martyrdom at Carthage. Vibia Perpetua, a young wife and mother, wrote the story of her experiences from the time of her arrest almost down to her actual martyrdom, when other hands completed it. He must have a hard heart indeed who can read these memoirs without being moved to tears.

It had come to the ears of the authorities that the noble lady Perpetua, contrary to the edict of Septimius Severus, was receiving instruction in the Christian religion with several members of her household, among them her brother Saturus and the slaves Felicitas and Revocatus. Armed soldiers entered her house and arrested all who professed themselves as Christians.

"When I was in the hands of the persecutors," she writes "my father, who was an obstinate pagan, in his tender solicitude tried hard to pervert me from the faith.

" 'Father,' I said, 'you see this pitcher. Can we call it by any other name than what it is? Neither can I call myself by any other name than that of Christian.'

"So he went away, but, on the rumor that we were to be tried, wasted away with anxiety.

" 'Daughter,' he said, 'have pity on my gray hairs; have pity on thy father. Do not give me over to disgrace. Behold thy brother, thy mother, and thy aunt: behold thy child, who cannot live without thee. Do not destroy us all.'

"Thus spake my father, kissing my hands, and throwing himself at my feet. And I wept because of my father, for he alone of all my family would not rejoice in my martyrdom. So I comforted him, saying:

" 'In this trial, what God determines will take place. We are not in our own keeping, but God's.' So he left me, weeping bitterly."

Perpetua was allowed to keep her little boy with her in prison, and she nursed him with such motherly tenderness and such resignation to God's will that the captain of the prison guard was moved to pity and made her prison days as pleasant as possible for her.

Three days before the time set for the execution, Felicitas gave birth to a child. She suffered intense pain, which she could not hide from the rude soldiers on guard.

"If you lament and cry out now," one of them said to her, "what will you do when you are thrown to the wild beasts?"

"I am suffering alone," she replied, "what I am suffering now; then Another will be with me, who will suffer for me, because I will suffer for Him."

The dreadful day arrived. The little band of Christians was led into the arena, Perpetua singing a hymn, and the men proclaiming aloud to all the spectators the coming judgment of God. First they were scourged; then leopards, bears and wild boars were let loose upon the men. Perpetua and Felicitas were tossed and gored by a mad cow; but in spite of cruel manglings yet survived. Perpetua seemed in a trance. "When are we going to be tossed?" she asked, and could scarcely believe that she had suffered, until she saw the ugly gash in her thigh. Presently all were stabbed to death. Perpetua had to guide to her own throat the unsteady hand of the young gladiator.—The noble woman Perpetua and the slave-woman Felicitas are commemorated together in the Canon of the Mass. Their feast is celebrated on the 6th of March.

After the year 203 the Church enjoyed nearly fifty years of tranquillity, broken only for a brief space by the brutal Maximinus Thrax (235-238). The emperors of this period were mostly Syrians, who cared little about the religion of Rome. Alexander Severus (222-235) permitted the Christians as a body to own property and to erect houses of worship. It is related that he placed an image of Christ among his collection of gods and heroes. His mother, the famous Julia Mamaea, displayed great interest in the Christian teaching. She invited Origen to Antioch and listened attentively to his lectures on Christianity. The learned Roman presbyter Hippolytus dedicated a treatise on the Resurrection to her.

The long peace was not an unmixed benefit for the Christians. A spirit of worldliness was beginning to manifest itself not only amongst the laity, but even in the ranks of the clergy. Then a storm of persecution swept over them, which exceeded in violence all that had gone before.

2. The Persecutions of Decius and Valerian, A.D. 250-260

The Edict of Decius.—Septimius Severus and Maximinus Thrax tried to stop the further spread of Christianity; Decius was determined to annihilate it. Severus forbade the preaching of the Gospel of Christ and the reception of Baptism; Decius promulgated an edict of extermination against Christianity itself. By virtue of this edict, all persons suspected of being Christians were obliged to present themselves before the local authorities and clear themselves of the accusation by sacrificing to the gods; if they failed to appear, the magistrates were to seize them and force them by every means in their power to abjure their faith. Those who remained firm were visited with exile or death and the confiscation of their property. The governors of the provinces were threatened with severe punishment if they condemned any one to death without having made every effort to obtain from him an act of abjuration. The Christians formed at this time about one-third of the population of the Empire, and Decius saw right well that to kill them all, even if that had been possible, would spell ruin for Rome. Wholesale apostasy would answer his purpose better. Hence the extreme measures adopted, especially against the bishops and priests, to break down their resistance.

The Attitude of the Christians.—There were apostates, fugitives and martyrs among the Christians.

The number of *apostates* was very great, especially in Africa and Asia, as we learn from the writings of St. Cyprian of Carthage and St. Dionysius of Alexandria. Even bishops and priests were found amongst them. The apostates were divided into two classes: the *thurificati* or *sacrificati,* those who had actually fulfilled the edict by offering incense or sacrifice to the gods, and the *libellatici,* those who evaded the consequences of their faith by procuring documents—*libelli*—through bribery or otherwise, which certified that they had satisfied the authorities of their submission to the edict.

One of these *libelli* was found in 1893 in the Fayum district in Egypt. It is on a papyrus leaf and reads as follows:

"To the Commissioners of Sacrifice of the Village of Alexander's Island. From Aurelius Diogenes, the son of Satabus, of the village of Alexander's Island, aged 72 years:—scar on his right eyebrow.

"I have always sacrificed to the gods, and now, in your presence, in accordance with the edict, I have sacrificed, and poured the drink offering, and tasted of the sacrifices, and I request you to certify the same. Farewell! Handed in by me, Aurelius Diogenes.

"I, Aurelius Syrus, certify that I saw Diogenes sacrificing.

"Done in the first year of the Emperor, Caesar Gaius Messius Quintus Trajanus Decius, Pius, Felix, Augustus: the second of the month Epiphi" (Nov., 250).

Many Christians evaded death by flight. "Some," says St. Cyprian, "embarked on the first ship that hove in sight: others wandered about in the deserts and the mountains, at the mercy of brigands and beasts of prey, exposed to hunger and thirst and the extremes of heat and cold."

St. Dionysius of Alexandria, surnamed "the Great," retired into a wild country district. His hiding-place was discovered, and a troop of soldiers was sent to capture him; but a band of peasants liberated him, placed him on an ass and led him away into the Libyan Desert, where he remained concealed till the end of the persecution.

St. Gregory Thaumaturgus (Wonderworker), bishop of Neo-Caesarea, advised his people to save their faith and their lives by flight; he himself withdrew with a portion of his flock into the neighboring mountains.

St. Cyprian of Carthage hid himself near the city, and from his place of concealment governed his Church for nearly a whole year, thus doing a greater service to the cause of Christianity than if he had died a premature death.

Amongst those who suffered martyrdom were Pope Fabian and the bishops of Jerusalem, Antioch and Toulouse. In Smyrna the aged priest Pionius was seized whilst he was offering up the Holy Sacrifice on the anniversary day of the martyrdom of St. Polycarp.

"What is thy name?" the judge asked him.

"Christian," he replied.

"What God dost thou adore?"

"The Almighty God, who made heaven and earth."

Immediately afterwards the judge asked another Christian who had been arrested with Pionius: "What God dost thou adore?"

He answered: "Christ."

"What," said the judge, "is that another God?"

"No, He is the same God whom Pionius has confessed."

All efforts on the part of the judge and the people to make Pionius deny his faith were in vain. He was repeatedly tortured and then burned at the stake.

Origen.—The most noted of all the victims of the Decian persecution was Origen, surnamed *Adamantius,* "the man of steel." After the martyrdom of his father Leonidas, the support of the family fell to him. Though only seventeen years old, he began to teach both in public and in private. He showed such marked talent, learning and ability that he was soon placed, with the sanction of Bishop Demetrius, at the head of the *Catechetical School* of Alexandria. This school, of which the origin is unknown, was the first and for a long time the only institution where Christians could receive instruction simultaneously in the Greek sciences and the doctrines of the Holy Scriptures. About A.D. 180 it had already reached a high degree of efficiency under the head-mastership of the learned and pious Pantaenus; but it was under Clement and his pupil Origen that its fame spread throughout the world. Clement, to whom we owe a truly epoch-making work, *An Introduction to Christianity,* left Alexandria in 203, owing to the persecution of Septimius Severus. Origen succeeded him and remained in charge of the school until 230. In this year, while on a journey to Athens, he stopped at Caesarea in Palestine and was ordained priest by his friend Alexander, bishop of Jerusalem, without the knowledge of his own bishop. He was recalled to Alexandria and deposed from the presidency of the School by a synod held in 231. A second synod, which met in the following year, degraded him from the priesthood, because of the irregularity of his ordination. He returned to Cæsarea, where he opened a school, which soon became even more famous than that of Alexandria. Here he continued his learned labors till the Decian persecution.

Known far and wide as the intellectual leader of the Christians, Origen was one of the first to be arrested in Caesarea. Every means was tried to make him recant, because the persecutors were convinced that if he proved an apostate, multitudes would follow his example. He was cast into the darkest and filthiest part of the prison and for days subjected to every imaginable torture. But in spite of his sixty-seven years he bore it all unflinchingly. After the death of Decius he regained his liberty. Broken in body, he lingered on for two years more. He died in 253 at Tyre, in Phoenicia, where his grave was still shown in the Middle Ages. Thus he attained in his old age the crown of martyrdom which he had desired so ardently in his youth.

Origen was one of the most prolific writers of whom there is record. "Which of us," asks St. Jerome, "can read all that he has written?" The number of his books was estimated at 6,000, but that is evidently an exaggeration. St. Jerome numbers about 800 titles. We possess but a small remnant of his writings, and of this remnant one-half is known only through Latin translations. His most important work was the *Hexapla* (sixfold), so called from the fact that it contained in six columns the Hebrew text of the Bible in Hebrew letters and Greek letters, the Septuagint, and three other Greek translations made in the second century. His book against the pagan philosopher *Celsus,* which has been completely preserved in the original text, is undoubtedly the most perfect piece of Apologetic literature of the early Church. His most popular works are the *"Admonition to Martyrdom,"* which was written during the persecution of Maximinus Thrax and dedicated to his friends Ambrosius and Protoctetus, who had been cast into prison, and his beautiful treatise *"On Prayer,"* which contains the first exposition of the Lord's Prayer that has come down to us.

Nearly three centuries after his death, Origen was condemned by the Fifth General Council (553), because it was found that his writings contained a number of heretical doctrines, such as the pre-existence of souls and the final salvation of all men.

During the reign of the Emperor Gallus (251-254) a great
pestilence broke out and spread rapidly over the whole Empire.
The Emperor ordered sacrifices of expiation to be offered to
Apollo in order to obtain relief from the dreadful scourge.   In
consequence Christian blood flowed once more.   When Pope Cornelius was taken prisoner, hundreds of Roman Christians appeared
before the tribunal of the Prefect and fearlessly declared that they
were ready to die with their bishop.   Cornelius died in exile, as did
also his successor Lucian.

Pope St. Sixtus and His Deacon St. Lawrence.—The Emperor Valerian (254-260) was at first very friendly to the Chris-

Fra Angelico

THE ORDINATION OF ST. LAWRENCE

tians, but towards the end of his reign, goaded on by jealousy and cupidity—his counsellors made him believe that the Church was a powerful organization possessed of great wealth—he played the rôle of a persecutor. In 257 he issued an edict ordering all bishops, priests, and deacons to sacrifice to the gods under pain of banishment, and forbidding all Christians under pain of death from assembling in public or in private, and from visiting the cemeteries. Pope Sixtus II was surprised in the Catacomb of Callistus, whilst celebrating the Sacred Mysteries, and was beheaded on the spot with six of his deacons (Aug. 6, 258). St. Lawrence, the seventh deacon, was reserved for greater sufferings before he joined his master. The details of his martyrdom, legendary in part, are recorded by St. Ambrose.

Lawrence was called upon by the judge to bring forth the treasures of the Church, which had been committed to his charge as chief deacon. He thereupon produced a multitude of poor people whom the Church had maintained. Seeing Pope Sixtus being led to the place of execution, he ran after him, crying: "Father! whither goest thou without thy son? Holy Priest! whither goest thou without the deacon?" Sixtus prophesied that Lawrence would follow him after three days. The prophecy was fulfilled. Lawrence was sentenced to be burnt alive on a gridiron. In the midst of his torments he addressed the judge with the words: "I am roasted enough on this side; turn me round."—His name appears with that of St. Sixtus in the Canon of the Mass. His great basilica in Rome in still visited by pilgrims from every land. Philip II of Spain built the Escurial in honor of St. Lawrence, on whose feast day his troops had won the battle of St. Quentin (Aug. 10, 1557).

St. Cyprian of Carthage.—Caecilius Thascius Cyprianus was of patrician family, wealthy, highly educated, and for some time occupied as a teacher of Rhetoric at Carthage. Caecilius, a learned and zealous priest of Carthage, was the instrument of his conversion, which took place about the year 245. He devoted all his wealth to the poor and other pious causes, and gave himself up, with all the enthusiasm of his ardent nature, to the defense and spread of the Church. In 249 he was raised to the episcopal see of Carthage by the unanimous voice of the clergy and the laity.

When those who had apostatized during the Decian persecution asked to be received back into the Church, Cyprian granted their request, just as Pope Cornelius had done in Rome, on condition that they did penance for the remainder of their life. This ruling caused a schism both in Rome and in Carthage. A party of rigorists, headed by the Roman priest Novatian, advocated the permanent exclusion of all apostates from the Church. Claiming that Cornelius had betrayed his trust, Novatian had himself elected as Pope by his followers—the first Anti-Pope in history. Cyprian thereupon wrote the beautiful treatise *On the Unity of the Catholic Church*. In it he compares the Church to the seamless robe of Christ and says: "Outside the Church there is no salvation. He cannot have God as his Father, who has not the Church for his Mother."

Cyprian was a great admirer of Tertullian and never passed a day without reading some portion of his works; he used frequently to say to his servant: *"Da Magistrum,"* Give me my master, meaning Tertullian (St. Jerome). Like Tertullian, however, he was impetuous and inclined to go to extremes. "This feature of his character is brought out strongly in his dispute with Pope Stephen regarding the re-baptism of converted heretics. He contended that those who had returned to the Church from heresy should be re-baptized in all cases, and when the Pope refused to accept his opinion, casting to the winds all that he had previously written about the authority of the Holy See, he insisted on his right to decide the question for himself without the interference of Rome." A rupture between Rome and Carthage would have taken place, since both parties held firmly to their standpoint, had not the persecution under Valerian intervened. St. Stephen died in 257, and St. Cyprian was martyred in the following year.

Brought before the Proconsul and asked who he was, Cyprian replied: "I am a Christian and a Bishop." When the sentence of death was pronounced, he said: "Thanks be to God." At the place of execution he bandaged his eyes with his own hands and ordered twenty-five pieces of gold to be given to the executioner. The Christians spread linen cloths under his feet in order to catch some drops at least of his blood, and in the night carried off his body in procession, bearing lighted torches and singing hymns of praise and thanksgiving. In his controversy with Pope Stephen, St. Cyprian was in the wrong; his contention was, in fact, heretical. "But," as St. Augustine, his great countryman and admirer, says, "he merited to attain the crown of martyrdom, so that any cloud which had obscured the brightness of his mind was driven away by the brilliant sunshine of his glorious blood." It is significant that St. Cyprian, in spite of his dispute with the Pope, is commemorated in the Mass by name, an honor which he shares with two other African martyrs, Perpetua and Felicitas.

3. The Persecutions of Diocletian and Galerius, A.D. 303-311

After the defeat and capture of Valerian by the Persians in the year 260, the Church enjoyed another long period of peace. The exiled bishops returned to their sees, and the Christian communities received back their confiscated property. The struggle between paganism and Christianity was not officially renewed till the nineteenth year of the reign of Diocletian, A.D. 303.

How Diocletian Became a Persecutor.—A new epoch in the history of Rome began with the accession of Diocletian to the throne in 284. The last traces of the ancient Republican institutions were abolished, and the Empire became an oriental despotism. On account of the menacing attitude of the Germans on the Rhine and the Persians in the East, Diocletian in 286 associated Maximian with himself in the government. When further dangers arose in the East and the West, he created two Caesars in 292: the one, Galerius, to act as his own subordinate in the East; the other, Constantius Chlorus, to divide the government of the West with Maximian. Each of the four rulers was placed at a separate capital—Nicomedia, Milan, Treves, and Sirmium.

Diocletian, though extremely superstitious, was tolerant by nature and indulged no hatred towards the Christians. Constantius Chlorus was averse to the popular idolatry and friendly towards the Christians; whilst Maximian and Galerius, brutal by nature and, like all tyrants, suspicious of any one who was not ready to bow before their will in all matters, hated the Christians and were eagerly awaiting an opportunity to exterminate them. It was Galerius who, in the year 303, obtained from Diocletian an edict by which the churches of the Christians were to be demolished, their Sacred Books committed to the flames, and themselves deprived of all their civil rights and honors.

This first edict spared the lives of the Christians; yet it caused many to be put to death, particularly those who refused to give up their Sacred Books to the magistrates. Many Christians, on the other hand, especially in Africa, voluntarily surrendered the books in their possession, but they were regarded by their more uncompromising brethren as guilty of sacrilege. They are known in history as *traditores*.

Not long after the publication of this first edict a fire broke out in the palace at Nicomedia, and the enemies of the Christians persuaded Diocletian that Christian hands had kindled it. He therefore ordered many Christians to be tortured and punished as incendiaries. About the same time there were insurrections in Armenia and Syria, and the blame for these was also charged to the Christians. Thereupon, by a second edict, Diocletian ordered all bishops, priests, and deacons to be cast into prison; and by a third edict, soon after, he commanded that all these prisoners should be compelled by torture to sacrifice to the gods. A great multitude, in every part of the Empire, Gaul only excepted, which was subject to Constantius Chlorus, were in consequence either punished with death or condemned to the mines—a punishment worse than death.

The Extermination of the Christians Decreed.—In the second year of the persecution a fourth edict directed the magistrates to force all Christians to offer sacrifice, and as these orders were strictly carried out, the Church was reduced to the last extremity. Almost to a man the Christians rose to the highest heights of heroism. The prisons were soon filled to overflowing; there was no room left for fresh chain-gangs in the mines; the populace, sickened by the daily butcheries, no longer crowded the places of execution. Constantine the Great later declared before the Fathers assembled at Nicaea that, if the Romans had slain as many barbarians as they had slaughtered Christians during the reign of Diocletian, there would be no barbarians left to threaten the safety of the Empire. In one district of Egypt, an eye-witness tells us, from ten to thirty and sixty victims were put to death daily for more than a year. A Christian town in Phrygia was burned to the ground with all its inhabitants, because they had refused to sacrifice to the idols.

Many saints, whose names have become household words throughout the world, suffered during this persecution: Sebastian, Tarcisius, Cosmas and Damian, Nabor and Felix, Vincent, Agnes, Lucy, Catherine, Margaret, etc. The great veneration in which these martyrs were held is responsible for the legends woven about them by the pious imagination of their admirers, so that it is by no means easy to extract the kernel of historical truth from their *Acts* as they have come down to us. We are best informed about the persecution of the Christians in Palestine. Eusebius of Caesarea, the "Father of Church History," who was about forty years old at the time, devoted a whole book to the martyrs of his native province: *The History of the Martyrs of Palestine.* It contains most touching details of Christian heroism. Thus, he tells of Paul of Gaza, who begged the executioner to permit him to say a prayer before he was beheaded. The permission being granted, he prayed with a loud voice for all the Christian brethren, that God might shorten the time of their trial; for the Jews, the Samaritans, and the pagans, that the grace of faith might be vouchsafed to them; for the judge who had condemned him to death; for the executioner who was to behead him; and, finally, for the rulers of the Empire. "What an infinite wealth of love lies in this prayer!" the historian cries out. It was this wealth of love that finally conquered the world.

4. *The Triumph of the Cross*

On the 1st of May, 305, Diocletian and Maximian abdicated. The sovereignty now devolved on Galerius in the East, and in the West on Constantius Chlorus, who in the following year was succeeded by his son Constantine. Constantine was very favorably disposed towards the Christians, but in the East the persecution raged with greater severity than before, until the death of Galerius in 311. Before his death, which was brought on by a dreadful and protracted disease, Galerius issued a decree in which he acknowledged the total failure of his policy of persecution and granted the Christians the free exercise of their religion, if they did not otherwise break the laws and would pray for the emperor and the empire.

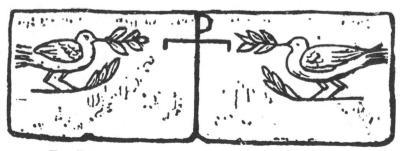

The Earliest Inscription of the Monogram of Christ

In Hoc Signo Vinces.—The long struggle between Christianity and paganism was decided in the year 312 before the walls of Rome. Maxentius, a brutal and debauched tyrant, who had made himself master of Italy and Africa after the death of Galerius, determined to make war on Constantine, in order to bring all the West under his authority. Constantine anticipated his design and marched into Italy with an army of 25,000 men. When he was approaching Rome he saw, as he later assured his biographer Eusebius under oath, about midday, a cross of light in the heavens, around which were woven the words: *In hoc signo vinces*—"In this sign thou shalt conquer." The following night Christ appeared to him in a dream and told him to adopt the cross as his standard instead of the Roman eagle. Thereupon he ordered the monogram of Christ (☧) to be painted on the shields of his soldiers and a standard, made after the pattern of the cross which he had seen, to be borne before him (Eusebius, *Life of Constantine*, I, 28-31. Lactantius, *On the Deaths of the Persecutors*, n. 44, speaks only of Constantine's dream. Since Eusebius in his *Church History* [IX, 9], which he wrote in 314-315 A.D., does not mention the appearance of the cross, some historians have declared the vision of the cross to be legendary, and the dream alone historical).

Confident of divine aid, Constantine awaited the attack of the enemy. Maxentius had caused the Sibylline books to be consulted, and the ambiguous answer had been, "The foe of Rome shall perish miserably." Thus blinded, he crossed the Tiber by the Milvian Bridge, north of Rome, and risked a decisive battle (Oct. 27, 312). After a severe struggle, his army fled in wild disorder. Thousands perished in the waters of the Tiber, among them Maxentius himself.

The impression which this victory made on the pagan world was tremendous. The God of the Christians had proved His superiority over the gods of the Capitol. Constantine entered the city amid the rejoicings of the people. Upon the triumphal arch which the Senate and people erected to him, and which is still standing amongst the ruins of the City of the Caesars, his great victory is ascribed to the "decree of God." Constantine himself caused his own statue to be set up, holding in his hand the standard of the cross (*Labarum*), with the inscription, "Through this saving sign have I freed your city from the tyrant's yoke."

In the following year Constantine and his colleague Licinius, the ruler of the East, met in conference at Milan and agreed to concede to the Christians throughout the Empire unrestricted free-

THE ARCH OF CONSTANTINE, ROME

dom of worship and to restore to them all the property which had been confiscated during the persecutions. This agreement is known as the *Edict of Milan*.

The victory of Christianity over paganism was "the purest ever won. For it was won by witnessing and enduring, by loving and suffering, by pouring out innocent blood. It was won by weak men and women, slaves often, opposed to the mightiest of governments and all the social and intellectual pride and prejudice of the civilized world."

Digitus Dei est hic.—"The finger of God is here." We are in the presence of a divine work. The victory of the Gospel is a proof of its divinity.

Let us see how the Church honored the heroes and heroines who suffered and died that she might live.

5. *How the Martyrs Were Honored*

The Privileges of Martyrdom.—We, in the present day, says a modern Church historian, can form only a faint conception of the intimacy of that union which subsisted between the primitive Christians, and was cemented by a community of danger as well as of faith and hope. The love which they bore to each other excited the astonishment, though it could not subdue the hostility, of their heathen persecutors. But they naturally regarded with feelings of peculiar affection and respect those members of the Church who were called to suffer in its cause, to be "witnesses" (*martyr* is the Greek word for witness) of the divine power operating in her.

The Christian, says Tertullian, when imprisoned on account of his Religion, was supported by the reflection that his brethren anxiously watched over his fate, and that no exertion would be wanting on their part to mitigate its severity; that he would be maintained during his confinement by their voluntary contributions; that devout men and women would flock to his prison to kiss his chains, and penitents to obtain through his intercession a speedier restoration to the communion of the Church. If he escaped with his life, he knew that he would become the object of the most reverential regard; that he would be held up by the Church as an example to all its members, and possess a prior claim to all its dignities and honors. If he was destined to lose his life, he had been taught that martyrdom was a second Baptism, which washed away every stain, and that the soul of the martyr was secure in immediate admission to the perfect happiness of heaven.

The Feasts of the Martyrs.—Special honors were paid to the Martyrs at the place of their burial. On the anniversary day of their martyrdom, which was called their *natalitium*, the day of their birth into eternal life, the faithful assembled in the cemetery, where their remains rested amidst those of their departed brethren. The Holy Eucharist was celebrated, hymns were sung in their honor, and the Acts of their martyrdom were read and commented upon by the bishop or a priest. Usually a "love-feast," at which the poor were fed at the expense of the rich, concluded the celebration.

The "Memoriae" of the Martyrs.—Even during the persecutions chapels in memory of the Martyrs (hence called *memoriae*) were built over their tombs. They became especially numerous since the time of Constantine.

"We do not build temples to our Martyrs," writes St. Augustine, "as though they were gods, but memorials or shrines (*memoriae*), as to dead men whose spirits live with God. Nor do we set up altars, to sacrifice to the Martyrs, but to God alone, God of the Martyrs and our God. In this sacrifice all the men of God, who in confession of their allegiance to Him have overcome the world, are named in due place and order, but are not invoked by the sacrificing priest. The reason is, because he is sacrificing to God, not to them, because he is God's priest, not theirs, although it is in their Memorial Shrine that he sacrifices" (*City of God*, XXII, 10).

God, too, glorified His champions, not only by admitting them to the abode of the blessed in heaven, but also by performing miracles through their relics here on earth. St. Augustine gives a list of miracles which happened before his own eyes at the Shrines of the Martyrs or when their relics were carried in procession (*City of God*, XXII, 8).

The Catacombs.—In many places, especially in Rome, the Christians adopted the ancient Jewish custom of burying their dead in underground cemeteries, afterwards known as catacombs. Originally the word catacombs (Greek *kata* and *kymbas*, "by the hollows") was applied to the district round the tomb of Cecilia Metella and the Circus of Romulus on the Appian Way. Throughout the Middle Ages "ad catacumbas" meant the subterranean cemetery adjacent to the great basilica of St. Sebastian in the above-mentioned district. It was the only cemetery of this kind known in the later Middle Ages. When many others were discovered in the sixteenth century, the term catacombs was applied to all the ancient underground cemeteries near Rome and to similar burying-places in other parts of the world. About seventy Roman catacombs are known, and have been more or less carefully examined; many others, blocked up with earth and rubbish, are still inaccessible.

The Christian cemeteries were not secret hiding-places. Even during the persecutions they enjoyed the protection of the Roman law, so that the faithful could celebrate the memorial days of the Martyrs without interference. Under Valerian, as we have seen, these assemblies were forbidden under pain of death, and it was only then that the Christians tried to conceal the entrances to the various catacombs. Staircases were destroyed, passages blocked up, and new exits and entrances devised, so as to defeat as much as possible the myrmidons of the law.

When the persecutions ceased, the catacombs, in which many Martyrs had perished and many more had been buried, became a place of religious reverence, the goal of countless pilgrims from all parts of the Christian world. Different Popes, especially St. Damasus (366-384), did much to make the catacombs more accessible and to decorate the interior. They caused old staircases to be enlarged and new ones to be made, and openings for admitting air and light to be broken through from the chambers or vaults to the surface of the ground. Burial in the catacombs gradually died out, and entirely ceased with the sack of Rome by Alaric, A.D. 410. In the succeeding centuries Gothic, Vandal, and Lombard invaders plundered and partly destroyed the catacombs. This induced the Popes of the seventh and eighth centuries to remove all the relics of the principal Martyrs and Confessors for greater safety to the churches of Rome. After that the catacombs were abandoned and in great part closed. Their very existence was hardly suspected till the close of the sixteenth century.

The Catacomb of San Callisto.—The earliest account of the catacombs is that of St. Jerome, who visited them about A.D. 354.

"When I was a boy," he writes, "receiving my education in Rome, I and my schoolfellows used, on Sundays, to make the circuit of the sepulchers of the Apostles and Martyrs. Many a time did we go down into the catacombs. These are excavated deep in the earth, and contain, on either hand as you enter, the bodies of the dead buried in the wall. It is all so dark there that the language of the prophet seems to be fulfilled, 'Let them go down quick into hell.' Only occasionally is light let in to mitigate the horror of the gloom, and then not so much through a window as through a hole. You take each step with caution as, surrounded by deep night, you recall the words of Virgil (Aen. II, 755) : " *'Horror ubique animos, simul ipsa silentia terrent.'* (Everywhere there is horror, at the same time the silence itself terrifies the mind)."

A description of the most important portion of the Catacomb of San Callisto will give the reader some idea of the present state of subterranean Rome,—not much different from what it was sixteen hundred years ago.

"Entering it from a vineyard near the Appian Way, the visitor descends a broad flight of steps, fashioned by Pope Damasus, and finds himself in a

kind of vestibule, on the stuccoed walls of which, honeycombed with *loculi*
(oblong niches large enough to hold from one to three bodies), are a
quantity of rude inscriptions, some of them thirteen and fourteen centuries

THE CATACOMB OF SAN CALLISTO

old, scratched by the pilgrims who visited out of devotion the places where
the Popes and Martyrs who had fought a good fight for Christ, lay in
peaceful gloom, awaiting the resurrection.

"By following a narrow gallery to the right, a chamber is reached which
is called the *Papal Crypt*; for here beyond all doubt the bodies of many
Popes of the third century, after Zephyrinus (203-217) had secured this
cemetery for the use of the Christians and committed it to the care of his
deacon Callistus, were laid, and here they remained till they were removed
by Pope Paschal (817) to the Vatican crypts. A passage leads out of the
crypt into the *cubiculum* (chamber or vault) of St. Caecilia, where the body
of the Saint was originally deposited, though it was afterwards removed
by Paschal to her church in the Trastevere, where it now lies under the
high altar. In this *cubiculum* are paintings of St. Caecilia and of Our
Lord, dating back to the tenth century. Besides the Papal Crypt and the
chamber of St. Caecilia, there are in this part of the cemetery several
cubicula interesting for their paintings, chiefly referable to Baptism and
the Eucharist, the fish being the principal emblem of the latter. In one
of these crypts is a painting of four male figures with uplifted hands, each
with his name placed over an *arcosolium* (an arched vault above the

loculus with a flat surface beneath on which Mass could be celebrated); in another are representations of peacocks, the emblem of immortality; in a third, Moses striking the rock, and ascending to the mount; in a fourth, a grave-digger (*fossor*) surrounded with the implements of his trade; in a fifth, the Good Shepherd, with the miracle of the paralytic taking up his bed; in a sixth, a banquet of seven persons, supposed to be the seven disciples alluded to in the twenty-first chapter of St. John's Gospel. These paintings, as well as the greater part of the catacomb, are referred to the last half of the third century" (*Catholic Dictionary,* Art. *Catacombs*).

Hints for Study

1. Draw up a list of all the Martyrs mentioned in this chapter; tell what their station in life was, in what persecution they suffered, and the place of their martyrdom.
2. What is meant by an *apologist?* Name the great apologists of the Early Church and their works.
3. What is the difference between *heresy* and *schism?* What heresies are mentioned in this chapter? Who was the first schismatic and anti-Pope? Was St. Cyprian a schismatic?
4. What is meant by the *Acts* of the Martyrs? Are they all of equal value? Name six genuine *Acts* and two legendary ones.
5. Name some instruments of torture employed during the persecutions.
6. Can you quote a text from the New Testament which justifies flight during persecution (Matt. 10, 23). ˙
7. Some Christians presented themselves voluntarily at the tribunals of the magistrates; were they justified in doing so?
8. What is meant by: *Martyr, Natalitium, libellatici, apostate, traditores, catechetical school, Monogram of Christ, Labarum, Hexapla, memorial, catacomb?*
9. Read Wiseman's *Fabiola* and Newman's *Callista,* and prepare a report on one or both.

CHAPTER IX

EARLY CHRISTIAN LIFE AND WORSHIP

We have already spoken of the organization of the early Church, and much too has been said of the social, religious, and moral life of the Christians during the first three centuries; but it will be well to sum up the scattered remarks and to bring out some points more clearly.

Baptism.—Membership in the Christian Church was acquired by Baptism. In the earliest days of the Church, Baptism was conferred without delay on those who professed their faith in Christ Later on, however, perhaps even before the death of the last Apostle, a period of preparation, called the *Catechumenate* and extending over a period of two or three years, regularly preceded the administration of Baptism. The catechumens (Greek *katechoumenoi*, "hearers," those receiving oral instruction) assisted only at the first part of the Divine Service up to the Offertory, which was afterwards called on this account the *Mass of the Catechumens.* During the weeks immediately preceding Baptism the catechumens were required to present themselves repeatedly in the church. Each time the bishop or one of his priests laid his hand upon their heads, and an Exorcist prayed over them that they might be delivered from the power of the devil in the name of the Blessed Trinity. Special instructions were also given them at this time on the Apostles' Creed; but the wording of the Creed itself—we do not know what the exact wording was in the third century—and the Lord's Prayer were made known to them only during the baptismal ceremony just as they were about to descend into the *piscina*, or baptismal font. The great mysteries of our Religion, especially the Sacrament of the Holy Eucharist, were explained to them only after Baptism.

Discipline of the Secret.—The practice of only gradually initiating the catechumens into the more important mysteries of Christianity, and of secrecy in speaking and writing of them, is known as the *Disciplina Arcani,* the "Discipline of the Secret." **This** practice prevailed especially during the third and fourth centuries. Origen refers to the Eucharist as a "certain holy body." A very ancient Greek inscription discovered at Autun in France in 1839 reads in part as follows: "Take the food sweet as honey of the Savior of the holy ones and eat it hungrily, holding the fish in thy hands." These words were intelligible to Christians, among whom the *fish* meant "Jesus Christ, Son of God, Savior," but mere jargon to those outside the Church. Since both Justin and Tertullian speak very openly of the Creed and the Eucharist, the Discipline of the Secret must not have been as binding as some historians think it was. But to return to the candidates for Baptism.

Tertullian tells us that the catechumens were required to make a solemn renunciation of Satan and all his works, and pomps, and wicked angels. They then recited the Creed and the Our Father and descended into the *piscina.* Baptism was administered by triple immersion, but in case of necessity aspersion or infusion were also allowed. The minister of Baptism was the Bishop, who was assisted by priests and deacons, and in the case of women by deaconesses. *The Sacrament of Confirmation* was conferred immediately after Baptism, as is still done in the Eastern Churches. In the Apostolic Age there was no special time set apart for Baptism; later on, however, it was solemnly administered only on Holy Saturday. On the Sunday after Easter—*Dominica in Albis,* "White Sunday"—the neophytes (newly baptized) removed the white robes of their Baptism.

Infant Baptism was rare until the beginning of the fifth century. Perhaps it was the dread of incurring the responsibilities of the Christian life, that led many to defer their own Baptism or that of their children except in danger of death. But it was always regarded as valid and as an apostolic institution, as we know from Irenaeus, Origen and St. Cyprian. Sponsors at the Baptism of children are mentioned as early as A.D. 200 by Tertullian.

The Holy Eucharist. —By Baptism the catechumens were incorporated with the Church and henceforth enjoyed all the rights and privileges of the faithful. The greatest of these were the assistance at the whole Eucharistic Service and the reception of Holy Communion. In the Apostolic Age the Eucharistic Service took place in the evening in conjunction with the *Agape*, or love-feast, in memory of the Last Supper. In the beginning of the second century the Eucharist was transferred to the early morning hours, which gave rise to the Eucharistic fast. The *Agape* continued for a time as a separate institution; but when it became the occasion of more or less serious abuses, it was entirely abolished.

During the first three centuries the Eucharist was celebrated, as a rule, only on Sundays, but towards the end of this period we already hear of daily Mass both in Rome and in Africa. Being for the most part converts from Judaism, the first Christians,

From a fresco in the Church of San Clemente, Rome (11th cent.)
MASS IN THE EARLY CHURCH

when they ceased to frequent the synagogues, quite naturally began their assemblies with a sort of Christianized synagogue service. This consisted of readings from the Bible, sermons on what had been read, singing of psalms and hymns, public recitation of prayers, and a collection for the poor. Then followed the Eucharist proper. There were as yet no fixed prayers for this part of the service, the celebrant "giving thanks" (Eucharist is the Greek for thanksgiving) in words chosen by himself. The Consecration consisted of a prayer in memory of our Lord's passion and the words of Institution as we have them in the Mass to-day. The people answered *Amen*, and received Communion under both kinds. Deacons carried the Blessed Sacrament to those who were unable to be present. In times of persecution it was customary to keep the Sacred Species in the houses of the faithful; people even took them along with them when they went on a journey. "No one is richer," says St. Jerome, "than he who carries the Body of Christ in a little wicker basket and His Blood in a glass."

Penance.—The Church was to be a Communion of *Saints.* Those who sinned grievously were excluded from her communion, —"excommunicated." In order to gain readmission they had to submit to a long period of public penance imposed upon them by the bishop. Dressed in a distinctive penitential garb, they took their place among the catechumens in the vestibule of the church and with them left the church before the Offertory of the Mass. Absolution was given publicly by the bishop on Holy Thursday. Those who relapsed into the same sins were denied readmittance. Three sins, idolatry, murder, and adultery, were visited with perpetual excommunication. When Pope Callistus (217-222) declared that those guilty of adultery could be absolved after they had performed the prescribed penances, Tertullian and other rigorists opposed him bitterly for what they called his criminal laxity. In the second and third centuries it frequently happened that Christians who were in prison awaiting martyrdom sent "letters of peace" (*libelli pacis*) to the bishop in favor of some brother under penance for apostasy, and the bishop, if satisfied with the sinner's contrition, restored him to the peace of the Church. We also hear of Councils mitigating penances that seemed too long and severe. In the fourth century it became the established rule to give Communion in the hour of death to all penitents, however great their previous crimes may have been. The Church was so severe in her penitential discipline, because she wanted to remit not only the sins of the penitent, but *all* the punishment, eternal and temporal, due to them. For this reason the Sacrament of Penance was called in those days a "second Baptism."

Fasts and Feasts.—The early Christians fasted on Wednesdays and Fridays. These days were called *dies stationis* (station days), because, like a true soldier of Christ, the Christian "stood on guard" and touched neither food nor drink till after midday. Those who were able abstained entirely from food and drink during the two days preceding Easter, because our Lord had said: "The days will come when the bridegroom shall be taken away from them, and then they shall fast." (Matt. 9, 15). During the third century it became the custom throughout the Church to fast during the forty days before Easter. The Wednesday and Friday fast was gradually discontinued. Our Friday abstinence is all that is left of this earliest penitential practice of the Church. In the fifth century the Ember Days were introduced into the Roman Church. The East never adopted them, perhaps because from the earliest times Saturday was regarded as a holyday by the Christians of those parts.

In remembrance of the Resurrection of our Lord the first day of the week was kept holy from the days of the Apostles. In the language of the Church, Sunday, the *dies solis* of the pagans, was called the Day of the Lord, *dies Dominica*. The anniversary of the Resurrection—Easter, *Pascha*—and of the descent of the Holy Ghost—*dies Pentecostes*—are the most ancient festivals of the Church. Since both Jews and Romans began their day at six in the evening, the Christians began their Easter celebration with a *Vigil*, or all-night service, during which the catechumens received their last instructions and were baptized. Every new feast as it was introduced was preceded by a vigil.

Easter was not celebrated on the same day throughout the early Church. In Asia Minor the day of the Lord's Death and Resurrection was kept on the 14th of the month Nisan (our March-April), that is, on the same day that the Jews celebrated their Passover, no matter on what day of the week it happened to fall. Nearly everywhere else Easter was kept on the first Sunday after the first Spring full moon and never on the same day as the Jewish Passover. Hundreds of years elapsed before absolute uniformity was achieved in this matter.

Early in the third century the Feast of the *Epiphany* (Jan. 6) began to be celebrated in Egypt, whence it spread rapidly throughout the East. Its purpose was to commemorate the manifestation of Christ's glory when the Magi adored Him, at His Baptism in the Jordan, and at the wedding-feast of Cana.

Holy Places.—The religious services of the early Christians were held in private houses. The first church of which there is record is that of Edessa in Syria, erected A.D. 201. Simple as these primitive houses of worship were, they already consisted of an apse, a nave, and a vestibule. The vestibule was reserved for the catechumens and the penitents. Mass was also said, as we have seen, in the memorial chapels built over or near the remains of the martyrs, and in the catacombs. Christian art could develop to a certain extent in the narrow crypts of the catacombs, but it

THE CONFERRING OF HOLY ORDERS IN THE EARLY CHURCH

was not until freedom of worship was granted that Christian architecture began its glorious progress through the centuries.

Social Life.—Aside from the worship and discipline imposed upon them by their Religion, the daily life of the early Christians was not outwardly very different from that of their pagan neighbors. "We reject no creature of God's hands," writes Tertullian, "though certainly we exercise restraint upon ourselves, lest of any gift of His we make an immoderate or sinful use. So we sojourn with you, abjuring neither the forum, nor the shambles, nor the baths, nor the booths, inns, and fairs, nor any other places of commerce. We sail with you, and go to war with you, and till the ground with you—even in the various arts we make public property of our works for your benefit." But the Christian spirit ennobled and elevated the Christian's daily life. His family life was exemplary; unnatural sins were abhorred; divorce was unknown; the modesty of the Christian virgins excited the admiration of the great pagan philosopher-physician Galen; the chastity of the Christian young man was an inexplicable riddle to the depraved votaries of the immoral pagan rites. At a time when slaves were treated worse than cattle by their pagan masters, the Christians recognized the human dignity and the rights of their slaves and regarded their emancipation as a work pleasing to God. Justice and charity were the Christian's guide in his dealings with his fellow-men. At a time when usury was rampant and the prisons were filled with its victims, the Christians neither gave nor took interest.

Asceticism.—In all parts of the Church there were numerous Ascetes, that is, men and women who sought the secret of the more perfect life in the practice of the evangelical counsels. They lived in perpetual poverty and chastity, prayed and fasted much and practised other austerities. They considered it their duty to visit and assist the sick, the poor and the prisoners. The great Origen was a perfect model of the ascetical life, and many of his friends and pupils followed his example. From the earliest times young women consecrated their virginity to God. In the third century this was done solemnly in the presence of the bishop, from whom they received the veil which they wore whenever they appeared in public. They enjoyed universal esteem, and at the religious services places of honor were reserved for them. St. Cyprian calls the consecrated virgins the "élite of the faithful, who have found the pearl of great price and though still living on the earth belong to the family of the Angels." During the Decian persecution Paul, a rich young man of Thebes in Egypt, retired to a cave at the foot of a mountain and for ninety years led the life of a *hermit*. He spent his days in prayer and contemplation; a palm-tree furnished him with food and clothing. Shortly before his death (A.D. 340) he was visited by St. Anthony, the "Father of Monasticism," an institution which was to play such an important part in the subsequent history of the Church. In these men and women the spirit triumphed over the flesh, grace over nature, the divine power of Christianity over a world steeped in vice and luxury.

An Early Christian Instruction on Baptism and the Holy Eucharist

In the Didache, (or "Teaching of the Twelve Apostles," as it styles itself), an early Christian manual written probably before the end of the first century, we find the following instruction on Baptism and the Holy Eucharist:

"Baptize in the name of the Father, and of the Son, and of the Holy Ghost in living (i.e., flowing) water. If you have no living water, use other water. If you cannot baptize in cold water, do so in warm water. If you have neither, pour water three times over the head in the name of the Father, and of the Son, and of the Holy Ghost. Before Baptism the minister as well as the person to be baptized, and others, too, if they can, should fast; but you must command the person who is to be baptized to fast for one or two days before the Baptism takes place.

"On the Lord's Day assemble together and break bread and give thanks, having confessed your transgressions, in order that your sacrifice be not defiled. For this is that sacrifice which was spoken of by the Lord: 'In every place and time offer Me a pure sacrifice: for I am a great King, saith the Lord, and My Name is wonderful among the nations.' "

—Didache, IV, VII.

A Eucharistic Service in Rome, A.D. 150

"On the day called Sunday there is a meeting of all who live in town or country, and the memoirs of the Apostles or the writings of the prophets are read, as long as time allows. Then when the reader has ceased, the president delivers a discourse in which he admonishes and exhorts all present to imitate these excellent things. Then we all rise together and send up prayers. And when we have ceased from prayers, bread and a cup of water and tempered wine is brought to the president of the brethren, and he takes it and sends up praise and glory to the Father of all things through the name of the Son and of the Holy Spirit, and gives thanks at great length for our having received these favors from Him. When he has completed the prayers and the thanksgiving, the whole people present responds, saying 'Amen.' Now the word Amen in the Hebrew language signifies 'So be it.' When the president has given thanks and all the people have responded, the deacons, as we call them, give to each of those present to partake of the consecrated bread and wine and water, and they take some away for the absent.

"And this food is with us called *Eucharist,* and it is not lawful for any man to partake of it but him who believes our teaching to be true, and has been washed with the washing which is for the forgiveness of sins, and unto a new birth, and lives as Christ commanded. For it is not as common bread or common drink that we receive these, but as by God's word Jesus Christ our Savior became flesh and blood for our salvation, so also we have been taught that the food made Eucharist by the word of prayer that comes from Him is both Flesh and Blood of that Jesus who was made flesh. For the Apostles in the memoirs which they composed, which are called Gospels, have thus recorded that they were given command—that Jesus took bread and gave thanks and said 'Do this in remembrance of Me; this is my Body'; and took the cup likewise and gave thanks and said, 'This is My Blood,' and gave of it only to them. . . ."

—Justin Martyr, *First Apology*, 65-67.

Hints for Study

1. Read Matt. 7, 6. Do you think these words of our Lord had anything to do with the introduction of the *Discipline of the Secret?*
2. What is meant by a *Vigil* in the liturgy of to-day? How does it differ from a Vigil in the early Church?
3. What is the difference between a *catechumen* and a *neophyte?* Where do we still hear of catechumens and catechumenate?
4. Describe the life of a Roman Christian of the third century (call him Maximus) : *a.* his conversion; *b.* preparation for Baptism; *c.* Baptism, Confirmation, First Communion; *d.* his daily life as a Christian; *e.* he commits a grievous sin; he does penance; a Christian awaiting martyrdom intercedes for him; he is absolved and readmitted into the Church; *f.* he falls into the same grievous sin; *g.* his death and burial.
5. In the selection from St. Justin's First Apology the following expression may have puzzled the reader : "And when we have ceased from prayers, *bread* and *a cup of water* and *tempered wine* is brought to the president of the brethren, and he takes it. . . ." Why the *two* chalices, one with water, the other with tempered wine; that is, wine mixed with water? The purpose of the second is evident. The reason for the first is simple enough: the Mass described by St. Justin is a Baptismal Mass; that is, a Mass following the administration of Baptism. At such Masses, in Justin's time, *two* chalices were used, the first containing water, the second wine mixed with water. The neophytes drank of the water to add, as it were, an inner washing to the external one which had just taken place: "the inner man, who is a living soul, was to receive what the outer man had already received." Later on, a third chalice was added, filled with milk and honey. Drinking of this symbolized the neophytes' entrance into the Church, the Promised Land, flowing with milk and honey. (See Albert Ehrhard, *Die Kirche der Märtyrer. Ihre Aufgaben und Ihre Leistungen.* Koesel and Pustet, Munich, 1932, pp. 334-335.)

From the Decree of Milan to the Beginning of the Pontificate of Gregory the Great, A.D. 313-590

Character of this Period. —By the Decree of Milan Christianity secured freedom and legal recognition. Placed at first on an equal footing with paganism, it became in time the official religion of the Empire. Although the days of bloody persecution were past, dangers and obstacles threatened her both from within and from without. Julian the Apostate's attempt to revive the dying paganism of ancient Rome was, it is true, only an episode, a "little cloud that hurried by"; but the Arian heresy was a raging flood to which the indefectible Church of God seemed for a time to have succumbed. Whilst the Church was fighting against heresy and schism for the truth and life given to her by her Divine Founder, countless barbarians poured in upon both Empire and Christendom. It is the age of the great heresies and heresiarchs, of the great Councils and the great Fathers and Doctors of the Church, of the Migration of the Nations and the Decline and Fall of the Roman Empire of the West.

CHAPTER I

THE ROMAN EMPIRE BECOMES CHRISTIAN

1. *Constantine and His Sons*

Constantine's Attitude towards Christianity.—The Decree of Milan was based on the principle of religious tolerance. Complete freedom of worship was guaranteed to pagans and Christians alike, and Constantine saw to it that the rights conceded to the Christians did not remain a dead letter. By a series of enactments the clergy were exempted from taxation and from all municipal functions; the churches were empowered to receive donations and legacies; public business and servile work were forbidden on Sunday, the Christian holyday, to both Christians and pagans, and crucifixion was abolished as a penalty. Personally Constantine inclined more and more towards Christianity. He began to take an active interest in ecclesiastical affairs and greatly enhanced the influence of the bishops. He no longer took part in pagan worship, though he still retained the dignity of *Pontifex Maximus* (pagan high priest) and exercised the rights and duties connected with this office.

Licinius, who ruled over the eastern half of the Empire, did not carry out the provisions of the Decree of Milan. He never made a secret of his hostility to the Christians, but it was not until 321 that he began an active persecution, which was especially directed against the bishops and the clergy. In the spring of 324

Mosaic of Xth Cent., Church of St. John Lateran

St. Peter and Constantine Receiving Their Powers From Jesus Christ

he declared war on Constantine. He was twice defeated, once at Adrianople and afterwards before the walls of Byzantium, and was finally captured at Nicomedia. His life was spared, and he was interned at Thessalonica, where he was executed in the following year on the charge of treasonable correspondence with the enemies of the Empire.

Constantine now reigned as sole emperor in East and West. Though he still put off the reception of Baptism, he manifested in various ways his love and veneration for the Christian religion. At Rome, Nicomedia, Antioch, Tyre, and Jerusalem he built magnificent churches and endowed them with rich gifts of money and landed property. The official life was gradually shorn of its pagan character. Pagan symbols disappeared from the coinage, and the monogram of Christ became a prominent device; all licentious and cruel pagan rites were prohibited; the highest offices in the State were conferred upon Christians. The Emperor's personal attitude towards paganism was one of contemptuous toleration, and he openly expressed his desire that all his subjects should embrace the Christian Religion.

The Founding of Constantinople.—In 326 Constantine carried out his long-cherished plan of removing the seat of empire from Rome to the East. Sardica and Troy were considered before his choice fell on Byzantium. The site was admirably suited for an imperial residence, being on the threshold of Asia, which was constantly threatened by the Persians, and within easy reach of the Danube, where the northern barbarians were always swarming. Before the end of the year the foundation-stone of Constantinople was laid, and on the 11th of May, 330, the new city, which equaled Rome in splendor and was soon to surpass it in population and wealth, was solemnly dedicated to the Blessed Virgin.

It is very probable, says a modern historian of Rome, that the founding of Constantinople was connected with Constantine's decision to make Christianity the official religion of the Empire. Rome was naturally the stronghold of paganism, to which the great majority of the senate clung with fervent devotion. Constantine did not wish to do open violence to this sentiment, and therefore resolved to found a new capital for the new empire of his creation.

The founding of Constantinople is one of the turning points of history—not in itself, but in its consequences. By transferring the center of gravity, as it were, of the Empire to the East, the emperors prolonged the existence of a part at least of the old Roman world and its civilization for many centuries, and thus saved the precious relics of Roman Law and Greek science, literature and art until the new nations of the West were ready to receive them. For the Church the consequences were more far-reaching still. By fixing their residence in the East, the emperors practically gave up Rome to the Popes, with the result that the Church in the West could develop more freely and exercise its spiritual authority without too much interference on the part of the secular power; whereas in the East the emperors allowed themselves to be drawn more and more deeply into the religious controversies which followed one another in rapid succession, and by throwing the weight of the imperial power now on one side and now on the other, prolonged them almost indefinitely. As the rule of the emperors became more despotic, the Church in the East lost every semblance of real independence. Under the circumstances it was inevitable that the two sections of the Church should draw farther and farther apart. It is not too much to say that the estrangement between the East and the West, which culminated in the great Eastern Schism, was begun on the day when Constantine laid the foundation-stone of New Rome on the shores of the Bosporus.

Death of Constantine.—In 336 Sapor II of Persia declared war on Constantine. The Emperor was preparing to lead his army in person against him when he was taken ill, and after a vain trial of the mineral waters at Helenopolis, died at Nicomedia, on the 22nd of May, 337. On his deathbed he received Baptism at the hands of his friend Eusebius, the Arian bishop of the city. One of his last acts was to recall several persons whom he had unjustly exiled; his last words were a prayer of praise and thanksgiving to God. His remains were buried in the great church of the Apostles which he had built at Constantinople. The Greek Church honors him as a saint; the Roman Church, while refusing him this distinction, has always revered him as her liberator from the iron hand of pagan Rome, and has joined with the East in giving him the title of "Great"—not so much in virtue of what he was, for he was by no means a model Christian ruler—but rather in virtue of what he did for Christianity and the world.

First Systematic Attempts to Abolish Paganism.—Of the three sons of Constantine, Constantius reigned longest (337-361); during the last ten years of his life he governed the whole Empire. He did all in his power to abolish paganism and to propagate Christianity. "The accursed tolerance shall cease," he declared in one of his edicts. He prohibited all heathen sacrifices under penalty of death and in 353, after his victory over the pagan usurper Magnentius, ordered all the pagan temples to be closed, dismantled, or converted to other purposes. These severe measures did not have the desired effect; they only gave dying paganism a new lease of life. By a strange inconsistency Constantius permitted those arch-enemies of Christianity, the pagan rhetoricians, sophists, and Neo-Platonic philosophers to teach in all the higher institutions of learning throughout the Empire. These men exhausted all their ingenuity to arrest the progress of the Christian religion. How much harm they did, appears from numerous examples mentioned in the writings of the Fathers, and especially from the apostasy of Julian, the successor of Constantius, who was seduced by men of this stamp. During his reign a short but sharp pagan reaction set in.

2. *Julian the Apostate and the Pagan Reaction*

How Julian Became an Apostate.—Julian was the youngest son of Julius Constantius, the half-brother of Constantine the Great. In the general massacre of the younger line of the Flavian family (the family of Constantine, who was called Flavius Constantinus) after the death of Constantine, Julian was spared because of his extreme youth. The remembrance of the murder of his father and brothers, a remembrance which his pagan tutor Mardonios took care to keep alive, caused Julian to hate Christianity, the faith professed by the perpetrators of these wrongs. Therefore, though instructed in the Christian religion and baptized, he readily accepted the heathen philosophy of his teacher. Grown to manhood, he pursued his studies at Athens, where he openly joined the Neo-Platonic school of philosophers, which was notorious for its opposition to Christianity. In 355 he was summoned to Milan to assume the rank of Caesar and the command of the armies of Gaul and Italy.

Julian Becomes Emperor. The Pagan Reaction.—Julian was successful in his wars against the Franks and the Alemanni, who had invaded the Gallic provinces. In addition to displaying unexpected capacities as a general, he showed himself a forceful and upright administrator, and thereby won the admiration of the people and the army. Therefore, when Constantius ordered away his best troops to serve against the Persians, all his soldiers revolted and proclaimed Julian emperor (April, 360). With 3,000 picked troops he set out for Constantinople. On the way he heard of the sudden death of Constantius. He immediately proclaimed himself both emperor and pagan, sacrificed to the gods, and ordered the dismantled pagan temples to be rebuilt. These measures were soon followed by more drastic ones. He forbade the Christians to teach classical literature in their schools, forced them to surrender many pagan shrines which they had occupied, deprived the clergy of their immunities, and stimulated a literary war against Christianity in which he himself took a prominent part. He next attempted to combat Christianity with its own weapons, and tried to establish a universal pagan church with a clergy and liturgy on the Christian model. He also sought to vitalize paganism by infusing into it the morality and missionary zeal of Christianity. But all his efforts were of no avail; paganism in any form had lost its appeal for the masses, and the only converts were those who sought the imperial favor by abandoning the Christian religion.

In July, 362, Julian went to war with the Persians, establishing at Antioch his base of campaign. While here he thought to confute the prophecy of Christ (Matt. 24, 2) by rebuilding the Temple of Jerusalem. The attempt was a failure. Whilst the work of laying the foundation was in progress, relates the pagan historian Ammianus Marcellinus (XXIII, 1, 3), "fearful globes of fire, bursting forth repeatedly from the earth close to the foundations, scorched the workmen, and rendered the place, after frequent trials on their part, quite inaccessible."

After long preparations Julian began his attack on the Persians early in 363 A.D. After some notable successes, he was compelled to retreat. On the march up the Tigris valley he was mortally wounded in a skirmish with the Persian cavalry. As he was falling from his horse and saw the blood spurting from the wound, he is said to have exclaimed: "Thou hast conquered, O Galilean." (Theodoret, *Ecclesiastical History*, III, 25). With his death the pagan interlude came to an end.

3. *From Julian to Justinian*

Extinction of Paganism.—Under Julian's successor, the mild and prudent Jovian (363-364), Christianity was re-established as the religion of the Empire, and the Labarum of Constantine again became the standard of the army; against the pagans, however, no measures of repression were enacted. The same policy was pursued by Jovian's successors, Valentinian I (364-375) in the West, and his brother Valens (364-378) in the East. Under the following emperors energetic steps were again taken for the complete suppression of paganism. Gratian (375-383) refused to wear

From an old Mosaic.
THE EMPEROR JUSTINIAN

the insignia of the Pontifex Maximus as unbefitting a Christian. He removed the altar of the goddess of Victory from the senate-house in spite of the remonstrances of the pagan members of the senate; forbade legacies of real property to the Vestal Virgins, and abolished all the privileges of the heathen priests.

Theodosius the Great (379-395), a highly cultured, thoroughly Christian ruler, who towards the end of his life for the last time united all the provinces of the Empire under one scepter, forbade all pagan sacrifices and ordered all the temples "throughout the world" to be closed forever. The Catholic faith was declared to be the faith of the Empire, and no other was to be tolerated. Paganism celebrated a short-lived triumph in the West when the young emperor Valentinian II was murdered (392) at the instigation of Arbogast, a Frankish officer in the Roman army, and the pagan grammarian Eugenius was set up in his stead. After a reign of two years Eugenius was defeated by Theodosius and slain by his own soldiers near Aquileia in North Italy; Arbogast committed suicide. From this time on, paganism steadily declined. In the year 423 the emperor Theodosius II declared that there were hardly any pagans left in his dominions.

The emperor Justinian the Great (527-565) took away all civil rights from the unbaptized, and in 529 closed the philosophical schools of Athens, the last stronghold of paganism. In the remote country districts the ancient gods were, however, still worshiped for a century or more. The last pagans were converted on the islands of Sardinia and Corsica through the efforts of Pope Gregory the Great.

4. The Church and the Christianization of the Empire

It is evident that the imperial edicts in favor of the Christian religion and the continued efforts of the emperors to discourage and suppress paganism were largely responsible for the rapid Christianization of the Empire. Yet no one who knows the history of this period will ascribe the expansion of Christianity to these causes alone. The untiring zeal of the bishops and of other holy and learned men, the pure and devout lives which so many of the faithful exhibited, and the manifest truth and beauty of the Christian religion itself were far more efficient motives with all honest and sincere pagans for joining the Church than all the pressure brought to bear on them by the secular power. It may be justly doubted whether all the imperial laws put together were directly responsible for even one true conversion. The wholesale conversions effected by these laws created a gigantic problem for the Church. She had to try to make true Christians of these pagans of yesterday. Such a work of regeneration could not be accomplished in a decade or two; it was hardly begun when it was interrupted by the barbarian invasions, which put an end to the Roman Empire in the West. The Church was, moreover, hampered in her efforts by numerous religious controversies and heresies in her own fold, which taxed all her energies for more than a hundred years. And yet during all this time she did not forget the task given her by her Divine Founder of preaching the Gospel to all nations.

5. Christianity beyond the Borders of the Empire

Christianity in Persia.—The most dangerous enemies of the Empire in the East were the Persians, who in the fourth century occupied all the lands between the Caspian Sea and the Euphrates, as well as the southeastern portion of Mesopotamia. In this vast domain a number of flourishing Christian communities had been established in the course of the third century. Mares, the first bishop of Seleucia, is said to have erected more than three hundred churches. As long as the Christians were persecuted by the Roman emperors, they were left unmolested by the Persian kings; but when Constantius undertook to suppress paganism in his dominions, a long and cruel persecution was begun against the Christians in those of his neighbor. Sapor II (310-380) commanded all the Christians to worship the Sun and to accept the religion of the "king of kings," or pay with their lives for their "madness." Bishop Simeon of Seleucia was the first victim; with him died nearly a hundred of his priests. Then thousands of Christians of every age and condition were tortured and executed. The Greek historian Sozomen says that the names of 16,000 Persian martyrs were on record in his day. By a refinement of cruelty, those who denied the faith were compelled to be the executioners of those who remained faithful. But there were very few apostates. Ustazades, an aged courtier, who in a moment of weakness had renounced his faith, afterwards repented and was immediately led off to death. As a last favor he asked the executioner to proclaim publicly that he was suffering death not because he was a traitor to his country, but because he was a Christian.

During the reign of Isdegerdes I the Christians enjoyed a long period of peace. They were permitted to practice their religion openly and to rebuild their churches. The imprudent zeal of Abdas, bishop of Susa, who in 418 set fire to the temple of the sun-god Ormuzd, was the signal for a second general persecution. Abdas was beheaded and thousands of Christians shared the same fate. Bahram V (420-438) was the most barbarous of all the Persian persecutors. His favorite manner of punishing the Christians was to have them sawed in pieces. Jacob Beth-Lapat, general of the Persians under Isdegerdes, had bartered his faith for the royal favor. When the persecution under Bahram broke out, he boldly proclaimed himself a Christian and was ordered by the tyrant to have his arms and legs sawed off. He is known as the *Megalomartyr*, the great martyr, of the Persians. During the reign of Bahram the Nestorian heresy (see p. 153) invaded Persia, found favor at court, and gradually perverted the Christian remnant from the true faith.

Armenia, the First Christian Nation.—St. Gregory, surnamed *Illuminator*, is the Apostle of the Armenians. As a little child he was saved by his nurse from the general massacre of the royal family of the Arsacids to which he belonged, and educated in the Christian Religion at Caesarea in Cappadocia. On his return to his native land (A.D. 286) he succeeded in converting King Tiridates III, most of the nobility and great numbers of the people to the Christian faith. By royal decree Christianity was declared the religion of the State. Thus, the honor of having been the first Christian nation belongs to the Armenians. A rich Christian literature began to develop about the year 400, when St. Mesrop invented the Armenian alphabet and translated the Bible and many Greek writings into the Armenian language. When the greater part of Armenia became a Persian province in the fifth century, the Armenians vigorously and successfully resisted every attempt to supplant Christianity by the Fire-worship (Parsism) of the Persians. Nestorianism tried in vain to gain entrance; but unfortunately, towards the end of the fifth century, the whole nation drifted into the Monophysite heresy.

Conversion of the Abyssinians.—In the year 316 Meropius, a Christian philosopher of Tyre in Phoenicia, undertook a voyage of exploration along the coast of Africa. In his company were two boys, Frumentius and Aedesius, whose education had been entrusted to him. The vessel was stranded on the coast of Abyssinia and attacked by a band of natives, who slew all the travelers except Frumentius and Aedesius, whom they brought to the royal palace at Axum. Here the youths were not only treated kindly, but also given positions of trust at the Court. They remained faithful to their religion, practiced it as best they could, and soon made conversions amongst the officials and even in the household of the king. After the death of the sovereign, Frumentius was appointed regent of the realm by the queen, and instructor of her young son. Some years later Aedesius returned to Tyre, where he entered the priesthood. About the same time (340) Frumentius went to Alexandria in Egypt in order to consult with St. Athanasius on the future of Christianity in Abyssinia. It was decided that a bishop should be sent to that country, and as Athanasius insisted that no one was better fitted for this office than Frumentius himself, he received episcopal consecration and immediately returned to Axum to begin the work of organization and to continue the work of evangelization. He baptized King Aizana and many of his subjects. Constantius tried in vain to win him over to the Arian heresy (see p. 104). Frumentius lived and died in the true faith and is numbered amongst the saints of the Church. But the Abyssinians escaped one heresy only to fall into another. About a hundred years after the death of their apostle they adopted Monophysism (see p. 155) to which Alexandria and all Egypt had also succumbed. Cut off from the center of unity and orthodoxy and left, by their political and geographical isolation, to their own resources, they evolved in the course of the centuries that curious medley of Christianity, Judaism, paganism, and Mohammedanism which is their religion today.

How the Christians Resisted Julian the Apostate

When Julian was at Antioch in 362 he ordered the great church which Constantine had built to be closed. During the translation of the remains of St. Babylas, the martyr-bishop of their city, the Christians sang the words of the 96th Psalm: "Let them all be confounded that adore graven things, and that glory in their idols." At the same time Julian ordered the temple of Apollo in Daphne, which the Christians had burned down, to be restored and the pagan sacrifices to be resumed; but only one pagan priest could be found to do honor to the god, and he could obtain only a goose to sacrifice to him.

One day as Julian was passing through the streets of Antioch he heard the Deaconess Publia with her band of consecrated virgins singing the words: "The idols of the Gentiles are silver and gold, the works of the hands of men. Let them that make them become like unto them." The enraged Emperor ordered them to stop, but they forthwith intoned the 67th Psalm: "Let God arise, and let His enemies be scattered," whereupon he commanded the fearless matron to be publicly maltreated.

When Julian asked the aged and blind bishop Maris of Chalcedon whether he thought that his Galilean God would heal him of his infirmity, the man of God replied: "I thank God for having permitted me to become blind, so that I do not have to look upon the face of an apostate."

A few days before Julian's death, his friend, the pagan sophist Libanius, asked a Christian what the Carpenter's Son was doing; to which the Christian replied: "He is making a winding-sheet for your master."

—St. John Chrysostom, *Homily on St. Babylas.*
—Theodoret, *Eccl. Hist., III,* 6, 14, 18.

Hints for Study

1. Draw up a chronological table showing the steps taken by Constantine the Great and his successors to Christianize the Roman Empire.
2. Compare the persecution of the Christians by the pagan emperors with the persecution of the pagans by the Christian emperors.
3. What was the real cause of the rapid decline of paganism?
4. Why was Julian's attempt to revive paganism doomed to failure from the outset?
5. Was the great influx of pagans into the Church an unmixed benefit?
6. The founding of Constantinople by Constantine has been called a "stroke of genius"; why?
7. Read the articles on *Persia, Armenia,* and *Abyssinia* in the *Catholic Encyclopedia.*

CHAPTER II

THE CHURCH IN CONFLICT WITH HERESY

Cardinal Newman calls the eventful fourth century a drama in three acts, "each marvelous in itself, each different from the other two." The first act, the Roman Empire becoming Christian, we have just passed in review; we now come to the second, the conflict of the Church with Arianism and the heresies that followed in its wake. We can do no more than give a brief outline of this momentous struggle.

A. *Arianism*

1. *The Forerunners of Arius*

The Trinity and the Incarnation are the fundamental doctrines of Christianity. The Church has always believed that Christ is both true God and true Man. The opening words of the oldest Christian sermon that has come down to us, by their very simplicity, bear eloquent witness to this faith: "Brethren, we must so think of Jesus Christ as of God, as of the Judge of the living and the dead" (Homily wrongly ascribed to St. Clement of Rome). In the same matter-of-fact manner St. Ignatius of Antioch writes to the Romans: "Suffer me to be an imitator of my God's sufferings," and in his letter to the Ephesians he speaks of "God's Blood." The early Christians drew the consequences from their faith and paid divine honors to Christ. Pliny, as we have seen, informs the Emperor Trajan that the Christians of Bithynia were wont "to sing hymns to Christ as a God"; and we must remember that most of these Christians had received the faith from the Apostles themselves or their immediate disciples. Later on it became the fashion in Rome and elsewhere to deride the Christians for worshiping a crucified God. One of the rude scratchings on the walls of a Roman palace on the Palatine represents a man with the head of a donkey upon a cross, while another stands by his side in prayer to him.   It is inscribed, "Alexamenos worships his god."

Such was the faith of the Church from the beginning, the faith of the Apostles and their disciples, of the Martyrs and the Confessors; and it was in keeping with this faith when Pope St. Victor, in the last decade of the second century excommunicated Theodotus the leather-dealer for declaring that Christ was a mere man. This Theodotus, we are told, was the first to deny the divinity of Christ.   Both before and after him many Christian teachers, who had no intention of departing from the faith of the Church, set themselves to inquire in what sense was Christ God?   Was He God as the Father was God?   Was He of the same substance and nature as the Father, eternal as the Father, and equal to Him in power and glory?   In other words, they began to *speculate*, to reason on the mysteries of the faith; they endeavored to reconcile the apparent contradictions which they involve, in order to recommend them as reasonable to those outside the Church.   In their speculations they often used inaccurate language, and some of them even introduced theories that were absolutely erroneous.

Sabellius, an African, and his followers in the third century denied that there were three distinct Persons in God: the Persons, they said, were only like stage characters assumed on different occasions to represent the Godhead to men.   This doctrine was rejected by the whole Church because it was clearly opposed to Scripture and Tradition.   In his anxiety to establish the distinction between the Divine Persons, St. Dionysius of Alexandria, in the year 260, asserted that the Son was "made by God," and "did not exist till He was made"; in other words, he *subordinated* the Son to the Father, just as Justin Martyr and Origen had done before him.   As soon as it became known in Rome that Dionysius was holding such views, his namesake Pope Dionysius summoned a synod and issued a memorable document to the bishops of Egypt and Libya.   "Had the Son," writes the Pope, "been created, there would have been a time when He was not; but the Son always was."   Thereupon, the bishop of Alexandria, in two letters which he sent to Rome, explained away his former inaccurate language, and distinctly confessed the Son's eternity.   About the same time, Paul of Samosata, bishop of Antioch, taught that Christ was not the real, but only the *adopted* Son of God. He was condemned and deposed by a council of bishops which met at Antioch in 269.

Paul of Samosata was a heretic, because he taught a false doctrine, and *obstinately* persisted in holding it, even after it had been condemned by the Church. *Obstinacy* is the distinctive note of the heretic. St. Dionysius of Alexandria was not a heretic.

Lucian, the founder of the great school of theology and Holy Scripture at Antioch, was a disciple of Paul of Samosata and imbibed some of his master's errors concerning the Trinity and the relation of the Son to the Father. He held that the Son was subordinate to the Father, and that Christ was neither perfect God nor perfect man. Lucian died a martyr's death in 311. His most noted pupils were Eusebius of Nicomedia and *Arius,* a native of Egypt or Libya.

2. *The Rise of Arianism*

Arius was still a layman, or at most in Minor Orders, when he settled down in Alexandria in the first decade of the third century. Bishop Peter raised him to deaconship, but was forced to excommunicate him soon afterwards for supporting a turbulent schismatic party called the Meletians after the Egyptian bishop of that name. Peter was martyred in 311, and his successor Achillas not only freed Arius from the sentence of excommunication, but also ordained him priest and put him in charge of one of the great churches of the city, which bore the name of Baucalis. Arius is described as very tall and thin. "His dress and demeanor were those of a rigid ascetic. He always wore a long coat with short sleeves, and a scarf of only half size, such as was the mark of an austere life; and his hair hung in a tangled mass over his head. There was a wild look about him, which at first sight was startling. He was usually silent, but at times broke out into fierce excitement, which gave the impression of madness. Yet with all this there was a sweetness in his voice and a winning, earnest manner which fascinated those who came across him." His reputation for sanctity, learning and eloquence, coupled with his skill in disputation, soon made him the center of religious thought and activity in the second church of Christendom. He might have done a great work in the Church; but, inflamed by his own opiniativeness, by

pride and ambition, he proved a curse from which she suffered
long and cruelly.

Alexander, the successor of Achillas, held Arius in high repute,
until suddenly, in 318 or 319, on the occasion of a clerical conference at which the bishop presided, Arius threw off the mask
and revealed his true character. He had been informed, the
bishop said, that erroneous opinions concerning the Trinity were
being disseminated in the city, and that Arius was one of the chief
offenders; he had called the conference in order to give the priest
of the Baucalis church an opportunity to justify himself. Arius
arose and briefly exposed his views on the question at issue: "If
the Son is a real Son," he said, "then a Father must exist before
a Son; therefore the Divine Father must have existed before the
Divine Son. Therefore there was a time when the Son did not
exist. Therefore He is a creature; the greatest indeed and the
eldest of all creatures and Himself a God, but still created; therefore, like all creatures, of an essence or substance (Greek *ousia*)
which previously had not existed."

Alexander, on his part, set forth the true Catholic doctrine and
commanded Arius to retract his blasphemous assertions. Deeply
wounded in his pride, Arius persisted in his error. He accused his
bishop of being a Gnostic and a Sabellian, and posed as the champion of pure doctrine against heresy. Blinded by obstinacy, he
did not see that his own brand of monotheism "was hardly to be
distinguished from that of the pagan philosophers, and that his
Christ was nothing but a Greek demi-god."

3. *Arianism Spreads*

From this time on, events followed one another to a speedy
conclusion. Arius wrote to several bishops in Greece and Asia
Minor, who like him had passed through the school of Lucian, and
asked them to examine his enclosed profession of faith and to
intercede for him with Alexander. The most influential of his
friends was Eusebius, bishop of Nicomedia, a kinsman of the
Emperor Constantine. On him Arius especially set his hopes, and
he was not disappointed; for Eusebius entered the lists energetically in his behalf and sought to win as many bishops as possible
for his old school-fellow. What had been a local controversy thus

became an affair that concerned the whole Empire. Nine bishops, two of them suffragans of Alexandria, seven priests and twelve deacons of the episcopal city, and seven hundred consecrated virgins openly sided with Arius.

Alexander too was active. When he saw that all his efforts to bring Arius to his senses were fruitless, he summoned the bishops of his province to a synod (A.D. 320). Nearly a hundred responded and unanimously anathematized Arius and his adherents. Still Arius would not submit. He continued his propaganda more vigorously than ever, and even went so far as to arouse the pagan rabble of the city against his opponents. Alexander then called another synod, which, by a circular letter, made known the excommunication of Arius and his followers to all the bishops of the world.

Arius now left Egypt, repairing first to Palestine, where he succeeded in deceiving several bishops, then to Nicomedia, the residence of his powerful friend Eusebius. From here he propagated his false teachings by means of a book, written partly in prose and partly in verse, which he called *Thalia* ("a goodly banquet"), and with greater success still through numerous hymns and songs intended for the common people. When about this time Licinius renewed the persecution of the Christians in the East, Arius took advantage of the general confusion which ensued and returned to Alexandria.

Licinius was defeated in 323. Constantine, the official protector of the Church, was sole emperor. His first care was to secure the unity and harmony of his vast empire, and he realized at once how dangerous religious dissensions might prove to this ideal. Through Hosius, the influential bishop of Cordova (Spain), his personal friend and adviser, he sent a letter to Alexander and Arius, bidding them cease disturbing the peace of the Church, at the same time giving them to understand that such questions, the meaning of which could be grasped only by the few, had better not be brought into public discussion. This well-meaning attempt at reconciliation, betraying as it did no very deep understanding of the tremendous importance of the issue, came to nothing. On the advice of Hosius, and with the active concurrence of Pope Sylvester, Constantine then summoned a synod of all the bishops of the Church in the imperial palace at Nicaea in Bithynia.

4. *The Council of Nicaea*

When the First Oecumenical Council was opened on the 20th of May, 325, the number of bishops present was 250; before it held its last session this number had grown to 318. Each bishop was accompanied by two priests or deacons, and in many cases by several clerics of inferior rank. These took no active part in

THE FIRST COUNCIL OF NICAEA

the deliberations of the Council, but some of them, especially Athanasius, the archdeacon of Alexandria, were prominent in private conferences and semi-public disputations.

"From all the churches which are spread over Europe, Africa and Asia, the most renowned servants of God came together," writes Eusebius of Caesarea in his *Life of Constantine* (III, 7). "One house of prayer received them all: Syrians and Cilicians, Phoenicians and Arabians, Palestinians and Egyptians, Thebans and Libyans, as well as the men from Mesopotamia. There also appeared at the Synod a Persian bishop, and a Scythian was not missing. Pontus and Galatia, Pamphylia and Cappadocia, Asia Minor and Phrygia had sent the flower of their episcopacy. Yea, Thracians also, and Macedonians, Achaeans and Epirotes, and such as lived much farther away still, were present. Even from Spain a world-renowned man (Hosius of Cordova) took his place with the multitude of the others in the assembly. The Supreme Bishop, however, of the Imperial City (Pope Sylvester) was prevented by the infirmities of old age from coming; but his priests appeared and represented him." Hosius of Cordova, as the legate of the Pope, and the Roman priests Vitus and Vincent—precursors of the later cardinals—presided at the Council.

The Emperor opened the first session with a discourse, a summary of which has been preserved by Eusebius. "I consider dissension in the Church," he said, "more dreadful and more painful than any other war. When I had triumphed, with the help of God, over all my enemies, I believed there remained nothing for me to do but to unite with you in returning thanks to God. But when I heard of your dissensions, I was convinced that this matter required my attention before all others, and therefore, in the hope of being of some service to you, I called you together to this meeting." As soon as the Emperor's address had been translated into Greek, the Council was formally opened by Hosius of Cordova. Constantine was present at all the sessions, but only as an interested listener and, when the occasion required it, as an authoritative peacemaker.

The Emperor's intervention was occasionally required. Feeling ran high at times, and the vast majority were incensed at the endless quibblings and subterfuges of the followers of Arius and Eusebius. An Arian profession of faith was first brought forward and read. It aroused such a storm of indignation that an immediate condemnation of Arius seemed imminent. But as the great Council had not met merely to pronounce sentence against Arius, it was necessary to define its position with reference to the controversy by means of a clear-cut statement of the Catholic faith in the Divinity of Christ.

Several symbols of faith (creeds) were presented, but none was found acceptable, because none unequivocally professed the essential unity of the Father and the Son. It was proposed to introduce the word *homo-ousios*, which means "of the same essence or substance." Eusebius of Nicomedia objected that it was a technical term not found in Scripture. But his objection was overruled: for if Scripture is interpreted in different ways, the Catholics rightly maintained, the Church must explain Scripture by a term outside it. The word *homo-ousios* (Latin: *consubstantialis*) was therefore eagerly taken up as just the word wanted: and from that moment it became the watchword of the Catholics

Dürer

THE HOLY TRINITY

In this painting executed in 1511, the artist portrays the adoration of the Holy Trinity by various classes of the blessed in heaven and the hierarchy and laity on earth, the latter led by the Pope and the Emperor.

in their struggle against Arianism. Constantine himself advised its insertion in the Creed.

On June the 19th, 325, after nearly four weeks of deliberation, the deacon Hermogenes, who acted as secretary of the Council, read the Creed which had finally been agreed upon and has since been known as the *Nicene Creed*. Literally translated, it reads as follows:

"We believe in One God, the Father Almighty, Creator of all things visible and invisible; and in One Lord Jesus Christ, the Son of God, begotten as the only-begotten of the Father, that is, from the essence (*ousia*) of the Father, God from God, Light from Light, true God from true God, begotten, not created, *consubstantial* (*homo-ousios*) *with the Father*, through Whom (viz., the Son) all things were made, both in heaven and earth; Who for us men and for our salvation came down and was incarnate, was made Man; Who suffered and rose again on the third day, ascended into heaven, and shall come again to judge the living and the dead; and in the Holy Ghost.—But those who say, 'There was a time when He was not, and before he was begotten He was not, and He came into existence out of what was not'; or who say, 'He is of a different nature and essence from the Father,' or 'the Son of God is created or capable of change,' let them be anathema."

This Creed was signed by all the bishops except two—Theonas of Marmarica and Secundus of Ptolemais, who with Arius were exiled by the Emperor to Illyria. Three months after the Council, Eusebius of Nicomedia and Theognis of Nicaea were also banished, because, in spite of their signature, they refused to recognize the condemnation of Arius, gave hospitality to Arians, and openly professed Arian errors.

The work of the Council did not end with the condemnation of Arius and the definition of the eternal Sonship of Christ; important matters concerning the liturgy and discipline of the Church were discussed and the decisions embodied in a number of *Canones*.

A brilliant banquet in the imperial palace marked the close of the First Oecumenical Council, the model of all those that were to follow. With earnest admonitions to peace and concord, Constantine dismissed the bishops to their homes.

5. *The Arian Reaction.   St. Athanasius the Great*

The peace which Constantine had hoped would be restored to the Church by the Council of Nicaea was still a long way off. Nicaea was only the preface to the great Arian struggle, which was to last for nearly half a century.

Constantia, the sister of Constantine and widow of Licinius, had been an ardent follower of Arius from the very beginning. Her adviser in all spiritual matters was Eusebius of Nicomedia. When Eusebius was banished, his place was taken by an Arian priest. On her deathbed Constantia recommended this priest to her brother's special care. We do not know his name, but he must have been a past master in dissimulation and intrigue. Before long, he succeeded in persuading the Emperor that Arius was no heretic at all, but had been wrongfully condemned from personal enmity. Eusebius and Theognis were recalled from exile and reinstated in their Sees.

Eusebius, once more in Court favor and thirsting for revenge against those who had caused his discomfiture, organized and directed the Arian reaction. He stooped to the vilest means to attain his purpose. An Arian synod slandered and deposed Eustathius of Antioch, one of the chief opponents of Arius at Nicaea, and set up an Arian bishop in his place. Arius, summoned to Constantinople by the Emperor, presented an ambiguous profession of faith, and was allowed to return to Alexandria. But here his triumph ended. Athanasius, who had succeeded Alexander as bishop in 327, absolutely refused, in spite of strict orders from Constantinople, to restore him to his former ecclesiastical standing. This courageous act raised the fury of the Arian party to the highest pitch. They swore to rid themselves at all costs of such a stubborn adversary. From this time on, the history of Arianism is largely the history of Athanasius.

Born in Egypt in 295, Athanasius when still a child attracted the notice of Alexander, the future bishop of Alexandria. Alexander found him baptizing other children on the seashore, and decided after careful inquiry that the baptisms were valid. Seeing the signs of a higher vocation in the precocious child, he took him into his house and trained him for the priesthood. Athanasius was only twenty-five years old when he wrote his famous treatise *On the Incarnation of the Word of God*, and he was not yet thirty when he exercised such a far-reaching influence at the Council of Nicaea. He is described at this time as a little, almost insignificant man, with an auburn beard, and a very beautiful countenance. Julian the Apostate called him a "despicable mannikin"; but, as the infidel Gibbon observes, "he was much better qualified to rule the Empire than Constantius." During the whole period of his long episcopacy he was undoubtedly the outstanding personality in the Roman world.

When neither threats nor promises availed to bend Athanasius to their will, the Arians had recourse to calumny. All sorts of

Domenichino

St. Athanasius

ridiculous charges were raised against him: that he had sent a box of gold to a rebel; that he had broken the chalice and spilt the Precious Blood at an Arian Eucharistic service; that he was immoral and given to magical practices; that he had murdered a bishop, Arsenius, and used his dead hand for magic. Eusebius demanded a synod to examine into these and other charges. It met by order of Constantine at Tyre. Athanasius had no difficulty in clearing himself. The woman who had accused him of immorality, when confronted by him, did not even recognize him. Arsenius appeared at the council alive and with both hands on. Still, foreseeing that his enemies would condemn him in spite of his innocence, Athanasius secretly left the Council and hastened to Constantinople. Meeting the Emperor as he was entering the city with his retinue, he stopped him by seizing the bridle of his horse, and demanded a just inquiry into his case, which was granted, though reluctantly.

Summoned from Tyre to Constantinople, the Arians dropped all the former charges against Athanasius and raised a new one— that he had tried to stop the corn-ships from sailing from Alexandria to Constantinople. There was no truth in the accusation, but Constantine believed it, as it was testified to by several schismatic bishops, and banished Athanasius to Treves, the capital of the Gallic Prefecture (335).

In the same year the Emperor, at the urgent request of Eusebius, called Arius to Constantinople and ordered Alexander, the bishop of the city, to receive him back into the communion of the Church. Alexander refused, and Arius threatened to use force. Alexander prayed that either Arius or himself might die rather than that such a sacrilege should be perpetrated. A few days after, Arius died suddenly as he was on his way to church surrounded by a group of his followers. The aged Alexander died in the same year (336). His Catholic successor, Paul, was deposed and an Arian appointed in his place. Arianism had triumphed in the East. It was the Arian Eusebius who baptized Constantine on his deathbed. Egypt and the West remained faithful to the Creed of Nicaea.

Of the three sons of Constantine two, Constantine II and Constans, were Catholics, whilst the third, Constantius, was an out-and-out Arian. In the division of the Empire the East fell to Constantius. Immediately on his accession to the throne in the West, Constantine II permitted Athanasius to return to Alexandria. The Arians protested against his resuming his See after being deposed by a Council, and Eusebius, who had in the meantime usurped the See of Constantinople, assembled a Synod at Antioch, deposed Athanasius once more and with the aid of State troops intruded an Arian into his See. Athanasius, accompanied by two monks—the first to appear in the streets of the Eternal City—went to Rome to lay his case before Pope Julius I.

Julius invited the Eastern bishops to a Council at Rome. When they refused to come, he called a Council of fifty bishops who unanimously acquitted Athanasius of all charges lodged against him (341). A Council held two years later at Sardica again acquitted Athanasius and upheld the Nicene Creed. But it was not until the year 346 that Constantius, alarmed at the strong opposition to Arianism in the West and in Egypt, permitted Athanasius to return to Alexandria. For the next ten years Athanasius enjoyed, to use his own words, a period of "deep and wondrous peace," although the storm raged all round him, and at one time he was abandoned by almost all the Churches of Christendom.

The Triumph of Arianism.—After the death of Constans in 350 Constantius became sole Emperor, and under his influence the West, and even Italy, was infected with Arianism. During the next ten years the fortunes of the Catholics steadily declined. In 355 a council convoked by the Emperor at Milan and completely dominated by him condemned Athanasius and agreed to receive the Arians into the Church. Pope Liberius, Hosius of Cordova, Eusebius of Vercelli, Lucifer of Cagliari (in Sardinia) and Dionysius of Milan, who refused to comply with the imperial command, were exiled. Hilary of Poitiers, who called the council "a synagogue of the malignant," was scourged and then banished to Phrygia, where he wrote his profound work *On the Trinity in Twelve Books,* which has gained for him the title of Father and Doctor of the Church. An anti-Pope was set up in Rome. A band of soldiers was sent to arrest Athanasius during divine service. When the soldiers entered the church, he ordered the service to proceed, and the choir continued to chant: "For His mercy endureth forever," till the soldiers reached the apsis; then he mysteriously disappeared. For some years he was in hiding in a monastery on the banks of the Nile and in a grotto in the desert, ruling his diocese all the while and writing his eloquent and trenchant *Addresses to Constantius,* the *Discourses against the Arians,* the *History of the Arians,* and the remarkable *Life of St. Antony.* He was hunted down like a criminal. The whole country was scoured to discover his hiding-place. Once, coming down stream, he met his pursuers sailing up the Nile. Not recognizing him, they asked him where Athanasius was. "Not far from here," he replied; and glided past them to safety.

After the expulsion of Athanasius and the other champions of orthodoxy, Constantius and his counsellors judged that the time had come for making a decisive attack on the faith of Nicaea and imposing Arianism on the whole Church. But which brand of Arianism? For the Arians had in the meantime split into three distinct sects: the *Semi-Arians*, who wished to replace the word *homo-ousios* (of the same substance) in the Nicene Creed by the word *homoi-ousios* (of like substance) ; the *Extreme Arians*, who maintained that the Son was unlike (*an-homoios*) the Father; and the *Middle Party*, who proposed to reconcile the other two and also win over the Catholics by leaving out all reference to substance, and simply affirming that the Son was *like* (*homoios*) the Father.

The Middle, or Compromise, Party embodied their views in a new Creed, which immediately won the approval of Constantius. It was this diluted and mutilated creed that he determined to force upon the Church. His first step was to gain the signature of Pope Liberius and Hosius of Cordova. "Liberius," says St. Athanasius, "after he had been in banishment two years, gave way, and from fear of threatened death was induced to subscribe. Hosius was confined so straitly that, at last broken by suffering (he was over a hundred years old), he was brought, though with great difficulty, to hold communion with the Arians." They were both permitted to return to their Sees. Both afterwards repented and refused to abjure the Nicene faith.

The so-called "fall of Liberius" has always been given great prominence by the opponents of Papal Infallibility. But his case does not really bear on the question at all. "Liberius, at the time of his fall, taught nothing and imposed no belief. Besides, if the Pope is to teach *ex cathedra*, common sense requires that he should be free. Liberius, on the contrary, subscribed the Semi-Arian formula separated from his friends and counsellors and in terror of death. . . . What the case does prove is the extreme importance attached to the judgment of Liberius. They knew his zeal and energy, and the impious, writes Athanasius, said to themselves, if we persuade Liberius, we shall quickly master all" (*Catholic Dictionary*, Addis and Arnold, Art. *Liberius*).

The Emperor's next step was to convoke a General Council at Nicomedia; but an earthquake destroyed the episcopal church and part of the city (360) and the plan was abandoned. It was determined instead to hold a Western Council at Rimini (Italy) and an Eastern Council at Seleucia (Asia Minor). The Homoean

Creed was to be presented for acceptance at both Councils. At Seleucia the majority of the bishops signed it without much discussion; at Rimini 320 out of 400 at first declared their adherence to the Nicene Creed, but all were subsequently forced by threats of imprisonment and exile to sign the Semi-Arian formula. The formula was then sent to all the bishops of the Empire, and only a few refused to accept it. It was the time of the deepest humiliation of the Church; the time of which St. Jerome wrote: "The world groaned and was astonished to find itself Arian."

The Catholic Reaction.—Arianism had reached its zenith; its decline was more rapid than had been its rise. The Catholic reaction set in almost immediately. Pope Liberius refused to sign the Homoean formula and in a public letter condemned the action of the Council of Rimini. Many bishops retracted their signatures as soon as they returned to their Sees. Hilary of Poitiers, who had been allowed to return to Gaul after the Council of Seleucia, made the first decided step towards purifying the West from heresy by calling the Council of Paris (362) and proclaiming the Nicene Creed. Cyril of Jerusalem cast off his Semi-Arian sympathies and fearlessly stood up for the pure Catholic faith. Athanasius from his place of concealment and Lucifer of Cagliari sent forth tract after tract in defense of the *Homo-ousion*.

Constantius, who had been chiefly responsible for the triumph of Arianism, died on the 3rd of November, 361. Julian the Apostate permitted all the exiled bishops to return to their dioceses, with the sinister intention of thus causing greater confusion in the Church. Many Semi-Arians, disgusted by the excesses of the extreme Arian party and frightened by the appearance of an apostate on the throne, returned to the unity of the Church. Athanasius was so prominent in promoting the work of reunion and peace that Julian was exasperated and issued a decree of banishment against him and even threatened him with death. Athanasius left Alexandria with the prophetic remark that "this little cloud would soon pass." It did; for Julian was killed in battle shortly after. His successor, Jovian, summoned Athanasius to Antioch to receive instruction from him in the Catholic faith. After Jovian's sudden death, the West received a Catholic Emperor in Valentinian, while the East fell to Valens, who was as determined an Arian as Constantius had been. During the fourteen years of his reign he did all in his power to retrieve the declining fortunes of Arianism. He persecuted both Catholics and Semi-Arians, with the result that scores of the latter returned to the Church. A special decree of banishment was pronounced against Athanasius, but it was rescinded after four months, because the people of Alexandria threatened to bring him back by force. This was in 367. Athanasius spent the last six years of his life in the midst of his people, to the last a "pillar of Orthodoxy" and the center of Catholic life in the East. He died on the 3rd of May, 373.

6. The Victory of Catholicism over Arianism. The Three Cappadocians

In spite of prolonged and bitter persecution, the Catholics were marching on to final victory. New champions of the Nicene faith were rising up everywhere. In the East the most renowned of these were St. Basil, his brother St. Gregory of Nyssa, and his intimate friend St. Gregory of Nazianzus, who are known as the three Cappadocians.

St. Basil was born in 329 or 330 at Caesarea in Cappadocia. He received his early training from his grandmother, St. Macrina, who taught him the faith as she had learned it from St. Gregory Thaumaturgus, bishop of Neo-Caesarea. As a young man he frequented the schools of his native city, passed thence to Constantinople, where his teacher was the celebrated pagan orator Libanius, and in 350 to the University of Athens. At Athens his countryman Gregory of Nazianzus was his constant companion; Julian, the future Apostate, was his fellow-student. On his return to Caesarea in 357, Basil opened a school of rhetoric which soon attracted scholars from every part of Asia Minor.

Up to this time his life seems to have been rather a worldly one. It was his sister, St. Macrina the younger, who raised his thoughts to higher things by directing his attention to the study of the Gospels. "I awoke," he writes, "as from deep sleep, and cast my eyes on that admirable light of the truth, the Gospel. Long I wept over the misery of my life, and prayed that a hand should come and lead me, and teach me the lessons of piety" (Letter 223). He visited the solitaries and monks of Syria, Palestine and Egypt, and then retired to the family estate at Arnesi in Pontus, where he was later joined by his friend Gregory. He divided his time between prayer, study of the Scriptures, and manual labor. His mother St. Emmelia and his sister St. Macrina fixed their abode in the neighborhood on the opposite bank of the little river Iris. Disciples began to flock to Arnesi from all sides. Basil organized

St. Basil

them into a religious community, for which he wrote his celebrated *Rules*, a shorter one containing thirty-five, and a longer one containing three hundred and thirteen articles. This twofold Rule became so popular in the East that it soon supplanted all others; and to-day it alone is recognized and followed by the monks of the Greek Church.

In 364 Basil returned to Caesarea at the request of Bishop Eusebius, who desired his help in the administration of his vast diocese. He became at once the leading personality of the city and exercised an immense influence for good over Christians, Jews, and pagans. Every day he preached in the cathedral church, the working people coming in crowds in the early morning hours to hear him. On the death of Eusebius in 370, Basil succeeded him. The work which he accomplished during his episcopate, in spite of constant ill-health and much opposition from the Arians, was marvelous. He reformed the clergy so thoroughly that other bishops used to send for them to assist them in their dioceses. To relieve distress he founded hospitals and houses for the poor. In the sick he saw Christ, and in all humility often kissed their wounds and sores. His greatest achievement was the vast hospital and work house which he erected just outside the city. It was known as the New Town, and after his death as the *Basileiad*. It provided not only food and shelter for the homeless and treatment for all diseases, but also work for the unemployed. During these busy years he found time to write his splendid theological works: the *Hexahemeron*, or Account of the Six Days of Creation, and the treatises *On the Holy Ghost* and *Against Eunomius the Arian*. The 22nd of his 24 extant *Discourses* is addressed *To Our Young Men, How They Can Derive Benefit from the Study of Pagan Literature*. Pagan writings can be very useful to one preparing to study the Scriptures, he says, but they must be read with discretion. The student must act like the bee "which only takes the honey out of the flower, and leaves the poison."

Basil had not been long in his See when he was brought into open collision with the Arian Emperor Valens and his emissary, the Pretorian Prefect Modestus. St. Gregory of Nazianzus has preserved an account of the dramatic incidents.

"Valens was determined to reduce Cappadocia to the Arian level, and demanded from Basil the admission of Arians to communion. To enforce this he sent Modestus, who summoned Basil before his tribunal, first tried to bribe him, and then proceeded to threaten him with confiscation, torture, death. As for confiscation, Basil replied that he owned nothing but a cloak and a few books; as for torture, Modestus had threatened to tear out his liver, and Basil said there was nothing gave him more trouble; as for death, he would gladly welcome it. When Modestus complained that he was not used to such replies, Basil retorted that perhaps he had not met a real bishop before. So Modestus reported him to Valens as hopeless: 'We have been worsted, sir, by the prelate of this Church. He is superior to threats, invincible in argument, uninfluenced by persuasion. We must make trial on some feebler character.' He conceived a great respect for him, and ultimately became his friend and correspondent."

St. Basil died on the 1st of January, 379, at the age of fifty
It was only after his death that his true greatness was discovered.
He is known in history as Basil the Great. Another Father of
the Church called him "the light not only of Cappadocia, but of
the world"; and the Council of Chalcedon ranked him as the
"greatest of the Fathers."

St. Gregory of Nazianzus.—Basil died before any of the great
objects for which he had fought and suffered—the overthrow of
Arianism, the pacification of the Eastern Church and its reunion
with the West—had been realized. His friend Gregory of Nazianzus was more fortunate. Valens had fallen in battle against
the Goths (378). Better days dawned for the Church. Gratian,
who had been emperor of the West since 376, and now became
sole emperor, was a Catholic; and the man whom he associated
with himself in the East, Theodosius, was also a Catholic. Immediately after the accession of Theodosius, the Catholics of Constantinople invited Gregory of Nazianzus to become their bishop.

Gregory had already been consecrated bishop of Sasima in
Cappadocia by Basil, but he had never taken possession of his See.
When he accepted the invitation to Constantinople, there was a
mere handful of Catholics left in that bulwark of Arianism. The
city, says Gregory in one of his poems, "had passed through the
death of infidelity; there was left but one last breath of life."
He established himself in a small private house, which he turned
into a place of worship, and called it the *Anastasia*—the Resurrection. Here he began to preach the true doctrine. In his sermons, especially in the five so-called *Theological Orations*, he
dwelt continually on the Catholic Doctrine of the Blessed Trinity,
which he set forth with such marvelous clearness and eloquence
that he earned for himself the title of *the* Theologian and "Defender of the Godhead of the Word." In the short space of less
than two years and in the face of the fiercest opposition from the
Arian populace, he restored the ascendancy of Catholicism.

End of the Arian Troubles. Second General Council.—
On the 28th of February, 380, Gratian and Theodosius issued an
edict of uniformity which abolished all toleration of Arianism.
This famous edict, which marks the end of the Arian troubles and
the complete reunion of the East and the West, runs as follows:

"We will that all the peoples who are ruled by the authority of our
clemency shall hold to the religion which the Divine Apostle Peter delivered

to the Romans, and which is recognized by his having preserved it there until the present day, and which it is known that the Pontiff Damasus follows, and Peter, Bishop of Alexandria, a man of apostolic holiness, that is to say, that according to the teaching of the apostles and the doctrine of the Gospel, we should believe in one Godhead of the Father, Son, and Holy Ghost, in co-equal majesty and Holy Trinity. We order those who follow this law to take the name of Catholic Christians; all others, mad and insane, we condemn to the infamy of heresy, and they will be punished in the first place by Divine vengeance, and also by our penalties, wherein we follow the will of Heaven."

In November of the same year Theodosius restored all the churches of Constantinople to the Catholics. In the next May he convoked a Council at Constantinople. One hundred and fifty bishops from the East were present. Meletius of Antioch at first

THE FIRST COUNCIL OF CONSTANTINOPLE

presided; but he died shortly afterwards and Gregory succeeded him. The true faith was maintained against Arianism; and to meet the error of Macedonius, a former Semi-Arian bishop of Constantinople, who had denied the perfect Godhead of the Holy Ghost, the Council added to the Nicene Creed the words: "and in the Holy Ghost, the Lord and life-giver, who proceedeth from the Father, who with the Father and the Son is together worshiped and glorified, who spake through the prophets."

The Council of Constantinople had in itself no claim to be an Oecumenical or General Council, because the whole Church was not summoned, nor was it presided over by the Pope or his legates, but it was generally recognized as such since the sixth century, because its doctrinal definitions were accepted throughout the Church. Among the disciplinary decrees passed by the Council was one which was destined to be a source of conflict between the Sees of Alexandria and Constantinople, and between Rome, which would not accept the decree, and Constantinople, viz., that "the Bishop of Constantinople should be honored next to the Bishop of Rome, Constantinople being New Rome."

Gregory was confirmed by the Council as Bishop of Constantinople; but when opposition to his appointment was voiced by many of his fellow-bishops, he publicly resigned his See and retired to Asia Minor, where he spent the remainder of his life in prayer and study. He died in 391. The Breviary calls him the "keenest champion of the Consubstantiality of the Son"; and adds that "while no one surpassed him in virtue, so he easily surpassed all others in the solidity of his reasoning." He has left us fifty-eight dogmatic discourses, five eulogies or funeral orations, about eighteen thousand lines of poetry, two hundred forty-two letters, two Invectives against Julian the Apostate, a treatise on the Priesthood, the most charming perhaps of all his writings, and (in collaboration with Basil) an Anthology from the works of Origen.

St. Gregory of Nyssa.—Gregory, the younger brother of Basil, never enjoyed the advantages of a university education, and yet he was a greater philosopher and more original thinker than his brother or his namesake of Nazianzus. He was a Lector in the church of Caesarea, then a teacher of rhetoric. He married, but after the death of his wife, his sister St. Macrina induced him to re-enter the ranks of the clergy. When Basil was elevated to the See of Caesarea, he recognized the great intellectual gifts of his brother, but had no very high opinion of his practical ability; he therefore appointed him to the obscure See of Nyssa, hoping, as he said, that Gregory would give luster to the See, instead of receiving luster from it. His hopes were not disappointed. A Synod of Antioch sent Gregory on an important mission to reform the churches of Arabia. On his return he wrote his treatise on *Pilgrimages*, which is not always very complimentary to the pilgrims of those days. In 374 he was deposed from his See by Valens and retired till 378 to Seleucia. During this period he acted for some time as Archbishop of Sebaste in Armenia. At the Council of Constantinople he was a prominent figure, reading to the assembled Fathers a part of his celebrated work against the Arian Eunomius, and delivering the funeral oration over Bishop Meletius, who died during the sessions. He again came to the Capital to preach on the death of the Empress Flaccilla (385). He died before the end of the century, probably in 395.

The two works on which Gregory's reputation as a philosopher and theologian rests are the *Thirteen Books against Eunomius* and the *Great Catechism,* an exposition of the doctrines of Christianity addressed to atheists, pagans, Jews, and heretics. In his treatise *On Virginity* he insists on the necessity of detachment from the things of this world if we wish to be united with God. He does not condemn marriage, but he thinks that for many it is a hindrance to complete detachment. "Let no one think we depreciate marriage. We are well aware that it is not a stranger to God's blessing. But as the common instincts of man can plead sufficiently on its behalf, it is superfluous to formally compose an exhortation to marriage." One of his most pleasing works is the dialogue with his sister Macrina on *The Soul and the Resurrection.*

With the "Star of Nyssa" the story of the Arian controversy is closed. "Gregory of Nazianzus summed up the Catholic faith in five sermons; Gregory of Nyssa disposed of Arianism in detail in his thirteen books against Eunomius; the Second General Council put an end to it officially." In the meantime, however, it had been carried beyond the boundaries of the Empire to the Germanic tribes north of the Danube. The Goths, Vandals, Suevi, Burgundians, and the Longobardi embraced it, and with them it will reappear on Roman soil.

B. *The Truce in the Wars of the Lord*

The great controversies on the Trinity and the Divinity of Christ are known in ecclesiastical history as the *Theological* Controversies; they ended with the defeat of Arianism and Macedonianism. Forty years later the controversies on the relation of the Divine and Human Natures in Christ, the *Christological* controversies began, centering around the names of Nestorius, Eutyches, and Sergius. A modern historian has called these controversies the "Wars of the Lord" and the intervening period the "Truce in the Wars of the Lord." Four great Fathers and Doctors of the Church flourished during this period: St. John Chrysostom in the East, and St. Jerome, St. Ambrose, and St. Augustine in the West. The Church and Christian literature owe an inestimable debt of gratitude to them, and their names are dear to every Catholic heart.

1. *St. John Chrysostom, the Glory of the Christian Pulpit*

John, on account of his eloquence surnamed Chrysostom, the Golden-Mouthed, was born at Antioch about the year 344 of noble and wealthy parents. He was only a year old when his father died, and his education devolved entirely on his pious mother Anthusa. At the age of twenty he entered the school of the celebrated sophist Libanius, and his proficiency in all branches of learning was such that he would have been the successor of his pagan master had he not been "stolen away," as Libanius put it, to a life of piety through the influence of his mother. It was of this remarkable woman that Libanius said: "Ye gods, what women there are amongst the Christians!"

Abandoning the forum, the theater, the halls of learning, John began to devote himself exclusively to prayer and the study of the Scriptures under the guidance of Meletius, the saintly bishop of Antioch, and the priest Diodorus, who later became so famous as bishop of Tarsus. After three years' careful preparation he received Baptism and, after the death of his mother, retired to the mountains near Antioch. For six years he made his home among the monks who had settled there. For two years more he lived by himself in a cave; he slept, when he did sleep, without lying down; he exposed himself to the extremities of cold, and all this, as he tells us, in order to subdue the daintiness of his natural appetites; for in his youth he had loved fine wines, and costly foods, and the pleasures of the baths. At length he found that he was passing the bounds of discretion. Nature would bear no more. He fell ill, and was obliged to return to the city. He was ordained deacon by Meletius in 381, and priest by his successor, Flavian, in 386. It had required much persuasion to induce him to take upon himself the responsibilities of the priesthood. To this hesitation we owe the most popular of his works, the beautiful treatise *On the Priesthood*. It is in this work that the oft-quoted words on the absolving power of the priest occur: "What priests do here below, God ratifies above; the Master confirms the sentences of His servants."

During the next ten years Chrysostom preached those wonderful homilies on the Scriptures which established his fame as the

ST. JOHN CHRYSOSTOM

greatest pulpit orator of all times. In a fine passage Cardinal Newman tells us what was the secret of St. Chrysostom's success as a preacher:

"We shall be very wrong if we suppose that fine expressions, or rounded periods, or figures of speech, were the credentials by which he claimed to be the first doctor of the East. His oratorical power was but the instrument, by which he readily, gracefully, adequately expressed, expressed without effort and with felicity, the keen feelings, the living ideas, the earnest practical lessons which he had to communicate to his hearers. He spoke because his heart, his head, were brimful of things to speak about. His elocution corresponded to that strength and flexibility of limb, that quickness of eye, hand and foot, by which a man excels in manly games or in mechanical skill. It would be a great mistake, in speaking of it, to ask whether it was Attic or Asiatic, terse or flowing, when its distinctive praise was that it was natural. His unrivalled charm, as that of every really eloquent man, lies in his singleness of purpose, his fixed grasp of his aim, his noble earnestness" (*Historical Sketches*, II, 234).

Shortly after Chrysostom's ordination the people of Antioch broke out into open revolt on account of an extraordinary tax imposed on them by the Emperor Theodosius. During a riot the statues of the imperial family were torn from their pedestals and dragged through the streets of the city. How would Theodosius, who was known to possess a violent temper, punish this insult? Would he destroy the city? Would he give it up to be plundered by the soldiery? These questions were on the lips of all. During this trying period of suspense, when consternation and despair lay like a nightmare on the city, Chrysostom ascended the pulpit of the great basilica every day for twenty-one days and by his beautiful sermons *On the Statues* poured consolation and courage and hope into the hearts of the people. Bishop Flavian in the meantime hastened to Constantinople to implore forgiveness, which he ultimately obtained.

When the patriarch of Constantinople died in 397, Chrysostom was chosen to succeed him. To prevent opposition from the people of Antioch, who were determined to keep their beloved preacher at all costs, he had to be carried away by stealth. At Constantinople he was as popular as at Antioch. "The people flocked to him," says the historian Sozomen, "as often as he preached. They hung upon his words, and could not have enough of them; so that, when they thrust and jammed themselves together in an alarming way, every one making an effort to get nearer to him, and to hear him more perfectly, he took his seat in the midst of them, and taught from the pulpit of the Reader." Contemporaries have left us a description of his personal appearance. "He was short in stature, but his limbs were long; and so thin had his early austerities made him that he compared himself to a spider. His forehead was lofty and wrinkled; his head was bald; his eyes deeply set, but keen and piercing; his cheeks were pale and withered; he had a pointed chin and a short beard." It is said of him that he was a man to make both friends and enemies; to inspire affection, and to kindle resentment.

He was not long in making plenty of enemies. The gay Capital had wanted a famous preacher, but not a reformer and censor of its morals. The clerics whom he severely reprimanded for their laxity, the bishops whom he deposed for simony, the monks whom he denounced for leaving their monasteries and roaming about the streets, the magistrates, the court officials, the court favorites,

whose venality, servility and licentiousness he condemned in no
measured terms—all these conspired against the disturber of their
sinful peace.   Eutropius, the all-powerful, despicable minister
of the feeble Emperor Arcadius (395-408), openly violated the
right of sanctuary granted to the Christian churches by Constantine.   But he fell into disgrace through grossly insulting the
haughty Empress Eudoxia, and fled to the altar of St. Sophia for
protection against the soldiers and the mob.   Chrysostom shielded
him from violence and on this occasion delivered *ex tempore* the
eloquent sermon on the vanity of human greatness, which is
known in literature as the *Oratio pro Eutropio.*

Before long, the fearless Patriarch drew down upon himself the
resentment of Eudoxia, whom he gravely offended by a sermon
against the worldliness and frivolity of the court, with open allu-
sion to herself.   He had made a vain and revengeful woman his
bitter enemy, and this proved to be his undoing.   Eudoxia found
an ally in the proud and imperious Theophilus, bishop of Alexandria.   Chrysostom had been enthroned in Constantinople against
the wishes of Theophilus, which was an unpardonable offense.
Besides, Theophilus had a pet aversion—Origen.   Whoever was
known to defend that great Christian scholar was persecuted by
him with fanatical zeal.   Chrysostom did not share this aversion.
He did not, it is true, defend the palpable errors found in some
of Origen's writings, but he stoutly refused to condemn a man
who had done so much for the Church, a hundred and fifty years
after he had died a martyr's death.   The slightest pretext was sure
to be seized upon by the overbearing successor of St. Athanasius
to bring about a conflict.   Theophilus had excommunicated and
ejected all the Origenite monks of the Nitrian desert.   Many of
them fled to Constantinople, where Chrysostom received them with
kindness, housed them, but refused to give them Communion, until
an explanation arrived from their own bishop.   The Emperor
summoned Theophilus to court to give an account of his high-
handed proceedings against the monks, and for other misde-
meanors, and Chrysostom was to try him.   But with the aid of
Eudoxia, Theophilus turned the tables on his appointed judge.
He called a synod of bishops hostile to Chrysostom, preferred
thirty frivolous charges against him, and when he refused to
appear, condemned him for contumacy.   The Emperor approved
the condemnation and sent Chrysostom into exile.   But as soon

as the people of Constantinople learned that their bishop had been transported across the Hellespont, they arose in revolt and forced the Court to recall him (403).

His return resembled a triumphal entry but, two months after, he was again in exile. Eudoxia had caused a silver statue of herself to be erected within the precincts of the Cathedral. The demonstration at the dedication ceremonies was so profane and noisy that divine service had to be interrupted. From the pulpit Chrysostom inveighed against such a desecration. It was reported to Eudoxia that he had begun his discourse with the words: "Herodias is again furious; Herodias again dances; she once more demands the head of John." The report was false, but it sealed the doom of the patriarch. Another synod was summoned by Theophilus, which pronounced sentence of deposition against Chrysostom on the pretense that he had resumed his episcopal functions before the former condemnation had been legitimately reversed.

On the 9th of June, 404, Chrysostom was hurried off to Cucusus, a desolate town in the bleak ridges of Mount Taurus. His enemies fondly hoped that either the long journey or the rough climate or the brigands who infested those regions would put an end to his frail life. But they were disappointed. For nearly three years he lived in Cucusus, honored and loved by the poor people. From here he wrote most of the 240 letters that have come down to us. From here he directed the evangelization of the Lebanon district, a last stronghold of paganism in the East. Here he made the plans, which were partly carried out, of reorganizing the Church in Persia and of converting the Goths. From here he appealed to Pope Innocent I against the bishops who had condemned him. The Pope took his part vigorously, declared the decree of deposition against him null and void, and interested Honorius, the Emperor of the West, in his case. But he accomplished nothing. We still possess the letters which he wrote to Chrysostom and the people of Constantinople deploring the injustice which had been done to them and encouraging them to be patient in their trials.

Eudoxia died soon after Chrysostom's banishment, but her death only served to increase the violence of the persecution against him. When his enemies learned that his influence in the Capital was more powerfully felt than ever before, and that the people were constantly clamoring for his return, and refused to recognize any one else as their bishop, they resolved to visit him with severer punishment. In the summer of 407 the Emperor published a rescript banishing him to Pityus on the northeast coast of the Black Sea. He never reached his destination. He died of the fatigues and hardships of the long journey at Comana in Pontus on the 14th of September, 407. His last words were: "God be praised for everything."

Thirty years later, Theodosius II ordered his relics to be brought back to Constantinople. "Great multitudes of the faithful," says Theodoret, "crowded the sea in vessels, and lighted up a part of the Bosporus, near the mouth of the Propontis, with torches. The Emperor laid his face upon the coffin, and entreated that his parents might be forgiven for having so unadvisedly persecuted the bishop."

With St. John Chrysostom we take leave of the last and greatest of the Greek Fathers. "Chrysostom," says the Abbé Martin, "was the supreme effort and last splendor of the Christian genius in the East. After him its fall was rapid, dragging everything with it into the tombs, the future as well as the past. There are still a few champions of orthodoxy to come, like Proclus, Cyril of Alexandria, and John of Damascus. But the grandeur, the strength, the fecundity, the genius disappeared from the worn-out and degenerate East with Chrysostom."

> Let heathens sing thy heathen praise,
> Fall'n Greece! the thought of holier days
>   In my sad heart abides;
> For sons of thine in Truth's first hour
> Were tongues and weapons of His power,
> Born of the Spirit's fiery shower,
>   Our Fathers and our guides.
>
> All thine is Clement's varied page;
> And Dionysius, ruler sage,
>   In days of doubt and pain;
> And Origen with eagle eye;
> And saintly Basil's purpose high
> To smite imperial heresy,
>   And cleanse the altar's stain.
>
> From thee the glorious preacher came,
> With soul of zeal and lips of flame,
>   A court's stern martyr-guest;

And thine, O inexhaustive race!
Was Nazianzen's heaven-taught grace;
And royal-hearted Athanase,
    With Paul's own mantle blest.
            —Cardinal Newman, *The Greek Fathers.*

2. St. Ambrose of Milan

St. Ambrose was rather a man of deeds than of words; an ecclesiastical statesman rather than a scholar. And yet we have St. Augustine's testimony that he was an orator of great ability, and his extant works prove that he fully deserves the place that has always been assigned to him among the Fathers and Doctors of the Church.

The father of Ambrose was Prefect of Gaul—a vast territory embracing modern France, Britain, Spain, Belgium, and parts of Holland, Germany, and Africa. His residence was at Treves on the Moselle, and here Ambrose was born about the year 340. After the death of his father he went to Rome to prepare himself for a public career. In 370 he was appointed Governor of Liguria and Aemilia, and soon won the respect and love of the people by his wise, clement, and just administration. In 374 Auxentius, the Arian bishop of Milan, died and a meeting of the clergy and the people was called to elect his successor. It was a tumultuous gathering, Arians and Catholics striving with might and main to obtain the nomination of their candidate. Ambrose appeared on the scene to restore order. Suddenly a voice, apparently that of a child, cried, *"Ambrosium episcopum!"*—Ambrose bishop! The people took up the cry; the clergy gave their assent; the Emperor Valentinian I, flattered because one of his officials was considered worthy of so high a dignity, made no objection to the election. One alone protested—Ambrose. He tried to evade the episcopacy by every means in his power. He insisted that he was only a catechumen; he pretended to be a cruel and immoral man; he fled from the city and hid himself. But it was of no avail: he was obviously the right man, and he was forced on to the episcopal throne. Within eight days he received all the necessary Sacraments, from Baptism to the plenitude of the Priesthood. Gifted by nature with a keen mind and a retentive memory, he soon made up for his want of theological training by the closest study of the Scriptures and the works of the Greek Fathers.

Ambrose' episcopate was remarkable in many ways. He was a true friend and supporter of the imperial power, but he never sacrificed one jot or tittle of the spiritual supremacy of the Church. The Empress Justina, who was an Arian, ordered him in the name of her young son Valentinian II to give up one of the churches of Milan to the Arians. Ambrose refused to comply.

"Churches," he said, "cannot be alienated or surrendered."

"Yes," Justina replied, "to the Emperor: his rights are absolute."

"No," said Ambrose, "the Emperor is not above, he is within the Church."

Justina tried to exile him; but he took refuge in his cathedral, which the people guarded day and night, while he taught the congregation to sing antiphonally and expounded the Scriptures to them. Perhaps it was during these days of voluntary imprisonment, from Palm Sunday till Holy Thursday, that he composed those beautiful hymns which are still sung by the Church at the Divine Office and are found in every Catholic hymn-book. St. Augustine was at Milan at this time and was moved to tears by the beauty of the music of the Church and the sweetness of Ambrose' preaching.

Ambrose built the great cathedral church, later named after him San Ambrogio. The dedication is memorable on account of the miracles which happened at the time. Wondering where he should find relics for the new church, he was shown in a dream the bodies of the Martyrs Gervasius and Protasius reposing under the altar of another church. St. Augustine relates what happened when the relics were dug up and with due honor translated to the Ambrosian Basilica: "Not only they who were vexed with unclean spirits were cured, but a certain man, who had for many years been blind, a citizen well known in the city, asking and hearing the reason of the people's confused joy, sprang forth, desiring his guide to lead him thither. Led thither, he begged to be allowed to touch with his handkerchief the bier of Thy Saints, whose death is precious in Thy sight. Which when he had done and put it to his eyes, they were forthwith opened" (*Confessions* IX). Ambrose describes the same miracle in a letter to his sister Marcellina.

In 390 occurred the dramatic scene between Ambrose and the Emperor Theodosius the Great. Theodosius had ordered a wholesale massacre at Thessalonica in revenge for the murder by the mob of the unpopular governor. Ambrose refused him Communion or even admission to the church until he had done penance. Theodosius nevertheless presented himself at the cathedral and was about to enter with his retinue, when Ambrose faced him at the door, and is said to have actually laid hands on him to prevent his proceeding any farther. "Theodosius remained for some time

Murillo

St. Ambrose Prevents Theodosius from Entering the Church

in his palace in deep grief, and at last, in preparation for the Christmas Communion, divested himself of the imperial robes, prostrated himself on the pavement of the vestibule of the church, spread out his arms in the form of a cross and, like the humblest penitent, repeated the words of the Psalm: 'My soul hath cleaved to the pavement; quicken Thou me according to Thy word'" (Ps. 118, 25).

Theodosius died in 395; two years later Ambrose followed him. The great bishop's death was beautiful as his life had been. He was writing his commentary on the 43rd Psalm; he had to break off at the second last verse. It was Good Friday, and for five hours he lay with his arms extended in the form of a cross, and then died.

Of the ninety-one letters of St. Ambrose that have come down to us a few are of great historical importance, but all reveal the strength and beauty of his character. If we wish to look into the hidden depths of his soul and touch the mainspring of his every word and deed, we have only to read the letter to his friend Irenaeus in which he discourses on the *Beauty of Christ*. His funeral oration on his brother Satyrus and his discourse on Virginity are masterpieces of Christian eloquence. Out of the many so-called Ambrosian hymns modern critics only allow twelve or fourteen as authentic. These, however, include the two world-famous pieces *Deus Creator omnium* and *Aeterne rerum Conditor*, which moved St. Augustine so deeply. All his hymns are written in iambic meter, and are remarkable for clearness of expression and sublimity of thought. In his *De Officiis* (modeled after Cicero's treatise of the same name) he has left us a system of Christian moral philosophy. He shows how Christianity perfected the ancient notion of charity and added three new virtues to the moral code: faith, humility, and chastity. His reverence for the Apostolic See summed itself up in the famous expression: *Ubi Petrus, ibi Ecclesia*—"Where is Peter, there is the Church."

3. St. Jerome, the Doctor of Sacred Scripture

The life of St. Jerome is the life of an ascetic, a scholar and controversialist. There are no dramatic scenes in it, unless it be his sudden abandonment of the pagan classics for the study of the Sacred Scriptures—the sudden substitution of one absorbing passion for another.

Jerome (Eusebius Hieronymus Sophronius) was born between 330 and 340 at Stridon in Dalmatia of wealthy Christian parents. In 354 we find him in Rome, studying literature under the famous grammarian Aelius Donatus, and Rhetoric under Victorinus. He also attended the schools of philosophy and listened to the Roman lawyers pleading in the Forum. His Sundays, he tells us, were spent in visiting the Catacombs and the churches of Rome. For a brief period he succumbed to the seductions of the Capital and joined in the dissipations of the young men of his age. Disgusted with this manner of life, he entered the Catechumenate and after serious preparation was baptized by Pope Liberius, probably in the year 360.

When his student days were over, he returned to Stridon, but did not stay there very long. From 366-370 he traveled through Gaul, studying, and observing, and noting down his impressions. At Treves he formed the resolution of embracing the monastic life. For this purpose he betook himself to Aquileia, where there was a colony of monks. Here he formed a friendship with Rufinus, the historian and translator of the works of Origen, with whom in later life he engaged in bitter controversy. His first experience of Western monasticism was not very satisfactory, and he turned his face towards the East, the home of the monastic life.

Dürer

St. Jerome

At Antioch he fell seriously ill, and resolved to renounce forever all that kept him back from God. He was passionately fond of the old Latin Classics and disliked the uncouth style of the Scriptures. In a dream, which he has described for us in minute detail, Christ appeared to him in the form of a stern judge, who reproached him severely and scourged him unmercifully for caring more to be a good Ciceronian than a good Christian. When he awoke he vowed to devote his intellect henceforth to the study of the Scriptures. For five years he lived as a hermit in the Syrian desert, practicing the most intense asceticism and striving, with the aid of an old monk, to acquire a knowledge of Hebrew. This was no easy task. "The study of Hebrew," he afterwards wrote to a friend, "caused me the greatest difficulties. How often I lost courage, how often I cast the book aside and took it up again, spurred on by the violent desire to perfect myself in knowledge. But I thank God for having given me the courage to persevere, for I have gathered the sweetest fruits from this bitter sowing."

His health finally broke down, and in 379 we find him in Antioch, where Bishop Paulinus, whose side he espoused in the schism which had divided that city for many years, persuaded him to receive Holy Orders. In the following year he journeyed to Constantinople in order to gratify his ardent desire of hearing St. Gregory of Nazianzus. After the Council of Constantinople, at which he assisted, he was summoned to Rome by Pope Damasus to report on the troubles at Antioch. He eventually became the Pope's private secretary and close friend. It was St. Damasus who suggested to him to revise the Old Italian translation of the Bible, which was very unsatisfactory in many respects. Before the Pontiff's death (384) he published a revised text of the New Testament and a translation of the Psalms made from the Septuagint.

This labor, however, did not take up Jerome's whole time. A number of high-born Roman ladies, among them Marcella, Paula, and Paula's four daughters Blesilla, Eustochium, Paulina, and Rufina, had formed a kind of religious community, Marcella having fitted up her spacious mansion for this purpose. On their urgent invitation Jerome became their spiritual adviser, initiated them into the monastic life, expounded the Scriptures to them, and even taught them Hebrew. Jerome's influence over these wealthy women aroused a storm of indignation against him, especially when Blesilla took sick and died, as it was rumored, from over-much fasting. Jerome returned blow for blow; but soon tiring of the constant opposition, open and secret, he decided to turn his back on Rome and spend the rest of his days in the Holy Land. His brother Paulinian and the priest Vincent accompanied him. Paula and Eustochium met them at Antioch, and together they visited the great monasteries of Egypt, attended for four months the lectures of the celebrated Didymus the Blind, the head of the Catechetical School of Alexandria, and, finally, in 386, settled down at Bethlehem. Paula built four monasteries, three for nuns and one for monks. Though nominally presiding over the monastery for men, Jerome spent most of his time in a little cell hewn out of a cliff, which was just large enough to shelter himself and his books.

Jerome seldom, if ever, left his beloved Bethlehem; but all the world seemed to find their way to the great scholar's cell. By his translation of the Bible, which he completed in 404, by his numerous letters, which were all "intended for publication," and by his treatises on the most varied subjects, he was a living power in the Church. He was always in controversy with some one, and in the heat of the fight his quick temper only too often got the better of him. Only once did he acknowledge himself beaten, and that was in a debate with St. Augustine on the dispute between St. Peter and St. Paul at Antioch (Gal. 2), which Jerome had treated as a feigned dispute, thus throwing doubt on the sincerity of the Princes of the Apostles. His *Dialogue on Pelagianism*, the finest of his controversial writings, cost him dear. The Pelagians had made Jerusalem their headquarters, and they replied to Jerome's arguments by attacking and partly destroying the monasteries at Bethlehem (416). Shortly after, his health broke down and his eyesight failed him. He was busily at work on his Commentary of the Prophet Jeremias when the end came, September 30, 420.

St. Jerome is one of the most original and striking figures in Church History. Endowed with a vivid imagination, a keen and clear intellect, a style as personal as that of Tertullian, and possessing an indefatigable ardor for study and research, he takes rank among the very greatest ecclesiastical writers of all time. The most important work that he accomplished and which has merited for him the title of Doctor of Sacred Scripture is his translation of the Bible, known as the *Vulgate*. "The Latin translation of the Bible," says Professor Mackail, "is on its own merits, and still more if we give weight to its overwhelming influence on later years, the greatest masterpiece of the Lower Empire. The *Vulgate* of Jerome was for Europe of the Middle Ages more than Homer was to Greece. The year 405, which witnessed its publication, may claim to be held, if any definite point is to be fixed, as marking the end of ancient and the complete establishment of mediaeval Latin" (*Latin Literature*, p. 278).

4. *St. Augustine, the Doctor of Grace*

"St. Augustine," writes Dom Leclercq in his work on Christian Africa, "is probably the man who since his death has been more than all others admired and loved. He is also, perhaps, the one who most fully understood Christianity, who has felt it the most passionately; and in the twenty centuries of its history, we can see none but St. Paul to whom he may be compared."

But what a long and thorny road he had to travel before he reached these heights! How fiercely he had to wrestle with the demons in his own breast, with pride, and ambition, and sensuality, till these false idols were shattered and "God and the Soul" were found!

Augustine has taken us into his confidence and in his *Confessions* made us witnesses of every stage of the long and grueling battle until the final victory was won. His life falls into two parts: the God-seeker and the God-finder. He has summed it up in the immortal words: "Thou hast made us for Thyself, and our heart is restless, till it finds its rest in Thee."

I

Augustine (Aurelius Augustinus) was born at Tagaste, a small town in Numidia, November 13, 354. His father, Patricius, a pagan of somewhat loose morals, was converted to Christianity before his death; his mother was the far-famed Monica, whose tender piety, beautiful faith, and persevering prayer for both her husband and her son have made her one of the most revered women of all times. Monica instilled into her son a deep conviction of God's providence and fear of His judgment, and above all a love for the sweet name of Jesus. "The Name of Thy Savior and Son," Augustine writes in his *Confessions*, "had my tender heart, even with my mother's milk, devoutly drunk in and deeply treasured; and whatsoever was without that Name, though never so learned, polished and true, took not entire hold on me." Following a widespread custom of the time, which was afterwards forbidden by the Church, Monica did not have Baptism conferred on her son in his childhood, though, in a dangerous illness he earnestly begged for it.

Augustine received his elementary training at Tagaste and his secondary education at the neighboring city of Madaura. His father not having the means to send him at once to the University at Carthage, Augustine spent his sixteenth year in fatal idleness at Tagaste, flinging himself into dissipation of every sort, so much so that the Christians shrugged their shoulders and said: "Let him do as he likes: he is not yet baptized!"

Botticelli

St. Augustine

In 370 he made his way to Carthage. In this half-pagan city sensuality reigned supreme, especially amongst the University students; Augustine became its delighted slave: "banqueted upon iniquity" as he expresses it. Two years later a son, Adeodatus, whom he passionately loved, was born to him of a mother to whom he consecrated, for fourteen years, at least "fidelity in sin."

In the midst of the dissipations of university life Cicero's *Hortensius* fell into his hands. Its glowing description of the pleasures of philosophical study fired his imagination and, disgusted as he was with the life of self-indulgence which he had been leading, turned his thoughts to the "conquest of immortality by the acquisition of true wisdom." It was the first step towards his conversion. "Every vain hope," he says, "at once became worthless to me; and I longed with an incredibly burning desire for an immortality of wisdom, and began now to arise, that I might return to Thee."

His conversion, however, seemed indefinitely distant, for he thought to find the true wisdom which he sought in the teachings of the *Manichaeans*, who professed to have received from their founder, Manes, a higher form of truth than that taught by Christ.

Manes, or Mani (215-276), a Persian, formed a new religion out of the ancient Persian doctrine of the two kingdoms of Light and Darkness. Light is Good; Darkness is Evil. Light is a kingdom ruled by a spirit called God; Darkness is a godless kingdom that gave birth to Satan. There is a ceaseless struggle going on in this world between the two elements of Light and Darkness. Man is especially the scene of this conflict. Satan produced Adam, in whose descendants there are, however, some sparks of Light imprisoned in the mass of Darkness. Christ and St. Paul were sent to set free the imprisoned Light. The means to accomplish this is the abstention from all that is allied with Darkness: flesh meat, wine, sexual desires, marriage. Those who took upon themselves this rigid asceticism were called the "Elect" or "Perfect"; the others the "Hearers" or "Catechumens." The Elect could merit for the Hearers, and even redeem them from Evil. The organization and ritual of the Manichaeans closely resembled those of the Christian Church. Mani was crucified by order of the Persian king, and his followers were persecuted by Diocletian, but they multiplied rapidly and were found in all parts of the Empire. Their doctrines were revived in the 12th century.

For nine years Augustine abandoned himself to this oriental sect, attracted especially by its very simple, but false solution of the problem of Evil, and by its claim, so welcome to the sinner, that not man, but the Darkness in him is responsible for sin. Nor was he a Manichaean merely in name; he openly attacked the Catholic Church and strove to make as many converts as possible.

When Augustine finished his studies at Carthage, a brilliant career began for him, first at Tagaste, where he taught literature, and then at Carthage, where he trained young lawyers in the art of pleading.

Horrified at her son's godless opinions, Monica would not for a while even eat with him. But she soon received him back to her table. She had a dream, in which she was told that where she stood, there her son would one day be with her. At another time a bishop, whom she had asked to try to convert Augustine, said to her: "Go thy ways, and God bless thee, for it is not possible that the son of so many tears should perish." So she went on hoping, and praying, and weeping. . . .

A keen mind like that of Augustine was bound in time to turn away in disgust from the shallow teachings of the Manichees. He found that they "destroyed, but built up nothing"; that the Catholics had the better of them in nearly every encounter; that their flagrant immorality belied their boasted purity, and, above all, that their renowned champion and head-bishop, Faustus of Mileve, was as impotent as the rest to answer his questions. Faustus, he says, "could speak fluently and in better terms than the rest, but still the selfsame things; and what availed the utmost neatness of the cup-bearer to my thirst for a more precious draught?"

Thoroughly disillusioned, he left Carthage secretly for Rome in 383. But he soon found that he could not make a living in a city where he was unknown, and where the few pupils who attended his lectures refused to pay the lecture fees. He therefore eagerly accepted an offer made to him by Symmachus, the pagan Prefect of Rome, to fill the professorship of oratory in the public schools of Milan. Here he passed through an agonizing period of mental darkness. He fell a prey to the skepticism so fashionable with the pagan intellectuals of that time. Manichaeism had deceived him, the Scriptures were still a closed book to him, and in his pride he scorned to bow to the authority of the Catholic Church. He despaired utterly of ever being able to attain truth. From this dark abyss he was drawn towards the light by reading some works of Plato which had accidentally fallen into his hands. He was ravished by the beauty and sublimity of the Platonic conception of God and of man's ascent to God.

He learned from Plato that the "aim of all philosophy is to know, to copy, and lovingly to exult in God; that God is a spiritual Being, and that we are consequently bound to check our imagination and to silence our senses if we would reach Him; that God is ultimate Being, Truth, and Goodness, and the source of these created qualities in the universe; that evil is not a substance but only a negation or defect" (C. C. Martindale, *Hist. of Religions,* Vol. III, p. 8). Platonism had overthrown the last vestiges of Manichaeism and skepticism and brought him a step nearer to the Church.

The study of Plato had lifted Augustine out of the slough of despair, but it had not completed his deliverance, had not changed his will. He discovered that there is something wanting in philosophy—a personal Ideal and a religious authority. He found the one in Christ, the other in the Church, and both personified, as it were, in Ambrose, the saintly bishop of Milan. He had an introduction to Ambrose from a friend, and the bishop received him as a son. "I loved him," he says, "not at first as a teacher of the truth (which I utterly despaired of in Thy Church), but as a person kind towards myself. And I listened diligently to him; I hung on his words attentively, but of the matter I was careless and a scornful looker-on; . . . and yet I was drawing nearer by little and little unconsciously. And while I opened my heart to hear how eloquently he spoke, there also entered how truly he spoke." For the first time he heard the doctrines of the Church exposed in literary form and the Scriptures spiritually interpreted. The result was that he passed from the study of Platonism to the study of the Epistles of St. Paul. He cut himself off from Manichaeism by returning to the state of a catechumen in the Catholic Church into which he had been admitted in his early youth by his mother.

And yet his conversion was delayed. An unseen power was drawing him, and "to resist was agony." He was intellectually convinced, but he still shrank from the supreme sacrifice of bidding farewell to all secular ambitions and sensual joys. He sent away the mother of Adeodatus, but soon after, when the marriage which had been arranged for him by his mother had to be delayed on account of the extreme youth of the bride, he resumed his illicit relations with another companion. "I had found the good pearl, and, at the price of all I had, I should have bought it; and I hesitated. Two wills, one old, one new; one of the flesh, one of the spirit, fought angrily together, and my soul was on the rack."

Some one read to him the *Life of St. Antony,* by St. Athanasius, and it marked a crisis in his life. "I saw," he says, "how foul I was, how distorted and filthy, how soiled and ulcered. And I saw, and shuddered, and could not flee from myself. . . . The day had come when I lay naked to myself." Then he hears of the sudden conversion of two Roman officers, who had abandoned their military career and embraced the monastic life. The effect produced on him was nothing short of miraculous. "What ails us?" he cried out to his friend Alypius. "The unlearned start up and take heaven by violence, while we with all our learning, all our want of heart, see where we wallow in flesh and blood!" He could no longer bear to be inside the house; in terrible excitement he rushed into the garden, Alypius, marveling and terrified, at his side, and sat for a while in bitter meditation on the impotence and slavery of the human will. "The empty trifles, and the vanities of vanities, my loves of old, still held me back, plucking softly at my robe of flesh, and softly whispering, 'Wilt thou dismiss us? And from this moment shall not this and that be allowed to thee any more forever? Thinkest thou to do without these things?' On the other side there arose up before him the army of the pure, youths and maidens, men and women, and Chastity herself in all her serene cheerful majesty, who seemed to mock him with the words, 'Canst not thou do what these have done, these boys and girls?' He tore himself from Alypius, ran to the farthest part of the garden, flung himself under a fig-tree, and wept and poured out his heart to God. Suddenly he heard the voice of a child singing from a house near-by some trifling song with the refrain: 'Take up and read! Take up and read!' He left off weeping, returned to Alypius, opened the volume of St. Paul's Epistles at random and read in silence the following:

"*Not in riotings and drunkenness, not in chamberings and impurities, not in contention and envy, but put ye on the Lord Jesus Christ, and make not provisions for the flesh and its lusts*" (Rom. 13, 13-14).

"I had neither desire nor need to read farther," he says. "The miracle of grace was worked in calm and silence." He went straight to his mother and told her what had happened. "She leaped for joy, and triumphed, and blessed Thee, Who art able to do above that which we ask or think; for Thou hadst given her more for me, than she was wont to beg by her pitiful and most sorrowful groanings."

II

After his baptism Augustine went to Rome, and from there to Ostia. Just as they were about to embark for Africa, his mother fell ill. Only a few days before her death they discussed the eternal happiness of the Saints of God. Augustine never soared higher in all his writings than in the Ninth Book of his *Confessions* in which he describes how "in the hush of all creation their souls were rapt in God":

"We said: If the tumult of the flesh were hushed, hushed the images of earth, and waters, and air, hushed also the poles of heaven, yea if the very soul were hushed to herself, hushed all dreams and fantasies, every tongue and every sign, and whatsoever comes and goes, and we could but hear their last word: 'We made not ourselves, but He made us that abideth forever,' if they too should then be hushed, and He alone spoke, not by them, but by Himself, that we may hear His word, not through any tongue of flesh nor Angel's voice nor sound of thunder, not in the dark riddle of a similitude, but might hear Him whom in these things we love, might hear His very self without these, could this be continued on and on, and all other visions be withdrawn, and this one alone ravish and absorb and wrap up its beholder and plunge him into the innermost depths of joy, so that life might be forever like that one moment of understanding when we two strained ourselves and in swift thought touched on the Eternal Truth, and which now we sighed after, were not this, 'Enter into thy Master's joy'?" (Translation based on that of Pusey.)

Monica died peacefully a few days later. Her last request was for a daily *memento* at the altar "from which she knew that Holy Sacrifice to be dispensed, by which the hand-writing that was against us is blotted out." Augustine concludes his own prayer for his mother by asking his readers to remember her too at the altar, "that so her last request of me may be more fully granted through the prayers of many than through my own poor prayers."

On his return to Tagaste in 388 Augustine retired with a number of friends into a monastic seclusion. They cast their property into a common stock, whence distribution was made according to the needs of each. Fasting, prayer, and Scripture study were their daily occupations. On a visit to Hippo in 391 Augustine was practically forced into taking Holy Orders. To

THE ORDINATION OF ST. AUGUSTINE

compensate him for leaving his beloved retreat in Tagaste, Valerius, the bishop of Hippo, gave him a garden belonging to the church to build a monastery upon. He made this monastery a school, or as we would now say, a seminary, which gave many excellent priests and no less than ten bishops to the African Church. In word and writing he defended the Catholic faith and fought against various heresies, especially Manichaeism, whose chief exponent, Fortunatus, he routed so completely that he fled from Hippo.

In 395 Augustine became coadjutor to Valerius and shortly afterwards bishop. He had to leave his monastery, but immediately formed a religious and clerical community in the episcopal residence. It consisted chiefly of priests, deacons, and sub-deacons, who gave up all personal property and were supported upon a common fund. He himself strictly conformed to the rule he imposed on others. Although he lived in poverty, his self-respect required great cleanliness and neatness of person and dress; and although his diet was of the simplest, he did not, we are told, abstain altogether from wine, and his spoons were of silver. Hospitality was religiously observed. Every one was welcome in his house and at his table except the gossiper, the whisperer, and backbiter. On the wall of his dining-room he had the following distich engraved:

Quisquis amat dictis absentum rodere vitam,
Hanc mensam vetitam noverit esse sibi.

(Whoever finds pleasure in gnawing at the lives of the absent, let him know that there is no room for him at this table).

During the thirty-five years of his episcopacy Augustine took a leading part in the activities of the Church in Africa, and gradually became the outstanding figure in all Christendom. Still, the care of his diocese and the writing of his books formed his chief occupation. A large part of his literary activity was devoted to controversy with the heretics and schismatics of his time, first the Manichaeans, his own former sect, then the Donatists, and finally the Pelagians. We have already referred to his successful fight against the Manichaeans. The Donatist schism had existed for nearly a century when he became bishop. The Pelagians propagated their heresy during his episcopacy.

The Donatists.—The year 311 saw the birth of the Donatist schism at Carthage. It grew out of the erroneous doctrine of St. Cyprian that Baptism depended for its validity on the *faith* of the minister. The Donatists maintained that the validity of the Sacraments depended on the faith and even the *moral character* of the minister. Moreover, with the Novatians they taught that sinners could not be members of the Church. Although there were some good men among them, the Donatists were, on the whole, a bad and mischievous sect. Their origin was bad, and their subsequent history one of hatred, intolerance, and violence.

In 311 Mensurius, the saintly Archbishop of Carthage, died, and the clergy and people of the city duly elected the Archdeacon Caecilian as his successor. This aroused the ire of a certain Lucilla, a wealthy but very meddlesome widow, who harbored a grudge against the Archdeacon for having upbraided her for superstitious practices. For a consideration—and a very small one, it seems—she prevailed upon a number of Numidian bishops to declare the election and consecration of Caecilian invalid and to consecrate her servant, the Lector Majorinus, as Archbishop of Carthage. In order to justify their conduct the schismatics charged that Bishop Felix of Aptunga, who had consecrated Caecilian, was a *Traditor*, (i.e. one who had given up copies of the Scriptures and the sacred vessels to the heathens in time of persecution) and consequently, he being an unworthy minister, that the consecration was invalid. Majorinus died in 313, and was succeeded by *Donatus,* surnamed the Great, from whom the sect took its name. The schism spread rapidly, and in a very short time there were rival churches and rival bishops in every town and city of Africa.

The Governor of Africa, at the command of Constantine, to whom the Donatists had appealed, examined into the accusation against Felix and found it false. A similar verdict was handed down by Pope Melchiades, and in 314 the Council of Arles, after pronouncing Felix innocent, declared that even if he had been guilty the consecration of Caecilian would still have been valid.

The schismatics remained irreconcilable, and even went so far as to set up a rival bishop in Rome itself. Constantius deprived them of their churches and sent their bishops into exile. They countered by organizing wild and fanatical bands of peasants and slaves which spread terror and death throughout Africa. Armed force had to be employed to repress them. When Julian the Apostate became emperor, they appealed to him, and he not only recalled their bishops from exile, but restored all the churches and other property to them which had been confiscated by previous decrees. From this time on they were paramount in Northern Africa. Their fanaticism knew no bounds. When they seized a Catholic church, they scraped the walls, burnt the altar, and threw the Sacred Species to the dogs. Their marauding bands, known as the *Circumcellions,* whose battle-cry was "Praise the Lord," fell upon the Catholics, and murdered and mutilated them.

At first St. Augustine sought to win over the Donatists by friendly discussions and interviews. But they redoubled their violence, refused all discussion, and attempted to murder the Bishops of Calama and Bagaia, and even Augustine himself. It was only then that he agreed to call in the aid of the Emperor Honorius to suppress them. A series of imperial edicts provoked further resistance. Time and again Augustine begged the authorities not to punish the heretics with death if they were not guilty of any other crime. At the instance of Augustine, the Emperor, in 411, ordered a conference between the Catholic and Donatist bishops at Carthage. Augustine was the chief spokesman on the Catholic side. Marcellinus, the imperial delegate, who acted as judge of the debate, gave the victory at all points to the irrefutable arguments of the Bishop of Hippo, and his decision was affixed to the walls of the churches throughout Africa. The discomfited Donatists afterwards murdered Marcellinus for his share in bringing about their defeat. From this time on, conversions were rapid, but repression was still severe, and it was not

until the Saracen invasion of Africa that Donatism disappeared
entirely from the scene.

In his writings against the Donatists and in his famous debate
at Carthage Augustine constantly insisted on the following truths:
There is but one Church of Christ, which is His Body, and outside this Church there is no salvation. All who are validly baptized are members of the Church. Even those who have fallen
into mortal sin belong to her, although whilst in the state of
mortal sin they are only dead members. The Sacraments receive
their validity, not from the minister, who may be a sinner, but
from the invisible head of the Church, Jesus Christ: it is Christ
who baptizes, confirms, etc., through his ministers.

Pelagianism.—The leading thought throughout the *Confessions*
of St. Augustine is the wonderful way in which he had been
led by the grace of God out of darkness into "marvelous light."
Entering into the depths of his own soul, he found, like St Paul,
that there was no power except divine grace when "could bring
rest to human weariness, or pardon and peace for human guilt."

And now, just as he was putting the finishing touches to his
Confessions—it was about the year 400—a British monk named
Pelagius came to Rome and began to spread opinions which struck
at the very heart and center of the Catholic doctrine of grace.
Pelagius was a learned man, a linguist, an eloquent speaker, and
of unblemished character. With the aid of the Roman lawyer
and monk Coelestius he soon won a considerable following. The
main points of his teachings were: that man by his *natural* powers
could merit the Beatific Vision; that Adam's sin was purely personal, and affected none but himself; that, consequently, each
man is born into this world with powers as incorrupt as those
of our first parents before the fall; that children who die in
infancy, being untainted by sin, are saved without Baptism; that
it is possible to live altogether without sin.

In order to deceive their hearers and readers, Pelagius and
Coelestius made use of Christian terms, such as baptism, original
sin, grace, redemption, but attached entirely new meanings to
them. They would say: "God gives us His grace," but understood by grace merely the gift of free will and the moral law;
"Christ redeemed us," but only by the example of His holy life;
"Children are baptized," but only that they may become members

of the Church; "Adam transmitted his sin to his descendants," but all that he handed on was his own bad example.

After the sack of Rome by Alaric in 410 Pelagius and Coelestius fled to Carthage, where Coelestius remained for some years, whilst Pelagius passed over to Palestine. Coelestius was condemned by a council held at Carthage in 411, Pelagius succeeded in deceiving a number of Eastern bishops and for a time maintained his ground against all opposition. In Jerusalem he won over hundreds of monks who were ready even to use violence to propagate his errors or to quash the arguments of his opponents.

As soon as Augustine's attention was drawn to the erroneous opinions of Pelagius, he undertook their refutation. He wrote in all, during the years 412 to 427, no fewer than fifteen treatises dealing with the all-important questions of man's original state of justice, of the fall of our first parents, of Original Sin, of the necessity of Baptism, of final perseverance, and of the mysterious working-together of man's free will and the grace of God. It is these profound writings which have won for Augustine his supreme title, *Doctor of Grace*. His doctrine on justification may be summed up as follows: Justification takes place not through man alone, as Pelagius taught, nor through man and God, as the more moderate amongst his followers (Semi-Pelagians) maintained, but through *God and Man,* as the Catholic Church teaches.

In 416 the Councils of Carthage and Milevi once more condemned the doctrines of Pelagius, and excommunicated both Pelagius and Coelestius. Pope Innocent I confirmed the decision of the Councils. Augustine was overjoyed. Rome had spoken; the question was settled, he told his people in a sermon. The heresiarchs, however, appealed to Innocent's successor Zosimus, and succeeded in deceiving him by two ambiguous professions of faith. But he soon saw through their trickery, and in an encyclical (418 A.D.) subscribed to by nearly all the bishops of the world condemned them as heretics and defined the dogma of Original Sin and the universal necessity of Grace. Banished by Honorius from the Western Empire, Pelagius and Coelestius found an asylum with Nestorius, Bishop of Constantinople, and along with him they were condemned by the Council of Ephesus in 431.

The City of God.—On August 24, 410, Rome was taken and pillaged by the Visigoths under Alaric. The pagans laid the blame for this catastrophe on Christianity. Century after century, they said, the ancient gods of Rome had been victorious; one century of Christianity had sufficed to bring ruin on the Eternal City. "These reproaches and blasphemies," says St. Augustine, "set my heart on fire with zeal for the house of God, and I commenced to write the books *Of the City of God* against the blasphemies and errors of the pagans. This work occupied me for a number of years owing to numerous interruptions of businesses that would not brook delay and had a prior claim on me. At last this large work was brought to a conclusion in twenty-two books." The first part of the *City of God* is the the most grandiose defense of Christianity against paganism ever written. In the second part (Books 11 to 22) he deals with the history of the "City of Man," founded upon love of self, and of the "City of God," founded upon love of God and contempt of self. Through all the ages these two cities move side by side, each to its destiny. Christianity is the key to the world's history. It is the divine light that illumines and explains the story of humanity.

The Great Teacher, though Dead, yet Speaks.—St. Augustine died on the 18th of August, 430. Whilst he was breathing his last, Genseric and his Vandals were besieging the city of Hippo. Roman Africa was breaking up after it had given to the Church her greatest teacher. Shortly after his death the Vandals entered the city and burned it. "The desolation which at that era swept over the face of Africa, was completed by the subsequent invasion of the Saracens. Hippo has ceased to be an episcopal city; but its great Teacher, though dead, yet speaks; his voice is gone out into all lands, and his word unto the end of the world. He needs no dwelling-place, whose home is the Catholic Church; he fears no barbarian or heretical desolation, whose creed is destined to last unto the end" (Newman, *The Church of the Fathers,* Pocket Edition p. 137).

C. The Christological Controversies

The Catholic doctrine of the Blessed Trinity emerged triumphant out of the long and bitter Arian controversies. Arianism was dead so far as the Roman Empire was concerned. All who called themselves Christians professed the Nicene Creed and confessed that the Son of God is true God, "consubstantial with the Father." There was a comparatively long period of peace in

Raphael

THE MOTHER OF GOD

This famous painting called the "Sistine Madonna" because originally painted for the Church of San Sisto, Piacenza, now hangs in the Dresden Gallery.

the Eastern Church. Then a new controversy arose, which turned on our Lord's Nature and Person.

The Catholic Church teaches that Jesus Christ is God and Man in One Person. Jesus Christ is only *One* Person, the Second Person of the Blessed Trinity, which inseparably united the human nature with Itself. This union is called a *hypostatic,* that is, a *personal* union. The divine and human natures in Christ were not blended together; after their union they remained "unmixed, unconfused, unchanged." On account of the unity of Person in Christ we can say: "The Son of God suffered and died for us," and "Mary is the Mother of God"; for the same reason the Human Nature of Christ can be adored. Since there are two distinct natures in Christ, it follows that there are two distinct *wills* in Him: a divine will and a human will; the human will of Christ was, however, always in perfect accord with the divine will.

For nearly three hundred years the Church had to defend this teaching against various heretics; first against the Nestorians, the *two-person* heretics; then against the Monophysites, the *one-nature* heretics; and finally against the Monotheletes, the *one-will* heretics. The true doctrine was defined at three General Councils. Monotheletism disappeared, but the other two heresies gave birth to heretical and schismatical Churches which still exist.

The Nestorian Heresy.— Nestorius, a monk of Antioch, a man of great eloquence and of austere life, being chosen patriarch of Constantinople in 428, preached that the Man Christ was not God; that God only dwelt in Him as in a temple. and that He became God by degrees; in other words, he taught that there were *two persons* in Christ, the one human, the other divine. Logically he had to deny that Mary is the Mother of God. He said she should be called *Christotókos* (Mother of Christ), but not *Theotókos* (Mother of God). Christotókos became the watchword of the Nestorians; Theotókos, that of the Catholics.

Copies of the sermons of Nestorius were sent to St. Cyril, patriarch of Alexandria, who lost no time in refuting them. Nestorius appealed to the Emperor Theodosius II (408-450) against the attacks of Cyril; Cyril, on his side, appealed to Pope Celestine I (423-432). Celestine condemned the teaching of Nestorius and appointed Cyril his legate for the settlement of the controversy. If Nestorius did not retract within ten days after notification of his condemnation, he was to be deposed. Far from submitting, Nestorius labored only the more to sustain himself and his false teaching. He declared that his doctrine was correct, and that his condemnation was the work of the Church of Alexandria, which was jealous of that of Constantinople. The remembrance of the unjust persecution to which St. John Chrysostom had been subjected by Theophilus, the uncle of Cyril, lent color to his charge. Unfortunately he was encouraged in his resistance by John of Antioch and most of the other Syrian bishops, who openly espoused his cause.

In order to end the controversy the Emperor convoked a General Council to meet at Ephesus on the Feast of Pentecost, 431. At the appointed time about two hundred bishops assembled in the church of the Theotókos, (Mother of God), but, owing to the absence of John of Antioch, the opening of the Council was deferred. The heat and unhealthiness of the season soon caused great suffering and sickness among the bishops, several of whom died. At last, with the consent of the legates of John of Antioch, the council was opened on the 22nd of June. St. Cyril, as plenipotentiary of the Pope, presided. At the first session the teachings of Nestorius were carefully examined and unanimously condemned, and the heresiarch himself, after three refusals to appear before the assembly, was excommunicated and deposed. The people of Ephesus, who had been eagerly waiting from early morning till night, were wild with joy. Everywhere the shout was raised, *Theotókos! Theotókos!* Torchlight processions were formed and the bishops were escorted in triumph to their lodgings. All night long the city was brilliantly illuminated. When at last John of Antioch arrived he called a meeting of the bishops friendly to Nestorius, declared the action of the Council null and void, and excommunicated Cyril and his friend Memnon, bishop of Ephesus.

Theodosius at first decided that Nestorius, Cyril, and Memnon should all be deposed; but through the influence of his pious sister Pulcheria he afterwards ratified the Council of Ephesus and exiled Nestorius. Free to choose his retreat, Nestorius withdrew to a monastery in Antioch; but, continuing here to maintain and spread his errors, he was banished to Egypt, where he died in 450 or 451.

Many Syrian bishops continued to defend Nestorius. In two synods they declared his deposition to be unjust. Eventually the west Syrian bishops submitted to the decision of Ephesus. But at Edessa, in eastern Syria,

Nestorianism was so strongly entrenched that it was not dislodged until the Emperor Zeno, in 489, closed the famous theological school of that city and banished the heretics. They fled across the border into Persia, where, under the protection of the Persian king, a separate Nestorian Church was formed. In the course of time Nestorianism spread into Arabia, India, China, and even to the island of Java. It attained its greatest expansion in the 14th century. Then the Mogul Timur-Leng swept with his hordes over all Asia and fiercely persecuted the Christians. From that time on, Nestorianism declined rapidly. At present the Nestorians are found only in Kurdistan, on the frontier of Turkey and Persia, and around Lake Urmia. They do not number more than about 150,000 souls (Adrian Fortescue, *Eastern Churches,* in *The History of Religions,* Vol. IV).

The Monophysite Troubles.—Many of those who took part in the struggle against Nestorius went to the opposite extreme. The Nestorians had divided Christ into two persons; against them St. Cyril had insisted on His unity. Eutyches, Archimandrite (Archabbot) of a monastery in Constantinople, carried away by his anti-Nestorian zeal, denied that Christ had a true human nature. The human nature, he maintained, was absorbed in the Divinity as a drop of wine in an ocean. Hence there was really only *one nature* in Christ, and that His divine nature. This heresy is called Monophysism, from the Greek words *mone*, one, and *physis*, nature. There were other defenders of this false doctrine, especially in Egypt, where people believed it to be the teaching of their great hero St. Cyril against Nestorius. Flavian, the Patriarch of Constantinople, immediately took steps to root out a heresy which was so absolutely subversive of the Catholic doctrine of the Redemption. Eutyches was deposed and excommunicated. But he refused to submit, and he was confirmed in his obstinacy by Dioscurus, St. Cyril's successor in Alexandria. Dioscurus prevailed upon the Emperor Theodosius to summon a council. Only 130 bishops were present when it opened at Ephesus on the 8th of August, 449. It was completely dominated by Dioscurus. Eutyches was acquitted of heresy and reinstated in his office. Flavian and other bishops were deposed, the legates of the Pope grossly insulted, and all opposition was overborne by intimidation or actual violence. Flavian died on the way back to Constantinople as a result, it is said, of injuries received in the synod. When Pope Leo the Great (440-461) heard of what had happened at Ephesus, he called the synod a *latrocinium,* a "Robber Synod," a name which has clung to it ever since.

The Robber Synod called forth vigorous remonstrances throughout Christendom. Pope Leo excommunicated Dioscurus and demanded a new and greater general council. The demand was ignored by Theodosius II, but granted by his successor Marcian (450-457). Nearly six hundred bishops assembled in Chalcedon, opposite Constantinople, on the 8th of October, 451. When the *Dogmatic Epistle* of Pope Leo to Flavian, in which the Catholic doctrine of the two natures in the one Divine Person of Christ was expounded with admirable clearness, was read at the first session of the council, all present arose and exclaimed: *"That is the faith of the Fathers; that is the faith of the Apostles! So we all believe! Peter has spoken through Leo!"*

In the third session sentence of deposition was solemnly pronounced against Dioscurus by the Papal Legatee: "The most holy and blessed Archbishop of great and ancient Rome, Leo, by us and by the Holy Synod here assembled, in union with the Blessed Apostle Peter, who is the cornerstone of the Catholic Church, has deprived Dioscurus of episcopal dignity and has forbidden him all sacerdotal functions."

The definition of the Council of Chalcedon was not accepted by the whole Church. The Monophysite controversy went on for nearly a hundred years. Finally all those parts of the Eastern Empire in which Greek was not the language of the people severed themselves from the Church and have remained in schism to the present day: viz., the Copts in Egypt, the Jacobites in Syria, the Armenians, and the Abyssinians—about four million in all. The Catholics form but a small minority in these countries.

The Three Chapters and the Fifth General Council.—Many attempts were made by the emperors of the East to end the Monophysite Schism. Only one of them had even a temporary success. Theodora, the wife of the Emperor Justinian (527-565), was a Monophysite at heart, and used all her influence to protect the schismatics from persecution. She told Justinian that he could easily reconcile the Monophysites to the Church if three stumbling-blocks were removed. At the Council of Chalcedon, she said, Theodoret of Cyrrhus and Ibas of Edessa had been restored to their sees; but they had really been Nestorians, and must therefore be condemned together with Theodore of Mopsuestia, the teacher of Nestorius and the spiritual father of Nestorianism. Justinian readily agreed to her proposal, and in a "theological edict"—Justinian loved to dabble in theology—issued in 544 anathematized three things, or *Chapters,* as they were called, viz., the person and the writings of Theodore of Mopsuestia, the writings of Theodoret against St. Cyril, and the Letter of Ibas of Edessa to Maris, bishop of Hardashir in Persia. After some hesitation the majority of the Eastern bishops signed the imperial anathemas; but the bishops of the West, Pope Vigilius at their head, refused their signatures. To break down the opposition of Vigilius, Justinian summoned him to Constantinople. After having been kept in durance for nearly three years, and plied with threats and persuasions and promises, Vigilius at last consented, for the sake of the peace of the Church, to confirm the condemnation of the Three Chapters. When the West resented his action, he retracted his condemnation, and it was agreed between him and the Emperor to refer the whole dispute to a general council. When the council met at Constantinople in 553, Vigilius refused to be present at the sessions and to ratify the condemnation of the Three Chapters. Thereupon Justinian accused him of Nestorianism and sent him into exile. To prevent the Emperor from intruding an anti-pope in the See of Rome, Vigilius finally sanctioned the acts of the Council, and as his successor Pelagius I also sanctioned them, it took rank as the Fifth Oecumenical Council. The Egyptians were won over, for a while at any rate; but to offset this triumph the opponents of the Council in the West, above all in North Italy and Africa, started a schism which lasted for over half a century.

The Monothelete Heresy.—The last effort made to conciliate the Monophysites led to a new heresy. Sergius, since 610 Patriarch of Constantinople, thought that by declaring that there was only *one will* in Christ, the Syrians and Egyptians would be satisfied and give up their schism. Sophronius, the saintly and learned Patriarch of Jerusalem, opposed this teaching as heretical. Monotheletism (Gr. *monon,* one, and *thelema,* will), he rightly maintained, was nothing but disguised Monophysism. Anxious to prevent Rome from interfering on the side of Sophronius, Sergius wrote to Pope Honorius I (625-638), misrepresenting his own teaching and that of his opponents. "Honorius, who believed that the opponents of Sergius held that there were two conflicting wills in Christ, responded by asserting that there was only one will in Christ, meaning thereby that there could not be a conflict between the divine will and the human will," and agreed with **Sergius** that the expressions, "one principle of action" or "two principles of action" (one will or two wills) were in future to be avoided as mere grammatical subtleties.

Honorius' successors strenuously opposed Monotheletism. which was finally condemned by the Sixth General Council at Constantinople (680). Thus ended the last great doctrinal dispute in the East. It was only among the Maronites in the fastnesses of the Lebanon that the heresy lingered on. During the Crusades the Maronites made their submission to Rome, and they have been most faithful Catholics ever since. They number about 300,000.

The Condemnation of Honorius.—The Fathers of the Sixth General Council condemned Honorius as a heretic. But in confirming the decrees of the Council—and it must be remembered that no council has any infallibility unless its definitions are confirmed by the Pope—Pope Leo II declared that Honorius was guilty of heresy only in so far as he had permitted himself to be duped by Sergius and, through his negligence, had been largely responsible for the spread of the heresy. The action of Honorius cannot be urged as an argument against Papal Infallibility. A careful reading of his two letters to Sergius—one is preserved entire, the other in part—leaves the impression on an unprejudiced mind that he was no Monothelete, although he uses expressions that could be easily misinterpreted, especially if torn from their context. He adopts the words of Sergius, but understands them in an orthodox sense. It is true that he forbids the use of the expressions "one will" and "two wills," but he nowhere says that he requires all the faithful to accept this decision under pain of separation from the Church. Hence he did not intend to teach *ex cathedra.*

Hints for Study

1. Draw up a chronological sketch of the Arian Controversy from 318-381 A.D.
2. If you were writing an historical novel dealing with the Arian Controversy, what major and minor characters would you introduce, and where would you lay the scenes?
3. Thomas Carlyle says: "If Arianism had not been conquered, Christianity would in time have dwindled into a legend." Comment on these words.
4. Read Cardinal Newman's *The Church of the Fathers* (Longmans, Green & Co., N. Y.). You will find charming and vivid accounts of SS. Basil, Gregory of Nazianzus, and St. Augustine.
5. Draw up a list of the General or Oecumenical Councils mentioned in this chapter and tell what doctrine was defined by each.
6. Draw up a list of the Popes mentioned in this chapter and tell in what connection they are mentioned, for example: *Pope St. Julius* (341-352) defended St. Athanasius and condemned Arianism.

7. Why is St. John Chrysostom called the "Glory of the Christian Pulpit," St. Jerome, the "Doctor of Sacred Scripture," and St. Augustine, the "Doctor of Grace"?

8. What is the historical significance of the penance of the Emperor Theodosius the Great? (The moral and spiritual power of the Christian Church). Theodosius voluntarily submitted to the public penance imposed upon him by St. Ambrose for the Thessalonica massacre. The scene at the cathedral door in Milan is legendary, though already described by Theodoret in his *Ecclesiastical History*, V, 18.

9. Draw up a list of the great heresies that disturbed the peace of the Church and the State from the 4th to the 7th century. Name the authors of these heresies and the Saints who combated them. Which heresies started permanent schisms?

10. How did the rivalry between Constantinople and Alexandria begin? Mention some of the consequences of this rivalry.

St. Leo the Great Meets Attila, the "Scourge of God"

In the spring of 452, Attila had recovered sufficiently from the effects of his defeat in the Catalaunian Plains to invade Italy. He took and destroyed Aquileia, burned the cities at the head of the Adriatic, plundered Milan and Padua, and prepared to descend upon Rome. The Romans, unable to offer effective resistance, resolved to sue for peace. A contemporary historian, *Prosper of Aquitaine* (c. 400-c. 463), tells us the outcome in his *Epitoma Chronicon* (ad annum Chr. 452):

"The most blessed Pope Leo, trusting in the help of God, who never deserts His friends, took this difficult enterprise upon himself. He was accompanied only by the ex-consul Avienus and the ex-Prefect Trygetius. His confidence in God was rewarded; for the deputation was respectfully received, and the king (Attila) was so well pleased with the presence of the Sovereign Pontiff that he gave orders to cease from war, promised to make peace, and withdrew beyond the Danube."

In time the impressiveness of this event was enhanced by the well-known legend immortalized by Raphael's brush in the Stanza d'Eliodoro. The legend is told by Paul the Deacon, the Lombard historian (c. 750), in his *Historia Romana* (XIV, 12, 2):

"After the departure of the Pontiff, Attila was asked by his followers why he had, contrary to his custom, shown such reverence to the Roman Pope and acceded to his every demand; the king replied: 'I did not fear the person of him who came to me, but at his side I saw another man, clothed in sacerdotal vestments, of imposing stature and venerable age, who with drawn sword menaced me with death unless I agreed to carry out all that was demanded of me.'"

A still later legend associated St. Paul with St. Peter in the apparition. In St. Leo's own writings we find only a single reference to the Attila incident. In a letter to Bishop Julian of Kios he speaks of the deliverance from the "scourge" as a special gift of the divine mercy" (*Ep.* 113, 1).

CHAPTER III

SOCIAL, RELIGIOUS, AND MORAL LIFE OF THE CHURCH

Before considering the last act of the dramatic history of the ancient Church—the Barbarian Invasion and the Fall of the Empire—we must pause for a moment and pass in review the development of the social, religious, and moral life of the Church from the time that she ascended the throne of the Caesars, and her future was linked with the destinies of Rome.

The Hierarchy.—As the Church grew in numbers, influence, and wealth, her organization developed apace. New clerical orders were introduced to assist the bishops, priests, and deacons in the liturgical functions and in the care for the poor. Thus arose the five Minor Orders: sub-deacons, acolytes, exorcists, lectors, and doorkeepers. Since the twelfth century the sub-deaconship has been numbered among the Major Orders.

When Christianity spread from the cities to the country districts, "country bishops" (*chorepiscopi*) were placed in charge of these scattered communities; they were, however, subject to the jurisdiction of the nearest "city bishop." St. Basil's vast diocese of Caesarea counted no less than fifty chorepiscopi. Later on, priests took the place of the chorepiscopi, and the custom of confining episcopal sees to the cities has been maintained to this day. In the cities the Sacred Mysteries were celebrated only by the bishops, assisted by the priests, deacons and sub-deacons. In Rome in the fourth century the consecration of the Holy Eucharist took place only in the papal basilica, from which the Sacred Species were carried to the other churches.

The bishops continued to be elected by the clergy and the people, but the share of the people soon became a mere matter of form. The number of episcopal sees increased to such proportions that they were grouped into *eparchies,* or provinces. These provinces corresponded, as a rule, to the political divisions of the Empire. In the East a number of eparchies were grouped together into *exarchies.* At first there were only two exarchies—Alexandria and Antioch; the Council of Constantinople (381) added Constantinople, and the Council of Chalcedon (451), Jerusalem. The bishops of these cities were later known as *patriarchs*—a title

A REPRESENTATION OF THE HIERARCHY IN THE EARLY CHURCH

which they still bear. In the West there were no exarchies. Carthage, Milan and Arles were illustrious Sees, but the Pope alone was the "Patriarch of the West."

Clerical Celibacy.—In the West clerical celibacy was no longer merely a general custom as in the earlier centuries; before the end of the fourth century it had become a rigorous obligation, as we know from the letters of several Popes and from the decrees of Italian, Gallic, African, and Spanish synods. Celibacy was binding on all bishops, priests and deacons. In the East the discipline was different. Here married men could advance to deaconship and the priesthood and continue to live as married men; but no one was allowed to marry after the reception of one of the major orders. We still hear occasionally of a married bishop; but after the fifth century no married priest ever advanced to the episcopacy. This is still the rule in the East.

The Papacy.—The exercise of the Primacy by the Popes increased with the growth of the Church. Many powers latent in the Primacy were not fully realized, much less exercised, by the Popes until the welfare of the Church demanded it. This is true of all governmental powers, and was therefore to be expected in the Church. We saw how, in the great doctrinal controversies, the Popes stood forth as the guardians of the faith and of ecclesiastical unity. Even heresiarchs, such as Pelagius, Nestorius, and Sergius sought to win over the Popes to their side. The Council of Sardica (Sofia in Bulgaria) declared that every bishop deposed by a provincial synod had the right to appeal to the Pope, and that no successor could be appointed to an accused bishop until Rome had given a final decision. The General Councils during this period were, it is true, convoked by the emperors, but the Popes always presided at them through their legates and confirmed their decrees—and only such decrees as they confirmed were binding on the whole Church.

Penitential Discipline.—The repressive measures against paganism had brought vast numbers of pagans into the Church. But most of these were not seriously desirous of living as Christians. They put off the reception of baptism, and remained catechumens the greater part of their lives. Even Christian parents deferred the baptism of their children, and it was not until the beginning of the fifth century that infant baptism became universal. The number of fervent Christians was still very great, but moral laxity was widespread, and it became practically impossible to carry out the prescriptions of the ancient penitential code. It was necessary, above all, to be more lenient towards those who relapsed into grievous sins after baptism. In the fifth century private confession and private penance became general throughout the Church. In the East the last vestiges of the primitive system of public confession and public penance disappeared, while in the West Pope Leo the Great declared that private confession to a priest was sufficient in all cases, and limited public penance to the three capital sins, properly so called, viz., murder, fornication and apostasy (*Letter 168*).

The Liturgy.—Solemn public functions took the place of the private devotions with which the early Christians had been obliged to content themselves. The people met in the churches, not only for the Eucharistic service, but also for evening prayer (Vespers and Compline), night prayer (Vigil, Matins), morning prayer (Lauds and Prime), and at the third, sixth and ninth hour during the day (Terce, Sext, None). The clergy and the ascetics kept up the custom of saying these prayers even after the faithful had ceased to take part in them. In the Breviary of the priest and the choir service of the monks and nuns the primitive Christian manner of prayer has been preserved to this day.

During the fourth century daily Communion was almost the rule in the West; in the East this custom never existed, because there Mass was celebrated only on Sundays and feast days. In the beautiful little work *De Sacramentis* (On the Sacraments) written by a friend or pupil of St. Ambrose, we read: "If it [the Eucharist] is the daily bread, why do you receive it only once a year as the Greeks do? Receive it daily in order that it may profit you daily. Live in such a manner that you may be worthy to receive it daily" (V, 4, 25).

In the early ages there was only one altar in every church, and this is still the case in the East. The altar stood in front of the apse. It did not lean up against a wall, as it usually does now, but stood out with a space round it. The altar looked in the same direction as the portals of the church, and as a rule both faced

THE APSE OF ST. JOHN LATERAN, ROME

the East. When the bishop celebrated, he faced the people. The altar was either in the form of a table or of a sarcophagus, or sepulcher. Since the fifth century that part of the altar on which the Eucharist was consecrated was of stone or marble. It was surmounted by a canopy, supported by columns between which veils or curtains were often hung, and on great festivals it was decorated with the sacred vessels placed upon it in rows, and with flowers. The altar was held in great veneration by the faithful. They called it the "divine table," the "altar of Christ," or the "table of the Lord." They bowed towards it as they entered the church. Before it was used, relics were placed in it, and it was consecrated by the bishop with chrism. The linen cloths with which it was covered were also blessed and consecrated. A cross was placed on the altar table or over the canopy (see *Cath. Dictionary*, Art. *Altar*).

No special vestments were worn by the bishop and the clergy at divine service. The ordinary garb which they used was gradually altered and ornamented until our present vestments grew out of it. One vestment, the Pallium, was reserved to the Pope and those bishops to whom he sent it as a special mark of distinction. Originally a loose upper garment, it dwindled down in time to a band of white wool worn on the shoulders.

When more sumptuous churches began to be built, the liturgical functions were carried out with great pomp and splendor. This was especially the case in Jerusalem. Pilgrims came here from all parts of the world, and what they saw moved them deeply and encouraged them to introduce similar solemnities in their own churches.

Ecclesiastical Architecture.—As soon as the peace of the Church was secured by Constantine, the Christians began to erect churches on a magnificent scale. Eusebius of Caesarea describes in detail the great church built at Tyre in Phoenicia between 313 and 322. He tells us of "its great wall of enclosure; of its portico opening into the atrium (quadrangle) in the center of which there was a fountain for the purification of the worshipers before they entered—the precursor of our Holy Water fonts; of the great doors, the vast nave, the aisles with galleries above them; of the thrones [chairs] for the clergy, and of the most holy altar surrounded with railings of the most exquisite work."

The earliest type of Christian church was the *basilica*, a combination of the earlier Memorial Chapels, which terminated in one or three apses, and the ancient Roman basilicas, or large oblong three-aisled halls used for purposes of justice or commerce. On account of their general resemblance to these Roman public halls the Christian churches were called basilicas.

A valuable fourth century work, the *Apostolic Constitutions,* contains a very interesting account of the interior arrangements of a Christian church. The church, the writer says, was to have the sanctuary at the east end, because the Christians in church were thus enabled to pray as they were accustomed to pray in private, that is, facing the East. The altar was placed in the apse, or *concha*; the bishop's throne was behind the altar; the priests occupied seats which formed a semicircle around the bishop; both priests and bishop faced the people. Of the deacons some stood in the sanctuary, others were stationed in the body of the church to keep order. The laity occupied the nave of the church. Nearest to the sanctuary places were reserved for the consecrated virgins, the widows, and aged women. The next part of the nave was divided into two spaces, each with a separate entrance; one of these portions was for the men, the other for the women. Door-

THE INTERIOR OF SANTA SABINA, ROME, A TYPE OF THE BASILICA STYLE
OF CHURCH ARCHITECTURE

keepers (*ostiarii*), the lowest clerical grade, guarded the men's entrance, deaconesses that of the women. The deacons had to see that each one as he entered took his proper place; it was also his duty to prevent whispering, sleeping, laughing, or making signs; "for it is proper," our author says, "to observe discipline and self-control in church and to listen with attentive ear to the word of the Lord" (*Apostolic Constitutions*, II, 57).

The Basilica style was not confined to Rome and the West. Basilicas were erected in Constantinople and in Palestine by Constantine and his mother St. Helena. But in the East a new style, the circular, or central type of building, was developed. It was called Byzantine, from Byzantium, the ancient name for Constantinople. The most perfect example of the Byzantine Style is the *Hagia Sophia* (Holy Wisdom) in Constantinople built by the

THE CHURCH OF SANTA SOPHIA, CONSTANTINOPLE

Emperor Justinian after the church of the same name had been destroyed by fire in 532. Unfortunately this marvel of Christian art and architecture has been used as a Mohammedan mosque since 1453. The Turks have added nothing to the original building except the slender turrets for their muezzins when they call the people to prayer; but they have disfigured its interior splendor by covering the gorgeous mosaics on the walls and vaults with plaster.

Works of Christian Charity.—Every work and institute of mercy existing in the world to-day is of Christian origin. In Rome and the West the revenues of the Church were divided into four parts, one each for the bishop, the clergy, the public worship, and the poor. Public institutions for the relief of sickness and poverty were not possible as long as the Church was an outlawed society. But as soon as better times dawned, the bishops began to erect homes for the reception of strangers, of the sick, of the poor, of orphans and foundlings, and of the aged. We have already spoken of St. Basil's vast hospital at Caesarea. St. Chrysostom spent all the spare revenues of his church in restoring old hospitals and building new ones. St. Paulinus of Nola founded a hospital for the poor, the sick, and the widows. In fact, there was scarcely an episcopal city to be found anywhere which did not have some institution devoted to charity. Nor were the laity remiss in promoting works of mercy. Fabiola, the friend of St. Jerome, founded the first hospital in Rome, and, with the help of the senator Pammachius, a hospice for poor sea-voyagers at the mouth of the Tiber. After the death of his wife Paulina (396), Pammachius divided the fortune which he inherited from her among the poor and the sick.

Melania the Younger was perhaps the wealthiest heiress of her time. She was the only child of the senator Publicola. In obedience to his wishes she married the rich and noble Pinianus. After the early death of their two children, husband and wife embraced a life of charity and self-denial. "They visited the sick and tended them," says Gerontius, Melania's biographer; "they welcomed the homeless stranger and dismissed him with rich presents; they visited the prisons and the metal-mines in various parts of Italy, and whenever they found any one who had been imprisoned for debt, they purchased his liberty. The doors of their palace always stood open to the poor." Then they began to sell their possessions, which was so vast and complicated a task that officials of the Empire had to be summoned to help them. With the proceeds they built churches and monasteries and hospitals. In Jerusalem they gave away their last pieces of gold and silver, and had their names entered on the poor-lists. Melania spent her days in monastic seclusion. Her favorite book, which she studied daily and copied and re-copied many times, was the Holy Scripture.

The Church not only founded institutions of charity; "she infused into her children a spirit which made them count it an honor to tend their suffering brethren and, if need be, to sacrifice life itself in their behalf." Bishops like Basil and Gregory of Nazianzus found time to minister to the sick with their own hands. How the pagan philosophers must have stared and wagged their heads in wonder, when they saw Flaccilla, the wife of Theodosius the Great, enter the huts of the poor and the hospitals, and with her own hands prepare meals for the sick and wash the dishes! . . .

Monasticism.—The fourth century saw the rise of monasticism and its marvelous expansion. The father and most illustrious representative of early monasticism was St. Antony, a detailed account of whose life, written by his friend St. Athanasius, has come down to us. He was an Egyptian by birth, and the son of noble and wealthy Christian parents. At the age of twenty he lost both his parents. Not long afterwards he heard in a church the words of the Gospel, "If thou wilt be perfect, go sell what thou hast." He applied them to himself, and acted upon them. He sold his three hundred acres of fertile land, gave the money to the poor and began to lead the life of an ascetic in a retired spot near his native village of Heracleopolis. After fifteen years he withdrew to a deserted fort on the east bank of the Nile. Here he lived for twenty years in absolute seclusion, never seeing the face of man. His retreat was discovered, and people flocked to him from all sides asking his advice and his prayers. Others, following his example, took up their abode in the caves and among the rocks that surrounded his hermitage. In response to their urgent appeals for guidance in the path of life they had chosen, Antony assembled them at stated times for prayer and singing of psalms and spiritual conferences. This was the origin of Christian monasticism. Antony left his solitude but rarely; once to encourage the Christians of Alexandria during the persecution under Maximinus Daïa, and again, at the request of St. Athanasius, to combat the Arian heresy. Towards the end of his life, in search of more complete solitude, he retired to the mountains by the Red Sea, where now stands the monastery that bears his name. Here he died in 356, at the age of 105 years. The effect produced by

Antony's example even during his lifetime is thus described by St. Athanasius:

"Among the mountains there were monasteries, as if tabernacles filled with divine choirs, singing, studying, fasting, praying, exulting in the hope of things to come, and working for almsdeeds, having love and harmony one towards another. And truly it was given one there to see a peculiar country of piety and righteousness. Neither injurer nor injured was there, nor chiding of the tax-collector; but a multitude of ascetics, whose one feeling was towards holiness. So that a stranger, seeing the monasteries and their order, would be led to cry out, 'How beauteous are thy homes, O Jacob, and thy tabernacles, O Israel; as shady groves, as a garden on a river, as tents which the Lord has pitched, and as cedars by the waters'!" (Newman, *The Church of the Fathers*, p. 122).

The monasticism of St. Antony, growing as it did out of the hermit life, always remained more or less eremitical. There was no organized community life, no living according to a fixed rule. The monks lived either alone, or two or three together, or in communities, as they chose. The founder of monasticism, as now understood, was St. Pachomius. He was born in Upper Egypt about the year 292, of pagan parents. After his conversion in 314 he began to lead an eremitical life at Tabennisi on the Nile. In 318 he felt himself called by God to establish a monastery of cenobites, that is, monks living in common. In the course of time he founded eight other monasteries. The life of his monks was regulated in all details by minute rules. Prayer and meals were always in common. Work was an integral part of the monastic life, and so well organized and so profitable that the Pachomian monasteries might almost have been called agricultural and industrial colonies.

St. Pachomius was not only the founder of the cenobitical life, but he also created the first religious order. "The abbot of the head monastery was the superior general of the whole institute; he nominated the superiors of the other monasteries; he was visitor and held provincial visitations of all of them; he exercised universal supervision, control and authority; and every year a general chapter was held at the head house" (Dom Cuthbert Butler in *Encyclopedia Britannica*, Art. *Monasticism*). When St. Pachomius died in 346 the number of monks who lived according to his rule already amounted to several thousand.

St. Pachomius had a sister named Mary. One day she came to Tabennisi, and asked to speak with her brother. But he refused her request, telling her through a messenger that if she cared to lead a life similar to his own, the monks would build her a monastery. She took him at his word, and not long afterwards she became the first superioress of the first monastery for women.

Monasticism in the Orient and in the West.—Early in the fourth century monasticism, both in its Antonian and Pachomian types, was imported from Egypt into Syria and Asia Minor; before the end of the century it had spread into Eastern Europe, Persia, and Arabia. We have already seen how successfully it was promoted by St. Basil and his friend St. Gregory of Nazianzus.

The knowledge of Egyptian monasticism was brought to Western Europe by St. Athanasius, who in 340 went to Rome accompanied by two monks. The *Life* of St. Antony, translated at an early date into Latin, was not only instrumental in the conversion of St. Augustine, but also gave a mighty impulse to monasticism in Italy, Northern Africa and Gaul.

The chief propagator of monasticism in Gaul was *St. Martin of Tours.* He was born of heathen parents in the Roman province of Pannonia, the modern Hungary, about the year 316. When ten years old he became a catechumen against the wish of his parents, and at fifteen was forced by his father to enter the army. As a soldier he came to Gaul. While stationed at Amiens he encountered, one bitter-cold winter day, at the city gate a half-clad beggar. Martin had nothing on him but his military cloak and his arms. Without a moment's hesitation he took his sword, cut the cloak in two, and gave half to the poor man. On the following night he had a dream: he saw our Lord clad in the half cloak, and heard Him say to His angels that "Martin, still a catechumen, had wrapped Him in this garment." Soon afterwards Martin received baptism and left the army. On a visit to his home he gained his mother, but his father remained an obstinate pagan. Driven out of Pannonia by the Arians, he lived for several years as a hermit in Italy. He finally returned to Gaul and, with the encouragement and aid of St. Hilary, founded the first monastery on Gallic soil near the city of Poitiers.

In 371 Martin was made bishop of Tours. By his preaching and his miracles he did much to extirpate idolatry from his diocese. As bishop he remained faithful to his ascetical ideals, and in order to be able to spend at least a part of his time as a true monk, he established a monastery on the banks of the Loire near Tours, which afterwards became so famous as the abbey of Marmoutiers (*Martini Monasterium,* Monastery of St. Martin). Here he died in 397. When the Franks, who conquered Gaul, became Christians, they chose St. Martin for their patron saint. Numerous churches dedicated in his honor throughout Western Europe testify to the high esteem in which the humble monk and bishop is held to this day. His life was written by his disciple Sulpicius Severus, one of the most charming and scholarly writers of the late fourth and early fifth century.

Palm Sunday in Jerusalem A.D. 385

Between the years 380 and 386 A.D. Aetheria, a Gallic lady of rank, perhaps a nun or abbess, made a pilgrimage to the Holy Places in Palestine and the neighboring countries. For the benefit of her friends at home she noted down her observations and experiences. Only fragments of this work have come down to us. They were discovered at Arezzo in 1883 by J. F. Gamurrini and published at Rome in 1884 under the title: *Peregrinatio Silviae ad loca sancta* (Pilgrimage of Silvia to the Holy Places). The pilgrim's name, however, as has since been proved, was not Silvia, but probably Aetheria or Egeria. The *Peregrinatio* contains amongst other highly interesting things a detailed account of the Holy Week ceremonies at Jerusalem. The following is a literal translation of the account of the liturgical celebration of Palm Sunday:

"On the Day of the Lord with which the Great Week begins, the usual Sunday services are held at an early hour in the church of the *Martyrion,* which stands on Golgotha behind the Cross on which the Lord suffered. Before the dismissal the archdeacon raises his voice and says: 'During the coming week, that is, from to-morrow on, we shall all meet at the ninth hour (3 P.M.) in the church of the Martyrion!' Then he raises his voice a second time and says: 'To-day at the seventh hour (1 P.M.) we shall all be at the church of the *Eleona* on the Mount of Olives.' When the dismissal has taken place in the Martyrion, the bishop is conducted with singing of hymns to the church of the *Anastasis* (Resurrection, Holy Sepulchre) where the Sunday service is concluded as usual. Then all go to their homes and eat a hasty meal in order to be in the church of the Eleona at the seventh hour.

"At the seventh hour the bishop and all the people assemble in the church on the Mount of Olives, where appropriate hymns and antiphons are sung and extracts from the Scriptures read. At the beginning of the ninth hour all go in procession, singing hymns, to the *Embomion,* the scene of the Ascension, and there they sit down—the people must always be seated in the presence of the bishop; only the deacons remain standing. Here also hymns and antiphons are sung; Scripture passages are read and prayers said between the hymns. At the eleventh hour the passage from the Gospel is read which tells how the children with olive branches and palms go to meet the Lord, and cry: 'Blessed is He that cometh in the name of the Lord.' Immediately the bishop and all the people rise and go down from the Mount of Olives. The people march in front of the bishop and answer all the hymns and antiphons with the response: 'Blessed is He that cometh in the name of the Lord!' And all the children, even the little ones in their mothers' arms, hold olive branches or palms in their hands. And thus the bishop is conducted just as the Lord was long ago. From the top of the Mount of Olives to the city all go on foot, the venerable matrons also and the noble lords, but slowly, so as not to cause too great fatigue. It is almost night when the procession arrives at the church of the Resurrection, where, no matter how late it may be, Vesper service is held and prayers are said before the Cross. Then the people are dismissed."

—Peregrinatio Aetheriae ad loca sancta, cap. 30-31

Pope Gelasius on the Relations between the Civil and Ecclesiastical Powers

St. *Gelasius I* (492-496) was the first Pope to state in clear and unmistakable terms the relations between the civil and ecclesiastical powers. This statement, contained in a letter to the Emperor Anastasius (491-518), was of such far-reaching importance for the relation between *Sacerdotium* and *Imperium* during the Middle Ages that a translation of at least the main part of it will be welcomed by the reader:

"There are two above all, August Emperor, by whom the world is ruled: the sacred authority of the Bishops and the regal power. Of these the burden of the Bishops is all the heavier because they must give an account of human rulers also before the judgment seat of God. You know right well that, although you occupy a position of pre-eminence amongst men, you nevertheless bow your head before the Bishops and expect from them the means of eternal salvation, and you are well aware that in regard to the reception and the administration of the heavenly Mysteries you must submit to the prescriptions of Religion, and not pretend to dictate in these matters. In things which concern public order and discipline the Bishops also obey your laws, because they know that the imperial power has been conferred upon you by divine ordinance. . . . If it is proper that the hearts of the faithful should be subject to all the Bishops who dispense the divine Mysteries in a right manner, *how much more necessary is it for everyone to yield obedience to the Head of that See which the Divine Will established as the first of all, and which has ever since been venerated as such with filial homage by the whole Church."*

—Epistolæ Romanorum Pontificum Genuinæ, ed. Thiel, 1867, pp. 350-351.

Hints for Study

1. How is the Catholic Church organized to-day? Does this organization differ much from that of the fourth century? Specify the differences.

2. Read the following articles in the *Catholic Encyclopedia: Patriarch, Pallium, Parish, Celibacy, Basilica, Cenobite.*

3. For a graphic account of St. Antony and the rise of Monasticism in Egypt read Newman, *The Church of the Fathers,* Chs. V and VI.

4. Do you think that the cessation of persecution and the moral laxity that invaded the Church in the fourth century had anything to do with the rapid spread of Monasticism?

5. Write a brief account of Monasticism, showing that it is in accord with the teaching of Christ and a proof of the holiness of the Church.

6. Chapter X of Newman's *Church of the Fathers* presents a fine sketch of St. Martin of Tours. An English translation of the Life of St. Martin by Sulpicius Severus is published by Benziger Brothers.

CHAPTER IV

THE CHURCH AND THE BARBARIAN INVASION

1. *The Migration of the Nations*

The Roman Empire, with which the Church had become so intimately bound up since the days of Constantine, seemed built for eternity, and its capital destined to be the mistress of the nations for all time. Even the Christians shared the belief in the eternity of Rome and the Roman civilization. "How could we," says a Christian Apologist, "desire the end of the Empire, since thereby we should desire the end of the world?" This was a delusion. The huge fabric of the Empire fell before the repeated onslaughts of the Germanic tribes from the north of the Danube and east of the Rhine. The southward and westward movements of these tribes began in the second century; by the westward advance, in the latter half of the fourth century, of the Asiatic hordes known as the Huns, these sporadic attacks on the outposts of the Empire became a veritable migration of nations.

The Migration of the Nations!—What a medley of images this word calls up in our mind. It carries us back to the sunset of the old civilization; we rest for a while in the twilight, then grope about in the night, and emerge at last into the dawn—grey, indistinct, undefined—of a new social order.

As the great St. Benedict was one day seated at the gate of his monastery on the hill of Cassino, he saw approaching him a figure clad in royal robes. It was Totila, the greatest of the Ostrogoths after Theodoric, who came to the prophet of the Apennines, as Odoacer had come to the Austrian hermit, St. Severinus, to ascertain what destiny Heaven had in store for him. "You have done much evil," answered the Saint, "you do it still every day; it is time your iniquities should cease. You shall enter Rome; you shall cross the sea; you shall reign nine years, and the tenth you shall die."

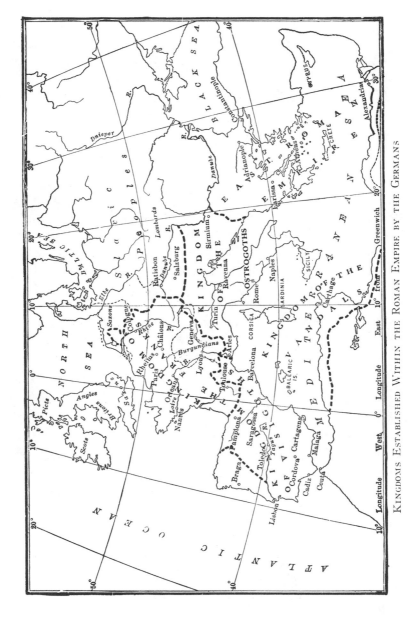

Kingdoms Established Within the Roman Empire by the Germans

History tells us how the prediction came true. Totila fell in battle against Narses in 552. Teias snatched the sword from the hands of the dying hero, but he too fell, and with him the Gothic Empire. When Benedict beheld in vision the fall of the Goth, there loomed up, in the background, the dim outline of a fierce barbarian horde. Long beards swept their bosoms. Over the Alps they poured. Italians and Greeks were blown before them like chaff before the whirlwind.

The invasion of the Lombards (568) was the last, but in many respects also the most tremendous, scourge with which the fair provinces of Italy were visited. It was the most terrible, as Newman remarks, because it was the last; because the Visigoth and the Hun and the Vandal and the Herulian and the Ostrogoth and the Byzantine had devastated the land before him, the Lombard could in so short a time make the desolation so complete.

There was scarcely a province of the Roman world, but shared the fate of Italy. Asia Minor had been ravaged by the Goths; the Huns had poured down upon Cappadocia, Cilicia and Syria, and the Goths and Huns had spread terror and desolation over Greece and Illyria, Pannonia, and Noricum. The Goth and the Hun had driven the Burgundian and the Alemannian, the Frank, the Sueve, the Vandal, and the Alan before them into Gaul and Spain, and then followed them to finish the work of destruction. When the barbarian torrent had spread from the banks of the Rhine to the pillars of Hercules, it had overleaped the barrier of the sea: the Vandals had overrun Africa, and the Angles, Jutes, and Saxons had descended on the southern coast of Britain, and had gradually enslaved the Celt, or driven him into the mountain fastnesses of Wales and Cornwall or across the Channel into Armorica.

When the last wave of the barbarian invasion had spent its force, the face of Europe had been transformed. Independent Germanic kingdoms had been established on the ruins of the Roman Empire, and there was everywhere a bewildering mixture of races, institutions, and religions. There was a Lombard kingdom in Italy, a Visigothic kingdom in Spain, a Frankish kingdom in Gaul, and there were no less than seven Anglo-Saxon kingdoms in Britain. The generals of the Emperor Justinian had wiped out the Vandal kingdom in Africa and the Ostrogothic kingdom in

Italy, and the Frankish king, Clovis, and his sons had overthrown the Alemannian, Burgundian, and Visigothic kingdoms in Gaul.

2. The Church and the Invaders

The Church was the only institution that outlived the ruin of the Western Empire—"the heir of the glory and dignity of Rome, and the greatest influence making for the peace and unity of the western world." The barbarian invaders needed the Church as the only source of the inestimable blessings of religion, order, and culture; and the Church, faithful to her trust, resolutely set to work to win the rude and proud warriors of the north to the religion of the Cross.

Christianity amongst the Goths.—The Goths and their neighbors, the Vandals, Lombards, and Burgundians, were converted to Christianity in the fourth century, chiefly through the missionary efforts of Theophilus, bishop of the Crimea, one of the Fathers of the Nicene Council, and of Wulfila (d. 383), the son of Cappadocian parents who had been captured by the Goths in one of their raids into Roman territory. Wulfila translated the Bible into the Gothic language. This Gothic Bible, the earliest literary document in any Teutonic language, has been preserved in part in the famous *Codex Argenteus,* the Silver Manuscript, so called because it is written in letters of silver on purple vellum.

As Arianism was in the ascendant in the East in the latter half of the fourth century, it was Arianism, and not Catholic Christianity that had been preached to the Goths. In their migrations they were accompanied by their own bishops and priests. This difference in religion was a constant source of friction and even of open hostility between the invaders and the Catholic Romans. The Goths and Burgundians were in general tolerant towards their Catholic subjects, but in Africa the Vandals under Genseric and Hunneric cruelly persecuted the faithful, confiscated the property of the Church and turned it over to their own Arian clergy.

The Conversion of the Franks.—Unlike the Goths and Burgundians, the Franks were still pagans when they established themselves in Roman Gaul (485). In 493 the Frankish king Clovis married Clotilda, a Burgundian princess, who, though of Arian parentage, was herself a devout Catholic. It was mainly due to her example, her admonitions and her prayers that Clovis

embraced Christianity in spite of various attempts made by his
Arian neighbors to win him over to their heresy.   With three
thousand of his warriors he was baptized on Christmas day in the

THE BAPTISM OF CLOVIS

year 496 by St. Remigius, bishop of Rheims.   The bulk of the
nation followed the example of their leader.

The Franks were proud of their new religion—though they did
not always live up to its teachings—and were ready at all times to
draw the sword in its defense   This is attested by the prologue
of the ancient law book of the Franks.   Here Christ is represented
as the special protector of the Franks, who loved them and gave
them the victory over all their enemies, especially the Romans.
It was not only political ambition, but also zeal for the true faith
and hatred of heresy that urged on Clovis and his sons to drive
Arianism from the Gallic soil.

Before the middle of the sixth century Gaul from the British
Channel to the Pyrenees had been re-conquered for the Catholic
faith; but the rest of Europe, with the exception of Ireland, and
a remnant of Britain, was still either in the power of Arian rulers
or enveloped in the night of paganism.   Its conversion was reserved by Divine Providence to the sons of St. Patrick, to the
great Pope St. Gregory, and to the monks and nuns of the glorious
monastic family of St. Benedict.

3. *St. Patrick and the Conversion of Ireland*

Situated "in the ultimate places of the earth," Ireland had escaped the political and social revolutions of the rest of Europe.
No Roman proconsul had ever trod her soil; no Roman tax-
collector had drained the life-blood of her children: she had remained a stranger to Roman civilization, but also to Roman
degradation. It was not until three hundred years after the death
of the last Roman emperor, when she had fulfilled her providential
mission, that Erin felt the tread of the conqueror's heel.

The commercial relations of Ireland with Britain, Gaul, and
Spain, the Irish settlements on the west coast of Britain; the periodic invasions of Wales and Scotland; and, above all, the slave
trade, not only brought the Irish into touch with Christianity in
foreign parts, but must have also been the means of propagating
it in their own land. At all events, there must have been Christian
communities of some importance in the island, for in the year
431 Pope Celestine sent Palladius, a deacon of the Roman church,
"to the Scots (i.e., the Irish) that believed in Christ, to be their
first bishop." It would, however, be a grave mistake to suppose
that the work of evangelization had already been far advanced
in the year 431, for we know from the authentic writings of St.
Patrick that the greater part of the island was still pagan in the
second half of the fifth century. Palladius landed in Wicklow,
where he founded three little churches; but as his mission met
with little success, he retired to Britain or Gaul. He began and
ended his enterprise in a single year. It was not to him, but to
Patrick, as the Irish afterwards said, that God granted the conversion of Ireland.

St. Patrick was born probably at Caerwenr on the Severn
about the year 389. In his seventeenth year he was captured by a
band of Irish freebooters and carried off into captivity in Ireland.
During his six years of bondage "near the wood of Fochlad, nigh
to the western sea," a great change came over him. Though he
had been brought up a Christian, he had never given much serious
thought to his religion; but now the Lord, as he tells us in his
Confession, opened the sense of his unbelief. The fear of God
daily grew more and more in him, and in a single day he said as

many as a hundred prayers.   Escaping at last from his master, he was taken on board a trading vessel bound for Gaul, and after many wanderings found himself once more in his native place among his relatives in Britain.   But he did not remain long with them.   "In a vision of the night," he says, "I saw a man who seemed to have come from Ireland, and in his hand he held innumerable letters.   And he gave me one of these, and I read the beginning of the letter, which contained the *voice of the Irish*. And as I read the beginning of it, I fancied that I heard the voice of the folk who were near the wood of Fochlad, nigh to the western sea.   And this was the cry: 'We pray thee, holy youth, to come and walk among us as before.'   I was pierced to the heart and could read no more; and thereupon I awoke."

Convinced that he was called by God to go as a missionary to Ireland, Patrick earnestly set to work to prepare himself for his life-work.   After spending some time in the monastery of St. Honoratus at Lerins, he settled at Auxerre, in northern Gaul. Here he remained nearly fifteen years, devoting himself to prayer and study and the exercise of the functions of the deaconship under the holy bishops Amator and Germanus.   He was on his way to Rome, it seems, when news of the premature death of Palladius reached him.   St. Germanus, no doubt with the consent of Pope Celestine, consecrated him bishop and sent him to Ireland with a few chosen companions.   Patrick landed in Wicklow (432), near the place where Palladius had begun his mission, but he soon made his way northward to Ulster, where he succeeded in converting the powerful chief Dichu, and founded the church of Sabhall Patrick, afterwards called Saul.   His knowledge of the language, customs, and political organization of Ireland stood him in good stead.   He knew that the petty kings and chieftains were not only the political lords of the land, but also the sole possessors of the soil, and therefore alone in a position to make grants of suitable sites for ecclesiastical foundations.   Hence we find him everywhere attempting their conversion before preaching to the common people.   The conversion of the chief was usually the signal for the conversion of the whole clan.   When the chiefs refused to listen to his preaching, he tried to win them over by giving them presents.   In Meath he met with an important success; for here he

baptized Conall, the son of Niall of the Nine Hostages, and
brother of Leoghaire, the Ardri, or High King of Ireland. The
young nobleman gave Patrick a place, near his own fortress, for
the building of a church, which from its unusual size—twenty

ST. PATRICK LANDS IN IRELAND

yards from end to end—was known as the Great Church of Pat
rick. Leoghaire himself remained a pagan to the end, but he
seems to have permitted Patrick to preach freely throughout
Ireland.

After the nobles, the *fili* (poets and lawyers) were the chief
object of Patrick's solicitude. He succeeded in converting the
most celebrated poet and lawyer of his day, Dubtach, a member of
the commission that compiled the great Irish Law Book, the
Senchus Mór. A number of his pupils followed the example of
their master, one of them, Fiacc, surnamed the Fair, becoming
bishop of Sletty in Leinster.

Another feature of Patrick's method of evangelization, which
contributed in no small degree to the rapid propagation of Christianity, was his solicitude to create a native clergy. His first

fellow-laborers were of various nationalities, but he was soon joined by a number of zealous Irishmen whom he had sent to Auxerre to be trained for the sacred ministry. Thoroughly acquainted as he was with the monastic system on the Continent, it was natural that Patrick should establish monasteries in Ireland also. He himself speaks of "innumerable sons of Scots and daughters of kings who became monks and virgins of Christ." Monks are also mentioned by his biographers as pastors of early Christian communities. The first monasteries were in all probability mission stations rather than monasteries on a large scale. It was only in the generation after St. Patrick that monasteries constituted the main feature of the ecclesiastical system, and became powerful centers of religious, intellectual, and national life.

Two writings of St. Patrick have come down to us—the *Letter against Coroticus,* the ruler of a small independent principality in northern Britain, who, on one of his raids on the Irish coast, had carried off a number of newly-baptized Christians; and the *Confession,* written in his old age, in the very face of death, which contains the answer to a number of silly charges raised against him by some envious and uncharitable acquaintances in Britain. These writings enable us to gain a fair idea of the success of St. Patrick's labors and of his heroic and saintly personality. Humility, simplicity, candor of soul, unalterable trust in God, strength of will, energy in action, prudence in his dealings with all classes of men, sympathy for the corporal and spiritual ills of his fellowmen—these are the traits revealed in almost every line. We can imagine the influence such a strong, ardent, spiritual personality must have exercised over the minds of the Gaels. St. Patrick did not, it is true, convert all the pagans of Ireland; but, as Dom Gougaud, a keen student of early Christian Ireland, has justly remarked, "he won such multitudes for Christ, he founded so many churches, ordained so many priests and bishops, and inflamed the hearts of his converts with such fervor and love that it is not too much to say that the flourishing state of the Irish Church in the centuries following his death were the direct results of his apostolate" (*Les Chrétientés Celtiques,* p. 56).

Some years before his death St. Patrick resigned the See of Armagh, which he had founded in 444, shortly after he had received the approval of Pope Leo the Great for his work in Ireland. It is probable that he spent the remaining years of his life at Saul, in Ulster. Here he died in 461, and was fittingly interred in the first church which he had founded after his arrival on Irish soil.

Before the great Apostle closed his eyes in death, he begged God, the legend says, to show him the results of his labors. His prayer was heard. He was transported in spirit to the top of a very high mountain, and he saw the whole island spread out before him, and all the hills, and valleys, and rivers, and lakes aglow with the sacred fire of divine faith. It was the picture of Ireland in the sixth and seventh centuries. The hearths on which the fires burnt so brightly were the monasteries of men and women which spread like a net-work over the length and breadth of the land.

"During the sixth and seventh centuries," says Doellinger, "the Church of Ireland stood in the full beauty of its bloom. The spirit of the Gospel operated amongst the people with a vigorous and vivifying power; troops of holy men, from the highest to the lowest ranks of society, obeyed the counsel of Christ, and forsook all things, that they might follow Him. There was no country in the world, during this period, which could boast of pious foundations or of religious communities equal to those that adorned this far-distant land. The schools of the Irish cloisters were at this time the most celebrated in all the West. Whilst almost the whole of Europe was desolated by war, peaceful Ireland, free from the invasions of external foes, opened to the lovers of learning and piety a welcome asylum. The stranger who visited the island, not only from the neighboring shores of Britain, but also from the remote nations of the Continent, received from the Irish people the most hospitable reception, a gratuitous entertainment, free instruction, and even the books that were necessary for their instruction."

The most ancient of the monastic schools of Ireland is probably that of Arran, founded by St. Enda early in the sixth century. Many of the greatest saints and abbots of the time received their training here. The most important center of monastic life, however, was Clonard, in Meath, founded by St. Finnian about the year 527. So great was the fame of its school that at times several thousand students were in residence there. Clonmacnois was founded by St. Ciaran in 544; Glendalough by St. Kevin in 549; Clonfert in 552 by St. Brendan the Navigator; Durrow in 553 by St. Columba, and Bangor, in the Ards of Ulster, by St. Comgall in 558. From these and numerous other institutions hundreds of devoted missionaries went forth towards the end of the sixth century to proclaim the faith, to establish or reform monasteries, and to found seats of learning in distant lands, and thus became the benefactors of almost every nation of Europe.

4. *St. Benedict of Nursia, Patriarch and Lawgiver of Western Monasticism*

Whilst the great saints of Ireland were girding their disciples for the struggle against paganism and barbarism, St. Benedict was doing a similar work on the Continent; he too was training martyrs and confessors, bishops and priests to hand on the faith and to win new nations for Christ. Before long, the sons of St. Patrick and the sons of St. Benedict will join their forces and together renovate the face of Europe.

Benedict was born about 480 A.D. of noble Roman parents at Nursia in the Sabine country. In his early youth he was sent by his parents to frequent the Roman schools. Shocked by the prevailing looseness of morals, he left the city before completing his studies and retired to the solitude of Subiaco. For three years he lived in a cave near the ruins of Nero's palace, giving himself

Holbein

SCENE FROM LIFE OF ST. BENEDICT

up exclusively to prayer, contemplation, and ascetic practices. His retreat was discovered, and the monks of a neighboring monastery induced him to become their abbot. But the firmness and severity of the youthful superior aroused such a storm of opposition among the majority of the monks that Benedict soon laid down his office. He returned to his cave, determined to spend the rest of his life as a hermit. But the fame of his sanctity was noised abroad, and in a short time numerous disciples flocked to him. He became their spiritual father, and in time formed them into twelve communities, with twelve monks each; he himself retained a general control over all. The Roman nobility entrusted their sons to him to be brought up as monks. Among these Roman youths were Maurus and Placidus, whose fame later on rivaled that of St. Benedict himself.

The jealousy and hostility of a neighboring priest driving him at last from Subiaco, Benedict, accompanied by a small band of youthful monks, journeyed south until he came to Cassino, a town half-way between Rome and Naples. On the high mountain that overhangs the town he established the great monastery with which his name has ever since been associated. A temple of

A VIEW OF THE MONASTERY OF MONTE CASSINO

Apollo had crowned the summit of Monte Cassino when Benedict arrived, and paganism still counted many adherents among the country people. Benedict destroyed the heathen fane and by his preaching and his example soon won over all the pagans to the faith of Christ. Loved by his monks as their father and venerated by his contemporaries as a prophet and miracle-worker, Benedict died March 21, 543, at the foot of the altar of the monastery church and was laid to rest in the chapel of St. John.

These few facts of St. Benedict's life have been preserved for us by St. Gregory the Great in the second book of his *Dialogues*. From the same source we learn something about St. Benedict's sister, St. Scholastica, who founded a monastery for women near Monte Cassino and died a few days before her brother.

The character and spirit of St. Benedict and the secret of the success of monastic foundation are revealed in the *Rule* which he composed shortly after his settlement at Monte Cassino. Being historically the most important of all monastic constitutions, a brief summary of its contents will not be out of place.

Government.—The government is strictly patriarchal. The abbot is the lord, teacher, and father of his monks. His authority is full and unquestioned. On important matters he must consult the whole community; on matters of less weight, only the senior monks; but in all cases the final decision rests with him. He must, however, bear in mind that he will have to render an account of all his decisions and to answer for the souls of all his monks before the judgment seat of God. He has to govern in accordance with the Rule, and "must endeavor, while enforcing discipline and implanting virtues, not to sadden or overdrive his monks, or give them cause for just murmuring." The abbot is chosen for life by the whole community. If it turns out that he is altogether unworthy of his high office, the diocesan bishop or the neighboring abbots have the right to annul the election.

The Divine Office.—Twelve chapters of the Rule are devoted to the regulations for the public celebration of the Divine Office, which St. Benedict calls the "Work of God" and his monks' first duty, "of which nothing is to take precedence." The Office is chanted throughout. Twelve psalms are prescribed for the night Office; the entire psalter is to be said every week. Private prayers and meditation are recommended, but they are to be short.

Faults and Punishments.—Punishments for transgressions of the Rule must always be measured by the gravity of the fault. Excommunication, that is, temporary exclusion of the culprit from the common exercises of the community, is the usual punishment for ordinary infractions of the Rule. Corporal punishment is also prescribed, but sparingly, and to be applied only to the "unruly, the hard-hearted, the proud, and to boys and those under age." The incorrigible are dismissed from the monastery.

Daily Life.—The monks are allowed proper clothes, sufficient food, ample sleep. "The only bodily austerities are abstinence from flesh meat and unbroken fast till mid-day. Allowance is made for the weak and infirm, who are permitted the use of meat and other indulgences. The time for rising for the night Office varies from 1.30 to 3.00, according to the season, and the monks have unbroken sleep for seven and a half or even eight hours, except in hot weather, when in compensation they are allowed the traditional Italian summer siesta after the mid-day meal. The directly religious duties of the day take up hardly more than four or five hours— perhaps eight on Sundays. The remaining hours of the day are divided between work and reading. The "reading" is confined to the Bible and the Fathers. The "work" is ordinarily field work; but the principle laid down is that the monks should do whatever work is most useful" (Dom Cuthbert Butler, O.S.B.).

Admission of New Members.—When a new-comer applies for "con-version," as St. Benedict calls admission to his religious family, the Rule is read to him, and the following words are addressed to him: "Behold the law under which thou dost wish to serve; if thou canst observe it, enter; but if thou canst not, depart freely." A year's probation is provided for all candidates. At the end of that period each one who is accepted takes the following solemn vows: *Stability*—never to return to the world, but to remain in the monastery until death; *Obedience*—to obey without question the commands of his superior as if they were the commands of God; and *Conversion*—to show the change in his manner of life by humility, by the surrender of all his property either to the poor or to the monastery, and by giving up marriage and all family ties.

The Benedictine Rule is not only the work of a man of great prudence and moderation; its author was also possessed of an extraordinary talent for organization. Its eminently practical statutes could be applied to any association of monks. It is a masterpiece of spiritual legislation, and those who lived up to its letter and its spirit could not but become perfect Christians. And that was the purpose St. Benedict had in view. "Let the monks," he says, "mutually surpass each other in reverence. Let them most patiently tolerate their weaknesses, whether of body or character; let them vie with each other in showing obedience. Let no one pursue what he thinks useful for himself, but rather what he thinks useful for another. Let them love the brotherhood with a chaste love; let them fear God; let them love their abbot with a sincere and humble love; let them prefer nothing what-ever to Christ, who leads us alike to eternal life."

St. Benedict makes provision in his Rule for the reception of young boys into his monasteries. This necessitated the establish-ment of schools in which the elementary branches were taught. But it was the historian, statesman, and monk *Cassiodorus* who framed the code of monastic education which was followed in the Benedictine monasteries during the Middle Ages.

Born about 490 at Squillace in Bruttii, Cassiodorus was educated for the public service. At an early age he attached himself, as his father had done before him, to the Ostrogothic king, Theodoric the Great. For many years he was *quaestor,* or as we should now say, chancellor, to the king. At the death of Theodoric (526) he held the office of *magister officiorum,* chief of the civil service. About 540, when Belisarius captured Ravenna, the Gothic capital, Cassiodorus retired from public life and founded in his ancestral domains at Squillace the monastery of Vivarium. His avowed purpose was "to provide for the transmission of divine and human knowledge to later ages, and to secure it against the tide of barbarism which threatened to sweep it away."

In his famous encyclopaedic work, *Instructions in Sacred and Profane Literature,* he enjoins on his monks as a special duty the acquisition of ecclesiastical and secular knowledge and the copying of manuscripts, not only of the Scriptures and the Fathers, but also of the classical writers. He himself collected many valuable manuscripts and superintended the translation of various Greek works into Latin. In his ninety-third year he compiled a Latin Grammar for the use of his monks from the works of twelve Grammarians. Before his death, which occurred after 580, he resigned the headship of his monastery in order the better to prepare himself by prayer and meditation to appear before God.

Forty years after the death of St. Benedict, Monte Cassino was sacked by the Lombards, but the lives of the inmates were spared. The whole community migrated to Rome and was established in a monastery attached to the Lateran Basilica. When Gregory the Great became a monk and turned his palace on the Caelian Hill into a monastery, the Rule which he adopted was that of St. Benedict. With Gregory, in 590, the first monk and the first son of St. Benedict ascended the throne of Peter. His pontificate marks the beginning of the Middle Ages.

How Little Boys Became Benedictine Monks

"If by chance any one of the nobles offers his son to God in the monastery: if the boy himself is a minor in age, his parents shall make the petition for admission, and, with an oblation, they shall enwrap that petition and the hand of the boy in the linen cloth of the altar; and thus they shall offer him. Concerning their property, moreover, either they shall promise in the present petition, under an oath, that they will never, either through some chosen person, or in any way whatever, give him anything at any time, or furnish him with the means of possessing it. . . . And let all things be so observed that no suspicion may remain with the boy, by which being deceived he might perish—which God forbid—as we have learned by experience. The poorer ones shall also do likewise. Those, however, who have nothing at all shall simply make their petition, and, with an oblation, shall offer their son before witnesses."

—*Rule of St. Benedict,* Ch. 59 (Henderson, *Historical Documents of the Middle Ages,* p. 305).

Hints for Study

1. Draw up a list of the Germanic tribes that invaded the Roman Empire; locate them before and after their migration.
2. Read the article on *Ulfila* in the *Cath. Encyclopedia.*
3. The Most Rev. J. Healy has written a very interesting account of the Early Irish Church: *Insula Sanctorum et Doctorum—Ancient Irish Schools and Scholars,* which is well worth reading.
4. St. Gregory the Great characterizes the Rule of St. Benedict as "Conspicuous for its moderation." Comment on these words.
5. Read Newman, *Historical Sketches.* Vol. II, pp. 365-430, and Vol. III, pp. 105-129.

SUMMARY

Turning Points in the History of the Ancient Church

A.D.

50 In the *Council of Jerusalem* the Church takes the bold step of breaking away from the Jewish religious traditions and customs. She emphasizes her catholic, that is, her universal, character.

70 The government of the Church passes from the Apostles to their successors, the *bishops*. The martyrdom of the Princes of the Apostles at Rome and the destruction of Jerusalem shift the center of ecclesiastical life and government from Jerusalem to Rome.

130 By her triumph over *Gnosticism* and other heresies centering about
to the problem of evil, the Church turns back from her fold the tide of un-
200 Christian influences which had threatened her very life. This conflict brings forth the first great work on Catholic Doctrine, the *Adversus Haereses*—The Refutation of All Heresies—by St. Irenaeus of Lyons. The great *Apologists,* St. Justin, Minucius Felix, Clement of Alexandria, Tertullian, the Author of the Epistle to Diognetus, and Origen prepare the way for the propagation of the faith among the educated classes in the Empire.

250 The conflict between paganism and Christianity is decided. The *Mar-*
to *tyrs* strengthen the faith of the Christians and gain new members for
305 the Church. *Semen est sanguis Christianorum*—The blood of the Christians is a seed.

313 *The Decree of Milan* grants tolerance to Christianity. During the
to fourth century Christianity gradually supplants paganism in public and
476 private life. The *foundation of Constantinople* (330) is the first step in the estrangement of the Eastern from the Western Church. After a long struggle *Arianism* is overthrown and Catholic Christianity becomes the official religion of the Empire. It is the age of the great Councils and of the great Fathers and Doctors of the Church. The fourth century also sees the rise and rapid development of *Monasticism.*

476 After the *fall of the Western Empire* the Church, conscious of her
to eternal mission and inheriting all that was best in ancient culture, sets
590 to work to Christianize and civilize the Barbarian invaders. Her chief instruments for the accomplishment of this task are prepared by the conversion of Ireland through the labors of *St. Patrick* and the foundation of Benedictine monasticism by *St. Benedict* of Nursia. With St. Gregory the Great the first monk ascends the throne of Peter.

SECTION II

The Church in the Middle Ages
A.D. 590-1517

INTRODUCTION

The term "Middle Ages" is applied to that period of European history which lies between what are known as ancient and modern times, or, more specifically, between the fall of the Western Roman Empire in the fifth and the revival of ancient Greek and Roman art and literature in the fifteenth century. The term itself is false—there are no middle ages, no intermediary epochs, no long stretches of centuries separating two distinct civilizations—but long use has made it practically inevitable.

Some historians make the Middle Ages begin with the founding of Constantinople A.D. 330; others fix their beginning at the year 410, when Alaric and his Visigoths sacked Rome; others prefer 476, the year in which the Germanic chieftain Odoacer deposed the last Roman emperor of the West, or 496, the year in which Clovis, king of the Franks, was baptized at Rheims. Much may be said in favor of each of these dates—and much against them. In reality, as a modern historian remarks, it is impossible to assign any exact dates for the beginning and close of such a period. One thing, however, seems certain: when Gregory the Great began his pontificate in 590, the Middle Ages had set in. "In his time," says Monsignor Mann, the historian of the Popes of the Middle Ages, "it became clearly realized that East is East and West is West, that Greek is Greek and Latin is Latin, that the Empire had definitely been driven to the East, and that in the West barbarism was triumphant once again. The old order, in every sense of that word, had passed away; the old classical learning had all but perished in every province of the West."

If we begin the Middle Ages with Gregory the Great and extend them to the Protestant Revolt in the sixteenth century, which broke up Europe's unity of faith, they naturally fall into three periods:

I. The Early Middle Ages (590-1048).—The five centuries which elapsed from the beginning of the pontificate of Gregory the

Great to the formation of the Christian Commonwealth of Europe in the second half of the eleventh century. It was a period of marvelous missionary activity amongst all the Germanic and Slavic nations of Europe. It witnessed the last barbarian invasion that seriously affected the life of Western Europe. The Moslem Saracens and Moors stamped out Christianity in Northern Africa, raided all southern Europe, and gained a firm foothold in the Spanish Peninsula. The Popes had to struggle for their God-given ecclesiastical supremacy against the ambition of the patriarchs of Constantinople; and in Rome itself, in order to maintain their civil independence against the Lombards, they had to accept the temporal authority which the force of circumstances and the good-will of the Franks put into their hands. In the tenth century the Papacy became enveloped in the darkness that settled upon Europe after the collapse of the Carolingian Empire, and passed through a period of ghastly degradation at the hands of the rude Roman barons. It was saved by the Holy Roman Empire which it had itself created, and forthwith placed itself at the head of the Christian Commonwealth of Europe and ushered in the most glorious period of the Church's history.

II. The Central Period of the Middle Ages, from Hildebrand to Boniface VIII (1048-1294).—It is the age of the Papal Monarchy and its struggle with the Holy Roman Empire; the age of the Crusades, of the great Christian Schools and scholars, of the Military Religious Orders and the Mendicant Friars; the age of Romanesque and Gothic art and architecture; the age of the Troubadours and the Minnesingers; the age during which the dream of St. Augustine of a Kingdom of God on earth under the rule of the Church was for a time all but realized.

III. The Later Middle Ages (1294-1517).—The period of disintegration and transition. The great revolution begins which was to end in the disruption of the union between the Temporal and the Spiritual. This period is marked by the shattering of the political power of the Empire and the vigorous development of national states; by the struggle between the Papacy and the French monarchy, the disgraceful captivity of the Popes in Avignon, the Great Schism of the West, the decline of Christian Philosophy and Theology, the revival of ancient classical art and letters. It is an age of unrest, political and religious. The Protestant Revolt is casting its shadows before.

The Church in the Early Middle Ages
A.D. 590-1048

CHAPTER I

THE PONTIFICATE OF ST. GREGORY THE GREAT, A.D. 590-604

1. The Father of His Country

Gregory I sprang from the most illustrious of the later Roman Houses, the *Anicii*, who had long been Christian and had given to the Church Pope St. Felix and several other holy men and women. He entered public life and in 573 was made Prefect of the City of Rome. Upon the death of his father he renounced the career to which his wealth and talents entitled him, became a monk, and dedicated his ample patrimony to the foundation of seven monasteries, six in Sicily and one, that of St. Andrew, in Rome in his own splendid mansion on the Caelian Hill. After his ordination to the deaconship he was selected by Pope Pelagius II as *apocrisiarius*, or resident minister of the Apostolic See at Constantinople. In 585 he returned to Rome and to the solitude of his cloister, from which, on the death of Pelagius in 590, he was literally forced on the Papal Throne by the unanimous voice of the clergy and the people.

It was no light burden which he assumed, and we are not surprised that he sought to evade it by every means in his power. He himself, in a few vivid sentences, has described for us the state of Rome and Italy at this period. "Sights and sounds of war meet us on every side. The cities are destroyed; the military stations broken up; the land devastated; the earth depopulated. No one remains in the country; scarcely any inhabitants in the towns;

yet even the poor remains of human kind are still smitten daily and without intermission. Before our eyes some are carried away captive, some mutilated, some murdered. She herself, who once was the mistress of the world, we behold how Rome fares; worn down by manifold and incalculable distresses, the bereavement of citizens, the attack of foes, the reiteration of overthrows, where is her senate? Where are they who in former days reveled in her glory? where their pomp, their pride? Now no one hastens up to her for preferment; and so it is with other cities also; some places are laid waste by pestilence, others are depopulated by the sword, others are tormented by famine, and others are swallowed up by earthquakes."

St. Gregory the Great

The Lombards, whose Arian faith not less than their cruel mode of warfare made them detestable to the Catholic Italians, had subdued the greater part of Italy and were constantly threatening Rome. Gregory had no arms with which to resist them. Yet on him fell the task of defending the city and feeding its people. The Exarch of Ravenna, the representative of the Eastern Emperor, had neither money nor troops to help him. The Roman Church was endowed with large domains in Italy, Sicily, Corsica, Sardinia and the more distant provinces, which went by the name of the "Patrimony of St. Peter." Twice a year the rent or produce of these estates was transported to the mouth of the Tiber at the risk and expense of the Pope. With these resources Gregory time and again bought off the Lombard hordes, so that he called himself with a smile the "paymaster of the Lombards"; with them he fed the Romans at the doors of the basilicas, maintained the clergy, the churches, the monasteries, the almshouses, and cemeteries, ransomed captives, set up hospitals for pilgrims, and helped to relieve distress in every part of Italy. The temporal power over Rome had practically passed into his hands. He alone signs the treaty with the Lombard king; he raises troops, repairs the walls of the city, and gives advice as to the defense of Corsica and Sardinia; he defends the officials who appeal to him against the corruption and rapacity of the Byzantine Court, legislates in regard to the treatment of slaves, and, in the face of an imperial prohibition, insists on the right of a soldier to become a monk. From the Court of Constantinople he earned nothing but reproach and insult for having saved Rome from starvation and pillage, but his grateful fellow-citizens bestowed upon him the well-merited title of Father of his Country.

2. *The Apostolic Pastor*

Bossuet says of Gregory the Great that he gave to the world the most perfect model of ecclesiastical government. Universal pastoral vigilance is one of the outstanding characteristics of his pontificate. Though always feeble in health and frequently confined to his bed, his energy and activity was nothing short of marvelous. He was never idle. Prayer, preaching, writing, filled his days and the greater part of his nights. His 840 extant Letters furnish us with ample proof of his truly apostolic solicitude for the welfare of the Church in every part of Christendom. Wherever an abuse crops up he strives to repress it; wherever a bishop or a priest, a monk or a nun, a king or a queen deserves a reprimand, he fearlessly administers it; but he is just as ready to condone, to counsel, to encourage, and to console. He vigorously defends the rights of the hierarchy and the Papacy against John the Faster, Patriarch of Constantinople, who had arrogated to himself the title of Ecumenical (Universal) Patriarch, and gives him an example of Christlike humility by calling himself "Servant of the Servants of God"—a title retained by the Popes to the present day.

Soon after his elevation to the Papacy Gregory wrote the work on which his fame as an author chiefly rests—the *Liber Regulae Pastoralis,* known to English readers as the Pastoral Rule. It is divided into four parts: (*a*) on the selection of men for the work of the Church; (*b*) on the sort of life the pastor ought to lead;

(*c*) on the best methods of dealing with various types of people; and (*d*) on the necessity that the pastor guard himself against selfishness and personal ambition. Throughout the Middle Ages this work was regarded as second in importance only to the inspired books of the Bible. Its influence upon the life and manners of the clergy was beyond estimate. At their consecration the bishops of France took their oath of office on the collection of the Canons of the Church and the Pastoral Rule of St. Gregory. It was translated into Greek at an early date; Alfred the Great translated it into the Saxon tongue and sent a copy to every bishop in his kingdom. No better book on the life and duties of the clergy has ever been written. If he had written no other work than this, St. Gregory would deserve to be ranked amongst the Fathers and Doctors of the Church.

3. The Apostle of England

Gregory was a systematic organizer of missionary enterprises. He caused the last vestiges of paganism to disappear from Sardinia and Corsica, overcame Donatism in Africa, and drove Manichaeism out of Sicily. During his reign the Arians of Spain were reconciled to the Church, and the first breach was made in the solid front of Lombard Arianism in Italy. But his greatest glory lies in his title of "Apostle of England."

Of the early history of the Church in Britain only shadowy outlines have come down to us. How or when Christianity was introduced into the island, whether it came from the East or from Rome, is a matter of conjecture. At the end of the second century Tertullian already speaks of Christianity as having penetrated to regions of Britain which the Roman legions had not reached. During the Diocletian persecution British soil was reddened with the ever-fruitful seed of martyr-blood. That the British Church was well organized and in touch with the rest of Christendom is evidenced by the fact that three of her bishops signed the decrees of the important Synod of Arles in 314. To this Christian land came the destroying scourge of heathen invasion and conquest.

About the middle of the fifth century the Angles, Jutes, and Saxons, the right wing of the Teutonic host that was overrunning the Roman world, invaded Britain. They came as allies and friends of the Britons, who had been left defenseless against the attacks of the Picts from the north by the withdrawal of the Roman troops in 410. They remained as conquerors; and seldom has conquest appeared more dreadful. The arts and religion, the laws and the language, which the Romans had so carefully planted, were extirpated. The bishops and priests were scattered with their flocks, the churches demolished or profaned by heathen rites. On the ruins of the Roman cities and colonies the invaders gradually set up seven kingdoms: Kent, Sussex and Wessex in the south; East-Anglia and Essex in the east; Northumbria in the north, and Mercia in the center of the island. Britain had lost even its ancient name; it was known henceforth as the land of the Angles, or England.

St. Augustine of Canterbury

Still, in spite of all their wildness, their cruelty, their paganism, the rude Anglo-Saxon sea-rovers possessed a natural disposition and temper of mind fitted, if we may so speak, to be attracted and riveted by the teaching and liturgy of the Church. The message of the Gospel might have been brought to them by the remnants of the Britons in Wales and Cornwall, or by the Gauls and Franks; but the Britons dreaded and abhorred the Saxon so much that they did not even attempt his conversion; and in the dominions of the Franks the missionary spirit had not as yet been awakened. From the capital of the Christian world the faith was to be brought to the English: an occupant of the Chair of Peter and an Italian monk were to win the glorious title of Apostles of England.

The story of England's conversion to the faith, so beautifully told in the pages of St. Bede the Venerable, is too well known to bear repeating in detail. "We all recollect," says Cardinal Newman, "how some of the pagan invaders of Britain were brought for sale in the slave-market at Rome, and were taken

as samples of their brethren by St. Gregory the Great, who succeeded at length in buying the whole race, not for any human
master, but for Christ. From his monastery on the Caelian Hill
the Pontiff selected forty monks, whom he had himself trained
in the spiritual life and, placing Augustine, the prior, at their
head, sent them forth to preach the word of God to the English
nation."

The missionaries left Rome in the autumn of 596. They spent
the winter in northwestern Gaul, where Augustine, at the command of the Pope, received episcopal consecration. Then they
crossed the channel and landed on the Isle of Thanet. They had
chosen their place of landing with prudent calculation. Ethelbert,
who ruled over Kent at that time, had as wife the Frankish
princess Bertha, an ardent Christian. It could be reasonably
supposed that he would not be hostile to the Christian religion.
The missionaries were not disappointed. Ethelbert granted them
an interview, gave them permission to preach everywhere in his
kingdom, and supplied them with all things necessary for their
maintenance. For divine service he placed at their disposal a
church outside the walls of Canterbury, built in Roman times
and dedicated to St. Martin. On Whit-Sunday, 597, Ethelbert
renounced his pagan gods and received the sacrament of Baptism.
The majority of his people soon followed his example.

After this encouraging beginning, the Christian religion spread
rapidly throughout Kent and the neighboring kingdom of Essex.
In 601 Pope Gregory appointed Augustine "Bishop of the English" and sent him the pallium. At the same time he dispatched
a fresh band of missionaries from Rome to assist in the work
of evangelization.

Augustine had just established episcopal sees in London and
Rochester, and completed the monastery of Sts. Peter and Paul
in Canterbury, when Gregory the Great died, March 12, 604.
Bede has preserved the inscription on his tomb, which admirably
sums up his life and character:

". . . In this tomb are laid the limbs of a great pontiff, who yet
lives forever in all places in countless deeds of mercy. Hunger and cold he
overcame with food and raiment, and shielded souls from the enemy by his
holy teaching. And whatsoever he taught in word, that he fulfilled in deed,
that he might be a pattern, even as he spake words of mystic meaning.
By his guiding love he brought the Angles to Christ, gaining armies for the

faith from a new people. This was thy toil, thy task, thy care, thy aim as shepherd, to offer to .thy Lord abundant increase of the flock. So, Consul of God, rejoice in this thy triumph, for now thou hast the reward of thy works for evermore."
          —Bede's *Ecclesiastical History of England*, tr. by Sellar, pp. 81, 82.

When Augustine died in 605, the seed of the word of God had taken deep root in the good soil and gave promise of steady growth. But the tender plant had to weather many a rough storm before it became a sturdy tree. Much depended on the zeal and prudence of the missionaries, but much also on the good-will of the rulers. One bad ruler could ruin in a day the work of many years, as was the case in Kent and Essex under the heathen successors of the first Christian kings. In Kent the apostasy was fortunately not general, and St. Lawrence, the successor of St. Augustine, quickly won back both king and people ; the East Saxons, however, obstinately resisted every attempt to reconvert them till the year 653.

The losses of the Church in the south were, in part at least, counterbalanced by important gains in the north. In 627, after years of fruitless labor, St. Paulinus succeeded in converting King Edwin of Northumbria and a considerable portion of his subjects. But already in 633 Penda, the pagan king of Mercia, aided by the Britons of Wales, put an end to Edwin's rule. Paulinus had to flee, and paganism was triumphant once more. Christianity was confined to the little kingdom of Kent. The work of conversion appeared to have come hopelessly to a standstill.

At this critical juncture the ranks of the missionaries were strengthened by fresh reinforcements. Irish monks from the famous monastery of St. Columba on the Island of Iona resolutely stepped into the breach, and a glorious era of spiritual conquest followed.

A Lesson in Missionary Methods

In the year 601 Gregory the Great wrote the following letter to Abbot Mellitus, one of the second band of missionaries sent by him to England :

"When Almighty God has led you to the most reverend Bishop Augustine, tell him what I have long been considering in my own mind concerning. the matter of the English people ; to wit, that the temples of the idols in that nation ought not to be destroyed ; but let the idols that are in them be destroyed ; let water be consecrated and sprinkled in the said temples, let altars be erected, and relics placed there. For if those temples are well built, it is requisite that they be converted from the worship of devils to the service of the true God; that the nation, seeing that their temples are not destroyed, may remove error from their hearts and, knowing and adoring the true God, may the more freely resort to the places to which they have been accustomed.

And because they are used to slaughter many oxen in sacrifice to devils, some solemnity must be given them in exchange for this, as that on the day of the dedication, or the nativities of the holy martyrs, whose relics are there deposited, they should build themselves huts of the boughs of trees about those churches which have been turned to that use from being temples, and celebrate the solemnity with religious feasting, and no more offer animals to the devil, but kill cattle and glorify God in their feast, and return thanks to the Giver of all things for their abundance; to the end that, whilst some outward gratifications are retained, they may the more easily consent to the inward joys. For there is no doubt that it is impossible to cut off everything at once from their rude natures; because he who endeavors to ascend to the highest place rises by degrees or steps, and not by leaps . . ."

—Bede, *Ecclesiastical History*, I, 29.

Hints for Study

1. Read Godfrey Kurth, *What are the Middle Ages?* translated by Rt. Rev. Victor Day. It is only thirty pages in length but full of thought-provoking matter. It is printed as a supplement to the same author's *The Church at the Turning Points of History*, which should be carefully read by every student of Church History.
2. Why does Pope Gregory I deserve to be called the "Great"? What pope before him bears the same title?
3. For a detailed account of St. Gregory see Abbot Snow, *St. Gregory the Great*, F. Holmes Dudden, *Gregory the Great, His Place in History and Thought*, or Batiffol, *St. Gregory the Great*.
4. On the subjects treated in this chapter it will repay you to read Cardinal Newman, *Historical Sketches*, III, pp. 105-139.
5. What is meant by the "Patrimony of St. Peter"? Pallium? Exarch? Abbot? Basilica?
6. Read carefully the letter of Gregory to Abbot Mellitus quoted at the end of the chapter, and tell what characteristics of the writer it reveals.

CHAPTER II

WORK OF THE IRISH MISSIONARIES

1. St. Columba, Apostle of Scotland

We have seen that in their zeal for the spread of religion hundreds of Irish monks left their native land in the sixth and seventh centuries. The first and greatest of these "pilgrims" or voluntary exiles, as they called themselves, was St. Columba, the Apostle of Scotland.

Columba was born at Gartan in Donegal about the year 521. Both of his parents were of royal blood, his father being a member of the reigning family in Ireland and his mother a descendent of the kings of Leinster. In Baptism he received the name of Colum (Lat. *Columba*, dove), but he was afterwards known as Columcille, or Columba of the Cell or Church, no doubt in order to distinguish him from others of the same name; an ancient legend says that the name was given to him by his playmates. because he so often came from the little church in which he read his psalms to join in their games. He received his literary and religious training under two of the most distinguished Irishmen of his day, St. Finian of Moville and St. Finian of Clonard. Under these circumstances it was only natural that he became a monk himself, and a founder of monasteries. The famous monastery of Derry on the banks of Lough Foyle and numerous other churches and monasteries in various parts of the island revere him as their founder.

At the age of forty-two Columba left Ireland in order to preach the word of God to the Picts of northern Britain, who were still pagans. An Irish missionary band of those days presented a singular appearance. As a rule they traveled in companies of twelve. They wore a coarse outer garment, in color as it came from the fleece, and under this a white tunic of finer stuff. They were tonsured bare on the front of the head, while the long hair behind flowed down on the back, and the eyelids were painted or stained black. Each had a long stout *cambutta*, or walking-stick; and, slung from the shoulder, a leathern bottle for water, and a wallet containing his greatest treasure—a book or two and some relics (P. W. Joyce, *Smaller Social History of Ireland*, p. 148).

Of St. Columba himself his earliest biographer gives us the following portrait: "He had the face of an angel; his disposition was excellent, his speech brilliant, his deeds holy, his counsel admirable. He could not pass the space of even a single hour

St. Columba

without applying himself either to prayer, or reading, or writing, or also to some manual labor. By day and by night he was so occupied, without any intermission, in unwearied exercises of fasts and vigils, that the burden of any of these labors might seem to be beyond human endurance. And, amid all, he ever showed himself affable, smiling, saintly; he carried the joy of the Holy Spirit in his inmost heart." (Adamnan, *Life of St. Columba*, tr. Huyshe, p. 7.)

The little island of Hy or Iona, off the western coast of Scotland, was placed at Columba's disposal by the king of the Picts, and there he founded the monastery which for centuries was one of the most famous in Western Europe. It was a typical early Irish monastic settlement. Grouped about a number of small, unpretentious oratories of wood or dry-piled stone were dozens of wickerwork huts, circular or rectangular in shape. The larger ones served as guest-houses, workshops, kitchens, refectories, barns, etc.; the smaller ones were the cells of the monks, each affording accommodations for two or more persons. Somewhat apart from the rest, near the main oratory, stood the cell of the abbot. It was also of wood, but, being built on an eminence and raised from the ground on tree-stumps, it made more show than its fellows and commanded a good view of the surroundings. The whole group of buildings was enclosed by a strong rampart of palisades or stone.

St. Columba left Ireland with only twelve companions; but the number of his disciples increased from day to day. Other monasteries or hermitages had to be established on the neighboring islands and on the mainland. All these communities, together with those which the Saint had founded in Ireland, formed a vast monastic confederation known as the *Family of Columba*. Like the early Irish Church, the Church in Scotland was organized on a monastic basis. There were no dioceses ruled by bishops. Bishops performed all the episcopal functions, such as ordination, confirmation, dedication of churches and altars, but they lived in monasteries subject to the supreme authority of the abbot of Iona, who, unlike many abbots in Ireland, never received episcopal consecration.

In order to overthrow paganism in the land of the Picts, Columba resolved to attack it in its stronghold, the court of Brude, the Pictish king, at Inverness. There seems to have been a severe trial of strength between the Saint and the druids, the sworn enemies of Christianity, by whom the King was surrounded; but in the end, by his eloquent preaching, the manifest holiness of his life, and by the performance of miracles, he converted Brude and many of his subjects. All over northern Scotland and the Isles there remain to this day traces of the little cells or oratories that were planted by the monks of Iona. When Columba died on the 8th of June, 597, northern Scotland was a Christian country. The name of its apostle, says his biographer, was "venerated not only throughout Ireland and Britain, but even as far as

Spain, Gaul and Italy, and the City of Rome, the head of all cities."

2. St. Columban and Irish Missionaries on the Continent

Whilst Columba was engaged in winning the nation of the Picts for Christ, another great Irish saint, Columban, or, as he is sometimes called, Columba the Younger, left his cell in Bangor to preach the Gospel and to plant monasteries in the forests of France and Germany and in the mountains of Switzerland and Italy.

Columban was born in the west of Leinster about the year 542, and received his education first at a little monastic school on Cleenish Island in Lough Erne, and then in the far-famed monastery of St. Comgall at Bangor in the Ards of Ulster. About the year 589 he left Ireland with twelve companions, but without any well-defined purpose in view except to become an exile for the love of Christ, trusting that God would provide work for him to do in foreign parts.

In the Kingdom of the Franks.—Landing on the coast of Brittany, Columban advanced into the heart of the Frankish dominions. To one coming fresh from a land which was then the seat of a flourishing Church, abounding in fruits of sanctity, learning and zeal, the condition of Gaul must have appeared sad indeed. "Constant wars and the consequent negligence of the priests and bishops had caused religion to decay throughout the dominions of the Merovingian kings. The Christian faith indeed remained, but men hardly anywhere cared to practice self-mortification and penance." Such is the brief description which the monk Jonas, the biographer of St. Columban, gives of the state of religion in Gaul at the arrival of the Saint and his companions. But, far from discouraging him, the corruption of morals and the neglect of the saving remedy of penance aroused him to immediate and energetic action.

Pushing from place to place, Columban, like another John the Baptist, everywhere preached the Gospel of penance for the remission of sins. The people were delighted with his preaching and gathered in crowds to hear him. But the living example of the virtuous and mortified lives of the strangers made even a deeper impression on the luxurious and pleasure-loving Gallo-

Romans than the vehement eloquence of their leader. At the invitation of King Gunthram of Burgundy, Columban fixed his abode on the southwestern slope of the Vosges Mountains, near the headwaters of the Meuse, the Moselle, and the Saône, on the borders between Austrasia and Burgundy. On the ruins of a Roman fort to which the tradition of the day gave the name of Anagrates (now called Annegray) he erected his first monastery. This soon became too small, and he determined to build a larger one in the neighborhood. For this purpose Childebert II granted him the site of the once famous baths of Luxovium, or Luxeuil, as it was afterwards called. The sons of the Frankish nobility entered the new monastery in such large numbers that it, too, soon became full to overflowing. Columban accordingly founded a third colony about five miles to the north of Luxeuil, which he called Fontanae (Fontaines) from the numerous springs and rivulets with

10th Cent. MS. (St. Gall, Switzerland)
PART OF RULE OF ST. COLUMBAN

which the country was watered. It was for these three communities that he drew up his famous *Rule,* which was destined to play such an important part in the monastic history of the seventh century.

The *Rule of St. Columban* consists of two parts, which are quite different from each other in scope and character: the first part, what might be called the *moral code,* lays down the general principles on which the monastic life is based; the second part, or *penal code,* prescribes the penalties for various offenses against the rule. In the first part Columban tells his monks what virtues they must practice in order to attain perfection, insisting not so much on the reasons why they should be cultivated as on the degree in which they must be aimed at—obedience unto death, absolute poverty, daily fasting, chastity in thought and action, complete mortification of the will and the judgment, prayer without ceasing. But he was not content with the energy of command: in the second part of his Rule he displays an energy of punishment never equaled, much less surpassed by any monastic legislator. The high ascetical ideal which he had traced for his followers was not to remain a dead letter, but was to be realized at all hazards. Corporal punishment was freely meted out. Six, ten, twelve, or even fifty strokes of the lash were administered for coughing at the beginning of a psalm, or for omitting to pray before setting about the fulfillment of some task, or for offering an excuse when reprimanded. If we compare the Rule of St. Columban with that of St. Benedict, we must concede the palm of superiority to the latter. The Benedictine Rule not only has the advantage of greater moderation, but it also supplied what the Rule of St. Columban lacks, viz., eminently *practical statutes* for any association of monks. Even in his own monasteries the Rule of St. Columban was gradually supplanted by that of St. Benedict.

Preacher and Legislator of Penance.—Despite the severity of his discipline, or perhaps on account of it, the number of Columban's followers increased from day to day, and before he had been ten years in the Vosges country Luxeuil alone was peopled by more than two hundred monks. But a man of Columban's zeal and energy could not limit his activity to the direction of a few hundred monks. Men of every degree and condition sought his guidance and relief for their sin-burdened souls. The public penitential discipline still obtained in Gaul, but very few submitted to it. This system had never been introduced into Ireland. Confession and penance were private matters there. The monks accustomed the people to go to confession frequently, to confess not only their mortal sins but their less grievous offenses also, and to receive a penance from the priest. The confessor was called by the beautiful name *anam-chara* or soul-friend. "A man without an anam-chara," St. Comgall, the master of Columban, used to say, "is a body without a head." The frequency of confession naturally led to the regulation of the penitential discipline. In the absence of handbooks of Moral Theology as we have them today, the bishops and abbots compiled *Penance Books*, or *Penitentials*, which contained a detailed catalogue of sins and the appropriate penances that should be imposed by the confessors. When Columban saw how sadly in need of reform the discipline of penance was in Gaul, he immediately set to work to adapt the Penance Books of the Irish theologians to the special needs of the clergy and people.

The penalties prescribed by Columban were calculated not only to terrify the penitent by their severity but also to strike at the root of his sins. This was the purpose of the long fasts on bread and water, of the abstinence from flesh-meat and wine, of the injunction to leave home and kindred for a number of years, to free a serf or slave from bondage or to retire into a monastery. A homicide had to go unarmed into exile for three years and, after his return, to work for the parents of his victim and be as a son to them. Whoever had seriously injured or disabled another was bound to supply all his wants till his recovery.

When the Frankish bishops saw the good fruits produced everywhere by the new penitential system, they did not hesitate to give it their formal approval. Soon after Columban's death we meet with the title "father confessor" for the first time, and it is significant that it was a monk of Luxeuil who was the first to bear it.

In Conflict with Church and State.—Columban clung tenaciously to certain peculiarities of the Irish Church, such as the form of the tonsure, the liturgy of the Mass, and the date of celebrating Easter. He even went so far as to inveigh against the Easter cycle adopted by the Gallic Church and to make open propaganda for the reckoning in use in his native land. This brought him into serious conflict with the bishops. He was condemned by a synod held in 602, but no extreme measures were taken to enforce the decision.

His conflict with the notorious Brunhilde and her grandson Theodoric II, king of Burgundy, ended more disastrously. He had fearlessly reprimanded the young King for his sinful life and the Queen-Mother for encouraging him in it and for other crimes which her boundless ambition had led her to commit. An officer and a band of soldiers were sent by the enraged King to arrest Columban. They found him chanting the Office in the monastery church. "Man of God," they said, "we pray you to obey the King's orders and return whence you came." "No," answered the saint, "I left my country for the service of Jesus Christ, and I do not think that He desires me to return." He yielded at last to their entreaties, and left Luxeuil and Burgundy; all the Irish monks accompanied him. He was sent across the country to the sea, and at Nantes put on board a ship bound for Ireland. But a violent storm drove the vessel back to the coast. The captain thought that the monks he carried had brought him ill-luck, and he landed them all again at the mouth of the Loire.

The Pilgrim's Last Journey.—Columban found refuge for a time at the courts of the kings of Neustria and Austrasia. Then he withdrew with his companions to Switzerland, where he preached with some success to the pagan Alemannians and founded a little monastery at Bregenz on the shores of the Lake of Constance. When Switzerland passed into the hands of Theodoric and Brunhilde in 612, he retired to Italy. He was well received by the Lombard rulers, Agilulf and his Catholic queen Theodolinda, and at the request of the latter vigorously combated Arianism by word and writing. Although he did not succeed in converting the King, he nevertheless received from him a grant of land in one of the most beautiful parts of the Apennines, and there founded the celebrated monastery of Bobbio. Bobbio was the last stage of his long pilgrimage. Here he died on the 23rd of November, 615.

St. Columban's writings—the *Monastic Rule*, the *Penitential*, four *Homilies*, six *Letters*, and five *Latin Poems*—prove him to have been a man of learning, acquainted not only with the Scriptures and the works of the great Fathers of the Church, but also with the best Latin classics.

The Fruit of His Labors.—At the time of his death Columban bequeathed to Europe an army of spiritual sons who by their prudence, their indefatigable activity, their talent for organization, not only rescued his foundations from impending ruin, but brought them to the zenith of power and influence. If monasticism flourished in the seventh century as never before in the West, this was due in the first place to the mighty impetus given to it by the disciples of Luxeuil and Bobbio. Fourteen episcopal sees were occupied by men who had come under St. Columban's influence; they were all exemplary bishops, and ten of them are venerated by the Church as saints. At least forty monasteries of this period, both for men and women, adopted the Columbanian Rule. All these religious houses contributed their share to the revival of faith and culture in the Frankish dominions during the first half of the seventh century. "St. Columban," His Holiness Pope Pius XI wrote some years ago, "is to be reckoned among those distinguished and exceptional men whom Divine Providence is wont to raise up in the most difficult periods of human history to restore causes almost lost. This illustrious son of Ireland worked within no narrow confines. As scholarship throws an increasing light on the obscurity of the Middle Ages, the more clearly is it manifest that the revival of all Christian science and culture in many parts of France, Germany and Italy is due to the labors and zeal of Columban" (Pontifical Brief, August 6, 1923).

St. Gall, the Disciple of St. Columban.—St. Columban tarried only a little more than two years among the Alemannians. He did not accomplish much himself, but he left his ablest disciple, St. Gall, behind him to continue his work. Gall, a young Irish nobleman who had shared all his master's labors and trials, had become attached to the Alemannian people; he was acquainted with their language and their manner of life, and he hoped in time to reap a rich harvest of souls amongst them. Not wishing to remain in the deserted cloister of Bregenz after the departure of Columban, Gall explored the forest of Arbon for a suitable place in which to build a hermitage. He found it at the spot where the Steinach, an Alpine torrent, pausing for a moment in its mad rush, had formed a deep basin in the solid rock. After some time he was joined in his solitude by a number of young men from Chur and Arbon.

With immense labor [says the biographer of St. Gall] the monks rooted up trees, leveled the ground, and raised some crops. The rude huts, their first habitations, were improved and a neat little chapel, dedicated to the Blessed Virgin, was erected. Here they sang the divine praises and instructed the people who came to them. From time to time they quitted their solitude to preach in the villages and hamlets of Appenzell and Toggenburg. The wild beasts tendered their services to the man of God; snakes and other reptiles retired farther into the mountains; the demons, uttering lamentations and threats against the invaders of their ancient haunts, took to flight, and the water sprites, frightened by the ringing of the chapel bell, plunged headlong into the mountain streams and were seen no more by mortals. . . . What else do these legends tell us except that the valleys and mountainsides became the seats of culture, and that wherever the Cross is planted the power of the rulers of the world of darkness is broken forever?

The people of Constance desired to have Gall for their bishop, and the monks of Luxeuil sent a delegation to ask him to become their abbot. He declined both offers. As he grew older he left his hermitage but seldom; the last time on the feast of St. Michael in the year 641 to preach in the church of Arbon. Here he fell sick and, after a brief illness, died on the 16th of October, in the ninety-fifth year of his age. His remains were carried back to the little church on the Steinach and laid to rest "between the altar and the wall."

Many pilgrims from the surrounding countries as well as from Ireland and Britain later found their way to the tomb of the Saint, and about the middle of the eighth century the collection of hermit's cells was transformed into a regularly organized Benedictine monastery. For the next three centuries the monastery of St. Gall was one of the chief seats of learning and education in Europe. Its library was, and still is, one of the most renowned in the world by reason of its rich treasures of early manuscripts. About 954 the monastery and its far-flung subsidiary buildings were surrounded by walls as a protection against the wild Hungarian hordes, and this was the origin of the city of St. Gall, which is at present one of the most flourishing in Switzerland.

AN IVORY COVER WITH SCENES FROM LIFE OF ST. GALL

by the Monk Tuotilo. The center panel represents the Assumption of the Blessed Virgin, while in the lower one is shown St. Gall giving a piece of bread to a bear that had carried wood for him.

The Later Irish Pilgrims.—The monasteries that Columban and his Irish disciples founded on the Continent became an irresistible attraction for their countrymen. For more than three centuries such crowds of zealous and learned Irishmen swarmed

over the face of Europe that Eric of Auxerre could write to
Charles the Bald: "What shall I say of Ireland, which is migrat-
ing with almost her whole train of philosophers to our coasts?"
and Hermanrich of Ellwangen was but paying a just tribute of
admiration to Erin when he wrote: "I must not pass over in
silence the island of Hibernia whence such a flood of light went
out to us." Some of these later pilgrims occupied chairs of learning in the leading schools, others held positions of trust in the
courts of kings, and among the bishops of France and Germany
we find many a distinguished Irish name.

3. Irish Missionaries in England

The sons of St. Columba of Iona were at this time no less
active in promoting the cause of Christianity in England than
were the sons of St. Columban on the Continent. The Christian
Britons had refused to aid St. Augustine and his successors in
the work of converting the Saxon conquerors of England. When
a similar appeal was made later on to the monks of Iona, it was
responded to with alacrity.

St. Aidan, the Apostle of Northumbria.—We saw above that
Christianity, after a most auspicious beginning, was stamped out
in the north of England by the victory of Penda, the pagan king
of Mercia, over Edwin of Northumbria in year 633. But it
was not long before missionary enterprise was resumed. Oswald,
Edwin's nephew, who had passed his youth as an exile in Ireland
or in the Irish colonies in Scotland, returned in 634 to establish
himself as king of Northumbria. Anxious to restore the faith
in his dominions, he asked the monks of Iona to send him a
bishop. The first man they sent was of a harsh disposition, who
despised the Saxons as "intractable, stubborn, and barbarous."
He met with no success and returned to Iona. Another monk
was then consecrated bishop and sent to England in his place.
This was Aidan.

Oswald made a grant to Aidan of the island of Lindisfarne,
now known as Holy Island, in the North Sea, opposite the royal
residence of Bamborough. Here Aidan established his monastery
and his bishopric, he himself being both abbot and bishop but
still subject to the jurisdiction of the abbot of Iona. For thirty

years, till the Synod of Whitby (664), Lindisfarne was the most important center of religious influence in all England.

Zealously seconded by King Oswald, Aidan spread the faith with such marvelous success that some English historians do not hesitate to assert that it is St. Aidan not St. Augustine who should be called the apostle of England. He was indeed a man of truly apostolic caliber. His contemporaries dwell with delight on his sincere love of the poor, his simplicity, his straightforwardness, his austerity of life, his gift of gaining the hearts of all who came in contact with him. Love of the poor was a passion with him. King Oswin of Deira, relates St. Bede, "had given a beautiful horse to Bishop Aidan, though the Bishop was wont to travel ordinarily on foot. Some short time after, when a poor man met the Bishop and asked alms, he immediately dismounted, and ordered the horse with all his royal trappings to be given to the beggar. When this was told to the King, on the way in to dinner, he said to the Bishop, "What did you mean, my lord Bishop, by giving the poor man that royal horse? Had not we things of other sorts which would have been good enough to give to the poor?" Thereupon the Bishop answered, "What do you say, O King? Is that son of a mare more dear to you than that son of God?" When the King heard this, he fell down at the Bishop's feet, beseeching him to forgive him. "From this time forward," said he, "I will never judge of what or how much of our money you shall give to the sons of God."

St. Bede speaks very highly of the labors and virtues of Aidan. He reproaches him only with one thing: with having observed Easter after the manner of the Irish. But this disagreement, in a purely disciplinary matter, did not prevent other saints, who were his contemporaries, a Honorius of Canterbury, a Felix of East Anglia, both observers of the Roman Easter, from professing the greatest veneration for the apostle of Northumbria.

End of the Irish Mission in England.—Aidan died in 651. Finan, another Irishman, was sent from Iona to succeed him. Finan built a church in Lindisfarne worthier of an episcopal see than the original one. However, he did not use stone for the construction, but hewn oak, "after the manner of the Irish," and covered it with reeds. He did much for the diffusion of Christianity beyond the borders of Northumbria. He baptized two pagan kings, Peada, son of Penda, king of the Middle Angles, and

Sigebert, king of the East Saxons. He sent four priests to the Middle Angles, among them the Anglo-Saxon Cedd and the Irishman Diuma. Both were afterwards raised to the episcopacy, Cedd becoming bishop of the East Saxons, Diuma remaining in Middle Anglia. On his death Diuma was succeeded by Cellach, another Irishman from Iona.

St. Finan was succeeded in the see of Lindisfarne by Colman, a monk of Iona. It was during his episcopate that the dispute between the "Romans" and the Irish broke out regarding the date for the celebration of Easter. The whole country was divided into two hostile camps. There was division in the very household of the King: while the King was keeping Easter, the Queen, an ardent Roman, was still fasting and celebrating Palm Sunday. A great conference was held at Whitby (664) between the supporters of the rival systems. King Oswy of Northumbria presided. Bishop Colman defended the custom of his countrymen, and Wilfrid, a student of the monks of Lindisfarne, but who had gone over to the Roman customs after a prolonged visit to Rome and southern Gaul, was the champion of the "Romans." "Colman alleged in favor of his own view the authority of St. Columba, and made an impassioned appeal to the assembly not to abandon what had been inculcated by such a great servant of God. Wilfrid, however, weakened the effect of this appeal by opposing to the authority of St. Columba the authority of St. Peter, to whom Christ had said, "Thou art Peter, and upon this rock I will build my Church, and I will give to thee the keys of the kingdom of heaven." Oswy demanded of Colman whether these words were really spoken to Peter and if they were, could he point to a similar promise made by Christ to St. Columba. Colman was obliged to admit that to Peter alone was this promise given, whereupon Oswy promptly closed the discussion by deciding in favor of Rome; he did not dare, he said, to resist the Door-keeper, lest perhaps when he presented himself at the gates of the kingdom of heaven there should be none to open them to him. Colman and his monks, about thirty of them Northumbrians, rather than abandon the practice of their founder, returned to Lindisfarne, raised up the bones of their saintly dead, bade adieu to the monastery and the church they loved so much, and set sail for Ireland." Nearly a hundred years elapsed before all the Celts of Great Britain and Ireland conformed to the practice of the rest of Christendom in the celebration of Easter.

4. The Golden Age of the Anglo-Saxon Church

Roman and Irish missionaries had given the faith to the Anglo-Saxon race; a Greek monk completed the organization of the youthful Church and helped to give to its schools the high place which they held in Western Europe during the next two centuries.

In 668 Pope St. Vitalian (657-672) sent the Monk Theodore of Tarsus, and Hadrian, a countryman of St. Augustine, to England. "Both of them were distinguished for their classical, as well as their ecclesiastical attainments; and while Theodore had been educated in Greek usages, Hadrian represented the more congenial and suitable traditions of the West. Theodore, who was then in his sixty-seventh year, was made archbishop of Canterbury and primate of England, while Hadrian was placed at the head of the Abbey of St. Augustine. They immediately proceeded to found schools of

FACSIMILE OF PAGE FROM AN OLD IRISH ILLUMINATED MS.

The Latin words with contractions read: "Initium Avangelii Dni nri ihu chri filii di etc" (*Mark I, I: The Beginning of the Gospel Our Lord Jesus Christ, etc.*).

secular, as well as of sacred learning throughout the south of the island." Crowds of disciples gathered about them, and "rivers of wholesome knowledge," Bede enthusiastically assures us, "daily flowed from them to water the hearts of their hearers." Many of their scholars were as familiar with Greek and Latin as with their native tongue.

Out of the soil thus prepared by Roman, Greek, and Celt there burst forth the first spring of genuine medieval culture at a time when literary activity had all but ceased in the rest of Europe. The century that followed may be justly styled the Golden Age of the Anglo-Saxon Church. "There were never happier times," says Bede, "since the English came into Britain; for, having brave Christian kings, they were a terror to all barbarous nations, and the minds of all men were bent upon the joys of the heavenly

kingdom of which they had but lately heard; and all who desired to be instructed in sacred studies had masters at hand to teach them." St. Aldhelm and St. Bede are the chief representatives of the new era.

St. Aldhelm (*c.* 640-709), the father of Anglo-Saxon poetry and the greatest scholar of his time, was a West Saxon of royal blood, and born about 640. He studied first under the Irish hermit and monk, Malldub, whose cell he afterwards converted into the famous Benedictine monastery of Malmesbury, and then under Hadrian in the school of Canterbury. His versatile mind absorbed learning of the most varied kind. He was as familiar with the ancient classical as with early Christian literature, with the history of Greece and Rome as with the story of the Bible and the Church, with the legends of the saints and the principles of monasticism as with the rules of grammar and prosody, the science of numbers, the mysteries of astrology and the intricacies of ecclesiastical chronology and Roman Law. His style,

St. Bede

though always vivid and animated, is often turgid and full of extravagant conceits, and, owing to the high estimation in which he was held and the great popularity of his writings, his influence in this respect on contemporary letters was rather harmful than otherwise.

In *Bede* (673-735), whose home was in the north of England, we have a perfect type of the outward repose and intellectual activity—the "toil unsever'd from tranquillity"—of the Benedictine life. His works, which number no less than forty-five, embrace the whole compass of the learning of his age. His historical writings, especially his *Ecclesiastical History of England*, written as they are with scrupulous regard for the truth and in a simple and pleasing style, place him in the first rank among the writers of the Middle Ages. Everywhere in his works, says the translator of his *Ecclesiastical History*, we find the impress of a mind of wide intellectual grasp, a character of the highest saintliness, and a gentle refinement of thought and feeling. His lofty spirituality, his great learning and scholarly attainment are the more striking, when we reflect how recently his nation had emerged from barbarism and received Christianity and the culture which it brought with it to the British shores.

The conversion of England was one of the most important events in the history of Christianity. Supernatural faith and love burned too strongly in the hearts of the Saxon neophytes to brook confinement within the narrow bounds of their homeland. Their fierceness and boldness, now softened and subdued by grace, made them ready to do and to suffer for the sake of Him "in whose death they had been baptized." Hardly converted themselves, they already undertook to carry "the light of truth, the flame of love, the fertility of martyrdom" into the depths of the German forests still covered with heathen darkness. Their memory is still held in benediction by the people amongst whom they labored. The most illustrious of that heroic band was the apostle and martyr Wynfrid, whose second name *Bonifatius*, "the messenger of good tidings," expresses so exactly his glorious career.

The Death of St. Columba

St. Adamnan (624-704), seventh abbot of Iona, is the author of several books, but his fame rests on his *Life of St. Columba*, which is conceded by all historians to be one of the most interesting and valuable pieces of hagiology in existence. In the 23rd chapter of the third part, which describes the passing of St. Columba, we have, according to Mr. W. Huyshe, who translated the whole work into English, "one of the most exquisite pieces of pure biography ever written, not to be surpassed, indeed, in the whole range of ancient biography—simple, dignified, pathetic—a very gem of literature." The following extract is taken from this chapter:

"On Saturday (the 8th of June) the Saint, with his faithful attendant Diormit, ascended a little hill above the monastery and gave it his farewell blessing. Returning to the monastery, he sat in his hut transcribing the Psalter; and coming to that verse of the thirty-third Psalm, where it is written: 'But they that seek the Lord shall not want any good thing,' he said, 'Here I must stop at the foot of this page, and what follows let Baithene write.' After transcribing the verse, the Saint entered the church for the vespers of the vigil of the Lord's Day, and as soon as this was over, he returned to his cell and sat up throughout the night on his bed, where he had the bare rock for pallet and a stone for pillow, which to this day stands by his grave as his monumental pillar. When the bell began to toll at midnight, rising in haste, he went to the church and on bended knees fell down in prayer at the altar. Diormit, entering the church a little later, moaned out with mournful voice: 'Where art thou, Father?' And as the lights of the Brethren had not yet been brought in, groping his way in the dark he found the Saint lying before the altar, and, raising him up a little and sitting down by him, he laid the holy head on his bosom. And meanwhile the community of monks, running up with lights, began to weep at the sight of their dying Father. Diormit then lifted up the right hand of the Saint that he might bless the choir of monks. But the venerable Father himself at the same time moved his hand as much as he was able, so that what was impossible to him to do with his voice at his soul's departure he might still do by the movement of his hand, namely, give his blessing to the Brethren. And after thus signifying his holy benediction, he immediately breathed forth his spirit. And it having left the tabernacle of the body, the face remained so ruddy and wonderfully gladdened that it seemed not to be that of one dead, but of one living and sleeping. Meanwhile, the whole church resounded with sorrowful wailings. . . ."

Hints for Study

1. Adamnan's *Life of St. Columba,* translated with notes and illustrations by Wentworth Huyshe, may be had for a few cents and should be in every High School library (Universal Library, New York, Dutton and Co.).
2. An excellent account of the labors of the Celts for Christianity and civilization will be found in Gougaud, *Gaelic Pioneers of Christianity.*
3. Two works on St. Columban have been published in America: George Metlake, *Life and Writings of St. Columban* (Philadelphia, Dolphin Press), and Rev. E. J. McCarthy, D.S.C., *Montalembert's St. Columban* (The Society of St. Columban, St. Columban's, Neb.).
4. Bede's *Ecclesiastical History of England* translated by A. M. Sellar is the best and cheapest English edition of this invaluable work.
5. Summarize, in the form of a chronological table, the labors of the Irish missionaries, beginning with the birth of St. Columba and ending with the retirement of Colman from Lindisfarne.
6. What Missionary Society in the United States is named after St. Columban?
7. How did the penitential discipline of the Irish Church differ from that of the Roman Church?
8. Why is it so important that Easter should be celebrated at the same time all over Christendom? Look up *Easter* in the *Cath. Encyc.*

CHAPTER III

ANGLO-SAXON MISSIONARIES IN GERMAN LANDS

Of the German tribes which had been subdued by the Franks, the Bavarians alone were Christians; but the Bavarian Church lacked organization and stood in need of reform. The Alemannians and Suabians were gradually becoming christianized through the efforts of Irish and Frankish missionaries. The Thuringians and Hessians, who were only loosely subjected to the Frankish kingdom, still held fast to their pagan practices. The Frisians, who at this time occupied the coastland from the Maas to the region beyond the Ems, were fiercely defending themselves against the introduction of the Frankish rule and of Christianity. The Saxons retained their full independence as well as their paganism. This was the vast field which the Anglo-Saxons had chosen for their missionary enterprise. Amongst the Saxons and the independent Frisians their efforts were fruitless, because in those regions there was no one to protect them·against heathen malice and cruelty. Amongst the other tribes their labors were crowned with success, because, though protected by the rulers of the Franks, they did not belong to the hated race of the conquerors. Their mission also produced permanent results, because they remained in constant communication with the Pope, the Head of the Church.

1. The English Mission in Frisia. St. Willibrord

A happy accident drew the attention of the English Church to Frisia. When Wilfrid, whom we met at the Synod of Whitby, and who afterwards became archbishop of York, was expelled from his see in 668, he set out for Rome to plead his cause before the Pope. But his ship was driven by contrary winds on the coast of Frisia. He was honorably received by the Frisian ruler, Aldfrid, and permitted to preach the Gospel. His stay, however, was too short to enable him to do more than reap a hasty harvest. Several subsequent attempts made by Egbert, Wigbert, and other English monks residing in Ireland to continue the work begun by Wilfrid, failed utterly. Then in 689 Willibrord, a pupil of Wilfrid, set out for Frisia with eleven companions, among them St. Suitbert. With the sanction of Pope Sergius (687-701) and under the protection of Pippin I, the Austrasian Mayor of the Palace, Willibrord preached with extraordinary success among the Frisians south of the Rhine, who had been recently brought under Frankish rule. The missionaries chose the pious and gentle Suitbert for their bishop and sent him to England to be consecrated by Wilfrid. For some reason unknown to us Suitbert quitted Frisia and undertook the evangelization of the Bructeri on the Ruhr and Lippe. When the inroads of the pagan Saxons obliged him to abandon this promising field, Pippin gave him lands on the island of Kaiserswerth on the Rhine above Düsseldorf for the erection of a monastery. Here he died in 713.

After Suitbert's departure Willibrord received episcopal consecration in Rome and took up his residence in Utrecht. His success in Frisia tempted him to pass into other districts. He traveled as far as Denmark, and from there brought back thirty boys to be educated among the Franks. On his return he was wrecked on the holy island of Fosite (Heligoland); here he killed some of the sacred cattle of the god Fosite, a son of Balder, and baptized three men in his well. His boldness nearly cost him his life.

Although fresh recruits arrived at intervals from England and Ireland, Willibrord nevertheless took care to create a native clergy. For this purpose he founded the monastery of Echternach, in the present Grand Duchy of Luxemburg. His work seemed to be finished. But its stability depended entirely on the stability of the Frankish rule. When Pippin died in 714, Radbod, the pagan king of northern Frisia, took advantage of the confusion that ensued to regain possession of the lost Frisian territories. Direful times followed for the Frisian Church. The churches were desecrated or demolished and the worship of the false gods was everywhere renewed. Willibrord and his monks fled to Echternach. It was at this juncture that the greatest of the English missionaries, St. Boniface, arrived in Frisia.

2. St. Boniface, the Apostle of Germany

Wynfrid, a West Saxon of noble blood, was born about the year 675 at Crediton in Devon. At the age of seven he was sent by his parents to the Benedictine monastery of Exeter, where he passed the childhood and boyhood of his religious life. After studying for some years in other monastic schools, he entered Nhutscelle in Hampshire probably in the year 702 or 703. Here he was ordained priest in his thirtieth year and entrusted with the direction of the monastery school. He fulfilled his duties with such zeal and success that he attracted crowds of students from all parts of Wessex. But his heart was set on becoming a missionary, and in the spring of 716 he crossed to the Continent to assist Willibrord in evangelizing the Frisians. As we saw above, he could not have come at a more unfavorable time. Undeterred, however, by what he saw and heard around him, he went straight to the royal residence and sought an interview with Radbod himself, who had just returned in triumph from his victory over Charles Martel. The daring resoluteness of the Saxon monk did not fail to impress the king, who permitted him to preach in his kingdom as long as he pleased. Fruitful missionary work being out of the question under the circumstances, Wynfrid returned to Nhutscelle before the close of the year. But it was only for a short rest and in order to form new plans. Before choosing a definite field of labor, he resolved to go to Rome to receive the sanction and blessing of the Holy Father. He arrived there in the autumn of 718 and was most kindly welcomed by Gregory II (715-731).

Missionary Apostolic.—On the 15th of May, 719, Wynfrid had his last audience with the Pope. As a symbol of his intimate union with the Roman Church, Gregory gave him the name of *Boniface,* in honor of the holy martyr whose feast occurred on the previous day. He then appointed him by a special Brief, the first of its kind that has come down to us, missionary apostolic to all the heathen peoples to whom God might direct him; orally he commissioned him to proceed first to the Thuringians. But he had not been there many months, when the news of the death of Radbod determined him to attempt the conversion of the Frisians once more. For nearly two years he labored with great success under Willibrord, destroying heathen temples and sanctuaries, erecting churches and oratories, and bringing multitudes of pagans into the fold. From time to time he sent reports of his labors to his friends in England, who followed his fortunes with the deepest interest and assisted him with their prayers, with gifts of books, altar linen, and money.

Willibrord wished to make Boniface his coadjutor; Boniface, however, refused the proffered dignity and returned to his own

POPE GREGORY MAKES ST. BONIFACE MISSIONARY APOSTOLIC

mission field in central Germany. Crossing the Rhine at Mainz, he penetrated into the country of the Hessians between the Fulda and the Lahn. Here he made hosts of converts and at Amöneburg, the chief stronghold of the district, erected his first monastery on German soil. Then he passed on to the Saxon border. Here, too, numerous conversions rewarded his zeal, but only at the cost of the greatest perils and hardships.

Missionary Bishop and Archbishop.—When Gregory heard of Boniface's successes in Germany, he summoned him to Rome for a personal interview. His real object was to confer episcopal consecration upon him. The ceremony took place on the 30th of November, 722. After his return to Hesse, the Saint's first care was to administer the sacrament of Confirmation to his converts. Then he resumed his preaching among the pagan and semi-pagan inhabitants, many of whom were daily added to the Church. A bold deed which he performed at this time greatly increased his prestige and led to numerous conversions. At Geismar, near Fritzlar, there was a gigantic oak, called the "Tree of Thor," which the pagans of the whole country regarded with the deepest veneration. Mighty as the God of the Christians was, over the oak of Geismar, so they boasted, He had no power, and none of His followers would dare destroy it. This tree the Christians advised Boniface to cut down, assuring him that its fall would shake the faith of the pagans in the power of their gods. Boniface consented, and on the appointed day undertook to lay the ax to the tree with his own hands. A vast crowd of pagans stood around, intently watching to see some dire misfortune overwhelm the desecrator of their shrine. But when the mighty tree fell to the ground under the strokes of the Bishop's ax, they with one accord praised the God of the Christians and asked to be received among the number of His followers. Boniface baptized them, and out of the wood of the tree built a little oratory, which he dedicated to St. Peter. In order to insure a supply of priests for Hesse, he founded the monastery of Fritzlar in 725. Then he returned to his first mission field in Thuringia.

In Thuringia Boniface encountered violent opposition, not on the part of the pagans, but of some unworthy priests of Anglo-Saxon origin, who had labored in the Thuringian mission before him. But these men were no match for Boniface. The people, who are ever attracted by great and saintly personalities, soon turned their backs upon their seducers, and Boniface remained in possession of the field. At Ohrdruf, in the heart of the Thuringian Forest, Boniface founded a monastery, which he made his episcopal residence, or rather the place where he occasionally tarried; for in these years of intense missionary activity the saddle, the tent, and the huts of the scattered peasants were his home.

St. Gregory II, who had done so much to make Boniface's labors a success, died in 731. His successor, the learned and energetic Gregory III (731-741) raised Boniface to the archiepiscopal dignity, charging him at the same time "to consecrate bishops for those parts in which the multitude of the faithful showed the greatest increase." The Papal letter was accompanied with the Pallium, which, "according to the apostolic prescriptions, he was to use only for the celebration of the solemn service of the Mass or at the consecration of a bishop."

Help from Home.—It was ten years before Boniface could carry out the Papal plan of dividing up his mission field into dioceses. But if bishops could be dispensed with, more missionaries had to be supplied at once. Until Germany could furnish these herself, he had to look for them abroad. And where could he hope to obtain them if not from his native land? He was not disappointed. His call for help was eagerly obeyed by the best and holiest of his countrymen, by Burchard, Willibald, Wynnebald, Lullus, Wigbert, Denhard, John, Wiethbert, all of them venerated as saints of God. Among the women who gave their services to the German mission the most eminent was Boniface's cousin Lioba or Leobgytha, to whom the Bollandists have given the beautiful title of *Germaniae Apostola*—"the woman apostle of Germany." In the valley of the Main, Boniface and Lioba founded three monasteries for women. Lioba assumed the direction of the first and most important of these, Bischofsheim on the Tauber; her kinswoman Thecla was placed over the smaller houses in Kitzingen and Ochsenfurt. Other Saxon women, such as St. Walburga and St. Cynehild, founded monastic schools in other parts of the land. Lioba and her companions thus became a factor in the evangelization of Germany second in importance only to the missionaries themselves.

Papal Legate.—The year 738 marks a turning-point in the life of St. Boniface. Under his fostering care the Church in Hesse and Thuringia had grown like the mustard seed in the parable and become a great tree. He himself estimated the number of converts from paganism at about one hundred thousand. He had crossed the Alps in 737 and had returned in the following year as Papal Legate with practically unlimited powers over Austrasia, which were afterwards extended to Neustria also. The next ten years of his life were devoted almost exclusively to reform and organization work. He began in Bavaria. With the aid of Duke Odilo and the Bavarian nobility, he divided the country into four bishoprics (Passau, Salzburg, Freising and Ratisbon) with accurately defined limits, and selected fitting occupants for each. In his own mission districts he erected the sees of Buraburg, Erfurt, and Würzburg. Only Würzburg survived, Eichstädt later on taking the place of Buraburg and Erfurt. The consecration of the new bishops took place in 741. Before the end of the year a new and vaster field of labor was opened to Boniface. At an age when the life-work of most men nears completion, the most difficult and momentous part of his was to begin. He had founded one Church and reorganized another; he was now called upon to bring order out of chaos in a third.

Reform of the Church in the Kingdom of the Franks.— There are few darker pages in the history of the Church than those which describe the state of religion in the kingdom of the Franks under the last Merovingians, the notorious *rois fainéants*, the do-nothing kings, and their all-powerful Mayors of the Palace. Boniface's picture of the condition of the Church at the death of Charles Martel is not a whit overcharged. "For more than threescore years," he writes to Pope Zachary in 742, "all ecclesiastical order and discipline has been set at nought and trodden under foot; for more than eighty years the Franks have not held a synod nor had an archbishop, nor have the laws of the Church been enforced anywhere in all that time. The episcopal sees are for the most part in the hands of avaricious laymen or of dissolute ecclesiastics, who hold them as temporal possessions. No wickedness is a bar to the priesthood or the episcopacy."

Karlmann, who succeeded Charles Martel in Austrasia, resolved to take in hand the reform of the Church in his dominions, and asked Boniface to aid him in the work. "Karlmann, the Prince of the Franks," Boniface wrote to the Pope, "sent for me and desired me to take the necessary steps for holding a synod in that part of the Frankish dominions which is subject to his authority. He promised to reform as far as possible the abuses which have so long made havoc of all ecclesiastical order and discipline in these lands." The synod met April 21, 742. In Church History it is known as the First German Synod. Karlmann sanctioned its decrees, thus making them part of the civil law of the land.

The synod began its work by restoring the metropolitan constitution of the Church. The new bishoprics founded by Boniface were formally recognized, and steps were taken to fill the many vacant sees with worthy incumbents. Boniface was made archbishop and metropolitan of the whole Austrasian Church, and was at the same officially recognized as the *missus sancti Petri*—"the ambassador of St. Peter." All the church property that had passed into the hands of laymen was to be restored to its rightful owners. A synod was to meet once a year in the presence of the ruler.

Stringent laws were enacted for the diocesan clergy. Every year, during Lent, every parish priest must give an account of his ministry to his bishop, especially of the manner in which he celebrates Mass, prays, preaches, and administers the sacrament of Baptism. When the bishop comes to confirm the faithful, the priest must be ready to receive him, and present the candidates properly prepared for the reception of the Sacrament. On Holy Thursday he must go in person to the bishop for the Holy Oils, and at the same time furnish him with proof of the purity of his life, faith, and teaching. All false and unworthy priests, deacons, and other clerics are to be deposed, degraded, and subjected to punishment. Priests and deacons are not to dress like laymen. No women, except a mother, sister, or niece, are to live in the same house with a priest or deacon. All ecclesiastics are prohibited from hunting and hawking, carrying arms, or going to war. Two bishops and the royal chaplains are, however, to accompany the prince to the wars for the celebration of Mass and the custody of the Holy Relics; and one priest is to be appointed for each body of troops to hear the confessions of the soldiers. The Rule of St. Benedict is made obligatory on all monks and nuns, and the strictest discipline is enjoined on the members of the religious communities. Violations of the vow of chastity are to be visited with severe corporal punishment.

In spite of a thousand obstacles—an attempt was even made on Boniface's life—the decrees of the Synod did not remain a dead letter. Able and zealous men were immediately appointed to the vacant sees of Utrecht, Metz, Verdun, Speyer, and Liége. The most distinguished of the new prelates was *Chrodegang of Metz.* He was the son of a Rhenish nobleman, and had received the best education that could be got in those days. He spoke and wrote both German and Latin with equal facility. His talents and polished manners won for him the favor of Charles Martel, who made him his chancellor. As bishop he was noted for his piety and his great liberality to the poor, and became one of the chief promoters of the reform among the monks and the clergy. He introduced the Roman liturgy and plain chant into his diocese, and eagerly supported every movement whose object it was to bring the Frankish Church into closer union with Rome. Eventually he succeeded Boniface as metropolitan archbishop of Austrasia.

In 743 Pippin, who had succeeded Charles Martel in Neustria, invited Boniface to extend his reform labors into his dominions. As conditions in Neustria were similar to those which had prevailed in Austrasia, Boniface applied the same remedies. On March 2, 744, the first Neustrian synod was held in the presence of Pippin. The assembled bishops adopted nearly all the decrees passed by the German synod, with such modifications as local conditions required. A year later a joint council of all the bishops of Austrasia and Neustria was convened. Besides deposing Gewilip of Mainz and condemning two heretics to do penance in a monastery, the question of an archiepiscopal see for Boniface was discussed. The choice fell on Cologne, which had just become vacant. Though his appointment was ratified by Pope Zachary, Boniface never became archbishop of Cologne. In 746 he took up his residence in Mainz.

Union with the Holy See.—Not long after taking possession of the see of Mainz, Boniface scored one of the greatest triumphs of his life. By word and example he had gradually accustomed the Frankish authorities to regulate Church affairs in unison with Rome. The conviction that the Church could thrive only in union with Rome, had taken strong root in the Frankish episcopacy. Boniface resolved to bring about a public and solemn declaration of this conviction. For this purpose he summoned a general synod in the spring of 747. It was attended by thirteen bishops from both parts of the kingdom, and many auxiliary bishops, abbots, priests, and deacons. Boniface gained his end without any serious opposition. "In our synodal assembly," he wrote to Archbishop Cuthbert of Canterbury, "we decreed and declared that we would preserve the Catholic faith, and unity, and subjection to the Roman Church to the end of our life; that we would be subject to St. Peter and his Vicar; that the metropolitans should apply to the Apostolic See for their palliums, and in all things should strive to follow the precepts of St. Peter, in order that they might be numbered among the sheep entrusted to him. This confession we all consented to and subscribed, and sent to the body of St. Peter, the Prince of the Apostles."

After the synod Boniface composed a treatise on the *Unity of the Catholic Faith* for the use of the clergy, and sent it, together with the declaration of the bishops, to the Holy Father. Zachary expressed his joy and satisfaction in a letter to Boniface and to all who had taken part in the synod. The Pope had reason to rejoice. At a time when the East was rapidly becoming estranged from the West, when the signs of the Great Schism were already visible, it was of the highest importance that the youthful Frankish Church so unmistakably declared its obedience to the Holy See. It was the prelude to still closer relations, and a guarantee that the Frankish episcopacy would never again drift away from the center of unity as it had done in the course of the seventh century.

The Foundation of Fulda.—While Boniface was bending all his energies to bring about the reform of the Church in the land of the Franks, he did not forget his own mission field. He had long planned the erection of a monastery on a larger scale than he or his predecessors had as yet attempted in Germany. It should become the monastic metropolis of the country, the strategic center for the evangelization of the North, a training school for priests and missionaries, a nursery of the arts of peace. His beautiful dream was realized in 744 by the foundation of Fulda. Year after year, as often as his affairs permitted him, he repaired to Fulda both to refresh his own soul and body by solitude and prayer, and to edify the Brethren by his example and his holy conversation. In numerous conferences he explained to them the Rule of St. Benedict, urging them to observe both its letter and its spirit. After one of these conferences, in which he had spoken to them of the holy Patriarch's wish that monks should not drink wine, all the brethren with one accord solemnly pledged themselves to abstain from all intoxicating beverages—a promise which Boniface himself had made on the day of his ordination.

Fulda remained the special object of Boniface's care and affection. He sought to throw around it all the safeguards in his power. He caused a deed to be drawn up recording the founding of the Abbey and the exact limits of its territory. From Pope Zachary he obtained the privilege of exemption from the jurisdiction of the Ordinary and subjection only to that of the Holy See.

Boniface's loving solicitude for the newly-found abbey was abundantly rewarded. Before the death of the first abbot, St. Sturm, in 779, Fulda numbered about four hundred monks. Under their busy hands the forests were rapidly cleared away, the morasses drained, the watercourses regulated, the valleys and hillsides turned into smiling fields and gardens. Under the protection of religion the arts flourished. Scarcely half a century after its foundation Fulda was already one of the chief centers of religious and ecclesiastical life north of the Alps. Among the men of letters who graced the reigns of Charlemagne and Louis the Pious, not a few were monks of Fulda. The fifth abbot was the great Rhabanus Maurus, the most learned man of his age, who made Fulda famous as a seat of learning throughout Europe. His most celebrated pupils were Walafrid Strabo, a poet of no mean ability and the immortal author of the interlinear glosses to the Scriptures; Servatus Lupus, whose extant letters are invaluable to the student of Carolingian history; Haimo of Halberstadt, whose name will live on in German literature as the author of the *Heliand*, the first religious epic in the German tongue, and Otfrid of Weissenburg in Alsace, whose metrical harmony of the Gospels is the earliest and best specimen of the Frankish dialect. The renowned Eginhard also, the biographer of Charlemagne and the builder of the minster of Aix-la-Chapelle, received his early training in Fulda. During the first century of its existence no less than twenty-two bishops and archbishops and fourteen abbots were pupils of Fulda.

The Martyr's Crown.—In the course of the year 752 Boniface fell so ill that he believed himself to be at death's door. But his illness did not prove fatal. He soon felt strong enough to carry out a long-cherished wish. This was nothing less than the resumption of the evangelization of Frisia, which had been interrupted by the death of St. Willibrord in 739. Boniface had never forgotten Frisia. He had left it with his body, as his biographer says, but not with his heart. Here he had suffered his first reverses and won his first victories; he was resolved that it should also be the last scene of his conflict with the powers of darkness.

Towards the end of June, 753, he set out for Utrecht with a numerous train of followers. He chose the east coast of the Zuider Zee for the scene of his labors. Almost unexampled success attended his preaching. Thousands of men, women, and children were baptized; the heathen fanes were demolished and replaced by Christian chapels. The fifth of June, which in 754 fell on Wednesday of Whitsuntide, was set for the confirmation of the neophytes. In the meantime the pagans, whose fanaticism increased as they saw the power of their false gods diminish, were concerting the destruction of Boniface and his companions. They made their preparations with such secrecy that no sign of their barbarous purpose was seen before the day fixed for the administration of the sacrament. Boniface had spent the greater part of the night in prayer, and the rising sun found him still poring over the pages of a holy book. Suddenly the sound of approaching multitudes was heard. But they were not peaceful Christian men and women coming to be enrolled in the army of the Prince of peace. The brandished lances and unsheathed swords flashing in the morning light revealed their deadly design. In haste, with such weapons as they could find, some of the attendants rushed forward to interpose themselves as a defense between the murderers and their prey.

The confused sounds, each moment growing louder, roused

Boniface and his companions. With some holy relics, which he never failed to carry about with him, in his hand, he came forth at their head out of the tent and besought those who would have fought for him to lay by their swords. He had scarcely finished speaking when the murderers were already upon him. He was one of their first victims. A woman, who was a witness of the tragic scene, afterwards told a priest of Utrecht that the Saint placed a copy of the Gospels on his head just as the fatal blow

THE MARTYRDOM OF ST. BONIFACE

descended. The sword of the barbarian pierced through the book and cleaved the head of the martyr. The work of carnage was soon ended. Boniface and fifty-two of his followers slept in peace. The good shepherd had given his life for his sheep; the brave soldier, for his "Captain Christ, under whose banner he had fought so long." His body was carried to Fulda and laid to rest in the chancel of the abbey church.

St. Boniface's Place in History.—If we wish to assign to Boniface his proper place in history, we must keep in mind the scope and dimensions of his work. When he began his labors on the Continent, Southern Germany was already christianized, but without ecclesiastical organization; what there was of Christianity in Central Germany was in danger of extinction through predominant paganism; in Frisia missionary enterprise, after a period of bloom, had come to a standstill; all attempts to introduce the faith among the Saxons had failed; in Austrasia and Neustria, in what is today the Rhineland, Alsace-Lorraine, Belgium, and Northern France, political and ecclesiastical chaos reigned: relations with the center of Christendom had been suspended for nearly a hundred years, the metropolitan constitution had collapsed, the clergy were undisciplined, the monks woefully fallen from their first fervor. When he fell under the strokes of the Frisian battle-axes, what a wonderful change had been wrought!—The German Church was firmly established, the Frankish Church thoroughly reformed and reorganized, and vigor, life, and unity secured to both by their union with the Apostolic See. The Saxons alone remained entrenched in their paganism, but their outworks were already taken, and their submission was only a question of time.

Not less significant, though often overlooked, is the rôle which Boniface played in the founding of the German nation. By uniting the numerous warring German tribes religiously and ecclesiastically with one another and with Rome, he laid the foundations for their political union and consequently for Germany's existence as a nation and its subsequent greatness. In a double sense, therefore, he justly deserves to be called the *Apostle of the Germans.* "The German people," says a Protestant historian, "owes more to him than to any of its kings or emperors."

What Boniface's labors meant for a great part of modern France, a writer in the French weekly, *Ami du Clergé,* has expressed in a few pregnant sentences: "What would have become of the Church in the northern provinces of our country without St. Boniface? After ten generations of Catholic kings, the Franks at the dawn of the eighth century were returning to paganism; without the Carolingian renaissance they would have retained perhaps only some faint recollection of the Gospel—a fable more in the mythology of the Edda. St. Boniface ought on this account to be as dear to us as he is to the Catholics of Germany." (Vol. 24, p. 844).

"The importance of the work of Boniface," writes G. W. Robinson, in his Introduction to his translation of Willibald's *Life of St. Boniface* (p. 19), "in the ecclesiastical and, indeed, in the general history of Europe cannot easily be exaggerated. His activities may be viewed under several aspects, according as we consider him as one of the foremost scholars of his time; introducer of learning and literature and to a large extent of the arts of civilized life into the German lands; or as the great champion of Rome and of ecclesiastical uniformity in Central Europe; or as a missionary of God, a soldier, and leader in the great Christian warfare against the heathen of the North."

Letter of St. Lioba to St. Boniface

While still a pupil of the holy and accomplished Eadburga in the convent of Our Lady on the Isle of Thanet, Lioba wrote to her famous kinsman on the Continent, reminding him of their relationship, offering him her friendship and begging for his in return. Nearly twelve hundred years have passed away since this little letter was written, but it might have been written yesterday, so akin to our own are the sentiments it expresses. There is something inexpressibly charming in the childlike confidence with which the maiden turns to the man:

"I beseech your goodness to call to mind the friendship that united you long ago with my father Dynne. It is eight years since he was taken away from the light of this life. May it please you to offer up your prayers to God for his soul. I also commend my mother Aebba to you, who, as you well know, is bound to you by the ties of blood relationship. She is still alive, but oppressed by the weight of years and bodily ills.

I am my parents' only child and should like to deserve, unworthy as I am of such a favor, to be allowed to call you my brother, for I place greater trust and hope in you than in any other man.

I have enclosed a little present, not as though it were worthy of your regard, but only as a remembrance of me, lest the great distance that separates us cause you to forget me. May it serve to knit the bond of true affection between us forever.

More earnestly still I entreat you, beloved brother, to protect me with the shield of your prayers against the poisoned darts of the hidden enemy.— I have still another request; kindly correct this awkward letter of mine, and send me some friendly words from you, for which I long so much, and which will serve as a model for me.

The subjoined verses [four hexameters] I have attempted to compose according to the rules of poetical tradition, not in order to make a vain show of my abilities, but merely to exercise the poor little poetical talent given to me. I learned this art from Eadburga, who, however, does not for its sake neglect to study unceasingly the Divine Law.

Farewell! I wish you a long and happy life and commend myself to your prayers."

—*Bonifatii et Lulli Epistolae* (ed. Tangl., 1916), ep. 29.

Hints for Study

1. For an account of the labors of the Anglo-Saxon missionaries in Frisia see the *Ecclesiastical History* of Bede, Bk. V. cc. IX-XI. Chapter XIX of the same book contains an account of St. Wilfrid.

2. The life of St. Boniface was written about ten years after his death by the priest Willibald of Mainz; it was translated into English by G. W. Robinson (Harvard University Press, Cambridge, Mass., 1916).

3. Summarize, in the form of a chronological table, the missionary labors of the English monks on the Continent to the death of St. Boniface.

4. Write a brief character sketch of St. Boniface. (Deduce his character from his deeds.)

5. What were the duties of army chaplains in the time of St. Boniface?

6. Read carefully the letter of St. Lioba to St. Boniface. What does it tell you about the writer and about Anglo-Saxon womanhood?

7. Locate on the map all the places mentioned in this chapter (p. 254).

8. What parts of modern Europe were comprised in Frisia, Austrasia and Neustria?

CHAPTER IV

MOHAMMEDANISM AND THE CHURCH

While the Church was planting the Cross in the countries of the Northwest and handing on the culture of the ancient world to the new nations, vast hordes of fanatic warriors were marching out of the Arabian Desert to lay waste the cities and lands which had so long been the centers of Christian civilization. *Islam* was the new religion which had set the Arab tribes in motion, and *Mohammed* was its prophet and lawgiver.

Mohammed's Life.—Mohammed was born at Mecca in western Arabia about the year 570. Mecca was not only the most important city of Arabia; it also enclosed within its walls the national sanctuary, the far-famed *Caaba*—the small and nearly cubical stone building which contained the "black stone" fabled to have come down from Paradise whiter than milk, but to have changed to black by the sins of the children of Adam who have touched it. Originally dedicated to the one Supreme Being, the Caaba had in time become a veritable pagan Pantheon, harboring no less than 360 idols of all shapes and forms. From every part of the Arabian peninsula pilgrims came year after year in vast numbers to the Caaba. The inhabitants of Mecca and, above all, the clan of the Koraish, to whom the guardianship of the Caaba was entrusted, profited mightily by these pilgrimages and the great fairs which were held in connection with them.

Mohammed himself belonged to the Koraish, but his family was poor. Left an orphan when still a child, he would no doubt have lived and died in poverty if he had not attracted the attention of a rich elderly widow, Chadija, who first employed him to trade for her, and subsequently married him. The penniless orphan was now a man of wealth and social standing, and could devote his time to other matters than driving camels and herding sheep.

Paganism was rapidly declining in Arabia. There were strong colonies of Jews and Christians, the latter mostly heretics, scat-

tered throughout the land. Even in Central Arabia, the stronghold of idolatry, there was at least one Christian community.
The doctrines of Judaism and Christianity were thus known to the
Arabs and naturally made a deep impression on the finer minds
among them. Towards the end of the sixth century some men
from Mecca, Medina, and Taif, in search for a purer religion
than the dominant polytheism, took over from Jews and Christians the doctrines and practices that suited them and built up
from them what they termed the pure religion of their great
ancestors, Abraham and Ishmael. These were the *Hanifs*. They
were strict monotheists, believed in a future life, with its eternal
punishments and rewards, abstained from wine and practiced other
austerities. Mohammed's uncle Waraka joined the new movement, and through him Mohammed himself came under its
influence.

From now on, Mohammed spent much time in quiet and contemplation in the hill caves near Mecca. During one of these
periods of solitary contemplation—he was then about forty years
of age—he received, he tells us, his prophetic mission. He had
been commissioned by God, he said, through the Archangel
Gabriel, to destroy idolatry and to restore the true worship of
God. His wife Chadija was his first convert. Soon, however,
others gathered around him, and when the wealthy and influential
Abu-Bekr declared his belief in his revelations, he began to make
open propaganda for his new religion. He called it *Islam*, that
is, "resignation to the will of God," and his followers *Moslems*,
"those who have surrendered themselves to God."

The ruling aristocracy, fearing for their wealth and their influence if idol worship was wiped out, refused to listen to Mohammed's preaching and began a bitter persecution of his adherents.
Moslem slaves were tortured by their masters and the freemen
were disowned by their clans. This led to the first *Hegira*, or
migration, to Abyssinia in 615. Some years later Mohammed himself resolved to emigrate. An attempt to gain a footing in the
neighboring city of Taif failed. In Medina conditions were
more favorable. The Jews, who lived in great numbers in that
city, had told the inhabitants of a Messias, an ambassador, whom
God had promised to send into the world. And then pilgrims from
Mecca brought the news that a prophet had arisen in their midst,
an Arab like themselves, to whom God had made revelations in

their own tongue. Was not this man the long-expected Messias? Islam gained ground rapidly in Medina, and an invitation was extended to Mohammed to take up his abode there. Many Moslems left Mecca immediately for Medina, Mohammed himself on July 6, 622. His departure from Mecca is known as the second *Hegira*. The Mohammedan calendar is reckoned from the day of his arrival in Medina.

In Medina Mohammed perfected his religious system. Before long, by fair means and foul, he had made himself complete master of the city and the surrounding country. In the war against Mecca and the Koraish, which dragged on for several years, neither side gained a decisive advantage. After an unsuccessful attack on Medina in 627, the Meccans gave up further resistance as useless and admitted Mohammed and his army into their city. They did not suffer in wealth and prestige by their submission, for Mohammed made their city the holy city of Islam, and the Caaba its sacred shrine. Central and southern Arabia followed the example of Mecca. The few tribes that resisted were quickly subdued by the sword. In the midst of warlike plans for the conquest of Persia and Syria, Mohammed died at Medina, June 8, 632.

Character of Mohammed.—"In judging of Mohammed's moral character," writes Father Power, a careful student of Islam, "we must distinguish between the Mohammed of Mecca and the Mohammed of Medina. The hostility to Jews and Christians, the introduction of heathenism into Islam, the institution of the Holy War, the violation of his own lax marriage laws, the instigation of robberies and murders, the defense of his crimes and schemes by pretended revelations—all force us to the conclusion that at Medina we have to do with an unscrupulous politician. At Mecca, on the other hand, as he shows a profound and persevering conviction of the truth of his revelations, the materials for which he had already assimilated, and as his actions are not incompatible with that subjective persuasion, we prefer to attribute his prophetic experiences to his general nervous condition and the epileptic fits with which he was frequently visited." Illusion and hallucination were the causes of his early so-called revelations; thirst for power and uncontrolled sensuality dictated the later additions made to them.

Duties and Dogmas of Islam.—During his lifetime Moham-med's teachings were propagated by word of mouth; only a small number of his "sayings" were committed to writing. After his death his successor, the Caliph Abu-Bekr, intrusted to his secre-tary Zaid the task of collecting and putting into some sort of system all his "revelations" that had survived. The collection was called *Al-Koran*, or "the reading." About A.D. 660 Zaid's collection was revised, officially recognized, and all others destroyed.

The Koran contains 114 chapters, called *Suras*, which are subdivided into verses (*Ayat*). There is no attempt at orderly arrangement either according to time, place, or subject-matter. The style is just as irregular as the arrangement. While some portions abound in splendid imagery and lofty conceptions, others are extremely prosaic and monotonous. Many passages are so obscure that their meaning has not yet been discovered.

A second source from which Islam is derived is the *Sunna*, or tradition, by which is meant the "customary way of doing things" as observed by Mohammed and his companions. Many of these traditions are taken over from Jewish and Christian writings; others were invented to support politi-cal and religious views. The *Sunna*, from which the orthodox Mohamme-dans call themselves *Sunnites*, is rejected by the Persians, who are known on this account as *Shiahs*, "sectaries."

The four chief duties of the Moslems are Prayer, Almsgiving, Fasting, and Pilgrimage. Every Moslem must pray five times a day with his face turned towards Mecca. The prayer used most frequently is the first *sura* of the Koran:

> "In the name of Allah, the Compassionate, the Merciful.
> Praise be to Allah, the Lord of the Worlds,
> The Compassionate, the Merciful,
> The King of the day of Judgment.
> Thee do we worship, and of Thee seek we help.
> Guide us in the right way,
> The way of those to whom Thou hast been gracious,
> Not of those with whom Thou art wroth, nor of the erring.
> Amen! O Lord of Angels, Jinns, and men!"

Works of charity play a prominent part in early Islam. The Koran enjoins almsgiving on every true believer as a strict duty. It is specially to be practiced towards poor relations, orphans, beg-gars, and slaves. All who are over fourteen years of age, except the sick, the travelers, and those engaged in war, must abstain from eating, drinking, smoking, and using perfumes during the whole month of Ramadan from sunrise to sunset. In the twelfth month of the year, every free Moslem whose means allow him is bound to make the *Hadj*, the pilgrimage to Mecca, at least once in his life.

Among other duties imposed upon the Moslem we may mention the "holy war" against all non-Moslems; the abstention from wine, pork, games of chance; the performance of ablutions before prayer, before entering a mosque, and on other occasions; and the prohibition of representing in stone or painting any living beings. Marriage within certain degrees of kindred is forbidden, and the number of legal wives restricted to four. Mohammed himself was exempted from these restrictions by a "special revelation"; he had fifteen wives. Slaves are left completely at the disposal of their masters. A man can divorce any one of his wives at will on pay-

A VIEW OF MECCA

ing her a small sum of money; and he may punish infidelity on her side, if proved by four witnesses, by starving her to death. Women could take no part in public or social life; they remained shut up in the house and had to wear a thick veil in the presence of all men except their husbands.

The Mohammedan faith is summed up in the short formula which has always been in use amongst the Moslems and which the Muezzin sings five times daily from the lofty minaret of the mosque: "There is no God but Allah, and Mohammed is the messenger of Allah." The existence of the Trinity is expressly denied. There is no such thing as a Redemption in the Christian sense, though God did send prophets into the world from time to time to teach mankind "the right way." Moses and Christ were such prophets; but the last and greatest is Mohammed. The world is not governed by Divine Providence. Every human being is subject to the immutable decrees of Fate (*Kismet*). The court of Allah consists of angels, created out of fire, winged and mortal. Their "trial" was the command to acknowledge by homage their inferiority to Adam. All obeyed except *Iblis*, the devil, who in consequence was cast out of paradise. The *Jinn*, malicious spirits, are the helpers of Iblis in his efforts to lead men astray. Mohammed's teaching in regard to the resurrection, the last judgment and the state of the soul in eternity is borrowed mostly from Christian sources, but distorted in the borrowing. The happiness promised to the Moslems in paradise is wholly sensual, consisting of fine gardens, rich furniture, delicious fruits, and wines that neither cause headache nor intoxication; but, above all, gazelle-eyed maids, pure as pearls in their shells, and gifted with eternal youth, shall be their brides. The punishments threatened to the wicked are hell-fire breathing hot winds, the drinking of boiling and stinking water, eating briars and thorns, and the bitter fruit of the tree of Ez-Zakkoom, "which in their bellies will feel like burning pitch."

The Rapid Expansion of Islam and Its Causes.—The Caliphs (i.e., the successors of Mohammed) continued the efforts for the spread of Islam which Mohammed had initiated. Aided by the treason and the cowardice of the decadent Roman governing classes, Abu-Bekr, Omar, Othman and their generals, subjugated Syria, Egypt, and Persia. Soon after 650, Armenia was taken, and the victorious armies of Islam pushed on to Turkestan and India. In Asia Minor the armies of the Greek emperor successfully resisted the invaders. Blocked in their advance on Europe from the east, the Saracens sought to gain entrance from the south. From Egypt they extended their conquests along the north coast of Africa. Marmarica, Cyrenaica, Carthage, Numidia, and Mauretania were overrun, and in 700 the last Christian stronghold, Ceuta, on the Strait of Gibraltar, fell. From here a mixed horde of Arabs and Moors crossed over into Spain, and in the memorable battle of Jeres de la Frontera (711) put an end to the Gothic kingdom which had endured for three centuries. The remnants of the Goths fled into the fastnesses of the Asturias, from which the Saracens strove in vain to dislodge them.

When they had completed the conquest of Spain, the Saracens determined to extend their sway over the neighboring country of the Franks. Crossing the Pyrenees, they soon succeeded in making themselves masters of southern France and in 731 encamped on the banks of the Loire. Here they encountered "a lion in the path" in the person of Charles Martel. "Charles' signal victory over the arrogant invaders proved to be the turning-point in the Moslem career of conquest. The question whether the Crescent or the Cross, Mohammed or Christ, should rule Europe and the western world was decided forever upon the bloody field of Tours." Mohammedanism, however, retained the greater part of its conquests, and continued the most threatening and dreaded enemy of Christendom.

The losses suffered by the Church through the Mohammedan conquests were great and far-reaching in their results. Countries which had belonged to her for centuries, in fact the oldest centers of Christianity—Jerusalem, Antioch, Alexandria, Carthage—were torn from her, and the way to their reconquest barred, as it seemed, for all time.

As a rule the political subjugation of a nation meant its islamization. The conquered nations were not indeed, as is popularly believed, given their choice between the Koran and the sword, but their conquerors ruled them with such an iron hand and levied such high taxes upon them that multitudes in every land sought a remedy for their ills by professing the faith which secured for them equality with their oppressors. The apostasy was, however, by no means universal. In the face of the direst persecution millions of Christians held fast to their faith with heroic loyalty.

The rapid expansion of Islam was due in great measure to its appeal to the uncivilized, the poor, and the ignorant. It requires blind faith, presents no difficult problems to the intellect, and satisfies the natural religious instincts without forbidding the gratification of the baser passions. For the pagans of Arabia and Africa Islam proved a boon, for "it corrected many abuses, admitted every class to its ranks, enforced religious equality, and preached the great truths of Monotheism, Revelation, and Eternal Life." No Christian nations submitted peacefully to its yoke. The Persians, the only brave and cultured race that went over to Islam in a body, were not Christians, and they were the first to attempt to put a more deeply religious content into the crude system of Mohammed.

Origin of the Mohammedan Call to Prayer

In an ancient Life of Mohammed, ascribed to Mohammed Ibn Ishaq (d. 708), we read the following account of the origin of the famous Mohammedan call to prayer:

"When Mohammed came to Medina, the people assembled around him for prayer without any special summons. Then Mohammed, following the custom of the Jews, called the faithful to prayer by means of a trumpet. Becoming displeased with this method, he thought of introducing a bell, and one was actually cast. In the meantime Abd Allah had a vision in which the call to prayer was taught to him. He came to the Prophet and said to him: "This night a wandering spirit in the form of a man who had on two green garments and carried a bell in his hand, passed by me. I said to him: 'Servant of God, will you sell me your bell?' He asked me: 'What do you want with it?' I answered: 'We are going to use it to summon the faithful to prayer.' Then he said: 'I will teach you a better way: Cry four times: God is the greatest; then: I confess there is no God but Allah, and Mohammed is a messenger of Allah. Come to prayer! Come to prayer! Come to salvation! Come to salvation! God is the greatest! God is the greatest! There is no God beside Him!'" When Mohammed heard this, he said: "That is a true vision; go and teach Bilal to call to prayer in this way, because he has a better voice than thou." When Bilal called to prayer, Omar heard it in his house, ran quickly to Mohammed and said: "O Prophet of God, by Him who of a truth hath sent thee, I had the same vision as Bilal." Mohammed said: "God be praised!"

Hints for Study

1. A brief but adequate account of Mohammed and his religion will be found in *Lectures on the History of Religions,* Vol. IV, Lecture II, by E. Power, S.J. (Herder Book Co., St. Louis, Mo.)
2. We regard the rapid spread of Christianity as a proof of its divine origin; why does not the rapid spread of Islam prove its divinity?
3. Why is it so hard to convert a Mohammedan?
4. Why do you think God permitted the dreadful scourge of Islam to afflict the Christian world?
5. Read the description of the battle of Tours in Creasy, *Fifteen Decisive Battles of the World.*
6. What Eastern nation has always been distinguished for its loyalty to Christianity under Mohammedan tyranny and persecution?

CHAPTER V

THE ALLIANCE BETWEEN THE PAPACY AND THE FRANKS. THE BEGINNINGS OF THE TEMPORAL SOVEREIGNTY OF THE POPES

Turning from the sad spectacle of the Mohammedan devastation in the East to the Church in the West, we find that momentous changes have taken place here. In the kingdom of the Franks the scepter of the Merovingians has passed to the son and successor of Charles Martel, Pippin the Short. The Pope, who up to this time had exercised jurisdiction only over souls, has become also a temporal ruler, with possessions and subjects like other kings. The Papacy has entered into an alliance with the Franks which is destined to exert a profound influence on the history of Europe and of the Church. In order to understand how this change in the status of the Papacy came about, we must pass in review, step by step, the events which led up to it. Perhaps it will be best to group these events in the form of a chronological list.

154 B.C. The Romans complete the conquest of Cisalpine Gaul and thereby establish the *unity of Italy*.

67 A.D. St. Peter dies at Rome, as its first bishop and pope.

313. By the agreement of Milan the Christian religion is officially recognized. Constantine the Great confers on the Church the right to acquire property by legacy or donation. Through the generosity of Constantine and his successors the Popes gradually acquire much landed property in all parts of Italy, Sicily, etc. This is later known as the *Patrimony of St. Peter*.

330. Constantine the Great transfers the imperial residence to Constantinople. Rome thus becomes the *City of the Popes*.

395. Division of the Empire into Eastern and Western. The Western Emperors do not reside at Rome.

452. *Pope Leo the Great* saves Rome from the hordes of Attila, and greatly enhances the prestige of the Apostolic See.

476. Fall of the Roman Empire of the West. Odoacer, "king of the Germans," as he styles himself, rules over all Italy as lieutenant of the Eastern Emperors.

493. Theodoric the Great, king of the Ostrogoths, defeats Odoacer and rules over Italy for twenty-nine years. The Goths being Arians and foreigners, the influence of the Popes, "the heirs of Augustus and Constantine," in Italian affairs increases.

555. Narses, general of the Eastern Emperor Justinian, puts an end to the Gothic kingdom. *Italy is merged into the Eastern, or Byzantine, Empire.* It is ruled by a representative of the Emperor known as the *Exarch*, who resides, not at Rome, but at Ravenna. The Emperor Justinian claims and exercises the right to sanction the election of the Popes.

569. The Langobards or Lombards under their king Alboin conquer Northern Italy (Lombardy) and parts of Middle and Lower Italy. In the rest of the peninsula the Byzantine rule continues to be recognized. The unity of Italy receives a mortal blow. *Henceforward there are two Italies—the Lombard and the Byzantine.* Lombard Italy soon splits up into a number of almost independent duchies, the most important of which are Spoleto and Benevento.

590. Gregory the Great ascends the Papal Throne. He adopts a peaceful policy towards the Lombards, whereas the Byzantines refuse to treat with them, hoping against hope to reconquer Italy. Pope Gregory enters into friendly relations with the Lombard rulers Agilulf and his Catholic queen Theodolinda. Many Lombards abandon Arianism.

601. Pope Gregory concludes a treaty of peace with Agilulf, who had threatened Rome, without consulting the Exarch of Ravenna. *Gregory is practically both bishop and secular ruler of Rome.*

643. Rothari, the last Arian king of the Lombards, greatly extends the Lombard domain. After his death Arianism dies out among the Lombards.

712. Liutprand attempts to unite all Italy under his scepter. He conquers Byzantine Italy with the exception of Venice, the much reduced exarchate of Ravenna, and Rome with the surrounding country known as the *Roman Duchy.*

719. Pope Gregory II commissions St. Boniface to preach the

Gospel to the pagans of central Germany. Later he consecrates him bishop and assists him in every way in the work of conversion.

726. Leo the Isaurian, the Byzantine emperor, issues an *edict against the Veneration of Images.*

730. Leo the Isaurian prohibits the veneration of images and orders their destruction throughout the Byzantine Empire. Gregory II protests vigorously, and Romans as well as Lombards rally round him. The Exarch Paul invades Rome with orders to put the Pope to death; but the Lombards come to the assistance of the Pope, and Paul has to retire to Ravenna. Byzantine Italy threatens to make itself independent of Constantinople. Gregory refuses to be a party to the plot, and the Byzantine rule is secure in Rome for a few years more.

731. Pope Gregory III, whose election is the last confirmed by an Eastern Emperor, calls a council at Rome which condemns the Iconoclasts (Image Breakers). Leo the Isaurian retaliates by confiscating the property of the Holy See in Sicily and Southern Italy, and subjects the bishops of these districts to the Patriarch of Constantinople.

738. The Lombard Dukes of Spoleto and Benevento rebel against King Liutprand. The Romans side with the Dukes. Liutprand defeats the Duke of Spoleto, who flees to Rome. The Romans refuse to give him up to Liutprand. Thereupon Liutprand seizes several towns belonging to the Roman Duchy, and his soldiers ravage the Roman territory to the very gates of Rome. In this extremity Gregory III seeks help from the Franks.

Messengers, bearing eloquent letters and rich presents, and the golden keys of the Confession (Tomb) of St. Peter, are despatched to Charles Martel. The impression made on the people north of the Alps by this event is profound. They realize in some vague fashion its vast significance. It is even rumored that the Pope promised to break with the Emperor of the East and to make Charles consul of Rome. Charles receives the messengers with due respect, but declares his resolve to remain neutral in the conflict between Rome and the Lombards. Liutprand is his ally, who stood faithfully by him in the recent war against the Saracens; he will not turn his arms against him. Besides, he knows that the Romans have themselves to blame for the predicament in which they find themselves.

741. Death of Gregory III, Leo the Isaurian, and Charles

Martel. Pope Zachary succeeds Gregory III. He concludes a twenty years' treaty of peace with Liutprand. *Through St. Boni-face the Franks are brought into ever closer union with Rome.*

743. Liutprand marches against Ravenna. Pope Zachary inter-venes, and Ravenna remains, for the time being, under Byzantine rule.

744. The long reign of Liutprand comes to an end. He is succeeded by Ratchis.

747. Karlmann, who had succeeded Charles Martel in Aus-trasia, becomes a monk in Monte Cassino, leaving his brother *Pippin sole master of the Franks.*

749. Ratchis abdicates the Lombard throne and enters the monastery of Monte Cassino. Aistulf succeeds him.

751. Pippin, the Frankish Mayor of the Palace, sends Bishop Burchard of Würzburg and Abbot Fulrad of St. Denis to consult Pope Zachary on the subject of the Merovingian kings, "who bore only the name of king without enjoying even a tittle of authority." Zachary replies that "he who had the kingly power should also receive the kingly title." On Nov. 11th, in the presence and with the assent of the general convocation of nobles and bishops, Pippin is proclaimed king of the Franks, and receives from the hand of St. Boniface the sacred anointing, a ceremony which is new to the Franks and gives the sovereign immense prestige; henceforth the king of the Franks calls himself *Gratia Dei Rex Francorum*— "By the grace of God King of the Franks."

752. Pope Zachary dies and is succeeded by Stephen II. Aistulf, king of the Lombards, threatens the Roman Duchy. Pope Stephen brings about a treaty of peace which is to last for forty years.

753. Aistulf violates the treaty, besieges Rome and levies a poll tax on the inhabitants. Stephen appeals in vain for help to the Eastern Emperor. Aistulf, who has in the meantime seized Ravenna and put an end to the Exarchate, proposes to annex Rome also to his dominions, but to leave to the Romans a degree of self-government under the protection of the Pope. The Ro-mans must now either resign themselves to annexation, or prevent it by calling in the help of the Franks. Neither the Pope nor the Romans wish to be Lombard subjects. They want autonomy, but they want it established, not under the protection of an out-side monarch, but under the supervision of the Pope himself.

This is the solution of the problem required by the pontifical dignity.

Negotiations with King Pippin are begun. Pippin sends Chrodegang of Metz and Duke Autchar to Rome. Pope Stephen sets out with them for Pavia, where he makes a last vain effort to induce Aistulf to give up his designs against Rome. From Pavia, he proceeds to the court of Pippin.

754. Interview between Pope Stephen and Pippin at Ponthion. Pippin requests Aistulf to avoid any display of enmity against Rome "out of respect for the Apostles Peter and Paul." Aistulf refuses the overtures of peace. A Frankish national convocation is held at Kiersy on the Oise, April 14th. It is decided to make war on Aistulf, and force him to yield to the Pope's demands. Pippin crosses the Alps. Aistulf, utterly defeated in the field, is obliged by solemn treaty to deliver up Ravenna and to guarantee the safety of Rome. Pippin receives from the Pope the title of "Patrician (Protector) of Rome," and is solemnly crowned a second time by the Pontiff himself.

756. Aistulf violates the treaty, invades the Roman Duchy, and invests Rome. Summoned by the Pope, Pippin again crosses the Alps and defeats Aistulf. Envoys of the Eastern Emperor try to induce Pippin to restore Ravenna and the other former Byzantine territories to the imperial government. Pippin refuses; he protests that he has undertaken the campaign out of love for St. Peter, and to gain remission of his sins, and that no amount of bribery can make him change his mind. *By a deed of gift deposited in the Confession of St. Peter, Pippin makes over to the Apostle St. Peter, to his Vicar, and to all his successors Ravenna and the other cities which Aistulf had been forced to give up.*

Thus originated the temporal sovereignty of the Papacy, the guarantee of its independence in the exercise of its spiritual power. Nominally Rome itself, which had not been conquered by Aistulf, and hence did not belong to Pippin by right of conquest, still belonged to the Byzantine Empire, and the Popes continued for some years to use the Byzantine coinage and the Byzantine mode of reckoning dates.

Extent of the Papal Territory.—The Papal Territory, later known as the Papal States, embraced at this time (*a*) the Duchy of Rome, that is, the city of Rome, Roman Tuscany, and the Roman Campagna to Terracina; (*b*) the Exarchate of Ravenna;

(c) the Pentapolis, or five cities southeast of Ravenna. After the time of Pope Stephen we hear no more of a Roman Duke. The Pope is the head of the government; the army, like the rest, is subject to his command. "He claims no other dignity than that which accrues to him from his ecclesiastical position, and it is as head of the *Ecclesia Dei*, the Church of God, that he, at the same time, assumes authority over the *Respublica Romanorum*, the Roman Commonwealth" (Duchesne).

Military and Ecclesiastical Organization.—We know very little of the military organization of the Roman State at this period. The population of the city on the left bank of the Tiber was divided into twelve groups (*scholae*); the rest of the city formed two other groups. Besides the native population there were groups of foreigners—Greeks, Saxons, Frisians, Franks, and Lombards. At the head of each group there was a *patronus*, or military commander. The headquarters of the military were at the Palatine, in the old imperial palace. Here the general of the army and his staff resided.

The ecclesiastical organization consisted of the *Cardinal Priests*, generally twenty-five in number, who constituted a kind of Senate of the Church. They were of less importance, however, than the *Cardinal Deacons*, always seven in number, who were the permanent assistants and ordinary servants of the Pope. Most of the temporal affairs of the Church were committed to them. The Archdeacon was the director of the whole ecclesiastical organization. Next to the deacons came the *subdeacons*, divided into two groups of seven. Some of them were attached to the district government, others were in the immediate service of the Pope.

The financial administration was presided over by the *Arcarius*, or chief cashier, and the *Saccelarius*, or paymaster-general. Connected with them were the *Advocates* of the courts of justice. The pontifical finances were drawn, in the main, from the landed property of the Church around Rome, the greater part of the former immense estates of the Holy See having been confiscated by the Eastern emperors. Some of these lands had been leased, others were cultivated under the direct supervision of the Pope. The peasants who worked on the latter estates were regarded as Papal employees, and formed a rural militia, which proved of great service to the Popes in the internal difficulties which beset their temporal government.

The government of the Lateran Palace, which was the usual residence of the Popes, was controlled by the *Vice-Dominus*, the official representative of the Pope. Below him were the chamberlains, the cellarers, the equerries, the guardian of the Papal treasures, the librarian, etc. The chancellor's office was manned by a corp of *notaries*, the most important of whom, called the *Primicerius* and the *Secundicerius*, were numbered among the great ecclesiastical dignitaries; they were often clerics in minor orders, and married.

"The Roman clergy were recruited from two sources: those belonging to the lower classes were trained in a kind of seminary, the *Schola Cantorum*, which was situated not far from the Lateran. It was also known as the Orphanage. The children of

THE OLD LATERAN PALACE

the nobility were received into the palace among the Chamberlains. Both classes received the tonsure at the outset of their careers, a rite which admitted them to the ranks of the clergy, and gave them the much appreciated privilege of decorating their horses with white saddle cloths. During their period of preparation they took the position of Acolytes; the other Minor Orders, owing to their practical disuse, had fallen into insignificance. The Acolytes were, as a rule, married. It was not until after promotion to the Major Orders that they bound themselves to a celibate life" (Duchesne, *Beginnings of the Temporal Sovereignty of the Popes*, p. 65).

There were many religious and charitable institutions at Rome: hospices for strangers and pilgrims, hospitals, asylums for foundlings, for the aged, and various benevolent societies known as deaconries. They were founded on endowments, and had their own incomes and official staff. The monasteries were numerous, but of no great importance. The really influential monastic houses were in other parts of Italy—Monte Cassino, Monte Amiata, St. Savior of Rieti, and Santa Maria of Farfa.

From this brief survey of the organization of the little Roman State we see that it comprised two great rival bodies, the clergy and the army, the ecclesiastical aristocracy and the lay aristocracy. Until the formation of the Papal State the army had enjoyed the political supremacy and all the prestige and the emoluments that were connected with it. It was quite natural that the transfer of this supremacy from the army to the Church would not tend to improve the strained relations which had long subsisted between them. They vied with each other to win the favor of the people and the good will of the Franks, Lombards or Byzantines. Both sought by every means to secure the highest offices for their adherents. Political and ecclesiastical intrigues became the order of the day. This state of affairs must be borne in mind if we wish to understand the tragic history of the Papacy during the next three centuries.

The Forged Donation of Constantine

In the Middle Ages it was generally believed that Constantine the Great, by a solemn "Edict of Donation," had conferred on Pope Sylvester I and his successors dominion over all Italy and the islands of the West. The Donation document is first quoted in the middle of the ninth century. It was composed about the year 800 A.D. Even in the Middle Ages it was occasionally doubted, e. g., by the Emperor Otto III and Arnold of Brescia. Gregory VII quotes it, and Urban II claimed Corsica by virtue of it. According to John of Salisbury, Pope Adrian IV relied on it in claiming the right to dispose of Ireland in 1155. The Donation document was seriously attacked in the fifteenth century and its falseness proved by Cardinal Nicholas of Cusa and Laurentius Valla. The following extracts reproduce the most important features of the *Donation*:

"We decree that the Holy Roman Church shall be honored with veneration; and that, more than our empire and earthly throne, the most sacred seat of St. Peter shall be gloriously exalted; we give to it the imperial power, and dignity of glory, and vigor and honor. . . . We have constructed within our Lateran palace, to the Savior our Lord God Jesus Christ, a church with a baptistry from the foundations. We have also constructed the churches of St. Peter and St. Paul, chiefs of the apostles, which we have enriched with gold and silver. . . . On these churches we have conferred estates, and have enriched them with different objects; and through our sacred imperial decrees, we have granted them our gift of land in the east as well as in the west; and even on the northern and southern coast;—namely in Judea, Greece, Asia, Thrace, Africa and Italy and the various islands: under this condition indeed, that they all shall be administered by the hand of our most blessed father the pontiff Sylvester and his successors. . . . In order that the supreme pontificate may not deteriorate, but may rather be adorned with power and glory even more than is the dignity of an earthly rule: behold we give over to the oft-mentioned most blessed pontiff, our father Sylvester the universal Pope, as well our palace, as has been said, as also the city of Rome and all the provinces, districts and cities of Italy or of the western regions; and relinquish them, by our inviolate gift to the power and sway of himself or the pontiffs his successors. . . ."

From Henderson, *Select Historical Documents of the Middle Ages*, p. 319 ff.

Hints for Study

1. Two very thorough accounts of the beginnings of the Temporal Power of the Popes are available in English: Duchesne, *The Beginnings of the Temporal Sovereignty of the Popes*, tr. from the French by Arnold Harris Mathew (Kegan Paul, London), and William Barry, *The Papal Monarchy from St. Gregory the Great to Boniface VIII* (Story of the Nations Series, T. Fisher Unwin, London).

2. Note the deep veneration in which St. Peter was held in the early Middle Ages. Give instances from the life of St. Boniface and of Pippin. What is meant by the "Confession of St. Peter"?

3. How many Italies were there after 756? Was Italy ever again united?

4. Why should the Pope be independent of any earthly power? Is temporal sovereignty necessary for this independence? How is this problem solved at present?

5. Was the temporal sovereignty of the Popes founded on the forged Donation of Constantine?

CHAPTER VI

THE AGE OF CHARLEMAGNE

Immediately after the death of Stephen II (in 757) the rivalry between the clergy and the aristocracy came to a head. His brother the Deacon Paul, was elected to succeed him, but not without strong opposition from the Archdeacon Theophylact, who belonged to one of the most powerful noble families of Rome. Paul ruled with a firm hand, which brought down upon him the enmity of all evil-doers. He was on his deathbed in 767 when Toto (Theodore), Duke of Nepi, a rapacious and cruel aristocrat, broke into the city with an armed band, and proclaimed his brother Constantine Bishop of Rome. Constantine was a soldier, not a cleric A bishop was forced to ordain him on the spot. A few days later he received episcopal consecration and was enthroned as Pope. The Primicerius Christopher with the aid of the Lombards crushed Toto and his party. According to the atrocious Greek custom, which was becoming common in Italy also, Constantine and several of his adherents had their eyes put out. Stephen III, a good but feeble man, was elected Pope. His reign is notable chiefly for the Council held in the Lateran Palace in 769, which was attended by thirteen bishops from the kingdom of the Franks. Constantine's election was declared illegal, and his ordinations null and void. The acts of his pontificate were publicly burnt. Stephen died in 772, and Hadrian I, the future friend and counselor of Charlemagne, ascended the Chair of Peter.

1. *Charlemagne and Pope Hadrian I*

Hadrian I (772-795), who reigned longer than any Pontiff since Sylvester I, belonged to one of the noblest families of Rome. He had been educated at the Lateran, and was distinguished for his piety and learning, his high principles, and edifying morals. His supporters hoped, by electing him, to please both the clergy and the nobility by giving them a Pope who was an eminent representative of both bodies. Hadrian was, besides, a man of action, and such a man was sorely needed.

During the reign of Stephen the Lombard party, led by the Papal Chamberlain Paul Afiarta, had governed Rome with a high hand. No help had been received from the Franks. Pippin had died in 768 and been succeeded by his two sons Karlmann and Charles, the former holding the southern, the latter the northern half of the kingdom. The brothers were on no friendly terms, and civil war was constantly threatening. They had neither time nor inclination to antagonize the Lombards. To make matters worse for the Papacy, Charles married a daughter of Desiderius, and an alliance between the Franks and the Lombards seemed imminent. Then Karlmann died (Dec. 771), and Charles was at once recognized as sole king of the Franks. Karlmann's widow, Gerberga, fled with her two infant sons to the Lombard king for protection. Desiderius welcomed them all the more readily because Charles had, in the meantime, r e p u d i a t e d his Lombard wife and sent her back to her father. He considered the time ripe for carry-out the plans of Liutprand and Aistulf, which had been so

CHARLEMAGNE

rudely crossed by the Franks. He requested Pope Hadrian to recognize the sons of Karlmann as the lawful Frankish kings and to crown them in St. Peter's. When the Pope refused to assent to this demand, Desiderius invaded the Papal territory from the north, whilst the Dukes of Spoleto and Benevento ravaged it in the south. Hadrian immediately appealed to the Frankish king for help. Charles crossed the Alps in the summer of 773, defeated Desiderius, and shut him up in Pavia.

Leaving his army before Pavia, Charles proceeded to Rome for the Easter festivals. He was received with royal honors. At St. Peter's the Pope, surrounded by his clergy, waited at the head of the great staircase to welcome his protector. Charles ascended it on his knees, kissing each step on the way, as pilgrims still do when going up the Scala Santa. Arrived at the top, he embraced the Pope, accepted his right hand, and accompanied him into the Basilica amid the singing of joyful hymns. During his stay in the city Charles renewed and enlarged the donation which his father Pippin had made to the Holy See, but with the understanding that the supreme civil authority remained in his hands as protector of Rome. Then he returned to Pavia to press the siege. In June the city opened its gates. Desiderius was deposed and sent to a monastery. He had staked all on one decisive throw, and had lost. Charles now took the title of "King of the Lombards," to which the Pope added that of "Patrician of the Romans." He was to mount higher still, but not in the lifetime of Hadrian.

2. *Charlemagne and the Saxons*

Charles was engaged in his first campaign against the Saxons when Hadrian's cry for help reached him. For many years the Saxons, who had stubbornly resisted all attempts to convert them to Christianity, had made periodical raids into the Frankish dominions, pillaged the towns and villages and burnt the churches to the ground. On one raid alone they destroyed thirty mission stations founded by St. Boniface in Thuringia and Hesse. Charles Martel, Karlmann, and Pippin had contented themselves with repelling and punishing these incursions. Charlemagne determined to put an end to them by conquering Saxony and annexing it to his dominions. It was between the Christianity of the Franks and the national paganism of the Saxons that the struggle took place. For thirty years, from 772 to 803, such was its character. Charlemagne, as Guizot remarks, regarded the conquest of Saxony as indispensable for putting a stop to the inroads of the Saxons, and the conversion of the Saxons to Christianity as indispensable for assuring the conquest of Saxony. The Saxons were defending at one and the same time the independence of their country and the gods of their fathers. Here was wherewithal to stir up and foment, on both sides, the profoundest passions; and they burst forth, on both sides, with equal fury. Whithersoever Charlemagne penetrated he built strong castles and churches; and at his departure left garrisons and missionaries. When he had gone, the Saxons returned, attacked the forts, and massacred the garrisons and the missionaries. There were only two pitched battles fought throughout the whole war. Exasperated by the perfidy and cruelty of the Saxons, Charlemagne resorted to the utmost severity. After the great Saxon revolt in 782, led by the famous chieftain Widukind, he had 4,500 Saxons condemned to death and beheaded in a single day at Verden on the Aller. Three years later Widukind gave up the struggle and asked to be baptized.

In order to hasten the work of conversion and to stamp out the remnants of paganism among the converts, the Frankish assembly held at Paderborn in 785 adopted measures that were disapproved by Pope Hadrian and by some of Charlemagne's own advisers. Death was to be the penalty for eating meat during Lent, if done out of contempt for Christianity, and death also for causing the body of a dead man to be burned in accordance with pagan rites. Even for merely scorning to be baptized a man could forfeit his life. The harshness of these regulations was, however, considerably diminished in practice. The priests were admonished to exercise care and to take circumstances into account in judging a man's guilt or innocence. In 797 the national assembly at Aachen issued another *Capitulary,* as the edicts of the Frankish kings were called, because they were divided into *capitula,* or chapters, for the Saxons, in which the severest features of the earlier decree were considerably relaxed. It was not these edicts, but the establishment of abbeys and bishoprics in the conquered territories and the self-sacrificing labors of such missionaries as St. Sturm of Fulda, St. Ludger, the first bishop of Münster, and St. Willehad, the first bishop of Bremen, that christianized and civilized the Saxons. "A man can be drawn to the Faith," Alcuin wrote to Charlemagne, "but he cannot be forced; you can be forced to receive Baptism, but it avails nothing for the Faith."

3. *Charlemagne Receives the Imperial Crown*

In 799 Charlemagne received, at his palace in Aachen, news of serious disturbances which had broken out at Rome. Pope Leo III (795-816), who had been unanimously chosen to succeed Hadrian I, had been attacked by a troop of armed conspirators during the solemn procession on St. Mark's Day. The ruffians pulled him off his horse, flung themselves upon him, and did their best to tear out his tongue and his eyes. Not succeeding in this, they dragged him into a church, beat him till he fainted, and left him for dead in front of the altar. He revived as by a miracle and, with the aid of the Duke of Spoleto, fled out of the city, announcing his intention of repairing to the court of Charlemagne. The latter, who was at Paderborn in Westphalia at this time, received the Pontiff with the greatest kindness and respect, and sent him back to Rome with a bodyguard of Frankish counts and bishops. Leo's return resembled a triumphal entry. The ringleaders of the sacrilegious conspiracy, nephews of Pope Hadrian, were arrested, tried, and imprisoned.

A year later, on November 23, 800, Charlemagne himself arrived at the gates of Rome. "The Pope," says the ancient chronicler, "received him there as he was dismounting; then, the next day, standing on the steps of the basilica of St. Peter and amid general alleluias, he introduced the king into the sanctuary of the blessed Apostle, glorifying and thanking the Lord for this happy event." Some days were spent in examining into the accusations lodged against the Pontiff by his enemies, and in receiving from the envoys of the patriarch of Jerusalem the keys and the banner of the Holy Sepulcher. "Then, on Christmas Day, the king came into the basilica of St. Peter, to attend the celebration of Mass. At the moment when, in his place before the altar, he was bowing down to pray, Pope Leo placed on his head an exceedingly precious crown, and all the Roman people shouted: 'To Charles the Augustus, crowned by God, great and pacific Emperor of the Romans, long life and victory.' " Then the Assembly burst forth into the imperial *laudes*, or songs of praise, while the Pope anointed with chrism the forehead, not of the new Emperor, who had long been consecrated, but of his young son Charles, who had accompanied him to Rome, and was standing by his side."

The Roman Empire of the West had been restored after the lapse of more than three hundred years. Such a restoration was to be expected at that time. Under Charlemagne the kingdom of the Franks had attained dimensions similar to those of the former Western Empire. Rome itself, which was universally regarded as the Capital of the World, belonged to it. Charles was emperor in fact; why should he not also bear the title and the crown?

Einhard, in his *Vita Karoli Magni*, attributes to Charlemagne the statement that he would not have entered St. Peter's on Christmas Day if he had known the intention of the Sovereign Pontiff. But it was evidently the time or manner of the act rather than the act itself that aroused his temporary displeasure. The coronation had no doubt been discussed during Leo's stay in Paderborn in 799; but Charles had begun negotiations with the court of Constantinople, and it seems that he wished to bring them to a satisfactory termination before assuming the imperial title. In 812 an embassy from Constantinople arrived at Aachen, when Charles was finally acknowledged as emperor, and in return agreed to cede Venice and Dalmatia to Byzantium.

Much has been written on the significance of the coronation of Charlemagne. Bryce calls it "the central event of the Middle

THE CORONATION OF CHARLEMAGNE

Ages." And such indeed it was. In the minds of medieval men the new Empire was *a universal Christian Monarchy*. The Roman Empire and the Catholic Church were, to use the words of Freeman, two aspects of one society, a society ordained by the divine will to spread itself over the whole world. Of this society Rome was marked out by God as the predestined capital, the chief seat alike of spiritual and of temporal rule. At the head of this society, in its temporal character as an Empire, stood the temporal chief of Christendom, the Roman Caesar. At its head, in its spiritual character as a Church, stood the spiritual chief of Chris-

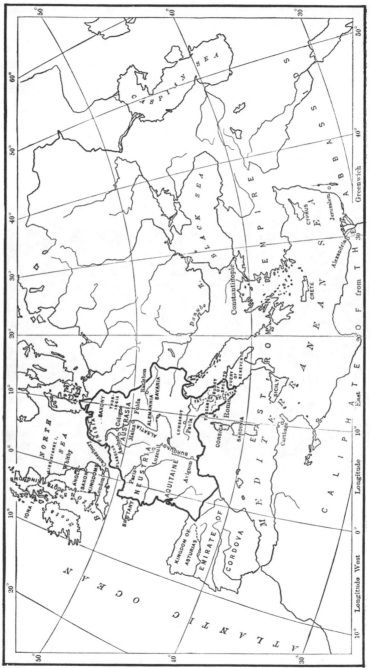

EUROPE IN THE TIME OF CHARLEMAGNE

tendom, the Roman Pontiff. Caesar and Pontiff alike ruled by divine right, each as God's immediate Vicar within his own sphere. Each ruler was bound to the other by the closest ties. Caesar was the Advocate of the Roman Church, bound to defend her by the temporal arm against all temporal enemies. The Pontiff, on the other hand, had the right of admitting the Emperor to his office by placing the imperial crown on his brow. "The sway alike of Caesar and of Pontiff is universal; to each alike in his own sphere, God has given the heathen for his inheritance, and the utmost parts of the earth for his possession. The Lord of the World has all mankind alike for the object of his paternal rule; the Successor of St. Peter welcomes all alike, from the east and from the west, from the north and from the south, within one universal fold over which he has the commission to bind and to loose, to remit and to retain. Here is a conception as magnificent as it was impracticable. No wonder indeed that such a theory fascinated men's minds for ages, and that in such a cause they were willing to spend and to be spent. That it never was carried out history tells us at the first glance. Still no theory, as a theory, can be more magnificent" (Freeman, *Select Historical Essays, I*).

It is easy to see why this grandiose conception which originated in the mind of St. Augustine was impracticable. The universal Christian monarchy was a divided monarchy, both Pope and Emperor were not angels but human beings, and the Pope was both a temporal and a spiritual ruler. The Christian Emperor could not be, as in pagan times, Pontifex Maximus, head of Church and State at the same time, and this distinction of persons should have warned Pope Leo, as a modern historian remarks, that a Charter, or Concordat, was necessary to prevent misunderstandings. None had been devised, and the result was that the two powers, which were designed to work in harmony, were often found engaged in bitter conflict. When the Emperor thought himself powerful enough, he tried to domineer over the Church after the manner of the Eastern Emperors; then, in order to prevent the enslavement of the Church, the Pope asserted his right to excommunicate and depose such tyrannical rulers, to absolve their subjects from their oath of allegiance, and to bestow their dominions on others. This right was based on the general belief in the Middle Ages that the power of the Pontiff was above that of all temporal sovereigns, and on the received public law of those ages, that emperors and kings had to profess the true Faith and to be in communion with the Pope, as essential conditions of their ruling lawfully.

4. The Carolingian Revival of Learning

Great as Charles was as conqueror and ruler, he was no less great as a patron of learning. He loved science, literature, and such studies as were then possible, and he cultivated them as far as his multifarious duties permitted. He strove painfully, and without much success, to write a good hand; but he spoke Latin as fluently as German and had a practical knowledge of Greek. He caused the first German grammar to be drawn up, collected the ancient songs and ballads of his people, gave German names to the months of the year, distinguished the winds by twelve special terms, paid great attention to astronomy, and took a deep interest in theological discussions. His favorite author was St. Augustine, whose *City of God* was read aloud to him as he sat at table. About him were grouped the best intellects of the time, as his own habitual advisers, or assigned by him as tutors and advisers to his sons, or sent by him to all parts of his dominions as his commissioners (*Missi Dominici*). Those whom he did not employ at a distance formed the faculty of the *Palace School* (*Schola Palatina*) and at the same time an *Academy of the Arts and Sciences*. All Europe supplied the members of this learned body. From Italy came the rhetorician Paul of Pisa, Paul Warne-fried, the historian of the Lombards, and the Grammarian Paul of Aquileia; from England, the great theologian and Latin scholar Alcuin; from Spain, Theodulf, the most important poet of his time; from Bavaria, the learned deacons Arno and Leidrad; from Middle Germany, Einhard, the biographer of the Emperor; and from Ireland, the mathematician Dungal. Of this select circle two names have remained justly celebrated in the literary history of the Carolingian age: Alcuin and Einhard.

Alcuin was born at York in 735. He received his education at the Cathedral School of York under the celebrated Master Aelbert. On a journey to Italy in 780 he met Charlemagne, who persuaded him to take up his residence at his Court. From 781 to 796 Alcuin was Charlemagne's chief helper in his efforts to create schools and to revive learning. He became director of the Palace School, and was the life and soul of the

Academy. "If your zeal were imitated," he said one day to the king, "perchance one might see arise in the land of the Franks a new Athens, far more glorious than the ancient—the Athens of Christ." His talent for poetry earned for him the name of "Flaccus" (Horace). It was under his inspiration that Charlemagne wrote his famous letter to Abbot Baugulf of Fulda *De Colendis Litteris*, on the cultivation of learning, and it was he who founded the fine library in the palace at Aachen. In 796 Charlemagne

PALACE CHAPEL BUILT BY CHARLEMAGNE AT AACHEN
The crown of lights was afterwards added by Frederick Barbarossa.

gave him the Abbey of St. Martin at Tours, and there he passed his last years—he died in 804—far from the noise of the Court, but remaining to the end the confidant and adviser of his sovereign. The Abbey School, which he made into a model of excellence, soon became the foremost educational institution in the Empire.—Alcuin wrote many books—works on grammar, rhetoric and logic in the form of dialogues, several theological treatises, and numerous poems—but his 232 letters, written to friends in England, to Arno, bishop of Salzburg, and to Charlemagne himself, are his most important literary legacy.

Einhard, a younger contemporary of Alcuin, was born about 770 and educated at Fulda. Owing to his literary and artistic skill, he was summoned to the palace between 791 and 796. Here he soon won the friendship of the king and his family, and was entrusted with the charge of the public buildings. He was probably the architect of the Cathedral at Aachen, portions of which are still standing. After Charlemagne's death he enjoyed the special friendship of Louis the Pious, and was the tutor and counselor of the future Emperor Lothar I. In 830 he retired from court life, entered the clerical state, and founded the abbey and church of Seligenstadt, the "City of the Blessed," so called from the relics of the holy martyrs Peter and Marcellinus, which he had procured—by a pious theft, it seems—from Rome. He died in 840, after a visit from Louis the Pious.—Einhard's most famous work is his *Vita Karoli Magni.* It was written as an expression of the author's gratitude to his imperial friend and patron, though it was not published till some years after the Emperor's death. In spite of some inaccuracies which later historians have pointed out, the fact remains that "almost all our real vivifying knowledge of Charles the Great is derived from Einhard, and that the *Vita Karoli* is one of the most precious literary bequests of the Middle Ages" (Hodgkin, *Charles the Great*, p. 222).

In order to carry out his plan of giving all his subjects an opportunity to obtain an education, Charlemagne established three kinds of schools: the village schools, in charge of the parish priests, for the most elementary studies; schools of singing and Church music, for clerics; Monastic and Cathedral schools, in which the Seven Liberal Arts—grammar, rhetoric, logic, arithmetic, geometry, astronomy, and music—as well as theology—were taught. Higher education was not to be a privilege of the clergy or the nobility, but open to all. "In the monastic and cathedral schools," the Emperor told the abbots and bishops, "there is no distinction to be made between the sons of serfs and of freemen, so that they may come and sit on the same benches to study grammar, music and arithmetic."

The educational system as planned by Charlemagne was never fully put in operation. After his death civil wars and the long-continued ravages of the Hungarian and Norse invaders interfered with the work which he had begun so well. Still, much of what he had done remained, and bore fruit in due time.

5. Death of Charlemagne. His Place in History

In 813 Charlemagne summoned his only remaining son Louis, whom he had made king of Aquitaine in 806, to his Court at

Aachen, and before a general assembly of the clergy and laity, and with their approval, solemnly declared him his successor, and heir of all his dominions. In the beginning of the following year he was taken ill of a violent fever. A few weeks later pleurisy set in, of which he died on the 28th of January, fortified with the Holy Viaticum and pronouncing the words of the Psalmist: "Into Thy hands, O Lord, I commend my spirit." He was buried in the basilica which he himself had built. Above the tomb was put a gilded arcade with his image and this inscription: "In this tomb reposeth the body of Charles, great and orthodox Emperor, who did gloriously extend the kingdom of the Franks, and did govern it happily for forty-seven years. He died at the age of seventy years, in the year of the Lord 814, on the 5th of the Kalends of February."

By consolidating all the Germanic peoples of western continental Europe under the leadership of the Franks, by consistently and powerfully championing the cause of the Christian religion and of Christian culture, by welding Church and State into what long proved to be indissoluble bonds, by uniting northern vigor with the culture of the South, Charlemagne proved himself the beginner of a new era—in fact, as some historians declare, of modern history itself.

Few heroes of the world's history to whom the title of "the Great" has been given so well deserve it as Charlemagne, and he is the only one, as Gibbon remarks, who has retained it as a permanent addition to his name.

Charlemagne's Interest in Religion and the Church

"Charles cherished with the greatest fervor and devotion the principles of the Christian religion, which had been instilled into him from infancy. Hence it was that he built the beautiful basilica at Aachen, which he adorned with gold and silver and lamps, and with rails and doors of solid brass. He had the columns and marbles for this structure brought from Rome and Ravenna, for he could not find such as were suitable elsewhere. He was a constant worshiper at this church as long as his health permitted, going morning and evening, even after nightfall, besides attending Mass. He took care that all the services there conducted should be held in the best possible manner, very often warning the sextons not to let any improper or unclean thing be brought into the building, or remain in it. He provided it with a number of sacred vessels of gold and silver, and with such a quantity of clerical robes that not even the door-keepers, who filled the humblest office in the church, were obliged to wear their everyday clothes when in the performance of their duties. He took great pains to improve the church reading and singing, for he was well skilled in both, although he neither read in public nor sang, except in a low tone and with others.

He was very active in aiding the poor; so much so, indeed, that he not only made a point of giving in his own country and his own kingdom, but when he discovered that there were Christians living in poverty in Syria, Egypt, and Africa, at Jerusalem, Alexandria, and Carthage, he had compassion on their wants, and used to send money over the seas to them. The reason that he earnestly strove to make friends with the kings beyond seas was that he might get help and relief to the Christians living under their rule. He cared for the Church of St. Peter the Apostle at Rome above all other holy and sacred places, and heaped high its treasury with a vast wealth of gold, silver, and precious stones."

—Einhard, *Vita Karoli Magni*, 26-27, tr. by S. E. Turner in
Harper's School Classics.

Hints for Study

1. There are several good lives of Charlemagne in English; Davis, *Charlemagne*; Mombert, *A History of Charles the Great*, and Hodgkin, *Charles the Great*. Before reading any of these books it will be well to consult the article on Charlemagne in the *Catholic Encyclopedia*.
2. A. F. West has written a good life of *Alcuin* (Scribner, N. Y., 1916).
3. Could a heretic or schismatic be emperor or king during the Middle Ages? If not, why not?
4. Why were misunderstandings bound to arise between Church and State?
5. Charlemagne was canonized by an antipope in the 12th century. Do you think he deserved this honor? Did he deserve it more than Constantine the Great?
6. State briefly the medieval conception of the Christian Roman Empire. With whom did this conception originate?
7. What is a *Capitulary?*
8. Name some kings who became monks.
9. What countries of modern Europe were embraced in Charlemagne's Empire?
10. Name four celebrated Monastic Schools of the Middle Ages.

CHAPTER VII

DECLINE OF THE CAROLINGIAN EMPIRE AND OF THE PAPACY. THE IRON AGE. LIGHTS AND SHADOWS

1. *Disruption of the Empire*

No arm but the arm of Charlemagne could support such an empire as he had created, no hand but his could keep its parts together. From the death of his son and successor Louis the Pious (814-840) a state of division begins. At first there are three kingdoms of the Franks—an Eastern, a Western, and a Middle Kingdom. Kings and emperors rise and fall; the Empire itself is sometimes nominally, always practically, without a head. For a moment the whole Empire is reunited under Charles the Fat; but with his deposition in 887, the Eastern and the Western Franks—in modern language, Germany and France—dividing the Middle Kingdom between them, are parted asunder forever. Germany, France, Burgundy, Italy are ruled for the most part by kings who are only distantly related to the great Charles. The Carolingian line dies out in Italy in 875; in Germany in 911 with Louis the Child; in France, though for a long time shorn of all power, it lingers on till 987. For nearly a hundred years, when there was an emperor at all, he was at most king of Northern Italy, and his title was always disputed by several claimants.

New Barbarian Invasions.—The weakness of the kingdoms into which the Empire had split up, left them almost defenseless against their foes in North, East, and South.

The *Northmen*—Danes, Swedes, Norwegians, who called themselves Vikings—urged on by land-hunger and the natural love of adventure common to all Germanic peoples, not only scourged all the coasts of Europe but penetrated, harrying and burning, far inland up the great waterways. Before the end of Charlemagne's reign they had appeared in Friesland, and with his own eyes the Emperor saw their light vessels off the coast of Southern Gaul.

"They are not merchants, but pirates!" he exclaimed to those around him, and he wept as he looked forward and pictured the evils they would bring upon his descendants and his people. Their ravages in Germany came to an end in 891 after their crushing defeat at Louvain at the hands of the German king, Arnulf of Carinthia. Their raids on France continued until 912, when Charles the Simple ceded to their chieftain Rollo a large tract of territory along the northern coast, since known as Normandy. Meanwhile they had harried England and Ireland, penetrated Russia, settled in Iceland and Greenland, and were soon to take a firm foothold in Southern Italy.

The *Saracens,* with Northern Africa as their base of operations, infested the seas, attacked Sardinia, seized Palermo, landed at the mouth of the Tiber, pillaged and desecrated the churches of Rome, and then took possession of Sicily.

Towards the end of the ninth century the *Magyars,* or Hungarians, a people of Tartar origin, put an end to the powerful Moravian kingdom, and made periodic incursions into the very heart of the Frankish lands, spreading desolation far and wide. It was not until Otto the Great gained his splendid victory over them in 955 that they retreated eastward and settled down in the country which still bears their name.

2. The Rise of Feudalism

It was under stress of all these assaults from without and the growing disruption from within that the Franks, grown too feeble to defend themselves as Charlemagne would have done, by marching out and pursuing the invaders to their own homes, developed instead a system of defense which made the later Middle Ages what they were. "All central authority seemed lost; each little community was left to defend itself as best it might. So the local chieftain built himself a rude fortress, which in time became a towered castle; and thither the people fled in time of danger. Each man looked up to and swore faith to this, his own chief, his immediate protector, and took little thought of a distant and feeble king or emperor. Occasionally, of course, a stronger lord or king bestirred himself, and demanded homage of these various petty chieftains. They gave him such service as they wished or as they must. This was the *feudal system.*" It seemed likely at this time that instead of being divided into three or four kingdoms, the Frankish Empire would break up into thousands of little castled states. Gradually, however, the more powerful nobles extended their overlordship over the weaker ones, took the titles of dukes and counts, and thus prevented the total disintegration of the states of Europe. For centuries there were no kingdoms ruled by one monarch, but rather as many states as there were duchies or counties. In every country of Europe, in France, Italy, Christian Spain, Germany, in England after the Norman conquest, in the parts of Ireland conquered by the English, in southern Italy and Sicily, in the Latin states of the East, Feudalism became the acknowledged form of government. Feudal government has been well described by William Stubbs, one of the masterly writers on this subject, as a "graduated system of jurisdiction (i.e., the right to exercise legal authority) based on land tenure, in which every lord judged, taxed, and commanded the class next below him; of which abject serfdom formed the lowest, and irresponsible tyranny the highest grade, and private war, private coinage,

A FEUDAL CASTLE

private prisons, took the place of the imperial institutions of government."

3. *The Church and Feudalism*

By force of circumstances the Church was drawn into the feudal organization. In the early Middle Ages kings and princes had been very generous to the Church. There was not a monastery or cathedral which they had not made the owner of valuable property and invested with all the social prestige which rich estates gave in those days. Many of these abbeys and bishoprics became in this manner real powers, especially from the days when kings, outdoing their nobles in generosity, actually divided their authority with the Church and granted her in fief entire counties, with all the political and civil rights, and made her prelates temporal princes, the first personages of the state after themselves. Europe became covered with ecclesiastical principalities, veritable buttresses of the thrones which had created them. (Kurth, *The Church at the Turning Points of History,* p. 60.)

So much wealth and social prestige necessarily became a supreme danger to the Church. Whenever a *benefice,* that is, a bishopric, an abbacy, or any other high office in the Church, became vacant, all the nobles of the land were on the watch to secure it for themselves, for one of their younger sons, or for someone to whom they owed a debt of gratitude for services rendered in war or private feud. There was no longer any canonical election of the bishops by the clergy and the faithful, or of the abbots by the monks; the kings and dukes had acquired almost everywhere the habit of selecting the holders of the principal ecclesiastical dignities in their states, and the landed proprietors of appointing the pastors of the churches on their estates. "When a bishop died, his chapter at once took possession of the insignia of his priestly dignity: the *ring,* which represents his marriage to his diocese, and the *crosier,* which is the symbol of his authority over his flock, and sent them to the king. When the monarch had made his selection of a successor, the lucky candidate was sent for, and, in a distinctively feudal ceremony, received at the hands of the king the crosier and the ring. There was no longer anything canonical in the whole procedure, there was no longer anything ecclesiastical in the ceremony; the *investiture,* that is to say, the act by which the new bishop was supposed to be endowed with his powers, was exclusively a lay ceremony." Feudalism had made the Church rich and powerful, but it had also enslaved her.

And now let us glance at the results of this enslavement. From the moment the selection of candidates for the highest ecclesiastical offices depended solely on the will of the kings, men were appointed bishops and abbots for other reasons besides their priestly virtue or learning. If they could give guarantees to the sovereign of their fidelity to his dynasty and to his politics, that was considered more important than if they could interpret Scripture, preach a sermon, or write a learned treatise. Usually, in order to be successful, the aspirant to office had to be endorsed by some powerful courtier. But the courtiers did not give their patronage free of charge; they sold it to the highest bidder. "Most of the bishops, therefore, bought their office, and in their turn sold the dignities of secondary order; and the lower clergy, to reimburse themselves, sold the sacraments and the sacramentals." And thus the pest of *simony* which had been all but stamped out in the Church, began its ravages anew. The consequences of this traffic in sacred things can be readily imagined. A simoniacal clergy is bound to be an ignorant and immoral clergy. It is said on good authority that, in the tenth and eleventh centuries, half of the priests, and in some countries more than half, disregarded the law of celibacy and lived openly as fathers of families. And when the clergy fell from their high level, when many bishops were totally indifferent and paid no attention to their spiritual duties, is there any wonder that demoralization set in rapidly among the people? *Qualis rex, talis grex*—as the ruler, so the people.

4. Decline and Enslavement of the Papacy

In the partition of the Carolingian Empire (843) Italy passed under the rule of a prince of its own, Louis II, son of Lothar I, who, with the title of emperor which he shared with his father, made his authority felt in political matters and exercised the right granted to Louis the Pious in 824 of ratifying the Papal elections. Shortly after his death the power of the Carolingian princes was reduced to nought. The Papacy became involved in the party strife of Italy and of the city of Rome, and was plunged in consequence into such an abyss of degradation that it was in danger of forfeiting every shred of its moral authority over Christendom. It is the darkest period in the annals of the Papacy. The great Catholic historian Baronius called it the "Iron Age," and the designation has clung to it. Though the task is not a pleasant one, we must pick our way through the gloom; fortunately some rays of light will not be wanting.

Formosus and Stephen VI.—Charles the Fat, the last Carolingian to rule over the whole Empire of Charlemagne, was succeeded in Germany by his nephew Arnulf. In Italy the two most powerful vassals, Duke Berengar of Friuli and Duke Guido of

Spoleto, contended for the crown. Guido was victorious, and in 891 Pope Stephen VI had to crown him Emperor. In 892 Pope Formosus was forced to confer the same dignity on Guido's son Lambert. In order to rid himself of the intolerable oppression of the Spoletan party, Formosus called King Arnulf to his aid. Arnulf came, was crowned Emperor in the spring of 896, but returned to Germany after a brief sojourn. Immediately after his departure Pope Formosus died—a violent death, it was rumored. The Italian party was furious because he had dared to confer the imperial dignity on a foreigner, and would not be denied their revenge. They intruded two popes on the Apostolic See: Boniface VI, an excommunicated priest, who died after fifteen days, and Stephen VI, whose reign lasted only thirteen months. It was Stephen who served as the instrument of vengeance against the deceased Formosus. In 897 the body of Formosus was disinterred by Stephen, treated with contumely as that of a usurper of the Papacy, and denied Christian burial. Several of Stephen's successors rehabilitated Formosus, declared his Pontificate valid and confirmed all his acts: one alone, Sergius III (904-911), upheld the iniquitous proceedings against him.

The House of Theophylact.—Sergius was the protégé of one of the great Roman families: the senator Theophylact, who presided over the Papal treasury and was commander-in-chief of the Papal army, his wife, Theodora, and their two daughters, Marozia and Theodora the younger—a family notorious for the sacrilegious abuse it made of its power by enslaving the Papacy for nearly fifty years. Sergius III, elected pope by one of the factions of Rome in 898 simultaneously with John IX, was expelled from the city by his adversaries. After his party, headed by Theophylact, gained the upper hand, he reappeared in Rome in 904 with a bodyguard of Tuscan soldiers, seized the two claimants, Leo V and Christopher, who were disputing the succession of Benedict IV, and had them strangled. During the pontificate of Sergius, which lasted till 911, Theodora ruled supreme. The confusion and disorders which marked her ascendancy over Sergius baffle all description.

John X, who succeeded to the Papal Throne in 914 by the grace of Theodora, displayed remarkable though not priestly qualities. The Saracens were threatening Rome once more. They had taken up a strong position on the Garigliano, pillaged the

Abbey of Farfa, and laid waste the Campagna with fire and sword. Pope John called to his aid the aged Berengar, king of North Italy, whom he crowned Emperor in 915, and the imperial vassals of Tuscany and Spoleto, commanded by the youthful Alberic, Marquis of Camerino. The Saracens were completely defeated on the Garigliano (916). All Italy acclaimed the youthful conqueror, soon to be conquered himself by the charms of Marozia.

Alberic and Marozia had two sons, John and Alberic the Younger. After Alberic's death Marozia married Guido of Tuscany. When Pope John sought to free himself from the tyranny of Guido and Marozia, they had him flung into a dungeon and smothered (928). Marozia now did what she pleased with the Chair of St. Peter. Two Popes followed each other in rapid succession, Leo VI and Stephen VII. Guido of Tuscany vanished from the scene in 931, and Stephen VII about the same time. Then Marozia, who styled herself *Domina Senatrix et Patricia*, Lady Senatress and Patrician, raised her own son by her first marriage to the Papal Throne as John XI. In order to consolidate her power, Marozia married Hugh of Provence, who had become king of Italy after the tragic death of Berengar in 924. But her other son, Alberic the Younger, raised the standard of revolt against this new stepfather. Hugh had to flee; Marozia and Pope John were imprisoned in the Castle of St. Angelo, and then disappeared; and for twenty-two years Alberic exercised absolute rule as Prince and Senator of all the Romans. Alberic's rule, though autocratic, was a boon to the Papal States. The Popes set up by him were all good men and were permitted to exercise their spiritual duties without too much interference on his part. Personally he was deeply religious, and listened humbly to the counsels of the great monastic reformer St. Odo of Cluny. But he made one ghastly and unpardonable mistake: before his death he gathered the Romans in St. Peter's and made them swear that, on the death of the reigning Pope, Agapitus II, they would choose his son John Octavian to succeed him. And so it happened that John XII became Pope in 955, when yet a mere boy of sixteen, and for nine years disgraced the Chair of Peter as no occupant before or after him.

Otto the Great and the Papacy.—Some years after his unsuccessful Roman adventure Hugh of Provence, hard pressed by

Berengar of Ivrea, at the instance of St. Odo of Cluny surrendered his Italian domains to his son Lothar, whom he had married to Adelaide, daughter of Rudolph II of Burgundy. He died in 947; his son Lothar three years later. Then Berengar seized the crown of Lombardy and in order to legitimize his usurpation tried to force Adelaide to marry his son Adalbert. When she refused, she was imprisoned in a castle on the Lake of Garda; but she managed to escape and called the German King Otto I (936-973) to her aid. Otto crossed the Alps, defeated Berengar, had himself crowned king of Italy at Pavia, and on Christmas Day, 951,

THE CASTLE OF ST. ANGELO

married Adelaide. A revolt among his vassals hastened his return to Germany. During his absence Berengar made himself master of North Italy once more, deposed the Archbishop of Milan and several other bishops, and threatened to invade the Roman territory.

It was in this crisis that Pope John, perhaps in order to forestall a similar action on the part of his own subjects, who were by this time thoroughly disgusted with his monstrous and scandalous behavior, begged Otto to come to the aid of the Romans, promising him at the same time the imperial crown as an inducement.

His petition was seconded by the exiled Archbishop of Milan, by many other bishops and princes, and by the Romans themselves.

In the autumn of 961 Otto crossed the Alps a second time, entered Pavia without opposition, and then started for Rome, where he was crowned on the 2nd of February, 962. "Thus by his valor," says the contemporary chronicler, "Otto transferred the Roman Empire to the Eastern Franks." Thenceforward the imperial dignity was reserved to the German kings, and with the coronation of Otto begins the *Holy Roman Empire of the German Nation,* which lasted, at least in name, for eight hundred and forty-four years.

After the coronation, the Pope and the Emperor signed an agreement by which John XII swore to be loyal to Otto and never lend his support to Berengar and Adalbert; Otto, for his part, guaranteed to the Pope all his temporal possessions, and at the same time stipulated for the imperial rights over Rome and the Papal elections which had been granted by Leo III to Charlemagne.

Otto had hardly left Rome, when Pope John entered into conspiracy with Berengar, and in the following year welcomed his son Adalbert to Rome. Otto returned and called a Council at St. Peter's. The gravest charges were preferred against John, who had hastily fled into the open country at the approach of the Emperor. He was summoned to appear, but sent a disdainful reply. A second summons proved equally futile. Finally, on December the 4th, after a month of waiting, the Council deposed him and elected Leo VIII in his stead. After the Emperor's departure John returned at the head of a formidable company of friends and retainers, and wreaked cruel vengeance on his opponents. Leo sought safety in immediate flight. Otto determined to restore Leo to the throne, but before he reached the city John had died a shameful death, and the Romans had elected Benedict V to succeed him. Otto entered the city after a brief resistance and convened a new synod, which deposed Benedict and sent him for safekeeping to the Archbishop of Hamburg in Germany.

The Crescentii.—All historians agree that Otto the Great sincerely desired to put an end to the humiliations to which the Holy See had been so long subjected. This was to be expected from the son of St. Mathilda, the husband of St. Edith and St. Adelaide, and the brother of the great St. Bruno of Cologne. But

long-standing abuses cannot be removed in a day. No sooner had
Otto closed his eyes in death than the Papacy became once more
the plaything of Italian factions. Crescentius, the son of Theodora the Younger, took possession of the Temporal Power of
the Holy See, called himself Patrician of the Romans, and violently opposed every Pope elected under the auspices of the successors of Otto. He expelled some and caused others to be put
to death. One of these unfortunates, John XIV, was the second
Pope to change his name after his election; he had before been
known as Peter of Pavia, and it was no doubt out of reverence
for the Prince of the Apostles that he did not retain his baptismal
name.   John XV (985-996), protected by the Empress Theophano, who administered the Empire during the minority of her
son Otto III, shed some luster on the See of Peter. Through his
legates he prevented a threatened schism of the French Church
after the usurpation of the French crown by Hugh Capet. Under
his pontificate we also meet with the first complete process of a
canonization, the object of which was St. Ulrich, bishop of Augsburg. Up to that time the canonizations had been made by the
bishops or the synods. Wearying at last of the dictatorship of
Crescentius, Pope John invited the young German king Otto to
come to Rome, where his presence was indeed greatly needed. He
died, however, before the king's arrival.

Crescentius did not dare to appoint John's successor, and an
embassy was despatched to Otto, asking him to undertake the
responsibility. Otto selected one of his cousins, the saintly Bruno
of Carinthia, a man of only twenty-three, to fill the vacant post.
Bruno took the name of Gregory V. He was the first Pope of
transalpine origin to occupy the Chair of Peter. Crescentius was
deprived of his dignities, but saved from banishment by the intervention of the Pope. He showed his gratitude by intruding an
anti-pope and driving Gregory from Rome when Otto left for
the North. Otto brought Gregory back to Rome, imprisoned the
anti-pope, and captured and executed Crescentius. When Gregory
died in 999, from poison, it was whispered, Otto raised to the
pontificate his former tutor and friend, Gerbert of Aurillac, at
that time archbishop of Ravenna, who ruled the Church as
Sylvester II till the year 1003.

Gerbert was the most remarkable man of his time. Born of poor parents
in Auvergne, he was educated at the Benedictine monastery at Aurillac.

When he had learned all that his masters could teach him, he passed into Spain and for three years studied arithmetic, geometry, and astronomy at the famous Cathedral School of Vich in Catalonia. From Spain he went to Rome, where he attracted the attention of Otto the Great by his proficiency in music. We next hear of him in Rheims, where he was first a student of philosophy and then master of the Cathedral School. Otto II made him abbot of the once renowned, but now degenerate Irish-Italian monastery of Bobbio in the Appenines. Driven from there by the corrupt monks, he taught for ten years with great success at Rheims. On his deathbed Archbishop Adalbero designated him as his successor. Hugh Capet, however, the new king of France, supported another candidate, the Carolingian Arnulf, and it was not till Arnulf was deposed for treason that Gerbert became archbishop of Rheims, only to be deprived a few years later through the intervention of Pope Gregory V. Gerbert protested vehemently, but finally yielded and set out for the court of Otto III. Otto had built a palace in Rome on the Aventine, and there Gerbert taught him arithmetic and filled his mind with the splendid vision of a restored Roman Empire, of Pope and Emperor ruling in harmony from the Capital of the world, a world at peace. In 998 Gerbert was appointed Archbishop of Ravenna, and early in the next year succeeded Gregory V in the Chair of Peter. As Supreme Pontiff, Sylvester II showed the same energy that had characterized his former life, and zealously promoted the reforms begun by his predecessor. But all his plans for the advancement of the Church and the Empire were cut short by the untimely death of Otto III in 1002, and by his own death in the following year.

The extant writings of Gerbert, which cover the whole range of human knowledge, place him in the forefront of the scholars of his age. He was a distinguished theologian and philosopher, knew canon law as well as any professional canonist, excelled in music, arithmetic, geometry and astronomy; he passionately loved the classical writers of Rome, and spared no expense to collect manuscripts of their works. Fables soon began to cluster round his name. The poor lad of Auvergne, who was so far in advance of his generation in knowledge, who became the intimate friend of kings and emperors, who occupied in succession two of the great metropolitan sees of the West, and, finally, ascended the Papal Throne—how else could his phenomenal rise to power and influence be accounted for except that he must have been a magician, a necromancer, and in league with the devil. . . .

The Tusculan Dictatorship.—After the death of Sylvester II, the younger Crescentius, son of the executed Patrician, terrorized the Papacy for ten years. Then the Counts of Tusculum, descendants of Theophylact and the elder Theodora, took possession of the Temporal Power in Rome. They forced Gregory, the candidate of the Crescentian party, to flee from the city, and raised a member of their own family, Benedict VIII, to the Pontificate. Benedict (1012-1024), in spite of his antecedents, proved to be a very capable Pontiff. He defeated the Saracens, crowned St. Henry II and his wife St. Cunegunda, and worked hand in hand with them for the reform of the Church. A General Council of the Western Church was planned, but both Pope and Emperor died before it could be convened.

Benedict was succeeded by his brother Romanus, who took the name of John XIX (1024-1033). The old abuses flourished more luxuriantly than ever. They reached their climax when, at John's death, his nephew Theophylact, a boy of ten or twelve, was thrust upon the Papal Throne by the Tusculan masters of Rome as Benedict IX (1033-1045). To say that he was a fit successor to John XII, characterizes him sufficiently. He was driven from his throne in 1044, and Sylvester III elected in his place. Benedict, however, returned shortly afterward, and forced Sylvester to take refuge in his native Sabine Hills. Then an event occurred which has no parallel in the history of the Church: Benedict abdicated in favor of the Archpriest John Gratian for a good round sum of money. The highest office in Christendom had been bought and sold. Simon Magus had achieved his greatest triumph. John Gratian, who took the name of Gregory VI, was a simple, pious man whose sole purpose in the infamous transaction had been to rid the Papacy of a scandalous intruder. But a Pope branded with the mark of simony could not, with the best intentions in the world, successfully undertake the sorely needed work of reformation. He made some laudable efforts in this direction, but failed utterly. To make matters worse, Benedict retracted his abdication and attempted to ascend the Papal Throne once more. Thus there were three Popes in Rome, each claiming to be the true head of Christendom: Gregory at the Vatican, Benedict in the Lateran, and Sylvester in the Church of Santa Maria Maggiore.

It was at this juncture that Henry III, the young and zealous German king, arrived on the scene. He summoned a great council at Sutri, which received the voluntary resignation of Gregory VI and decreed the deposition of Sylvester III. A second synod at St. Peter's declared that Benedict had forfeited all right to the Papacy by his abdication.

At last the Temple had been cleared of the buyers and sellers, of those who had made it a den of thieves and a reproach among the nations. From this time on, the Chair of Peter was occupied by men of saintly lives and high aspirations, who labored zealously and with increasing success for the reformation of the Church and her liberation from the tyranny of the secular powers. The first of these "reform Popes" were the German Popes nominated by Henry III: Clement II (1046-1047), who crowned Henry and his wife Agnes; Damasus II (1048), whose brief reign was troubled by the reappearance of Benedict IX, and St. Leo IX (1048-1054), a cousin to the Emperor, a man of "stately bearing, famed for virtues and miracles," who made his entry into Rome accompanied by the monk Hildebrand.

How a Papal Letter Was Received in Constantinople
A.D. 968

Liudprand of Cremona (b. about 922, d. 972), belonged to a noble Lombard family, and was brought up at the court of King Hugh at Pavia. He entered the service of King Berengar in 945, and was sent by him on an embassy to the Byzantine court. Later he attached himself to the Emperor Otto the Great, accompanied him to Italy and was raised by him to the bishopric of Cremona. In 968 he was sent to Constantinople to seek for the younger Otto the hand of Theophano, daughter of the Emperor Nicephorus Phocas. His account of this embassy is the "most graphic and lively piece of writing which has come down to us from the 10th century. The detailed description of Constantinople and the Byzantine court is a document of rare value—though highly colored by his ill reception and offended dignity." The following extract shows how unfriendly were the relations between East and West at this period, and that the Eastern rulers and ecclesiastics never forgave the Popes for having conferred the title of Roman Emperors on the Frankish and Saxon "barbarians":

". . . And these perils tried my soul at Constantinople from the second day before the Nones of June (June 4), until the sixth day before the Nones of October (Oct. 2)—one hundred and twenty days. But to increase my calamities, on the day of the Assumption of the Virgin Mary the Holy Mother of God, there came—an evil augury for me—envoys of the Apostolic and Universal Pope John, through whom he asked Nicephorus 'the Emperor of the Greeks' to close an alliance and firm friendship with his beloved and spiritual son Otto 'august Emperor of the Romans.' Before the question as to why this word, this manner of address, sinful and bold in the eyes of the Greeks, did not cost its bearer his life—why he was not annihilated before it was read, I, who in other respects have often shown myself enough of a preacher and with words enough at my command, seem dumb as a fish! The Greeks inveighed against the sea, cursed the waves, and wondered exceedingly how they had been able to transport such an iniquity and why the yawning deep had not swallowed up the ship. 'Was it not unpardonable,' they said, 'to have called the universal emperor of the Romans, the august, great, only Nicephorus: Emperor of the Greeks;—

and a barbarian, a pauper: 'Emperor of the Romans'? Oh sky! Oh earth! Oh sea!' 'But what,' they said, 'shall we do to those scoundrels, those criminals? They are paupers, and if we kill them, we pollute our hands with vile blood. They are ragged, they are slaves, they are peasants. If we beat them we disgrace, not them, but ourselves. They may continue to live; and, until the holy Emperor of the Romans, Nicephorus, learns of this atrocity, they may languish in narrow confinement.'

The Papal messengers, therefore, were thrown into prison, and that offending epistle was sent to Nicephorus in Mesopotamia."

—*Relatio de Legatione Constantinopolitana* (tr. in Henderson's *Select Historical Documents of the Middle Ages,* pp. 465-466).

Hints for Study

1. For a more detailed account of the decline of the Carolingian Empire and the Papacy read Bryce, *The Holy Roman Empire,* Ch. VI; on the revival of the Empire under Otto the Great, the same, Chs. VIII & IX; and Msgr. William Barry, *The Papal Monarchy,* Chs. X-XII.

   Feudalism is well treated by Betten, *Ancient and Medieval History,* Chs. XXXIII & XXXIV.

   For the Papacy of the period see Mann, *Lives of the Popes in the Early Middle Ages,* and the articles on the various Popes in the *Cath. Encyclopedia.*

   For contemporary accounts of the ravages of the Vikings, see Ogg, *Source Book of Medieval History,* pp. 158-180.

2. Sum up briefly the causes that led to the decline of the Papacy in the tenth century.

3. Why are the pontificates of such Popes as Sergius III, John XII, and Benedict IX no argument against the Primacy and Infallibility of the successors of St. Peter?

4. The decay of the Papacy in the 10th century shows that there is a very strong human element in the Church—how does it prove the divine origin of the Church?

5. Who was the first German Pope? the first French Pope?

CHAPTER VIII

NEW NATIONS WON FOR THE CHURCH

Even during the darkest period of her history, when her records seem to yield "no light but only darkness visible," the Church was carrying out the commission given to her by her Divine Founder to preach the Gospel to all nations. It was during the ninth, tenth, and eleventh centuries that one of the greatest transformations in the history of the western world took place: the Danes, Swedes, Norwegians, Poles, Moravians, Bohemians, Hungarians, Serbs, Bulgarians, and Russians put from them their paganism with its horrid superstition and cruelty, and bowed their necks under the yoke of Christ.

In the history of the Church, by a kind of spiritual law, the people last to be converted becomes the next instrument for the propagation of the faith. We have seen this law in operation in the case of the Irish and the English; and now it is the turn of the Germans.

1. *Christianity among the Scandinavians*

By the subjugation of the Saxons the barrier which had so long separated Scandinavia from the Franks was broken down, and Christianity could penetrate unhindered into the realms of the Vikings.

In 826 King Harald of *Denmark*, who had been driven out of his kingdom by a rival faction, sailed up the Rhine to the court of Emperor Louis the Pious at Ingelheim near Mainz. Louis promised him the help he sought against his adversaries, but only on condition that he would receive baptism and promote the spread of the Christian faith among his people. Harald accepted the proposal, and was baptized with his wife, his son Godfred, and four hundred of his suite. *Ansgar,* a young monk of the newly founded Benedictine Abbey of Corvey on the Weser, encouraged by a vision, volunteered his services as a missionary. For nearly forty years he labored with indefatigable zeal and varying success for the conversion of the Danes and the Swedes. Honors and dignities came to him without his asking—he was made first Archbishop of Hamburg, Archbishop of Bremen-Hamburg after the union of these two sees, Imperial Ambassador to the kings of Denmark and Sweden, and legate of the Holy See to the countries of the North—but he accepted them only in the interests of his mission, personally remaining to the last an humble son of St. Benedict and a faithful observer of his Rule. He died in Bremen in 865. His only regret was that he had not been found worthy of the martyr's crown. Although he did not convert all the Danes, and although many of the churches, hospitals, schools,

St. Ansgar

and religious houses which he had founded were afterwards destroyed by the fury of the pagans, he nevertheless fully deserves the title bestowed upon him by the grateful Scandinavians—*Apostle of the North.*

During the apostolate of St. Ansgar and his immediate successors, the Viking raids were at their height, and it was not until they had subsided that Adalhag, Archbishop of Hamburg, could open a new and successful mission in Denmark, which resulted in the erection of the bishoprics of Schleswig, Ripen, and Aarhus in 948. The conversion of King Harald Bluetooth after his defeat by Otto the Great in 965 was the prelude to the final triumph of Christianity under Canute the Great (1014-1035). The Danish Church formed a part of the Archdiocese of Hamburg till 1104, when Pope Paschal II erected the Archdiocese of Lund.

About the year 829 St. Ansgar made his first expedition to *Sweden.* The vessel in which he sailed was captured and plundered by pirates, who even robbed him of his books. Nothing daunted, he made his way, by land and water, to Birca on the

Mälar. He came not only as a missionary, but also as the ambassador of the Emperor Louis, and as such was honorably received by King Björn. His preaching met with considerable immediate success, but the churches which he founded did not long survive his death, and no serious missionary enterprise was attempted for more than a century afterwards. Under King Olaf III, who had been baptized by the English bishop Siegfried about the year 1000, Christianity was firmly established in the Lowlands, but the Uplanders held out against it for many years more. Several English priests who had tried to convert them suffered martyrdom. King Stenkil (1060-1066) was an ardent Christian and ready at all times to use more than persuasion to win over the pagans to Christianity; but even he declared that it would be folly to try to destroy the great heathen sanctuary at Upsala. Stenkil's son Inge did try, and was driven from the throne for his pains. For three years the intruder Svend, called the Bloody, because he renewed the old pagan sacrifices, subjected the Christians to a violent persecution. Then Inge returned and slew Svend, and his fall marks the final fall of the old religion (1078). The temple at Upsala was dismantled and replaced by a Christian church, and in 1163 this ancient stronghold of paganism became the Christian metropolis of Sweden.

Adam of Bremen, the historian and geographer (11th cent.), whose *History* is a primary authority for all the North German and Baltic lands, and for the Scandinavian colonies as far as America, describes the pagan temple at Upsala as one of great splendor and covered with gilding. "In it stood the statues of the three chief gods Thor, Odin and Freya. Every nine years a great festival was held there to which embassies were sent by all the peoples of Sweden. A large number of animals and even men were sacrificed on such occasions. In the neighborhood of the temple was a grove of peculiar sanctity, in which the bodies of the victims were hung up." Owing to its intimate associations with paganism the Christian kings no longer resided at Upsala, and its importance steadily declined until it was made the residence of the Swedish archbishop and the seat of a university.

Norway was converted earlier than Sweden, although missionaries began their labors there much later. The work of evangelization was begun when Haakon the Good (938-961), who had received a Christian education in England, ascended the throne and invited English missionaries to preach the Gospel to his people. His work was, however, in great part destroyed by his pagan or half-pagan successors. Then Olaf Tryggvasen began his short but brilliant reign, and within the space of five years Norway was transformed from a pagan into a Christian country (995-1000). Olaf was known in every land of the West. He had spent his youth in Russia, where his countrymen had founded the kingdoms of Novgorod and Kiev; had fought for Otto III under the Wendish king Burislav, whose daughter he had married, and then, following the example of his countrymen, had turned freebooter and harried the coasts of Europe from Greece to Ireland. From the German priest Dankbrand he had received a massive shield adorned with the gilded image of the crucified Redeemer which he carried with him as a talisman, and to which he ascribed his deliverance out of a thousand perils on land and sea. Converted to Christianity by a hermit in the Scilly Islands, he had given up his marauding expeditions, married the daughter of the Danish king of Dublin and spent his time in administering her estates in England and Ireland. Reports of the unpopularity of the Norwegian ruler having reached him, he sailed for Norway, was unanimously accepted as king, and at once set about the conversion of the country to Christianity. His zeal was sincere, but the means he employed were not always praiseworthy. By the force of his character, by his fearless disregard of his numerous enemies, but, above all, by the popularity which his deeds of daring had won for him, he succeeded in treading down paganism and establishing the Christian religion on its ruins. While engaged on an expedition against his old companion in arms, the Wendish king Burislav, he was waylaid by the combined Swedish and Danish fleet off the island of Ruegen. Surprised and outnumbered, Olaf fought bravely to the last on his great ship, the *Long Snake,* and finally leapt overboard in order to escape falling into the hands of his enemies. His heroism reconciled his adversaries and made the religion which he had professed and fought for more popular than ever.

Olaf II (1016-1029) completed the work begun by Olaf Tryggvasen. With the aid of English and German missionaries he spread the faith into every part of Norway and to the Orkney, Shetland, and Faeroe islands. He built the church of St. Clement at Drontheim (Nidaros), procured the establishment of bishoprics, opened schools in various places, and caused a code of laws in harmony with the teachings of the Gospel to be drawn up. He fell in battle against the rebellious pagan nobility leagued with the

Danes. He was canonized in 1164 and declared the patron saint of Norway. His tomb at Drontheim was for centuries the goal of pilgrims from all Scandinavia.

Iceland had long been inhabited by a colony of Irish Culdees before its discovery by the Scandinavians in 850. Towards the end of the ninth century, Norwegian adventurers established an independent state in the island. They were pagans like their compatriots who were settling about the same time in England and Ireland. The first attempt to convert them was made by a Saxon priest named Frederick. He had been brought to Iceland by the sea-rover Thorwald, who had received baptism on the occasion of a visit to Saxony in 980. Being ignorant of the language of the people, he accomplished little and soon left the island. It was to Olaf Tryggvasen, who made an expedition to Iceland in 997, and to the missionaries whom he sent there, that the island owed its conversion. In the year 1000 the national assembly declared Christianity to be the religion of the land, but the pagans were permitted to practice their religion in private. This concession was revoked by St. Olaf II. Monastic foundations were made soon after by the Benedictines and Augustinians. The first bishop of the island was Isleif, who died in the odor of sanctity in 1080. A second bishopric was founded in the twelfth century. Till far into the thirteenth century Iceland was the principal center of Scandinavian culture, producing such well-known poets and historians as Snorri Sturleson, the author of the *Heimskringla,* and Eystein Asgrimsson, the singer of the *Lilja.* At this time Iceland counted 220 churches, 9 monasteries, and 290 priests.

Greenland was discovered in 982 by Eric the Red. Eric was a pagan, but his son Leif Ericsson embraced Christianity in 999 and at the instance of Olaf Tryggvasen introduced Christianity into Greenland in the year 1000, the year in which he discovered the North American continent. In 1055 Archbishop Adalbert of Bremen sent the first bishop to Greenland. He established his see at Gardar, near the present Eskimo station Igoliko. His diocese numbered about ten thousand souls, sixteen churches, one monastery, and one convent. Seventeen bishops were appointed to Greenland during the Middle Ages, but most of those appointed never reached their diocese; the last bishop who resided in Greenland died there in 1377. With the cessation of immigration from the mother country the Norwegian settlements decayed rapidly. After 1448 we hear no more of them. The settlers either died of some contagious disease, or were exterminated or absorbed by the pagan Eskimos.

The Northmen who settled on the northwest coast of France were converted in 912 with their famous chieftain Rollo, who took the name of Robert at his baptism. Those who had founded the "Danish" kingdom of Dublin embraced Christianity about the middle of the tenth century, while the Danes in England were brought into the Church chiefly through the efforts of Alfred the Great (871-901) and Canute the Great (1014-1035).

2. *The Conversion of the Slavs*

In the early Middle Ages the Slavs occupied all the territory in the East of Europe from the Elbe and the Saale to the Don and the Ural and from the Baltic to the Adriatic. They were divided into four groups: the central group, comprising the various Slavic tribes who dwelt within the present limits of Germany; the eastern group, formed by the Russians; the northwestern, composed chiefly of Czechs (Bohemians), Moravians (Slovaks), and Poles; and the southern group, also known as Jugo-Slavs, which included the Slovenes, Croatians, and Serbs. The Bulgarians, an Asiatic tribe, so completely lost their racial identity that they were reckoned as a Slavic people. The religion and the morality of the Slavs were no better and no worse than the religion and the morality of most other pagan nations. Slavery, polytheism and polygamy flourished amongst them; human sacrifices were offered to Perun, the god of thunder; the mother had the right to expose or kill an undesirable girl-child; the wife was nothing but the drudge of the husband, and often she was obliged to immolate herself on the funeral pyre of her husband. The priests were honored like princes, and the administration of justice was entirely in their hands.

Sts. Cyril and Methodius, the Apostles of the Slavs.—In 850 the Moravians, who had until then formed part of the empire of Charlemagne, asserted their independence and formed an alliance with the Eastern Empire. This alliance resulted in their conversion to Christianity through the efforts of two Greek monks of noble birth and high attainments, the brothers Cyril and Methodius. Cyril had been sent by the Emperor Michael III to the Chazars, a Tartar tribe living northeast of the Black Sea, in answer to their request for a Christian teacher, but had not remained long among them. After his return he worked with his brother for several years among the Bulgarians. About the year 863 the brothers went to Moravia on the invitation of Duke Ratislas. Their preaching was successful from the very beginning.

STS. CYRIL AND METHODIUS RECEIVE THEIR MISSION FROM THE POPE

This was due, in large measure, to the fact that they had a perfect command of the Slavonic language and celebrated the liturgy in the vernacular. Cyril is even said to have invented the modified form of the Greek alphabet known as the Cyrillic characters, which are still used by the Russians and other Slavic peoples.

A serious conflict with some German priests, who had been in Moravia before them and who objected to their use of the Slavonic language in celebrating Mass, led to their being called to Rome by Pope St. Nicholas I. Nicholas died (in 867) before their arrival. His successor Hadrian II received them kindly and gave them many marks of his good will. Cyril presented the Pontiff with the relics of the Martyr-Pope St. Clement of Rome, which he had discovered at Kherson during his mission to the Khazars and had borne with him in all his journeyings. Before the date set for their departure, Cyril fell sick and retired to a Roman monastery, where he died in 869. Methodius, having obtained permission to continue the use of the Slavonian liturgy—a permission renewed in 880 by Pope John VIII, but recalled by later Popes—went back to his labors among the Moravians, as archbishop of the Moravians and Pannonians. The Hungarian invasions, which began about this time, hampered his missionary work, and the last years of his life were embittered by constantly recurring ecclesiastical disputes between the Latin and Greek priests. He died on the 6th of April, 885. After his death the Slavonian liturgy was supplanted by the Latin, but some of his disciples introduced it among the Jugo-Slavs, where it is still in limited use. The old Slavonic language is also used in the liturgy of the schismatic churches of Russia, Bulgaria, and Jugo-Slavia. —In 973 Moravia was included in the archdiocese of Prague; it had no bishops of its own until the erection of the see of Olmütz in the 11th century.

The Czechs Become Christians.—Moravian missionaries preached with some success in Bohemia, the land of the Czechs. It is said that St. Methodius himself baptized Ludmilla, the wife of Duke Borziwoi. She became an ardent Christian and did much to spread the faith amongst her people. She was murdered (in 927) by her daughter-in-law Drahomira, a fanatical pagan, and is venerated as a martyr by the Church. During the reign of her son St. Wenceslaus, the Christians multiplied rapidly in spite of the fierce hostility of the pagan nobility and priesthood. He too was assassinated (935). Boleslaus the Cruel, his brother, murderer and successor, drove out all the Catholic priests and put many Christians to death. At last Otto the Great, after a bloody war, compelled Boleslaus to restore the Christian religion. Boleslaus himself became a Christian before his death, and his son Boleslaus II, surnamed the Good (967-999), brought about the final triumph of Christianity.

But pagan customs and vices were harder to root out than belief in idols. St. Adalbert, the second bishop of Prague, contended in vain against polygamy, incest, divorce, slave traffic, and ignorance and immorality amongst the native clergy. What he could not accomplish during his life, he achieved, in a measure, after his death. Martyred by the Prussians (in 1000), to whom he had gone to preach the Gospel, his glorious death wrought a salutary change in the hearts of many of his countrymen. Fired with admiration for the heroism of their blessed father, they made almost incredible efforts to obtain possession of his remains, and vowed to live henceforth more in accord with his teachings.

How Poland Became a Christian Nation.—The Poles obtained their first knowledge of the Gospel through Moravian immigrants; but Christianity made little progress among them until their land was placed under the overlordship of Germany by Otto the Great. Duke Miecislaw (962-992) married, as his eighth wife, Dombrowka, daughter of Boleslaus I of Bohemia, who persuaded him to become a Christian. His strict orders to cast all the idols into the rivers were almost universally obeyed, and before long most of his subjects had become Christians, at least in name. Boleslaus I, Chrobry (992-1025), the national hero of the Poles, made stringent laws against pagan practices and the violation of the precepts of the Church. He purchased the body of St. Adalbert from the Prussians and solemnly laid it in the church of Gnesen. St. Adalbert had been the intimate friend of Otto III, and in the year 1000 the young Emperor traveled from Rome to Gnesen to pray at his shrine. On this occasion he bestowed the title of king on Boleslaus and made the Polish Church independent of Germany by the establishment of the Archbishopric of Gnesen.

After the death of Boleslaus direful times followed for Poland. With the aid of the Emperor Henry III, King Casimir I (1040-1058), who had been educated at the great monastery of Cluny in France, succeeded in putting down a strong pagan uprising, and from this time on, Poland appears as a Christian nation. Boleslaus II (1058-1079) walked at first in the footsteps of his father, but later gave himself up to a life of cruelty and debauchery. When St. Stanislaus, Bishop of Cracow, called him to account and excommunicated him, he slew him with his own hand at the foot of the altar in the cathedral church (1079). The people were so enraged at this foul deed that Boleslaus had to flee for his life to a monastery in Carinthia, where he died three years later.

St. Olga and Vladimir the Great Convert the Russians.— About the middle of the ninth century Scandinavian Vikings of the Swedish-Finnish tribe of the Rus, under their leader Ruric, settled in the Ukraine and on the Dniepr, and founded an independent principality with Kiev as the seat of government. They called the country Russia, after their native district. Frequent dealings, both friendly and hostile, with the Eastern Empire brought the Russians into contact with Christianity. By the middle of the tenth century many of the Norse nobles of Kiev

THE MARTYRDOM OF ST. STANISLAUS

were Christians. Olga, widow of the Grand Duke Igor, Ruric's son, was baptized in 957, probably in Constantinople, and during the rest of her life lent her powerful influence to the spread of the faith. During the reign of her grandson Vladimir (d. 1015), known as the "Great and Apostolic Prince," who received baptism on the day of his marriage with Anna, sister of the Greek Emperor Basil II, the bulk of the Russian people embraced Christianity. Mouravieff, a Russian historian, tells us how this was brought about:

"After his return to Kiev, the 'Great Prince' caused his twelve sons to be baptized, and proceeded to destroy the monuments of heathenism. He ordered Perun to be thrown into the Dniepr. The people at first followed their idol, as it was borne down the stream, but were soon quieted when they saw that the statue had no power to help itself.—And now Vladimir, being surrounded and supported by believers in his own domestic circle, and encouraged by seeing that his boyars and suite were prepared and ready to embrace the faith, made a proclamation to the people, 'That whoever, on the morrow, should not repair to the river, whether rich or poor, he should hold him for his enemy.' At the call of their respected lord all the multitude of the citizens in troops, with their wives and children, flocked to the Dniepr; and without any manner of opposition received holy baptism as a nation from the Greek bishops and priests. Some stood in the water up to their necks, others up to their breasts, holding their young children in their arms; the priests read the prayers from the shore, naming at once whole companies by the same name.—Vladimir erected the first church—that of St. Basil, after whom he was named—on the very mount which had formerly been sacred to Perun, adjoining his own palace. Thus was Russia enlightened."

Kiev with its gorgeous cathedral of St. Sophia, erected early in the eleventh century, became the seat of an archbishop, who was, however, subject to the patriarch of Constantinople. For more than two hundred years the Russian patriarchs were almost without exception Greeks. Hence it was quite natural that the Russian Church should be drawn into the great schism which, in 1054, cut off the Eastern from the Western Church.

The Southern Slavs.—The Croatians, who had settled in Dalmatia about 640, joined the Church in great numbers under Prince Porza before the end of the seventh century; the conversion of the rest took place early in the ninth century. The Slovenes in Carniola, Carinthia and Styria were converted in the course of the eighth century chiefly through the efforts of the bishops of Salzburg. We still possess an interesting document belonging to the end of the eighth century, which describes the labors of the missionaries sent by St. Virgil, the Irish bishop of Salzburg (d. 782) to the pagan Slavs settled on the borders of his bishopric.

The Serbs, who had settled southeast of the Croatians at the beginning of the seventh century, were compelled by the Emperor Heraclius (610-641) to receive baptism. Their conversion lasted only as long as their subjection to the Greek Empire. In 827 they declared themselves independent and returned at the same time to the worship of their ancient gods. When they were again subdued by the Greeks forty years later, they resumed the practice of the Christian religion. Christianity was brought to the Bulgarians by Byzantine missionaries. Prince Boris received baptism in 864, the Emperor Michael III acting as his sponsor, and ordered his subjects to follow his example, which most of them did. Boris long wavered between Rome and Constantinople. At his request Latin missionaries, Bishop Ermanrich of Passau at their head, appeared at his court in 866, and about the same time he was in correspondence with Pope Nicholas I, whose advice he asked on some of the difficult moral and social problems which naturally arise during a transition from paganism to Christianity. The Pope's reply to his one hundred and six questions and petitions is one of the most important ecclesiastical documents of the early Middle Ages. Boris also corresponded with Pope Hadrian II in regard to the appointment of an archbishop; but he finally yielded to the importunities of the Greeks, and accepted an archbishop of their choice (870).

The Conversion of the Wends.—The Slavs who dwelt within the limits of the present German Republic and went by the name of Wends, became Christians as they were incorporated with the German Empire. The Emperor Otto the Great founded seven bishoprics among them. Their conversion was completed by St. Otto of Bamberg, one of the most successful missionaries of all times. In one year (1124) he founded eleven churches and baptized 22,165 pagans. The Prussians and Lithuanians were not converted till the thirteenth and fourteenth centuries.

3. *Christianity in Hungary*

After their crushing defeat at the hands of Otto the Great in 955 the wild Magyars gave up their raids into the neighboring countries and displayed their readiness to welcome the Christian teaching. Under Duke Geisa (972-997) St. Wolfgang, later bishop of Ratisbon, and other Bavarian missionaries preached with considerable success among them, especially after Geisa himself and all the members of his family had received baptism. Geisa's son, St. Stephen (997-1038), who married Gisela, the sister of the Emperor St. Henry II, is the real apostle of the Hungarians. He declared war on idolatry, procured the establishment of ten bishoprics, founded several monasteries, placed his country under the special protection of the Blessed Virgin, and drew up a Christian code of laws for his people. In 998, after putting down a formidable pagan insurrection, he assumed the royal title. Two years later he obtained from Pope Sylvester II and the Emperor Otto III confirmation of this act of sovereignty. Sylvester at the same time sent him a consecrated crown and conferred on him the title of "Apostolic King."

Unfortunately for the welfare of his country, Stephen died without an heir. The talented and saintly Emmerich, the only one of his five sons to reach manhood, was killed by a wild boar in 1031. During the civil strife which followed on the death of Stephen, paganism got the upper hand once more, and much of the great king's work was undone. Churches were devastated or destroyed, the priests exiled, and heathen temples set up. Martyrblood, too, flowed for a time. It was not till the reign of St. Ladislas (1077-1095) that the power of paganism was completely broken and the triumph of Christianity assured.

An Ordeal by Hot Iron

The method of trial called *ordeal*, or *judgment of God*, had its origin in the times when the Germanic tribes were still pagan, but it was retained long after they had been Christianized. It was based on the belief "that God would not permit an innocent person to suffer by reason of an unjust accusation and that when the opportunity was offered under certain prescribed conditions the divine power would indicate who was in the right and who in the wrong." Under Christian influence wager of battle, the commonest form of the ordeal in pagan times, was discouraged and even positively prohibited, but other forms such as the trials by hot or cold water, by fire, by red hot iron, etc., had to be tolerated and were frequently carried out under the supervision of the ecclesiastical authorities. They were never approved by the Holy See and were never practiced in Rome. The following account of an ordeal by hot iron is taken from the monk Widukind's *History of the Saxons*. The same incident is related, though in a somewhat different setting, by two other ancient chroniclers, Thietmar of Merseburg and Adam of Bremen, so that there is no reason to doubt its historical character:

"The Danes were already Christians in name, but they still worshiped idols in heathen fashion. Now it happened that, at a banquet at which the king was present, a contention arose in regard to the worship of the gods. The Danes maintained that Christ was indeed a god, but that there were other gods, whose power was greater than his, because they made themselves known to man by greater signs and wonders. Against them a certain priest named Poppo, who is at present a holy bishop, asserted that there is only one true God, the Father with the Only-begotten Son Jesus Christ our Lord, and the Holy Ghost, and that the idols are devils and not gods. King Harald, who is described as a man eager to hear but slow to speak, asked him whether he was ready to prove in his own person the truth of his faith. Without a moment's hesitation the priest declared his readiness. Thereupon the king gave orders to guard him carefully till the following day. At daybreak he caused a heavy piece of iron to be heated, and commanded the priest to carry the red hot mass in his hands in proof of the truth of the Catholic faith. The confessor of Christ seizes the iron

ORDEAL BY HOT IRON IN PRESENCE OF THE EMPEROR OTTO

and carries it as long as the king commands: then he shows his uninjured hands to all, and thus proves to the whole assembly the truth of the Catholic faith. After this trial the king was converted, and commanded his pagan subjects to disown their idols and to worship Christ alone as God. . . ."—*Widukindi Monachi Corbeiensis Rerum Gestarum Saxonicarum Lib. III Cap. LXV.*

Hints for Study

1. In the Roman Empire Christianity was first received by the lower classes, and from them made its way to the upper classes—what was the process among the Germanic and Slavic peoples?
2. Make a list of the men and women who played an important part in the conversion of the Scandinavians, Slavs, and Hungarians.
3. What events recorded in this chapter happened in the year 1000?
4. There is a good account of the origin and nature of the Medieval Ordeals in F. A. Ogg, *Source Book of Mediaeval History,* Ch. XII.

CHAPTER IX

THE GREEK SCHISM

The gains of the Church in the West were offset almost immediately by most painful losses in the East. In the middle of the eleventh century the disastrous schism known as the Greek, or Eastern, Schism broke the unity of Christendom and cut off an appalling large fragment from the Catholic Church.

Origin of Estrangement between East and West.—There had been misunderstanding and jealousy between the East and the West long before the fateful schism. Ever since the removal of the capital of the Empire from the banks of the Tiber to the shores of the Bosporus, East and West had tended to drift apart. The real authors of the Greek Schism, as Duchesne remarks, were neither Michael Cerularius, by whom it was consummated, nor yet Photius, by whom it was ushered in, but Eusebius of Nicomedia and his accomplices, in their opposition to the Council of Nicaea. It was under the guidance of this party that the autonomy of the Byzantine bishops was first organized and established. This autonomy revealed itself from the first under two most unfortunate aspects: from the dawn of its history the Greek Church was at war with Christian tradition concerning the divinity of Christ, and at the same time was on the best of terms with imperial despotism. The doctrinal war came to an end, to break out later, alas! on other points; but the cringing to imperial despotism continued, and ended in that sad alliance known by the name of Caesaro-Papism.

Caesaro-Papism.—We must clearly understand what this monster Caesaro-Papism was, for it was the main cause of the catastrophe that overtook the Church in the eleventh century, and again in the sixteenth.

The pagan conception of the secular power, viz., that the Emperor is supreme in spiritual as well as in temporal matters, did not entirely disappear after the Empire had become Christian. The Christian emperors, with few exceptions, sought to carry on

the pagan tradition. In their eagerness to interfere and to dictate in doctrinal matters many of them fell a prey to the heresies
which were forever cropping up in the East. These Arian, Monophysite, Monothelete, and Iconoclast Emperors found the Pope of
Rome very irritating to their pride; for his condemnations in the
end always triumphed over their pet heresies. "They wanted a
Christianity more submissive to their caprices or their passions, a
Church of which they themselves might become the actual heads;
in place of Peter's successor, they wanted an episcopate nominated
by themselves and immediately depending on them; they wanted
councils they could rule after their pleasure. The supreme head
of the hierarchy and bearer of the keys must be, in spiritual things
as in temporal, the most gracious sovereign of the state; the Emperor, *Pontifex Maximus,* as in pagan times" (Bishop d'Herbigny,
The Separated Eastern Churches). This is Caesaro-Papism.

The Court Bishops of Constantinople.—The servility and
ambition of most of the bishops of Constantinople prepared the
way for the triumph of the imperial despotism in religious matters. Nearly all of them owed their elevation to the emperor,
whose choice was not necessarily guided by the Gospel law. If
the emperors were weaklings, these court bishops made them the
tools of their ambition; if the emperors were strong men, the
bishops were completely at their mercy; in either case religion was
the sufferer.—On the part of their colleagues, the imperial bishops
were the objects of the most profound respect. Were they not the
bishops of New Rome? Did they not bask in the light of the
Caesar's countenance? Did not so much depend on their smile
or their frown? They were simple bishops at first, subject to the
Metropolitan of Heraclea. Soon, however, they were given a
number of suffragan bishops. Then the Council of Constantinople
(381) decreed that they should be honored next to the Bishops
of Rome, Constantinople being "New Rome," and bestowed the
title of Patriarch upon them; the Council of Chalcedon (451) made
them Patriarchs in fact, which permitted them to exercise their
authority over a large number of bishops; when Alexandria and
Antioch lost their importance through the Nestorian and Monophysite heresies, the Patriarchs of Constantinople came to be without a rival in the East, especially after they had usurped all Asia
Minor, which until then had belonged to no Patriarchate; by the
end of the sixth century they had arrogated to themselves the

fantastical title of "Ecumenical (Universal) Patriarchs," and continued to bear it in spite of the protests of Rome. Rome was too far away to detect their intrigues in time to frustrate them. The Papal condemnations and excommunications appeared to them, at a distance, less formidable, especially since they were sure that they could count on the support of the Court and the countenance of their fellow-bishops.

The Council in Trullo. The Rift Grows Larger.—The growing estrangement between East and West was accentuated by the diversity in national character, language, rites, and discipline. Since the time of Justinian the Great the Eastern Church had sunk into a state of stagnation and rigid adherence to the forms and traditions of the past; and because *she* adhered to them, she looked askance at those who did not; because *she* was stagnant, she was suspicious of those who moved. If she had been satisfied to hold on to her traditions, all might have been well; but she insisted on imposing them on the West also. Any ritual and disciplinary practices not in harmony with those in vogue in the East she declared "contrary to the apostolic tradition," and therefore to be abolished.

The Greek Council *in Trullo* (692), so called from the shell-like dome of the church in which it was held, presumed to dictate in matters of discipline to the Church of Rome, and to pronounce sentence of excommunication or deposition against such as refused to accept its ruling. "We have learned," says the 55th Canon of this Council, "that in the city of the Romans, people fast on the Saturdays of Lent contrary to ecclesiastical tradition: it hath accordingly seemed good to this Holy Synod to decree that amongst the Romans also the canon should be enforced which says: If a cleric be found to fast on Sunday or Saturday he shall be deposed; if a layman be guilty of the same offense, he shall be excommunicated!" According to this, even the Pope himself could be dispossessed of his See and of his sacerdotal dignity, if he insisted on fasting on Saturdays during Lent! The Emperor Justinian II, at whose wish the council had assembled, sent the canons to be signed by the Pope, who indignantly refused to sanction such a piece of impertinence, and was bullied and terrorized for his constancy, as were also several of his successors.

The Iconoclast Heresy.—Soon after the death of the tyrannical Justinian there broke out a terrible schism, caused by an

emperor who was both a despot and a heretic. In 726 Leo the
Isaurian (717-741), urged perhaps by Mohammedans and Jews,
ordered the destruction of all images in the churches. This decree was the beginning of the iconoclast (image-breaking) schism,
which for more than a hundred years filled the East with confusion, desolation, and death. The destruction of the famous
image of Christ over the brazen door of the palace led to an uproar
among the people. Leo was condemned by Pope Gregory II.
St. John of Damascus, the last of the Greek Fathers and Doctors,
who was living under the rule of the Chalifs, published three discourses in defense of images. The emperor threatened to destroy
the image of St. Peter at Rome, and to take the Pope captive. A
fleet was sent to Rome to carry out this threat, but the attack
failed utterly in the face of the armed resistance of the Italians
and the Lombards. Leo's successors · continued his policy. A
council of Constantinople anathematized those who venerated
images, and this anathema was the excuse for additional severity.
Monasteries were razed to the ground, and many monks died as
martyrs for the faith and traditional usage of the Church.

The Empress Irene, who held the regency after the death of her
husband Leo IV in 780, set herself to restore the veneration of
images and to bring back peace to the Church. She was sup·
ported by the Patriarch St. Tarasius. Irene and Tarasius convoked a General Council, to which Hadrian I was invited to send
legates. The Council—the Seventh Ecumenical—met at Nicaea in
787, the Papal legates presiding. In the seventh session the
Catholic doctrine on the question of the veneration of images was
defined. "The figure of the cross," the Council declares, "and
holy images, whether made in colors or of stone, or of any other
material, are to be retained. They are not to become objects of
adoration in the proper sense, which is given to God alone, but
they are useful because they raise the mind of the spectator to
the objects which they represent. It is right to salute, honor, and
venerate them, to burn lights and incense before them, not only
because this is in accordance with the tradition of the Church, but
also because such honor is really given to God and His saints, of
whom the images are intended to remind us."

The Iconoclast spirit was revived by Leo the Armenian in 813,
and Theophilus (829 842) violently persecuted the monks who
adhered to the definition of the Nicene Council. Theodora, widow

of Theophilus, brought the images back in triumph to the church of St. Sophia and in agreement with the Patriarch St. Methodius instituted the "Feast of Orthodoxy," which is still kept by the Greeks on the 19th of February.

The Coronation of Charlemagne.—Peace had scarcely been restored between the East and the West by the Council of Nicaea when an event occurred which not only greatly complicated, but also embittered their relations. This event was the coronation of Charlemagne as Roman Emperor by Pope St. Leo III on Christmas Day of the year 800. No single event, some historians claim, alienated the East so forcibly from the West. By it the age-long rivalry was turned into positive hatred. It was not a question of religion, but of national pride. That Rome should be detached from the Roman Empire; that Rome should be placed under the yoke of barbarians; that Rome should be no longer Roman—this appeared a monstrous thing indeed to the Eastern mind; and the Pope of Rome was responsible for this unpardonable crime! The Eastern Emperors retaliated by definitively detaching the provinces of Illyricum from the jurisdiction of the Roman See, and also the bishoprics of Sicily and lower Italy. "These provinces," says a Greek writer of the ninth century, "have been annexed to the Patriarchate of Constantinople *because the Pope of Ancient Rome is in the hands of barbarians.*" From now on, it was only a question of time when the whole East would refuse to obey the "barbarian" head of Christendom.

The Photian Schism.—In the middle of the ninth century a patriarch of Constantinople made the first deliberate attempt to sever the Greek Church from the West by appealing to the national pride of his countrymen. This man was Photius.

We saw above that St. Theodora re-established the Catholic faith in the East in 842. All went well until her son Michael, known in history as "the Drunkard," came of age and began to reign. This sensual prince fell entirely under the influence of his uncle Bardas, a profligate of the most despicable character, who lived in sin with one of his near relatives. On the feast of the Epiphany, 857, St. Ignatius, who had succeeded St. Methodius as patriarch of Constantinople in 846, refused to give Bardas Holy Communion. Ignatius was arrested and imprisoned, and upon refusing to resign his office was illegally deposed, while Photius, a layman, was installed as patriarch in his place.

Photius was easily the most learned man of his time, as his monumental work, the *Bibliotheca*, which consists of abridgments of and extracts from 280 volumes of classical authors, amply testifies. But even his greatest admirers admit that he was worldly, crafty, ambitious, and unscrupulous. When he saw that his usurpation caused discontent among the clergy and the people, he persuaded the Emperor to send ambassadors with costly presents to Pope St. Nicholas I in order to secure his approbation. In spite of false statements made by the ambassadors—they said

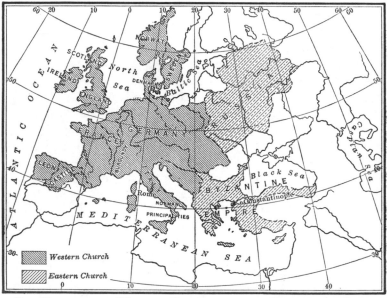

THE EASTERN AND WESTERN CHURCHES AT THE TIME OF THE GREAT
SCHISM

that Ignatius had resigned his see because of his advanced age, and voluntarily retired into a monastery—the Pope refused to decide until he had investigated the matter. The legates whom he sent to Constantinople for this purpose, yielding to threats of bribery, acknowledged Photius as lawful patriarch. But Nicholas saw through their deceit, and in a letter to the Eastern bishops condemned and deposed Photius. The rage of the proud intruder knew no bounds. "In a letter addressed to all the patriarchs and bishops of the East he railed against all claim to spiritual authority on the part of the Holy See, declaring it intolerable, above all, since the imperial crown of the West had been set by Leo III on the head of Charlemagne, a barbarian Frank." He accused the Latin Church of heresy for adding the word "Filioque" ("and from the Son") to the Nicene Creed, and attacked the discipline and the usages of the Latins, particularly their practice of fasting on Saturday, their use of milk and cheese on fast days, and the enforced celibacy of the clergy. His hatred of Rome at last led him to do what none of his predecessors had dared to do: he excommunicated the whole Latin world and pronounced sentence of deposition against Pope Nicholas (867).

The triumph of the arrogant patriarch was short-lived. The drunken and vicious Emperor over whom he had held sway so long was murdered in 867. Basil, his murderer and successor, cast Photius into prison and reinstated Ignatius. A Council—the Eighth Ecumenical—which assembled at Constantinople in 869, condemned Photius and his sacrilegious acts, and restored union under the authority of the Apostolic See. After the death of Ignatius in 877 Photius again ascended the patriarchal throne, and in order to be approved by Pope John VIII professed in express terms to acknowledge the Roman Primacy. He soon broke his word and was excommunicated once more. He ended ingloriously. In 886 the Emperor Leo the Philosopher deprived him of his office and banished him to a monastery in Armenia. After this, we hear no more of him.

The Final Separation.—For the next hundred and fifty years there was almost unbroken communion between Constantinople and Rome, but no real peace. The disreputable state into which the Papacy fell during this period did much to impair its prestige in the East. It only required another Photius to kindle the smoldering ashes of the old dissension into a devastating flame. This new Photius appeared in the person of the Patriarch Michael Cerularius. Cerularius was as proud and ambitious as Photius, but with none of his learning and cleverness. It was he who inspired the infamous letter sent by Bishop Leo of Achrida to the West. In this letter the use of unleavened bread in the Holy Eucharist is declared to be Jewish and invalid, and the Latins are reproached in unmeasured terms for fasting on Saturdays, for eating things strangled and blood, for omitting the Alleluia during Lent, for shaving their beards, and for other divergencies from Eastern customs. Cerularius himself closed the churches of the

Latins in Constantinople and impiously ordered the Blessed Sacrament to be cast out and trodden under foot as invalid. At the request of the Emperor Constantine Monomachus, who earnestly desired peace, Pope St. Leo IX sent three legates to Constantinople, but Cerularius obstinately refused to receive them. Thereupon they laid the document containing his excommunication on the altar of St. Sophia in the presence of the clergy and the people with the words "Let God be the Judge," and immediately left the city. It was the 16th of July, 1054.

All attempts made in later times by Popes, Emperors, and Councils to reunite the East and West were frustrated by the incurable narrow-minded hatred of the Eastern bishops, clergy, and people.

Hints for Study

1. For a more detailed account of the Eastern Schism see Adrian Fortescue, *The Orthodox Eastern Church,* London, Cath. Truth Society, and Louis Duchesne, *The Churches Separated from Rome,* London, Kegan Paul. There is a very good article on *Iconoclasm* by Fortescue in the *Catholic Encyclopedia.*
2. Briefly summarize, in the form of a chronological table, the steps in the progress of the Greek Schism.
3. On the addition of the word *Filioque* to the Creed see the article *Creed* in the *Catholic Dictionary* or the *Catholic Encyclopedia.*
4. Review the history of the Church in the East during the first four centuries and sum up in writing the reasons why we should venerate and love it.
5. What lessons does the history of the Greek Schism teach us?

The Christian Commonwealth of Europe from Hildebrand to Boniface VIII. A.D. 1048 to 1294

CHAPTER I

THE AGE OF HILDEBRAND

During the tenth century Rome and Western Christendom had sunk into an appalling state of corruption. A thorough reform "in head and members" was absolutely necessary. The Church had to be purged of the deadly pest of simony and the equally noxious pest of an ignorant, worldly-minded and incontinent hierarchy; she had to win her independence of the secular power; and if the constantly mounting tide of anarchy and violence which threatened to engulf both Church and State was to be effectively stemmed, she had to place herself at the head of the European nations and guide their destinies. This program of reform, conceived and inaugurated by the great Hildebrand, was carried out in successive stages. After Innocent III, who brought the Papacy to its highest power, the Church maintained her commanding position, though not without much opposition, for nearly a hundred years; the fourteenth century witnessed the decline of the Papal supremacy in temporal affairs and the gradual disruption of the European family of nations.

1. The Beginning of the Reform

"If Rome does not come back to a better way," wrote St. Peter Damian from his monastery at Fonte Avellana, "the world will remain plunged in error. The reform must start from Rome as from the cornerstone of salvation." As the Emperor Henry III put an end to the degradation of the Papacy and was responsible for the elevation of men of high character and spiritual ideals, the much-needed reform of the Church might be said to have been begun by him. It was indeed carried on at first almost entirely by his authority. "He was the pitiless opponent of simony and Nicolaitism," says Kurth; "no one branded these abuses with more bitterness, no one fought them with more vigor. He took care to intrust episcopal sees only to men above reproach; and those whom his influence raised to the Chair of Peter were worthy of it beyond contradiction." But the original sources of the reform movement lay much farther back.

Cluny.—It has been well said that the history of Medieval Europe is the history of its monasteries. They were its educators and civilizers, and from them, in times of decay, went forth the ideas of reform and the men who carried them into effect. The

ABBEY CHURCH OF CLUNY BEFORE IT WAS DESTROYED

monasteries, it is true, had shared in the general corruption; but they were the first to arise from it.

From the beginning of the tenth century an active reform movement began in the monasteries of Upper and Lower Lorraine, in Southern Germany, and Burgundy. Its center was the Burgundian Abbey of Cluny, founded by Duke William of Aquitaine in 910. Cluny was from the beginning exempt from all secular and episcopal control, and directly subject to the Holy See. The first abbot was Count Berno, who introduced such a splendid religious spirit into the new foundation that a number of other monasteries placed themselves under his guidance. Thus was formed the far-famed Congregation of Cluny. Before the middle of the eleventh century three hundred Benedictine monasteries all over Europe looked to Cluny as their mother-house. Other religious houses, without putting themselves under obedience to Cluny, began to imitate its example. Monastic life had its "second spring." The most famous abbot of Cluny was St. Odilo (994-1049), "friend of emperors, educator of popes and countless bishops." All the Spanish monasteries reformed themselves under his influence. His successor St. Hugh, the ally of every reform Pope, built the magnificent abbey at Cluny, which remained the largest building in Christendom till St. Peter's at Rome excelled it.

Allies of Cluny.—At the same time that Cluny began to grow in importance, holy men in other countries took an active part in the work of reform. *St. Romuald,* scion of the ducal house of Ravenna, forsook the bright prospects held out by the world in order to devote himself entirely to the service of God. For many years after his conversion he wandered through Europe preaching penance. In 1012 he settled down in a hermitage at Camaldoli in a picturesque valley of the Apennines about thirty miles east of Florence. His reputation for holiness attracted numerous disciples. He built separate hermitages for them, but all, with the exception of the recluses, had to repair to a common chapel for Mass and the singing of the Divine Office. They wore a white habit, abstained perpetually from meat, and observed two strict Lenten fasts during the year. Romuald's extreme austerity, his lofty religious idealism, and his fiery eloquence exerted a lasting influence for good on all who came in contact with him. Emperors, kings, and nobles, as well as the common people, revered him as a saint and consulted him as an oracle.

The most famous disciple of St. Romuald was *St. John Gualbert.* John's only brother had been murdered in a quarrel with another nobleman. It happened on Good Friday that John, attended by his men-at-arms, met his brother's murderer. As he was about to draw his sword to kill him, the murderer fell upon his knees and, holding up his arms in the form of a cross, besought him by the Passion of Christ to spare his life. Deeply affected by this appeal, John held out his hand to his enemy, and meekly said to him: "I cannot refuse what is asked in the name of Jesus Christ. I give you not only your life, but my friendship forever. Beg of God that he may pardon me my sin." John was from this moment a new man. After spending three years in the monastery of San Miniato in Florence and three more in the strict school of St. Romuald at Camaldoli, he withdrew to a lonely valley, deeply shaded by willows—hence known as the *Vallis Umbrosa,* the shady valley—and here founded a monastery which rivaled in austerity and fervor even that of Camaldoli.

A contemporary of Romuald and John Gualbert was *St. Peter Damian,* who deservedly takes rank amongst the greatest champions of the purity and liberty of the Church of all times. Peter was born at Ravenna in the year 1007, of a poor and numerous family. One day, while tending his brother's swine, he found a piece of money—a real fortune for the poor and hungry boy. He began to deliberate upon the use to which he should put his treasure; but at length he said within himself: "The pleasure it could procure for me would soon pass away; I will give it to a priest that he may offer up a Holy Mass for my father's soul." He did so, and God blessed his pious deed. His eldest brother, who had become archpriest of Ravenna, took charge of his education and sent him first to Faenza, and then to Parma, where the celebrated Ivo was attracting disciples from all parts of Italy. The pupil soon became a teacher himself, and wealth and honors came to him unsought. They might have proved his undoing, so he relinquished them and withdrew to Fonte Avellana, a monastery near Gubbio in Umbria, which had been hallowed for some years by the presence of St. Romuald. About 1043 he was chosen prior of the monastery, which, under his rule, quickly attained celebrity, and became a model for other institutions. His zeal for monastic and clerical reform, which he championed in word and writing, made his name known throughout Europe. He was a determined foe of simony, but his fiercest invectives were directed against immorality in the ranks of the clergy. He entered into communication with the Emperor Henry III, and in 1049 addressed to Pope Leo IX a treatise against the vices of the clergy. Every pope, king, or bishop who labored for the reform of the Church could count on Peter as his staunchest ally. His 158 *Letters* and other writings are a most valuable source of information on the history and manners of the troubled times in which he lived.

Not only in Italy, but in every part of Europe, Cluny had its admirers, disciples, and imitators. St. Dunstan and Lanfranc in England; the learned and saintly bishops Ulrich, Bruno, Wolfgang, Conrad, Gebhard, Bernwart, Godehard, Burchard, and Willigis in Germany; Notker and Wazo in Belgium, and many others of lesser renown, stood for the same cause as the great abbots of Cluny, and helped to prepare the way for the life work of Hildebrand.

2. *Hildebrand, the Counselor of Popes*

Hildebrand, whose "imperial mind" was to direct, for half a century, the series of campaigns for the purification and liberation of the Church, was born of poor parents about the year 1020 at Soana in Tuscany. Both his own name and his father's name suggest Lombard or German descent. When still a boy he was called to Rome by his uncle Lawrence, Abbot of the Cluniac monastery of St. Mary on the Aventine, and educated at the Lateran Palace. His intense love for Rome dates from this period. "The Prince of the Apostles," he wrote long afterwards to a German bishop, "nourished me from my infancy and kept me in the lap of his kindness." One of his instructors was John Gratian, who, when he became Pope Gregory VI, conferred Minor Orders on his former pupil and made him his secretary. When Gregory VI was banished to Cologne, Hildebrand followed him across the Alps. When his patron died in 1047 he passed into France and visited the Abbey of Cluny. There Pope Leo IX found him and took him with him to Rome.

St. Leo IX.—Leo entered Rome as a simple pilgrim and would not don the pontifical insignia until he had been elected in accordance with the rules of canon law. He ordained Hildebrand subdeacon and made him a member of the College of Cardinals and administrator of the property of the Roman Church. From this time on, Hildebrand was one of the most influential men in Rome. Not only in economic affairs but in all others as well, he was the soul of Leo's reforms. On his advice a Roman Synod (1049) made strict laws against simony, and deposed all bishops, cardinals, and abbots who had attained their dignities by bribery. During the next five years Leo traveled over a great part of Europe, holding councils, correcting abuses, deposing unworthy bishops, making peace between warring factions, dedicating churches and monasteries, receiving everywhere the homage of rulers and people.

In 1053 Hildebrand was sent as Papal Legate to France to settle the controversy begun by Berengar, a canon of Tours, who had publicly denied the Real Presence in the Eucharist. Before he returned to Rome Leo was dead (April, 1054). The Romans wanted to elect Hildebrand as his successor. He refused, but agreed to provide a worthy Pope. His choice, and that of the Emperor Henry III, was Bishop Gebhard of Eichstädt.

The Last German Popes.—Gebhard took the name of Victor II. During his brief reign of less than three years (1054-1057) he walked faithfully in the footsteps of his predecessor. In 1056 Henry III died at Goslar in the arms of Victor, whom he had summoned to his bedside in order to receive the Last Sacraments at his hands and to recommend to his protection his wife Agnes and his son and successor, a child of five—the future Henry IV. Victor himself died in the following year. Hildebrand was absent in France at the time, and the Romans elected Cardinal Frederick, Abbot of Monte Cassino and brother of Duke Godfrey of Lorraine, to succeed him. Stephen IX showed his zeal for reform by elevating Peter Damian to the bishopric of Ostia and the Cardinalate, and by enforcing the reform decrees of his predecessors. In the midst of far-reaching plans for the welfare of the Church, after a reign of less than a year, he died at Vallombrosa, attended in his last moments by St. John Gualbert. His dying request was that the Romans should not elect a successor till Hildebrand, who was absent in Germany at the time, should return to the city.

Nicholas II Regulates the Election of the Popes.—The Romans paid no attention to Stephen's last wishes. The familiar factions appeared on the scene. The Tusculan party set up John, Bishop of Velletri, as Pope with the title of Benedict X. Hildebrand, hurrying back from Germany, arranged a canonical election at Siena, and by his advice the Burgundian Gerhard, Bishop of Florence, was chosen and became Nicholas II (1058-1061). The German Court declared in favor of Hildebrand's candidate, and Benedict X was deposed.

The new Pope was as zealous for reform as his predecessors, and even more disposed than they had been to listen to the counsels of Hildebrand, whom he made Archdeacon of the Roman Church. It was at Hildebrand's suggestion that Nicholas published his famous *Constitution on the Election of the Sovereign*

Pontiff, which freed the Papacy not only from its temporal oppressors, the Roman and Tuscan barons, but also from its protectors, the German Emperors. The following are the chief provisions of the Constitution:

1. The election is to take place in Rome; but if for some reason it cannot
be held there, the electors may repair elsewhere.
2. The candidate must be a member of the Roman clergy, if there is a
suitable one; if not, the electors must look elsewhere for one.
3. The Cardinal-bishops, that is, the bishops of the suburban sees, take
the lead in the election by choosing a candidate, after which the other
Cardinals are called in to vote. The rest of the Roman clergy and people
are then given the opportunity to express their consent by acclamation.
4. King Henry of Germany, the future Emperor, and those of his successors who shall have obtained this privilege personally from the Apostolic
See, shall be asked to confirm the election.
The concession made to the emperors soon fell into disuse. The rest of
the Constitution, with some important modifications, is still in force.

This new regulation of the Papal elections called forth a storm
of opposition both in Germany and Italy. In order to check the
malcontents, Pope Nicholas entered into an alliance with Robert
Guiscard and his Normans who had established a strong independent principality in Southern Italy. By the Treaty of Melfi
(1059) Robert received in fief from the Apostolic See Apulia,
Calabria, and Sicily, and promised in return to pay an annual
tribute to the Pope, to guarantee the freedom of the Papal elections, and, if called upon, to defend the Holy See against its
enemies.

After the death of Nicholas, the Cardinals, carrying out the
electoral decree, chose Anselm, Bishop of Lucca, who called himself Alexander II (1061-1073). For three years the new Pope
was opposed by the anti-pope Honorius II, set up by the Roman
barons and supported by the Empire. Then Archbishop Anno of
Cologne, who assumed the administration of the affairs of the
Empire for the youthful Henry IV, declared against the intruder,
and the rightful Pope was acknowledged everywhere. Alexander
continued the work of reform. He made Hildebrand Papal
Chancellor and Peter Damian Legate in Germany. These two
were his advisers and guides throughout his pontificate. One of
his last acts was to excommunicate certain counselors of Henry IV,
who were chiefly concerned in that ruler's simoniacal proceedings.
It was the prelude to the great conflict that was coming.

3. *Hildebrand as Pope Gregory VII*

Hildebrand had been the guiding spirit of the Papal government for twenty-three years. He had evaded election at nearly every vacancy in all that time; but when Alexander II died in 1073 the feeling in his favor was too strong. The people demanded him, and the Cardinals acceded to their demand. Hildebrand took the name of Gregory VII—or perhaps it was given to him by the electors, as was often done at that time.

POPE GREGORY VII

During the twelve years of his pontificate (1073-1085) Gregory carried on a relentless war against simony, clerical marriage, and lay investiture. In that war his opponents were all those who were guilty of these offenses—a powerful coalition of kings, dukes, barons, bishops, abbots, clerics of all ranks, with Henry IV at their head. His allies were Cluny and all the Cluniac monasteries; the better elements amongst the clergy in every land; the generality of the common people, who are always attracted by virtue and holiness; the Normans in Italy, not because they were enthusiastic about reform, but from fear of the Empire; the Saxons and Suabians in Germany, who were in a continual state of rebellion against the tyranny of Henry IV. But his most faithful friend and ally was the Countess Matilda of Tuscany. This Lady, a Lombard by birth, "shared all the Pope's views, worked for his interests, and developed an enthusiastic devotion for him. When her husband died, the revenues, influence, and territory of Tuscany were always at the service of the Holy See." At her own death she made the Popes heirs of all her possessions.

The Lenten Synod of 1074. The War against Simony and Clerical Incontinence.—The year after his election Gregory held a great Synod in Rome which confirmed all the laws of his predecessors against simony and violations of clerical celibacy: No married priest may henceforth say Mass or administer the sacraments; the faithful may not, under any circumstances, assist at the Masses celebrated by such priests or receive the sacraments at their hands; simony is punished by excommunication of all concerned in it. There was much, and in many cases very violent, opposition to these laws in every country of Europe, but Gregory's Legates saw to it that they were carried out, and great numbers of disobedient bishops and priests were deposed without mercy. Not infrequently, as at Milan and Florence, the people took the law into their own hands, despoiled, and drove out the priests who defied the commands of the Pope. Celibacy was sure to triumph ultimately. The war against simony was more difficult. Lay investiture was the root of this evil, and against lay investiture Gregory now directed his attack.

Gregory Proscribes Lay Investiture. Conflict with Henry IV.—It was at the Lenten Synod of 1075 that Gregory made the momentous proclamation against lay investiture which was to plunge him into an abyss of suffering and misery, but which was to give liberty to the Church and to save her future by tearing her away from the deadly embrace of Feudalism. In one peremptory decree he abolished the whole right of investiture: "lay investiture makes all appointments null and void; whoever receives a spiritual office at the hands of a layman, whether he be baron, duke, king or emperor is to be deposed, and a layman who dares to confer a spiritual office, is to be excommunicated." This decree brought on a long and bitter conflict with the secular rulers and the Church dignitaries devoted to them, especially with Henry IV of Germany.

At the court of the young German King ecclesiastical offices were unblushingly bought and sold. Henry was a talented prince, but notoriously immoral, dishonest, and tyrannical. In spite of the Papal prohibition he continued the practice of nominating bishops and abbots and investing them with the crosier and the ring. Pope Gregory was not the man to overlook such conduct. In a letter written in December, 1075, he exhorted Henry to confess his sins and to do penance. If the King remained obstinate, the bearers of the letter were empowered to cite him, under threat of excommunication, to appear on the 22nd of February in Rome before an ecclesiastical tribunal. Henry neither heeded the Pope's exhortation nor obeyed his summons. Instead he gathered his bishops at Worms on Septuagesima Sunday and proceeded to depose the Pope on the ground that he had been unlawfully elected, that he was a disturber of the peace of the Church, that he had arrogated to himself authority over temporal rulers, and that he had threatened to take the royal and imperial authority away from him. The decree of deposition was sent to Rome with an insulting letter addressed to "Hildebrand, not Pope, but false monk." Gregory replied by pronouncing sentence of excommunication against Henry and formally releasing his subjects from their oath of allegiance.

Gregory's action created a tremendous sensation in Europe. In Germany it had the effect of detaching many influential bishops from the imperial cause and encouraging the political enemies of the King to renewed activity. In October the princes of the empire met with the Papal Legates at Tribur near Mainz and decreed that Henry should be judged by the Pope himself in a council to be held at Augsburg on Candlemas day, 1077. Meanwhile he was to go to Speyer and live in retirement, because it was a universally recognized law that no excommunicated person could hold any office in Church or State. Thus the right of the Pope over the Empire, his power of deposing unworthy and disobedient rulers, was officially acknowledged. A momentous revolution had taken place: kings and emperors had wanted the State to rule the Church; Gregory claimed for the Church authority over all things, even the State, and his claim was allowed. The Christian Commonwealth under the overlordship of the Pope was born.

Henry IV at Canossa.—Bonitho, the biographer of Gregory VII, describes Henry IV as "a man of deep counsel and remarkable sagacity." These qualities now stood the King in good stead. He knew that he was lost if the Pope came to judge him publicly. The council at Augsburg must not take place. Gregory must not cross the Alps. In the dead of winter—and the winter of 1077 was a terrible one—Henry fled from Speyer with his wife Bertha and his three-year-old son Conrad, crossed the Alps amid the greatest hardships and perils, and at last arrived at the castle of

Canossa southwest of Reggio, where Gregory, on his way to Germany, was being entertained by his devoted friend and ally, the Countess Matilda of Tuscany. He was determined to be released from the ban of excommunication at any cost. For three days he voluntarily did penance within the precincts of the castle "in the snow, barefoot, in penitential garb, holding a lighted candle." Gregory did not care to end the conflict at this point.

HENRY IV BEFORE POPE GREGORY VII AT CANOSSA

He would have preferred to enter German territory and to settle all the questions at issue in a general assembly. But what could he do? As a priest and bishop he could not refuse absolution to a repentant sinner; had he done so, he would have forfeited all his influence as the spiritual head of Christendom. Accordingly he admitted the apparently sincere penitent to his presence, absolved him from excommunication, and gave him Holy Communion. All that he required of Henry was the solemn promise to submit to the decision of the Pope in the conflict with the princes, and not to hinder him from entering Germany or traveling to any part of the world. "Henry rode away from the Tuscan castle, bound, indeed, by promises for the future, but, in reality, a free man—free to labor and consult for his own interests. At the price of a deep personal humiliation he had gained an undoubted diplomatic victory."

Perfidy of Henry; Death of Gregory.—Henry had hardly been absolved by the Pope whose pity he had abused when he violated all his promises. Even before he left Italy he made common cause with Gregory's enemies in Lombardy. No Diet was held at Augsburg. Instead the princes of the empire met at Forchheim, declared Henry deposed, and elected Rudolph of Suabia King of Germany. In the civil war which followed, Gregory at first remained neutral; but when Henry continued to defy the laws of God and of the Church, he again excommunicated him in 1080, and acknowledged Rudolph as the rightful king. Henry retaliated by setting up Bishop Wibert of Ravenna as anti-pope and marching against Rome. When the city was finally taken in 1084, Gregory took refuge in the Castle of St. Angelo. In this dire extremity his Norman vassal, Robert Guiscard, came to his aid with a powerful army and forced Henry to retire to Northern Italy. Robert released the Pope and conducted him to the Lateran. But when the wild Norman hordes and their wilder Saracen allies desolated the city with fire and sword and committed unspeakable outrages against the inhabitants. Gregory withdrew with a few friends, first to Monte Cassino, and then to the rugged castle of Salerno. Here he died on the 25th of May, 1085. His last words—the epitaph of one of the greatest Popes—were: *Dilexi justitiam et odivi iniquitatem: propterea morior in exilio*—"I have loved justice and hated iniquity, therefore I die in exile." He lies buried in the cathedral of Salerno, not far from the crypt of the Apostle St. Matthew. He was canonized in 1606 by Paul V.

Gregory VII was the "marvel of his century," and in some respects the greatest of all the Popes. He was not only the instrument of Providence for the reform of the Church, but also the savior of European society. By establishing the supremacy of the spiritual authority over the secular power —the *Sacerdotium* over the *Regnum*—he held in check the passions of the great ones of earth, the violent and lawless feudal aristocracy, who, if given free rein, would have thrust Europe back into barbarism. His death did not compromise his work. His ideals and ideas lived after him and triumphed under his successors. The glories of Christianity in the twelfth and thirteenth centuries are the direct results of the policy of Hildebrand. "The victory of the unarmed monk," says the Protestant historian Gregorovius, "challenges the admiration of the world with more right than all the conquests of Alexander, Caesar, or Napoleon. The Popes of the Middle Ages did not wage their wars with lead and iron, but with moral force alone. Compared with a Gregory VII a Napoleon is nothing but a sanguinary barbarian."—*Geschichte der Stadt Rom im Mittelalter*, IV, p. 198.

4. End of the Investiture Struggle

Gregory died while the battle was raging, but he had really won his cause. His successors had still to wrestle with Henry IV and his successor Henry V in Germany, Bungundy, and Italy, and with William Rufus and Henry I in England and Normandy; the final victory, however, was not doubtful. The rulers of France had of their own accord renounced the right of investiture, and the bishops who held royal benefices were permitted to pay feudal homage to the king. Lanfranc and St. Anselm fought the battle to a successful issue in England, and in 1106 Henry I resigned the claim to investiture by ring and crosier and allowed free election to all ecclesiastical offices on condition that the bishops should take the oath of homage for the temporal possessions of their sees.

In the Empire a satisfactory solution was not reached so quickly. In 1111 an agreement was made at Sutri between Pope Paschal II and Henry V: The king was to grant absolute freedom of election and to give up all investiture; the Church, on her part, was to divest herself of all her temporal possessions; the bishops and abbots were, in future, to be spiritual rulers only; the clergy were to take as their only means of support the tithes and voluntary offerings of the faithful. This agreement was never carried out, owing to the general opposition to it. The times were not ripe for such a sweeping reformation, but had it been adopted, the Church would have passed out of the entire feudal system and would have undoubtedly been spared many subsequent afflictions and humiliations.

The long struggle was finally settled by the *Concordat of Worms* (1122). Both parties made important concessions. "Pope Callixtus II grants that the elections of bishops and abbots may take place in the presence of the Emperor, or of his agents, and that the Emperor should have the right to invest them with the scepter, i.e., with their dignity as princes of the Empire. Henry, on his side, agrees to give up investiture with the ring and the crosier, i.e., with spiritual functions, to allow free elections, and to aid in the restoration of church property which had been confiscated during the long struggle now drawing to a close." The Concordat of Worms was confirmed in the following year by the Ninth General Council, which convened in the Lateran Palace.

Gregory VII Deposes Henry IV

This famous decree, which marks a new era in the history of the Papacy, is couched in the form of an address to St. Peter, Prince of the Apostles. In the first part Gregory defends himself against the charge that he had mounted the Papal throne through the employment of unbecoming means. Then he continues:

"Confident of my integrity and authority, I now declare in the name of the omnipotent God, the Father, Son, and Holy Ghost, that Henry, son of the Emperor Henry, is deprived of his kingdom of Germany and Italy. I do this by thy authority and in defense of the honor of thy Church, because he has rebelled against it. He who attempts to destroy the honor of the Church should be deprived of such honor as he may have held. He has refused to obey as a Christian should; he has not returned to God from whom he had wandered; he has had dealings with excommunicated persons; he has done many iniquities; he has despised the warnings which, as thou art witness, I sent to him for his salvation; he has cut himself off from thy Church, and has attempted to rend it asunder; therefore, by thy authority, I place him under the ban. It is in thy name that I bind him with the chain of the anathema, that all people may know that thou art Peter, and upon thy rock the Son of the living God has built His Church, and the gates of hell shall not prevail against it."

—Translated in *Source Book for Mediaeval History* (Thatcher and McNeal), pp. 155-156.

Hints for Study

1. Be sure that you know the meaning of the following terms: *simony, Nicolaitism, celibacy, benefice, fief, fealty, homage, investiture, vassal, ban, excommunication, cardinal, concordat.*
2. The triumph of the Church in the Investiture quarrel has been called a turning point in the history of civilization; why?
3. Read carefully the decree in which Gregory VII deposes Henry IV, and state briefly the grounds on which the Pope bases his deposing power. Is the deposing power claimed by the Popes of the Middle Ages part of Catholic doctrine? Consult the article *Deposing Power* in the *Catholic Dictionary* (Addis and Arnold).
4. The principal documents relating to the Investiture quarrel can be read in English translation in E. F. Henderson, *Select Historical Documents of the Middle Ages,* pp. 365-410.
5. Two good lives of St. Gregory VII are available in English: A. H. Mathew, *The Life and Times of Hildebrand, Pope Gregory VII* (London, Griffiths, 1910), and Miss E. W. Wilmot-Buxton, *The Story of Hildebrand, St. Gregory VII* (London, Burns, Oates, 1920).

CHAPTER II

KNIGHTS AND MONKS IN THE SERVICE OF CHRISTENDOM

1. *The Crusades and the Military Orders*

Chivalry.—In feudal times the people were divided into three classes: the churchmen or clergy, the fighters or nobles, and the peasants or workers. Each class had its own traditions, customs, and ideals. The system of ideas prevalent among the fighting men of the Middle Ages is known as *chivalry,* from the Latin word *caballarius,* a horse-soldier. *Caballarii,* mounted men-at-arms, knights, are already mentioned in the capitularies of Charlemagne, but it was not until the disruption of the Empire of Charlemagne that nobleman and horse-soldier became practically identical. During this period, as we have seen, there was no strong central government in the various countries, and civil and military power was divided among thousands of principalities, counties, and fiefs. The holders of these believed that they had no other means of deciding which should be lord of the other except by going to war. Horses and heavy armor were found to give an advantage to those using them over the light-armed foot-soldier; hence those who could afford it went to battle on horseback and encased in as much armor as they could bear.

The feudal wars of the tenth and eleventh centuries were characterized by ferocity and rapacity, cruelty and injustice. The Church would have been untrue to her mission of christianizing and civilizing the world if she had not endeavored by every means in her power to transform and consecrate that rough struggle for superiority which was everywhere going on. To accomplish her purpose she set to work with consummate tact and prudence. She did not ask the knight to give up war altogether; she gradually imbued him with the salutary truth that constant fighting and violence were not consistent with the teaching of Christ. If he must fight, she told him, let him at least observe the *Pax Dei,* the "peace of God," and spare the lives and property of the defenseless; if he must engage in private warfare, let him at least desist from it on the days and during the seasons hallowed by the commemoration of the great mysteries of our Redemption; let there be a *Treuga Dei,* a "truce of God" on Fridays, Saturdays, and Sundays, and during the sacred seasons of Advent and Lent. If he must fight, if he is not fit for much else, let him fight to protect the weak and the innocent and to prevent injustice; let him defend the Church against her enemies; for the honor and service of the Blessed Mother of God, whose faithful vassal he is to be, let women, who are unable to fight for themselves, find in him an honorable, fearless, and virtuous protector.

A high standard of self-respect—the Church continued in her instructions of the knight—must accompany the consecration to these lofty ends: the honor of the knight must be without stain, his word once given must be irrevocable; he must take no unfair advantage of his enemy; he must support his liege lord according to his oath; he must be immovable in his faith, obedient to the Church, respectful to her ministers, submissive to the Vicar of Christ, the Roman Pontiff.

The Church crowned her work of educating the knight by raising the reception of knighthood to the dignity of a sacred function. Prayers and ceremonies of deep significance were to impress upon the mind and heart of the candidate the duties which he was to perform as a true Christian knight.

On the eve of the ceremony, which usually took place on one of the solemn festivals, the young noble took a bath, a symbol of purity of soul. He spent the night in the church in prayer and meditation, while the arms that he was to put on lay at the foot of the altar. The following morning he received the Body of the Lord. His sword was placed on the altar, and the priest said the following blessing over it: "Hear, O Lord, our prayers and bless this sword with which Thy servant is to be girded, so that he may defend and protect the widows and the orphans, the Church and all the servants of God against the heathen, and become a terror to all who contemplate evil against him."

Christian chivalry was an ideal, and, like all ideals, seldom fully realized in practice. A counterfeit chivalry accompanied genuine chivalry through the ages. Chivalry did not banish cruelty, immorality, treachery, and brutal disregard of the rights of others from European society, but it exercised a powerful influence in softening the harsh character of the times and preventing society from sinking back into barbarism.

The Crusades.—One of the most remarkable results of the alliance between Christian knighthood and the Church was the Crusades. A religious ideal—the eager desire to snatch from the hands of persecuting infidels the places made sacred by our Savior's sojourn and suffering—was their impelling motive, and the Popes who launched them, and blessed and aided them were but doing what Christendom expected them to do.

Since the time of Constantine the Great the Holy Land was the goal of countless pilgrims from the West. When the Holy Places fell into the hands of the Saracens in the seventh century, the pilgrims had very little to suffer from them. There was a change for the worse; however, after the Seljuk Turks captured Jerusalem in 1070. The sacred places were wantonly desecrated by the unbelievers, and the pilgrims were exposed to insult and persecution. It was Gregory VII who first conceived the idea of a Holy War. When Christian Europe was united it was to move towards the East, the Pope at its head, put an end to the Greek Schism and plant the cross again above the Holy City. That was his plan, but the unfortunate Investiture Struggle prevented him from taking any active measures to carry it out. It was reserved for another monk of Cluny, Pope Urban II, to launch the Crusades.

An embassy from the Emperor Alexius Comnenus appeared at the Council of Piacenza (1095) asking for aid from the West against the advancing hordes of Islam. In November of the same year Pope Urban II held a great council of prelates and nobles at Clermont in Auxergne. The occasion was the renewal of the ban against King Philip of France for flagrant violation of the marriage laws, and the further attempt to establish and extend the Peace and Truce of God. When these matters had been discussed, the Pope made an eloquent appeal for a great pilgrimage to recover the Holy Places from the infidels. "He dwelt upon the requests for aid which had come from the East, the sufferings of pilgrims and Christians there, and the need of giving assistance against the advancing Moslems. The evil private wars of Christian against Christian, which the Church was trying to curb, should be replaced by this holy war against the infidel, who could not hope to withstand the brave men from the West. The hardships of living in Europe would be exchanged for the pleasures of a land flowing with milk and honey. To those who took the cross, to their families and property, the Church extended its protection.

Within the jurisdiction of the episcopal courts they could gain
respite from their debts, a suspension of the payment of interest,
and some exemption from feudal and secular control. For sinners
the expedition offered the chance of a Plenary Indulgence. 'You,
oppressors of orphans and widows; you, murderers and violators
of churches; you, robbers of the property of others; you, who,
like vultures are drawn to the scent of the battlefield, hasten, as

CRUSADERS ON THE MARCH

you love your souls, under your Captain Christ to the rescue of
Jerusalem. All you who are guilty of such sins as exclude you
from the kingdom of God, ransom yourselves at this price, for
such is the will of God!' And, when Pope Urban had said these
and very many similar things in his urbane discourse, he so
influenced to one purpose the desires of all who were present that
they cried out, 'God wills it! God wills it!' " (R. A. Newhall,
The Crusades, p. 38.)

Itinerant preachers, foremost among them Peter the Hermit of Amiens, hurried from city to city, urging the crusade upon the people. The Pope himself toured France and aroused such tremendous enthusiasm that hundreds of thousands declared their readiness to take part in the proposed pilgrimage by fastening a cross of red material on their right shoulders.

It is true that self-interest, love of adventure, the possibility of worldly advantage in a new land, the hope of political conquest urged on many of the princes and nobles who took the cross; still the rank and file of the crusading armies were actuated by genuine religious enthusiasm. The words of the preachers stirred up in countless hearts an ardent love of the Savior—a love that was ready to suffer and to die for Him. From the prince to the lowest serf the eyes of all turned to Jerusalem and Bethlehem and Nazareth, and He who had lived and taught and died there—the poor, suffering Jesus—became a living reality once more.

The First Crusade was a popular movement from which the kings of Europe held aloof. Henry IV of Germany and Philip of France were under the ban of excommunication, and the king of England, William Rufus, who refused to recognize either Urban II or the anti-pope Clement II, was not interested in an enterprise inaugurated and directed by the See of Rome. The crusading armies were divided into three groups: the Lotharingians from the Rhinelands, among whom the most prominent leader was Godfrey of Bouillon, Duke of Lower Lorraine; the Provençals of Southern France under Count Raymond of Toulouse; and the Normans led by Boemund, the son of Robert Guiscard.

The Christian armies assembled at Constantinople in 1096; in the spring of 1097 the campaign began with a successful siege of Nicaea; Antioch was taken in 1098, and Jerusalem in 1099. Urban, the man who had set all Europe in motion towards the East, died before the news of the fall of Jerusalem reached Rome.

This is not the place to tell the story of the Crusades; the details will be found in the text-books of General History. A word must, however, be said on the effects of the Crusades. Their main object—the deliverance of the Holy Land and the reunion of the Eastern Schismatics with the Church—was not attained; but the sacrifice of millions of lives was not in vain. The Crusades held back the Turk from Europe for four hundred years and weakened his power considerably. They united Christendom in a lofty enterprise and thus helped to rid the West of some of the worst features of feudalism. By bringing the West into contact with the civilization and learning of the East, they exercised an enormous influence on the intellec-

tual life of Europe. The age of the Crusades was the golden age of
Medieval art, philosophy, theology, and literature.—These good effects were
counterbalanced by evil ones. The Crusades produced religious indifference
and widespread moral corruption. The south of France, which sent forth
so many brave knights to battle for the Holy Sepulcher, was also the
breeding ground of one of the most disastrous and horrible heresies with
which mankind was ever afflicted—the heresy of the Albigenses.—The Papacy,
too, suffered a diminution of its influence from the Crusades. Its prestige
was greatly enhanced at the start; but the Fourth Crusade, which ended
with the capture of Constantinople, showed that even an Innocent III could
not control the movement. In the thirteenth century some Popes permitted
the holy war against the Moslems to lag while crusades were preached and
waged against the Hohenstaufen Emperors in Italy. The Moslem victories
were regarded as judgments of God upon the Christians and the blame was
laid upon the Popes. Even when the danger to Europe from the Turk
was very real in the fifteenth century, the attempts of the Popes to re-
kindle the religious ardor of 1095 ended in complete failure. . . .

The Military Orders.—The recovery of the Holy Places, and
the necessity of defending them, stimulated travel from Europe
to Syria. Pilgrims by thousands visited Palestine each year, and
from time to time expeditions would be organized to bring assistance when the Latin Kingdom of Jerusalem was threatened. The
situation produced by this influx of pilgrims from Europe and
the military weakness of the Latin Kingdom brought into existence the three great Military Orders: the Knights of St. John
of Jerusalem, the Templars, and the Teutonic Knights. They
were religious congregations of soldier-monks, bound by the three
vows of poverty, chastity, and obedience, and devoted to the care
and defense of pilgrims. Their members were divided into
knights, priests, and lay brothers. Composed of nobles who had
renounced their worldly interests in their homeland, these orders
became a permanent force in the East, and, as their chapters
multiplied all over Europe, they formed a most important link
between the East and the West.

The oldest of the Military Orders, the *Knights of St. John,*
also known as Hospitallers, dates from the First Crusade. The
knights wore a black cloak adorned with a white cross. After the
fall of the last Christian stronghold in Palestine in 1291 they retired to Rhodes, which they held for two centuries against the
Turks. After the capture of Rhodes in 1523, the Emperor Charles
V bestowed upon them the island of Malta, from which Napoleon
expelled them in 1798.

The *Knights of the Temple,* or Templars, were founded in 1118 at Jerusalem by nine French knights. They were called Templars because their first quarters were in the Palace of King Baldwin of Jerusalem, which was built on the site of the ancient Temple of Solomon. They received the approval of the Pope at the Council of Troyes (1128). St. Bernard, who was present at the council, wrote a rule for them based on the Cistercian Rule, and did much to spread their order by his little treatise: *In Praise of the New Knighthood.* "In this Order," the Saint writes, "knighthood has blossomed forth into new life: warriors whose sole aim in life it once was to rob, to plunder, and to kill, have now bound themselves by solemn vow to defend the poor and the Church." During the Crusades the Templars rendered valuable service to the Christian cause, and on the fall of Acre they withdrew to the estates which they held in the different countries of Europe. Their wealth excited the cupidity of Philip the Fair of France. He trumped up charges of heresy against them, persuaded Pope Clement V to suppress them, burned the last Grand Master at the stake (1312), and appropriated a large share of their property.

In 1190 a number of crusaders from Bremen and Lübeck joined with the members of the German Hospital in Jerusalem to form the Order of the *Teutonic Knights,* or the Brothers of the Hospital of St. Mary of Jerusalem, as they were officially called. They maintained their headquarters at Acre until the city's fall, but as early as 1226 they had already turned their attention away from the Holy Land. Invited by the King of Hungary and the Bishop of Prussia to aid against the heathen Slavs and Tartars, they concentrated all their efforts on the subjugation and conversion of Prussia and the neighboring Baltic lands. At the time of the Reformation their Grand Master passed over to the Lutheran camp and converted the territories of the Knights in East Prussia into an hereditary principality.

The successes of the Almohade Moslems against the Christians of Spain in the last quarter of the twelfth century led to the organization of the Military Orders of Santiago, Calatrava and Alcantara. The most decisive victory gained by the Christian chivalry of the West during the age of the Crusades was that of Las Navas de Tolosa in 1212. On this memorable field the Moorish rule in Spain received a blow from which it never recovered.

Orders for the Ransom of Captives.—The Crusades gave birth to two Religious Orders which, in a quiet way, without the clash of swords and the shock of battle, did an incalculable amount of good: the Trinitarians, founded at Rome in 1198 by St. John of Matha and the aged hermit St. Felix of Valois for the ransom of captives taken by the Saracens, and the Order of Our Lady of Mercy, established at Barcelona in 1223 by St. Peter Nolasco and St. Raymond of Pennafort for a similar object. It was a fundamental rule of the Trinitarian Order that at least one third of its revenues and all the alms collected should be set apart for the ransoming of captives. The members of the Order of Mercy took a fourth vow, viz., to take the place of the captives if these could not be freed in any other way. Both Orders had at one time more than three hundred houses in various countries of Europe. It has been estimated that from their foundation till the end of the eighteenth century through their combined efforts more than a million slaves were ransomed.

2. *St. Bruno of Cologne and the Carthusians*

Amongst the many monastic foundations of the Middle Ages the Carthusians occupy a unique place. All the others either answered to a special need of the times or were attempts to introduce much-needed reforms into already existing institutions. The Carthusians, on the other hand, undertook to revive in western Europe the austere life led by the early Egyptian monks under the guidance of St. Antony.

St. Bruno, the founder of the Carthusians, was born at Cologne about 1030. He was educated in the Cathedral School of his native city and at Rheims and Tours. After his ordination in 1057 he was recalled to Rheims, where he was made a cathedral canon, chancellor, *scholasticus,* or head of the cathedral school, and supervisor of all the schools of the diocese. Among his pupils were many of the leading men of the age; one of them, Odo de Lagary, afterwards ascended the Papal Throne as Urban II. Having vigorously protested against the misdoings of the unworthy Archbishop Manasses, he was deprived of all his offices, and had to flee for safety (1076). When Manasses was deposed in 1080, Bruno was presented by the Papal Legate and the clergy of Rheims for the see; but King Philip of France succeeded in having him set aside. Bruno was now at liberty to carry out a resolution he had long since formed.

With six companions he presented himself to St. Hugh, Bishop of Grenoble, and explained to him his desire to lead an ascetical life in some solitary place. The Bishop led them to the desert of the Chartreuse, "an upland valley in the Alps to the north of Grenoble, more than 4,000 feet above the sea, and only to be reached by threading a gloomy and difficult ravine. High crags surround the valley on all sides; the soil is poor, the cold extreme—snow lies there most of the year—and the air is charged with fog." Here Bruno laid the foundation of his order (1084). The first "Charterhouse" consisted of three poor huts and a little oratory. In 1090 Bruno was summoned to Rome by Urban II to assist in the government of the Church. He never returned to the Chartreuse; but after founding monasteries in Southern Italy, he died at Torre in 1101. Of his writings only his *Commentaries*

St. Bruno

on the Psalms and the *Epistles of St. Paul,* a *Sermon on Contempt of the World,* and a number of *Letters* have been preserved.

Peter the Venerable, the celebrated Abbot of Cluny, writing about forty years after St. Bruno's death, describes in a few vivid sentences the mode of life of the early Carthusians:

"Their dress is meaner and poorer than that of other monks; so short and scanty, and so rough, that the very sight affrights one. They wear coarse hair-shirts next their skin; fast almost perpetually; eat only bran bread; never touch meat, either sick or well; never buy fish, but eat it if given them as an alms; eat eggs and cheese on Sundays and Thursdays; on Tuesdays their fare is pulse or herbs boiled; on Mondays, Wednesdays and Fridays they take nothing but bread and water; and they have only one meal a day, except within the octaves of Christmas, Easter, Whitsuntide,

Epiphany, and some other festivals. Their constant occupation is praying, reading, and manual labor, which consists chiefly in transcribing books. They say the lesser hours of the Divine Office in their cells at the time when the bell rings, but meet together at Vespers and Matins with wonderful recollection." (See Addis and Arnold, *Catholic Dictionary,* Art. *Carthusians.*)

To this austere life the Carthusians have faithfully adhered even to the present day, except that the regulations in regard to food are not quite so stringent. It was not to be expected that

IMPORTANT MONASTERIES OF WESTERN EUROPE

an Order of such severity would expand rapidly; still, there were fifty charterhouses in the thirteenth century, and one hundred and seventy at the time of the French Revolution. It is the only ancient Order in the Church which has never been reformed and never needed reform. It is also the only Order from which no one can pass to any other Order, although any other religious can exchange his Order for that of the Carthusians.

Among the many saintly and learned sons of St. Bruno the best known are St. Hugh, Bishop of Lincoln; Denis the Carthusian, whose writings are still much consulted; Walter Hilton, whose mystical work "The Ladder of Perfection" deserves the popularity which it still enjoys; Laurentius Surius, whose splendid "Lives of the Saints" places him in the forefront of the precursors of the Bollandists, and John Lansperger, one of the ablest and most fruitful ascetical writers of the early sixteenth century.—The heroism with which the English Carthusians defied Henry VIII and met death on the scaffold, or from jail fever, or starvation, forms one of the most glorious pages of the English Church.

3. The Monks of Citeaux

Cluny and the Cluniac monasteries reached the zenith of their renown under St. Hugh the Great, the friend of Gregory VII. Then they began to decline. First one concession, then another, was made to the spirit of the world, and before long the need of reform became evident to the more earnest among the monks. Their cry was: "Back to the primitive rule of St. Benedict!" The founding of the Cistercians was the answer to this demand.

On the feast of St. Benedict, 1098, the holy abbot Robert left the Cluniac monastery of Molesmes and with twenty chosen companions founded a new monastery in the solitude of Citeaux, near Dijon in Burgundy. The new monastery became the cradle of a new Religious Order, the Cistercians (from *Cistercium*, the Latin form of Citeaux). At the command of the Pope, Robert returned to Molesmes in 1099. Alberic, his successor at Citeaux, drew up the first code of Cistercian statutes; he changed the habit from black to white and dedicated the Order to the Blessed Virgin. Since his time the Blessed Mother of God is the principal patroness of every Cistercian house and church. The third abbot, the Englishman St. Stephen Harding, gave the Cistercian Rule its definitive form. The monks lived in extreme poverty; sickness carried off many of them; no new subjects presented themselves, and for a time it seemed as if the order, too severe for human weakness, must die out. At this critical moment the young nobleman Bernard of Fontaines, with thirty of his kinsmen and friends, presented himself at the monastery gate and applied for admission (1112). It was the austerity which had repelled others that had drawn him to Citeaux.

4. St. Bernard of Clairvaux, the Arbiter of Christendom

Bernard was born in 1091 of a noble Burgundian family in the castle of Fontaines near Dijon. In spite of his fiery temperament he loved study, prayer, and solitude from his earliest years. When his pious mother died, the only bond that attached him to the world was broken. His father, his sister, and his five brothers tried to dissuade him from his purpose to renounce the world; but he described to them the beauty of the religious life in such glowing colors that four of his brothers, his uncle, and many of his friends resolved to follow him to Citeaux.

The Perfect Monk.—At Citeaux Bernard practiced almost superhuman austerity. To keep ever alive in his heart the first fervor of his vocation he often repeated within himself: *Bernarde, ad quid venisti?*—"Bernard, why hast thou come hither?" Though really unfitted by his delicate constitution for hard work, he shared with the rest, as the Rule commanded, the arduous labors of the field. In later years he often said: "Beeches and oaks were my teachers."

The example of the young and gifted nobleman soon bore fruit. The three years which followed his arrival at Citeaux brought so great an increase of candidates that the foundation of a new monastery became a necessity. A wild, untilled valley, situated in a mountain gorge and known as the Valley of Wormwood, was chosen for the purpose. Bernard was appointed first abbot. Under the busy hands of the monks the savage waste was soon transformed into a smiling garden, which deserved the name it has borne for eight hundred years: Clairvaux, *clara vallis*, the "valley of light." Thanks to Bernard's fame and influence, Clairvaux soon became the most important of the Cistercian houses. It counted its members by the hundreds, and in less than forty years, seventy other monasteries in all parts of Europe had branched off from it. Since the days of the early Church there has been no greater miracle-worker than St. Bernard. From far and near the sick were brought to Clairvaux to be healed by his touch and his prayers. It was the name and fame of St. Bernard that gave the Cistercians subsequently so great a power in Christendom; their abbeys spread everywhere, and their agricultural success brought them immense wealth.

The Counselor of Popes and Princes.—Before long the holy abbot was drawn against his will into the affairs of the great world. He became the most influential supporter of Pope Innocent II (1130-1143) in his long struggle against the anti-popes Anacletus II and Victor IV. While Rome itself was held by

Anacletus, who was supported by Roger of Sicily, Germany France, and Spain were won over to Innocent through Bernard's efforts. Henry I of England was still wavering between the two obediences, when Bernard met him at Rouen. "Prince," asked the Saint, "what do you fear in submitting to Innocent?" "I fear," replied the king, "that I may commit a sin." "If that be your only obstacle," Bernard replied, "set your mind at rest. Think of the means by which you may satisfy the justice of God for your other sins; this one I take upon myself." Henry was satisfied, and acknowledged the authority of Innocent.

As a peacemaker St. Bernard stands unrivaled in history. He made peace between rival bishops, between bishops and their clergy, between warring cities, between the Emperor Lothar and his rebellious vassals. Pisa and Genoa had long been at variance; the man of God appears; the soldiers break their weapons and throw the fragments at his feet. When the anti-pope Anacletus died in 1138, his adherents elected Victor IV to succeed him. Bernard met the usurper in a secret conference at night, and persuaded him to lay aside the pontifical robes and to sue for pardon from the rightful Pope, thus ending the long and disastrous schism. "I return home," he wrote to the prior of Clairvaux, "laden with the fruits of peace."

The Champion of Orthodoxy.—Among the philosophers and theologians of the twelfth century Peter Abelard (1079-1142) was by far the most popular. Not so much by the solidity and extent of his learning, but rather through his oratorical powers, his readiness and boldness as a controversialist, and his adventurous career—every reader knows the story of his unfortunate infatuation for Heloïse—he attracted thousands of students to his lectures on the Hill of St. Genevieve in Paris. Serious-minded scholars, who were not blinded by his brilliant rhetoric, soon discovered in his lectures and writings, especially in his work *On the Divine Unity and Trinity*, doctrines opposed to the teaching of the Church. St. Bernard examined some of his writings and found no less than thirteen censurable propositions. Among other things Abelard held that "everything should be challenged, and all truths thrown into dispute." To defend this position he was driven to maintain that "a thing could be true in theology and false in philosophy, could be proved untrue, and yet have to be believed." A private conference between Bernard and Abelard proved fruitless, Abelard demanding the privilege of defending his teachings before a council. But when the council met at Sens in 1141, Abelard feared to face the abbot and appealed to Rome. Condemned by Pope Innocent, he retracted his errors and ended his stormy life in the practice of works of charity and penance.

The Preacher of the Second Crusade.—In 1144 the Saracens captured Edessa in Syria, and threatened Antioch and Jerusalem. Pope Eugene III (1145-1153), a former monk of

ST. BERNARD IN THE CATHEDRAL OF SPEYER

Clairvaux, commanded Bernard to preach a second crusade. The abbot threw himself into his task with all the energy and fervor of his nature. The whole of France rose up as one man at his call.

On the feast of Easter, 1146, he preached with such impassioned eloquence before a vast assembly of prelates, knights, and commons at Vezelay, that everyone present shouted, "The Cross! the Cross!" The crosses prepared for the occasion were soon exhausted, and the preacher tore his own cloak in pieces to supply the demand.

Then the Saint came into the Rhine country. When he entered the Cathedral of Speyer on Christmas Day, the throng was so great that the Emperor Conrad III took the abbot on his shoulders and carried him to the sanctuary. During the Mass, at which the Emperor assisted, Bernard arose and addressed these words to him: "What are you going to do for Christ, who gave you the royal crown, health, wealth, and wisdom?" The Emperor seized the Cross and exclaimed: "Now I see what gifts the Lord has bestowed upon me, and I shall never again be found ungrateful." With tears of deep emotion he promised to take part in the crusade, and all the prelates and princes present followed his example.

From Speyer Bernard sailed down the Rhine to Cologne. Miracles everywhere accompanied his preaching. His companions carefully noted down the cures wrought during this journey: sight was restored to 172 blind persons, and nearly 200 cripples were healed. In the churches of Cologne the crowds that welcomed him were so great that the sick had to be smuggled into his presence through the windows.

Whilst Bernard was summoning the chivalry of Germany to the defense of the Holy Land, another Cistercian monk, Radulf by name, advocated the destruction of the Jews as the worst enemies of the Gospel. As soon as Bernard heard of this, he wrote a severe letter against the misguided preacher to the Archbishop of Mainz. "The Jews," he said, "are the living figures and letters, which remind us of the mysteries of our religion. Besides, they dwell peacefully in our midst. In warring against the unbelievers, we repel force by force, but it ill befits a Christian warrior to strike an unarmed foe."

The Second Crusade ended disastrously. This was a hard blow to St. Bernard. People held him responsible for the catastrophe. He himself found it difficult to understand this "manifestation of the hidden counsel of God." His only consolation and his only defense was, as he wrote to Pope Eugene, that, in preaching the crusade, he had not acted on his own initiative, but in obedience to the command of the Sovereign Pontiff, and therefore of God Himself.

St. Bernard and the Irish Church.—The fame of Clairvaux and its abbot spread as far west as Ireland. The Irish Church was much in need of reform at this time. Two great Irish churchmen took this work energetically in hand: *St. Celsus* and *St. Malachy,* both archbishops of the ancient See of Armagh.

In the interest of the reform, Malachy undertook a journey to Rome during the pontificate of Innocent II. On his way he stayed at the monastery of Clairvaux, and was so charmed by the exemplary lives of the monks that he wished himself to become a Cistercian. The Pope, however, would not give his consent to such a step, and Malachy had to content himself with leaving some of his companions to be trained at Clairvaux. On their return to Ireland these monks established the first Cistercian house at Mellifont (1142). On his second journey to Rome in 1148 Malachy again visited Clairvaux. Here he took sick and, surrounded by St. Bernard and his monks, breathed his last (Nov. 2, 1148). St. Bernard preached the funeral sermon over his friend's remains and, later, aided by some of the Irish Cistercians, wrote a beautiful sketch of his life. St. Malachy was canonized in 1190. The so-called *Prophecies of St. Malachy*, consisting of 111 short characterizations of the Popes from Celestine II (1143) to the last Pope, were not written by St. Malachy; they are a fabrication of the last decade of the sixteenth century.

The Last of the Fathers.—Broken by his austerities and by ceaseless work, Bernard died at Clairvaux on the 20th of August, 1153. Twenty-one years later he was canonized by Pope Alexander III; in 1830 Pius VII bestowed upon him the title of *Doctor of the Church*; but for centuries he had been known as *Doctor Mellifluus,* and as the "Last of the Fathers of the Church."

If we ask what was the secret of Bernard's extraordinary sanctity and of his equally extraordinary power over his fellowmen, the answer is, that his soul was at all times firmly anchored in God. The crucified Savior was the center of his every thought and act; his "light, his food, and his medicine." And out of this all-pervading love for Christ was born a tender love for the Mother of Christ. The sermons of St. Bernard on the prerogatives of the Blessed Virgin have never been surpassed. . . . The works of St. Bernard, which are a true mirror of his life, above all his *Sermons,* his numerous *Letters* to all classes of persons, and his last book *on Meditation,* written at the request of Pope Eugene III, appeal to the present-day reader just as much as they appealed to the men and women of the twelfth century.

5. *St. Hildegard of Bingen*

Among the letters of St. Bernard there is one addressed to Hildegard, abbess of Rupertsberg, near Bingen on the Rhine.

Perhaps no figure in early medieval history, says a modern writer, combined so many kinds of greatness as St. Hildegard. She was the counterpart of the great abbot of Clairvaux among the women of the twelfth century.

Born in 1098 of noble parents at the castle of Böckelheim near Bingen, Hildegard was educated at the Benedictine cloister of Disibodenberg by the pious Jutta, sister of the Count of Sponheim. Her training in Latin was very imperfect, but she made extraordinary progress in sanctity. In 1136 she succeeded Jutta as abbess of Disibodenberg. Twelve years later she migrated with eighteen of her nuns to a new convent on the Rupertsberg at the junction of the Nahe and the Rhine, over which she presided till her death in 1179.

Through her gift of prophecy, her mystical writings, her voluminous correspondence, and her extensive journeys, Hildegard wielded an influence upon her contemporaries second only to that of St. Bernard himself. Rich and poor, nobles and peasants knocked at the cloister gates seeking counsel and aid, consolation and instruction. Messengers came to her from popes and emperors, bishops and abbots, and her answers were jealously guarded as precious treasures.

From earliest childhood Hildegard was accustomed to see visions and to receive revelations, but she kept them secret for many years. Not until a voice imperiously cried out to her "Write!" did she begin to divulge them. They are contained in the remarkable work entitled *Scivias* (i.e., *Sci Vias Domini*, "Know the Ways of the Lord").

Hildegard was also a genuine student of nature, possessing a knowledge of facts which was, for her time, most unusual. Her two books *Physica* (Nature Studies) and *Causae et Curae* (Causes and Cures of Diseases) have gained for her the reputation of having been the first German botanist, zoologist, and physician. Her *Physica* contains the names of no less than a thousand animals, plants, and minerals, each of which is described with the aid of personal observation and popular tradition.

Finally, the holy abbess was a poet and musician. She wrote a spiritual melodrama, "The Dance of the Virtues," and composed the music herself, although, as she assures us, she had never learned the art of musical composition. Of her other poetical compositions, seventy hymns, sequences, antiphons, and responsories have been preserved. As a literary curiosity it may be

mentioned that Hildegard invented a secret language—*lingua
ignota*, she called it—of 900 words.

Before publishing her visions and revelations Hildegard wrote
to St. Bernard, whom she calls "the eagle that gazes into the
sun," for advice. In reply the abbot expressed his joy at the
extraordinary gifts and graces given to her by God, encouraged
her to persevere, and recommended himself to her prayers. At
the Synod of Trier (1148), at which St. Bernard was present
and Pope Eugene presided, one of the questions discussed was
the life and writings of the "prophetess" of Bingen. The report
of the commission sent to Bingen by order of the Pope was so
favorable that St. Bernard begged the assembly to approve the
writings of Hildegard; this the Holy Father did in a personal
letter to her.

6. *Reforming the Secular Clergy. St. Norbert of Xanten and the Premonstratensians*

Another contemporary of St. Bernard, who rivaled the abbot of
Clairvaux in fame and influence, was St. Norbert, founder of the
celebrated Order of Regular Canons known as the Premonstratensians.

Canons and Regular Canons.—The clergy of every large church in the
Middle Ages were called *Canons,* because their names were entered on the
List (*canon* is Greek for list) of ecclesiastics serving the Church. In order
to revive a stricter discipline among the clergy, St. Chrodegang of Metz
(8th cent.) formed them into a community, bound by a *rule* (*canon* is also
Greek for rule). A council held at Aachen in 816 made this rule obligatory
on all cathedral priests in the Frankish empire. But grave abuses crept in
during the ninth and tenth centuries, and Popes Nicholas II and Alexander II, aided by Hildebrand and Peter Damian, tried to enforce the rule
of St. Chrodegang by obliging all canons to live in community and to
renounce private property. Those who followed this injunction were
known as "regular canons" (*regula* is Latin for rule) ; those who did not
were called "secular canons," or "secular priests" (from the Latin *saeculum,*
world). The rule which the regular canons followed was also known as
the Rule of St. Augustine, because it was made up chiefly from two letters
of St. Augustine. These regular canons formed a new class of monks who,
in order to distinguish them from the Benedictines, were called Augustinian
monks or canons. They were found not only at the cathedral churches, but
also as independent societies, such as the Canons of the famous Abbey of
St. Victor, outside Paris, and the Canons of the Hospice on the Great

St. Bernard in the Alps, who had the care of the souls and bodies of men high up amidst the eternal snows.—It was this Augustinian monasticism which St. Norbert undertook to reform at the beginning of the twelfth century. His Order was to the Augustinians what the Cistercians were to the Benedictines.

St. Norbert was born at Xanten on the Lower Rhine in 1082. His early years were spent at the court of Henry V, in the unrestrained enjoyment of worldly pleasures and vanities. Even when he was made a canon of St. Victor's Church at Xanten, his manner of life underwent but little change. One day while riding through a narrow valley near Cleves, he was overtaken by a violent storm. A thunderbolt, falling close before him, overthrew both horse and rider. For a whole hour Norbert lay stretched on the ground without sense or motion. He rose up a new man. After a retreat in the monastery of Siegburg, he was ordained priest by the Archbishop of Cologne, and, with the approbation of the Pope, led the life of an itinerant preacher after the example of the apostles (1115). His sharp, eloquent style of preaching, full of energy and fire, carried away the multitudes who flocked to hear him on his mission tours through Germany and France. Before long, his reputation was as wide as the bounds of Europe. It was commonly said that "Charity spoke to men under the form of Bernard; Faith, under the form of Norbert."

His unsuccessful attempts to reform the canons of Xanten and Laon inspired Norbert with the resolution to found a new Religious Order. For this purpose the Bishop of Laon, who wished to keep the holy preacher within his diocese, made over to him a lonely valley in the forest of Coucy. Several other sites had been offered to him in vain; but as soon as he saw this valley he said: "Here is the place which the Lord has chosen"; and he called it *Praemonstratum*, "foreshown." He was soon joined by thirteen companions, all canons like himself, to whom he gave the Rule of St. Augustine, with certain constitutions framed by himself (1120). His monks were to live in the strictest poverty, abstain entirely from meat, and fast practically all the year round; they were to combine the active with the contemplative life, fulfill the duties of monks as well as of parish priests, to pray and meditate, to study, preach, and hear confessions; the country districts were to be the special field of their ministry.

Some of the most illustrious men of the day begged the favor of living under Norbert's direction. The youthful Count of Champagne, Theobald IV, offered to give up to him all his estates—the counties of Blois, Chartres, Meaux and Troyes—and enter the monastery as a simple Brother. Norbert refused. "You shall bear the yoke of the Lord in the married state," he said to Theobald, "and your offspring will possess your great estates and administer them with the blessing of God for the welfare of the people."

The new institute spread with astonishing rapidity especially after it had obtained the approbation of Pope Honorius II (1126). Less than thirty years after its foundation, the Order counted one hundred abbeys; a century later there were one thousand, and five hundred houses of nuns. The services of the Premonstratensians for the christianization and civilization of the Slavic tribes east of the Elbe cannot be overestimated.—In 1126 Norbert was raised to the archiepiscopal see of Magdeburg. Here he died in 1134. "I have had the happiness to see his face," wrote St. Bernard, "and to drink in abundance from his lips, which are the channels of heaven."

Among the many illustrious sons of St. Norbert two deserve very special mention: *Bl. Hermann Joseph* (d. 1240), who was one of the first promoters of devotion to the Sacred Heart and the author of the first hymn to the Sacred Heart; and *Leonard Goffine* (d. 1719), whose popular devotional and catechetical work, *Explanation of the Epistles and Gospels for the Sundays, Holydays, and Festivals* was translated into every European language and is still widely read. Both belonged to the Abbey of Steinfeld in the Eifel.

The Solitude of Clairvaux

The biography of St. Bernard was written by three of his contemporaries: William, abbot of St. Thierry of Rheims; Arnold, abbot of Bonneval, near Chartres; and Geoffrey, a monk of Clairvaux and former secretary of the Saint. The following description of Clairvaux is from the pen of William of St. Thierry, who wrote it about 1140:

"At the first glance as you entered Clairvaux by descending the hill you could see that it was a temple of God; and the still, silent valley bespoke, in the modest simplicity of its buildings, the unfeigned humility of Christ's poor. Moreover, in this valley full of men, where no one was permitted to be idle, where one and all were occupied with their allotted tasks, a silence deep as that of night prevailed. The sounds of labor, or the chants of the brethren in the choral service, were the only exceptions. The orderliness of this silence, and the report that went forth concerning it, struck such a reverence even into secular persons that they dreaded breaking it— I will not say by idle or wicked conversation, but even by proper remarks.

The solitude, also, of the place—between dense forests in a narrow gorge of neighboring hills—in a certain sense recalled the cave of our father St. Benedict, so that while they strove to imitate his life, they also had some similarity to him in their habitation and loneliness. . . .

As regards their manual labor, so patiently and placidly, with such quiet countenances, in such sweet and holy order, do they perform all things, that although they exercise themselves at many works, they never seem moved or burdened in anything, whatever the labor may be. Many of them, I hear, are bishops and earls, and many illustrious through their birth or knowledge; but now, by God's grace, all distinction of persons being dead among them, the greater anyone thought himself in the world, the more in this flock does he regard himself as less than the least."

—*Life of St. Bernard*, Bk. I, Ch. 7 (tr. in Cutts,
Scenes and Characters of the Middle Ages).

Hints for Study

1. For more detailed information on Chivalry and the Crusades see F. W. Cornish, *Chivalry* (Macmillan), and Archer and Kingsford, *The Crusades* (Putnam), or Harold Lamb, *The Crusades* (Doubleday, Doran & Co.).
2. Read G. H. Miles, *The Truce of God* (My Book Case Series) and write a brief report on it.
3. Read the articles in the *Catholic Encyclopedia* on St. Bruno the Carthusian, St. Bernard, St. Norbert, St. Hildegard and the other saints mentioned in this chapter. For St. Hildegard see Francesca M. Steele, *The Life and Visions of St. Hildegard*.
4. Of all the orations delivered by famous men at various times which one, do you think, had the most wonderful results?
5. A modern historian says that one of the beneficial results of the Crusades was "to give Europe the undying memory of a spiritual romance." Comment on these words.

CHAPTER III

THE HUNDRED YEARS' WAR BETWEEN THE POPES AND THE HOHENSTAUFEN

At the Council of Clermont the Pope had placed himself at the head of Western Christendom; his legate marched at the head of the crusaders who wrested Jerusalem from the Turks; the long and bitter Investiture Struggle had ended in a victory for the Papacy; with the approval and the blessing of the Popes, knights and monks had extended the boundaries of Christian civilization in North, South, and East; the Papacy alone held all Christendom together during the turbulent feudal age; "it alone was the visible pledge of Christian unity; it was the only symbol of a common Europe and no mere symbol, but an undying fact: the only power each sovereign State accepted was the jurisdiction of the Pope." Thus, by the middle of the twelfth century, the Papacy had attained a supremacy even in temporal matters which was generally acknowledged throughout the western world. From all sides princes and peoples appealed to the Pope to settle disputes, to regulate successions, to act as mediator between warring factions. Powerful rulers did not think it a disgrace to hold their lands in feudal dependence upon the successor of St. Peter.

What was the attitude of the Empire, the highest temporal authority in Europe, in the face of this extraordinary increase of Papal influence and power? Under the Emperors Lothar (1120-1137) and the first Hohenstaufen, Conrad III (1138-1152), there was peace, if not harmony, between the heads of Christendom. But it was the calm before the storm. With the accession of Frederick Barbarossa (1152-1190) a desperate struggle began between the Papacy and the Empire, which lasted, with occasional intervals of peace, for over a hundred years and ended with the utter defeat and extermination of the great house of Hohenstaufen. Religion had no direct interest in the contest; "the Ghibelline, the supporter of the Emperor, was no heretic, nor was the Guelf, the adherent of the Pope, a saint."

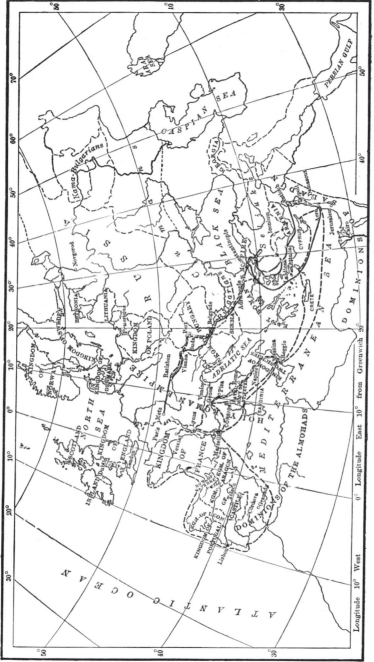

EUROPE AT THE TIME OF THE THIRD CRUSADE

"The Investiture Struggle," says a modern historian, "had been between Pope and Emperor over bishops and abbots; the conflict with the Hohenstaufen was between Pope and Emperor over each other's supremacy. All the elements of a quarrel were present. The Popes had crowned the Emperors, and the coronation of the Emperors had seemed needed before the king, elected by the dukes and prelates of Germany, could assume his imperial titles. On the other hand, the Emperors had nominated some of the Popes, and nearly all the Popes, up to the time of Urban II, even Gregory VII, had waited for the Imperial approbation before being consecrated Bishops of Rome and thereby holders of the apostolic powers." The Emperors had been gradually forced to give up both their right of nomination and of approbation; but the Popes had continued to exercise their right of bestowing or refusing the imperial crown and title. The Hohenstaufen Emperors strove to regain the powers exercised by Charlemagne, Otto and Henry III; they wanted to be Emperors, not merely in name, but in fact. The Popes fought to retain what they had gained—the recognition of the supremacy of the *sacerdotium* over the *regnum*, of the spiritual over the temporal power. The conflict was all the keener because the ablest and most energetic of the Emperors—Barbarossa, Henry VI, and Frederick II— were opposed by Popes of no less energy and ability—an Alexander III, an Innocent III, and a Gregory IX.

1. *Prelude to the Great Struggle. Barbarossa and Hadrian IV*

Frederick Barbarossa had been king of Germany for two years, when Hadrian IV (Nicholas Breakspear), the only Englishman to sit on St. Peter's throne, became Pope. The first clash between Pope and Emperor occurred on Frederick's first journey to Rome in 1155. Frederick refused to hold the Pope's stirrup, as the Emperor Lothar had done, till Hadrian's threat that he would withold the imperial crown from him, forced him to yield.

Two years later, at the Diet of Besançon, the Papal Legate, Cardinal Roland, presented to Barbarossa a letter from Hadrian, which alluded to the *beneficia* conferred upon the Emperor by the Pope. This word *beneficia*, which in its usual legal sense meant a "fief," and thus implied that the Pope claimed feudal authority over the Emperor, provoked angry shouts from the assembled nobles; and when Roland answered, "From whom, then, if not from our Lord the Pope, does your king hold the Empire?" he barely escaped with his life. Later Hadrian declared that by *beneficium* he did not mean a "benefice" of "fief," but merely a *bonum factum*, a benefit. The breach was thus closed for the moment; but it was opened anew, and wider than before, when Barbarossa, on the occasion of his second visit to Italy (1158), formulated his claim to be the source of all feudal rights, of all lay authority in Italy, the supreme governor of all cities, including Rome.

The Pope demanded that Rome should be left entirely to his government. Frederick, in reply, appealed to the Roman civil law, and closed with the words: "Since by the ordination of God I both am called and am Emperor of the Romans, in nothing but name shall I appear to be ruler if the control of the Roman city be wrested from my hands." Hadrian's answer shows how irreconcilable were the views of Pope and Emperor: "What were the Franks till Pope Zacharias welcomed Pippin? What is the Teutonic king now till consecrated at Rome by holy hands? The Chair of Peter has given and can withdraw its gifts." (Bryce, *Holy Roman Empire*, p. 170.)

Hadrian was about to excommunicate the Emperor and to organize armed resistance against his encroachments, when he died at Anagni, September 1, 1159.

2. Barbarossa and Alexander III.   The Seventeen Years' Schism

The disputed Papal election that followed Hadrian's death produced a second and more momentous conflict. Cardinal Roland, the storm-center at Besançon, was the choice of the majority of the Cardinals; he took the name of Alexander III. The minority, who favored the Emperor, chose Cardinal Octavian. Barbarossa now claimed the rights of Justinian, Charlemagne, and Otto, and declared that it was for him to decide who was the rightful Pope. "Divine Providence," he said, "had specially appointed the Roman Empire as a remedy against continued schism." Alexander refused to listen to his suggestion that a council should be called at Pavia to settle the dispute. "No one," he said, "has the right to judge me, who am the supreme judge of the world." Thereupon Frederick gave his support to the anti-pope Victor IV. Alexander promptly excommunicated him and all his adherents. The schism which followed lasted for seventeen years.

Alexander had the moral support of France, Spain, and England, and the material support of the kingdom of Sicily and of the powerful league of the Lombard cities, which he had helped to establish. More pernicious to Frederick's cause than the Lom-

bard swords and spears were the fevers of Rome, by which, at
the height of his power (1167), his conquering host was suddenly
annihilated. After the defeat at Legnano, which was caused by
the refusal of Henry the Lion, Duke of Saxony, to bring help
into Italy, Frederick began negotiations with Alexander, which
ripened into the Peace of Venice in August, 1177.

BARBAROSSA AT THE FEET OF THE POPE

"At Venice, which, inaccessible by her position, maintained a sedulous
neutrality, claiming to be independent of the Empire, yet seldom led into
war by sympathy with the Popes, the two powers whose strife had roused
all Europe were induced to meet by the mediation of the Doge Sebastian
Ziani. Three slabs of red marble in the porch of St. Mark's point out the
spot where Frederick knelt in sudden awe, and the Pope with tears of joy
raised him, and gave the kiss of peace. A later legend, to which poetry
and painting have given an undeserved currency, tells how the Pontiff
set his foot on the neck of the prostrate king, with the words, 'The young

lion and the dragon shalt thou trample under foot.' It needed not this
exaggeration to enhance the significance of that scene, even more full of
meaning for the future than it was solemn and affecting to the Venetian
crowd that thronged the church and the piazza. For it was the renunciation by the mightiest prince of his time of the project to which his life had
been devoted: it was the abandonment by the secular power of a contest in
which it had twice been vanquished, and which it could not renew under
more favorable conditions." (Bryce, *The Holy Roman Empire*, p. 171.)

The Peace of Venice was followed, in 1179, by the Third Council of the Lateran, which was attended by more than three hundred
bishops and six hundred abbots. Twenty-seven disciplinary decrees were promulgated, the first of which was an amendment to
the decree on the election of the Sovereign Pontiff of the year
1059: henceforth, a two-thirds majority in the College of Cardinals
was necessary to make valid the choice of a Pope. There was no
mention of the clergy and people of Rome, nor of the right of
confirmation on the part of the Emperor.

With Alexander III the Emperor remained on friendly terms;
but the great Pope died in exile in 1181, having been forced by
the faithless Romans, as Gregory VII had been a century before,
to flee from the city.

With the Lombard towns Frederick signed articles of peace at
Constance in 1183. The municipal liberties for which they had
fought so long were now accorded them; the Emperor gave up
his right to appoint the governors of the cities, and recognized
the Lombard League. His dream of becoming a second Charlemagne had not been realized.

The years immediately following the Peace of Venice were the most brilliant period of Frederick's reign. After the fall of Jerusalem in 1187, though
nearly seventy years of age, he put on the cross, and by his ever firm and
powerful will collected an army of fifty thousand Crusaders. After defeat-
ing the Turks in the desperate battle of Iconium, he was drowned while
attempting to swim the rapid mountain stream of the Seleph in Cilicia
(1190).

3. St. Thomas à Becket, the Champion of the Liberty of the Church

Like many German Emperors, the Norman kings of England
wanted to keep the control of ecclesiastical affairs to a great extent
in their own hands. We have already seen how Henry I was

forced to abandon investiture and to allow free election of bishops
and abbots. When Henry II (1154-1189), an able ruler, but of
a violent and capricious temper, ascended the throne, he was
determined to assert the supremacy of the State once more. He
would have succeeded but for St. Thomas à Becket, who resolutely withstood his designs.

Thomas à Becket was born in London about 1118, of Norman parents.
He was educated at Merton Abbey and in the schools of London and
Oxford. When his father died, Theobald, Archbishop of Canterbury and
Primate of England, took the youth into his house, superintended his further
training, and sent him on various missions of study or diplomacy to France
and Italy. His talents and accomplishments were fully recognized, and
preferments followed rapidly until he became Archdeacon of Canterbury,
a dignity second only after a bishop and an abbot. On the recommendation
of Theobald he was appointed Lord Chancellor of England, and as such
assumed great splendor and magnificence in his retinue. King Henry II
regarded him as his personal friend and the ablest and most trustworthy of
his advisers. Thomas attended Henry on his war in France, and his chivalric
exploits in Normandy at the head of a large body of knights were more
befitting the career of a military adventurer than that of a churchman.

On the death of Theobald in 1161, Thomas was raised, in spite
of his protests, to the archiepiscopal see. From that day he became
a new man. He laid aside the former pomp and splendor, took
the habit of the monks of his cathedral, was present at all the
night-offices in the cathedral, and became by the austerity of his
life, his zeal for discipline, and his pastoral energy, the model of
prelates. Convinced that he could not at the same time serve
both the Church and Henry Plantagenet, he resigned the Chan-
cellorship, a step which at once cost him the friendship of the
King. A conflict between two such men was inevitable.

At the Parliament of Westminster (1163) Henry demanded
that ecclesiastics charged with certain crimes should be degraded
from their office and handed over for trial to the secular tribunals.
This demand was in direct violation of one of the most ancient
rights enjoyed by the clergy throughout Christendom. The bishops
refused. Would they at least pledge themselves, Henry then
asked, to observe the "ancient customs" of the realm? After
much persuasion Thomas agreed to do this, and a meeting was
convoked at Clarendon (1164) to formulate in writing these
supposed ancient customs to which the King had appealed. A list
of sixteen statutes, known as the "Constitutions of Clarendon,"

were presented to the bishops for their signature. The most obnoxious of these were: (*a*) that no election should be held for vacant bishoprics or abbacies without the king's permission; (*b*) that during the vacancy the revenues should go to the royal exchequer; (*c*) that no archbishop, bishop, or other ecclesiastic should leave the kingdom without the king's permission; (*d*) that no one should be allowed to appeal to Rome without the king's license; (*e*) that all disputes concerning ecclesiastical offices should be decided in the king's court.

St. Thomas à Becket

Thomas hesitated to accept such "customs," but finally, yielding to pressure brought upon him from all sides, he took the oath with the rest of the bishops. But he had no sooner returned to Canterbury, than he regretted his act of weakness, and heroically redeemed it by sincere repentance and severe penance. He immediately dispatched deputies to Pope Alexander III, who was then in exile at Sens in France, to solicit forgiveness; and on the following day sent to the King a recantation of his oath. Henry was furious, and swore that he would be avenged on the "traitor."

Deserted by his fellow-bishops and his life in danger, Thomas fled to France and placed himself under the protection of Louis VII. Alexander III annulled the Constitutions of Clarendon in public consistory, but took no further steps against Henry. Thomas thereupon tendered his resignation, but the Pope refused to accept it. Meanwhile Henry did all in his power to bend the exiled Archbishop to his will. He confiscated all his property and banished his dependents and kinsmen. At last, in 1170, when threatened with excommunication and interdict, Henry agreed to be reconciled with Thomas; but one thing he could not be induced to do—to give the customary kiss of peace to his enemy. On the Archbishop's return to England (December 1, 1170), the people, who had been all along ardent in his support, gave him an enthusiastic welcome.

One of Thomas' first official acts was to excommunicate a number of prelates who had sided with the King and accepted benefices from him. When this was reported to Henry at one of his castles in Normandy, he exclaimed in a fit of irritation: "Is there no one who will rid me of this insolent priest?" Four knights, who were present when the King uttered the fatal words, immediately crossed the channel, rode to Canterbury, forced their way into the cathedral, and murdered the Archbishop on the stone floor of the north transept (December 29, 1170).

The whole Catholic world was roused to indignation by the sacrilegious crime. Pope Alexander would not suffer Henry's name to be pronounced in his hearing, and solemnly excommunicated all who had any part in the murder. Henry, who expressed sorrow for what had happened, cleared himself by oath from any complicity in the murder, consented to do public penance for his rash words, and was absolved in the cathedral of Avranches in 1172. In the following year Alexander raised the martyred Archbishop to the honors of the altar. In spite of his public penance, his pilgrimage to the shrine of St. Thomas at Canterbury, and his promises to the Pope, Henry did not change his policy towards the Church. We shall find it continued by his worthless son, John Lackland.

"The passion of Thomas à Becket, which scattered his brains on the floor of his own cathedral, is perhaps the most dramatic episode in English history. After seven hundred and thirty years we can see it all with our eyes as it was enacted on that dark winter's evening. The champion of his order and the people, a saint in self-denial, an Athanasius against the world, who had overcome his king by sheer tenacity of principle, and conquered the venality, the waverings, of Cardinals in Rome and Bishops in England; at whose feet the country lay prostrate in a trance of worship and religious dread; shone forth in one moment with a martyr's crown. The vision filled every imagination, the tragedy melted all hearts. Within three days miracles of healing began to be reported from a distance. They multiplied as years went on; the pilgrimage to Canterbury did not yield in renown to Rome or Compostella; and Alexander canonized, not unwillingly, the defender of Church liberties who had poured out on himself rebukes the most scathing nor wholly undeserved. In his death Thomas had subdued friends as well as enemies. But it is only the historian who, looking back, can perceive that the great popular saint and churchman had delayed the Reformation in England by more than three hundred years" (Canon Barry, *The Papal Monarchy*, p. 277).

4. The Papacy at the Noontide of Its Power. Pope Innocent III

Henry VI. The Empire at Its Zenith.—During the reign of the Emperor Henry VI, son of Barbarossa, it looked as though the Empire would triumph over the Papacy. Henry was a born statesman; he had inherited all his father's valor, ambition, and severity, but none of his father's generosity and nobility. By his marriage with Constance, the heiress of the Norman kings of Southern Italy, he had become master of Naples and Sicily, and a treaty with the Lombard League had secured for him the balance of power in North Italy. The Patrimony of Peter was thus hemmed in from all sides. The Papacy, as a temporal power, was left isolated and impotent. Henry governed his wide domains with brilliance and success. He forced Richard Coeur de Lion to acknowledge his supremacy, married his brother Philip to Irene, daughter of the Greek Emperor, and persuaded the majority of the German princes to accept his scheme of annexing Sicily to the Empire and of making the imperial crown hereditary in his family. Pope Celestine III (1191-1198) would not give his consent to such a step. and Henry had, for the time, to content himself with getting his infant son Frederick II crowned king of the Romans. Skillfully taking advantage of every fresh success, the Emperor was about to realize the Hohenstaufen dream of imperial sway over Europe and the East, when his untimely death ruined his cause (1197). He was only thirty-three years old.

On Henry's death the election of Frederick II was set aside, Sicily was once more separated from the Empire, and the contest which followed between the Guelf, Otto of Brunswick, and the Ghibelline, Philip of Suabia, threw all Germany into war and confusion. At one stroke the Papacy was freed from the incubus of the imperial power in Italy. The way was clear for the man in whose pontificate the Papacy attained the flood tide of its power and influence—Innocent III (1198-1216).

Early Career and Election of Innocent III.—Innocent III (Lothario of Segni) belonged to a noble Italian family, his father being descended from the Lombard Dukes of Spoleto. He received his early education at Rome, then studied philosophy and theology at Paris, and law, both civil and canon, at Bologna. Returning to Rome, he immediately entered upon that career in the Church for which he was so eminently fitted by his genius and his brilliant training. At the age of twenty-seven he was already Canon of St. Peter's, and two years later he was raised to the cardinalate by Pope Clement III (1187-1191). As the most trusted of the Papal advisers, he gained a thorough knowledge of the details of ecclesiastical organization and government. After the death of Celestine III in 1198 he was elected, on the first ballot, to the Supreme Pontificate. He was only thirty-seven years old. Those who did not know him had some misgivings because of his youth; but his actions soon dissipated all doubts as to the wisdom of the Cardinals' choice.

Fresco at Subiaco

INNOCENT III

Rome and Italy.—The first task which confronted the new Pope was the restoration of the Papal power in the city of Rome and in the Papal States. The Prefect and the Senate of Rome tendered their oaths of submission to him on the day of his enthronement; but nearly ten years elapsed before he could be said to be complete master in his own city. He overawed the turbulent nobility by his firmness and fearlessness in the face of uproar and rebellion, and won the hearts of the common people by his generosity, especially during the famine years of 1202, when he fed 8,000 persons at his own expense. In 1204 he founded the great Hospital of the Holy Spirit, which ministered to the Romans, man, woman, and child, saint and sinner, itself the pioneer among such municipal institutions, and the model for similar ones in the rest of Europe.

The Papal States in Central Italy had been almost entirely lost to the Popes during the ascendancy of the Hohenstaufen. By skillful diplomacy, by espousing the cause of the people against their imperial oppressors, by excommunicating the dukes who had been set up by Henry VI, and absolving their subjects from allegiance, Innocent III established the States of the Church on a permanent footing in the very first year of his pontificate. The effect of such an achievement in such a brief space of time upon the public opinion of Europe was incalculable.

Innocent was equally successful in Sicily. From Queen Constance, who had become regent of Sicily and Naples on the death of Henry VI, he obtained the recognition of the Papal suzerainty over the kingdom. Later, on her deathbed, Constance entrusted to him by testament both her infant son Frederick II and her kingdom.

Innocent III and the Empire.—In Germany Philip of Suabia and Otto of Brunswick were meanwhile engaged in a bitter struggle for the right to succeed Henry VI. Both appealed to the Pope, who, after hesitating for more than a year, decided in favor of Otto. Philip's party would not yield, and there was civil war until Philip was assassinated in 1208, following a private quarrel. Otto then journeyed to Rome and was crowned in St. Peter's by the Pope. But the imperial crown had scarcely touched his brow when he showed himself as haughty and overbearing as any Hohenstaufen, and as regardless of the rights of the Church. He seized several of the most important strongholds in the Papal States, and prepared to snatch Southern Italy from Frederick II, the Pope's ward. Innocent remonstrated with him, and then excommunicated him. Thereupon the German princes chose Frederick II Emperor (1212). At Bouvines, July 27, 1214, the decisive battle was fought between the contending parties: Otto with the English troops of King John his uncle, and contingents from Holland and Brabant, Flanders, and Boulogne, was badly

beaten by the army of Philip Augustus of France, who, at the
invitation of the Pope, had rallied to the support of Frederick II.

The Champion of the Cross.—The one thought that was
always uppermost in the mind of Innocent III was to launch a
universal crusade for the complete recovery of Palestine and all the
Christian lands of the East. It proved to be the only purpose of his
life that was not attained. The Fourth Crusade was diverted from
its purpose and, instead of driving the Turks from the Holy Land,
the so-called crusaders, mostly French and Venetians, captured
and sacked Constantinople, and converted the Greek Empire into
a Latin one. Innocent condemned in the strongest terms this
war of Christians upon Christians and excommunicated the leaders.
In spite of this dismal failure, he spared no efforts to unite
Christendom against Islam. He kept calling for a crusade to the
day of his death. But his cries fell on deaf ears. The masses of
the people were willing, but they had no leaders.

In the year 1212 some fifty thousand children, mostly French and German, under the leadership of the shepherd boys Stephen and Nicholas, set
out for Palestine. A monk had persuaded them that the Holy Land could
only be reconquered by innocence, not by military valor and strategy. Those
of them who did not perish of hunger and fatigue were betrayed into the
hands of the Saracens and sold as slaves.

Another Crusade, for which Innocent was largely responsible,
proved a splendid success. The issue of the long and sanguinary
conflict between the Christians and the Moors for the possession
of Spain was as doubtful as ever at the end of the twelfth century. The five Christian kingdoms, Castile, Leon, Aragon,
Navarre, and Portugal, were carrying on feudal wars amongst
themselves while fresh hordes of fanatic Moslems were crossing
the Straits of Gibraltar. Innocent forced the quarrelsome rulers
to make peace and to unite their forces against the infidels. He
summoned aid for them from France and Burgundy, spurred
them on by frequent letters of encouragement, and offered up
public prayers for the success of their arms. The result was the
glorious victory on the field of Las Navas de Tolosa (July, 1212).

Champion of the Sanctity of Marriage.—In August, 1193,
Philip Augustus, King of France, married Ingeborg, sister of
King Knut VI of Denmark; but he soon conceived an aversion
for her and sought to repudiate her. A council of bishops, packed

with the King's own relatives and presided over by his uncle, the Archbishop of Rheims, annulled the marriage on the flimsy pretext of some distant relationship. Ingeborg and her brother appealed to the Pope. Celestine III reversed the decision of the bishops; but Philip refused to take back his lawful wife, and in open defiance of the Pope, married Agnes of Meran, daughter of a Bavarian nobleman. When Innocent III became Pope, he demanded that Philip separate from Agnes and submit the question of his first marriage to the judgment of the Church. This Philip would not do. Thereupon Innocent laid the Interdict on the whole French kingdom (Jan., 1200). The King was beside himself with rage. "I am going to turn infidel," he said; "how fortunate Saladin was; he had no Pope!" The Interdict was rigorously enforced. After nine months the discontent and indignation of his subjects forced Philip to yield. In 1201 a council examined the question anew and pronounced against the King in favor of Ingeborg. Agnes died in 1204; but Ingeborg was never more than queen in name. About the same time Innocent defended the sanctity and indissolubility of matrimony with equal vigor and success against Pedro II of Aragon and Alphonso IX of Leon.

An *Interdict* is "an ecclesiastical censure by which the inhabitants of a kingdom, province or city are barred from the use of certain sacraments, from participation in the usual religious services, and from Christian burial." "Let all the churches be closed," says Pope Innocent III in the interdict pronounced against France, "let no one be admitted to them, except to baptize infants; let them not be otherwise opened, except for the purpose of lighting the lamps, or when the priest shall come for the Eucharist and holy water for the use of the sick. We permit Mass to be celebrated once a week, on Friday, early in the morning, to consecrate the Host for the use of the sick, but only one cleric is to be admitted to assist the priest. Let the clergy preach on Sundays in the vestibules of the churches, and in place of the Mass let them deliver the word of God. On Easter morning let them hear the confessions of all who desire to confess in the portico of the church. Extreme Unction may not be given. . . ."

England Becomes a Papal Fief.—For fourteen years King John of England carried on a conflict with the Church in England, Ireland, and Normandy which has been justly characterized as "stubborn, virulent, and brutal."

The struggle with the Pope began in 1205. Anxious to have

a devoted follower as archbishop of Canterbury, John insisted on the election of John de Gray; but the younger monks of Canterbury gave their votes to their sub-prior Reginald. Both parties sent delegates to Innocent III, who for the sake of peace set aside the two candidates and appointed the learned Stephen Langton, a cardinal and an Englishman. When John would not allow the new Archbishop to land in England, Innocent laid the whole country under Interdict in 1208, excommunicated John in 1209, absolved his subjects from their oath of allegiance in 1211, and, finally, in 1212, deposed the stubborn King from the English throne and offered his crown to Philip Augustus of France. Fearing defeat at the hands of Philip and knowing that he could not depend upon the English clergy and nobility, who were tired of his tyrannical rule, John surrendered completely to the Pope. He not only conceded every disputed point, but handed over his crown to the Papacy, declared himself a vassal of the Pope for the territory of England and Ireland, and agreed to pay an annual tribute of one thousand marks to the Holy See (1213).

Two years later John was forced by his rebellious barons to sign the Great Charter of English liberty at Runnymede. Innocent III annulled the charter, not because he objected to its supposed innovations or because he was an enemy of liberty, but on account of the violent manner in which the royal signature had been obtained, and because the barons had not appealed to the Pope, who was feudal lord of England, before resorting to force.

The Fourth Lateran Council.—The General Council which convened in the Lateran in November, 1215, was a fitting climax of the memorable pontificate of Innocent III. It was the most brilliant gathering of churchmen since the days of Nicaea. About 1300 prelates were present, including seventy-one Primates and Archbishops, besides representatives from every Catholic kingdom of Europe and the East. The Council discussed the question of raising men and money for a fresh Crusade, passed many important decrees of reform, imposed the precept of annual communion, defined the doctrine of confession, condemned the Albigensian heresy, and, for the first time, made official use of the word *transubstantiation*. Eight months after the close of the great Council on July 16, 1216, Innocent III died at Anagni. He was buried in the basilica at Perugia. His body was removed to Rome by Leo XIII and now rests in the basilica of St. John Lateran.

5. *The Popes and Frederick II. The Fall of the House of the Hohenstaufen*

Frederick II, whose title to the imperial crown was recognized by the Lateran Council, was, as the historian Freeman says, "the most wonderful man in a most wonderful age—not the greatest, still less the best, man of his time, but, as the ancient chronicler Matthew Paris calls him, the most wonderful man. Warrior, statesman, lawgiver, scholar, there was nothing in the compass of the political or intellectual world of his age which he failed to grasp."

THE FAÇADE OF ST. JOHN LATERAN, THE POPE'S CATHEDRAL

Frederick had promised his protector Pope Innocent III that the Sicilian kingdom should be held separately from the Empire. Innocent made this demand in order that the Papacy might not again be hemmed in between a hostile and imperial North and South, as in the days of Henry VI. Frederick had also promised to embark on a Crusade. When Innocent died and Honorius III became Pope, Frederick repudiated both these promises. He occasionally talked of taking the cross, but he never made any positive step to fulfill his oath. Under Gregory IX (1227-1241), an aged but energetic Pontiff, a Crusade was at last launched, and Frederick joined it with his fleet. A fever broke out on his ships, and the Emperor returned to Sicily. Gregory, who believed that Frederick was simulating, promptly excommunicated him, thus depriving him of the status of a crusader. In spite of the ban Frederick now set sail for Palestine with a small army, obtained possession of Jerusalem, and as no bishop would crown an excommunicate, crowned himself in the Holy Sepulcher. With the Sultan of Egypt he concluded a treaty of peace, whereby for ten years the Christians were to hold Jerusalem, Bethlehem, and Nazareth on the sole condition of leaving the mosque of Omar in the hands of the Saracens. On his return to Europe Frederick was again excommunicated for disregarding the former ban and for coming to terms with the infidel.

When things went wrong in Germany, and his presence was required there, Frederick made peace with Gregory and was released from the ban. The quarrel began anew under Gregory's successor Innocent IV (1243-1254). It revolved around the Papal and Imperial claims in Lombardy and Sardinia. When Frederick invited Innocent to a personal interview, the Pontiff, fearing treachery, fled first to Genoa, and then to the imperial free city of Lyons; and called a General Council in 1245 to pass judgment on the Emperor. Only 140 bishops, mostly from France and Spain, were present when the sessions began. Frederick was charged with perjury, sacrilege, heresy, and unjust and cruel conduct. Innocent solemnly deposed him, offered the imperial crown to Robert of France and several other princes, who all refused to accept it, and finally gave it to the ambitious Henry Raspe, the brother-in-law of St. Elizabeth of Thuringia. There was civil war in Germany. Guelfs and Ghibellines laid Italy waste from the Alps to the Straits of Messina. Frederick died in the midst of the strife, A.D. 1250, repentant and absolved from the ban of excommunication.

Conrad IV, Frederick's son, survived his unhappy father only a few years. Manfred, another son, maintained his title over Sicily till his defeat and death at Benevento in 1266. Conradin, son of Conrad IV, a gallant boy of fifteen, then crossed the Alps with four thousand knights and his inseparable friend Frederick of Austria, to assert his rights to Sicily, which the Pope had given to Charles of Anjou, brother of St. Louis IX of France. Rome opened its gates to him; but at Tagliacozzo he was defeated and captured. With his death on the scaffold at Naples, August 26, 1268, the House of Hohenstaufen ended. . . .

The strife between the *Regnum* and the *Sacerdotium* will be renewed, but the antagonist of the Papacy will not be a German Emperor; a French King will play the rôle of the Hohenstaufen, and play it more tyrannically and more brutally than Barbarossa or Frederick II.

Hints for Study

1. Many of the documents relating to the events dealt with in this chapter will be found in E. Henderson, *Select Historical Documents of the Middle Ages*, pp. 410-430; others in F. A. Ogg, *Source Book of Medieval History*, pp. 297-311, 380-383, and 398-409.
2. What is meant by *Guelfs* and *Ghibellines*? Look up these words in a dictionary or encyclopedia.
3. What is the difference between *excommunication* and *interdict*? Give examples of each from this chapter.
4. Summarize the hundred years' conflict between the Hohenstaufen and the Papacy in the form of a chronological table.
5. The Crusade of the Children is well treated by W. Scott Durand, *Cross and Dagger* (London, 1910).
6. There is a good French biography of St. Thomas à Becket available in an English translation: Msgr. Demimuid, *St. Thomas à Becket* (Benziger).
7. Read the article on Innocent III in the *Cath. Encyclopedia*.

CHAPTER IV

MEDIEVAL HERESIES AND HERETICS

The disorder and moral relaxation prevailing almost universally during the tenth and eleventh centuries favored the rise and rapid expansion of numerous extravagant and scandalous sects. Nearly all of them had a socialistic or anarchistic tendency. The trait common to all of them was a boundless aversion for the clergy. It would take us too far afield to describe each sect and its vagaries; it will suffice to fix our attention on one of them, the head and center of them all—the New Manichaeans; directly or indirectly, all the other heresies were tributary to them.

1. *The New Manichaean or Albigensian Heresy*

The Manichaeans (see p. 141), who had caused so much trouble in the early Church, had never completely died out. Defeated in the fourth century, chiefly through the efforts of St. Augustine, they reappeared in Armenia in the seventh century under the name of Paulicians, and in the ninth century spread throughout the Greek Empire. In the tenth century they invaded Bulgaria, where they were known as Bogomils; about the same time we find them in Constantinople. From the Balkan Peninsula we can follow them to the seaport towns on the Adriatic, and from there to Northern Italy, Spain, the Rhineland, and Southern France. Their headquarters were at Toulouse in Languedoc.

Easy-going and dissolute, in constant touch with the Jews and Moslems of Spain, governed by counts and barons who were indifferent to religion, and by bishops who cared very little about the spiritual welfare of their subjects, the south of France was especially favorable to the progress of the new Manichaeans. A council held at Albi in 1165 failed to stop their propaganda; an attempt made by an army of crusaders commanded by Cardinal Henry, a former abbot of Clairvaux, proved equally fruitless: the heretics, cowed for the moment, raised their heads again as soon as the danger was past. At the beginning of the reign of Innocent III more than a thousand towns in Languedoc were in their power.

The New Manichaeans called themselves *Cathari*, the pure; but because their principal forces were concentrated about Albi in the County of Toulouse, they were generally known as *Albigensians*. A glance at their principal tenets will show us why they were a serious menace to Church and State alike.

The Albigensians believed in two gods, one good and one evil, the one in control of the spirit and the other in control of the flesh; and both in perpetual conflict one with the other. The whole visible world, they said, was the work of the evil god and therefore evil in itself. Whatever tended to the preservation of the human race—marriage, motherhood, the family—was sinful; all animal food—flesh-meat, eggs, milk—defiles the soul. Whoever married or partook of animal food could not be saved. Those who lived strictly according to these teachings were called the "perfect"; the rest, the "believers." When a "believer" was at the point of death, one of the "perfect" was called in to lay his hands and the book of the Gospels on the head of the patient. This was called spiritual baptism, or *consolamentum* (consolation), and was believed to free the sinner from all the consequences of his sinful life. If the patient recovered, he was as often as not smothered or starved to death (*endura*) in order to assure his salvation, because the consolamentum could be given only once. The possession of private property was regarded as sinful and therefore to be abolished. Christ was only a man, and as such subject to the control of the evil god and incapable of redeeming mankind. The Church was called the "synagogue of satan," and the masses were encouraged to insult her ministers, to desecrate and pillage her temples and monasteries. Such, in broad outline, was Albigensianism. Professor Kurth was not exaggerating when he described it as "a dark night which came down with the weight of lead and with the coldness of ice upon the mind and the heart, a chancre of death which ate at all the luminous and elevated faculties of the human soul, a deadly folly that choked the joy of living and made existence here below like a bad dream" (*The Church at the Turning Points of History*, p. 68).

Even many pious Christians were drawn to this doctrine of

darkness and despair. They mistook the fanaticism of the "perfect" for Christian self-denial. In the ranks of the Cathari they
hoped to find what they often looked for in vain among their
own bishops, priests, and monks. It was the worldly-mindedness,
the abuse of wealth, the luxury, the moral corruption, so much
in evidence among certain sections of the clergy, that "opened
the door through which the multitudes rushed headlong out of
the Church."

2. *The Waldensians*

In the last quarter of the twelfth century the Albigensians
were strengthened both morally and numerically by the Waldensians. The founder of the Waldensians was Peter Waldes (or
Waldo), a rich merchant of Lyons. He made over all his possessions to the poor and devoted himself to the study of the New
Testament, which two priests had translated for him into the
vernacular. In 1176 he began to preach in public, his avowed
intention being to restore the apostolic life in all its primitive
poverty and simplicity. His followers, who went about the country, two by two, poorly dressed, barefooted or wearing wooden
sandals, were called the "Poor Men of Lyons." They expounded
the Scriptures to all who would listen to them, and occasionally
declaimed against the wealth and luxury of the clergy. When
some of them appeared at the Third Lateran Council (1179),
their zeal and piety were commended, but as they were for the
most part ignorant and illiterate they were forbidden to preach
the Gospel to the people. In spite of this prohibition Waldes and
his disciples continued their preaching. The excommunication
pronounced against them at the Council of Verona (1184) by
Pope Lucius III brought many of them back to the Church, but
the vast majority remained obstinate. Passing from schism to
heresy, they openly attacked the fundamental dogmas of the Christian faith, the divine institution of the hierarchy, the priesthood,
the Sacrifice of the Mass, Purgatory, Indulgences, the veneration
of Saints and Relics, the indissolubility of marriage. . . . The
Waldensians carried their errors to every country of Europe, even
to Bohemia and Poland. Those who remained in France were
absorbed by the rising flood of Albigensianism.

3. *How Church and State Combated Heresy*

In the heresy of the Albigensians contemporaries saw not only a sin against the faith, for which they would have had to answer only before God and the Church, but also a public crime, an attack on the existing social order; for it was evident to everyone that the new Manichaeism, if it proved triumphant, would bring down in a common ruin both Church and State. To the powers, secular and religious, of the Middle Ages, heretics appeared precisely such as anarchists appear to us now—as revolutionaries who, if they do not listen to reason and mend their ways, must be cut off by the strong arm of the law. Toleration was out of the question; it was never even mentioned; and if it had been, it would have been scouted alike by the orthodox and the heretic, by the civil and religious authorities. No one in those days dreamed of questioning the lawfulness of putting down dangerous and subversive heresies by force. "If a crusade were holy which aimed at delivering the Lord's Sepulcher from the infidels, was it not as holy when it took up arms in defense of the priesthood, Sacraments, the Commandments themselves, and the social order?" It is not surprising, therefore, that Pope Innocent III, after all other means had been tried in vain to convert the Albigensians, should have proclaimed a crusade against them.

On the twelfth of January, 1208, the Papal Legate Pierre de Castelnau was murdered by a follower of Count Raymund VI of Toulouse on the banks of the Rhone. This sacrilegious act, in which Raymund was supposed to have had a hand, excited the greatest indignation throughout Europe. Innocent III at once released the subjects of Raymund from their allegiance and invited the warriors of Christendom to occupy his lands and to suppress the Albigensian heresy. An army of two hundred thousand crusaders, chiefly from the north of France, responded. The war which followed was waged with the utmost ferocity on both sides. The religious motive which had brought the crusaders together was soon relegated to the background by their leader Simon de Montfort. The holy war became a war of extermination and political conquest. It dragged on amidst unspeakable cruelties for twenty years. Pedro of Aragon, the hero of Navas de Tolosa, marched to the assistance of his kinsman of Toulouse. He was defeated and slain in the battle of Muret (1213). De Montfort himself was killed while besieging Toulouse (1215). Then Louis VIII of France threw his armies into Languedoc and gathered in the spoils. By an inheritance treaty all the lands of Toulouse were given to the French crown in 1229.

4. *The Inquisition*

The Albigensian wars were over, but the Albigensian heresy still counted many secret adherents. For the detection and punishment of these heretics the Council of Toulouse (1229) established a special ecclesiastical tribunal known as the *Inquisition* (Lat. *inquisitio*, an inquiry). But neither the bishops who met at Toulouse, nor Pope Innocent III, nor St. Dominic, as has sometimes been incorrectly stated, were the founders of the Inquisition. The name was perhaps new, but the thing itself was old. The Inquisition of 1229 was but one step in a process, the beginnings of which can be traced back to Apostolic times. In order to form a correct estimate of the much-maligned Inquisition it will be profitable to outline the stages of this process. We shall then see how it came about that the Church, which was for centuries opposed to bloodshed, in the end permitted and even commanded the secular princes to inflict the death penalty on obstinate heretics.

1. St. Paul "delivered up to Satan Hymeneus and Alexander, that they might learn not to blaspheme" (1 Tim. 1, 20). This penalty was called excommunication, and was the only one inflicted on heretics during the first three centuries. The earlier fathers of the Church, especially Origen, St. Cyprian, and Lactantius, expressly reject the idea of any other punishment.

2. The pagan emperors of Rome exercised absolute authority over their subjects even in matters of religion; every emperor was also *summus pontifex*, high priest. Hence, when the emperors became Christians they constituted themselves protectors of the Church and often interfered in religious matters. Arian emperors persecuted the Catholics, and Catholic emperors repressed the Arians. Valentinian I and Theodosius the Great enacted laws against heresies: Heretics were subjected to exile, their possessions were confiscated, they were disqualified from inheriting property.

3. In 382 the death penalty was decreed against certain heretics (Encratites) whose doctrines were regarded as dangerous to the State. Later on, the same penalty was applied to the Manichaeans and the Donatists. Only one bishop, St. Optatus of Mileve, approved of this violent repression of the Donatists. St. Augustine, after much hesitation, would admit only scourg-

ing, fines, or exile. When the Spanish heretic Priscillian was put to death by order of the Emperor Maximus (385), this act was strongly condemned by St. Ambrose and St. Martin of Tours. St. John Chrysostom called the killing of a heretic an "inexpiable crime," but he did think that heretics should be deprived of liberty of speech, and that heretical assemblies should be dissolved.

4. Under the later Greek Emperors, the Church and the Empire were regarded as one institution, and the ecclesiastical canons and the political laws were entered on the same statute books, so that it was often difficult to distinguish one from the other.

5. During the early Middle Ages, from the sixth to the end of the tenth century, we hear little of heretics and their punishment. Scourging and incarceration, the punishments to which recalcitrant monks were subjected by their Rule, were also applied to heretics, such as Aldebert and Clement in the time of St. Boniface, and the monk Gottschalk in the ninth century.

6. In the eleventh century we find the first examples of death by fire as a punishment for heresy in the West; in the East the Emperor Justinian had decreed this penalty against the Manichaeans. The pagan Germans had burned at the stake those found guilty of sorcery or witchcraft. The common people looked upon heretics such as the Cathari as worse than sorcerers, and insisted on their being delivered to the flames. In 1022 thirteen Cathari were burnt at Orleans by order of King Robert of France. After this there were numerous cases of the execution of heretics, either by burning or hanging, in England, France, Germany, and Italy.

Till the beginning of the thirteenth century the Church had no part in these executions. The people and the civil magistrates were alone responsible for them. The mob frequently took the law into its own hands, broke open the prisons and "lynched" the heretics. It was the mob who, infuriated at seeing him tear down and set fire to crosses, burnt the heresiarch Peter de Bruys in 1140. We hear of only one bishop in the eleventh century who affirmed the necessity for the punishment of heretics by the secular arm. Bishop Wazo of Liége expressly condemned capital punishment and recommended resort to peaceful conversion. St. Bernard demanded excommunication, imprisonment or exile, if persuasion and refutation proved fruitless, but flatly disapproved of the death penalty. *Fides suadenda est, non imponenda,* "Faith is to be produced by persuasion, not imposed by force," was his motto.

In the Acts of the Councils of the eleventh and twelfth centuries which treat of the combating of heresy there is never even a suggestion of capital punishment. Neither did any secular law before 1197 demand the death penalty for heresy. But there were not wanting canonists who, basing their opinion on the Roman Law, the study of which was then much in vogue, declared that impenitent heretics may, and even should, be punished by death.

7. Peter II of Aragon was the first ruler to decree death by fire against heretics found in his kingdom after a given time (1197). During the Albigensian crisis Pope Innocent III exhorted the secular rulers to proceed against the Cathari. He calls heresy high treason against God and puts

it on a par with high treason against temporal rulers, which was punishable with death. Still in all his legislation and in the Acts of the Fourth Lateran Council (1215), which organized the method of procedure against heretics, the death penalty is never mentioned. For punishment Innocent had in mind the confiscation of property, banishment, and exclusion from burial in consecrated ground, not death. He was the first of the Popes, however, to rely extensively upon the secular arm in the repression of heresy and was therefore the first to discover, as one of his biographers remarks, how difficult it is to call back the hounds of violence once they are unleashed.

8. When the Emperor Frederick II, who was anything but an ardent Catholic, in 1224 decreed death by fire against obstinate heretics in Lombardy, Gregory IX sanctioned the imperial legislation, but *reserved to the organs of the Church the right to decide the all-important question as to who was to be considered an obstinate heretic and consequently to be delivered to the secular arm for punishment.* Thus the two authorities, the temporal and the spiritual, after they had worked separately for a long time, united their efforts to stamp out the anti-christian, anti-social and anarchistic heresies which had for over two hundred years troubled the peace of Christendom and menaced the foundations of Church and State.

Until the year 1231 the duty of detecting and repressing heresy had devolved upon the bishops. In 1231 Pope Gregory IX appointed a number of Papal Inquisitors (*Inquisitores haereticae pravitatis*), mostly Dominicans and Franciscans, for the various countries of Europe. The Inquisition was thus regularly established; but in the course of time more or less important changes were made in its mode of procedure. Pope Gregory IX was opposed to torture, but Innocent IV approved its use for the discovery of heresy, and Urban IV confirmed this usage, which like the death penalty for heresy, had its origin in the Roman Law. Although intended for the whole of Christendom it was only in the Latin countries that the Papal Inquisition was permanently active.

The Inquisitors at first traveled from place to place. "On arriving in a district they addressed its inhabitants, called upon them to confess if they were heretics, or to denounce those whom they knew to be heretics. A 'time of grace' was opened, during which those who freely confessed were dispensed from all penalties, or only given a secret and very light penance; while those whose heresy had been openly manifested were exempted from the penalties of death and perpetual imprisonment. But this time could not exceed one month. After that began the inquisition properly so called." Denunciations were received, the accused brought before the inquisitors, the witnesses examined. The sentences were solemnly pronounced on a Sunday, in a church or public place. This was known as the *sermo generalis* (in

Spain Auto-da-fé—"act of faith"). Those who had confessed were reconciled and various penances imposed, such as fasting, prayers, pilgrimages, public scourging; the obstinate heretics and the renegades were for the last time called upon to submit, to confess, and to abjure. If they consented, they were condemned to perpetual imprisonment; if they did not consent, they were handed over to the secular arm, which was equivalent to sentence of death by fire. The number of those delivered over to the secular power has been grossly exaggerated. Even H. C. Lea in his *History of the Inquisition in the Middle Ages*—a bitter Protestant account—admits that comparatively few people suffered at the stake in the Middle Ages, probably not more than three or four per cent of those convicted of heresy.

The Spanish Inquisition, and the Inquisition in Venice and other countries, must not be identified with the ecclesiastical Inquisition. They were mixed tribunals, with the civil element predominating, and their excesses cannot be charged to the Church. The Spanish Inquisition, established in 1481 by Ferdinand and Isabella, was intended primarily for the Mohammedan converts to Catholicism, in the old Arab kingdoms, who were suspected of wishing to return to their old religion, and for disguised Jews, many of whom had succeeded in becoming priests and even bishops. The tribunal, once established, also directed its activity against murder, immorality, smuggling, usury, and other offenses. The king appointed the Grand Inquisitor and the other officials, and also signed the decrees; and the penalties were inflicted in his name. Pope Sixtus IV approved the Spanish Inquisition, because he was under the impression that an ecclesiastical Inquisition was to be established; when the true state of the case was brought to his knowledge, it was too late; all that he and his successors could do was to protest against its excesses. The Spanish kings made extensive use of the powers of the Inquisition against obnoxious prelates and nobles who were not subject to the jurisdiction of other tribunals. On one occasion the Pope had great difficulty in rescuing Cardinal Caranza, Primate of Toledo, from the hands of the Inquisitors.

The Protestant Reformation did nothing to change the traditional views in regard to the persecution of heretics. In Protestant as well as in Catholic countries heretics were imprisoned, tortured, and put to death by fire or otherwise. It was not until 1677 that the death penalty against heretics was removed from the statute books in England. Philip of Spain considered heresy to be no less dangerous to the state than Elizabeth of England considered Catholicism to be; and Philip's prisons were no more unsavory and noisome than the English prisons of the time. Luther, Melanchthon, Calvin, and Theodore of Beza explicitly approved of capital punishment for obstinate heretics. Calvin even wrote a special work in defense of the principle that "Heretics are to be coerced by the sword," after he had burned Michael Servetus at the stake.

We shall not attempt to defend the Inquisition. We cannot approve of the extreme measures adopted, not only on account of their cruelty, but because they undoubtedly led to hypocrisy and the simulation of orthodoxy. Some writers blame the fundamentally unchristian Roman Law, which was revived in the eleventh century, for the Inquisition with all its by-products. "The persecuting era of the Inquisition," writes Father Bede Jarrett, O.P., in his *History of Europe*, "coincided with the recovery of Roman Law and was an inevitable consequence of it." This is perhaps too sweeping an assertion; it explains only one phase of the Inquisition. Father Bernard Duhr, S.J., has put his finger on the deeper motives behind the institution.

"In the last analysis," he says, "the introduction and aggravation of the Inquisition was mainly influenced by two ideas, or, more correctly, the exaggeration of these two ideas. The Middle Ages by the power of the Faith accomplished great things in all spheres of social life and art, produced saints, and erected architectural monuments before which we bow our head in awe and admiration. But this glowing faith concealed a danger which not all the men of that time were able to escape: I mean the danger of overdoing a good thing. This tendency to exaggerate led to fanaticism, which deadens the brain and petrifies the heart that loves the faith above everything, but does not glow with charity, having lost sight of the Apostle's dictum: If I had faith strong enough to transfer mountains, without love I should be nothing. Those who were thus affected loudly demanded the stake: many laymen even outdid the clergy, and so the Inquisition found open doors. Closely connected with the exaggerated enthusiasm for the faith was the overemphasis given to another idea, namely, that to the clergy belonged superiority and leadership in all domains of social, nay, even political life. Though the underlying idea was perfectly correct, when exaggerated it was bound to divert the ecclesiastical authorities from their own proper sphere and to urge them to adopt material measures which were not essential to their spiritual mission" (*Fortnightly Review*, Nov. 1929, p. 279).

What an Inquisitor Should Be

One of the most important sources of our knowledge in regard to the functioning of the Inquisition is the *Practica Inquisitionis Haereticae Pravitatis,* a practical manual or directory for Inquisitors, drawn up in the first quarter of the fourteenth century by *Bernard Gui,* a Dominican Friar, who exercised inquisitorial functions in various parts of Europe from 1307 to 1324. In the fourth part of his Manual, which consists in a "short and useful instruction" concerning the power of the inquisitors, their excellence, etc., he draws the following portrait of what an inquisitor should be, and what he himself, and no doubt many other inquisitors, tried to be:

"He, the Inquisitor, ought to be diligent and fervent in his zeal for religious truth, the salvation of souls, and the extirpation of heresy. In presence of difficulties and reverses he ought to remain calm, and never give way to anger or indignation. He ought to be fearless, facing danger up till death; but while not flinching in the presence of peril, he ought not to hasten it by unreflecting boldness. He must be insensible to the prayers and advances of those who endeavor to persuade him; nevertheless he must not harden his heart to the point of refusing delays or relaxations of punishment, according to circumstances and places. . . . In doubtful matters he must be circumspect, and not give easy credence to what seems only likely and often is not true, for often that which seems unlikely ends by being true. He must listen, discuss, and examine with all zeal, in order patiently to attain to the light. Let that love of truth and mercy, which ought always to dwell in the heart of a judge, shine on his countenance, so that his decisions may never seem to be dictated by envy or by cruelty."

—See Jean Guiraud, *The Mediaeval Inquisition*, p. 75.

Hints for Study

1. Note the difference between the medieval heresies and those in the Early Church.
2. Pope Gregory IX said of the heresies of his time: "They have different faces, but their tails are bound together." Comment on these words.
3. What conditions favored the spread of the Albigensian and Waldensian heresies?
4. Explain the following: *Paulicians, New Manichaeans, Cathari, Bogomils, Consolamentum, Endura, Poor Men of Lyons, Albigenses, Inquisition, Sermo Generalis, Auto-da-fé.*
5. Be careful not to judge the Inquisition by the ideas of our time. Have the Protestants any right to throw stones at the Catholics because of the Inquisition?
6. The best book on the Inquisition available in English is Maycock, *The Inquisition—From Its Establishment to the Great Schism.*

CHAPTER V

THE RISE OF THE MENDICANT ORDERS

Christian Europe could never have overcome by violence alone the revolutionary and anarchistic heresies with which it was flooded. What gave these heresies their driving power was the worldly life led by so many of the ministers of the Church. The steadily increasing power and influence of the hierarchy in secular affairs had alienated many bishops and priests and abbots from their spiritual functions. Not all of them had been able to resist the temptation of seeking after the things of the world, and had thus become more and more unlike their Divine Master. The common people felt this opposition between the poor Jesus of the Gospels and His worldly-minded representatives, and eagerly listened to the words of the Poor Men of Lyons and the Cathari of Toulouse. If society was to be healed, the healing had to begin within the Church herself. Christ living in His Church had to become visible again in His ministers.

1. *The Church and the New Middle Class*

The great changes that took place in the social and economic life of Europe during the twelfth and thirteenth centuries necessitated changes in the pastoral care of souls. The Crusades had promoted a lively exchange of goods between the East and the West. The towns lying on the trade routes increased in wealth and population, and new centers of trade were springing up everywhere. The burghers of these flourishing towns sought to gain political rights corresponding to their growing wealth and social importance. Where these rights were denied them, they rebelled against their feudal lords and overlords. Where the bishops were the lords of the cities, as in Cologne, Milan, and Laon, the burghers directed their fight for liberty against them. The higher clergy, recruited as a rule from the ranks of the nobility, sided with the bishops in these quarrels, and in consequence became estranged from the people, which made a fruitful care of souls very difficult if not altogether impossible. The monasteries, situated as they were outside the towns on their own broad acres, exercised very little influence over the religious life of the townspeople. What the Church needed was preachers of the Gospel, guides of souls, who, taken from the people and living among the people, could sympathize with them and win their confidence— men who, shorn of the trappings of feudal nobility and the pomp and luxury engendered by wealth, could walk among them as living models of the Gospel which they preached.

The Church heeded the call of the new age. She did all in her power to preserve the rapidly growing burgher class from the contagion of heresy and to imbue it with the true Christian spirit. The chief instruments which she employed for this all-important task were the Mendicant Orders: the sons of St. Dominic and St. Francis. To them, in the first place, must be ascribed the marvelous period of bloom which the Church enjoyed during the thirteenth century.

2. St. Dominic and the Preaching Friars

When the Abbot of Citeaux, with a gorgeous retinue and much display of feudal magnificence, was endeavoring to convert the Albigenses by his preaching, he fell in with the Spanish bishop Diego of Osma and the canon Domingo de Guzman, who were returning from Rome through southern France. The Abbot complained bitterly of the fruitlessness of his preaching; the Spaniards reminded him that the Lord's disciples were sent to preach barefoot, without scrip, without staff, and set him an example which, for a time at least, he tried to follow. For two years Diego and Domingo (Dominic) preached in the towns and villages of Languedoc, confirming the Catholics in their fidelity to the Church and vanquishing the heretics in public discussions; for they were both learned men, well versed in the lore of the great Spanish universities and in the art of debate. Although they confounded the heretics, they did not succeed in converting all too many of them. Their success was greatest among the women, who had been especially easy prey of the Albigensian agitators. Many of those whom they brought back to the Church were placed in a convent at Prouille near Toulouse founded for that purpose.

When Diego was obliged to return to his diocese, Dominic remained at his post. A few zealous priests joined him and shared his arduous and oftentimes perilous labors. When they were not engaged in preaching, they lived together like monks in a house in Toulouse. Being a canon himself, it was but natural that

Dominic should adopt the Rule of St. Augustine for the community which had almost accidentally grown up around him. He borrowed many of the statutes from the Premonstratensians, and St. Francis supplied him with the idea of absolute poverty. The new Order was approved by Pope Honorius III in 1216. Because their chief purpose was to preach the Gospel, the members were called *Fratres Praedicatores*, Preaching Brothers, or Friars (abbr. O.P., i.e., Ordo Praedicatorum). At first they wore the dress of the Regular Canons— a black cassock and rochet—; but Dominic changed this later to a white habit and scapular, with a long black cappa or mantle. Hence they came to be known in England as Black Friars.

When Dominic saw that a war-torn country like Languedoc offered no field for fruitful labor, he sent his Friars, in groups of two and three, into the towns and cities of the neighboring countries. Those who did not already possess the

St. Dominic

necessary philosophical and theological training were told to proceed first to Paris, which was at that time the seat of the most famous university in Christendom. They came as humble and docile pupils, but before many years had passed, the poor preaching Friars furnished the university with its most brilliant professors.

The little we know about St. Dominic's life shows him as a man of boundless love and compassion. When a student, he sold his books in a season of famine to give to the poor; he once offered to sell himself to redeem a captive, and his "frequent and special prayer" to God was for the gift of true charity.

At St. Dominic's death in 1221, his Order already numbered sixty convents, distributed into eight provinces, each under a provincial. Under subsequent Masters-General it spread far and wide, and the white robe of the Dominicans became a familiar object in Poland, where the Order was introduced by St. Hyacinth, in Denmark, Greece, and the Holy Land.

The Second Order of St. Dominic, which grew out of the convent for women which the Saint had founded in Prouille, was one of the strictest in the Church. Besides the perpetual abstinence from meat and other austerities which they practiced in common with the brothers of the First Order, the nuns were bound to strict cloister and to long hours of prayer. They were intended to be contemplatives, but later undertook the education of girls. Many canonized saints belonged to this Order, among them the far-famed St. Agnes of Montepulciano.

The Third Order of St. Dominic developed out of the institution of the "Soldiery of Christ," which St. Dominic founded in his lifetime for men and women living in the world, but anxious to assist in the combating of heresy and in defending the rights and property of the Church. St. Catherine of Siena and St. Rose of Lima belonged to this Order.

3. St. Francis of Assisi and the Order of Friars Minor

Francis of Assisi was a different type from the stately and learned Spanish hidalgo and Canon of Osma. Of all men who have borne the Christian name, none resembled Christ Himself so much as the *Poverello*, the "dear poor man" of Assisi, and of all the saints whom the Church has canonized, none has been so unanimously canonized by all succeeding generations.

Francis was the son of Bernardone, a rich merchant of Assisi in Umbria. He was baptized John, but he was later called Francesco, "the Frenchman," because he spoke French fluently, having learned it from his mother, who was a native of Provence. The gay and impetuous boy showed no inclination to follow his father's trade; he loved merry feasts, but scorned all that was low and common; he was fired with enthusiasm for poetry and adventure by the wandering minstrels who sang of Charlemagne and his paladins. As a lad of sixteen he took part in the uprising against Conrad of Suabia, who held the castle of Assisi. He marched out with his townsmen against the Perugians, was wounded and taken prisoner. A lingering illness gave a more serious turn to his thoughts. At twenty-two he underwent the great spiritual crisis which he calls his "conversion." He began to give much time to prayer and other religious exercises. Once, as he was praying in the ruins of the little church of St. Damian, he heard a voice: "Francis, go and build up my house again!" He took the words literally, and in order to carry them out sold his horse, his best garments, and even some bales of cloth from his father's storeroom. Disowned by his father for squandering his goods on the poor, Francis broke entirely with the world, stripped himself of the clothes he wore in the presence of his father and the bishop of Assisi, and was wedded to his "bride" Poverty: henceforth he would have none of the goods, honors, or privileges of this world (1206). To test his spirit of renouncement, he attended on the lepers, of whom there were many in his native town, and brought himself to wash their sores and to eat out of their dishes.

Francis lived for several years in a cottage near Assisi, in the practice of almost continual prayer accompanied by severe bodily discipline. When he went out it was to collect alms for the restoration of several ruined churches. In a little church dedicated to Our Lady of the Angels he heard a priest preach on the words of Christ: "Take nothing for your journey, neither staff, nor scrip, nor bread, nor money, neither have two coats" (Luke 9, 3). "That is what I want," said Francis, and laid aside his staff and his shoes, and instead of a girdle tied a leather thong about his loins. Then he went forth to preach to the poor in their squalid huts and in the narrow, filthy alleys and courts, where poverty and disease were constant companions. "Assisi, Umbria, Italy, were stirred as though never before had Christ been announced to them. Umbria became the Italian Galilee; Francis the beneficent shadow of the Son of Man."

In 1209 Bernard of Quintavalle, a wealthy tradesman of Assisi, and Peter of Catana, a canon of the cathedral, openly threw in their lot with Francis. This is regarded as the date of the foundation of the Franciscan Order; for three make a community. A fourth member soon appeared in Giles of Assisi, who was afterwards beatified. His rule, the founder said to his disciples, was the life of Christ. He exhorted them to manual labor, but would have them content to receive for it things necessary for life, not money. He bade them not to be ashamed to beg alms, remembering the poverty of Christ; and he forbade them to preach in any city without the bishop's leave. *Fratres Minores*, Friars Minor (abbr. O.F.M., Ordo Fratrum Minorum), was the name by which they were to be known, for their apostolate was to be by preference among the *minores*, the lesser people, as the lower classes were called in those days. The habit which he gave them was a grey gown of coarse cloth with a pointed hood or capuche attached to it, and a knotted cord round the waist—a costume which closely resembled that worn by the poor shepherds in the Umbrian hills.

The cottage in Assisi was soon found too small to harbor the growing community. The Benedictines of the Monastery of Subasio offered Francis a little plot of ground near Assisi called *Portiuncula*, on which stood the Church of Our Lady of the Angels. Francis would not accept the land as an absolute gift, but agreed to hold it as "a tenant-at-will by the tenure of rendering yearly to the Benedictines a basket of little fish caught in the stream that flowed hard by." The Portiuncula became the cradle of the Order from which so many blessings were to go forth to all the world.

Francis was ordained deacon, which gave him the right to preach; but he never would consent to become a priest, thinking himself unworthy of such an honor. "He remained entirely a stranger," says Canon Barry, "to the learning, classic or theological, of his time; with Canon Law he was unacquainted; but his reverence for the clergy, his devotion to the Holy Eucharist, saved him from the perilous conflicts in which Waldo and the Paterines had gone down."

In 1210 Francis went to Rome with a few companions to obtain the confirmation of his institute. The cardinals demurred; the Pope hesitated; the aims of the new Order were considered too lofty, too impossible of attainment. But who could resist the sweetness and joy that lighted up the countenance of the humble pleader? It is perhaps Innocent's highest title to fame that he seized the outstretched hand of the Poverello with joy and gave him and his bride, Holy Poverty, the rights of citizenship in the Church.

One night, so the story went, Pope Innocent dreamt that the Lateran basilica, the head and mother of all churches, was tottering to its fall.

Terror seized the dreamer. Then the scene changed. A poor, despised
man approached, set his back against the wall, and propped it up. On the
following day Innocent saw the man of his dream standing before him.
It was Francis, who had come to seek approbation for his brotherhood.

Innocent III gave only a verbal approbation to the rule which Francis
had drawn up. Some years later Francis composed a more detailed rule
containing twenty-seven precepts. This second rule, as it was called, was
revised and supplemented under the guidance of Cardinal Ugolino, afterwards Gregory IX, and solemnly ratified by Honorius III in 1223.

Giotto

ST. FRANCIS OF ASSISI BEFORE POPE HONORIUS III

The story of the founding of the Second Order of St. Francis
known as the Poor Ladies, or *Poor Clares*, is full of high romance. St. Clare belonged to the noble family of the Sciffi,
whose mansion stood in Assisi. When very young she heard of
the seraphic life led by her townsman Francis in his little convent
of the Portiuncula, and aspired to imitate it. Her parents sternly

opposed her plan, so "she fled from her home under cover of
night, hurried out of the slumbering old town and down by the
silent woods below it to the wayside chapel of the Portiuncula
in the plain. St. Francis and his companions, who had been
keeping vigil there, advanced with lighted torches to meet her,
and St. Francis, having cut off her hair before the little altar of
Our Lady of the Angels, clothed her with the coarse grey-colored
habit and knotted cord which had been adopted by his Friars. All
this took place shortly after midnight on Palm Sunday, which, in
the year 1212, fell on the 18th of March; and it is from that date
the Poor Clares reckon the foundation of their Order" (Paschal
Robinson, O.S.F., *The Rule of St. Clare*, p. 9). The Benedictine
monks gave the venerable sanctuary of St. Damian to St. Francis
as a suitable retreat for St. Clare and the women who were
already gathering around her. The rule which St. Francis prescribed for them was one of great austerity. They fasted much,
slept on boards, wore a coarse habit, and, like the Friars, possessed no landed property. Within a few years the Order had
spread into France, Spain, Bohemia, and Germany.

Long before the rule of St. Francis had been approved, the
Friars Minor had made their way into the principal European
centers of population, preaching penance and founding convents.
"Let your behavior in the world," Francis said to them as he
sent them on their way, "be such that everyone who sees or hears
of you may praise the heavenly Father. Preach peace to all; but
have it in your hearts still more than on your lips. Give no
occasion of anger or scandal to any, but by your gentleness lead
all men to goodness, peace, and union. We are called to heal the
wounded and to recall the erring. For there are many who appear
to you limbs of the devil, who will be one day the disciples of
Jesus Christ."

In 1219 Francis made a pilgrimage to Jerusalem and established
a little community of his Order at the Holy Sepulcher. From
the Holy Land he went to Egypt, where the Crusaders were besieging the fortress of Damiette on the Nile. He also fed on
visions of chivalry, but as a true knight of the Cross his call was
not to battle, but to the imitation of Christ. In his zeal for souls
he advanced fearlessly into the camp of the Moslems and in glowing words conjured the Soldan to forsake Mohammed and embrace the religion of Christ. The Soldan was not converted, but

he treated Francis kindly and made over to him the guardianship of the Holy Sepulcher in Jerusalem, which the Franciscans have retained to this day.

Towards the end of his life Francis voluntarily resigned the headship of his Order, which already numbered over five thousand Friars, so that he might have more time to devote to prayer and works of penance. His favorite place of retreat was Mount Alverna. On the feast of the Exaltation of the Cross, September 14, 1224, as he was contemplating the passion and death of Christ, he saw a seraph flying towards him. There was the figure of a man attached to a cross between the wings. After the vision disappeared, the hands and feet of the Saint were found to be marked with nails, and there was a wound in his side. He had received the sacred *stigmata,* the impress of the nails and the lance as a testimony to his oneness of spirit with Christ. Two years later, on the 4th of October, 1226, he died at Assisi amid scenes of touching simplicity, poor and bare like his Divine Master. He was canonized in 1228 by Pope Gregory IX.

4. A Franciscan Saint in the World: St. Elizabeth of Hungary

Wherever St. Francis and his Friars preached, the hearts of their hearers turned with renewed love to God. Not all who were seized with the ardent longing to serve God more perfectly could put on the habit of the Franciscans or the Poor Clares. For these chosen souls, who lived in the world, but did not want to be of the world, St. Francis instituted, in 1221, a Third Order, as a sort of middle term between the world and the cloister. The members were bound by vow and rule "to dress more soberly, fast more strictly, pray more regularly, and practice works of mercy more systematically than ordinary persons living in the world." Francis called them the "Brothers and Sisters of Penance," but they are better known as Tertiaries, or members of the Third Order of St. Francis. Among the tertiaries of the 13th century two stand out most prominently: St. Louis of France and St. Elizabeth of Hungary. The charming, brave, just, tender Louis, who wore the cord and rough habit of St. Francis under his royal robes, the last and best of the crusaders, belongs to general history, where his deeds and virtues are recorded; but we must pause a moment to contemplate the no less charming picture of "dear St. Elizabeth."

Elizabeth was the daughter of Andrew II of Hungary and his first wife, the Bavarian duchess Gertrude of Andechs-Meran. At four years of age she was betrothed to Louis, Landgrave of Thuringia, and conducted to the Wartburg, near Eisenach, to be educated with her future husband. The Wartburg was at this time the seat of a boisterous court to which minstrels and wandering folk of all description streamed night and day. It was here that in 1207, four years before it became the home of Elizabeth, took place the minstrels' contest (*Sängerkrieg*) immortalized in Wagner's *Tannhäuser*. In spite of these worldly surroundings, Elizabeth evinced from her earliest years a decided aversion for all frivolous amusements and pleasures, and, stimulated by the wise counsels of the Landgravine Sophie and the example of her mother's sister, St. Hedwig of Silesia, she devoted all her free time to prayer and works of charity. The tragic death of her mother, who was murdered by a rebellious band of Hungarian nobles in 1213, turned her thoughts still more from worldly pomp and ambition.

She was married to Louis at the age of fourteen, and acquired such an influence over him that he zealously assisted her in all her works of charity. Her love for him was true and tender. When he was away fighting for the Emperor in Lombardy or Sicily, she laid aside all her finery and dressed in mourning garments; when he returned, her heart was filled, says the chronicler, with "unutterable joy." They had built a hospital at the foot of the Wartburg, and here, during the epidemic and famine that swept over central Europe in 1226, Elizabeth cared for the sick-poor with her own hands. She devoted her whole income to the relief of the poor and suffering, and when that proved too small, she sold all the jewels and valuables which she had inherited from her mother.

After the death of her husband, who had joined the crusade of Frederick II in 1227, Elizabeth left the Wartburg with her three infant children, because under Henry Raspe, the new Landgrave, she could not continue her life of prayer, penance, and charity. For a time she lived in great hardship in a delapidated stable. When the crusaders returned with the body of Louis, they forced Henry to reinstate Elizabeth in her rights as regent for her oldest son. But she preferred to live in seclusion at Marburg. Here she became a member of the Third Order of St. Francis and, under the direction of the priest Conrad of Marburg, she spent the remainder of her days in penances of unusual severity, and in daily ministrations to the sick, especially those afflicted with the most loathsome diseases. She died in the poor hut which had been her home, November 17, 1231, only twenty-four years of age.

Four years after her death Elizabeth was canonized by Gregory IX. In the following year, in the presence of the Emperor Frederick II, her body was disinterred and laid in a costly shrine; Frederick himself placed a golden crown on her head. Over this shrine the Grand Master of the Teutonic Knights erected the church of St. Elizabeth, a veritable gem of the purest Early Gothic style. Her remains were visited by millions of pilgrims until the Protestant Landgrave Philip of Hesse—he to whom Luther permitted two wives—desecrated her shrine and removed her relics. Some of these relics are at present preserved in the convent chapel of the Elizabethine Sisters in Vienna.

No saint in the calendar of the Church has been so deeply enshrined in the affections of the German people as St. Elizabeth, the docile pupil of St. Francis.

The Canticle of the Sun

St. Francis looked upon all creatures with the eyes of God and loved them with the heart of God. He lived in the finest intimacy with nature. The birds of the air flew confidently to him, and the wild beasts approached him without fear. The sun became his sister and the wind his brother. His world-wide love inspired him to write a song of praise to God, which is one of the oldest specimens of Italian poetry: the *Canticle of the Sun*. It is said that he dictated the last verses as he lay on the bare ground waiting for "his Sister Death" to summon him. The following is a literal translation of the famous canticle:

"Most high, omnipotent, good Lord,
  Praise, glory and honor and benediction all, are Thine.
  To Thee alone do they belong, Most High,
  And there is no man fit to mention Thee.
  Praise be to Thee, my Lord, with all Thy creatures,
  Especially to my worshipful Brother Sun,
  The which lights up the day, and through him dost
      Thou brightness give;
  And beautiful is he and radiant with splendor great;
  Of Thee, Most High, signification gives.
  Praised be my Lord, for Sister Moon and for the Stars,
  In heaven Thou hast formed them clear and precious and fair.
  Praised be my Lord for Brother Wind
  And for the air and clouds and fair and every kind of weather,
  By the which Thou givest to Thy creatures nourishment.
  Praised be my Lord for Sister Water.

The which is greatly helpful and humble and precious and pure.
Praised be my Lord for Brother Fire,
By the which Thou lightest up the dark.
And fair is he and gay and mighty and strong.
Praised be my Lord for our Sister, Mother Earth,
The which sustains and keeps us
And brings forth diverse fruits with grass and flowers bright.
Praised be my Lord for those who for Thy love forgive
And weakness bear and tribulation.
Blessed those who shall in peace endure,
For by Thee, Most High, shall they be crowned.
Praised be my Lord for our Sister, the bodily Death,
From the which no living man can flee.
Woe to them who die in mortal sin;
Blessed those who shall find themselves in Thy most holy will,
For the second death shall do them no ill.
Praise ye and bless ye my Lord, and give Him thanks.
And be subject unto Him with great humility.

Amen."

—From *The Ideals of St. Francis of Assisi*, by
Hilarin Felder, O.M.Cap., trans. by Berchmans Bittle, O.M.Cap.

Hints for Study

1. There should be one or more lives of St. Francis and St. Dominic in every High School library. There are excellent lives of St. Francis by Jörgensen, Cuthbert, Felder, Chesterton, and Egan; and of St. Dominic by Jarrett, Drane, and Guiraud.

2. If you want to know what the greatest Christian poet, Dante, thought of St. Francis and St. Dominic, read Dante's *Paradiso*, Canto XI. One of the most delightful books ever written about any Saint is the *Fioretti*, or Little Flowers of St. Francis of Assisi, of which there is a first-class English translation by Lady Georgiana Fullerton, edited by Cardinal Manning.

3. Dante says of St. Francis and St. Dominic: "The one was all seraphic in his ardor, the other by his wisdom was on earth a splendor of cherubic light." Comment on these words.

4. Are the Dominicans and Franciscans still doing the work they did during the Middle Ages? Are the Tertiaries still in existence?

5. In Thatcher and McNeal, *Europe in the Middle Ages*, p. 243, we read the following sentence: "One of the main principles on which the Franciscan Order was founded was the *sinfulness* of property." Criticize this statement.

CHAPTER VI

SCHOLASTICISM AND MYSTICISM

1. *Rise of the Medieval Universities*

The twelfth and thirteenth centuries, remarkable for their holy wars, their social and economic upheavals, their gigantic struggles for power, their armies of monks and nuns, their saints in the world and in the cloister, were also rendered forever memorable by their unbounded intellectual activity.

In the Early Middle Ages the work of education was carried on by the monastery and cathedral schools. In the course of the twelfth century the monastic schools were outstripped by the cathedral schools, in which not only the seven liberal arts, inherited from the Roman days, were taught, but also such new subjects as philosophy, astronomy, civil and canon law, and medicine. Students in ever increasing numbers flocked to those places where exceptional opportunities for instruction in the various branches of learning were offered. A common faith and a common language— Latin—made them feel at home wherever they went.

Three cities were especially renowned for their schools: Salerno for Medicine, Bologna for Law, and Paris for Philosophy and Theology. The school of Salerno was already in existence in the tenth century, but it was under Robert Guiscard and his secretary, the celebrated physician Constantine the African, that it attained the reputation which it enjoyed throughout the Middle Ages of being the leading School of Medicine in Europe. Bologna owed its fame to the jurist Irnerius and the monk Gratian. Irnerius, at the instance of the Countess Matilda of Tuscany, revived the study of Roman Law; Gratian reduced Ecclesiastical (Canon) Law to a system and thus facilitated its study. Paris had three famous schools: Notre Dame, St. Genevieve, and St. Victor.

The schools of these three cities received special favors and privileges both from the Church and the secular authorities. Salerno received a grant of privileges from Robert Guiscard and his son Roger, both of whom showed themselves liberal patrons of learning. In 1168 Frederick Barbarossa, by a special edict, guaranteed security of travel and residence for scholars and students, and in any legal proceedings against a scholar the defendant could not be haled before a civil magistrate, but was given the privilege of choosing whether he would be tried before his own professors or before the bishop of the city; "for we think it fitting," the document says, "that those should enjoy our peace and protection, by whose learning the world is enlightened to the obedience of God and of us, His ministers, and the life of the subject is molded; and by a special consideration we defend them from all injuries." The same privileges were conferred in 1200 on the students of Paris by King Philip Augustus.

Before the close of the twelfth century the students of Salerno and Bologna, in order to acquire legal recognition, formed themselves into corporations (*universitates*) modeled after the guilds of the workmen. In Paris it was the masters who organized themselves into a corporation and thus managed to retain all power in their own hands. Bologna became the pattern of most of the Spanish and Italian universities; Paris for the German universities and Oxford and Cambridge in England. It was not until about the year 1230 that all the branches of learning were taught at one and the same university. When completely equipped, a university was called a *Studium Generale,* comprising four faculties: *Theology,* including Philosophy and all the ecclesiastical sciences with the exception of Canon Law; *Law,* both Civil and Canon; *Medicine,* which was called Physics; and *Arts,* that is, Latin Grammar, Rhetoric, Logic (the *trivium*), Arithmetic, Geometry, Astronomy, and Music (the *quadrivium*).

Rising into prominence in the twelfth century through such teachers   William of Champeaux, Peter Abelard, and Hugh of St. Victor, Paris in time became the greatest university of the Middle Ages. Everyone, no matter to what country he belonged, regarded his education as incomplete unless he had spent at least some years in Paris, followed the lectures of its professors, and obtained a master's or doctor's degree. It is a rather curious phenomenon, that during the latter half of the twelfth century and all of the thirteenth, when Paris boasted of being the Capital of Intelligence, its most renowned professors were not native Frenchmen, but men from other countries: the Lombard Peter, the

Englishman Alexander of Hales, the Germans Hugh of St. Victor and Albertus Magnus, the Italians Bonaventure and Thomas Aquinas, the Irishman John Duns Scotus, and the Scotchman Richard of St. Victor.

Protected by the State and liberally endowed by the Church, under whose jurisdiction they were all placed, the medieval universities enjoyed a prosperity nothing short of marvelous. From the twelfth to the sixteenth century thirteen universities were founded in France, seventeen in Italy, five in Great Britain, seventeen in Germany, ten in Spain and Portugal, and several in the other countries of Europe. Thousands of students frequented these seats of learning. At one time Paris had nearly as many students as inhabitants; ten thousand were constantly in attendance at Bologna, and according to some authorities Oxford counted even more.

2. Scholasticism and Mysticism

During the Early Middle Ages the theologians of the Church had been content to assimilate the teachings of the Fathers and to communicate them without comment to their hearers. Few attempted to study the truths of faith with the aid of their own reasoning powers; those who did so, fell into error. Beginning with the dawn of the twelfth century a great change took place. Questions of philosophy and theology occupied the leading minds in every land. New ways were sought by which to penetrate more deeply into the truths of revelation; instead of repeating over and over again the opinions handed down from antiquity, determined efforts were made to throw light on the doctrines of the Church with the aid of Greek philosophy, especially that of Aristotle, whose works were gradually becoming known in Europe through translations from the Arabian. This new theology, which used philosophy and the conclusions of the natural sciences insofar as they were known at that time, as its handmaids, is called *Scholasticism,* that is, "Science of the Schools" (Lat. *schola,* school), because it had developed out of the instructions given in the Cathedral and Monastic Schools. Scholasticism did not attempt to add anything to Divine Revelation or to teach new doctrines, but only to furnish a rational basis for Christianity by showing the harmony which exists between faith and reason, and also to reduce the doctrines contained in Scripture and Tradition to an orderly and definite system. This is called the Scholastic Synthesis.

St. Anselm of Aosta in Lombardy, who died as archbishop of Canterbury in 1109, is regarded as the "Father of Scholasticism," because he was the first who systematically studied the truths of faith in the light of reason alone, and in the same light defended them against heretics.

"St. Anselm expressed the relation of philosophy to theology in the formulas, *Credo ut intelligam* ('I believe that I may understand, i.e., I do not seek to understand things in order to justify my faith; on the contrary, I find my faith a light without which I cannot acquire full science of other things') and *Fides quaerens intellectum* ('Faith seeking to understand'). In his book *Cur Deus Homo*? (Why a God-Man?) he seeks to prove from reason alone that the Redemption and all facts incidental to it had necessarily to occur just as Revelation shows that they did occur" (Paul J. Glenn, *History of Philosophy*, p. 194).

Peter, called the *Lombard* after his native country, contributed more than any other theologian of the twelfth century towards the development of Scholasticism. He studied in Paris under Hugh of St. Victor, taught theology at the Cathedral School, and died as bishop of Paris in 1160. In his four *Books of Sentences* he collected and discussed the opinions (*sententiae*) of the Fathers and the earlier theologians on all questions pertaining to Revelation. From this book he received the title by which he has been known ever since, "The Master of Sentences." It became immediately the handbook of theologians and the text of every professor. One hundred and sixty commentaries were written on it in subsequent years.

Mysticism.—The immense vogue which philosophical studies enjoyed during the twelfth century was fraught with elements of danger. The intellect was worshiped by many at the expense of the will, reason at the expense of faith. St. Bernard raised his voice in warning. "Of what use is philosophy to me?" he cried. "My teachers are the Apostles. They have not taught me to read Plato and to understand Aristotle. But they have taught me how to live. Do you think that to know how to live is a small matter? It is the most important of all." St. Bernard did not condemn Scholasticism, but he knew from experience that there was another and higher way to arrive at a deeper understanding of the truths of faith; namely, to train the soul by a holy life to seek and to achieve intimate union with God, and in the light of grace, which is given only to the clean of heart, to *see,* as it were, with the eyes of the soul, in God the truths revealed by God. In other words,

St. Bernard preferred *Mysticism* to Scholasticism. His favorite
theologians were not the professors of Notre Dame or St.
Genevieve, but the Mystics Hugh and Richard, who taught in the
Abbey School of St. Victor. Some Mystics, such as Walter of
St. Victor, went too far in their opposition to the philosophers,
denouncing them as heretics and their dialectics as the "devil's
own art."

Scholasticism and Mysticism are not opposed to each other.
They should go hand in hand. If theology is treated merely as an
affair of the intellect and the reason, it is devoid of all living and
life-giving warmth; if it lacks clear and precise notions, if there
is no method in its treatment, no logical classification, definition,
division, it will end in sentimentalism and heresy. Hence we find
that the leading theologians of the thirteenth century, a Saint
Albertus Magnus, a St. Bonaventure, and a St. Thomas, were at
once Scholastics and Mystics.

The Mystics of Helfta.—The German mind seems to have been
an especially fruitful soil for mysticism. A number of women
appear about this time, combining a spirit of mystical piety and
asceticism with a sturdy zeal for reforming the abuses of the
age. Three stand out prominently, all of them nuns in the Cistercian Convent at Helfta near Eisleben in Saxony: St. Mechtild of
Magdeburg (d. 1285), St. Mechtild of Hackeborn (d. 1310), and
her elder sister, St. Gertrude, surnamed the Great (d. 1302).
St. Gertrude's famous book, "The Herald of Divine Love," has
retained its popularity to the present day and has been translated
into many languages. Like St. Bernard, St. Gertrude had a special
devotion to the Humanity of our Lord. Like St. Francis, she saw
in all creatures the reflection of the Creator. She constantly felt
the nearness of God. She was one of the earliest propagators of
devotion to the Sacred Heart and the Blessed Sacrament.

In the country of St. Francis we meet with the celebrated mystic St.
Angela of Foligno (d. 1309). After living a worldly and sinful life for
many years, she joined the Third Order of St. Francis and edified all who
knew her by her humility and her spirit of penance. Her *Divine Consolations* was one of the favorite devotional books of the later Middle Ages.

3. *The Great Scholastics*

The credit of having made Paris the seat of a truly "classic"
system of philosophy and theology belongs to the Mendicant

Orders, to the Dominicans and Franciscans. The task which these Orders had set themselves, to preach the truths of faith to all classes of the people and to defend them against heretics, Jews and infidels, imposed upon them the duty of acquainting themselves thoroughly with the teachings of the Church; hence we find them in Padua, in Naples, in Bologna, but especially at the University of Paris, where they outstripped all their fellow-students in their devotion to study. When the first Dominican, Roland of Cremona, mounted the professor's chair in 1229, followed by the first Franciscan, Alexander of Hales, in 1231, the golden age of Scholasticism began. We cannot pass all the great leaders of the movement in review; a glance at the prince of them all, St. Thomas Aquinas, and his teacher, St. Albertus Magnus, must suffice.

Albertus Magnus.—Albert belonged to the family of the Counts of Bollstädt in Suabia. He was born at Lauingen before the close of the twelfth century. From his earliest years he evinced a love for study combined with a tender devotion to the Mother of God, the "Seat of Wisdom." At the University of Padua he became acquainted with the Dominican Order, which he joined in 1223. After obtaining his doctor's degree he taught in various cities of Germany and at Paris. At Paris one of his pupils was Thomas of Aquino, and a friendship sprang up between master and pupil which is unique in the annals of learning. In 1248 Albert became the first Lector in philosophy and theology at the Dominican general house of studies in Cologne. His fame as an interpreter of Aristotle, as a theologian and a scientist drew students from the most distant countries to Cologne. He was made bishop of Ratisbon in 1260, but resigned his see after three years. The remainder of his life he spent in preaching throughout Bavaria, and in teaching and writing at Cologne. In 1270 he preached the eighth Crusade in Austria. When the doctrines of his recently deceased pupil and friend, Thomas Aquinas, were fiercely assailed at the University of Paris, Albert did not hesitate, though nearly eighty years of age, to set out on foot from Cologne to Paris in order to defend him. He died at Cologne, November 15, 1280. He was beatified in 1622, and canonized and proclaimed a Doctor of the Church by Pope Pius XI in 1932. His feast occurs on November 14.

Albert was the most widely read and most learned man of his time. His works form a veritable library, covering the field of philosophy, theology, Scripture, and the natural sciences. His knowledge of physical science was extensive and for the age accurate. On account of the number and variety of his works and the vast erudition which they display, his contemporaries gave him the honorable surnames "Doctor Universalis" and "The Great," a distinction which no other man of learning enjoys. Dante places him with his pupil St. Thomas among the *Spiriti Sapienti* (the great lovers of wisdom) in the Heaven of the Sun (*Paradiso*, Canto X, 97-99).

St. Thomas Aquinas.—Thomas, born at Rocca Sicca, near Naples, in 1224 or 1225, was the son of Count Landulf of Aquino, a nephew of the Emperor Frederick Barbarossa. He received his elementary training at Monte Cassino and studied the liberal arts at Naples under Petrus Hibernus (Peter the Irishman). After the death of his father in 1244 he entered the Dominican Order. His brothers resented this action, and when Thomas was on his way to Paris to finish his studies, they kidnaped him and held him prisoner for a year in the parental castle at St. Giovanni. Regaining his liberty with the help of his sisters, Thomas continued his journey to Paris, where for three years he sat at the feet of Albert the Great. When Albert was sent to Cologne in 1248, Thomas followed him and spent four years more under his guidance. Ordained priest, Thomas taught with distinction at Paris, Rome, and Naples. Wherever he taught, crowds of students flocked to hear him. One of his early biographers has given us the secret of his success. "When Thomas had taken up his work as teacher," says Peter Calo, "and had begun the disputations and lectures, such a multitude of pupils flocked to his school, that the lecture room could hardly contain all who were attracted by the word of so renowned a master and inspired by him to progress in the pursuit of learning. Under the light of his teaching, many masters flourished, both of the Dominicans and of the secular clergy. The reason for this was the *synthetic, clear, and intelligible method of his lectures.*"

From 1261 to 1264 Thomas was at the Papal Court of Urban IV. During this time he composed the Mass and Office for the feast of Corpus Christi, which had just been instituted, and the wonderful Eucharistic hymns: *Lauda Sion, Pange Lingua, Verbum Supernum, Sacris Solemniis,* and *Adoro Te.* Clement IV offered him the archiepiscopal chair of Naples, but by dint of prayers and tears he escaped a dignity which was so repugnant to his humility and his retired manner of life. After a second sojourn in Paris, where we see him at the height of his scientific achievement (1269-1272), he returned to Naples to organize the theological curriculum of the Roman Province of his Order. In 1274 Gregory X summoned him to attend the General Council of Lyons. He took sick on the way and stopped for rest at the Cistercian Monastery of Fossanuova, and there he died, March 7, 1274. Before he received the Holy Viaticum he made the following declaration: "I receive Thee, redeeming Price of my soul. Out of love for Thee have I studied, watched through many nights, and exerted myself; Thee did I teach and preach. I never said aught against Thee. Nor do I persist stubbornly in my views. If I have ever expressed myself erroneously on this Sacrament, I submit to the judgment of the holy Roman Church, in the obedience to which I now part from this world."

Reginald of Piperno, his inseparable friend and companion, and his confessor in his last illness, testified that at the time of his death Thomas was as pure and innocent as a child of five years.

Thomas was canonized in 1323, on the fiftieth anniversary of his death. Pope Leo XIII declared him the patron Saint of all Catholic schools and scholars.

St. Thomas bears the honorable title of *Doctor Angelicus,* the "Angelic Doctor," as a tribute not only to the purity and sanctity of his life, but also to his all but superhuman insight into the profoundest truths of our holy faith. He himself tells us that he owed more to prayer, to devotion to the Holy Eucharist, and to loving contemplation of the Crucified Savior than to all his studies. His monumental work, the *Summa Theologica,* a summary of the whole of philosophy and theology, has been compared to the Pyramids, because of its majestic simplicity, and to a Medieval Gothic Cathedral, because of its wealth of material, its enormous scope, its wonderful construction, and its "concentration in one marvelous synthesis of all the fruits of theology and philosophy." St. Thomas is the Church's greatest theologian, but, above all, her chosen exponent and guardian of the doctrine of her central mystery, the Blessed Eucharist, about which he wrote so beautifully that Christ Himself, unable to contain His love for him, broke out from the silent crucifix: "Well hast thou written of Me, Thomas. What reward do you ask?" But he replied: "Thyself, O Lord:

> Ut te revelata cernens facie,
> Visu sim beatus tuae gloriae."

An Article from the Summa Theologica of St. Thomas

The *Summa* of St. Thomas consists of three parts; the second part is again subdivided into two parts. Each part contains a number of questions, and each question a number of articles. The heading of each article indicates in the form of an indirect question the matter to be treated, e.g., *Utrum confirmatio sit sacramentum*—Whether Confirmation is a sacrament. Every problem is handled in the same way: the opposing views are first given; then follows a counter statement, which is proved in the *corpus articuli,* the main body of the article, and finally the rejected views are criticized. In some of his works St. Thomas abandons this technic and presents his views and arguments with complete freedom of expression. The following translation of an article of the *Summa* will serve as an illustration of the "scholastic technic." It has been chosen because of its brevity.

BENE SCRIPSISTI
DE ME THOMA

St. Thomas Aquinas Lays His Writings before the Feet
of the Church

Whether God Has Free-Will?

We proceed thus to the Tenth Article:

Objection 1. It seems that God has not free-will. For Jerome says: "God alone is He who is not liable to sin, nor can be liable: all others, as having free-will, can be inclined to either side."

Obj. 2. Further, free-will is the faculty of the reason and will, by which good and evil are chosen. But God does not will evil. Therefore there is not free-will in God.

On the contrary, Ambrose says: "The Holy Spirit divideth unto each one as He will, namely, according to the free choice of the will, not in obedience to necessity."

I answer that, We have free-will with respect to what we will not of necessity, nor by natural instinct. For our will to be happy does not pertain to free-will, but to natural instinct. Hence other animals, that are moved to act by natural instinct, are not said to be moved by free-will. Since then God necessarily wills His own goodness, but other things not necessarily, He has free-will with respect to what He does not necessarily will.

Reply to Obj. 1. Jerome seems to deny free-will to God not simply, but only as regards the inclination to sin.

Reply to Obj. 2. Since the evil of sin consists in turning away from the divine goodness, by which God wills all things, it is manifestly impossible for Him to will the evil of sin; yet He can make choice of one of two opposites, inasmuch as He can will a thing to be, or not to be. In the same way we ourselves, without sin, can will to sit down, or not will to sit down.

—*S. Th. I, Q. 19., A. 10* (Summa Theologica, Part I, Question 19, Article 10). From the English translation of the *Summa* by the Fathers of the English Dominican Province.

Hints for Study

1. Cardinal Newman has some interesting chapters on Universities and University Education in *Historical Sketches*, Vol. II.
2. Dr. Martin Grabmann, *Thomas Aquinas, His Personality and Thought*, translated by Virgil Michel, O.S.B., is an excellent introduction to St. Thomas and Scholasticism. (Longmans, 1928.)
3. The life of St. Thomas is well told by Rev. Pius Kavanaugh, O.P., *Life and Labors of St. Thomas Aquinas.* (Benziger.)
4. James J. Walsh, *The Thirteenth the Greatest of Centuries*, should be in every High School Library. (Cath. Summer School Press, N. Y.)
5. How did our modern universities originate?
6. Can you tell in a few words the difference between Scholasticism and Mysticism?
7. There are several good English editions of the works of St. Gertrude the Great, e.g., *Life and Revelations of St. Gertrude,* by the author of "St. Francis and the Franciscans."

CHAPTER VII

THE ARTS IN THE SERVICE OF RELIGION

1. *Religious Poetry*

From the earliest times psalms and hymns were sung in Christian assemblies, in imitation of Christ and His disciples, who sang a hymn at the close of the Last Supper. St. Paul tells the Ephesians not to imitate the drunken revelry of the heathen, but to express their joy in "psalms and spiritual odes." Pliny mentions the custom of the Christians of singing a hymn to Christ as God in their early morning assemblies. Besides the canticles found in the Old and New Testaments, other songs of praise were introduced at an early period, such as the *Gloria in excelsis Deo,* known as the "Great Doxology," and the *Te Deum,* the sublime unmetrical hymn ascribed to St. Ambrose.

Early Religious Poetry.—The earliest religious poem adapted to be sung and written in meter is the "Hymn to Christ the Savior" by Clement of Alexandria (2nd cent.). From that time on, there is an uninterrupted stream of religious poetry down to our own day. Some of the most celebrated Fathers and Doctors of the Church in East and West applied their genius to the composition of hymns. Hymns from the pens of St. Ambrose, St. Hilary of Poitiers, Prudentius, Sedulius, are found in every hymn-book. Towards the end of the sixth century the use of hymns in the divine service was officially sanctioned; but it was not till the thirteenth century that the Roman Church admitted hymns to a place in her Breviary, which now contains about two hundred. From the sixth to the ninth century some of the loveliest of Christian hymns were written: the *Vexilla Regis Prodeunt* ("The Royal Banners Forward Go") by Venantius Fortunatus; the famous processional hymn for Palm Sunday, *Gloria, laus, et honor tibi sit, Rex Christe Redemptor,* in hexameters and pentameters by Theodulph of Orleans; the *Veni Creator Spiritus,* styled "the most famous of hymns," by Rhabanus Maurus; and the anonymous hymns in praise of the Heavenly Jerusalem, which are remarkable for "an attractive union of melody, imagination, poetical coloring, and faith."

Medieval Sacred Poetry.—In the ninth century a new kind of hymn, called a *sequence,* because it *followed* (or continued the melody of) the Alleluia after the Gradual, was introduced by St. Notker Balbulus, a monk of St. Gall (d. 912). The sequence was also called a "prose," because it was not written in regular meter. It is said that St. Notker, who was a "man of a gentle contemplative nature, observant of all around him, and accustomed to find spiritual and poetical suggestions in common sights and sounds," was moved by the sound of a mill-wheel to compose his sequence on the Holy Ghost, "Present with us ever be the Holy Spirit's grace." The most famous of the sequences ascribed to St. Notker, the *Media in vita,* "In the midst of life we are in death," was suggested to him, so the story goes, while observing some workmen engaged in constructing a bridge over an Alpine torrent near his monastery.

The invention of "sequences" gave a fresh impulse to hymn-writing. The simply rhythmical form employed by St. Notker and his immediate successors gave place in time to a metrical one. This transition is seen in the *Veni, Sancte Spiritus,* "Holy Spirit, Lord of Light," which was known as the "Golden Sequence," and is justly regarded as one of the masterpieces of sacred Latin poetry. It was written in the twelfth century by an unknown author. To the same period belongs the warm and passionately devotional *Jesu, dulcis memoria,* "Jesu, the very thought of Thee," long ascribed to St. Bernard.

The centers of Latin hymnology in the twelfth century were Reichenau and St. Gall, in Germany, Cluny in Burgundy, and St. Victor near Paris. At Reichenau Hermann called "the lame" wrote the *Alma Redemptoris Mater,* "Mother benign of our redeeming Lord," and the *Salve Regina.* At Cluny, Peter of Morlaix wrote the remarkable poem on "Contempt of the World" in 3000 long verses, from which the popular Protestant hymn, "Jerusalem the Golden" is taken. Adam of St. Victor (d. 1194) was the most fertile and, in the estimation of many authorities, the greatest of the Latin hymnographers of the Middle Ages. But it was the thirteenth century that produced the most widely celebrated hymns of all times, which have exercised the talents of the greatest composers, and the ingenuity of innumerable translators

—the *Dies Irae,* by Thomas of Celano, the companion and biographer of St. Francis of Assisi, and the *Stabat Mater,* usually ascribed to the Franciscan Jacopone da Todi (d. 1306). Sir Walter Scott translated the *Dies Irae* and recited the *Stabat Mater* on his deathbed.—We have already referred to the Eucharistic hymns of St. Thomas Aquinas, in which the doctrine of transubstantiation is set forth with such admirable precision. All critics agree that they are "works of genius, powerful in thought, feeling, and expression."

Dante and His Divine Comedy.—The century that produced the greatest philosopher and theologian also produced the greatest Christian poet—Dante Alighieri (b. at Florence 1265, d. at Ravenna 1321). Dante's masterpiece, the *Divina Commedia,* is a fine summary of the medieval spirit. The influence of St. Thomas is so much in evidence throughout that it has been called "Aquinas in verse." In the form of a journey through the three kingdoms beyond the grave—Hell, Purgatory, and Paradise—we are introduced to the whole world of spirits; the damned, the penitents, and the blessed; monsters of iniquity and he-

Raphael

DANTE

roes and heroines of every virtue; great and good men and women of all times; poets, philosophers, Roman Caesars, and German Emperors, French and English kings, and Norman dukes; Popes, Cardinals, priests, monks, and nuns; devils and angels intermingled with the fabulous creations of Greek and Roman mythology. The poet's purpose is to show us how all human actions are judged by God. "The whole work was undertaken," he tells us himself, "not for a speculative but for a practical end—to remove those who are living in this life from the state of wretchedness, and to lead them to the state of blessedness." By writing his great poem—undoubtedly one of the most splendid in the world's literature—in the Italian tongue, Dante became the creator of the Italian written language and literature. Longfellow, who spent so many years in translating the *Divine Comedy*, pays the following tribute to the poet and his song:

> Ah! from what agonies of heart and brain,
> What exultations trampling on despair,
> What tenderness, what tears, what hate of wrong,
>
> What passionate outcry of a soul in pain,
> Uprose this poem of the earth and air,
> *This mediaeval miracle of song!*

The Religious Drama.—The liturgy of the Mass contains in itself dramatic elements. At an early period living pictures illustrating the Gospel and accompanied by singing were introduced to make the service more intelligible and attractive to the worshipers. In the tenth century *tropes,* that is several verses of texts not forming part of the regular Mass formulary, were inserted after the Introit or the Gloria and recited by the two halves of the choir. This naturally led to dialogue chanting, which was frequently accompanied by fragments of action. Out of this practice arose the so-called *Liturgical Mystery,* the earliest form of the Christian drama.

The earliest *tropes* that have come down to us belong to the tenth and eleventh centuries. They are Easter and Christmas tropes. The Easter trope will serve as an illustration. After the Introit has been sung, three priests clad in hooded mantles and carrying censers walk slowly to the Holy Sepulcher, which may be seen on one side of the sanctuary. There two priests, who take the part of the angels, are sitting vested in albs and holding palm branches in their hands. As soon as the three priests, representing the three Holy Women, approach the Sepulcher, the singing of the trope begins:

The Angels: Whom seek ye at this tomb, O Christian women?
The Holy Women: O ye inhabitants of Heaven, we seek Jesus of Nazareth, the Crucified.
The Angels: He is not here, He is risen, as He foretold. Go and proclaim the good news that He is risen from the dead. Alleluia!
All: The Lord is risen!
The Angels: Behold the place where they laid him. (The Angels remove the cloth which covered the place of the sepulcher and spread it out before the people.)

When, in the thirteenth century, the vernacular supplanted the Latin, and new scenes and characters had been invented, the drama was removed from the sanctuary to the nave of the church, where it continued to be produced until abuses crept in and caused its removal to the churchyard or to the market-place. The mystery play ceased to be liturgical, without however losing its religious character. To the mystery plays there were soon added the *Miracle-Plays*, the plots of which were taken from the lives and legends of the saints, and the *Moralities,* or moral-plays, whose object was to cultivate Christian character by representing the different virtues and vices as human beings on the stage.

2. Medieval Architecture. Romanesque and Gothic.

One of the greatest glories of the Middle Ages is their architecture.

A ROMANESQUE BENEDICTINE CHURCH, MURBACH

From the fall of the Empire of the West till the eleventh century very little building that deserved the name of architecture w a s done. There was a brief revival under Charlemagne and his immediate successors, but the confusion that followed upon the break up of his Empire put a stop to any further development. A new period of building began shortly after the year 1000. "It was as if the world, throwing off its old garments, desired to reclothe itself in the white robes of the Church. . . . The Christian nations seemed to rival one another in magnificence, in order to erect the most elegant churches. . . . All the religious buildings, cathedrals, country churches, and village chapels were rebuilt and transformed into something better." Thus wrote the Burgundian monk, Raoul Glaber, who died in 1050. He refers to the new style of architecture that had just made its appearance in northern Italy, France, Burgundy, and Germany, and is called *Romanesque.*

Romanesque is characterized by the use of round arches and very heavy, thick walls. "The walls were made thick and heavy in order to meet a change in the construction and material of the ceilings. Instead of making the ceilings flat and of wood, as hitherto, architects began to arch them and to construct them of stone.   Thus the ceiling assumed the form of the 'barrel' vaulting, which of course was known to the Romans.   The great weight of the stones and the 'thrust' (as the side, or outward, pressure is called), caused by the heavy arched ceiling, tended to make the walls spread apart.   To resist this outward pressure, or thrust, the walls were made thick and, at regular intervals, strengthened by buttresses."—For nearly two centuries the Romanesque style reigned supreme.   The tourist still meets with excellent examples of cathedral and abbey churches in this style, especially in Lombardy, central France, and western Germany.

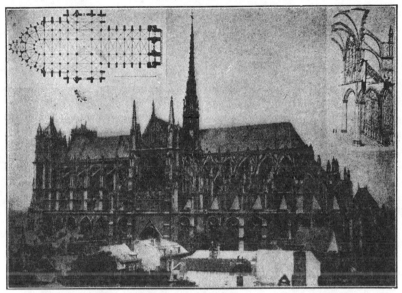

GOTHIC CATHEDRAL, AMIENS, WITH GROUND AND STRUCTURAL PLANS

In the first quarter of the twelfth century a new style was developed in Northern France, known since the fifteenth century as *Gothic*. Its main features are thinner and higher walls with larger windows topped by pointed arches instead of round ones, the substitution of the groined for the barrel vault, and the use of "flying" buttresses to concentrate the "thrust" on certain points of the wall. The great windows were filled with stained glass of most beautiful colors. Gothic spread rapidly through France and England, more slowly to Germany, where Romanesque long remained the favorite style; but, once firmly established, it held sway till the sixteenth century, when it was gradually supplanted by the art of the Renaissance.

Gothic is the most scientific and the most artistic style of architecture. It deserves to be called the "Catholic" style, because it was a creation of the ages of faith and embodied their highest aspirations. The Gothic monuments of the Middle Ages—such pictures of perfect beauty as the cathedrals of Rheims, Paris, Amiens, Chartres, Lincoln, Exeter, Westminster, Cologne and Freiburg—are at once the admiration and the despair of modern architects. To form some idea of the beauty of medieval stained glass—a beauty which has never been recaptured—"one has to sit at noon in the north transept of Notre Dame in Paris and see the sunlight stream through the great rose window of the south transept."

Hymn to Christ Our King

(By Clement of Alexandria (150-215 A.D.)

The authenticity of this hymn, formerly called in question, is now universally admitted. It consists, in the original Greek, of 65 verses, 57 of which are anapaestic monometers. The following extract will give some idea of its poetic inspiration and the depth of its symbolism:

Bridle of colts untamed,
Over our wills presiding;
Wing of unwandering birds. . .
Rudder of youth unbending,
Shepherd with wisdom tending
Lambs of the royal flock:
Thy simple children bring
In one, that they may sing
In solemn lays
Their hymns of praise
With guileless lips to Christ their
King.
King of saints, almighty Word
Of the Father, highest Lord;
Wisdom's head and chief;
Assuagement of all grief;
Lord of all time and space,
Jesus, Savior of our race;

Shepherd who dost us keep;
Husbandman who tillest,
Bit to restrain us, Rudder
To guide us as Thou willest;
Of the all-holy flock celestial wing;
Fisher of men whom Thou to life
    dost bring;
From evil sea of sin,
And from the billowy strife,
Gathering pure fishes in,
Caught with sweet bait of life:
Lead us, Shepherd of the sheep. . .
Life that never can decay,
Fount of mercy. . .
Let us sucklings join to raise
With pure lips our hymns of praise,
As our grateful offering,
Clean and pure to Christ our King.

(Tr. in The Ante-Nicene Fathers, Vol. II, pp. 295-296. Scribners, New York, 1913.)

Mary, the Mediatrix of All Graces

In the last Canto of the Divina Commedia St. Bernard supplicates the Blessed Virgin that Dante may have the crowning grace given him to contemplate the brightness of the Divine Majesty:

"Virgin Mother, daughter of Thy son, lowly and uplifted more than
    any creature, fixed goal of the eternal counsel,
Thou art she who didst human nature so ennoble that its own
    Maker scorned not to become its making.
In thy womb was lit again the love under whose warmth in the
    eternal peace this flower hath thus unfolded.
Here art thou to us the noon-day torch of love and there below
    with mortals art a living spring of hope.
Lady, thou art so great and hast such worth, that if there be who
    would have grace yet betaketh not himself to thee, his long-
    ing seeketh to fly without wings.
Thy kindliness not only succoreth whoso requesteth, but doth often-
    times freely forerun request.
In thee is tenderness, in thee is pity, in thee munificence, in thee
    united whatever in created beings is of excellence.
Now he who from the deepest pool of the universe even to here
    hath seen the spirit lives one by one,
Imploreth thee, of grace, for so much power as to be able to uplift
    his eyes more high towards final bliss;
And I, who never burned for my own vision more than I do for his,
    proffer thee all my prayers and pray they be not scant
That thou do scatter for him every cloud of his mortality with
    prayers of thine, so that the joy supreme may be unfolded
    to him.
And further do I pray thee, Queen who canst all that thou wilt,
    that thou keep sound for him, after so great a vision, his
    affections, and human passions quell."

           —Dante, *Paradiso,* Canto XXXIII, 1-37, tr. by
           Philip H. Wicksteed (The Temple Classics, 1904).

Hints for Study

1. In Britt, *Hymns of the Breviary and Missal* (Benziger), you will find
excellent translations of all the hymns used by the Church in her liturgy.
2. Slattery, *My Favorite Passage from Dante,* will serve very well as an
introduction to the great Florentine and his masterpiece. The *Temple
Classics* edition of Dante, Italian-English, should be in every High School
library.
3. On the *Mysteries, Miracle Plays,* and *Moralities* consult the articles in
the *Catholic Encyclopedia.*
4. Make a list of the most celebrated Catholic hymns written during the
Middle Ages.
5. What "Sequences" are still used by the Church? Consult your Missal.
6. Look up the articles on Romanesque and Gothic architecture in the
Catholic Encyclopedia. Mention five famous Romanesque and fifteen
famous Gothic churches built during the Middle Ages. Are there any
Romanesque or Gothic churches in your city?

The Church in the Later Middle Ages and the Renaissance. From Boniface VIII to the Protestant Revolt. A.D. 1294-1517

CHAPTER I

DESTRUCTION OF THE CHRISTIAN COMMONWEALTH OF EUROPE. PHILIP THE FAIR TRIUMPHS OVER THE PAPACY

Since the downfall of the Hohenstaufen, French influence had become predominant in Europe. The French monarchy had been the first to emerge from the swirl and confusion of Feudalism as a strong national state. By successful wars, by purchase and inheritance, the French monarchs had steadily increased their possessions and firmly established their sovereignty. Not Rome, but Paris, the home of Scholasticism and the seat of the great university, appears as the capital of the West in the thirteenth century.

With this powerful national state the Head of the Church had allied himself. Here the Popes had sought and found protection and help in their conflicts with the Empire. Charles of Anjou, a brother of St. Louis of France, had been invested with the kingdom of Sicily, which the Popes had wrested from the German emperors. Frenchmen ruled Italy. Frenchmen became cardinals and ascended the Papal Throne. Thus France had gradually supplanted Germany as the leading power in Christendom.

The close alliance between the Papacy and France was a blessing to the Church as long as the kings of France co-operated as Christian rulers with the Popes for the triumph of Christian principles and ideals. This was especially the case during the long and glorious reign of St. Louis IX (1226-1270). But this blessing was turned into a curse when kings arose whose sole ambition was to enhance the power of their country at any cost and to enslave the Church. Philip the Fair (1285-1314) was a ruler of this type —the first absolute monarch of Europe. The Papacy had triumphantly maintained its position as spiritual and temporal head of Christendom against the German emperors; in the conflict with the national French monarchy it was doomed to defeat. With the aid of the Roman Civil Law, Philip the Fair, the creator of absolutism, overthrew the medieval system, "under which no monarch could be absolute, and Rome was the ultimate Court of Appeal between the nations and their rulers."

Boniface VIII and Philip the Fair.—When Pope Nicholas IV (1288-1292) died of a broken heart on hearing the disastrous news of the fall of Acre, the last Christian stronghold in Palestine (1291), the Cardinals, after a long delay, elected the saintly hermit Peter Morone to succeed him. The new Pope, who took the name of Celestine V, saint though he was, showed himself so patently unfit to manage his high office that he voluntarily resigned after five months and returned to his sackcloth and his hermitage (1294). "From cowardice he made the great refusal," Dante says of him, and for this cowardice places him in the *Inferno*. St. Celestine was succeeded by Boniface VIII (1294-1303).

Boniface was advanced in years when he assumed the government of the Church—he was born about 1235—but still vigorous and indefatigable. He was noted as a canonist of exceptional ability and a man of wide learning. He was a patron of the fine arts, and attracted painters and sculptors from every part of Italy to his court. During his pontificate he founded the University of Rome and encouraged the painter Giotto. He planned to pacify Europe and then recover Palestine from the infidel. Unfortunately he lacked both the meekness and humility of a saint and the self-control of a statesman. His violent temper and his inconsiderate political measures created numerous enemies for him at Rome and abroad. He found himself almost at once in conflict with the two most powerful kings of the time—Edward I of England and Philip the Fair of France. The question at issue was the *taxation of the clergy*.

St. Thomas à Becket had fought and died for the exemption of the clergy from the jurisdiction of the secular courts; now the right of the clergy to be exempt from secular taxation was attacked. In accordance with the doctrine of the time, the possessions of the Church belonged to the poor and could not be taxed. "This did not mean that the Church did not contribute to the public expenses. Far from it! Only, it contributed in the form of voluntary donations, by giving over to the king, when he was in need of it, one tenth of its entire revenue. This was called the tithes. It has been calculated that in little more than half a century, from 1247 to 1300, the French clergy paid to the king thirty-nine tithes, almost four times its entire revenue, or one-fifth of all its possessions. These figures attest that the exemption from taxation was for the Church a purely honorary privilege, and that the patriotism of the clergy neutralized its immunities. Their *voluntary donations* were more burdensome than an obligatory tax would have been" (Kurth).

In 1296 Philip the Fair, who was a bad financier, and always in need of money and greedy for money, had taxed the possessions of the Church in order to prosecute his war against Edward I of England. Boniface, recognizing that the immunities and liberties of the Church were being destroyed, and wishing also to see the senseless war terminated as soon as possible, issued the famous Bull *Clericis Laicos,* in which he strictly forbade the clergy to pay taxes to any layman without Papal permission. Philip replied to the action of the Pope by forbidding money to be carried out of France and all foreigners to enter the country or carry on trade without license from the Crown. This was equivalent to cutting off the Papal revenues from France, which were considerable. Philip went even farther and publicly threw doubt on the validity of Boniface's election, claiming that Celestine V had been forced to resign and was being kept a prisoner in Rome. Circumstances obliged Boniface to suspend the Bull *Clericis Laicos* and to make far-reaching concessions to Philip. But the peace thus wrung from him was not of long duration.

The Great Jubilee.—The ten years of Boniface's pontificate were years of almost continual strife. But he enjoyed one year of triumph scarcely paralleled in all the experience of his predecessors. This was the closing year of the thirteenth century. About Christmas of 1299 crowds flocked both from the city and the country to St. Peter's. A general impression prevailed at that time that a great indulgence was granted in Rome at the beginning of each century. No document was found in the Roman archives to confirm the tradition, but Boniface sanctioned it by promulgating a Bull of Jubilee on February 22, 1300, which granted a plenary indulgence to those who repented and confessed their sins and visited the churches of St. Peter and St. Paul thirty times if Romans, fifteen times if strangers. A contemporary historian estimates the number of pilgrims from all lands at more than

200,000; according to others nearly two million men, women, and children visited Rome during the jubilee year. The bridge of St. Angelo was covered with booths, which divided it into two, and in order to prevent accidents it was enacted, as Dante tells us, that those going to St. Peter's should keep to one side of the bridge; those returning, to the other.

Boniface closed the memorable festival on Christmas Eve of the year 1300. Giotto painted the scene: the Pontiff, standing in

Giotto

POPE BONIFACE VIII PROCLAIMING THE END OF JUBILEE

the old loggia of the Lateran, surrounded by his cardinals and his court, pronouncing the Papal Benediction, *Urbi et Orbi,* on the City and the World. All this glory came to a sudden end in the tragedy of Anagni.

The Tragedy of Anagni.—Suspended for a moment, the conflict with Philip the Fair was speedily resumed. Philip had lorded it over all his subjects, lay and clerical, with a high hand. Boniface despatched a Legate to remonstrate with him. Philip had the Legate arrested and imprisoned because of his supposed "intemperate and insolent language." Boniface thereupon re-enacted the Bull *Clericis Laicos* and summoned the archbishops, bishops, and other leading ecclesiastics to Rome "to take counsel touching the excesses, crimes, and acts of violence committed by the King of France and his officers against the Church of God." At the same time he addressed to Philip himself the Bull *Ausculta Fili* ("Listen, my son") in which he set forth his grievances in dignified terms and cited the King to appear in Rome to answer

OLD ST. PETER'S BASILICA

for his conduct. In reply Philip summoned the States-General (Parliament) of France, obtained their support for his conduct towards the Pope, and then sent an embassy to Rome with a refusal and a warning. Boniface's righteous indignation found expression in the most celebrated of all medieval Bulls, the *Unam Sanctam,* in which he insisted on the subjection of the temporal sword of Christian rulers to the spiritual authority of the Church, and solemnly defined "that to be subject to the Roman Pontiff is for every human creature a necessity of salvation." If the King refused to submit, he was to be excommunicated and deposed. But before the Bull of excommunication was published, two of Boniface's most vindictive enemies, William of Nogaret, one of Philip's chief advisers, and Sciarra Colonna, with a band of hired ruffians surprised the aged Pontiff in his palace at Anagni, insulted him, hurled in his face the most infamous accusations, and brutally mistreated him; it is said that Colonna struck him with his iron glove. The Pope remained in their power for three days; the third day he was rescued by the citizens of Anagni and borne in triumph to Rome. A few weeks later (Oct. 11, 1303) he died of the pain and humiliation and the savage ill-treatment to which he had been subjected.

"This outrage at Anagni," says the French publicist Carrère in his book *The Pope,* "is without excuse because it is beyond all reason and devoid of any dignity. Otto, Henry III, Henry IV, Barbarossa, Frederick II treated the Popes as enemies, but at least as kings. Philip behaved, not as one of the powerful of the earth at war with another power, but like a vindictive boor preparing an ambush and hiring with gold the cut-throats charged to carry out his vengeance. . . . Whatever may have been the errors of this Pope, he was, none the less, the Vicar of Christ, recognized by all Christendom; he bore upon his forehead and upon his shoulders the insignia of his office, and he was an old man. . . ." We can understand the anger of Dante, even though he was an enemy of Boniface VIII. He has branded forever the perpetrators of the cowardly assault in the immortal verses:

> Lo! the fleur-de-lys
> Enters Anagni; in His Vicar Christ
> Himself a captive, and His mockery
> Acted again. Lo! to His holy lip
> The vinegar and gall once more applied;
> And He 'twixt living robbers doomed to bleed."
> —*Purgatorio,* XX, 86-90.

The Bull *Unam Sanctam* is the classical expression of the specifically medieval claim of the Papacy to absolute dominion over the Christian Commonwealth, its peoples, princes and kings. God gave *two swords* to the Church, the Pontiff argues, following St. Bernard's allegorical interpretation of Luke 22, 38: a *spiritual* one, which she herself wields, and a *material* one, which she hands over to the secular power to be used in her service and under her direction. The recalcitrant temporal ruler is judged by the possessor of the spirtual power, the Pope, who is judged by God alone. The concluding sentence of the Bull—the only one to which infallible teaching authority attaches (see p. 394)—repeats the ancient and obvious Catholic doctrine that outside the Catholic Church there is no salvation. (For Latin text and translation of the *Unam Sanctam* see Sister M. Mildred Curley, *The Conflict between Pope Boniface VIII and King Philip IV, the Fair.* Catholic University. 1927. Pp. 113-116.)

CHAPTER II

THE BABYLONIAN CAPTIVITY OF THE POPES (1309-1377)

All Europe was indignant at the sacrilegious outrage committed at Anagni, but no one was found to avenge it, no one was ever brought to account for it. France marched at the head of Europe, and Philip the Fair was master of France. With intense rancor Philip strove to bring into contempt the memory of Boniface VIII and clamored for a General Council which would sit in judgment upon him and condemn him as a heretic. Benedict XI, who succeeded Boniface VIII, was found dead within four weeks after he had excommunicated Nogaret and some of his accomplices. It was rumored that he had been poisoned.

The predominating influence of France in the affairs of the Church resulted in the removal of the Papal seat from Rome to Avignon, on the borderland of France, where for nearly seventy years (1309-1377) the Popes, all of them Frenchmen, were under the influence of the French kings. These seventy years are known in Church History as the "Babylonian Captivity," because the duration of the Papal residence was about the same as that of the Jews in Babylon.

1. *The Disastrous Reign of Clement V*

A vacancy of nine months followed the death of Benedict XI. Then, at the dictation of Philip, Bertrand de Got, Archbishop of Bordeaux, was elected. The new Pope, who took the name of Clement V, was crowned at Lyons, took up his abode in France, and surrounded himself with French cardinals. He never set foot in Rome. His reign of nine years (1305-1314) was an uninterrupted succession of blunders and of concessions to the insatiable avarice of the French King. He abrogated the Bull *Clericis Laicos,* and interpreted the *Unam Sanctam* in a purely spiritual sense, thus sacrificing the claims of the Papacy to temporal su-

premacy.   He aided Philip in the persecution of the Knights
Templars, and suppressed them in accordance with the decision of
the Council of Vienne (1311).   He sided with England in her
war against Scotland and excommunicated Robert Bruce.   In
1309 he fixed his residence at Avignon, nominally a free city, but
actually French in language and sympathy.   It was Clement who
began to levy those heavy contributions on all Christian countries
which called forth the severest criticisms on the Papal Court, and
led in Germany and England to open resistance.

2. *John XXII and Louis of Bavaria*

Clement V was dead two years before his successor, John XXII,
was elected.   Clement had lived in the Dominican Convent at
Avignon; one of the first acts of the new Pope was to set up a
magnificent establishment, out of which afterwards grew that huge
pile known as the Papal Palace of Avignon, which still stands in
somber grandeur on the left bank of the Rhone.   John's comparatively long reign (1316-1334) was largely taken up by his
quarrel with the German Emperor, Louis of Bavaria—the last
struggle between the Papacy and the Empire.   It began over the
old claim of the Popes to decide disputed elections to the Empire.
A disputed election had followed the death of Henry VII in 1313.
But it was only after Louis (1314-1347) had worsted his rival,
Frederick of Hapsburg, that Pope John made his claim.   Louis
refused to accept the decision, and was excommunicated and
deposed.   But no German or foreign prince undertook to make
the deposition effective.   Louis retaliated by marching on Rome,
where he received the imperial crown from the Roman people,
deposed John, and set up an anti-pope in the person of the Franciscan monk Pietro da Corvara (Nicholas V).   John XXII laid
the interdict upon every place in Christendom where the recalcitrant Emperor should tarry.

A heated discussion of the prerogatives of Popes and the rights
of kings followed.   It was a veritable battle of books and pamphlets.   The most prominent antagonists of the Papacy gathered
around Louis, offering him their assistance.   At the head of the
opposition we find not only laymen and representatives of the
secular clergy, but also many Franciscan Friars, who had long
been at odds with the Pope on the question of evangelical poverty.

Their chief spokesman was the Englishman William of Occam. He claimed that the Emperor had the right to depose the Pope should he fall into heresy; that both General Councils and Popes can err, and that Holy Scripture and the beliefs held by the Church at all times and in all places, can alone be taken as the unalterable rule of faith. Occam granted, however, that under certain conditions the Pope "can and ought to interfere in temporal matters, for he had a fullness of power which enabled him to supply all other powers, spiritual and temporal, when these had

THE PALACE OF THE POPES, AVIGNON

failed in their duty." Two other opponents of the Papacy went much farther than Occam. In their joint work called *Defensor Pacis* ("Defender of Peace"), Marsilius of Padua and John of Jandun declared that the people are the State and hence may decide on the form of government which they wish; the Church is subject to the State in all things; the Bishop of Rome has no more authority than any other bishop; the controlling power in the Church is a General Council convened by the State and composed of the whole body of Christians.

There were not wanting brave champions of the Apostolic See

and of the doctrine of the Church; and the literary war went on, both sides often going to extremes, and neither yielding to the other. A satisfactory settlement of the quarrel with Louis was impossible, because the interests of the kings of France were opposed to an understanding. John XXII bequeathed the quarrel to his successors. It came to an end only with the death of Louis during a boar hunt in 1347. Charles IV, who succeeded Louis of Bavaria, undertook to satisfy all the demands of the Papal Court. The triumph of the Papacy seemed assured; but it was a delusion: the temporal supremacy of the Popes was a thing of the past. The principles proclaimed by Gregory VII and upheld by his successors, after accomplishing their providential mission, had become unsuited to control the destinies of Europe. "The Papal power of judgment in political affairs (as Pius IX declared later) had been granted by the public consent of Christendom; it was now by that same public consent being refused."

The long-drawn-out conflict with Louis of Bavaria could not but diminish the prestige of the Holy See and shake the allegiance of thousands to its authority. The celebrated Mystic, St. Bridget of Sweden, who spent the last thirty years of her life in Rome, wrote to the Popes at Avignon and expressed the fear that, unless they soon returned to Italy, they would forfeit not only their temporal, but also their spiritual authority. When Urban IV, who had taken up his residence in Rome for two years (1368-1370), went back to Avignon, she prophesied his speedy death; which actually took place a few months later.

St. Bridget did not live to see the conclusion of the unnatural exile of the Papacy in France. It was another heroic woman, St. Catherine of Siena, "one of the most marvelous figures in the history of the world," who broke the spell with which Philip the Fair had bound the Papacy.

3. St. Catherine of Siena and Gregory XI. End of the Babylonian Captivity

Catherine was the youngest of the twenty-five children of Giacomo de Benincasa, a dyer, and was born March 25, 1347, at Siena. At the age of seven she made the vow of perpetual virginity. After a long struggle she persuaded her parents to allow her to become a member of the Third Order of St. Dominic. For

some years she led the life of a recluse in her own family, devoting all her time to prayer and works of penance, and speaking
to no one but her confessor.   It was during this period (about
1366) that she underwent the mystical experience known as the
"spiritual espousals" and was favored with many heavenly visions.
On the advice of her confessor she resumed her place in the family
circle, and after the death of her father (1368) lovingly assumed
the care of her sickly mother.   She also began her mission of
charity outside the family by seeking out and helping the poor and

Sodoma

OUR LORD APPEARS TO ST. CATHERINE OF SIENA
AND IMPRINTS ON HER HIS BLESSED WOUNDS

the sick.   Her extreme corporal austerities, her visions and miracles, her power to read the hearts of men and to convert the most
hardened sinners; above all, her superhuman heroism in the care
of the plague-stricken (1374), won for the simple maiden a
numerous following of devoted men and women who labored under her guidance for the reformation of the Church in her head
and members.

In 1375 we find Catherine entering on a wider stage.   No one
deplored the sad state of Christendom more deeply than she did,
and she was determined to do her utmost to remedy it.   There

was civil strife everywhere in Italy, and in 1375 war broke out between the powerful Republic of Florence and Pope Gregory XI. Catherine hurried from city to city as a "tireless dove of peace," and "in heart-stirring and heart-winning words spoke out her con-viction to all, even to the most powerful." In the summer of 1376 she went in person to Avignon and urged Gregory to return to Rome. Her burning words at last overcame all opposition, and on September 13, 1376, Gregory left Avignon for Genoa, and on the 17th of January, 1377, made his entry into the City of St. Peter.

The war with Florence dragged on. In 1377 Gregory sent Catherine on an embassy to that unhappy city. While she was urging the citizens to make peace with the Pope there came the news of his death. During the troubles that followed, Catherine nearly lost her life in a popular tumult, and "sorely regretted not winning her heart's desire, the red rose of martyrdom." Peace was made with the new Pope, Urban VI, and Catherine returned to Siena. When the Great Schism broke out a few months later, Urban VI summoned her to Rome. She heartily espoused his cause and wore herself out in restraining the Pontiff's impatience, calming the excited Roman populace, and trying to gain the sup-port of Christendom for the rightful Pope. Her efforts were vain. Broken in health, and after a long and painful illness she died on the 29th of April, 1380, at the early age of thirty-three years.

St. Catherine's writings—*The Book of Divine Doctrine* and nearly four hundred *Letters* addressed to kings, Popes, cardinals, bishops, convents of men and women, city corporations and private individuals—have secured for her in Italian literature a place beside Dante and Petrarch. Her lan-guage is the purest Tuscan of the golden age of the Italian vernacular; which is all the more remarkable because she learned to read and write comparatively late in life.

4. Missionary Enterprise in the Far East

The migration of the Popes to France was disastrous; but the dark points of the Avignon period have been greatly exaggerated. The Popes of those days were not all so weak as Clement V, nor so fond of wealth and luxury as Clement VI. Benedict XII, Innocent VI, and Urban V were poor politicians and diplomatists, but they were men of austere morals and reformers in the best sense of the word. If they accomplished little, it was not for want of good will and laudable efforts, but because the force of untoward circumstances nullified all their attempts. The brightest page in the history of this period is that which recounts the noble efforts of the Popes for the conversion of the heathen peoples of the Far East.

When the Knights of the Cross, despairing of success, sheathed their swords, daring monks took the field. They marched out, not to subject foreign nations, but to win them for Christ. They too followed the call of the East. But it was not the Mohammedan East to which they directed their steps—they knew from long experience that the task of trying to convert the Moslem was hopeless—; the farthest East, the vast Mongol or Tartar Empire, the creation of Jenghis Khan, which stretched from the Black Sea to the Pacific Ocean, was their goal.

The Missions to the Mongols (or Tartars) were inaugurated by Pope Innocent IV. In 1245 that Pontiff sent John de Plano Carpini, one of the most faithful companions of St. Francis of Assisi, to the court of the Tartar Emperor in Central Asia. In 1253 another Franciscan, William of Rubruk, went as ambassador of St. Louis IX to the Grand Khan at Karakorum. Other missionaries followed in the footsteps of these pioneers. Not being attached to any monastery, they were apostolic missionaries in the truest sense. Highly cultured and gifted with remarkable knowledge of men, they readily adapted themselves to the strangest surroundings and found the right ways and means of prosecuting their work with success. In the mission schools they rapidly learned the languages of the East. The material means for their daring undertakings were furnished them in great part by the "Society for the Travelers for Christ" in their home country.

The Tartar princes declined, as a rule, to become Christians themselves, but they placed no obstacles in the way of the missionaries. The most prominent of these fearless pioneers of Christianity were the Friars John of Monte Corvino, Blessed Odoric of Pordenone, and their companions Arnold of Cologne and James of Ireland.

John of Monte Corvino (b. about 1247; d. 1330) arrived in Cathay (China) with Arnold of Cologne in 1294. In two letters, written in 1306 and still extant, John tells of their friendly reception at the court of the Mongol Emperor and their successful missionary work in spite of the hostility of the Nestorians who had entered the field before them. John built two churches in Cambalu (Peking) and a monastery, preached in the

Tartar language and translated the New Testament and the Psalms into the vernacular. He baptized 6,000 pagans, among them the Emperor Ayur-Balibatra and his mother, and the Grand Kahn Haichan Our-Son. In 1307 he was made Archbishop of Peking by Pope Clement V, with Zaitun as suffragan See. Of the seven auxiliary bishops sent to him by the same Pope only two reached China.

The missionary journeys of *Odoric of Pordenone* were replete with adventures and perils of every description. On his way to China in 1318 he passed through Persia, India, Java, and Ceylon. He remained three years in Peking attached to one of the churches erected by Archbishop John. On his return he was the first European to penetrate into the Holy City of Lhasa, the capital of the Dalai-Lama of Thibet. Friar James, an Irishman, was his companion during at least a part of these long journeys. Shortly after his return to his native land (1330) Odoric related the story of his travels to Friar William of Solagna, who wrote it down in rather crude Latin. It became one of the most popular books of the later Middle Ages. The substance of Sir John Mandeville's book of travels is stolen from Odoric.

Unhappily, the seed sown by these and many other daring missionaries in China was ruthlessly trampled down and destroyed in 1368, when the rule of the tolerant Tartar princes was supplanted by the Ming dynasty, whose founder was an ex-Buddhist priest. More than two centuries elapsed before the missions in the Far East could be revived.

St. Catherine Begs Gregory XI to Return to Rome

"Be valiant and not fearful; answer God who calls you to come and to fill and defend the place of the glorious Pastor St. Peter, whose successor you are. Raise the standard of the Holy Cross, for as, according to the saying of the Apostle St. Paul, we are made free by the Cross, so by the exaltation of this standard which appears before me as the consolation of Christendom, shall we be delivered from discord, war, and wickedness, and those who have gone astray shall return to their allegiance. Thus doing, you shall obtain the conversion of the Pastors of the Church. Implant again in her heart the burning love that she has lost. She is pale through loss of blood which has been drained by insatiable devourers. But take courage and come, O Father; let not the servants of God, whose hearts are heavy with longing, have still to wait for you. And I, poor and miserable that I am, cannot wait longer; life seems death to me while I see and hear that God is so dishonored. Do not let yourself be kept from peace by what has come to pass in Bologna, but come. I tell you that ravening wolves will lay their heads in your lap like gentle lambs, and beseech you to have pity on them, O Father."

—*Tommaseo, Le Lettere di S. Caterina da Siena,* III, pp. 173-4 (tr. in Pastor, *History of the Popes.* I, p. 105).

CHAPTER III

THE GREAT SCHISM OF THE WEST
(1378-1417)

1. *Rise and Progress of the Schism*

The Babylonian Captivity was followed by the Great Schism, which disrupted ecclesiastical unity for forty years and brought untold misfortunes upon the Church. After the death of Gregory XI (1378) the cardinals had chosen an Italian Pope, Urban VI. During the absence of the Popes Rome had decayed rapidly. The French cardinals, who formed the majority in the Sacred College, were dissatisfied with the city and wished to return to Avignon, where there were no dilapidated basilicas and ruined palaces, no tumultuous Roman mobs and deadly Roman fevers; where life was, in one word, more comfortable. Urban VI refused to leave Rome, and his stern resolve, intimated to them in no mincing words, to reform the Papal court and break down the luxury of its life, gave deep offense to the cardinals. Despairing of otherwise escaping from the desolate city and the violent-tempered Pontiff, the French cardinals fled from Rome and, meeting together at Fondi in the Kingdom of Naples, declared Urban's election invalid, on the ground that the Roman mob had surrounded the conclave and threatened the cardinals with death unless they should elect a Roman or an Italian Pope. They proceeded to another election, which on September 20, 1378, resulted in the choice of the Cardinal of Geneva, who called himself Clement VII.

The rebel cardinals then wrote to the European courts explaining their action. Charles V of France and the whole French nation immediately acknowledged Clement VII, as did also Flanders, Spain, and Scotland. The Empire and England, with the northern and eastern nations and most of the Italian republics, adhered to Urban VI. Under threats from Wenceslaus, king of the Romans, son and successor of Charles IV, the schismatic Pope fled from

Naples to Avignon, where, under the protection of France, the rival Papacy was set up.

The schism was now an accomplished fact, and for forty years Christendom was treated with the melancholy spectacle of two and even three rival Popes claiming its allegiance. It was the most perilous crisis through which the Church had ever passed. Both Popes declared a crusade against each other. Each of the Popes claimed the right to create cardinals and to confirm archbishops, bishops, and abbots, so that there were two Colleges of Cardinals and in many places two claimants for the high positions in the Church. Each Pope attempted to collect all the ecclesiastical revenues, and each excommunicated the other with all his adherents.

When Urban VI died in 1389, the Roman cardinals elected Boniface IX to succeed him. Five years later, Clement VII died at Avignon. The schism might now have been healed, but the French cardinals chose the Spaniard Peter de Luna, who had been one of the ruling spirits in the election of Urban VI. He styled himself Benedict XIII. Voices were heard on all sides demanding that union be restored. The universities of Paris, Oxford and Prague took the matter up and began negotiations to end the schism. The University of Paris, or rather, its two most prominent professors, John Gerson and Peter d'Ailly, proposed that a General Council should be summoned to decide between the rival claimants. Many refused to accept this solution, rightly claiming that the Pope was supreme in the Church and could be judged by no one. But, as the situation grew worse from day to day, and no other way seemed possible, the two Colleges of Cardinals agreed to call a General Council. It met at Pisa in 1409, and was largely attended, especially by those of the Avignon obedience. After declaring its competency to try the rival Popes, it cited them to appear before it for trial. Neither of the Popes recognized its authority, and neither obeyed its summons. The cardinals then pronounced their deposition, and elected another Pope, Alexander V, fondly hoping that they had achieved the union of Christendom. But the scandal was only increased, for neither of the Popes yielded. There were now three Popes, and three Colleges of Cardinals, in some dioceses three rival bishops, and in some Religious Orders three rival superiors.

The Synod of Pisa was no Ecumenical Council; it has never been regarded as such by the Church. It was from the outset, as Pastor says, an act of open revolt against the Pope, a denial of the Primacy of St. Peter and the monarchical constitution of the Church. It was the first attempt to put into practice the theory of William of Occam, John Gerson, and Peter d'Ailly that a General Council is superior to the Pope.

Alexander V survived his election only eleven months. The Pisan cardinals, who had the support of the greater part of Christendom, continued the Pisan line of Popes by electing the warlike Cardinal Baldassare Cossa, who took the name of John XXIII.

2. Wycliffe and Hus

To the other trials of the Church was also added that of heresy. Whenever abuses against the moral and disciplinary teachings of the Church have been widespread, errors against her doctrinal truths have obtained a ready acceptance, especially if the cloak of zeal for moral reform was thrown over them. The Englishman John Wycliffe and the Bohemian John Hus were the chief heresiarchs of this period.

Wycliffe was born in Yorkshire about 1324, studied at Oxford, and entered the priesthood. He openly espoused the cause of Edward III when the latter refused the contributions levied on England by the Holy See. His lectures and sermons against the temporal power and the temporal possessions of the Church were loudly applauded. The Church must become poor once more, he said, as she was in the time of the Apostles. He next attacked the Catholic doctrine of Transubstantiation and the divine institution of the hierarchy, as well as Indulgences, Auricular Confession, Extreme Unction and Holy Orders. The Bible alone, without Tradition, was the sole rule of faith. The Church was composed only of the *predestined*; prayer and sacraments benefited only the predestined, and sins could not harm them. No temporal or ecclesiastical superior had authority when he was in a state of mortal sin. Here we have Calvinism a century and a half before Calvin.

At first Wycliffe enjoyed the favor and protection of the English court and the parliament; but when the common people carrying the teachings of the Oxford professor to their practical conclusions, raised the standard of revolt against the wealthy landowners and refused obedience to the secular and ecclesiastical authorities, his protectors turned against him. His heretical teachings were condemned by the Council of London (1382), and he was deprived of his professorship at Oxford by royal order. He died two years later.

The alliance between the royal houses of England and Bohemia—-Richard

II of England had married Anne, the daughter of the King of Bohemia—
!ed to an increase of intercourse between these countries. In this way
Wycliffe's ideas found entrance into Bohemia. *John*, surnamed *Hus* (from
the place of his birth, Husinec) professor at the University of Prague,
espoused them enthusiastically. He translated Wycliffe's chief work, the
Trialogus, into Czech, and helped to circulate it even after the ecclesiastical
authorities had condemned forty-five of Wycliffe's propositions in 1403. He
made all the errors of Wycliffe his own, except his rejection of the doctrine
of Transubstantiation; he preached, however, that the Holy Eucharist must
be received under both species by the faithful. Summoned to appear before
John XXIII, he sent representatives in his stead, and sentence of excommunication was pronounced against him (1411). When he continued to
propagate his errors—one of his favorite sayings was that a Czech can
teach nothing false—and to incite his countrymen to revolt, more vigorous
action was taken by the civil and ecclesiastical authorities. We shall meet
Hus again at the Council of Constance.

3. *The Council of Constance. End of the Great Schism*

A list of the Popes and Anti-popes during the Great Schism will
show how matters stood in the year 1414 when, at the instance of
the Emperor Sigismund, John XXIII summoned the Council of
Constance.

Roman Pontiffs	*Anti-popes at Avignon*
Urban VI, 1378-1389	Clement VII, 1378-1394
Boniface, IX, 1389-1404	Benedict XIII, 1394-1415
Innocent VII, 1404-1406	
Gregory XII, 1406-1415	*Line of the Council of Pisa*
	Alexander V, 1409-1410
	John XXIII, 1410-1417

John XXIII had consented not only to convoke the Council of
Constance, but also to attend it in person, because he hoped that it
would confirm him as Sovereign Pontiff.

The Council of Constance was one of the most memorable in
the history of the Church. It was in a sense an international
congress. Eighteen thousand ecclesiastics of all ranks took part
in it, besides hundreds of laymen from all parts of Europe. Although called primarily for the purpose of ending the Schism, two
other important matters were to be dealt with: the heresy of John
Hus and the reform of the Church in her head and members.

The case of the Czech heresiarch was settled first. In order
to put a stop to his revolutionary agitation in Bohemia, Sigismund had cited Hus to present himself before the Council at

Constance, giving him a verbal promise that he could return in safety to Bohemia. The written document—the so-called "safe-conduct" was nothing but a passport, which did not guarantee the inviolability of his person. At the Council Hus refused to retract his errors, was condemned as an obstinate heretic, and handed over to the secular arm. He was burned at the stake July 6, 1415. The bloody Hussite wars, which devastated Bohemia and parts of Germany for nearly two decades, were the aftermath of this execution.

When John XXIII saw that his hopes of being acknowledged as Pope were illusory, he fled from the city, disguised as a groom. He was captured, returned to the Council and deposed. Gregory XII, the true Pope, who had long promised to abdicate, now redeemed his promise, but first by a solemn act declared the Council true and legitimate. Sigismund, who had done all in his power to induce Benedict XIII, of the Avignon line, to abdicate, succeeded in detaching the Spaniards from his cause. Thereupon the Council declared his deposition, July 16, 1417. Benedict disregarded the sentence, and in his rocky Castle of Peniscola obstinately maintained his claim to be regarded as the only true Pope till his death, November 29, 1422, in his ninety-second year.

The next step of the Council was to elect a new Pontiff. The choice fell on Cardinal Otto Colonna, a Roman, who took the name of Martin V. When the Council addressed itself to the matter of reform, it was at once apparent that no thoroughgoing reforms could be made. There was no agreement as to whether the Council or the Pope should conduct the reforms; there was no agreement even as to what reforms should be undertaken. Finally, the question was left to the Pope, who promised to call another Council within ten years to reform the Church. The Council was dissolved in May, 1418. The new Pope approved "all that the Council had resolved as a Council in matters of faith," expressly rejecting the decrees of the fourth and fifth sessions, which had declared that the Council held its authority immediately from God, and that even the Pope was subject to it.

Martin V, true to his promise, called another General Council, to meet at Basel, in 1431; but he died before it began its sessions. Eugene IV (1431-1447) suppressed the Council at the end of the year; but it withstood the suppression and continued to hold its meetings. The chief business to come before it was the question of the Hussite heresy in Bohemia, which it finally settled by making a very sensible compromise (known as the famous *Compactata*) with the conservative wing of the Bohemian sectarians. Eugene, now finding that the Council was doing good service to the Church, again approved it and declared it ecumenical. It was not long, however, before the Council engaged in a quarrel with the Pope over the question of authority. It lost the support of public opinion and the prestige which it had gained by its laudable attempts at reform when it deposed the Pope and renewed the schism by electing an anti-pope—Felix V—the last in the history of the Church. In 1449 the Council yielded to Pope Nicholas V and dissolved itself. This practically ended the period which is known in Church History as the "Conciliar Epoch." In 1459 Pope Pius II forbade all appeals to a General Council. The best minds in Europe recognized that what Christendom needed most was a "spiritual rejuvenation," and that this depended for its success on the leadership of the divinely appointed head of Christendom, the Pope.

Whilst the refractory Council of Basel was in session, Eugene IV convoked another Synod, which was opened at Ferrara in 1438 and was transferred to Florence in the following year. This Council brought about a temporary reunion of the Eastern and Western Churches. The Greeks attended it in large numbers; the Emperor himself, John Paleologus, was present with the Patriarch of Constantinople. The chief promoter of reunion was the learned and virtuous Greek bishop Bessarion of Nicaea, who was later elevated to the cardinalate.

The Greeks accepted the *Filioque* of the Latin Creed (viz., the procession of the Holy Ghost from the Father *and* the Son) and the Primacy of the Pope, whilst the Council permitted the Greeks to retain all their ancient rites and customs.—Only fear of the Turks had induced the Emperor and his Patriarch to come to Italy and to sign the articles of reunion: they hoped that the West would help them in their impending struggle with Mohammed II. The reunion never was practically carried out. In 1453 Constantinople fell into the hands of the Turks. The Greek Empire had ceased to exist. "Rather Turks than Papists," has been the answer of the Greeks to every subsequent advance of the Latins. . . .

CHAPTER IV

THE CHURCH AND THE RENAISSANCE

1. *Humanism*

During the first quarter of the fourteenth century a new intellectual movement began in Italy which had for its purpose the study of the classical authors of antiquity. The Latin classics, and even some of the Greek, had not been unknown in the Earlier Middle Ages, but their study had been pushed into the background. When studied at all, they had been valued as a means to an end, as storehouses of information and as models of Rhetoric, not as "living literature to be enjoyed for the ideas that were contained in it and the form in which they were expressed." The Latin that was written and spoken in the Early Middle Ages was more or less barbarous. Later, especially during the Carolingian revival and again in the thirteenth century, it had improved considerably, but still lacked classical elegance. In the fourteenth century the reading of the classics became commoner. They began to be studied for their own sake, for the beauty of their style, and for the ideas of human life and of the world which they contained. The monastic libraries were ransacked for copies of Virgil, Horace, and Cicero, and every new manuscript that was unearthed was hailed with joy. Believing that a thorough training in the classical literature of Greece and Rome alone could form a perfect human being, the followers of the new movement called themselves "Humanists," while the subjects of their studies came to be known as *Litterae Humaniores,* or Humanities.

Humanism is the first phase of the *Renaissance,* the term used to designate the movement to revive the art and learning of classical antiquity, which became identified with the period of transition from the Middle Ages to modern times. The Renaissance is not a rejection but a ripening of the Middle Ages. "All the roots and stalks of medieval planting and growth come now to blossoming and flower." Humanism, the literary manifestation of this movement, may be said to have begun with Dante's *Divina Commedia*. It received a fresh impulse through Petrarch (d. 1374) and Boccaccio (d. 1375). The Council of Constance also played an important part in the movement. It was the rallying point for all the humanists of the time, many of whom did not scruple to pilfer treasures of antiquity from the famous libraries of the neighboring monasteries of Reichenau and St. Gall. The Council of Florence (1439) was a landmark in the revival of Greek studies. It brought many Greeks to Italy, who afterwards made their abode there and earned their livelihood by the teaching of Greek. The most learned of these visitors, Cardinal Bessarion, was directly responsible for the revival of the study of Plato and Platonic philosophy.

2. *Pagan and Christian Humanism*

Humanism had, almost from the first, both a pagan and a Christian aspect. Men like Dante, Petrarch, Vittorino da Feltre, Aleandro, Vegio, Vida, Pico della Mirandola, Rudolph Agricola, Cardinal Cusa, Hegius, Thomas More, Cardinal Fisher, John Colet, Linacre, Louis Vives, made free use of the treasures of antiquity without sacrificing Christian principles; they combined classical materials with Christian ideals, held fast to the teachings of Christ, and used the classics only as a means to embellish those teachings.

But there were others, such as Lorenzo Valla, Boccaccio, Beccadelli, Filelfo, and Ariosto, to mention only the most prominent, who in their infatuation for the classics absorbed the pagan conception of life which those classics embodied. They looked down with scorn upon everything that savored of the supernatural and the unworldly, and ridiculed the writings of the Scholastics for their barbarous Latin. "They gave themselves up," says a modern writer, "body and soul to the worship of the ancients. They were pagans because the ancients were pagans and, according to the energetic expression of Holy Writ, they became like to their idols."

Many pious and zealous men, alarmed at the rebirth of pagan immorality which accompanied the rebirth of pagan science, art, and poetry, condemned the whole movement as evil. But this was not the attitude of the Church; on the contrary, she undertook to direct the new movement; she proposed to create a revival that would be Catholic, and, in a measure at least, she succeeded.

3. *The Renaissance Popes*

The Popes from Nicholas V to Leo X are known as the Renaissance Popes. Following the trend of the times, these Popes collected manuscripts of the classical authors, pictures, statues, precious stones, and all kinds of works of art. They became munificent patrons of art and learning, and gathered about them a host of artists and men of letters. They erected magnificent buildings and adorned them with masterpieces of sculpture and painting. As lords of the Papal States their court was brilliant, and most of them lived in magnificent splendor. Statesmen and diplomats, poets and artists, scientists and philosophers, were always sure of a cordial welcome and costly entertainment. But many of those who found their way into the Roman court sought only wealth and luxurious living; and it was these voluptuaries who brought the Curia into ill-repute throughout Christendom. The maintenance of the princely court of the Popes required vast sums of money; to collect these the Papal revenues had to be increased from year to year. The whole of Europe was put under contribution by levying taxes of various kinds and under different names. That the highest ecclesiastics in the government of the Church only too often succumbed to the temptations which surrounded them on all sides; that they became "intoxicated with the wine of the Renaissance to the point of totally forgetting the Catholic spirit, forgetting that they were priests, bishops, cardinals, Popes, remembering only that they were humanists"—this is one of the reasons why the Protestant revolt was promptly popular and so largely successful.

The Renaissance Popes have also been styled the "political Popes." The circumstances of the time forced them to be political Popes. The Papal States had become an Italian national power from the moment that the Christian commonwealth of Europe was disrupted. The Popes were drawn into the political struggles of Italy, and much of their time, energy, and resources was consumed in the task of maintaining and increasing their territories and their power. They had to keep a standing army, like their neighbors, and were often engaged in warlike enterprises.

Owing to the great influence exercised by the Curia on European politics, the various States sought to win over as many cardinals as possible to their side, and those who succumbed to the temptation served their foreign patrons more faithfully than their own master, the Pope. In self-defense, the Popes surrounded themselves with members of their own families, nephews, as a rule, whom they raised to the highest offices and provided with incomes from the possessions of the Church. This system, known as Nepotism, did much to lower the prestige of the Holy See. Many of the *nipoti* were young and inexperienced and, being in most cases devoid of any sense of the responsibility that rested on them, gave themselves up to a life of self-indulgence and political ambition. They also exercised a baneful influence on the Papal elections, several of them by their intrigues attaining the height of their ambition, the Papal Throne. Of the thirteen Popes who reigned from 1431 to 1534 only three—Nicholas V, Innocent VIII, and Adrian VI—were not related to one of their predecessors or successors.

4. The Popes As Patrons of Art

Nicholas V (1447-1455), a man of learning and a classical scholar second to none of his time, aimed to make Rome the center of arts and letters. He founded the Vatican Library, planned to rebuild the basilica of St. Peter, employed Fra Angelico to paint his study in the Vatican Palace, and drew many noted literary men to his court. He is especially famous as a collector of ancient manuscripts, both of the pagan authors and of the Fathers of the Church. By means of translations, which he always paid for handsomely, he placed the treasures of Greek literature at the disposal of his contemporaries. He gave prizes for the discovery of rare manuscripts, and promised a princely reward to anyone who should discover a copy of the Hebrew text of St. Matthew's Gospel. The fall of Constantinople cast a shadow on his otherwise brilliant reign.

The following Popes—Calixtus III, Pius II, and Paul II—were too much occupied with vain efforts to unite Europe against the Turkish peril to do much for the encouragement of art and artists. Sixtus IV again walked in the footsteps of Nicholas V. He built the Sixtine Chapel in the Vatican Palace and was a liberal patron of the celebrated painters Ghirlandajo, Botticelli and Pinturicchio. Unfortunately Sixtus raised a number of very worldly men to the purple. It was these cardinals who, in 1492, bribed by his gold, placed the Spanish Cardinal Rodrigo Borgia on the Throne of Peter. Alexander VI, the "Borgia Pope," says a contemporary historian, seems to have no other aim than to aggrandize his children by fair means or by foul. "The name of Alexander VI was so infamous for the many evils of his reign—his own unsavory life, the scandals of the Papal court, the infamies of his son

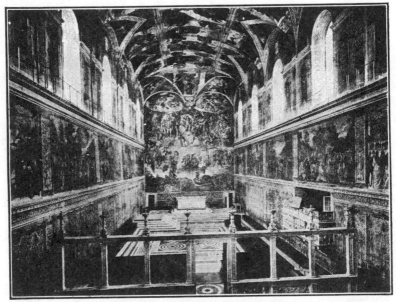

THE SIXTINE CHAPEL

Cesare Borgia, the ill-legend of Lucrezia, the persecution of Savonarola—that in his reign the secularization of the Papacy seemed to have been complete" (Bede Jarrett, O.P., *History of Europe*, p. 265).

5. *Girolamo Savonarola*

Florence, the home of the Medici and the Renaissance, was also the home of all the excesses of the new culture. Here arose, towards the end of the fifteenth century, a prophet and preacher of penance, a man of magnetic personality and singular power—

Girolamo (Jerome) Savonarola, Prior of the Dominican Convent of San Marco.

From the pulpits of San Marco and the Duomo, Savonarola preached to ever increasing crowds of eager listeners in the words and images of the Old Testament Prophets. "The Church will be chastised," he cried, "and then renewed, and this will come to pass quickly." The pagan-minded and pagan-lived humanists in high places were the peculiar object of his righteous anger, and he poured out upon them the vials of his scorn: "Go to Rome and through the length and breadth of Christendom: in the palaces of the high and highest ecclesiastics, you will find everyone busy with the books of the ancients, declaiming poetry, and turning elegant rhetorical phrases. As though they could guide souls with Virgil, Horace, and Cicero! They feed the ears of their hearers with Aristotle and Plato, Virgil and Petrarch. Why do they not teach the one thing necessary? Because it does not appeal to them, because the be-all and end-all of their existence is ambition and pleasure!"

Savonarola was a man of great austerity and moral purity, and animated by the holiest motives. In season and out of season he urged the need of reform in Church and State. Gradually, in his overzeal, he became involved in the party-strife of Florence and overstepped the bounds of moderation and Christian charity. When Charles VIII of France marched upon Florence, the Prior of San Marco greeted him as a new Cyrus, the instrument of God for the punishment of the wicked city. The Medici, the rulers of Florence, had to seek safety in flight. Under Savonarola's dictatorship,

Fra Bartolomeo

SAVONAROLA

a new constitution was drawn up, making Florence a democratic republic. The upper classes now turned against the friar. The followers of the Medici became his bitterest enemies and plotted his fall. They succeeded in poisoning the mind of Alexander VI against him. The Pope forbade him to preach to the people, and when he disregarded the prohibition, excommunicated him. Savonarola preached against the ban, declaring it to be null and void, since it was pronounced by a Pope whose own election was null and void—a fact which, he publicly declared, he was ready to prove by the ordeal of fire. The ordeal did not take place. The prophet was discredited, and his followers turned against him. An attack was made on San Marco, Savonarola was taken with two other Dominicans, tortured, hanged, and burnt (May 23, 1498). With the body of the great friar the soul of Medieval Italy went up in flame. . . .

Savonarola cannot be claimed as a precursor of the Reformation. He refused obedience to the Pope, and that was a grievous fault, even though that Pope was Alexander VI; but he never preached or wrote a word against the Catholic faith. In his chief work *Il Trionfo della Croce* ("The Triumph of the Cross") he says: "Whoever swerves from the unity of the Roman Church undoubtedly enters upon the path of error and turns his back upon Christ."

6. *On the Eve of the Protestant Revolt*

Julius II (1503-1513), a nephew of Sixtus IV, was a great statesman, patriot, and soldier, but not a great priest. His strong hand not only saved the Papal territories, but extended them considerably. He joined the League of Cambrai (1509) and later the Holy League (1511), to free Italy from the French rule. He achieved undying fame as a munificent patron of art. Donato Bramante designed for him the new St. Peter's; at his request Michelangelo, sculptor, painter, architect, and poet—one of the greatest geniuses and artists of all time—decorated the ceiling of the Sixtine Chapel with the immortal scenes from the Book of Genesis from the Creation to the Flood, and carved the majestic figure of Moses for the Pontiff's own sepulchral monument; and Raphael embellished the stanze (rooms) of the Vatican with the marvelous frescoes of the "Disputà" and the "School of Athens."

Leo X (1513-1521), the "Medici Pope," who said that he "intended to enjoy his Pontificate," was so absorbed in his patronage of art and artists that he took little interest in his duties as Father of Christendom. He allowed the Fifth Lateran Council, which Julius II had convoked in 1512, to dissolve without doing very much to reform the Church. He and his advisers failed to grasp the seriousness of the religious situation that was developing. The last session of the Lateran Council was held March 16, 1517. On

All Saints' Day of the same year Luther nailed his Ninety-five Theses on the door of the castle church of Wittenberg. Savonarola's prediction was to become true: the Church had to be chastised before it could be renewed.

A Gothic Hymn of Longing

Before the Middle Ages passed away they gave to the world "the most beautiful book ever penned by the hand of man"—the *Imitation of Christ*. The author, Thomas à Kempis, was born at Kempen in the Archdiocese of Cologne in 1380, and died at Zwolle in Holland in 1471. Educated by the Brothers of the Common Life at Deventer, he entered the monastery of the Canons Regular on Mount St. Agnes near Zwolle. He was ordained priest in 1413 and was subsequently appointed sub-prior. For seventy years Thomas knew no other life but that within the monastery walls. "The cell, constantly dwelt in," he writes, "groweth sweet . . . a dear friend and a most pleasant comfort." His favorite motto bears this out: "Everywhere have I sought for peace, but nowhere have I found it save in a quiet corner with a little book—*in angello cum libello*."—To follow Christ, to die to self, and to find salvation in union with God, this is his whole philosophy of life. His passionate longing for the heavenly fatherland is beautifully expressed in a passage of the Third Book of the *Imitation*, which has been well styled a "Gothic Hymn of Longing." With it we take leave of the Ages of Faith:

"O Light everlasting, surpassing all created lights, dart down Thy rays from on high to pierce the inmost depths of my heart.

"Give purity, joy, clearness, life to my spirit that with all its powers it may cleave to Thee with rapture passing man's understanding.

"Oh, when shall that blessed and longed-for time come when Thou shalt satisfy me with Thy presence, and be unto me All in all?

"Grant me, most sweet and loving Jesus, to rest in Thee above every creature, above all health and beauty, above all glory and

THOMAS À KEMPIS

honor, above all power and dignity, above all knowledge and skillfulness, above all riches and arts, above all joy and exultation, above all sweetness and consolation, above all hope and promise, above all merit and desire;

"Above all gifts and rewards which Thou canst give and pour forth, above all joy and jubilation which the mind is able to perceive and feel ;

"In a word, above Angels and Archangels and all the army of heaven, above all things visible and invisible, and above all that Thou art not, O my God.

"Hear the prayer of Thy poor servant, far exiled from Thee in the land of the shadow of death.

"Protect and keep the soul of Thy least servant amid the many dangers of this corruptible life, and by Thy grace direct me in the way of peace unto the home of perpetual light."

Hints for Study

1. Read the article on Boniface VIII in the *Catholic Encyclopedia*.
2. The Popes of the Avignon period are admirably treated by Pastor, *History of the Popes*, Vol. I, pp. 57-116.
3. The Great Schism of the West is fully treated by Pastor in the same volume, pp. 117-208, and by Salembier, *The Great Schism*.
4. There are at least half a dozen lives of St. Catherine of Siena in English, also a translation of her life written by her confessor Raymond of Capua.
5. On the Renaissance and the Church, see Kurth, *The Church at the Turning Points of History*, pp. 123-158, and the Introduction to Pastor's *History of the Popes*.
6. For Savonarola see Lucas, *Fra Girolamo Savonarola* (London, 1906).
7. No library should be without Brother Leo's edition of the *Imitation of Christ*. The Introduction records all that is known about Thomas à Kempis.
8. Draw up a chronological list of events from the accession of Pope Boniface VIII to the close of the Fifth Lateran Council.
9. Annotate the following: "The Hermit Pope," "Immunities of the Clergy," "Clericis Laicos," "The Great Jubilee," "Unam Sanctam," "Urbi et Orbi," "The Tragedy of Anagni," "Babylonian Captivity of the Popes," "Defensor Pacis," The "tireless dove of peace," "Odoric of Pordenone," "Great Schism," The "Pisan Line of Popes," "The Renaissance Popes," "Humanism" Christian and Pagan, "Humanities," "Nepotism," "The Great Friar of San Marco," "The last anti-pope."
10. Was the Renaissance a benefit or a detriment to the Church?

SUMMARY

Turning Points in the History of the Medieval Church

A.D.

596 Pope Gregory the Great sends the Prior Augustine with forty monks to preach the Gospel to the English. Beginning of the marvelous missionary activity of the Church among the Teutonic nations. Ire-

land sends forth St. Columcille and St. Columban; England, St. Willibrord and St. Boniface.

622 The *Hegira*. Mohammed begins his career of conquest, which is pushed to the limits of the known world by his successors. Eastern Christianity is decimated; North Africa and Spain are overrun. Islam's advance is checked in the West by the victory of Charles Martel at Tours (732).

754 The alliance of the Papacy, which has become also a temporal power, with the Carolingian rulers of the Franks leads to the restoration of the Roman Empire of the West. Charlemagne is crowned Emperor by the Pope on Christmas Day, A.D. 800.

888 The disruption of the Carolingian Empire is followed by the darkest period in the history of the Church. The gloom is relieved by the conversion of the Scandinavian and Slavic races and the spread of Christianity into Iceland and Greenland.

963 Otto the Great, king of the Eastern Franks (Germany) founds the Holy Roman Empire. His successors, especially Henry III, rescue the Papacy from its degradation at the hands of the Roman barons and begin the reform of the Church.

1054 The Separation of the Eastern Church from the West—the Greek Schism—is consummated.

1073 Gregory VII (Hildebrand) takes up the struggle for the liberation of the Church from secular control and establishes the supremacy of the Papacy over the Empire. The Popes are acknowledged as the judges not only in spiritual but also in temporal matters by the peoples of the West.

1095 The Crusades place the Pope at the head of a movement which unites all western Christendom against the Saracens.

1198 During the reign of Innocent III the Papacy attains the zenith of its power.

1245 The fall of Frederick II frees the Papacy from the Hohenstaufen, but forces it to seek an alliance with the French monarchy.

1303 Boniface VIII succumbs in the struggle with the French king. The Papacy loses its temporal supremacy. For seventy years the Popes reside far from Rome in the shadow of the French court.

1378 The attempt to restore the seat of the Papacy to Rome leads to the Great Schism of the West. The reunion effected at the Council of Constance (1417) leads to a sharp conflict for supremacy between Pope and Council. The Papacy triumphs in the Council of Florence (1439). The Primacy of the Pope is acknowledged by East and West.

1447 With Nicholas V the first Renaissance Pope ascends the Throne of Peter. For nearly a hundred years the Papacy is identified with the deep and widespread intellectual movement known as the Renaissance and attempts to guide its destinies. The Popes fail to heed the signs of the time, which point to an approaching religious revolution.

SECTION III

The Church in Modern Times, from the Protestant Revolt to the Present Day, A.D. 1517-1930

FIRST PERIOD

From the Protestant Revolt to the French Revolution 1517-1789

CHAPTER I

LUTHER AND LUTHERANISM

Luther's Early Years.—Martin Luther was born of poor parents at Eisleben (Saxony) in 1483. He received his elementary education at Mansfeld, Magdeburg, and Eisenach. At Eisenach young Martin was a "poor student," that is, a boy who lived rent-free and attended school without paying tuition, and for his board sang as a chorister in the church to which the school was attached. At eighteen he entered the University of Erfurt and took the various degrees in an unusually brief time. His father, whose fortunes had in the meantime improved, wished him to study law; but his fond hope of one day seeing his talented son a famous lawyer, was frustrated. Martin, who was harassed with constant fear for his soul's salvation, suddenly resolved to leave the world and become a monk. Without consulting his parents or notifying them of his intention, he entered the convent of the Augustinian Hermits at Erfurt (July 17, 1505).

In the convent Luther did not find the peace of soul and the assurance of salvation which he had come to seek. He fasted and scourged himself, practiced all kinds of mortification, and made frequent general confessions. All to no purpose. He advanced to the priesthood in 1507, received the degree of doctor of theology in 1512, and in the same year was sent by his superior to teach philosophy and Sacred Scripture at the newly founded University of Wittenberg. He plunged headlong into his duties; but no amount of work could allay the tumult of his morbid conscience. In 1510 he was despatched to Rome on some business connected with his Order. While there he made a general confession, hoping it would bring him peace. Just the contrary happened: he was more discontented than ever with the state of his soul. All his efforts to attain holiness seemed to him of no avail. His fear of hell and eternal damnation almost drove him to distraction. The prescriptions of the Rule became an intolerable burden to him. He fought hopelessly against the temptations that assailed him.

Tiring at last of this constant warfare, he persuaded himself that good works, since they had failed to give him the desired inward peace, were useless for salvation; that faith alone justified before God; that God's pardon could be won only by trusting to His promises. This false view of justification led to another equally false: that man has become, in consequence of Original Sin, incapable of willing or doing anything good: all his acts are sins; he became a rotten tree by Original Sin, and cannot bear good fruit. These doctrines, which he believed he had found in the

LUTHER AS A MONK

Epistles of St. Paul, and which became the fundamental dogmas of the New Gospel, were publicly taught by Luther in his lectures at Wittenberg as early as 1516, if not earlier. In 1517 an occasion presented itself of giving them still greater publicity.

Luther's Ninety-five Theses.—Pope Julius II (d. 1513), anxious to secure funds for the building of St. Peter's, had proclaimed a Plenary Indulgence throughout Europe which all could gain who confessed their sins, received Holy Communion, and contributed according to their means towards the erection of St. Peter's. Under his successor Leo X, the Archbishop of Mainz, Albrecht of Brandenburg, undertook to publish the Indulgence in Germany.

Half of the contributions was to go to him to pay a tax which he owed to the Holy See. When the Dominican John Tetzel, who had been commissioned by the Archbishop to preach the Indulgence in Saxony, approached Wittenberg, Luther, who had long since thrown indulgences along with all other good works overboard, nailed his famous Ninety-five Theses, most of which were directed against indulgences, on the door of the Castle Church of Wittenberg (Nov. 1, 1517), where everyone could see and read them. He

MICHELANGELO'S DESIGN FOR THE NEW ST. PETER'S

offered to defend them against all comers. The Theses were drawn up very skillfully and in a style likely to deceive the unwary. Many of them were quite orthodox, while not a few were clearly opposed to the teachings of the Church on Indulgences and Purgatory.

The publication of the Theses aroused great commotion in Germany. Everyone wanted to read them. In less than a fortnight they were known throughout the country. Within a month they had been heard of all over western and southern Europe.

All who were dissatisfied with the Papacy, especially many humanists, hastened to assure Luther of their approval. Tetzel himself, Professor Eck of Ingolstadt, and other Catholic theologians published very learned rejoinders; but while the defenders of the faith were wasting their time preparing erudite dissertations which only a few would read, Luther was employing his extraordinary powers as a popular orator and writer to win support. He succeeded beyond his expectations. In a short time he had secured an enormous following, most of whom, however, regarded him merely as a reformer anxious to put an end to abuses in the Church. The Elector Frederick the Wise of Saxony and Luther's own Provincial Staupitz openly sided with him. This increased Luther's self-confidence.

Intervention of Rome.—Informed by the Archbishop of Mainz of the disturbance in Germany, Pope Leo X did not take the matter very seriously. He thought that at worst it was only a dispute between two rival Religious Orders. A letter which Luther had written to him, and in which he had declared: "In your voice I recognize the voice of Christ, who lives in you and speaks through you," seemed to justify this view. He contented himself with asking the General of the Augustinians to keep his monks quiet. When the Emperor Maximilian finally succeeded in opening Leo's eyes to the gravity of the situation, Luther was summoned to Rome. At the request of Frederick the Wise this order was retracted, and a meeting was arranged between the Papal Legate, Cardinal Cajetan, and Luther at Augsburg in the autumn of 1518. The interview produced little effect. Luther refused to admit that the merits of Christ and of the saints constitute the treasury out of which the Church takes her indulgences, and insisted that the sacraments work merely in proportion to the faith with which they are received. He promised, however, to be silent if his opponents also remained silent. Before leaving Augsburg, Luther published two appeals—one from the Pope ill-informed to the Pope well-informed, and another to a General Council. The next year, however, he was induced by the Papal Chamberlain Charles von Miltitz to write a most respectful letter to the Pope, assuring him of his loyalty and devotion. How sincere these protestations were, may be judged from the fact that three days after he had written to the Pope, he wrote to Spalatin, the chaplain and private secretary of Frederick the Wise: "I am not sure whether the Pope is anti-Christ himself, or only one of his apostles."

The Leipzig Disputation.—In a controversy between Luther's adherent Andrew Carlstadt and Professor Eck of Ingolstadt, several of Luther's tenets were branded as heretical by Eck. Accordingly, when Eck and Carlstadt met in public debate in the ducal palace at Leipzig (June-July, 1519), Luther also presented himself in order to take part in the disputation. In the heat of debate Luther went so far as to defend the teachings of John Hus, which had been condemned by the Council of Constance. He had thus, as Eck forced him to admit, accused a General Council of teaching error. All those present, especially Duke George of Saxony, were highly indignant. Luther was branded as a heretic. Eck left Leipzig triumphant, and Luther returned to Wittenberg deeply mortified and depressed. The disputation had, however, served to give him and his theories the notoriety he desired, and won for him the man who was to be his ablest supporter, the learned, but pliant and vacillating, Philip Melanchthon, professor of Greek at Wittenberg.

Under the Ban of the Church and the Empire.—In the meantime Luther's doctrines had been thoroughly examined in Rome. A Papal Bull (*Exsurge Domine*) condemned forty-one of Luther's propositions, interdicted his writings, and threatened him with excommunication unless he retracted within sixty days.

The action of the Pope came too late. Luther had passed the stage when he feared even threats of excommunication. He posted a notice inviting the students and people of Wittenberg to witness the burning of the Bull, which took place Dec. 10, 1520. He then threw himself with renewed ardor into the struggle. In a series of pamphlets—"An Address to the Nobility of the German Nation," "On the Liberty of a Christian Man," "On the Babylonian Captivity of the Church of God"—written in a terse and popular style, he exposed the abuses rampant in the Church, but also attacked the divine foundations of her constitution. He declared that the priesthood and the episcopal office must be done away with; that the secular power must have the right to decide also in spiritual matters. "He appealed to the cupidity of the princes by offering to make them the heads of the Church in their own states if only they threw off the Pope, to the discontented nobility and peasantry by dangling before their eyes the wealth which would be ready for distribution among them if bishoprics and monasteries were suppressed, and to the university students and professors by proclaiming that he was the champion of liberty, who would save them from the ignorant rule of the Scholastics" (MacCaffrey).

Luther had proved himself an obstinate heretic. The Church had done her part to reclaim him. Nothing remained but an appeal to the secular power.

Charles V had been elected emperor in 1519, and had been crowned at Aachen in the following year. As ruler of Spain, the Netherlands, Germany, and the greater part of Italy, the young Emperor, who was devoted heart and soul to the Catholic C h u r c h, might have easily put an end to Luther's movement had he not been handicapped by revolts in Spain, by wars with France, and by the Turkish invasion of the Empire, and, above all, by opposition w i t h i n the E m p i r e itself. On January 22, 1521, he opened his first German Diet at Worms.

BVLLA

Decimi Leonis, contra errores Martini Lutheri, & fequacium.

Affiftit Bulla a' dextris eius, in veftitu deaurato, circumamicta varietatibus:

Videlector, opereprecium eft. Adficies ris, Cognofces qualis paftor fu Leo.

TITLE OF THE BULL AGAINST LUTHER

Luther was summoned under a safe-conduct to appear and stand trial. He was asked whether certain books had been written by him and whether he was prepared to maintain or to abjure what he had written against the Catholic faith. He answered the first question at once in the affirmative, but asked time to prepare an answer to the second. When he again appeared before the assembly—he had in the meantime received assurance of support from Frederick of Saxony and other German nobles—he refused to retract his doctrines unless they could be shown to be false by Scripture and reason. Thereupon Luther and his adherents were placed under the ban of the Empire; their writings were to be destroyed, and all books were in future to be censored before publication. Luther was ordered to leave Worms and to return to Wittenberg. His safe-conduct was

LUTHER AT THE DIET OF WORMS

to expire in twenty-one days. Then he was liable to be seized and executed as a heretic.

To save Luther from the possible consequences of the ban, the Elector of Saxony ordered some knights to seize him on his way and bring him to the Castle of the Wartburg near Eisenach. The report was spread that Luther had been slain by emissaries of the Pope, and that his body, pierced with a dagger, had been found in a silver mine. Luther remained ten months in the Wartburg. During this time he began his German translation of the Bible, which was completed in 1534.

Luther translated the Old Testament from the Hebrew, the New Testament from the Greek. As he was himself neither a Hebrew nor a Greek scholar of any note, he was much indebted to Philip Melanchthon for assistance. Luther was by no means the first German Bible translator, nor can his translation be called an independent work from the original Hebrew and Greek: there is no doubt that he had the old Catholic German Bible of 1475 before him when making his translation. He did not scruple to do violence to many passages in the original in order to make them harmonize with his own heretical views. Thus, to bolster up his false doctrine of justification he added the word "alone" after the word "faith" in Rom. 3, 28. He omitted the so-called deutero-canonical books—Tobias, Judith, Wisdom, Ecclesiasticus, Baruch, 1 and 2 Machabees and parts of Esther and Daniel —from the Old Testament, and from the New Testament the Epistle of St. James, which he contemptuously called "a straw Epistle," because it teaches that "faith without works is dead."

Private Judgment in Action.—The results of Luther's revolutionary teachings—his denial of free will, his assertion of the complete corruption of human nature by Original Sin, his doctrine of justification by faith alone, his stand on the Scriptures as the sole authority in religious matters, his wild onslaughts on all authority, both ecclesiastical and civil—soon made themselves felt. Tradesmen and day-laborers publicly interpreted the Bible, which had suddenly become intelligible to everyone. At St. Gall, in Switzerland, a crowd of people left the city and directed their steps to the four quarters of the globe to announce the kingdom of God to the nations: didn't the Bible say: "Go, teach all nations and preach the Gospel to them?" Thomas Münzer of Zwickau concluded from the Scriptures that all Christians baptized as infants must be rebaptized (Anabaptists), because Christ said: "He who shall believe and shall be baptized, shall be saved"; but infants do not believe. He also taught that an interior light is given by God to each one to interpret the Bible; that there is no spiritual or temporal authority; that all things must be possessed in common by all men, who form one large community of brethren enjoying equal rights and exercising conjointly both sacerdotal and royal powers. Two hundred Anabaptists gathered at Appenzell and patiently waited for a supply of food from heaven; for they had read in the Gospel: "Be not solicitous for your life, what you shall eat." Bands of barefooted men and women ran through the streets and preached from the roofs of the houses in order to obey the words of Scripture: "That which ye hear in the ear, preach ye upon the housetops." Others burned the Bible, because it is written: "The letter killeth, but the spirit quickeneth. . . ."

During Luther's seclusion at the Wartburg, the "reformers" were very active in Wittenberg. Private Masses were prohibited; Communion was distributed under both kinds, often without confession and without any preparation; the statues and paintings in the churches were demolished. Monks left their convents, students their books, and became preachers of the new Gospel. The confusion reached its height when hundreds of Anabaptists, driven from Zwickau, invaded Wittenberg. The Archdeacon Carlstadt was the leading spirit in this revolutionary movement. On Christmas Day (1521) he celebrated Mass in German, denied the dogma of the Real Presence, and took to himself a wife. Melanchthon was helpless in the face of all these excesses. Luther heard of them, hastened from his retreat to attack the daring innovators, and drove Carlstadt from Wittenberg. The parting scene between these two apostles of heresy was very edifying. It took place at Orlamünde. After several vain attempts to come to an agreement on points of doctrine and practice, they hurled the vilest epithets at each other. "Depart in the name of all the devils," the friends of Carlstadt shouted at Luther, "and may you break your neck before leaving our city." A few days after, Carlstadt was forced to leave Orlamünde by order of Frederick of Saxony. He wandered about from city to city, and died at Basel, "strangled by the devils," as Luther and his friends maintained.

The Peasants' War.—Roused by Luther's teaching and the example of his flagrant disobedience to the laws of Church and State, the lesser nobility, who were mostly impoverished, and the peasants rose against the princes, and a frightful war devastated Germany. The Anabaptists, under the leadership of Münzer, formed the backbone of the rebellion. As long as the rebels attacked only monasteries, convents, and churches, Luther did not interfere, although he had opposed their taking up arms from the first. But when Thomas Münzer, the Anabaptist, sent forth his fiery proclamations urging the peasantry to overthrow the thrones of the princes and "not to let the blood cool on their swords," he issued a violent pamphlet in which he hounded on the ruling classes to "whip, strangle, and kill these murderers and robbers like mad dogs." In the end the rebellion, formidable as it seemed for a few months, was crushed, and a heavier yoke than ever was laid on the shoulders of the peasants. One of the victims of the war was Thomas Münzer. He died reconciled with the Church.

The defeat of the peasants and the death of Münzer proved only a temporary check to the revolutionary Anabaptist movement. In 1532, under John Mathys of Haarlem, and the tailor John Bockelson, called John of Leyden, the Anabaptists gathered in Münster (Westphalia) from all parts of Europe, expelled the bishop, deposed the magistrates, and for three years held possession of the city. Their plan was to proceed from Münster as a center to the conquest of the world. Francis of Waldeck, the expelled bishop, besieged the city (1534). Mathys made a sally with only thirty men, under the fanatical idea that he was a second Gideon. He was cut off with his whole band. John of Leyden was now supreme. Giving himself out as the successor of David, he claimed royal honor and absolute power in the "new Sion." He justified all his tyrannical measures by the authority of visions from heaven. He legalized polygamy, and gave the good example by taking four wives himself, one of whom he beheaded with his own hand in a fit of frenzy. For twelve months the city was the scene of unbridled profligacy. At last it was taken by the bishop's forces, and John of Leyden and some of his followers were executed (1535).

Organization of the Lutheran State Churches.—While the horrors of the Peasants' War were being enacted, Luther, much to the disgust of his friends, laid aside his religious habit and married the ex-Cistercian nun, Catherine Bora, and urged all monks, nuns, priests, and even the Archbishop of Mainz, to follow his example. After he had thus definitely set himself against the whole Roman position, he began to organize his followers into a new church. He had discarded the original constitution of the Catholic Church, and had preached the "universal priesthood" of all the faithful; logically he now turned over to the individual congregations the management of their ecclesiastical affairs and gave the supreme control over all the congregations into the hands of the civil rulers. From now on, freedom of conscience was a privilege enjoyed only by the secular rulers; the subjects had to believe what he believed—*cuius regio, eius religio.* Religion was delivered over to the state. Not the bishops as the successors of the Apostles, but the princes as the absolute masters of their subjects ruled the Church. Before long, nearly every petty principality in central and northern Germany had its own "State Church," with the landgrave, margrave, duke, grand-duke, elector, or prince as its chief bishop—*summus episcopus.* The Church of Christ had lost, in these lands, all its characteristic marks—unity, Catholicity, apostolicity—and, of course, its sanctity also.

The first "State" churches were organized in Hesse and in the Electorate of Saxony. Albrecht of Brandenburg, Grand Master of the Teutonic Knights, adopted Lutheranism, secularized the lands of the Order, and proclaimed himself duke of Prussia, and head of the Prussian Church. After this, Lutheranism spread rapidly in northern Germany; the south and west, with the exception of Würtemberg and a few imperial free cities, such as Nürnberg and Strasburg, retained their allegiance to the Catholic Church.

Attempts to Restore Unity.—The defection of so many princes was possible only because the Emperor Charles V was taken up so much by the war with France and the defense of the eastern frontiers against the Turks that he was unable to give any attention to the course of affairs in Germany. At the Diet of Speyer (1526) he saw Germany divided into a Catholic and a Lutheran party. A compromise was all that could be arrived at. It was resolved that princes, clergy, and burghers "should live religiously as they hoped to answer for their conduct to God and the Emperor, and that the Word of God should be preached without disturbance." In the Diet held at Speyer in (1529) the Catholics were in the majority. The compromise of 1526 was abolished, because the Lutherans had interpreted it to mean that they could regulate ecclesiastical affairs to suit themselves, and it was decreed that no further alterations and innovations should be made till a General Council had been summoned, and that where the new doctrines had been introduced, no one was to be hindered from saying or hearing Mass. Against this decree the Lutheran minority (six princes and fourteen cities) protested vigorously. From this protest came the name *Protestants*.

In 1530 Charles V appeared in person in Germany and summoned both parties to meet at Augsburg. Melanchthon on behalf of the Protestants presented a résumé of their doctrinal views, which is known as the *Augsburg Confession*, the future symbol (creed) of the Lutheran church.

At the request of the Emperor, conferences were held between the Catholic and the Lutheran theologians to see whether the *Confession* could not be made the basis of a compromise. It was found that reconciliation was hopeless, and the Emperor announced his intention of upholding the Catholic faith. Everyone, he said, must return to the Catholic Church, otherwise he should be forced to act, as he was in conscience bound to act, as protector of the Church.

The Protestant princes replied to the decision of the Diet of Augsburg by forming the *League of Schmalkalden,* entering into negotiations with Francis I of France and with Henry VIII of England, and refusing to aid the Emperor against the Turks. Vienna was hard pressed by the armies of Soliman, and France was preparing to declare war. Charles was forced to give way. At the Diet of Nürnberg (1532) it was resolved that no prince was to molest the other on account of his religious doctrines, until a General Council should convene.

Luther's Last Years.—From the time of the formation of the Protestant League, Luther retired gradually from the forefront of the reformation movement. His last years were by no means happy. The Protestant princes confiscated the wealthiest bishoprics and monasteries for their own use, whilst the preachers often suffered the direst want. Irreligion and immorality and vices of all sorts flourished wherever the new gospel gained the ascendancy. "We experience it daily," he says in a sermon, "that the people are seven times worse today than ever before under the Papacy; they are more avaricious, more unchaste, more envious, more intemperate, more dishonest. . . ." He was especially dissatisfied with the state of things in his own Wittenberg. "Let us get out of this Sodom," he wrote to his wife in 1545. "I prefer to wander about homeless, and to beg my bread from door to door than to poison my poor last days by the spectacle of all these disorders." With the Landgrave Philip of Hesse he had a very disagreeable experience. In 1539 Philip, who was already married, besieged Luther with requests to give his sanction to taking a second wife, and threatened that if permission were not granted he would take no further part in the whole movement. Luther and Melanchthon at last sanctioned the bigamy on condition that it should be kept secret. But the secret was not long kept, and Melanchthon at least was thoroughly ashamed of his part in the disgraceful affair.

Against the Pope, Luther vented his rage to the last. In 1545 he wrote the coarsest of his pamphlets, *Against the Papacy Founded by the Devil,* in order to hinder his followers from attending the Council of Trent. He died of apoplexy on the 18th of February, 1546, in his sixty-third year.

The Peace of Augsburg.—The Protestant League of Schmalkalden was supposed to be only a defensive league; but it very soon took the offensive. In 1542 its army invaded the Duchy of Brunswick, deposed the Catholic sovereign, and introduced the Protestant reform. The next year it backed Hermann of Wied in his vain attempt to force Lutheranism upon the Archdiocese of Cologne. The Protestant League thus proved a standing menace to the Catholic states of Germany. In self-defense the Catholics formed the Holy League. In 1544 Charles V concluded an armistice with the Turks and imposed the Treaty of Crespy on Francis I of France. He now determined to take decisive action against the Protestants in Germany. John Frederick, elector of Saxony, and Philip of Hesse were declared traitors; their forces were annihilated in the battle of Mühlberg on the Elbe (1547). After this crushing defeat many Protestants declared their readiness to accept the decrees of the Council of Trent, which was then in session; Melanchthon himself was actually on his way to the Council with a deputation from Wittenberg, when all hope of peace was dispelled once more by an alliance between the Protestant princes and Henry II of France. Henry invaded Germany with a large army, whilst Maurice of Saxony, who had until then fought for the Emperor, suddenly turned traitor, threw his forces into Tyrol and threatened to break up the Council of Trent. Charles was obliged to take to flight. Toul, Metz, and Verdun were ceded to Henry II by the victorious Protestants in return for the aid which he had given them. It was Catholic France that prevented the triumph of the Catholic cause in Germany. A hundred years later it was to interfere once more on behalf of the Protestant princes of Germany and save them from destruction.

Charles V, discouraged by his inability to secure a real union of Christendom, determined to resign the Empire and to retire to a monastery. He was succeeded by his brother Ferdinand as Emperor and by his son Philip as King of Spain. In 1555 Ferdinand was obliged to sign the *Peace of Augsburg*, which sealed the triumph of heresy in the Empire. The princes could choose their own religion, and this religion their people were obliged to accept. Ecclesiastical rulers, who wished to become Protestants, had to resign their benefices before they passed over to the new religion.

In the free imperial cities, where both religions already existed side by side, both were to be tolerated.

The Peace of Augsburg was no real peace, for it contained the seeds out of which grew the terrible Thirty Years' War (1618-1648).

Lutheranism Beyond the Limits of the Empire.—Luther lived to see his doctrines accepted by all the German nations of the north. Lutheranism was forced upon Denmark by the tyranny of King Christian III (1534-1559) who saw in the new doctrine a means for increasing his authority and replenishing his exchequer at the expense of the power and the possessions of the Church. All the bishops were cast into prison on one day. Christian then offered them their liberty if they agreed to resign their sacred dignity and promised to abstain from all opposition to his policy. Only one had the courage to resist to the end. All were replaced by superintendents, or Lutheran bishops, who were absolutely dependent on the Crown. This measure was followed by others, whose purpose it was to stamp out every vestige of the old religion: the death penalty was decreed against every priest taken within the realm; Catholics were deprived of all political rights; every Lutheran who embraced the Catholic faith was subject to banishment. Catholicity was practically annihilated, for these penal laws were rigorously carried out and remained in force till 1849.

Sweden and Norway had been united since 1397 under the scepter of the Kings of Denmark. In 1521 Gustavus Wasa of Sweden succeeded in throwing off the yoke of the Dane. Raised to the throne by his grateful fellow-countrymen (1523), he determined to build up, with the aid of Lutheranism, an absolute temporal and spiritual monarchy. His chief instruments for accomplishing this end were the archdeacon Lawrence Anderson and the brothers Lawrence and Olaf Peterson. Partly by trickery—the Catholic vestments, candles, images, etc., were retained—partly by violence the people were robbed of their ancient faith. Two bishops were martyred, every show of resistance was mercilessly repressed, even some Lutheran preachers, who displayed too little zeal in propagating the new doctrines, were condemned to death. Within two decades the fate of the Catholic Church was sealed—there were no Catholics left in the country. With the Catholic faith the remnants of public and private morality seemed to disappear. To bring the people to their senses, Gustavus Wasa, in his capacity as supreme head of the Church, ordered a strict fast of eight days to be observed throughout the country (1544)—an experiment which was repeated in 1558, with what results we are not told.

Norway, which remained united to Denmark, was won over to Lutheranism by the defection of Archbishop Olaf of Drontheim under Christian II; the work of "conversion" was completed by Christian III. Iceland offered more determined resistance to the Danish tyrant; but the execution of Aresen, bishop of Holar, cast such fear into the hearts of the islanders that Lutheranism was silently accepted as the state religion (1551).

Zwingli and the Reformation in Switzerland.—Ulrich Zwingli, parish priest of Einsiedeln, was for Switzerland what Luther was for Germany. He was an eloquent preacher, and endowed with a lively and clear intellect, but without talent for philosophy and without solid learning. In 1516 he began to preach against the Blessed Virgin and against pilgrimages. Driven from his parish for his scandalous conduct, he passed on to Zürich, where the fame of his eloquence made him a welcome guest. Here in a series of sermons, he laid down the principle that the Bible was the sole rule of faith. From this principle, which he claimed to have discovered independently of Luther, he deduced a system of doctrine which, in its main outlines, agreed with that of Luther. He differed from the Wittenberg reformer in regard to original sin, which, he maintained, was nothing but an inclination to evil, and in regard to the sacraments, allowing only two—Baptism and the Eucharist—neither of them true sacraments producing grace, but merely *symbols* of grace.

In 1522 he requested the Bishop of Constance to suppress clerical celibacy, citing his own case as a proof that it was impossible for anyone to observe it. Shortly after, he married a widow with whom he had been living in sin for some years. After thus providing for his own reformation, he had recourse to violence to reform others. Supported by the town council of Zürich, he broke into the churches, destroyed the altars, statues, and pictures, and set up in place of the altars plain tables for the celebration of the Lord's Supper. This ridiculously simplified service—even the playing of the organ and singing was prohibited—was forced upon the whole Canton of Zürich.

About the same time Oecolampadius—a Greek rendering of his original name Hausschein—an apostate monk, introduced the reformation into Basel (1527), and set an example to other monks and priests by taking a wife. In 1529 the practice of the Catholic religion was interdicted by the city council. Switzerland was thus being rapidly "reformed" by men who disagreed with the reformer of Wittenberg in many important points of doctrine and practice. Luther was enraged. He denounced both Zwingli and Oecolampadius as liars, as men possessed by the devil, and as heretics for whose salvation it was useless to pray, because they dared to deny the Real Presence of Christ in the Eucharist. He himself was anxious to reject this doctrine in order to spite the Pope, but, on his own admission, the words of Scripture were too strong for him. He denied transubstantiation, however, and at last imagined the absurd theory of the ubiquity of Christ's body in order to explain its presence in the Blessed Sacrament in so many places at the same time. The Swiss reformers replied to Luther that they were merely following his own principle of interpreting the Scriptures for themselves. To refute them, Luther was finally forced to fall back upon the practice of the Church and the writings of the Fathers of the Church, who suddenly became his "well-beloved Fathers," forgetting that he had formerly, when it suited his purpose, denounced them as "fetid pools from which Christians had been drinking unwholesome draughts."

The Cantons of Switzerland which had accepted Zwinglianism were determined to force the other Cantons to follow their example. The Catholic Cantons, Schwyz, Uri, Unterwalden, Luzern and Zug, took up arms, and at Kappel gained a decisive victory over their oppressors (1531). Zwingli himself was killed; Oecolampadius died in the same year at Basel—two events which gave great satisfaction to Luther, who expressed his regret that the Catholic forces had not profited by their victory and exterminated Zwinglianism.

Decay of Education in Germany after Luther's Revolt

Luther himself, as well as many of his contemporaries who revolted from the Church, bears witness to the sad decay of education after the Reformation:

"Under the Popes not a child could escape the devil's broad nets, barring a rare wonder, so many monasteries and schools were there, but now that the priests are gone good studies are packed off with them. . . . When I was a child there was a proverb that it was no less an evil to neglect a student than to mislead a virgin. This was said to frighten the teachers."

"The devil has misled the people into the belief that schooling is useless since the exit of the monks, nuns and priests. As long as the people were caught in the abominations of the Papacy, every purse was open for churches and schools, and the doors of these latter were widespread for the free reception of children who could almost be forced to receive the expensive training given within their walls"

—*Martin Luther* cited by Janssen, *History of the German People at the close of the Middle Ages*.

"In the darkness of the Papacy everyone from the highest to the lowest, even servants and day-laborers, contributed to churches and schools; but now, in the clear light of the Gospel, even the rich grow impatient, if ever so little be asked, even for the repairing and maintenance of those on hand"

—*Konrad Porta of Eisleben* cited by Janssen.

Hints for Study

1. O'Hare, *Facts about Luther* (N.Y., 1916), gives a very readable account of Luther, the man and his teachings. See also article on Luther in the *Cath. Encyclopedia*. Janssen, *History of the German People*, Vol. II, should be consulted for the historical background of the Protestant Reformation. H. Belloc, *How the Reformation Happened*, should be in every library. It contains an admirable exposition of the remote and proximate causes of the Reformation. MacCaffrey, *The Church from the Renaissance to the French Revolution*, 2 vols., is the best general history of the Church in modern times available in English.

2. Draw up a chronological list of events from the birth of Luther to the Peace of Augsburg.

3. Which are the fundamental doctrines of Lutheranism? What sacraments did he retain? Why did he retain the Real Presence in the Eucharist?

4. What is meant by the doctrine of private judgment?

5. Which are the main features of Luther's ecclesiastical organization?

6. Write a brief character sketch of Luther.

7. In justice to Luther it must be said that he was right in the main in his criticism of the "traffic in Indulgences" carried on by Tetzel and others. Tetzel really did teach that "as soon as the Indulgence money is paid, the soul is liberated from Purgatory." The historical significance of Luther's 95 Theses lies rather in the fact that they contain utterly false doctrines in regard to Indulgences and Purgatory, that they seek to undermine the teaching authority of the Church, and that they usher in the so-called Reformation and its basic doctrinal errors.

CHAPTER II

CALVINISM

1. *Calvinism in Switzerland*

The first to give Protestantism a system of theology and a permanent ecclesiastical organization was John Calvin. It was through him that Protestantism became a world power. Calvinism invaded Switzerland, Holland, England, Scotland, and America, and for a time threatened the supremacy of the Catholic religion in France.

Calvin and His Doctrine.—Calvin was born at Noyon, France, in 1509. He was at first intended for the Church, receiving the tonsure at the age of twelve. Later he changed his mind and took up the study of law. At Bourges he made the acquaintance of the German Melchior Wolmar, professor of Greek, whom Margaret of Navarre, sister of Francis I, had invited to France. Wolmar was a Lutheran and had little difficulty, it seems, in making a "convert" of the young law student (1529). Calvin immediately became one of the leaders of the party in France that favored the Lutheran movement. When active measures were taken against the heretics, he fled to Basel, where he published his principal work, "The Institutes of the Christian Religion" (1535) in Latin; a French translation appeared in 1540 dedicated to Francis I.

"In their personal characteristics there was a great difference between Calvin and Luther. Luther, with all his faults, had a big heart and could be at times generous and sympathetic, but Calvin seems to have been devoid of human feeling and utterly incapable of appreciating the bright side of human nature" (MacCaffrey). The same difference may be noticed in their doctrinal systems. Calvin taught that man as a result of Adam's fall, has no freedom of will, but is an absolute slave of God; God has predestined each one of us, some to hell, and some to heaven from eternity, irrespective of our merits; if we are predestined for heaven, we cannot be lost; there are only two sacraments instituted by Christ: Baptism and the Lord's Supper; the Body of Christ is virtually present in the Eucharist, that is, the communicant, if he is predestined, receives something of the spiritual life and strength of Christ; there are two churches: the invisible, which is composed of the predestined; and the visible, which comprises all the believers. Unlike Luther, Calvin refused to give supreme control of his organization to the state. It was to be governed by a Consistory consisting of a certain number of representatives, called Elders (six ecclesiastics and twelve laymen), appointed by the different churches. After his death laymen were excluded from the Consistory, which was placed under the authority of the state.

Calvinism at Geneva.—Calvin arrived at Geneva in 1536. It was still largely Catholic, though the reform movement was being warmly supported for political reasons by the opponents of the Duke of Savoy. Calvin's first sojourn in the future "Rome of Protestantism" was neither very long nor very pleasant. His despotic tendencies did not suit the great body of the citizens and he was expelled (1538). He retired to Strasburg, married the widow of an Anabaptist, and paid a visit to Melanchthon at Frankfort. In the meantime public sentiment in Geneva had changed. Calvin was asked to return. He pretended to be indifferent to the flattering offers made to him, allowed deputations to wait on him, laid down conditions, and finally reappeared at Geneva (1541). He at once became the dictator of the city in spite of the opposition of the "Libertines," whom it took him nine years to subdue.

The laws which Calvin enacted for the government of Geneva were despotic in the extreme. Attendance at divine service, which was as cold and as bare as that of Zwingli at Zürich, was obligatory; severe penalties were decreed against dancing, gaming, and extravagance in dress; heresy, blasphemy, and adultery were punished by death. His spies were everywhere, and no man felt himself safe. His preachers, armed with the powers of the law, entered the homes of the citizens, catechized the members of the family, young and old, on their faith and their morals, and reported their findings to their master. The number of imprisonments and executions during Calvin's dictatorship is almost incredible: from 1542 to 1546 alone fifty-eight persons were put to death for various crimes, and during the same period seventy-three were banished and nine hundred imprisoned. Michael Servetus, a Spanish doctor, who had entered into controversy with Calvin on the doctrine of the Trinity, was seized while on a visit to Geneva, brought to trial for heresy and burnt at the stake

(1553). Calvin watched the execution from a window. Then he
wrote a book in defense of putting heretics to death; Melanchthon and other reformers approved both the execution and the
book.

Some years before his death Calvin founded a university at
Geneva in which philosophy, theology, Greek, and Hebrew were
taught. He placed the rectorship in the hands of the Frenchman
Theodore Beza, his ablest lieutenant, future biographer, and successor in the dictatorship. This school of higher studies soon
became the Mecca of all the followers of Calvin throughout
Europe. With the assistance of Beza and the graduates of his
university, Calvin succeeded, before his death in 1564, in having
his system adopted in many of the Cantons of Switzerland. Of
the Protestant Cantons Bern alone refused admittance to the
gloomy preachers of absolute predestination.

Because it inculcated unremitting thrift and discouraged every kind of
self-indulgence and extravagance, Calvinism promoted industrial activity.
As the money acquired in this way could not be spent in luxury, pleasure-
seeking, art, and the other refinements of culture, it was invested in new
industrial undertakings. It was thus that the economic system known as
"capitalism" was developed in the countries that adopted Calvinism as their
religion. Money for money's sake was its motto. It produced a race of
men "who spared neither themselves nor their employees" in the pursuit of
material wealth.

2. *Calvinism in France*

The Huguenots.—Lutheranism gained adherents in France at
a very early date. It found favor especially at the court and
amongst a certain class of intellectuals at the Paris University and
elsewhere who thought they saw in it a means of reforming abuses
and of furthering classical studies. At first the King, Francis I,
occupied as he was by his wars with the Emperor Charles V, paid
little attention to what seemed to him to be a dispute between the
Scholastics and the Humanists. Roused at last by the repeated
outrages against the Catholic religion throughout the country, he
took serious measures to suppress the heretics. Berquin, one of
the outstanding leaders, was beheaded in 1525. Some years later
twenty-four heretics were tortured and burnt at Paris. Still, the
King's desire of keeping on good terms with the Protestant princes

of Germany in order to use them against the Emperor, and the protection afforded to the heretics by his own sister Margaret of Navarre prevented him from doing what he personally felt inclined to do to stamp out the movement. This temporizing policy almost proved fatal to the Catholic cause in France. A number of persons of high rank openly professed the new religion, among them, Renèe, daughter of Louis XII, Jeanne d'Albret, queen of Navarre, and her husband Anthony of Bourbon; the Prince de Condé, and the three Coligny brothers, Dandelot, the admiral Gaspard, and Odet, cardinal and bishop of Beauvais. In 1559 the French Protestants were strong enough to hold a synod at Paris, in which they adopted Calvinism as their official creed. Because the reform movement was largely directed by Calvinistic emissaries from Switzerland, whose people were called "Eidgenossen" (confederates), the French Calvinists were known as "Eiguenots," a word which was gradually corrupted into *Huguenots.* In 1569 the Huguenots claimed one third of the French nobility and one thirtieth of the entire population of the country.

French Wars of Religion.—Wherever the Huguenots gained a foothold, they strove by persuasion or by force to suppress Catholic worship. They took possession of the churches, "purified" them by demolishing the images and statues of the saints, which they called "idols," and introduced their own services, which consisted of long prayers, long sermons, and monotonous singing without organ accompaniment. Monks and nuns were, of course, expelled from their monasteries and convents. Ecclesiastical art suffered irreparable damage at the hands of these "reformers." The cathedrals at Nimes, Bourges, Castres and Montpellier were stripped bare of every ornament, fifty large sculptures on the gable-side of the cathedral at Lyons were hammered to pieces, and the cathedrals of Orleans, Auxerre and Alet were completely demolished.

The struggle for supremacy in the towns and cities soon widened into a desperate struggle for supremacy in the state. Henry II, the ally of the German Protestants, died in 1559. He was followed by three youthful Kings, Francis II (1559-1560), husband of Mary Queen of Scots, Charles IX (1560-1574) and Henry III (1574-1589). The real ruler of France was, during these years, the queen mother, Catherine de Medici, a clever intriguer, who cared little about religion and was anxious only to maintain her own power by playing off the Calvinists against the Catholics. As the three Kings remained childless, the crown of France seemed inevitably destined to go to a side branch of the royal house, the Kings of Navarre, who were Huguenots. Civil war broke out between the Catholics and the Huguenots, with horrors committed on both sides. During the eighteen years between 1562 and 1580 the struggle was renewed no less than seven times. The outcome was that the Huguenots formed a state within the state. This Calvinist Free State, as it might be called, had its own religious laws, regulated its own political and financial affairs, maintained an army and a navy and its own courts of justice; four of the strongest fortresses of France were in its possession. In defense of their interests the Catholics organized the *Holy League*, under the leadership of the Duke of Guise and the Cardinal of Bourbon. It was the avowed purpose of the League to prevent a Huguenot from becoming King of France. Hostile feeling rose to fever-heat. The Massacre of St. Bartholomew's Eve (August 24, 1572), engineered by Catherine de Medici, with its destruction of two thousand Huguenots who had come to Paris to witness the marriage between Henry of Navarre and the sister of Charles IX, only increased the fury of the Calvinists. Wars and insurrections followed one another, and there appeared to be no hope of peace, when Henry III, the last of the sons of Catherine de Medici, was murdered by a mad Dominican friar (August 2, 1589). Henry of Navarre became King of France under the title of Henry IV.

The Edict of Nantes.—The triumph of Protestantism seemed imminent; but the new King, realizing that the vast majority of Frenchmen would not accept a heretic as ruler, announced his intention of receiving instruction in the Catholic faith. He abjured Calvinism in 1593, and was absolved from all censures by the Pope in 1595. To put an end to the religious troubles he published the *Edict of Nantes* (1598), by which liberty of worship, full civil rights and full civil protection were guaranteed to the Huguenots, and they were allowed to retain complete control of the 200 towns which they held. In no country of Europe did a Protestant majority grant such freedom to the Catholic minority.

3. *Calvinism in Germany, the Netherlands, and Scotland*

Calvinism never succeeded in gaining many adherents in Germany. Both princes and people who broke away from the Catholic Church preferred the Lutheran brand of Protestantism. Moreover, the Peace of Augsburg expressly forbade any other religion than the Catholic and the Lutheran. Still this Article was not vigorously enforced. Calvinists were tolerated in several of the southern and western states. The Electors of the Palatinate forced their subjects to abandon Lutheranism for Calvinism in 1563, then to return to Lutheranism in 1576, and finally settled on Calvinism as the religion of the state. Thus within sixty years the people had changed their religion four times.

Holland Is Lost to the Church.—The Netherlands, the "wealthiest, freest, and most populous country of Europe," were severed from the German Empire at the beginning of the 16th century and became an appanage of Spain. During the reign of Charles V they were not seriously troubled by heresy, though both Calvinists and Lutherans sought to spread their errors. Philip II (1555-1598) lost the sympathies of the people by his contempt for their constitutional privileges, by quartering Spanish troops in their towns, and by appointing Spaniards to most of the higher offices of State. Political opposition begot religious opposition. William of Orange, the governor of Holland, formed an alliance with the Calvinists. Thirty preachers arrived from Geneva and stirred up the people to revolt. Bands of iconoclasts, Calvinists, Lutherans, and Anabaptists, scoured the country "thirsting for the blood of the papists and the possessions of the rich"; they plundered four hundred churches, maltreated the priests, monks, and nuns, desecrated the Sacred Species, and committed other acts of sacrilege and violence. Philip recalled Margaret of Parma, who had been governor, and sent the Duke of Alva to put down both the heresy and the rebellion. Alva arrived in 1567 and inaugurated a reign of terror. His efforts were in vain; his severity only served to increase the opposition. After six years he was recalled; but it was too late. Not even that brilliant soldier, Don John of Austria, the victor of Lepanto, could win back the provinces to their former allegiance. Farnese, Duke of Parma, was more successful. By his skillful diplomacy he succeeded in detaching the ten southern provinces (Belgium) from the seven northern ones, which definitely accepted Calvinism and formed themselves into a separate state (Holland) under William of Orange. The new Calvinist state was supported by England, and Spain was compelled, after years of fighting, to recognize its independence.

THE MARTYRS OF GORKUM

In 1572 the Calvinists seized 17 priests and two lay brothers in Gorkum, threw them into prison, cruelly mutilated them, and finally hanged them for refusing to deny their belief in the Real Presence and the Papal Supremacy. They are known as the *Martyrs of Gorkum,* and were canonized in 1865.

The Triumph of Calvinism in Scotland.—"Of all the Churches of Europe," says Lingard, "none perhaps was better prepared to receive the seed of the new Gospel than that of Scotland." Through the influence of the Crown and the higher nobility, very unworthy men had for a long time been appointed to the most important offices in the Church, and as a result, discipline had broken down completely, especially in the monasteries. The wealth of the Church excited the cupidity of the greedy Scottish nobles, who, on account of the clan system then predominant in the country, could rely for support upon their people in their attacks on the lands of the Church. Another factor that promoted the Reformation movement was the division in Scotland between those who favored an alliance with France and those who advocated a union with England. The party favorable to England was also favorable to Protestantism, and hence had a double claim on English support, and their claim was fully recognized both by Henry VIII and Queen Elizabeth.

James V of Scotland took stern measures to prevent the spread of Lutheranism. In 1525 Lutheranism was interdicted by an Act of Parliament, and in the following years a number of Lutheran preachers were executed. When James V refused to follow the suggestions of his uncle, Henry VIII, who wished to involve Scotland in his own quarrel with Rome, Henry threw all his influence on the side of the Scottish nobles who had leanings towards heresy. Finally, it came to war, and James was beaten (1541). He died soon after, leaving as his successor a child of eight days, Mary, afterwards known as Mary Queen of Scots, one of the most beautiful, but also one of the most unfortunate, queens of history. The Earl of Arran, a Protestant, became regent. Cardinal Beaton, Archbishop of St. Andrews, who opposed his schemes to protestantize the country and to deliver it over to England, was arrested, and afterwards murdered (1546). The dastardly crime was publicly approved by John Knox, the Apostle of Calvinism in Scotland.

Knox was a priest and served as a private tutor when he joined the murderers of Cardinal Beaton. He was imprisoned, but escaped to the Continent. He spent several years at Geneva, where he imbibed the doctrines of Calvin and published (in 1558) "The First Blast of the Trumpet against the Monstrous Regiment of Women" (i.e., Mary the Catholic of England and Mary Queen of Scots). In the meantime, the Scottish nobles favorable to England had formed the "Solemn League and Covenant" for the overthrow of the Catholic Church in Scotland. Knox returned to Scotland and took charge of the anti-Catholic movement. He inveighed in the most violent terms against the Pope and all things Catholic. Everywhere serious disturbances broke out in the wake of his preaching. Churches, convents, and monasteries were pillaged; not even the superb Cathedral of St. Andrews escaped desecration. The Protestant party soon gained the ascendancy, and a parliament, called in 1560, proclaimed Protestantism the State religion, adopted the Calvinistic "Confession of Faith" drawn up by Knox, abolished Catholic worship, and decreed exile and death against anybody found celebrating or assisting at Mass. When Mary Queen of Scots returned to Scotland in 1561 to take possession of the throne, she found it difficult to get permission to have Mass celebrated even in her own private chapel. Scotland was lost to the faith. Mary could not even maintain herself on the throne. Forced to resign (1568) in favor of her young son James VI, she threw herself on the mercy of her cousin Queen Elizabeth of England; but instead of aid and protection, she found imprisonment and, finally, death on the scaffold (1587). Her last words were: "My faith is the ancient Catholic faith. For this faith I give up my life. In Thee I trust, O Lord; into Thy hands I commend my spirit." Nineteen of her forty-five years had been spent in prison. A little while before her tragic death, she wrote the following short poem:

> O Domine Jesu, speravi in Te!
> O care mi Jesu, hunc libera me!
> In dura catena, in misera poena,
> Languendo, gemendo et genuflectendo
> Adoro, imploro ut liberes me.

Hints for Study

1. Read the articles on *Calvin* and *Knox* in the *Catholic Encyclopedia*.
2. For Mary Queen of Scots see Mrs. M. Scott, *The Tragedy of Fotheringay* and Eric Linkwater, *Mary, Queen of Scots*. (Appleton, N. Y. 1933.)
3. A short but excellent account of the *Massacre of St. Bartholomew's Day* will be found in B. Conway, *The Question Box*, p. 199.
4. Show how in every country where Calvinism triumphed politics played an important part in its triumph.
5. Which are the main points of difference between Lutheranism and Calvinism?
6. Why are the Calvinists called Presbyterians?
7. What doctrine have the American Baptists in common with the Anabaptists and Calvinists?
8. Draw up a chronological table showing the rise and progress of Calvinism.

CHAPTER III

DISRUPTION OF THE CHURCH IN ENGLAND.
ANGLICANISM

1. *Henry VIII Repudiates the Papacy*

In 1509 Henry VIII succeeded his father Henry VII on the throne of England. In the same year he married his deceased brother's widow, Catherine of Aragon, after obtaining the Papal dispensation required for such a marriage. Handsome, intelligent, devoted to letters and skilled in outdoor sports, he seemed to possess all the qualities which make for a happy reign. His zeal for the doctrines of St. Thomas and his hatred of heresy added to his royal diadem the aureole of orthodoxy; he publicly burned the writings of Luther, and exhorted the German princes by letter to "cut off while it is time, that impure and tainted member from the noble Body of Christ." At the same time he composed an elegant defense of the Catholic doctrine of the seven sacraments, which won for him from Pope Leo X, to whom the book was dedicated, the title of *Defender of the Faith* (1521).

There was no trace of Luther's doubts and scruples in the soul of this self-satisfied monarch, nor was there any desire manifested by the English people as a whole to assault the edifice of Catholic Doctrine or to rid themselves of the "Yoke of Rome." And yet it was this King who tore the English Church from its Head in Rome and it was this people that in less than a hundred years turned Protestant almost to the last man. What sinister power was it that made Protestants of a King and a nation who did not want to be Protestants at all, that caused irreparable damage to so many souls, and brought hundreds of loyal Catholics to a cruel death? It was the demon of lust.

It is doubtful whether Henry VIII's married life was pure; from 1521 on it became positively immoral. Other women, besides Catherine, his wife, entered his life; his relations with some of them were a public scandal. In 1527 he conceived a violent passion for Anne Boleyn, maid of honor to the queen, and determined to marry her. He applied to Pope Clement VII for a declaration that his marriage with Catherine was null and void on the ground that marriage with a deceased brother's wife was forbidden by Divine Law (Lev. 18, 16), and consequently, that the dispensation given by Julius II was worthless. The royal theologian, or rather his advisers, forgot that the Ancient Law (Deut. 25, 5) authorized such a marriage, and that the Roman Curia had granted dispensations before in similar cases. Pope Clement appointed Cardinal Campeggio and Cardinal Wolsey to try the case in England (1529). Catherine refused to appear before such judges, and the Pope summoned both parties to submit the case to Rome. Wolsey's failure to secure a divorce caused his downfall. His place was taken by two very able but unprincipled men, Thomas Cromwell, son of a drunken brewer of Put-ney, and Thomas Cranmer, a Lutheran at heart, who, though a priest, had taken to himself a wife, whose existence he care-fully concealed. It was these two men who goaded Henry on to the rupture with Rome.

HENRY VIII   *Holbein*

On Cranmer's advice, Henry asked and by shameless brib-ery obtained from Oxford and Cambridge and from several French and Italian Universities a declaration that his marriage with Catherine was invalid, or at least doubtful. At the same time, in order to frighten the Pope into giving a favorable decision, Henry forced the convocation of the clergy to accept him as "su-preme head of the Church of England as far as the law of Christ allows" (1531). Shortly afterwards Archbishop Warham of Canterbury died, and Henry nominated Cranmer to succeed him. One of the first acts of the new Archbishop was to pronounce Henry's marriage with Catherine invalid. Anne Boleyn, who had been in the meantime secretly married to Henry by his court chaplain, was solemnly crowned by Cranmer (1533).

Clement VII could not defer his judgment any longer without appearing to approve of Henry's divorce; on March 23, 1534, he declared the King's marriage with Catherine of Aragon to be a valid marriage from which no divorce was possible. But this belated sentence only hastened the consummation of the schism. Henry broke completely and definitely with the Holy See. In November, 1534, a subservient Parliament enacted that "the King, his heirs and successors, should be taken and reputed the only supreme heads on earth of the Church of England." Thomas Cromwell was appointed "Vicar-General"; it was his task to force the bishops and the clergy to accept the new conditions by taking the "oath of Supremacy." Most of the cowardly bishops and priests proved unfaithful to their trust, took the prescribed oath, expunged the name of the Pope from the liturgical books, preached against the tyranny of Rome, and extolled the virtues and pre-rogatives of the new Vicar of Christ. Cranmer's favorite theme was that the Pope was anti-Christ, "the same who was to come at the end of the world."

Of all the bishops of England only one refused to bend the knee before the adulterous tyrant: *John Fisher*, Bishop of Rochester, a man of seventy-seven years. "If I were to consent," he declared, "that the King is the head of the English Church, I should be guilty of tearing the seamless robe of Christ, the *one* Catholic Church." For this fearless confession of faith he was imprisoned, tried, and convicted of high-treason, and executed by beheading (1535). Pope Paul III had raised him to the cardinalate whilst he was awaiting the death sentence in prison.

All the laymen of England set their loyalty to Henry VIII above their loyalty to Christ's Vicar, except *Sir Thomas More*. Thomas More was one of the most distinguished men of his age. He had written books that were read throughout Europe. He was the friend and patron of the famous painter Hans Holbein, and of the great scholar Erasmus of Rotterdam. He had held the highest offices in the kingdom, had been Chancellor of England and the trusted friend and Councilor of Henry VIII, who had often come to his house and walked arm in arm with him in his garden. His son-in-law expressed his astonishment at all this honor. Sir Thomas calmed him: "Be assured the King will have my head cut off if this brings him in but *one* castle in France."—When he refused to subscribe to the laws proclaiming the King's spiritual supremacy, he was thrown into prison, and when all attempts to make him change his mind proved unavailing, he was beheaded, July 7, 1535, and his head fixed upon London Bridge.

Most of the English monks also proved recreant; the London Carthusians, and some Brigittines and Franciscans upheld the honor of monasticism. These men stood firm and met death like heroes. Menaced with death by drowning in the Thames, two Franciscans replied: "Take your threats elsewhere; as far as we

Both by Holbein

BL. THOMAS MORE   BL. JOHN FISHER

are concerned, they do not frighten us; with the grace of God we know that the road to heaven is as short by water as by land, and it matters little which one you will make us take."—In 1888 Pope Leo XIII beatified John Fisher, Thomas More, and their fifty-four companions in martyrdom.

If the lives of his subjects were not sacred to Henry, their property was much less so. In 1536 a Bill was passed ordering the suppression of the lesser monasteries. The suppression was rigorously carried out. An insurrection that broke out in the north of the country served Henry as a pretext for dissolving all the English monasteries, and handing over their property to the greedy English nobility. Within the space of a few years 645 monasteries were suppressed.

Pope Paul III, despairing of a change of heart in the English King, excommunicated him, and released his subjects from their oath of allegiance (1538). But there was no one to carry out the sentence; both Francis I of France and Charles V were, at this very time, making overtures to Henry for an alliance. Henry did not mind being called a schismatic; but he hated heretics. To furnish the world with a proof of his orthodoxy, he passed (in 1539) the famous *Statute of the Six Articles* which laid down the "truth of Transubstantiation, the sufficiency of Communion under one kind, clerical celibacy, the validity of the vows of chastity, the utility of private Masses for the souls in Purgatory, and the necessity of auricular confession." The violators of these articles were punished as inexorably as the defenders of Papal supremacy.

All the world knows what happened to Anne Boleyn, for whose sake England was separated from the Holy See, and to the other wives of Henry; and how Thomas Cromwell lost his head for having advised the tyrant to marry the ugly Anne of Cleves. When Henry died (1547), the Court orators forbade the people to weep for him, "because such a pious King must have surely gone straight to heaven!"

2. Triumph of Protestantism Under Edward VI

Under Henry's son, the boy King Edward VI, a mere puppet in the hands of the Somersets and Cranmer, the English Church became out-and-out Protestant. Wholesale religious changes were undertaken at once. Henry's Six Articles were repealed; Lutheran and Calvinist professors were imported from the Continent to teach theology at Oxford and Cambridge; a communion service in English was inserted in the Mass; a new Prayer-Book "compiled with the assistance of the Holy Ghost" (1549) was introduced to take the place of the Missal; a second Prayer-Book (Book of Common Prayer) was later (1552) made obligatory on all; the Mass was abolished as idolatrous, and a new creed consisting of forty-two articles was drawn up as the official creed of the English Church. The work of pulling down altars, destroying ornaments, pillaging churches, went merrily on. . . . Foreign sectaries of every description, Lutherans, Calvinists, Zwinglians, Anabaptists, Waldensians, Arians, swarmed in London. "The common faith of England was submerged in strife. The majority of the people went about their work and endured the changes in religion. There is no evidence that any considerable number of the clergy welcomed the new religion. Generally they conformed, waiting for the storm to pass." It did pass, but a new one was brewing.

3. The Catholic Restoration under Mary Tudor

Mary Tudor's accession—Mary was the daughter of Henry VIII and Catherine of Aragon—brought back the old order. The monks returned and the Mass was said. The anti-Papal legislation was repealed, and many men who had been prominent in promoting the new religion were reconciled to the faith. As the nobles were allowed by Rome to keep the Church lands which they had stolen, they were perfectly willing, if a Tudor ordered it, to vote the reconciliation of England with the Pope. Cardinal Pole was sent into England as Papal Legate to absolve the country from censure and to restore it to communion with Rome. Then Queen Mary made her first mistake. Against the wishes of Cardinal Pole, and against the advice of her cousin, the Emperor Charles V, she had Archbishop Cranmer, and the three bishops appointed by Edward VI—Hooper, Latimer, and Ridley—burnt at the stake for heresy, as were also a large number (about 210 in all) of their friends. "There was no precedent for burning a bishop at the stake, and it shocked the people. Had Mary executed Cranmer for treason, as she might well have done, his fate would have attracted no pity. Had she put Hooper, Latimer, and Ridley in prison, as Edward's Council had put Gardiner and Bonner, and as Elizabeth put the Catholic hierarchy, no one would have complained. . . . The burning of the bishops struck at the respect for authority. The return of England to Catholicity was hindered by the fires of Smithfield" (Clayton, *The English Disruption in the 16th Century*, in Lattey, *The Church*, p. 283).

The marriage of Queen Mary with Philip II of Spain was her second mistake. "The fear that England was going to become a Spanish province ruled by Philip, for whom the English people entertained the greatest dislike, helped to turn the people against Mary and prepared the way for their acceptance of Elizabeth."

4. The Elizabethan Settlement. The Triumph of Anglicanism

On Mary's death (1558) Elizabeth, daughter of Henry VIII and Anne Boleyn, was proclaimed Queen. At her coronation she took the oath to uphold the Catholic faith. But her ministers, with the clever but unscrupulous Cecil at their head, had little difficulty in persuading her "to put down a religion which proclaimed her a bastard, and to support the reformed doctrines, which alone could give stability to her throne" (Lingard). With a majority of only three votes, her first Parliament (1559) passed an Act of Supremacy, which declared the Queen supreme governor in spiritual as well as in temporal matters. The Act of Uniformity prescribed the use of the Second Prayer Book of Edward VI, and ordered the attendance of the laity at the Protestant service. The altars were again destroyed, and the Mass proscribed. In 1563 the Forty-two Articles of Edward VI were cut down to Thirty-nine Articles and made the official creed of the Church.

This time the bishops were not so subservient as in the time of Henry VIII. They realized that they had to do with heresy, and refused to make any compromise. Of the sixteen Catholic bishops all except one steadfastly refused to submit. Two died in exile, one died in his home, the other twelve were imprisoned until death. They were replaced by invalidly consecrated Calvinistic laymen. Of the Catholic clergy one thousand resigned or were forcibly deprived of their parishes. Many priests conducted the Protestant service and said Mass afterwards for the faithful. This went on until Pope Pius V positively forbade Catholics to attend the heretical services in England. "In the years 1560-70," says Clayton, "England was lost to the faith. Lack of clergy, lack of guidance, compromise with the new order, help to explain the loss. Rome and Philip of Spain refrained from any show of hostility to Elizabeth, trusting to time to bring reconciliation. Elizabeth played with them till the Catholic cause in England was lost."

In 1570 Pope Pius V, against the advice of the Emperor Ferdinand and Philip of Spain, excommunicated and deposed Elizabeth. The English Parliament retaliated by making it high treason to declare the Queen a heretic, or to receive any Bull from Rome. A violent persecution of the Catholics set in, and great numbers of the clergy were fined, imprisoned, or put to death. The real era of persecution, however, began in 1581, when Parliament passed an Act making it high treason to return to the old religion, and felony to say or hear Mass, to go to confession, or to harbor a priest. It was in this year that the heroic Jesuit Blessed Edmund Campion was put to death.

BL. EDMUND CAMPION BEING LED TO PRISON
The inscription on his head reads: Campion the Seditious Jesuit

The intrigues carried on by some English Catholics with Spain, and Philip's attempt to invade England, roused the national patriotism, strengthened Elizabeth's position and enabled her to succeed in her plan of delivering up England to Protestantism. The English Catholics, several hundred thousand in number, were secretly ministered to by priests educated at the English college established by Cardinal Allen at Douai, in France, and by Jesuits and members of other Religious Orders. The laws against the Catholics remained in force until 1778, but they were not always strictly enforced. The Catholics suffered most during the reigns of William and Mary (1689-1702) and Queen Anne (1702-1714) when the most violent measures (Penal Laws) were passed against them, and their lives and their property were at the mercy of the spy and the professional priest-hunter.

The total number of men and women, priests, monks, etc., who suffered death in England for the Catholic faith from 1535 to 1681 is over six hundred, several hundred of whom have been beatified.

5. *The Reformation in Ireland*

The political conquest of Ireland, begun in the 12th century by Henry II, was completed by Elizabeth, who spent vast sums of money in the enterprise. The Irish were more successful in their resistance when England tried to conquer them spiritually also.

In 1536 a so-called Irish Parliament, composed entirely of Anglo-Irish nobles, accepted the religious supremacy of Henry VIII; but practically the whole nation, with the exception of Archbishop Brown of Dublin, an apostate Augustinian Friar, who owed his elevation to Henry VIII, remained faithful to the Pope. For the next six years a relentless war was waged on the Catholic chiefs, and one after the other submitted to the King and renounced the authority of the Pope. A Parliament was again summoned in Dublin, in which Irish and Anglo-Irish sat side by side, and Henry was proclaimed King of Ireland (1542).

The lay leaders had proved themselves cowards; the bishops, however, with three or four exceptions, were faithful to their oaths and refused to accept the royal supremacy. War was declared upon the property of the Church. Five hundred and forty abbeys, priories, and other religious houses were seized, and the monks were either put to death or dispersed. Many of the famous shrines were plundered, and their priceless relics destroyed. With the sacrilegious spoils Henry enriched his courtiers and the nobles, not forgetting himself. Still, all these measures did not produce the desired effect on the feelings of the people; if anything, they were more loyal to Rome than ever.

Edward VI made a vain attempt to introduce heretical doctrines into Ireland and to force the Book of Common Prayer upon the people in place of the Mass. Elizabeth determined to pursue the same policy in Ireland as she was pursuing in England. But all her measures failed to make Ireland Protestant. Then she tried persecution against the bishops and the clergy. Six archbishops and bishops were arrested and put to death after terrible torture; many other prelates were obliged to escape to the Continent. "Hundreds of the clergy, both secular and regular, underwent martyrdom for the faith, but, notwithstanding the persecution, priests were still found to minister to the spiritual wants of the people, the Franciscans and the Dominicans being especially active. In order to keep up the supply of priests many Irish seminaries were established on the Continent, at this time and at a later period, at Paris, Bordeaux, Nantes, Douai, Antwerp, Lisbon, Salamanca, Seville and Rome" (MacCaffrey).

Since they could not "convert" the Irish, the English monarchs resolved to exterminate them little by little. Elizabeth confiscated one hundred thousand acres of land in Ulster, and drove out the Catholics to make way for Scotch and English planters. James I extended the Protestant colonization by confiscating four hundred thousand acres more, and ordered all the Irish priests to leave Ireland under pain of death. Every effort made subsequently by the Irish people to win their rights was mercilessly put down, and the yoke that rested upon them made heavier. After the rising in 1690 the English set themselves deliberately to enslave three-fourths of the inhabitants of Ireland. Every Catholic was deprived of even a semblance of civil and religious rights. "These Penal Laws were made to put an end to the Catholic religion, and for a long time they were strictly enforced; but, instead of succeeding in their object, they succeeded only in impoverishing the Protestant landowners and the country generally, and in giving Catholicity a stronger hold than it ever had before on the great body of the people in Ireland" (MacCaffrey).

The loyalty of the Irish people to the Catholic faith is all the more remarkable because practically the same causes were at work in Ireland to bring about a decline in religion as in the other countries of Europe—the interference of the secular power in ecclesiastical appointments, the nomination of foreign clerics to most of the Irish sees, the break-down of episcopal authority, the heaping-up of ecclesiastical offices in one hand, the want of good schools for the education of the clergy, the heavy taxes levied frequently by the Papal Court, the loss of Papal prestige through the Great Western Schism, the undermining of faith and morality by the humanist movement. . . . About 260 persons died for the faith in Ireland between 1537 and 1719; of these the names of 4 archbishops, 11 bishops, 37 priests, 35 monks, 49 laymen and 6 lay women have been presented to the Pope for beatification.

Martyrdom of the Ven. Robert Southwell

Robert Southwell, the English poet, whose *Burning Babe, Mary Magdalen's Tears,* and *Triumphs over Death* are known to every student of English literature, was born in Norfolk in 1561. He studied at Douai, Paris, Rome and Tournai. In 1578 he joined the Jesuits at Rome. Ordained priest in 1584, he accompanied Father Henry Garnett to England in 1586. For six years he labored with great zeal and marked success among the scattered and persecuted Catholics. In 1592 he was betrayed by a woman into the hands of that unspeakable villain Richard Topcliffe, the confidant of Queen Elizabeth. For weeks Topcliffe tortured him most inhumanly. Transferred to the Gatehouse, he was treated so abominably that his father presented a petition to Queen Elizabeth begging that his son might either be executed or treated as a gentleman. Southwell was then lodged in the Tower, but he was not brought to trial till the beginning of 1595. His condemnation was a foregone conclusion. He was hanged at Tyburn on March 3, 1595. On March 4 Father Garnett wrote an account of his martyrdom to the General of the Society of Jesus in Rome, from which the following extract is taken:

"The Peace of Christ Jesus. At length I have a most beautiful flower to offer to your paternity from your garden, a most sweet fruit from your tree, an admirable treasure from your treasury, 'silver tried by the fire, purged from the earth, refined seven times.' It is Christ's unconquered soldier, most faithful disciple, most valiant martyr, Robert Southwell, formerly my dearest companion and brother, now my lord, patron, and king, reigning with Christ.

"He had been kept for nearly three years in closer custody than anyone ever was, so that no Catholic ever saw him or spoke to him. He was often tortured and that in a more cruel manner than even this barbarity is accustomed to inflict. He publicly declared that he had been tortured ten times, and that with torments worse than the rack or than death itself.

"Thus deprived of all human aid, at length they brought him forth that it might be clear to all how far the divine assistance exceeds all human help.

"For all this long time he could neither say Mass, nor go to the Sacrament of Penance, nor speak with anyone, nor receive consolation from any; yet he went to judgment and to execution with so calm and tranquil a mind that you would have said that he came from the midst of a monastery of religious men, and that he was passing of his own free will from the breasts of his mother to the sweetest of delights.

". . . Having been drawn to the gallows and lifted, from the hurdle on which he had been drawn, to the cart, he made the sign of the cross as well as he could (for his hands were bound) and began his speech. . . . As the cart was driven away he signed himself, saying, 'Into Thy hands O Lord.' Whilst hanging from the gallows he often made the sign of the cross (for the rope was badly placed on his neck) until the hangman pulled his legs (which is an unusual act of humanity with us) and then he closed his eyes which till then were open. An officer often tried to cut the rope but was prevented by Lord Mountjoy and by all the people, who three times cried out: 'Leave him, leave him.'

The hangman took him down from the gallows with much reverence and, with his attendants, carried him in his arms to the place of his disembowelling. Others they usually drag along the ground in a very inhuman way. One of the pursuivants declared that he had never seen a man die more piously, and some of the heretics wished that their souls might be with his. . . ."

—*The Triumphs Over Death* by the Ven. Robert Southwell, Appendix II. Edited by J. W. Trotman, p. 99-104.

Hints for Study

1. For detailed accounts of the Reformation in England and Ireland the following works may be consulted with profit: D'Alton, *History of Ireland;* Birt, *The Elizabethan Settlement;* Card. Gasquet, *The Eve of the Reformation;* Moran, *The Persecution of the Irish Catholics;* Cobbett-Gasquet, *A History of the Protestant Reformation in England and Ireland; The English Martyrs* (Herder, 1929).

2. Every student should read Robert Hugh Benson's historical novels *The King's Achievement* (Henry VIII), *By What Authority?* (Queen Elizabeth), and *Come Rack, Come Rope.*

3. Write a chronological outline of the disruption of the English Church from 1527 to 1590.

4. Good lives of Bl. John Fisher and Bl. Thomas More have been written by T. E. Bridgett (Cath. Publication Society, N. Y., 1888). The short life of Sir Thomas More by Bremond-Child (Benziger, 1913) and Louise Imogen Guiney's *Bl. Edmund Campion* are excellent.

5. Why is the English Protestant Church called the *Established Church,* the *High Church,* and the *Anglican Church?* Who were the *Puritans?* Why hasn't the Anglican Church any true bishops and priests? (See Art. *Anglican Orders* in *Cath. Encycl.*)

CHAPTER IV

THE CATHOLIC REACTION AND REVIVAL

1. *Nature and Scope of the Catholic Reformation*

Long before the Protestant revolt, all serious-minded Catholic men and women were convinced that the Church needed to be thoroughly reformed. Not the Catholic religion, as the Protestants maintained, but the people who professed that religion, required reformation. "Men must be changed by Religion," as one of the champions of true reform remarked, "not Religion by men." Reformation of the Church in her Head and in her members, this was the first part of the Catholic program of Reform. The spread of error by the religious innovators, who attacked the Divine Constitution of the Church and many of her fundamental doctrines, imposed upon the Catholic leaders the duty of setting forth in unmistakable and authoritative terms the true doctrines of Christianity contained in Scripture and Tradition.

There is no better proof for the divine origin and guidance of the Church than the fact that she not only survived the great apostasy of the 16th century, but emerged from the conflict rejuvenated and prepared to meet new ones.

2. *The End of the Roman Renaissance*

Leo X, the patron of the men of letters, artists, and worldlings who made the Papal Court a center of refinement, luxury, and amusement, was succeeded by the learned, austere, and reform-zealous Hadrian VI (1521-1523).

Hadrian Florensz (i.e., son of Florens) was born in the city of Utrecht, which at that time belonged to the German Empire. He is therefore reckoned among the German Popes—the last German Pope, and, in fact, the last non-Italian Pope. Educated by the pious "Brothers of the Common Life," he became vice-chancellor of the University of Louvain and, in 1506, tutor to the future Emperor Charles V. Charles was grateful to his teacher, obtained a Spanish bishopric for him and had him raised to the cardinalate.

458

As Pope he was determined to reform the Curia. He was convinced that the hierarchy was mainly responsible for the schism that was threatening Christendom.

The Pope's intentions were good, but his zeal outran his prudence. Surrounded by the luxurious culture of the Renaissance, he lived in monastic simplicity; he gave no time nor thought to artists and humanists; he did not even speak the language of the Italian Court. All his efforts at reform were met with opposition, and his appeal to the Christian rulers to oppose the advancing Turks fell on deaf ears. His death, it was said, was hastened by the fall of Rhodes. When he was laid to rest, after a reign of only twenty months, in the German national church Santa Maria dell 'Anima, the following words, often quoted by himself, were written on his tomb: *"Proh dolor, quantum refert, in quae tempora vel optimi cuiusque virtus incidat!"* ("Alas, how much it matters in what times the work of even the best of men happens to fall!")

Even before Hadrian's accession the work of reform had been quietly begun in Rome. Priests and laymen had founded the "Oratory of Divine Love." Their purpose was to labor for their own sanctification and that of their friends and acquaintances. They held meetings in a little church and gave themselves up to works of charity. The guiding spirit of this pious company was St. Cajetan of Tiene (1480-1547). Filled with the spirit of St. Francis of Assisi, he wrote: "I see Christ poor and myself rich; I see Him despised and myself honored; I want to draw a step nearer to Him and have therefore resolved to rid myself of all that I still possess."

In 1523 Cajetan founded the Congregation of Regular Clerks, known as Theatines, because John Peter Carafa, bishop of Theate and later Pope Paul IV, was its first Superior-General. The new Order set itself the task of recalling the clergy to an edifying life and the laity to the practice of virtue. Despite its severe rule, it developed rapidly and was a powerful agency for true reform in Italy and in every country of Europe.

The greatest obstacle to reform was the worldly, not to say pagan, spirit of the Renaissance which still reigned supreme in the Eternal City. A terrible catastrophe removed this obstacle. This was the sack of Rome at the hands of the Constable of Bourbon and the troops of Charles V (May 1527). Clement VII (1523-

1534, a cousin of Leo X, had, by his unfortunate alliance with Francis I of France, drawn down upon himself the anger and vengeance of Charles V. He had to witness the imperial invasion of Papal territory and the Bourbon's sack of Rome which ended the Augustan Age of the Papal City in a horror of fire and blood. Earnest-minded contemporaries saw in the *Sacco di Roma* a judgment of God and an impressive call to conversion and penance.

3. Spain Rises to World Power, and Promotes the Catholic Reform Movement

The Catholic Reform Movement became a European Movement when a great Catholic people placed all its enthusiasm and its resources in the service of the Church.

During the Middle Ages the Spaniards had been forced to fight for their national existence and for their faith against the Moors. Towards the end of the fifteenth century their power grew with unexampled rapidity. In 1492 the last remnant of Moorish rule in the Peninsula was destroyed by the Conquest of Granada. In the same year Christopher Columbus discovered America and presented his royal patrons, Ferdinand and Isabella, with a new world. Under Charles I (1517-1556) and his son Philip II (1556-1598) Spain reached the zenith of its power and influence.

Spain's rise to world-power was of paramount importance for the history of the Church. If the Protestant revolt in Germany was brought to a halt, this was due in the first place to the King of Spain, who as Charles V succeeded his grandfather Maximilian I to the Imperial Crown. Spain was the cradle of the Religious Order which was to become the chief instrument of reform—the Society of Jesus. The colonial policy of Spain (and of her sister-kingdom Portugal) brought the Church face to face with an entirely new problem—the evangelization of the pagans in every quarter of the globe.

During the Renaissance period ecclesiastical discipline was, as a rule, better observed in Spain than in any other country in Europe. This was due in the first place to Cardinal *Ximenes,* who attacked the existing abuses within the Church with the greatest energy, and when resistance was made, he succeeded in crushing it. He gave special attention to Biblical Studies and made the University of Alcala a center of learned studies from which all Spain profited. It was at Alcala that he published his famous *Polyglot*

Bible. Thanks to men like Ximenes, who were eagerly supported by the Spanish sovereigns, Spain found herself armed against the Protestant movement.

4. Pope Paul III Reforms the Papal Court

The reign of Clement VII marks the passing of the Renaissance. With Paul III (1534-1549) a new era in the history of the Papacy begins. Although his early life had not been beyond reproach, and his pontificate was not free from the blemish of nepotism, Pope Paul III saw the necessity of a prompt and efficacious reform of the Church. He began by reforming the Papal Court. He opened the portals of the Sacred College of Cardinals to men of solid learning and unblemished morals, to John Fisher of Rochester, who by his martyr-blood was to give back to the red hat and cassock of the cardinal their deeper meaning; to the Venetian statesman Contarini, a man whose high intellectual gifts and achievements were enhanced by his simple faith and piety; to Reginald Pole, an Englishman, whose loyalty to the Church shed greater luster on his name than the royal blood which flowed in his veins; to the noble-hearted Cervini, who later became Pope Marcellus II, and to John Peter Carafa, who excelled all his fellow-cardinals in enthusiastic devotion to the work of reform.

Seconded by such eminent men, Paul III strove for almost ten years (1535-1544) to convene a General Council. But during all these trying years he never lost sight of the needs of the Church and from time to time enacted laws of the highest importance for her welfare. The reform of the Roman Court was his work, and, by blessing and favoring with his protection the newly-established Orders of Theatines, Capuchins, Barnabites, Ursulines, and Jesuits, he helped to prepare the men and women who were to form the shock-troops of the Church's spiritual army.

5. St. Ignatius of Loyola and the Society of Jesus

Of the many new religious congregations founded in the time of the Church's direst need, the most illustrious was the Society of Jesus. By the "Spiritual Exercises" of its founder, St. Ignatius of Loyola, the Church was enriched with a new and most excellent method for the guidance of souls. In the field of modern education the sons of Ignatius were pioneers *par excellence*, and in the propagation of the faith they blazed a trail which missionaries have followed ever since.

Ignatius was born at Loyola Castle, Guipuzcoa, Spain, in 1491. He was educated to be a knight and served for fourteen years as

Rubens

ST. IGNATIUS HEALS THE POSSESSED

squire to the Grand Treasurer of Queen Isabella of Castile. Whilst fighting for the viceroy of Navarre against the French, he was severely wounded at the siege of Pamplona (May 20, 1521); a cannon-ball had grazed one of his legs and almost shattered the other. During his convalescence he asked for his favorite reading matter, the romances of chivalry, so popular at the time. There were none at hand, and the attendant gave him instead the Life of Christ by the Carthusian Ludolf of Saxony and the Golden

Legend (Lives of the Saints) of Jacobus de Voragine. Reading
the lives of St. Dominic and St. Francis of Assisi, the thought
came to him: "What if some day you were to do what these men
did?" He resolved to make a pilgrimage to Jerusalem.

Like a true Christian knight he first paid homage to his Lady—
the Madonna in the abbey church on Montserrat. He confessed
his sins, gave away his charger and his armor, laid his sword as
an *ex voto* on the altar, and spent the night in prayer. On his way
to the port of Barcelona he stopped at the little town of Manresa.
He wished to prepare himself for his pilgrimage by a few days
of solitude and prayer. The "few days" became a full year, rich
in penance and mortification, richer still in heavenly enlightenment. In Manresa Ignatius wrote the first draft of the "Spiritual
Exercises." Here he also became acquainted with the *Imitation
of Christ*, which he ever after regarded as the most excellent
of all books of devotion.

In 1523 Ignatius arrived in Jerusalem, where he wished to
spend the rest of his days in visiting the Holy Places and working
for the salvation of souls. The Franciscans dissuaded him from
carrying out this purpose, and he returned to Spain in the same
year. He was convinced now that he must become a priest if he
really wished to labor for souls. In spite of his thirty-two years
he took up the study of Latin in Barcelona. After two years he
was far enough advanced to begin the study of philosophy at the
University of Alcala. Here and in Salamanca his shabby clothes
and his efforts to influence his fellow-students to lead lives of
greater piety and mortification brought him into unpleasant connection with the Inquisition, which took him for one of the many
religious fanatics who were causing so much trouble in Spain at
the time.

From 1528 to 1535 Ignatius studied theology at the University
of Paris. Here he induced several of his fellow-students, among
them the Savoyard Peter Faber, and the talented Spanish nobleman, Francis Xavier, to make the "Spiritual Exercises," and
formed a circle of pious students imbued with his own spirit
and ideals. On the Feast of the Assumption, 1534, Ignatius and
six companions repaired to a little church on Montmartre. Peter
Faber, the only one in Holy Orders, celebrated Mass, and before
the Communion each one vowed to God to practice perpetual
poverty and chastity, to make a pilgrimage to the Holy Land, and

to labor there for the salvation of the infidels. If the pilgrimage to Jerusalem should not be possible within a year, or they should not be able to remain in Palestine, they agreed to place themselves at the disposal of the Pope.

In 1537 the friends arrived in Venice, prepared to take ship for the Holy Land. They called themselves the "Company of Jesus" (*Compañia di Gesù*). Venice was at war with the Turks, and for a whole year traveling at sea was impossible. So they carried out the second part of their vow, went to Rome, and offered their services to the Holy Father.

Paul III approved the new Order (1540), and Ignatius was elected the first General (1541). The "Constitutions," drafted

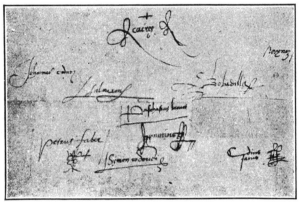

THE SIGNATURES TO THE VOWS TAKEN BY
ST. IGNATIUS AND HIS COMPANIONS
That of St. Francis Xavier appears under
the name of Bobadilla

by him and based on the Spiritual Exercises, were adopted in 1558. When the holy founder died on the 31st of July, 1556, the Society of Jesus numbered about a thousand members. He was beatified in 1609 and canonized together with his faithful friend and disciple Francis Xavier, March 12, 1622.

Defense of the faith at home and its propagation abroad—this was the purpose of the Company of Jesus. It saved or restored to the Church whole districts and provinces. From the time that it entered into action, the advance of the Protestant revolution was checked. With the Franciscans, Dominicans, and other older Orders it compensated the Church for her losses in Europe by the conquest of new and vaster territories beyond the seas.

6. Missionaries in the Wake of the Discoverers in the Far East

During the closing years of the 15th century daring European sailors had discovered and explored vast countries in the South, the East, and the West. The Portuguese, who had sailed south along the western coast of Africa, doubled the Cape of Good Hope in 1487 and, ten years later, under Vasco da Gama, reached India. The Spaniards, under Christopher Columbus, sailing west, had already touched the portals of the New World. A new task thus confronted the Church: the evangelization of the heathen inhabitants of the newly discovered Continents. In America and Africa it was mainly primitive peoples that had to be christianized and civilized; in East Asia the Gospel had to be brought to nations that had already reached a high level of culture.

The Franciscans were the first to follow in the trail of Vasco da Gama in India. They were soon joined by the Dominicans. For forty years they labored heroically, but without much success. The ambition, cruel avarice, and immorality of the Portuguese adventurers and colonists combined with the idolatry of the natives and the baneful influence of Mohammedanism to render their efforts abortive. Then St. Francis Xavier, the Apostle of India and Japan, came upon the scene.

St. Francis Xavier.—Francis was born in 1506 at the Castle of Xavier in Navarre, Spain. With his head full of ambitious plans for the future, the young Basque nobleman, who counted Kings of Navarre and Aragon amongst his ancestors, was pursuing his higher studies at Paris when Ignatius of Loyola weaned him from his worldly life and worldly aspirations by repeating to him over and over the words of Christ: "What doth it profit a man, if he gain the whole world, but suffer the loss of his soul?" We have already met him in the chapel on Montmartre taking the vows.

In 1540 Francis bade farewell to Rome and Ignatius, and in the following year set out on his long sea-voyage to India as Papal Legate. He landed at Goa, the capital of the Portuguese possessions. Ten years of intense apostolic labors followed, first at Goa, where in six months he accomplished the reformation of that corrupt city; then among the baptized but uninstructed pearl-fishers of Cape Comorin, and their neighbors, the fisher-folk of Travancore, ten-thousand of whom—their whole caste—he baptized in one month; then as apostolic explorer among the barbarous inhabitants of the distant Spice Islands (Moluccas), the farthest Portuguese outpost in the East; then as first messenger of the Gospel among the Japanese—as simple missionary, as pioneer, as founder, organizer, and first provincial of the flourishing Jesuit missions of the Far East, and as a shining model for all subse-

Rubens

St. Francis Xavier Preaching in India

quent preachers of the Gospel—until God called the indefatigable soldier to eternal rest on the 3rd of December, 1552, from the solitary island of Sanzian, just as he was preparing to begin the conquest of the teeming millions of China. Hundreds of thousands are said to have been converted by him. Since Paul traversed the Roman Empire God's Church had seen no greater apostle.

The great missionary lives on in his *Letters*. These Letters, whose every line reveals a heart aflame for Christ, have inspired thousands of his countrymen and of every nation with enthusiastic love for the apostolate among the heathens and the desire to lay down their lives for the Gospel—founders of Religious Orders like Philip Neri, Francis de Sales, Vincent de Paul and Gaspar del Buffalo, saints like Peter Canisius and Aloysius, and martyrs like Francis Mastrilli, John de Britto, Diego de Sanvitores, and hosts of others. "Master Francis Xavier," wrote one of his countrymen, "works in Spain and Portugal as fruitfully through his letters as he does in India by his preaching."

Christianity in Japan.—After the death of St. Francis Xavier Christianity made rapid progress in Japan. The number of Christians soon rose to two hundred thousand. During the reign of the Emperor Taikosama (1587) a persecution broke out which continued, with slight interruptions, for fifty years. In order to prevent Christian merchants from entering the country every visitor had to trample a crucifix under his feet. In 1862 Pope Pius IX canonized twenty-six men, missionaries and natives, who had been crucified in 1597 on a hill near Nagasaki. The last vestige of the once flourishing mission in Japan was destroyed in 1637. A handful of Christians alone remained in the country. They practiced their religion in secret and handed on their faith to their children and children's children, until the arrival of fresh missionaries more than two hundred years later.

The Jesuits in China.—St. Francis bequeathed to his Order his own ardent desire to enter and christianize China. For nearly thirty years insurmountable obstacles prevented the realization of this noble ambition; but at last, in 1578, some Portuguese merchants obtained permission to reside at Canton. They were immediately followed by three Jesuits, one of whom was the celebrated *Matteo Ricci*. Ricci became a thorough Chinese scholar. His command of the Chinese language was so perfect that his treatise on the "True Doctrine of God" found a place among the Chinese classics. He made himself useful to the learned world of China by his lectures and writings on Mathematics, Arithmetic, Astronomy, Geography, Music and Philosophy, gradually introducing into them instructions on the Christian religion. Instead of attacking the doctrines of the famous Chinese philosopher Confucius, he often made them the starting-point for his own teachings, and permitted the Christians to pay special honors to him.—In 1601 Ricci obtained an audience with the Emperor Wan-Li, and pre-

sented him with watches, music-boxes, and musical instruments
and finally also with his own writings on the Christian religion.
The Emperor asked him to write books on geography and to draw
maps for him, but never manifested any inclination to become
a Christian. Ricci died at Peking in 1611.

Some time after Ricci's death the German Jesuit *John Adam
Schall* (b. at Cologne in 1591), a learned mathematician and
astronomer, for a long time enjoyed the favor and confidence of
the Chinese Emperors. He had attracted the attention of the
court by calculating eclipses of the sun and moon which had
escaped the native scholars. The Emperor Shun-Chi appointed
him director of the imperial observatory and president of the
Mathematical Institute, raising him at the same time to the rank
of mandarin. During the reign of Shun-Chi Christianity was
tolerated and many high officials embraced it openly. Schall became their spiritual director. In 1664 the last Emperor of the
Ming dynasty was succeeded by a Manchu, a deadly enemy of
the Christians. Father Schall was thrown into prison and condemned to death, but pardoned at the last moment. After his
death (Aug. 15, 1666) his memory was held in high esteem by
the Chinese.

Ferdinand Verbiest, a Flemish Jesuit, for a time assisted and later replaced Father Schall in his astronomical labors at Peking. By his scientific experiments and inventions, and especially by demonstrating his
superiority as an astronomer, he succeeded in winning the favor of the
Manchu Emperors and secured the return of the missionaries after the
persecution of 1664. He was the author of several astronomical works in
Chinese.

Xavier Friedel, an Austrian Jesuit (1673-1743), made a cartographical
survey of China, traversing the whole Empire from south to north. The
work occupied him ten years from 1708 to 1718.

Not long after the Jesuits, the Franciscans and Dominicans entered the
Far Eastern mission field. Unfortunately the progress of missionary work
was retarded by ill-feeling between the Jesuits and Dominicans, growing
out of the controversy on Chinese customs. The Jesuits, as we have seen,
permitted their converts to pay honor to Confucius and to retain their
ancestor cult, regarding these practices as civil, not religious, ceremonies.
This the Dominicans opposed. The Popes, appealed to by both parties, decided in favor of the Dominicans.

Robert de Nobili, the Christian "Sanyasi."—In India great
difficulties were created for the missionaries by the caste system
and the peculiar customs of the Brahmans. For a long time the
converts to Christianity belonged almost exclusively to the lower

classes of society. This fact ripened in the Jesuit missionary, Roberto de Nobili (1577-1656), a Roman of noble birth, the resolve to lay aside European manners and live entirely like a Brahman "Sanyasi" (ascetic). He put on a dress of cavy or yellow color, put on his forehead the sandalwood paste used by the Brahmans, inserted rings in his ears, wore wooden sandals and always had about his neck the Brahman necklace of gold and silver threads. On his head, which was shaven except for a small tuft on the crown, he placed a turban of red silk. He lived in a hut and strictly observed the food laws of the Brahmans, drinking no intoxicants and eating no meat, fish, or eggs. He applied himself to the study of the Indian languages, especially Sanscrit, the sacred language, and became an adept in Indian literature and philosophy. A twenty-day debate with a Brahman philosopher on the "Way of Salvation" ended with a victory for Nobili. The philosopher received baptism, and crowds of Brahmans flocked to the missionary for instruction.

On account of his very liberal concessions to Indian rites Nobili was attacked by other missionaries, especially the Dominicans. He defended himself ably, maintaining that India could be converted in no other way. Gregory XV took his part and sanctioned caste regulations in India. Nobili then proceeded to establish a special mission for the despised caste of the Pariahs, which was rigidly separated from the Brahman missions. The controversy was renewed and carried on for over a hundred years after Nobili's death and caused irreparable damage to the Indian missions.

To give unity and solidity to the work of the missions a committee of cardinals was appointed by Gregory XV under the name of "Congregatio de Propaganda Fide" (June 2, 1622). Urban VIII supplemented the work of this congregation by founding a great missionary college and seminary, where Europeans might be trained for foreign labors, and natives might be educated to undertake mission work. At this college is the famous missionary printing-press, and its library contains an unrivaled collection of literary treasures bearing on every phase of mission work.

7. Missions and Missionaries in the New World

Spanish America.—In the new world discovered by Columbus missionaries followed as eagerly in the wake of the explorers as they did in the Far East. They followed Columbus to Haiti and Cuba and Porto Rico (1493), Ponce de Leon to Florida, Balboa

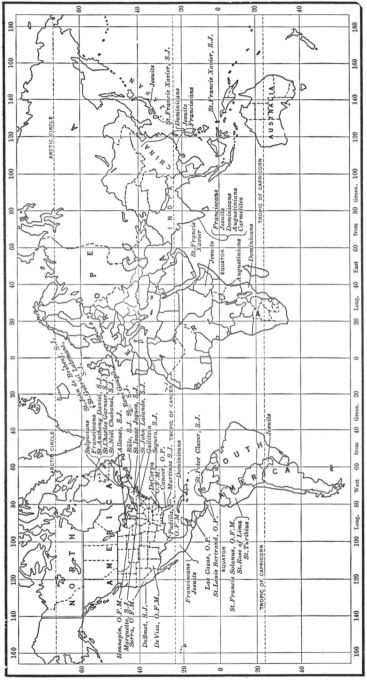

MISSIONARY ACTIVITIES OF THE 16TH AND 17TH CENTURIES

to the Pacific, Cortes to Mexico, Pizarro to Peru, Valdivia to Chile, De Soto to the Mississippi, and Coronado to New Mexico. Franciscans, Dominicans, and Carmelites were first in the field, and to these were soon added the Sons of St. Ignatius. Missions were established at once, thousands of natives were baptized, and in less than eighty years over thirty archdioceses and dioceses had been erected in the West Indies, in Mexico, Florida, Central America, and South America.

Great Saints added luster to the heroic bands of missionaries. *St. Louis Bertrand* (1526-1581) a Spanish Dominican, who landed in New Granada in 1562, baptized more than 25,000 pagans during the eight years that he labored along the coasts of Colombia and Panama. He is venerated as the Apostle of New Granada. *St. Francis Solanus* (1549-1610) a Franciscan of Andalusia, worked for twenty-seven years with wonderful success among the Indians of Peru, and no less successfully by his saintly life and his preaching of penance among the Spanish inhabitants of Lima and Truxillo. In 1610 the Catalonian Jesuit *St. Peter Claver* (1580-1654) landed at Cartagena, was ordained in 1616, and devoted his remaining days to alleviating the spiritual and bodily miseries of the Negro slaves, 300,000 of whom he baptized. He is the special patron of all the missions to the Negroes. The secular clergy were also represented among the saintly missionaries. *St. Turibius* (1538-1606), a Spanish noble and professor of law at Salamanca, was appointed Archbishop of Lima (Peru) in 1580. He traversed 50,000 miles in his diocese, teaching, baptizing, and confirming the natives. He founded the first American seminary. During his episcopate the first saint was born on American soil — *St. Rose of Lima* (1586-1617), whose name is so truly symbolic of the perfume of her virtue. She was canonized in 1667.

The identification of Christianity with the European conquistadores was a great drawback to the spread of Christianity. Both the Spanish and Portuguese adventurers, whom the tales of the fabulous wealth of the New World had attracted to its shores, were often cruel and unjust to the Indians, trampled upon their rights as human beings, and enslaved them. Pope Paul III, in two briefs, condemned the nefarious practices and cruelties of the conquerors, and the missionaries, foremost among them the Dominican *Bartolomé de las Casas* (1474-1566), championed the cause of the natives. It was through the influence of Las Casas that the "New Laws" for the Indies were promulgated in 1542, which saved the Indians from extermination and improved their condition considerably.

"The legislation of Spain in behalf of the Indians everywhere," says C. F. Lummis, "was incomparably more extensive, more comprehensive, more systematic, and more humane than that of Great Britain, the Colonies, and the present United States combined. Those first teachers gave the Spanish language and Christian faith to a thousand aborigines, where we gave a new language and religion to one. There have been Spanish schools for Indians in America since 1524. By 1575—nearly a century before there was a printing-press in English America—many books in *twelve* different Indian languages had been printed in the City of Mexico, whereas in our history John Eliot's Indian bible stands alone; and three Spanish universities in America were nearly rounding out their century when Harvard was founded. A surprisingly large proportion of the pioneers of America were college men; and intelligence went hand in hand with heroism in the early settlement of the New World" (*The Spanish Pioneers,* p. 24).

The "Reductions" of Paraguay.—In villages, generally called "reductions," composed exclusively of Indians, the work of civilization advanced far more rapidly than in colonial settlements. These reductions existed throughout all South and Central America, in Mexico, and as far north as California. The Franciscans formed some of them, but the most celebrated were those of Paraguay, whose founders and governors were Jesuits.

The first Reduction was established in 1609 in what is now southern Brazil, and by 1630 twelve more had been founded. The main part of the "Christian Indian State," as the Reductions were called, was formed by the thirty-two Guarani Reductions in Paraguay. The Spanish colonists opposed the Reductions, because they deprived them of cheap labor and potential slaves, but Philip III of Spain aided the Jesuits with subsidies and legal measures. The venture grew so successful that subsidies from the Crown were soon replaced by taxes to the Crown. "The site of a Reduction was chosen for its healthful climate and proximity to waterways. The plan of the village was square, with streets running in straight lines. In the center was the church, and nearby were the residence of the Fathers and the cemetery." The Indians, some of them, like the Caribs, just weaned from cannibalism, were taught to cultivate the soil, and, little by little, were instructed in all branches of industry. They cast bells and built organs; they made cannon; they were good carpenters, masons, blacksmiths, carvers, and printers; the women manufactured calicoes of the finest qualities. Commerce was developed. Education was general, so that illiteracy was practically unknown. Many Indians could read Spanish and Latin as well as their own tongue. Part of the land was set aside as the "property of God," which the whole community had to till, in order to make provision for times of stress and scarcity and for the maintenance of the sick and the aged.

The Indians were sincerely attached to their unselfish instructors and guides; they knew only too well that it was the missionaries alone who stood between them and abject slavery. Once—in 1631—12,000 Guarani Indians, under the leadership of two Jesuits, migrated from their ancestral lands before the Portuguese slave-hunters to the Reductions on the Paraná, a distance of nearly eight hundred miles.

Among the many Jesuits who labored in the Reductions the most successful were Maceta, De Mendoza, Mazetta, Baraza, and De Montoya. De Montoya composed a dictionary, grammar, and catechism in the Guarani language, and wrote an excellent history of the Paraguay missions. Martyrs, too, grace the annals of the Reductions: three priests, Rocco Gonzales, a native of Paraguay, Alfonso Rodriguez and Juan del Castillo, were killed at the instigation of an Indian wizard in 1628. The heroic missionaries were beatified on Jan. 28, 1934, in a brilliant ceremony attended by hundreds of South American pilgrims.

In the 17th century the Reductions were the object of numerous attacks by the "Paulistas" or Portuguese settlers of São Paulo, who disrupted many villages and carried the Indians off as slaves. The fatal blow was dealt to the Reductions in 1767, when Charles III of Spain signed the edict expelling the Jesuits from the Spanish colonies in America. Thus ended one of the most remarkable experiments in the history of Christian missionary enterprise. Voltaire called the Reductions "the triumph of humanity," and a modern English writer, R. B. Cunningham-Graham, entitled his history of the Paraguay Reductions "A Vanished Arcadia."

The Canadian Missions.—The first successful missionary enterprise in North America was launched in Canada. Jacques Cartier had taken possession of Canada in 1535 in the name of Francis I of France; but no effort was made to settle or evangelize the territory till nearly a hundred years later. Henry IV, stimulated by the example of Spain, which conquered immense territories through its missionaries, asked the Jesuits to begin the work (1608). Two set out, but were imprisoned two years after by the English. In 1615 the Franciscans settled at Quebec at the request of Champlain, the founder of that city, and began to evangelize the natives. In 1626 the Jesuits were called in to assist them. They founded a college at Quebec, and from there undertook missionary work on a large scale. The Hurons, the Algonquins, the Montagnais were converted; villages were established. The Iroquois alone remained obstinate; they refused to profess a religion which the Hurons, their despised enemies from time immemorial, had embraced. Montreal was founded in 1642. In 1657 Sulpicians came to the infant colony and labored both as pastors and teachers in the colony and as missionaries amongst the Indians.

Missions on the Atlantic Coast.—From Canada many missionaries penetrated into the territories now occupied by the United States, and carried the Gospel amongst the Indians who inhabited them.

On the Atlantic coast, within the limits of the present State of Maine, the first Holy Mass was said on Ste. Croix Island in 1604 by Nicholas Aubry, a French priest who had accompanied the Sieur de Monts in an expedition to acquire territory for France. The mission which he established was, however, soon abandoned. There still exists a map made by Samuel de Champlain on which the site of the first chapel in New England is indicated. In 1611 Mass was offered up on Mt. Desert Island by Father Peter Biard, S.J. Two years later a permanent settlement was attempted at St. Sauveur near the present Bar Harbor; but the colony was attacked by a band of Protestants from Virginia, and the missionaries were ruthlessly dispersed. The Capuchin mission on the Penobscot (1633) and the Jesuit mission on the upper Kennebec (1646) were more successful and permanent, many Indians embracing the faith. Both missions were destroyed by expeditions of English soldiers sent for that purpose from Massachusetts in 1704, 1722, and 1724. During the last attack the Ven. Sebastian Râle, a profound scholar of the Indian dialects, was brutally killed and scalped with several of his flock at Norridgewock by the English and their pagan Mohawk allies.

The Jesuit Martyrs of North America.—Martyr-blood had already been shed in other parts of the Indian mission field. *Isaac Jogues,* the first Catholic priest who ever came to Manhattan Island, and "one of the first missionaries," as Bancroft remarks, "to preach the Gospel a thousand miles in the interior," endured untold hardships and trials during his labors in the region of the Great Lakes (1636-1642). Captured by the Iroquois while returning to Quebec, he spent thirteen months in the most abject slavery until he was rescued by the Dutch of Fort Orange and sent back to his native France. On a visit to Rome Pope Urban VIII permitted him to say Mass in spite of the fact that two fingers of his right hand had been burnt off. "It is not fitting," the Pontiff declared, "that Christ's martyr should not drink Christ's blood." In 1644 Jogues returned to Canada, and in 1646 visited Auriesville (N. Y.) to negotiate peace with the Iroquois. It was in the course of this journey that he bestowed upon the charming lake now called after one of the Georges of England the far more appropriate name "Lake of the Blessed Sacrament." Returning to the Iroquois a third time, he was captured at Lake George, tortured most inhumanly, and finally put to death. *René Goupil,* a lay-brother and companion of Father Jogues, and *John Lalande,* a layman who assisted Jogues, received the crown of martyrdom about the same time as their heroic superior.

St. Isaac Jogues, S. J.

Three years after the death of Jogues two other Jesuit missionaries, *John de Brébeuf* and *Gabriel Lalemant,* fell victims to the cruelty of the fierce Iroquois tribe. *Charles Garnier,* whose angelic patience amid endless trials and sufferings had won for him the title of "lamb," was slain by the Iroquois in 1649, after having labored with unremitting zeal amongst the Hurons for fourteen years. *Noël Chabanel,* Garnier's companion among the Hurons, was murdered by a Huron renegade. *Anthony Daniel* was slain in an Iroquois attack on the Huron mission at Ihonatiria and his body thrown into the burning chapel in which he had just said Mass (1648).

This glorious band of Jesuit Martyrs of North America was beatified by Pope Pius XI on June 21, 1925, and canonized June

29, 1930. Their feast is celebrated in the United States on the 26th of September.

Two Missionary Explorers.—Among the Catholic explorers of North America who rendered such conspicuous service to civilization and religion in the most romantic period of American history two missionaries will ever occupy a prominent place—Jacques Marquette and Louis Hennepin.

Jacques Marquette was born at Laon, France, in 1636. Joining the Society of Jesus at an early age, he was sent to the Canadian Mission in 1666, where he labored successfully for several years on the southwest shore of Lake Superior. In 1673 he accompanied Louis Joliet on his voyage from Green Bay down the Wisconsin and Mississippi as far as the country below the entrance of the Arkansas. Having accurately studied the general course of the great stream, they returned to Green Bay by way of the Illinois River, Chicago, and Lake Michigan. Two years later Marquette returned to preach to the Illinois Indians. He established the Immaculate Conception Mission at the original village of Kaskaskia near the present Utica. Exhausted by his labors, he died near Luddington, Michigan, at the early age of thirty-nine years. The State of Wisconsin has placed his statue in the Hall of Fame at Washington.

Louis Hennepin, a Belgian Franciscan, came to Quebec in 1675 in company with Robert Cavalier de la Salle, the noted explorer, and Francis de Montmorency Laval, the first Bishop of Canada. After preaching at Quebec Father Hennepin went to the Indian Mission at Fort Frontenac, and visited the country of the Mohawks. In 1679 he joined La Salle's second expedition to the West. It was an epic voyage of adventure and discovery. "They journeyed from the Niagara River to Detroit, up Lake Huron, through the straits of Mackinac, and on to Green Bay, thence finally by the Kankakee and Illinois to Fort Crèvecoeur." At Peoria La Salle sent the missionary to make farther discoveries. With two companions Hennepin set out to explore the Illinois River and the Upper Mississippi. He was captured by a party of Sioux Indians on the Mississippi and during his captivity discovered the Falls of St. Anthony. After his rescue he went to Quebec by way of the Wisconsin River and St. Ignace. Returning to Europe to rest from his labors, Father Hennepin published a full account of his travels and discoveries. He was the first to describe the mighty cataract of Niagara, upon which he had come unsuspectingly in December of 1678. His death took place probably at Rome after 1701.

Fate of the Indian Missions.—The hunting grounds of the Mohawks, which had been fertilized by the blood of martyrs, were the birthplace of Catherine Tekakwitha, the "Lily of the Mohawks," who died in the odor of sanctity in 1680. She had been instructed by Jesuit missionaries at Fonda, near Auriesville, New York, in 1667 and later baptized. Going to the Indian Reservation at Caughnawaga, Canada, she lived with a Christian squaw a life of heroic sanctity. The Indians of Caughnawaga attribute their loyalty to the Faith to her patronage. The cause of her beatification has been introduced in Rome.

Widespread Indian uprisings led in 1658 to the abandonment of the missions in the present State of New York. They were restored under the protection of the powerful Onondaga chief, Garagonthié, in 1667. Two years later Garagonthié was baptized with great solemnity at Quebec, receiving the name of Daniel. When the Dutch colony of New Amsterdam passed into the hands of the English in 1664, the struggle between the English and the French for Indian allies began, and the missionaries were gradually forced out of the country. After 1709 no serious attempt was made to restore the once flourishing missions.

8. The Council of Trent

For years both friends and foes of the Papacy had demanded the convening of a General Council. Pope Paul III, as we have seen, was determined to give effect to this demand. After many difficulties and delays, the Council was opened at last in Trent (Tyrol) on the 13th of December, 1545. It was prorogued several times, and it remained suspended for ten years (1552-1562); so that it was not till the 3rd and 4th of December, 1563, that the last session was held, and the bishops were dismissed to their homes. On the 26th of January, 1564, Pope Pius IV confirmed the Council by the Bull *Benedictus Deus*.

At the beginning of the Council the question was warmly debated whether the reform of the Church should be taken in hand first, as the Emperor Charles V desired, in order to win over the Protestants, or whether the dogmatic decrees should take precedence. It was finally decided that the work of defining the faith and of reforming discipline should proceed side by side. In the dogmatic decrees the Catholic faith is usually first stated in a positive form called *Capitula* (chapters), and then the contrary errors are condemned in brief and precise terms (*canones*, canons). The *Capitula* and the *Canons* are of equal authority; both are *definitions* of faith.

Against the Protestants the Council declared that Scripture *and* Tradition are the two sources of Divine Revelation, that all the books of the Old and the New Testament are equally inspired

Titian

THE COUNCIL OF TRENT

because they have God for their author, and that the Scriptures, in matters pertaining to faith and morals, cannot be interpreted against the authoritative interpretations of the Church or against the unanimous consent of the Fathers. The Latin translation of the Bible, known as the Vulgate, is declared to be the only authentic Latin version, and the one to be used in public in the Western Church. The other dogmatic definitions concern Original Sin, Justification, the Sacraments in general and each Sacrament in particular, the Sacrifice of the Mass, Purgatory, the Invocation and Veneration of the Saints, the Relics of the Saints, Sacred Images, and Indulgences.

The Reform Decrees embrace a large part of Christian life and still form the basis of ecclesiastical discipline in the Latin Church. Some regard the laity exclusively. Thus, the indissolubility of the marriage bond is insisted upon, the matrimonial impediments are specified and classified, clandestine marriages are declared invalid, duelling is forbidden under pain of excommunication.

More important, still, is the legislation affecting the clergy. The College of Cardinals should be representative of the whole Church; bishops should be obliged to live in their own dioceses, to preach to their flocks, and to make periodical visitations of their parishes; diocesan and provincial synods should be held at regular intervals; priests in charge of parishes should instruct their people in Christain Doctrine; seminaries should be established in each diocese for the education of the clergy; no bishops or priests or other clerics should be allowed to hold more than one benefice. The medieval practice of Papal Indulgence preachers (pardoners, as they were called in England) is abolished. Strict laws regulate the admission of new members into a Religious Order, as well as the choice of Superiors and the observance of the vows.

The best comment on the work accomplished by the Council of Trent is contained in the Acts of the Vatican Council (1869) : "The salutary providence of Christ has been most clearly manifested in the abundant fruits which have accrued to the Christian world from the Ecumenical Councils, and especially from that of Trent, though it was held in evil times. For the result has been that the sacred dogmas of religion have been more exactly defined and more fully stated; errors have been condemned and repressed; ecclesiastical discipline has been restored and placed on a firmer basis; the cultivation of knowledge and piety has been fostered among the clergy; colleges have been founded to train youths for the clerical ranks, and morality has been revived among the Christian people by the more accurate instruction of the faithful and the greater frequentation of the Sacraments. Other results are the closer union of the members with their visible Head, and an increase of vigor throughout the mystical body of Christ, the multiplication of Religious Congregations and other institutes of Christian piety, and a zeal that is constant, even unto death, for the propagation of the kingdom of Christ throughout the world."

The decrees of the Council of Trent do not contain the complete Catholic faith, but only that portion of it which it was thought necessary to define in answer to the heretical attacks of Luther, Zwingli, Calvin, and the other so-called Reformers. The Council, however, ordered the preparation of a Catechism containing an exposition of Christian Doctrine, designed especially for the use of parish priests and other teachers of religion. It is usually called the *Catechism of the Council of Trent*, or the Roman Catechism, and was first published in 1566 by Pope Pius V. It brought about a much-needed uniformity in the teaching of Religion.

The Jesuit Vows

There are six grades of membership in the Society of Jesus: Novices, Formed Temporal Coadjutors, Approved Scholastics, Formed Spiritual Co-adjutors, the Professed of the Three Vows, and the Professed of the Four Vows.

At the end of his novitiate the Novice takes the following vows:

"Almighty everlasting God, although in every way unworthy in Thy holy sight, yet relying on Thy infinite goodness and mercy and impelled by the desire of serving Thee, I, N., before the most holy Virgin Mary and all Thy heavenly host, vow to Thy Divine Majesty Poverty, Chastity and Perpetual Obedience to the Society of Jesus, and promise that I will enter the same Society to live in it perpetually, understanding all things according to the Constitutions of the Society. I humbly implore Thine immense goodness and clemency, through the Blood of Jesus Christ, to deign to accept this sacrifice in the odor of sweetness; and as Thou hast granted me to desire and to offer this, so wilt Thou bestow abundant grace to fulfill it."

The formula of the vows taken by the Professed of the Three Vows is as follows:

"I, N., promise to Almighty God, before His Virgin Mother and the whole heavenly host, and to all here present; and to thee, Reverend Father General of the Society of Jesus, holding the place of God, and to thy successors (or, if the Father General is not present, to the Reverend Father in place of the General of the Society of Jesus and his successors holding the place of God), Perpetual Poverty, Chastity and Obedience; and according to it a special care in the education of boys according to the form of life contained in the Apostolic Letters of the Society of Jesus and in its Constitutions."

The Professed of the Four Vows form only a small class in comparison with the whole Society. The vows of this grade are the same as those taken by the professed of the three vows, with the following addition:

"Moreover I promise the special obedience to the Sovereign Pontiff concerning missions, as is contained in the same Apostolic Letters and Constitutions."

A Seventeenth Century Mission Ranch

Of the many brave and saintly men who labored for the spread of the Faith in the Southwest of the United States in the seventeenth century the most remarkable was the Jesuit *Eusebio Francisco Kino* (1644-1711), astronomer, geographer, explorer, colonizer, ranchman, but "first, last, and always" missionary to the Indians. Born near Trent in Tyrol in 1644, Kino was educated by the Jesuits in Ingolstadt (Bavaria). Entering the Society of Jesus in 1665, he volunteered for the vast Mexican mission field. For twenty-eight years, from 1683 till his death, he labored amid almost incredible hardships in Northern Mexico, Arizona and California. He is said to have baptized 50,000 Indians. His *Favores Celestiales,* an autobiography, is one of the most precious documents of early American history. Father Kino has left us a pen-sketch of his favorite mission, Dolores, which he founded in 1687:

"This mission has its church adequately furnished with ornaments, chalices, bells, choir chapel, etc.; likewise a great many large and small cattle, oxen, fields, a garden with various kinds of garden crops, Castilian fruit trees, grapes, peaches, quinces, figs, pomegranates, pears, and apricots. It has a forge for blacksmiths, a carpenter shop, a pack train, water mill, many kinds of grain, and provisions from rich and abundant harvests of wheat and maize, besides other things, including horse and mule herds, all of which serve and are greatly needed for the house, as well as for the expeditions and new conquests and conversions, and to purchase a few gifts and attractions, with which, together with the Word of God, it is customary to contrive to win the minds and souls of the natives." See Herbert E. Bolton, *The Padre on Horseback,* pp. 53-55.

Hints for Study

1. For more detailed accounts of the events, movements, and persons treated in this chapter consult the following books: Chapman, C. E., *A History of Spain.* Thompson, F., *Life of St. Ignatius Loyola.* Schurhammer, *St. Francis Xavier.* Carey, *History of Christianity in Japan.* Wolferstan, *The Catholic Church in China.* Cunninghame-Graham, *A Vanished Arcadia.* Wynne, *Jesuit Martyrs of North America.* O'Gorman, *A History of the Catholic Church in the United States.* Callan and McHugh, *Catechism of the Council of Trent.*

2. What is meant by the Catholic reaction? What problems did the Church have to solve in the 16th century?

3. Name the chief Religious Orders founded during the 16th century.

4. Name the great missionaries who labored in the 16th and 17th centuries. Tell where they labored and with what success.

5. Distinguish between the Congregation of the Propaganda, the College of the Propaganda, and the Society for the Propagation of the Faith.

6. Why were the missions of the 16th and 17th centuries not so successful as those in the Middle Ages and in the Early Church?

7. Which were the most important reforms enacted by the Council of Trent?

8. Familiarize yourself with the following: *Nepotism, Spiritual Exercises, ex voto, Company of Jesus, Sacco di Roma, Controversy on Chinese and Indian Rites, Sanyasi, Reductions, Caste System, The Lily of the Mohawks, Capitula and Canones, Roman Catechism.*

9. An interesting story dealing with the Japanese Missions is Lady Georgiana Fullerton's *Laurentia: A Tale of the Jesuit Missions in Japan.*

CHAPTER V

SOME LEADERS OF THE CATHOLIC REFORMATION

1. *St. Charles Borromeo, Cardinal and Archbishop of Milan*

The best reform decrees are useless if they are not carried out. The credit of having been the first churchman to enforce the reforms enacted by the Council of Trent both in his own person and in his diocese, belongs to St. Charles Borromeo, Cardinal-Archbishop of Milan.

St. Charles was born in the castle of the Borromeos at Arona, on Lake Maggiore, in 1538. He was destined for the Church from his childhood and received the tonsure at the age of twelve. The doctorate in civil and canon law crowned a brilliant course of studies at the University of Padua (1559). Upon the accession of his maternal uncle Giovanni Angelo Medici to the Papal Throne in 1559, Charles, though only twenty-one years old, was summoned to Rome, made Papal Secretary, elevated to the Cardinalate and entrusted with the administration of the Archdiocese of Milan. This was nepotism, but a nepotism that proved a boon, not a bane, to the Church. Charles was not a saint from the start. He still took part in worldly amusements, kept a princely retinue, and occasionally followed the chase. Gradually, however, he gave up every pursuit which was at variance with his spiritual office. When his older brother died, all the world believed that Charles, who was only a subdeacon, would relinquish his clerical profession and found a family. But Charles disappointed all these prophets. He made the Spiritual Exercises, and advanced to Holy Orders. From this time on, he lived the life of a model priest. A foreign ambassador reported to his government: "The life of Cardinal Borromeo is absolutely stainless. By his piety and his devotion to his duties he gives good example to all. His conduct deserves all the more praise because he is still in the prime of life, the favorite nephew of the Pope, rich in this world's goods, and attached to a Court where opportunities for amusements of all kinds are not wanting." Another eye-witness wrote: "Borromeo does more good by his example than all the decrees of a Council."

With his tender piety Charles combined an extraordinary talent for ecclesiastical organization and administration. He was the good angel of his uncle, Pius IV, whose measures for the welfare of the Church were nearly all inspired by him. The reassembling of the Council of Trent in 1562 and its successful conclusion was his work. He also had a large share in the composition of the Roman Catechism. When the death of the Pope freed him from his duties in Rome, he immediately took up his residence in his episcopal city of Milan, which had fallen into grave disorder through the absence of a resident archbishop for a period of eighty years. He devoted the rest of his life to reforming his diocese, creating parishes, establishing schools, colleges, seminaries, and religious houses of men and women.

ST. CHARLES BORROMEO MINISTERING TO THE PLAGUE-STRICKEN

It was the man behind these measures that made them fruitful. For this man was a saint. He daily renewed his strength in meditation and prayer, in works of penance and self-mortification. Pure love of God and of his neighbor was the mainspring of his every act. In him the Church had a bishop after the heart of the Good Shepherd. Nor did his influence stop at the borders of his archdiocese. By his vast correspondence—thousands of his letters are preserved—he remained in touch with the whole Catholic world and with all classes of society. His heroic sanctity shone forth most brilliantly during the dreadful plague which visited Milan in 1576. He turned his palace into a hospital, nursed the stricken with his own hands, heard their confessions, and gave them the Last Sacraments. The story of his struggles and victories and indefatigable zeal went abroad into all lands, and bishops vied with one another in imitating his example. At his death in 1584 everyone felt that the Church had lost one of her greatest servants. "A light has been extinguished in Israel!" Pope Gregory XIII exclaimed when the news was brought to him.

2. Three Pontifical Reformers

Among the Popes who did most to carry out the reforms of the Council of Trent, three, Pius V, Gregory XIII, and Sixtus V, stand out most prominently. Pius was a Dominican, Sixtus a Franciscan, and Gregory belonged to the secular clergy.

Pius V, the Dominican Pope.—Pius V (1566-1572) the last canonized Pope, had entered the Dominican Order in his early youth. From his first days of convent life he had been remarkable for the strict observance of the holy Rule, and he never relaxed in the least from his first fervor in this regard. With extreme reluctance he accepted the Papal dignity. He was deeply conscious of the heavy responsibility it laid upon him. It was not his ambition to be a great ruler, but, as a true "Servant of the servants of God" to labor for the salvation of souls. Everyone could see how truly spiritual a man he was, "how given to long prayers, to tears as well as to fasting, and to mortifications of the flesh, in spite of years and infirmities." Love for the crucified Savior was the impelling motive of all his actions. When he carried the Blessed Sacrament through the streets of Rome on the feast of Corpus Christi, he was so rapt in devotion, and his love for the Hidden God shone so clearly on his countenance, that the people whispered to one another: "We have a saint as Pope!"

Immediately on his accession Pius V undertook a thorough reform of the Papal household, of every branch of the Papal administration, and of the clergy and city of Rome. Every abuse was summarily corrected or punished. Scant allowance was made for sex, age, rank, or past services. All persons of bad life had to leave Rome. The Eternal City began to put on the appearance of a vast monastery. A new generation of zealous priests replaced the worldly-minded, pleasure-seeking benefice-hunters of old. The

Roman Catechism was placed in the hands of every priest; the Breviary was re-edited and its daily recital enforced.

Pius V failed in his efforts to bring back Scotland to the Catholic faith, and his *Bull of Excommunication* against Queen Elizabeth (25th Feb., 1571) aroused the English Catholics, it is true, from the lethargy which had hung over them since the reign of Henry VIII, but it also "procured," as Bl. Edmund Campion said, "much severity in England and the heavy hand of her majesty against the Catholics." A final triumph was, however, reserved to the great Pontiff. The victorious Ottoman armies, taking advantage of the disunion of Western Christendom, were threatening to overrun Europe. In this crisis the Pope formed an alliance between himself, Philip II of Spain, and the Venetians. Don John of Austria was given command of the fleet of the allies, and in the battle of Lepanto (Oct. 7, 1571) the power of the Turk on the seas was broken forever. On the day of the battle the Pope was discussing some business matters with his secretary. "Suddenly he lapsed into silence, went to his window, and opening the large shutters, was lost in thought as he gazed out into the void. Then, recovering himself, he turned to the secretary and said: 'It is not the time for doing business now. Let us return thanks to God. Our Armada has even now defeated the Turkish fleet.'"

Gregory XIII and the Catholic Restoration.—Gregory XIII (1571-1585), whom St. Charles Borromeo had converted from a worldly-minded man into an earnest Christian, advanced from the reformation of the Church to its restoration.

After the Protestant revolt had done its worst, the Catholic leaders, who had been taken by surprise by the suddenness of the onslaught, regained courage, and were now ready for the counterattack. It was Gregory XIII who organized this attack—the Counter-Reformation, as it is generally called. He raised the Roman (or Papal) Congregations, i.e., the administrative departments of the Roman Curia to fifteen. One of them was specially entrusted with the ecclesiastical affairs of Germany. Under Gregory the "Nunciatures" (official representations of the Holy See in the various countries) attained an importance which they never had before. The number of the Nuncios was considerably increased and their duties limited almost exclusively to spiritual matters, such as the reform of the clergy in accordance with the decrees of the Council of Trent, the erection of colleges and seminaries, the establishment of missions amongst the Protestants, etc. Of the greatest importance were the Nunciatures in the countries threatened by the Protestant revolt—Germany, Poland, Hungary, Switzerland, and the Netherlands. Two Nunciatures were erected in Germany, one for the South and one for the West, with its seat in Cologne. The men appointed to these posts were, almost without exception, admirably fitted by their prudence, piety, and learning to lead the Catholic forces in this most critical period of the Church's history. Hungary and Poland shook off the influence of the Protestant preachers; Belgium was secured to the Catholic Church, and Austria, Bohemia, Bavaria, and most of Western and Southern Germany remained loyal to the Holy See. One of his greatest services to the cause of religion in Germany was the establishment on a solid and permanent basis of the famous German College (*Collegium Germanicum*) in Rome (1578) which, in the course of the last three hundred years, has educated so many hundreds of zealous teachers and priests for every diocese of Germany. In order to help to keep the faith alive in England and to supply priests for the English mission Gregory founded the English College at Rome and entrusted it to the Jesuits.

An achievement for which Gregory's name will be famous for all time was the reform of the Calendar, which he ordered to be made and promulgated in 1582. The "Gregorian Calendar" is so nearly exact that there will be an error of one day only in thirty-five centuries. England refused to accept the reformed Calendar until 1752.

Sixtus V, the Franciscan Pope.—Sixtus V (1585-90) was born of poor parents near Montalto (Ancona). As a boy he herded cattle and in his free time took lessons from the Franciscans of the neighborhood. He became a Franciscan himself and was soon distinguished for his learning and his eloquence. Pius V, who had been one of the first to recognize the sterling qualities of the Friar, made him successively Vicar General of the Franciscan Order, Counselor of the Holy Office, bishop, and cardinal. As Pope he displayed, in spite of his sixty-five years, an astounding vitality and capacity for work. The reform work inaugurated by his predecessors was not permitted to lag for a moment. In order to acquaint himself thoroughly with the state of religion in the different countries, he decreed that all the bishops had to visit

Rome at regular intervals for a personal interview (*Visitatio liminum apostolorum*).

Sixtus gave proof of his eminent ability as a temporal ruler by exterminating the bandits—there were over 20,000 of them—in the Papal States. The carrying of arms was forbidden under pain of death, and this decree did not remain a dead letter. Captured bandits were promptly beheaded, and their heads fixed as a warning on the bridge of S. Angelo. It was a common saying that there were more heads on the bridge than melons in the market-place. The nobles who harbored or protected a bandit were punished as severely as the bandits themselves. In 1587 the Papal States, it is said, were the safest country in Europe to travel in.

INTERIOR OF ST. PETER'S, LOOKING TOWARDS HIGH ALTAR

The Pontiff's next task was to beautify Rome. In an incredibly short space of time the face of the city was renewed. New residence sections were laid out with broad, straight streets and spacious piazzas. To procure water for the higher parts of the city he constructed a new aqueduct—twenty-two miles in length. The work was completed in three years. It is still in use, supplying 21,000 cubic meters of water a day and feeding 27 fountains. The Lateran Palace and the Vatican Library were rebuilt, and the Vatican enlarged. The columns of Trajan and Antoninus Pius were restored and transformed into pedestals for the Statues of St. Peter and St. Paul. The gigantic Egyptian obelisk, which stood where Caligula had placed it, was moved to its present position in front of St. Peter's. Nine hundred men were required for the work; they prepared themselves for the difficult and delicate task by confession, Mass, and Holy Communion. The Pope had a bronze cross placed on the top of the obelisk bearing on its base the following inscription: "Behold the Cross of the Lord! Depart ye hostile powers! The Lion of the tribe of Juda hath prevailed! Christ conquers, Christ is King, Christ is Emperor! May Christ protect His people from all evil!"

There is something titanic about this Pope. No architect or contractor could work fast enough for him. The cupola of St. Peter's was still unfinished. It could not be completed in less than six years, the architects said. But six years was too long for Sixtus V, who feared he might be dead before then. He issued his orders; 800 workmen worked day and night to carry out the plan of Michelangelo. In twenty-two months the cupola, one of the marvels of architecture, rose triumphantly to the skies (May, 1590). A few months later the great Pontiff himself was called to rest forever from his labors.

3. St. Philip Neri, the Apostle of Rome

The work of reform required men of iron will and strong hands; and such were the great reforming Popes of this period—a Paul IV, Pius V, Gregory XIII and Sixtus V. These Pontiffs were feared rather than loved, and there was danger that a spirit of harshness and over-severity, a spirit infected with the gloominess of Calvinism, would predominate amongst the leaders of the Catholic revival. But the Spirit of God, who guided the movement, saw to it that joy and cheerfulness were not driven from their original home, the Catholic Church, and that the sun did not cease to shine during those long years of storm and stress. The sunshine of the Catholic Reformation was St. Philip Neri, whom the Romans called "Pippo buono," the good Philip.

Philip (b. 1515) belonged to an aristocratic, but not wealthy, family of Florence. A rich uncle induced him to enter his mercantile establishment near Monte Cassino, promising to make him his heir (1533). After two years Philip gave up all worldly prospects, went to Rome, and devoted himself to study and works of charity. He gained his livelihood as a private tutor. The nights he often spent in prayer in the vestibules of the churches or in his beloved Catacombs. He was soon known in every public place and in every workshop in Rome, and in every hospital, too, for all his free time was spent in trying to win souls for God. For years he was the butt and laughing-stock of the idlers and evil-livers at Rome, because they did not like to see a virtuous and conscientious man. But that did not disturb Philip; a simple smile was his only reply, and that sweet smile converted many a hardened sinner. In 1548 he founded the "Confraternity of the Blessed Trinity" for the care of needy pilgrims, and some years later the famous Hospital della Trinità.

After his ordination to the priesthood in 1551—his spiritual director had to command him to take this step—the sphere of Philip's influence increased. For thirty-three years he labored incessantly as the friend of youth, as confessor, as patron of Christian art and science. His room in the rectory of San Girolamo della Carità was the focus of spiritual life in Rome. Young men of all walks of life gathered about him. They met daily, first in his room, later in a more spacious apartment which he had turned into an *Oratory*, for silent prayer, spiritual reading, and conferences. The early days of Apostolic Christianity seemed to have returned. In time the number of those who took part in these meetings grew so large that they had to be transferred to the Church of Santa Maria in Vallicella. The priests who assisted Philip in this work lived in community but took no vows. This was the origin of the "Congregation of the Oratory of St. Philip Neri," which, approved by Gregory XIII in 1575, became the center of religious reform for the whole city, and soon spread to other cities and countries. The Oratorians pursued a two-fold object: to sanctify themselves by the exact performance of their priestly duties, and to work for the salvation of their neigh-bor, the young above all, by every means at their disposal. Philip was their guide and model. His zeal for the conversion of souls knew no bounds. He spent hours every day in the confessional, visited the sick in the hospitals, carried food and clothing secretly to the homes of the bashful poor, provided poor girls with mar-riage dowries and poor students with board and books. He could not bear to see children scantily clothed or suffering from hunger or disease. He had a particular anxiety about boys and young men. He was most anxious to have them always occupied, for he knew that idleness was the parent of every evil. He let them make what noise they pleased about him if in so doing he was keeping them from temptation. When a friend remonstrated with him for letting them so interfere with him, he made answer: "So long as they do not sin, they may chop wood upon my back." Sometimes he left his prayers and went down to sport and banter with young men, and by his sweetness and condescension and playful conversation gained their souls. He could not see anyone downcast or gloomy without making an effort to cheer him up. One day he restored cheerfulness to Father Bernardi by simply asking him to run with him, saying: "Come now, let us have a run together."

St. Philip's Oratory produced the first great modern Church historian, Cesare Baronio, the author of the monumental *Annales Ecclesiastici* (Annals of the Church). Here too originated the musical form known as the *Oratorio*—an elaborate composition for solo voices, chorus, orchestra, and organ set to a religious text, operatic in form but sung without action, scenery, or costume.

St. Philip died on the 26th of May, 1595, shortly after midnight. He had spent nearly the whole of his last day on earth in the confessional.

4. St. Peter Canisius, Second Apostle of Germany and Doctor of the Church

Whilst St. Philip Neri was edifying and converting the Romans and gaining for himself the title of Apostle of Rome, St. Peter Canisius was marching at the head of the Catholic forces of Germany, engaged in hand-to-hand conflict with Protestantism, never wearying in the long struggle, changing his tactics from time to time, but always aiming at the one goal—to save as much of the German Empire as possible for the Catholic faith. His success was ultimately so marvelous that he justly merited to be called the Second Apostle of Germany.

Peter Canisius was born May 8, 1521, at Nymwegen, in Holland, which at that time formed part of Germany. In 1536 he entered the University of Cologne. At the age of nineteen he took the vow of perpetual chastity. Two years later he met Bl. Peter Faber, the first companion of St. Ignatius, made the Spiritual Exercises under his direction, and then entered the Society of Jesus. A number of his fellow-students followed his example. The first Jesuit community in Germany was founded. After his ordination (1546) Canisius spent some time at Rome in the same house with St. Ignatius. In 1549 he took the four vows of the Jesuits in the presence of the holy Founder. The occasion, he tells us, was marked by such a flood of heavenly graces that it set its seal on his whole life. It was revealed to him, as clearly as if God's voice had spoken to him in human words, that he was destined to become the "Apostle of Germany." Full of joy, "clothed with the garment of peace, of love, and perseverance," he entered upon his apostolate. He spent most of the next thirty years in Bavaria, Tyrol, Bohemia, and Austria, laboring indefatigably at the restoration of the disordered ecclesiastical life, as university professor and instructor of little children, as cathedral preacher and village pastor, as representative of the Pope at the Imperial Diets and at the Council of Trent, as the opponent of Melanchthon in religious debates, as founder of great institutions

of learning and simple elementary schools, as the adviser of spiritual and temporal rulers, as spiritual director of kings and princes and their households. From 1556 to 1569 he was Provincial of the Jesuits of Tyrol, Austria, Bavaria, Bohemia, and Poland, which enabled him to carry out successfully his reform plans for that vast territory.

Whilst teaching at the University of Vienna, he published his three famous Catechisms—the larger one in 1555,

St. Peter Canisius, S. J.

the smaller one in 1558, and the smallest in 1556. Through these Catechisms Canisius became the "hammer of heretics." His contemporaries called them "banners of war, which gleamed in the religious struggles and won the most glorious victories." They were translated into every language of Europe and reprinted in countless editions—four hundred in Germany alone—so that the name *Canisius* became in time synonymous with Catechism.

Canisius spent the last seventeen years of his life in Freiburg in Switzerland, preaching, giving retreats, writing books, and promoting in every way the cause of Catholic reform. Here he died "full of years and merits" on the 21st of December, 1597. He was beatified in 1864, and canonized and at the same time declared a Doctor of the Church by His Holiness Pope Pius XI in 1925.

5. St. Angela Merici and St. Teresa of Jesus

The period of the Catholic revival produced an abundance of saints of both sexes. Amongst the holy women two deserve our special consideration—St. Angela Merici, the foundress of the Ursulines, and Spain's greatest woman, St. Teresa of Avila.

St. Angela was born March 21, 1474, at Desenzano on the shores of beautiful Lake Garda. From early childhood she was wholly given up to works of piety and charity. She spent many hours of the night in prayer. The poor were her special favorites, for whom she cared with motherly solicitude. She also loved to gather the children of the neighborhood about her and instruct them in their holy religion. Later she became a tertiary of St. Francis and founded a school for the instruction of young girls at Desenzano, and another at Brescia. In 1525 she made a pilgrimage to the Holy Land, but saw nothing of the Holy Places, having suffered the loss of her sight. A vision in which she saw a band of virgins escorted by angels bearing lilies in their hands and golden crowns on their heads and ascending a ladder which reached to heaven ripened in her mind the resolve to found the new order of women whose chief purpose should be the instruction of children. Twelve women in Brescia declared their readiness to join in the holy venture. They placed themselves under the patronage of the Virgin-Martyr St. Ursula, took no vows except that of chastity, chose a simple black dress as their habit, and continued to live in their families, meeting in common only for prayer and other spiritual exercises. They bound themselves to practice the spiritual and corporal works of mercy, to instruct children, especially poor girls whose parents could not afford to hire teachers, to care for the sick and to prepare them for the reception of the Last Sacraments. Angela herself was chosen Superior-General in 1537. The Ursulines were the first Order of women founded independently of any Order of men, and also the first non-cloistered Sisters—two things which for many years called forth much opposition. St. Angela died at Brescia in 1540. In her famous "Testament" and in her "Farewell Exhortations" she bequeathed to her foundation a "precious treasure of spiritual enlightenment, experience, and maternal love."

The Ursulines spread rapidly over Italy, thanks especially to St. Charles Borromeo, and into France and Germany. The Venerable Mary of the Incarnation introduced them into Canada in 1639, where they were the first women to take a direct share in the evangelization of the heathen. The first establishment in the United States was made at New Orleans in 1727. The Order numbers at present more than 300 monasteries with nearly 7,000 members.

St. Teresa's home was the mountain fortress of Avila in Spain. Here she was born of noble parents in 1515. As a child she was such an enthusiastic admirer of the martyrs of the early Church that she persuaded her brother Rodrigo to run away with her to Morocco to gain the crown of martyrdom. They did not proceed very far on their journey. Then Teresa wanted to become an anchoress. Romances of chivalry, which she read with avidity, turned her thoughts for a time from heavenly things, and when she entered the Carmelite convent of her native city, she accommodated herself to the worldliness of her surroundings. It was only after she began to read the

Bernini

THE HEART OF ST. TERESA
TRANSPIERCED BY A SERAPH

works of the great Fathers of the Church (Augustine, Jerome, Gregory the Great) that her mind was moved to loftier aspirations. She practiced living in the presence of God, and was soon rewarded with the gift of mystical contemplation. These spiritual experiences filled her soul with such heavenly delight that she felt impelled to communicate them to her fellow-men. No saint, man or woman, has grasped the deepest mystical experiences so clearly and described the mystical states of the soul so exactly as St. Teresa. Her sex alone has debarred her from being declared a Doctor of the Church.

At the instance of her confessor, Teresa wrote the story of her own life. Her "Way of Perfection" is a guide to meditation and contemplation. "In her *Castle of the Soul* she describes in bold imagery and highly figurative language the experiences of a soul striving after union with God. Before her eyes stands one of those proud feudal castles with which the tales of chivalry had made her familiar. The towering structure is surrounded by a moat, the home of poisonous reptiles. Seven apartments must be traversed, before the one is reached where the Bridegroom waits for His bride. The whole is an illustration of the various stages of the soul's progress towards perfection. As long as the soul lives enmeshed in distractions of the world, she remains a slave to the senses, in the castle moat, exposed to the deadly fangs of the serpents, i.e., mortal sins. Prayer is the gate through which the soul enters the castle. The seven apartments represent the different degrees of prayer. The soul traverses them all to celebrate at last the nuptials with Christ."

With all her high spirituality and mystic exaltation, Teresa was a woman of strong, practical good sense, full of natural shrewdness, and with unusual powers of organization. Few men have ever been braver in the face of difficulties and dangers. Convinced that the relaxation of discipline within the Religious Orders was the main cause of the spread of the Protestant Revolt, she formed the project of founding a house in which the Carmelite Rule should be observed in all its original severity. In spite of much opposition, she succeeded, and with the help of St. John of the Cross, another great Spanish mystic, she also reformed the Carmelite Order of men. She founded herself, or was instrumental in founding, no less than thirty-two houses of the Discalced Carmelites. The *Book of Foundations* tells the story of her activity as a foundress.

The writings of St. Teresa, and especially her *Letters,* are masterpieces of Spanish prose. She might have ranked amongst the classic poets of her native land had she developed her talent in that direction. The few specimens of her lyric power that have come down to us are exquisite, especially the *"Solos Dios Basta"* (God alone sufficeth). Her whole mystical theology is summed up in the lines—

> "The love of God flows just as much
> As that of ebbing self subsides;
> Our hearts, their scantiness is such,
> Bear not the conflict of these rival tides."

6. St. Francis de Sales and St. Jane Frances de Chantal

"St. Charles Borromeo," says Bossuet, "reawakened among the clergy the spirit of ecclesiastical piety; the illustrious Francis de Sales revived devotion amongst the laity. The interior and spiritual life had been relegated to the cloisters; Francis de Sales sought it out in its retreat and brought it back into the world. Nor did he disguise it in order to make it more agreeable to the eyes of the worldly-minded; he brought it as it was, with its cross, with its thorns, with its detachment and its sufferings."

The life of St. Francis de Sales (1567-1622) presents nothing sensational, no dramatic episodes, no marvelous occurrences. And yet few saints have exercised a deeper influence on their contemporaries or on succeeding generations. He touched the lives of thousands during his life; millions have been inspired by his wise and loving counsels since his death.

Francis was born at the Castle of Sales, near Annecy in the mountains of Savoy, studied the classics at Annecy, philosophy and theology at the college of the Jesuits in Paris, languages at Royal College, and received his doctorate in law at Padua (1592). Before returning home, he made a pilgrimage to Rome and Loretto.

At Paris he had passed through a long and terrible crisis; he had become obsessed with the thought that God had predestined him for eternal damnation. He had been able neither to eat, nor drink, nor sleep. He passed his days and nights in weeping and lamenting. At last, he asked the Blessed Virgin to obtain for him at least the grace of loving on earth with all his heart a God whom he was destined to hate for all eternity. When he had finished his prayer, the temptation vanished, and he regained his former tranquillity. This experience stood him in good stead in after life; he could sympathize with all who, under Calvinistic influences, suffered as he had suffered, and raise them gently out of the slough of despair.

Against the will of his father, Francis entered the priesthood and was ordained in 1593. After a year of zealous work as preacher and confessor, he was sent by the Bishop of Geneva, Claude de Granier, to win back the province of Chablais, which had embraced Calvinism when annexed by the Canton of Bern in 1535, and had retained it even after its restitution to Savoy in 1564. For four years (1594-98) Francis, amidst toil and privation, preached in every town and hamlet. At first the people refused to listen to him, but the spectacle of his virtues and his disinterestedness soon turned the tide of public opinion in his favor. More than 70,000 Calvinists returned to the Church. The re-erection of a wayside cross in Annemasse, at the very gates of Geneva, amid an enormous concourse of converts, brought his apostolate to a close. Shortly after, he was appointed coadjutor to the Bishop of Geneva, whom he succeeded in 1602. As no Catholic priest or bishop could live in Geneva, he took up his residence in Annecy. As bishop he walked faithfully in the footsteps of St. Charles Borromeo, whom he greatly admired and venerated.

While preaching the Lenten sermons at Dijon (Burgundy) in 1604, Francis made the acquaintance of Jane Frances de Frémiot, widow of the baron de Chantal. Together they founded the Order of the Visitation, "in favor of strong souls with weak bodies, deterred from entering the Orders already existing, by their inability to undertake severe corporal austerities." They were called Sisters of the Visitation because visiting and tending to the sick, especially the sick poor, was to be their first duty. For five years they carried out this program, then, against the will of St. Francis, they were cloistered. Prayer, the interior life, and a constant mortification of the will were to be the principal means of sanctification among the Sisters of the Visitation. The institution spread rapidly, counting twenty houses before the death of St. Francis and eighty-seven before that of St. Jane (1541.)

The care of his diocese and of his new foundation was not enough for the ardent charity of the Bishop of Geneva. Scarcely a day passed on which he did not write as many as twenty or twenty-five letters, mostly spiritual, to all classes of people in France and Savoy. In 1609 he published his famous *"Philothea, or Introduction to a Devout Life,"* a work which was at once translated into the chief European languages, and has retained its popularity ever since. In 1616 appeared his *Treatise on the Love of God,* which teaches that perfection of the spiritual life to which the *Philothea* was meant to be the introduction. It was dedicated to his faithful friend, Janes Frances de Chantal. He gave her a copy with the words: "I have written this book for you."

7. St. Fidelis of Sigmaringen, the First Martyr of the Propaganda

St. Francis de Sales died in 1622. In the same year, St. Fidelis of Sigmaringen, the first martyr of the newly founded Propaganda, met his death. Fidelis was born at Sigmaringen in Hohenzollern (Upper Germany) in 1577. After graduating from the University of Freiburg, he was admitted to the bar and began to practice at Ensisheim, where he was known as the "lawyer of the poor." Entering the Capuchin Order in 1612, he became famous both as a preacher and a writer against the Zwinglians and Calvinists. It was when Guardian of the Convent at Feldkirch in Austria that he was charged by the Roman Congregation of the Propaganda to attempt the conversion of the Protestants in the Grisons country (Switzerland). A most successful missionary tour (in 1622) brought many back to the Church, but also excited the anger of the Swiss Calvinists. Sallying forth in the same year on a second expedition, he was seized by the heretics, and, refusing to save his life by apostasy, was slain on the spot. His body rests at Feldkirch.

8. St. Vincent de Paul, Apostle of Organized Charity

When St. Francis de Sales paid his last visit to Paris in 1618-1619 one of his most ardent admirers, who scarcely ever left his side, was Vincent de Paul (1581-1660), private chaplain and tutor in the family of the Count of Gondi-Joigny. The two men had much in common, and yet were so different: the one a nobleman, the other the son of a poor peasant; one a prince-bishop, the other a simple priest in an uninfluential position; one died in the prime of manhood, the other at the ripe age of four score and four years. But both were saints, and both are amongst the greatest glories of the Church in modern times. We cannot do more here than touch on the "high lights" in the career of St. Vincent de Paul, the Apostle of organized charity, the founder of two Religious Orders, the reformer of the clergy, the promoter of home and foreign missions.

As a peasant boy in his Gascon village, watching his father's herds, Vincent loves to pray in the ruins of the shrine of Our Lady of Buglose. He saves all the pennies he can in order to help the poor. In the village school he studies so well that his parents decide to make a priest of him.

At college in Saragossa and Toulouse he gives private lessons for his board and tuition. He is ordained priest in 1600.

Sailing from Marseilles to Narbonne (1605), the young priest is seized by Mohammedan pirates, who sell him as a slave in Tunis. After a captivity of three years he succeeds in converting

his last master, a renegade Christian, and escapes with him to
France.

In 1609 he comes to Paris. He visits the hospitals daily and
serves the sick with his own hands. Temptations against the
faith assail him. He writes the Creed on a piece of paper and
carries it constantly on his heart. "Every time I place my hand

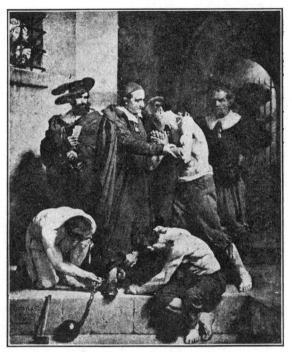

St. Vincent de Paul Ransoming the Slaves

on the paper, it is a protest against the temptations and a confession of my faith."

As chaplain to the Gondi family, he persuades the Count to
forgive a nobleman who had insulted him, and to refuse to accept a challenge to a duel.

A short stay in a country parish near Lyons convinces him of
the necessity of giving missions in all the villages of France to
combat ignorance and indifference in religious matters. A number
of secular priests offer him their services. This leads to the

founding of the *Congregation of the Mission,* usually called Vincentians (or Lazarists).

As parish priest he one day recommends to the charity of his parishioners a poor family, all of whose members are sick. Nearly the whole parish hastens to the house with gifts of food and money. "Behold noble but ill-regulated charity," St. Vincent exclaims. "These poor people, provided with too much now, must allow some to perish, and then they will be again in want as before." He calls together the ladies of the parish, suggests to them to club together to do the needful every day, not only for this poor family, but for others that might turn up in future. This was the beginning of the *Association of Charity,* the prototype of the modern St. Vincent de Paul Societies, and a host of similar institutions.

From 1632 till his death in 1660 St. Vincent lives as superior of his Congregation in the former hospital for lepers, St. Lazare. A poor, whitewashed cell serves as his study and bedroom. There is no carpet on the rough-tiled floor. A bare wooden table, two wicker chairs, and a straw mattress, are its only furniture; its only ornaments a holy picture and a wooden crucifix. The room is never heated. There is no stove in it. Vincent looked upon fuel as the property of the poor. It was too precious for himself.

From this poor cell he organized and directed a vast network of charitable enterprises. "He reformed the treatment of prisoners; he built free schools for working-class children, he founded houses for deserted children (Foundling Asylums); he arranged vocational training for young lads and girls; he established homes for the aged and anticipated the demands of the most advanced of modern philanthropists by providing that husband and wife should not be separated, as is the case in most institutions, but that each couple should spend their remaining days together. St. Vincent made such adequate provision for the regular relief of the destitute that there was left no excuse for street begging, which was accordingly abolished. He recruited and trained what have been called his armies of charity, lay men and lay women, as well as the consecrated Sisters of Charity, to visit and relieve the poor in their homes; and he organized a vast work for relieving provinces devastated by war" (H. Somerville).

This man of mighty deeds had a very poor opinion of himself. "I am only a swineherd and the son of poor peasants," he used to say; "people should not speak of such a contemptible man." Today the great works of organized Catholic Charity all the world over proclaim his glory, the glory of a man who took the words of Christ earnestly: "Thou shalt love thy neighbor as thyself."

How St. Philip Neri Cured a Scrupulous Nun

"A certain nun was sorely tormented with scruples. All trust in God, all joy in life had left her. Nowhere could she find peace, neither in prayer, nor in the tribunal of penance, nor in Holy Communion. The phantom of sin haunted her everywhere. She was convinced of her eternal reprobation.

"One day St. Philip Neri came to the convent. He asked to speak with the unhappy nun.

" 'What are you up to now, Sister Scholastica!' he said to her in his cheerfullest manner. 'Why these scruples? You are sure of going to Heaven, are you not?'

" 'On the contrary,' the nun replied, 'Hell is my lot!'

" 'And I tell you: Heaven is your portion,' Philip replied. 'Shall I prove it to you?

" 'Tell me: For whom did Christ die?'

" 'For sinners.'

" 'And what are you?'

" 'A poor sinner.'

" 'Well then, Christ died for you, and since you have washed your sins in His Blood and detest them from all your heart, you are sure of Heaven.'

"From this hour Scholastica's soul was free from fear and scruples. The words of the Saint 'You are sure of Heaven' ran ever in her mind and flooded her soul with peace."

—Girolamo Barnabeis in the contemporary *Life* of St. Philip Neri (*Acta Sanctorum Bollandiana*, May 26, col. 597).

Hints for Study

1. Of the Saints mentioned in this chapter, which ones founded new Orders and which ones reformed existing ones?
2. Of the books mentioned in this chapter, which ones were "best sellers"?
3. Who was the last Pope to be canonized?
4. Who was the oldest of the saints mentioned in this chapter? Who was the youngest?
5. In the sixteenth and seventeenth centuries a veritable witchmania broke out all over Europe and extended even to America—a frenzy of fear, ignorance and superstition; it was particularly violent in the countries of northern Europe; Protestants and Catholics alike were affected by it. The belief in witchcraft, i.e., "a power, real or supposed, of producing, in concert with an evil spirit, effects beyond the reach of

natural means and operations," has existed from the earliest recorded times. The Catholic Church does not deny the possibility, in rare instances, of human communication with evil spirits with the intention nomena of witchcraft imply, or ever implied, an actual diabolic compact." The whole question is excellently treated by Father Thurston, S.J., in the *Catholic Encyclopedia* and in Addis and Arnold's *Catholic Dictionary* Art. "Witchcraft."

6. Are you acquainted with the famous Italian scientist *Galileo* and the controversy centering around him? Here is a brief summary of the facts:

1564. *Galileo Galilei* born at Pisa. Educated at Pisa and Florence.

1589-1592. Professor of mathematics at Pisa. Attacks the natural philosophy of Aristotle, the basis of the natural sciences of his day. Forced to leave Pisa.

1592-1609. Professor at Padua. Advocates the Copernican System, viz., that the sun is the center round which the earth and other planets revolve. Returns to Pisa.

1611-1613. Named court astronomer to the Grand-Duke of Tuscany. In three open letters "On the Sun Spots" he espouses the Copernican System. In Rome and Florence his teaching is declared to be in contradiction with Scripture. He defends himself in a letter to the Benedictine Castelli; maintains (1) that the Sacred Authors do not pretend to teach science, and (2) that Scripture is a sure guide only in matters pertaining to salvation.

1615-1616. Denounced to the Congregation of the Index. His two propositions: the sun is the center of the universe; the earth moves round the sun, declared contrary to Scripture. The decision is communicated to him privately by St. Robert Bellarmine. His writings are placed on the Index. Silence is imposed on him, which he promises to observe. He is not asked to retract.

1632. In his *Dialogue on the Two Great Systems* he breaks his silence and expounds the Copernican System, not as an hypothesis, which it still was, but as conclusion of science.

1633. Summoned before the Holy Office (Roman Inquisition). Threatened with torture—torture was not actually applied—he abjures the Copernican System as false and contrary to Scripture. His book is placed on the Index; he himself is condemned to imprisonment, first in the palace of his friend the Archbishop of Siena, later in his own villa at Arcetri near Florence. In 1637 he becomes blind. Dies at peace with the Church on Jan. 8, 1642.

Galileo was condemned as "vehemently suspected of heresy," and not merely for transgressing a prohibition of the Index. This was a regretable mistake on the part of the Holy Office, which can be explained from the circumstances of the time and the character of Galileo. We must remember that the condemnation was the act of a Roman tribunal, which does not share the unique gift of infallibility. The Pope (Urban VIII) did not even sign the decree. In 1835 the works of Galileo were removed from the Index.

CHAPTER VI

JANSENISM

In the 17th and 18th centuries the Church in France was disturbed by religious controversies of various kinds, which at one time threatened to end in schism.

Baius.—The discussions with the Calvinists had brought the question of predestination, grace, and free-will again into prominence. *Michael de Bay,* usually called Baius (d. 1589), chancellor of the University of Louvain, advanced certain propositions on fallen human nature, which resembled those of Luther and Calvin. After Adam's fall, he said, man is incapable of performing any good work of himself; all he can do is commit sin; hence even the best actions of the pagans and of all persons who are not in the state of grace are sins and deserve damnation. Baius was condemned by Rome in 1560, whereupon he retracted.

Jansenius.—The teachings of Baius were adopted and elaborated by Cornelius Jansen, also a Louvain professor, and later bishop of Ypres. Jansen (Jansenius) died in communion with the Church (1638), but he left behind him a work which was published under the title *Augustinus,* because it professed to set forth the doctrine of St. Augustine on grace and free-will.

According to Jansenius the grace of God works in the human soul with irresistible power; whoever receives it is sure of salvation. God, however, does not give this grace to all men, but only to a small number of chosen souls, because He does not want to save all men. Man's free will has suffered greatly through Original Sin. Man dare not approach the severe Judge except with fear and trembling. He may receive the sacraments only after long and careful preparation. He may go to Holy Communion but very rarely and then with the greatest diffidence. Certain persons must be excluded altogether from the reception of the Holy Eucharist.

These teachings were directed in the first place against the theologians of the Society of Jesus. In the conflict with Lutheranism and Calvinism the Jesuits had emphasized the fact that man is free and capable of doing good. As directors of souls they made it a point not to repel the faithful by too great severity. This was construed as moral laxity, as an unwarranted concession to human weakness, by the Jansenists, who insisted on a return to the strictness and severity of the early Church in questions of morality. Their intentions were good. They wished to serve the cause of religion, but, at least amongst the masses of the people, they did great harm to religion. Zealous Catholics said to themselves: "If preparation for Confession and Communion is such a difficult matter, it will be best not to receive these sacraments at all." In their eyes it was a sign of special piety to remain away from the confessional and the Lord's Table. Others reasoned: "No one can resist grace. If God wants to save me, He will do so at all costs, for it is God, not we, who decides who is to be saved. Why trouble about our salvation? We cannot change the eternal decrees of God." Such reasoning was surely a more pressing invitation to lead a carefree, frivolous life than the supposed "moral laxity" of the Jesuit theologians.

Port Royal.—The teachings of Jansenius were assiduously spread in France by his old friend Saint-Cyran. They found fervent adherents in the Cistercian nuns of the Abbey of Port Royal, near Versailles.

Port Royal, especially after a number of pious priests and laymen who called themselves the "Solitaries" had settled in the neighborhood, became the great center for the dissemination of Jansenism in France. A book was published here against frequent Communion, which aroused a sharp controversy. The Jesuits attacked it vigorously. Pope Innocent X (1644-1655) condemned five propositions of the Jansenists as heretical. Whereupon the Jansenists, especially the nuns and Solitaries of Port Royal, declared that the condemned propositions were not to be found in the *Augustinus* of their master.

It was at this juncture that the famous Blaise Pascal, the author of the immortal *Pensées* (Thoughts), entered into the controversy, not by directly defending Jansenius, but by a violent attack on the Jesuits, in whom he rightly recognized the most dangerous enemies of Jansenism.

Blaise Pascal.—Pascal, born at Clermont in 1623, holds a distinguished place in the story of precocious children. He had learned Greek and Latin from his father, and mastered mathematics without book or teacher. At sixteen he wrote a treatise on conic sections, and at twenty-three discovered the laws of atmospheric pressure. In 1646 he and his accomplished sister Jacqueline came under the influence of Saint-Cyran and the Jansenists. Jacqueline became a nun at Port Royal, and Blaise, though a layman, bade farewell to all worldly joys and amusements, spent much time with the Solitaries of Port Royal, and, as we saw, took a leading part in the Jansenist controversy. His polemic against the Jesuits was in the form of letters addressed to a friend living in one of the provinces of France—*Lettres à un provincial de ses amis*—hence usually called the *Provinciales* (in English the *Provincial Letters*). The first was written in a single day. It was printed without the real author's name in 1656 and, being immensely popular and successful, was quickly followed by seventeen others.

The *Provincial Letters* are a severe indictment of the moral and political theories of the Jesuits. The author supports his accusations by quotations from Jesuit text-books, especially from Escobar's "Manual of Cases of Conscience," but the passages quoted, collected for him by his Jansenistic friends, for the most part are garbled, torn from their context, twisted and turned to suit the purpose. But all the world, especially the intellectual and social élite, devoured the *Provincial Letters* for their eloquence, wit, and brilliant style. Thus, through Pascal's masterpiece—the first prose masterpiece of the French language—one of the most difficult theological questions became the talk of the day in the salons and coffee-houses of Paris. No one read the learned and cumbrous refutations published by the Jesuits.

Pascal's *Letters,* it is not too much to say, did untold harm to the Catholic cause in France. The powerful Jesuit Order, the bulwark of the Church, was held up to ridicule and contempt in the name of Christian morality. The Jansenists exulted, but before long these same *Letters* furnished weapons of attack not only against a great Catholic institution, but against Christianity itself.

The Popes repeatedly condemned Jansenism, but the Jansenists always found some loophole of escape from these condemnations. Finally the publication of the Bull *Unigenitus* (1713) "made it clear that anyone who favored Jansenism was an enemy of the Church." From that time on, the Jansenists began to lose power and influence, and gradually sank into the condition of a schismatical sect. But the poisonous seed which they had sown flourished for many years. The last vestige of their rigorism was eliminated by Pope Pius X by his Encyclical on frequent and daily Communion (1905.)

Pius X on Frequent and Daily Communion

"Frequent and daily Communion, being most ardently desired by Christ Our Lord and by the Catholic Church, is open to the faithful of whatever degree or condition, so that no one who is in the state of grace, and approaches the altar with a proper and devout disposition, should be kept away from it.

"The proper disposition consists in this, that he who approaches the Holy Table does not do so through custom or vanity, or for merely human motives, but because he wishes to please God, to be more closely united to Him by love, and to apply the Divine Medicine as a remedy for his infirmities and defects.

"Although it is most expedient that those who go to Communion frequently or daily should be free from venial sins, at least fully deliberate ones, and from all attachment to them, it nevertheless suffices to be free from mortal sin and to have the sincere purpose of avoiding sin. With such a purpose, the result must be that daily communicants will little by little free themselves also from venial sins and from all attachment thereto.

"But since the Sacraments of the New Law, although they produce their effect *ex opere operato*, yet produce greater effects in proportion as they are received with better dispositions, assiduous preparation should precede and suitable thanksgiving follow Holy Communion, according to the ability, condition, and duties of each communicant. . . .

"After the promulgation of this decree, all ecclesiastical writers shall refrain from contentious discussions about the dispositions needed for frequent and daily Communion."

—*Decree on Frequent and Daily Communion*, Dec. 20, 1905.

Hints for Study

1. Show the relationship between Jansenism and Calvinism.
2. Read the Articles on Baius, Jansenius, Pascal, and Port Royal in the *Cath. Encyclopedia.*
3. Note that the Jansenists were so dangerous to the Church because they insisted on remaining in the Church.

CHAPTER VII

ROYAL ABSOLUTISM AND ITS OFFSPRING, GALLICANISM AND JOSEPHINISM

The life of St. Vincent de Paul was passed in one of the stormiest periods of ecclesiastical and secular history. The Wars of Religion were waged in France during his younger years, the terrible Thirty Years' War devastated Central Europe during his manhood, and when he died in 1660 Europe had been definitively divided into Catholic and Protestant States as a result of the Peace of Westphalia. He had been a witness of the tragedy that France, a Catholic country, under the leadership of two Cardinals of the Church, Richelieu and Mazarin, joined forces with the Protestant princes of Germany, Sweden, and Holland to overthrow the power of the Hapsburgs, and with it the ascendancy of Catholicity in Germany. The Treaty of Westphalia (1648) weakened and humiliated the Empire, and assured for a hundred and fifty years the preponderance of France in Europe; but at what a cost to the Catholic Church! Innocent X protested against the iniquitous Treaty, but no one listened to him.

1. *The Church and Royal Absolutism*

After the Thirty Years' War the Church in nearly all the States of Western Europe fell a prey to royal absolutism. The rulers arrogated to themselves unlimited power in religious as well as in secular affairs. The Protestant princes in all the Protestant countries were the acknowledged heads of the Church. The Protestant Churches in England, Scotland, Holland, Scandinavia, the German Lutheran States and the Protestant Cantons of Switzerland were State establishments pure and simple. Those who refused to acknowledge this arrangement were known as "dissenters" and subjected to persecution, imprisonment, exile, fines, and even death.

The Catholic princes in many cases laid claim to the same rights and powers in Church affairs as their Protestant fellows.

506

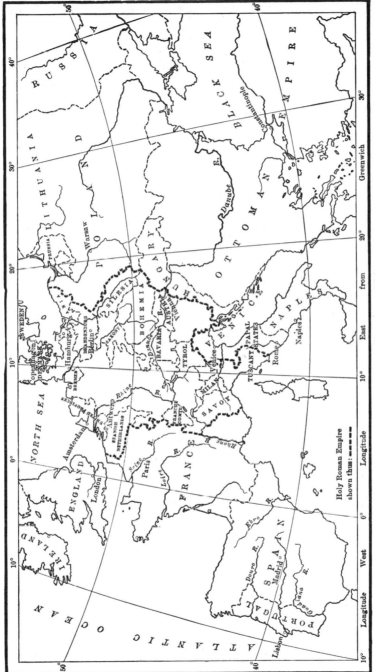

EUROPE AFTER THE PEACE OF WESTPHALIA

The liberty of the Church, for which the great Popes of the Middle Ages had fought so valiantly, was hardly more than a name. Everywhere it seemed to be the aim of the rulers to leave to the Pope only a shadow of power in religious affairs. Each prince wanted to be, as the Duke of Cleves expressed it, *"papa in terris suis,"* Pope in his own lands.

2. Gallicanism

It was in France under Louis XIV that this policy of absolutism was carried farthest. Louis dominated completely every department of the national life. In religion this domination included both the Catholics and the Huguenots. He dealt first with the Catholics, and, unfortunately, many bishops, among them the great Bossuet, were not unwilling to assist him. His plan was to isolate the French Church, as far as he could, from the Papacy. Nor were the people scandalized at his proceedings, for the worship of the Sovereign was one of their most cherished instincts. Louis supported Pope and bishops "as long as they took their marching orders from him; if they refused, he was perfectly ready to make war on the one and to send the others to the Bastille." In 1673 he began to confiscate for his own use the revenues of all vacant sees and to claim for himself the right of appointing new bishops, leaving to the Pope the formality of confirming his choice.

When the Popes resisted these claims, Louis summoned a General Assembly of the French Clergy (1681) and obtained from it the "Declaration of the Four Articles," known as the Four Gallican Propositions, namely that:

1. The Pope may not interfere directly or indirectly with the temporal concerns of princes.

2. In spiritual matters a General Council is superior to the Pope.

3. The rights and customs of the Gallican Church are inviolable.

4. The Pope is not infallible, even in matters of faith, unless his decision is confirmed by the consent of the Church.

The "Gallican customs, or Liberties," as they are usually called, were certain ancient rights, whose origin was lost in the mists of time. One forbade Papal Bulls to be published in France without the consent of the

Crown. Another exempted French subjects from the jurisdiction of the Inquisition and other Roman tribunals. A third claimed that the Gallican Church was independent of the Pope in its organization and elections.

Louis saw to it that this *Declaration* was afterwards sanctioned by the theological faculty of the Paris University (Sorbonne) and by many provincial parliaments. This subjection of the Church to the State in France is known as *Gallicanism*. Bossuet may not have drawn up the Four Articles, though some maintain that he did; but he defended them in a special treatise when they were attacked from many quarters, notably by Fénelon, Bishop of Cambrai. The Articles were immediately condemned by Pope Innocent XI, who declared them null and void. Adding deeds to words, Innocent refused to confirm the nomination to French bishoprics of any of those who had signed or approved the Articles. Louis retaliated by imprisoning the Papal Nuncio, and by seizing the Papal territory of Avignon; he even sent soldiers to Rome to overawe the Pope. It seemed as if Louis XIV was determined to plunge France into schism; but Innocent did not shrink from the task of defending the rights of the Holy See and the true liberties of the French Church. Alarmed at the dangers which threatened him in Europe at the time, Louis finally sought to bring about a reconciliation with the Holy See (1693). The thirty-six bishops who had been nominated by Louis expressed their regret for the part they had taken in the Assembly, and their nomination was confirmed by Innocent XII (1691-1700), while the King informed the Pope that the teaching of the Gallican Articles would not be enforced in the French seminaries. Peace was thus re-established, but more than once the Articles were revived by the successors of Louis to the great detriment of the authority of the Holy See. Gallicanism did not disappear entirely until after the Vatican Council (1870).

Revocation of the Edict of Nantes.—Whilst Louis XIV was employing his dragoons to invade the Papal territory at Avignon and bearding the Pope in his capital, he thought it a wise policy to manifest his zeal for the Catholic religion by driving the Huguenots from France. Cardinal Richelieu had put an end to the Huguenot State within a State, which the Edict of Nantes (1598) had created, when he brought about the fall of La Rochelle in 1628. The Huguenots had violated the Edict by refusing to tolerate the practice of Catholicism and by forming an alliance with England, France's hereditary enemy. But Richelieu had reaffirmed the Edict in 1629, and in the time of Louis XIV the Huguenots were an unarmed and peaceful body. The very existence of such a body that was not subject to his absolute control, was intolerable to the King. He ordered systematic efforts to be made to convert them. Bossuet held conferences with their leaders and wrote several books for their instruction. Their refusal to conform angered Louis, who was not used to meeting with opposition from his subjects. He determined to use force against them. At first the Edict of Nantes was interpreted in a sense unfavorable to the Huguenots, then it was brushed aside, and finally, on October 10, 1685, it was revoked altogether.

The revocation of the Edict of Nantes was a grave political mistake. Louis thought that there was only a small number of Huguenots in the country, and that these would now conform. But their number was much greater than he had dreamed, and very few consented under pressure to change their religion. More than 200,000 left the country and withdrew to England, to the Netherlands, to Brandenburg, to the Dutch Settlements in South Africa, and to the American colonies.

Pope Innocent XI had nothing whatever to do with the revocation of the Edict of Nantes. He was neither privy to the French King's design nor an abettor of it. On the contrary, he was strongly opposed to Louis's violent measures and asked King James II of England to intercede with the French King in favor of the persecuted Huguenots.

3. Josephinism

In 1763 John Nicholas von Hontheim, auxiliary-bishop of Trier, under the pseudonym *Febronius* published a book entitled *De Statu Ecclesiae* ("On the State of the Church") which was even more radical in regard to the Constitution of the Church than the Four Gallican Articles. According to Hontheim all bishops, including the Bishop of Rome, have the same powers. The Pope enjoys only a primacy of honor, no higher power; he is merely *primus inter pares*—"first among his peers." Hence the power of the Pope must be curtailed and that of the bishops extended. Hontheim's theories found ready acceptance in many quarters, and although the author withdrew his work fifteen years later, he could not undo its evil effects. The Electors of Mainz, Trier, and Cologne, and the Prince-Archbishop of Salzburg met in Congress at Ems in 1786, and issued a number of decrees—known as the "Punctation of Ems"—which, had they been acted upon, would have meant the foundation of a national church in Germany. The Emperor Joseph II (1780-1790) attempted to put them into practice, which led to an insurrection in Belgium and widespread dissatisfaction in the rest of the Empire among the clergy and the people. Joseph II and his minister Kaunitz spent most of their time suppressing monasteries, founding seminaries controlled by the State, drawing up curricula for the education of priests, nuns, and monks, revising prayer-books and hymnals, prescribing the number of candles to be lighted at Mass and how many Masses might be said at one time in the churches, working out sermon-plans for the parish priests, cutting down the feast days, pilgrimages, and processions, dissolving confraternities, restricting the number of candidates a monastery might receive. . . . No wonder Frederick II of Prussia spoke of the Emperor Joseph as "my Brother the Sacristan"!

Where all this interference of the State in Church affairs would have led to, it is impossible to say; three years after the Congress of Ems the French Revolution broke out, and the world had more important things to think of than Joseph's ecclesiastical "reforms."

4. Great Preachers, Scholars, and Saints

Sacred Orators.—The Church in France shared in the high culture for which the reign of Louis XIV was so remarkable. The royal autocracy of the *Grand Monarque* was applied to everything. It included a patronage of the arts and sciences, which enjoyed their Golden Age during the long life of Louis. It was but natural that a generation which produced a Pascal, a Corneille, a Racine, a Molière, should also hold up to the world masters of sacred eloquence. Jacques Bénigne *Bossuet* (d. 1704), Bishop of Meaux, a pupil of the Jesuits and a friend of St. Vincent de Paul, ranks high not only as a sacred orator of great brilliance, but also as an historian, a controversialist, and an ascetic writer. His eloquence earned for him the surname of "The Eagle of

Meaux." There is nothing in French, says a modern critic, that surpasses a fine page of Bossuet.

Louis *Bourdaloue* (d. 1704), a member of the Society of Jesus from his sixteenth year, is placed by his contemporaries even above Bossuet as a preacher. Time and again he was invited to preach before the Court of Louis XIV. He was called the "Preacher of Kings and the King of Preachers." But the palm of sacred eloquence, in the estimation of many, belongs to Jean Baptiste *Massillon* (d. 1742), member of the French Oratorians and Bishop of Clermont. His Lenten Sermons preached in Paris in 1699 established his reputation for all time, and have never lost their popularity. In moral earnestness he excels both Bossuet and Bourdaloue.

Catholic Scholarship.—Admirable work was accomplished in the field of ecclesiastical science by a number of French monks of the Benedictine Congregation of St. Maur.

The center of the literary activity of the Congregation was the abbey of St. Germain-des-Près, Paris. "The great claim of the Maurists to the gratitude and admiration of posterity is their historical and critical school, which stands quite alone in history, and produced an extraordinary number of colossal works of erudition which still are of permanent value." From 1645 to 1789 the Maurist scholars, chief among them Mabillon, Ruinart Montfaucon, Martène, Durand, Bouquet and d'Achery, published 199 great folio and 39 quarto or octavo volumes comprising editions of the works of the Fathers of the Church, collections of documents, monastic history, ecclesiastical histories and antiquities of France, and miscellaneous works of technical erudition. "The qualities that have made Maurist work proverbial for sound learning are its fine critical tact and thoroughness" (Butler).

About the same time as the Maurists in France, a group of Flemish Jesuits began to compile the monumental *Acta Sanctorum,* a hagiographical work comprising all the saints venerated throughout the Christian world, and containing a vast amount of material on Church History and kindred subjects in all countries and centuries. After John van Bolland, the editor of the first volume, the authors are called *Bollandists.* The 65th folio volume of the great collection was published in 1926.

Saints and Founders.—The era of royal absolutism did not produce many canonized saints. One known and venerated all over the Catholic world was *St. Margaret Mary Alacoque* (1647-1690,) apostle of the devotion to the Sacred Heart of Jesus.

Intense devotion to the Blessed Sacrament characterized her from early childhood. Her life in the Visitation Convent at Paray was distinguished for obedience, humility, and love of suffering. Favored with visions of Christ, who made known to her the favors in store for those practicing devotion to His Sacred Heart, she devoted her life to the spread of this devotion. She established the Holy Hour and the custom of receiving Holy Communion on the first Friday of each month. St. Margaret Mary's spiritual director for two years was the Bl. Claude de la

ST. ALPHONSUS LIGUORI   ST. PAUL OF THE CROSS

Colombière. Both he and St. John Eudes (1601-1680,) founder of the Congregation of Our Lady of Charity and of the Society of Jesus and Mary, did much to combat Jansenism and to spread devotion to the Sacred Heart.

St. Paul of the Cross (1694-1775), a Piedmontese, had from his youth a singular devotion to the Passion of Our Lord. To inspire his fellow-men with the same devotion, he founded the Congregation of the Passion in 1747, and thus gave to the Church a body of missionaries whose black habit, and badge of the Passion soon became known throughout the world.

The long career and varied labors of *St. Alphonsus dei Liguori* fill a great space in the Church history of the eighteenth century. Born at Naples in 1696, Alphonsus followed the profession of a lawyer until the age of twenty-six. Embracing the ecclesiastical state, he labored zealously for souls in Naples and in the country around. The sad spiritual condition of the country people inspired him with the idea of founding a Congregation to come to their assistance. He called it the Institute of the Most Holy Redeemer. He suffered almost incredible things to make and keep his Order regular and effective for good. He succeeded, and the Church is the richer for one of her most splendid preaching and missionary Orders. When St. Alphonsus could no longer preach in town and country, he began his fruitful career as a writer, and his great *Moral Theology* and his numerous ascetical works have gained for him an honored place among the Doctors of the Church.

A contemporary of St. Paul of the Cross and St. Alphonsus was the Franciscan *St. Leonard of Port Maurice* (1676-1751). For forty-four years he preached in every province of Italy, converting countless souls by his fiery and eloquent sermons, and then, worn out by his labors and exertions, came to Rome to die. Many a pious pilgrim still visits his tomb and his relics in the little Church of St. Bonaventure.

Armand Jean le Bouthillier de Rancè (d. 1700) was an accomplished courtier, and passionately fond of the chase. Falling into disfavor with Cardinal Mazarin, Minister of Louis XIV, he withdrew from the Court and began a new life. He gave all his possessions to the poor, renounced all revenues and inheritances, and lived a life of the strictest discipline in the Cistercian Abbey of La Trappe. When he entered the Abbey, the monks had fallen woefully from the true spirit of St. Bernard of Clairvaux. Chosen abbot, De Rancè thoroughly reformed the Abbey, and had his reforms confirmed by the Pope (1664). His monks are known as Trappists. Manual labor renders them self-supporting, but spiritual exercises and study occupy most of their time. Trappist houses are flourishing today in France, Germany, Belgium, China, Japan, Indo-China, Africa, Syria, the United States, Canada, England, and Ireland.

A name dear to countless schoolboys is that of *St. John Baptist de la Salle* (1651-1719). He was occupied, in 1681, with the direction of the Sisters of the Holy Infant, an Order devoted to the instruction of poor girls, when the resolve ripened in him to found a Congregation of men who would do the same service for poor boys. The members of his Congregation were to make teaching their sole profession, hence there were to be no priests among them. He called them "Brothers of the Christian Schools." In order to prepare teachers for the village schools he founded the first Normal School. He was also a pioneer in the field of Manual Training schools and reformatories. He has been universally recognized as the father of modern pedagogy.

"Who Then Will Be Saved?"

When Massillon delivered his famous sermon *On the Small Number of the Elect* before the voluptuous court of Versailles, the imagination of this august assembly, we are told, was so completely affected by his awe-inspiring description that, at length, terrified and struck as it were by an electric shock, they started involuntarily from their seats and, by their loud and continued murmurs of astonishment

St. John Baptist de la Salle

and applause, obliged him for a time to desist. The following extract is taken from this discourse:

"Who then will be saved? The man who, in these days of irreligion and vice, walks in the footsteps of the primitive Christian—'whose hands are innocent and whose heart is pure; who has not received his soul in vain'—; who has successfully struggled against the torrent of worldly example, and purified his soul; who is a lover of justice 'and swears not deceitfully against his neighbor'; who is not indebted to double dealing for an increase of fortune; who returns good for evil, and heaps favors on the enemy that has labored for his destruction; who is candid and sincere, and never sacrifices truth to interest, nor conscience to civility; who is charitable to all in distress, and a friend to all in affliction; who is resigned in adversity, and penitent even in prosperity.

"He, my brethren, will be saved, and he only.

"Now I ask you—I ask you with dismay, and without meaning to separate my lot from yours—Were the Son of Man to appear in this assembly, and separate the good from the bad, the innocent from the guilty, the penitent from the impenitent, how many would He place on His right hand? Would

He place the greater number of us? Would he place one half? Formerly He could not find ten just men in five populous cities; and could He find as many, do you think, in this assembly? You cannot give an answer, neither can I. Thou alone, my God, knowest Thy elect, Thy chosen few.

"But if we cannot say who will be placed on His right hand, we can say at least that sinners will be placed on His left. Who, then, are sinners? They may be divided into four classes. Let everyone attend and examine whether he may not be ranked in one of them:

"They who are immersed in vice, and will not reform;

"They who intend to reform, but defer their reformation;

"They who fall into their former habits as often as they pretend to renounce them;

"They who think they need not a change of life;

"These are the reprobate: separate them from the rest of this assembly, for they will be separated from them at the last day. Now, ye chosen servants of God—ye remnant of Israel, lift up your heads; your salvation is at hand: pass to the right: separate yourself from this chaff, which is destined for the fire. O God! where are Thy elect! . . .

—*Massillon's Sermons,* translated from the French by the Rev. Edward Peach, Dublin, 1867, p. 130-131.

Hints for Study

1. On the era of Absolutism, see H. O. Wakeham, *The Ascendency of France* 1598-1715 (Macmillan).

2. For more detailed information on Gallicanism, Gallican Liberties, and the Gallican Articles, see the *Cath. Encyclopedia.*

3. Brother Leo, of the Christian Brothers, has written an excellent life of St. John Baptist de la Salle—*Story of St. J. B. de la Salle* (N. Y. 1921).

4. For St. Paul of the Cross, see Ward, *The Passionists,* for St. Alphonsus, Stebbing, *The Redemptorists;* for St. Margaret Mary, either Bougaud or Demimuid.

5. Note the scarcity of great saints and founders of Religious Orders during this period. How can you explain this?

CHAPTER VIII

RATIONALISM AND "ENLIGHTENMENT"

The apostasy from the Catholic Church in the sixteenth century was followed in the seventeenth and eighteenth by wholesale apostasy from Christianity itself. The principle of Protestantism, that each one can and should interpret Holy Scripture according to his own individual judgment, not only struck a deadly blow at all ecclesiastical authority, but also made reason alone the ultimate criterion or standard in matters of religion. Many of those who accepted this principle began to question the very foundations on which Christianity rested, and ended by rejecting it altogether. This is known as Rationalism, or Free Thought in Religion; it is really nothing but Infidelity, or denial of all revealed Religion.

Rise of Rationalism.—Rationalism had its beginning in England. Lord Herbert of Cherbury (d. 1648) was the first to construct a system of "Natural Religion." Only what is common to all religions, he maintained, can be regarded as absolutely true. This common element he reduced to five points: (1) There is a Supreme Being. (2) It is man's duty to honor this Supreme Being. (3) The Supreme Being must be honored especially by a virtuous life. (4) Whoever offends the Supreme Being experiences a feeling of regret. (5) Because the Supreme Being is just, the good are rewarded and the wicked punished in this life and in the next. These propositions form the basis of so-called "Deism," that is, belief in a personal God founded on reason and not on revelation or authority.

According to Thomas Hobbes (d. 1679) science deals only with corporeal things and with motion. Hobbes is an outspoken materialist. In nature, he says in his *Leviathan,* everything happens with mechanical necessity. Man is a perfect mechanism, nothing more. The State, too, is a big machine.

John Locke (d. 1704) popularized Rationalism by his brilliant writings, especially his *Essay Concerning Human Understanding,* his *Reasonableness of Christianity,* and his *Letters on Toleration.* The individual, he said, must free himself from every external authority, also from that of the Church; he must divest himself of the influence of tradition and training, and be guided by his reason alone. David Hume (d. 1776) went a step further; he denied that certitude could ever be attained, and thus became the apostle of modern skepticism.

Freemasonry.—Rationalism found powerful support in the secret international fraternal organization known as *Masons* or *Freemasons.* In its present form Freemasonry dates from the first quarter of the eighteenth century, the first Grand Lodge having been founded in London in 1717. It is really a sectarian body having its own formulas of belief about God, the soul, conscience, etc., and its own secret as well as public ritual. It systematically promotes religious indifferentism, and its ultimate purpose is the "overthrow of the whole religious, political, and social order based on Christian institutions and the establishment of a new state of things based, in its principles and laws, on pure Naturalism." It claims religious toleration as one of its principles, but it has always, especially in the Latin countries of Europe and America, openly and secretly attacked Christianity. In 1738 Pope Clement XII condemned Freemasonry and forbade Catholics, under penalty of excommunication, to enter Masonic societies.

Rationalism in France.—Rationalism soon found its way into France, where the open and shameless immorality of the Court and of a large section of the nobility helped to carry it to extremes which it never attained in England. One of the ablest and most influential leaders of the movement in France was *Voltaire* (1694-1778). By his ready wit, his sarcasm, and his keen appreciation of the weak points of his opponents, Voltaire did more than any other man of his time to spread hatred of the Church and her ministers and institutions among the middle and lower classes of the people. His motto was: *Écrasez l'infame!* "Crush the infamous thing," that is, the Church. His last words were: "I die forsaken by God and men." The same year, 1778, also witnessed the death of *Jean Jacques Rousseau,* who in his *Émile* had written a catechism of Natural Religion and in his *Contrat Social* (Social Contract) the Gospel of the Revolution. He maintained that the right to govern came not from God but from the people, who could therefore unmake what they themselves had made.

The principal organ of French Rationalism was the *Encyclopedia* or Dictionary of the Arts and Sciences, begun by Diderot and d'Alembert in

1750. Most of the articles on religion and philosophy were written in a materialistic spirit. History was deliberately perverted, Christianity travestied. It was Diderot's pious wish that "the last king might be strangled with the entrails of the last priest." Scores of books and pamphlets were published by the "Encyclopedists," all breathing the spirit of infidelity and skepticism. Their style was pleasing, their humor coarse, and their irony incisive. Rationalism reigned supreme in the drawing-rooms of Paris and Versailles, and infidelity was the newest fashion of all France.

Rationalism and Enlightenment in the Other Countries.— From France the irreligious movement spread to the other countries of Europe. In Germany it made great progress especially during the reign of Frederick II of Prussia (1740-1786), at whose court the French Rationalists were always welcome guests. Freemasonry followed in the wake of Rationalism. The first lodge was founded at Hamburg in 1773, and it soon became fashionable in high society, in literary and artistic circles, to be initiated into the new sect. Goethe, Lessing, and Schiller, the leading German poets, were infected with Rationalism. The philosopher Immanuel Kant recognized no religion but Deism. Fichte's Pantheism attacked the foundations of all religion.

Nor were the religious views of numerous Catholics who still remained true to the Church, uninfluenced by the rationalist movement. In Germany the party of "Enlightenment" (the *Illuminati*) aimed at bringing about a complete transformation in the doctrines and discipline of the Church, in the hope of making the Catholic religion more palatable to their rationalist opponents. It was under the influence of these views that the Emperor Joseph II undertook his scheme of religious reform to which we referred above, and it was the same views that caused the prince-bishops of Germany and many of the higher clergy to show themselves so hostile to the Pope and all things Roman. The same movement fostered the anti-Catholic and anti-Papal spirit in all the Catholic countries of Europe, in Spain, Portugal, Venice, Naples, Parma, and Tuscany, and in the Spanish and Portuguese colonies.

Suppression of the Jesuits.—Jansenists, Gallicans, and Rationalists, so fundamentally opposed to one another in all other respects, had one pet aversion in common—hostility to the Society of Jesus, the most dangerous opponent of all of them. This feeling of enmity grew in intensity from year to year and led in the end to the suppression of the great Order by the Pope.

Portugal was the first to run down its prey. In 1750 Spain and Portugal exchanged parts of their colonies in South America. The Indians, who had been under the government of Spain, revolted against the despotic rule introduced by the Portuguese. The Jesuits were blamed for the rebellion and promptly expelled. Some time after, an attempt was made on the life of the King of Portugal at Lisbon. The Jesuits were accused of complicity in the conspiracy, and without a shadow of proof against them, their superiors were imprisoned and all the rest of the members were sent by ship to Civita Vecchia, a sea-port of the Papal States, "as a present to the Pope," as the Portuguese minister Pombal had the insolence to phrase it. Clement XIII gave them a fatherly welcome.

In France the imprudence of one of its members led to the expulsion of the Society of Jesus. Father la Valette, superior of the Jesuit missions in the island of Martinique, had taken part in an extensive mercantile enterprise which proved unsuccessful. In 1761 he became insolvent. The Society was held responsible for his debts, but refused to pay. The Parliament made the trial which followed, the excuse for a general inquiry into the Society's rules and constitutions. The result was a foregone conclusion. The existence of the Society was declared illegal in France. In November, 1764, Louis XV, who was entirely under the influence of his minister Choiseul and Madame de Pompadour, who had a special grudge against the Jesuits, signed the decree of expulsion.

In Spain the Jesuits thought they had a friend in King Charles III but his minister Aranda succeeded in poisoning his mind against them by means of the infamous "Jesuit Letters," an abominable forgery, in which the Fathers were accused of fomenting rebellion against the government. Completely deceived, the King signed an order for their expulsion (April, 1767).

Pressure was now brought to bear on Rome by all the Bourbon courts of Europe to dissolve the Society of Jesus altogether. Clement XIII refused; but his successor, Clement XIV, proved more pliable. Threatened by Spain with schism, he issued on July 21, 1773, the Brief of Suppression, *Dominus ac Redemptor,* "to remove a source of trouble and to restore peace to the Church." No blame was laid by the Pope on the Constitution of the Order, or on the personal conduct of its members, or the correctness of their teaching.   In Prussia the Order continued to exist till the death of Frederick II (1786); in Russia the Papal suppression was never published, and the Jesuits were left undisturbed.

Pope Clement XII Condemns Freemasonry

On April 28, 1738 Clement XII published the Constitution *In Eminenti* condemning *Freemasonry* as "fundamentally anti-Christian and immoral." If we remember that Voltaire, the Encyclopedists, the leaders of the French Revolution, and the instigators of all the revolts against the Holy See in Italy and in most of the Latin countries were members of that secret organization, the action of the Pope was fully justified.   The following extract from the Bull of condemnation contains the indictment of primitive Freemasonry, the grounds on which its prohibition was based:

"It has come to our knowledge and indeed it is a matter of public notoriety, that there has been a great development, spreading far and wide and growing in strength from day to day, of certain Societies, Meetings, Clubs, Reunions, Conventicles or Lodges, commonly known by the name of *Liberi Muratori, Francs Maçons,* or otherwise variously designated according to the local idiom, in which men of no matter what religion and sect, *content with a certain affectation of natural virtue,* are mutually banded together in a close and exclusive league, in accordance with laws and statutes which they have framed for themselves.   Further, *they concert measures in secrecy* and are bound under extravagant penalties by an oath taken on the Bible to shroud their activities in impenetrable silence.   Since, however, it is of the very nature of wrong-doing to betray itself and to give itself away by the outcry which it raises, hence the aforesaid associations or assemblies have excited such vehement suspicion in the minds of the faithful that to enroll oneself in these Lodges is in the judgment of men of sense and high principle tantamount to incurring the stigma of a libertine and a miscreant; for, assuredly, if such people were not doing evil they would never have so much hatred of the light.   Moreover *their ill-repute* has spread to such a degree that in very many countries the associations aforesaid have some time ago been *proscribed by secular rulers* and have been wisely suppressed as dangerous to the safety of the realm."

—*Bullarium Romanum,* XXIV, p. 366 (Cf. *Thought,* June, 1927, p. 135).

Hints for Study

1. On the Rationalist Movement read Kurth, *The Church at the Turning Points of History,* pp. 154-177.
2. For a very thorough account of the origin and progress of modern unbelief see A. Léman, *The Church in Modern Times,* Ch. IV (Herder, 1929).
3. Write a brief paragraph on each of the following: *Deism, Leviathan Encyclopedists, Illuminati, Freemasonry, Contrat Social, Dominus ac Redemptor.*

From the French Revolution to the Present Day
1789-1933

CHAPTER I

THE CHURCH IN THE STORMS OF THE REVOLUTION

Absolutism, free thought, infidelity, licentiousness, the sneers of Voltaire and the seductive democratic theories of Rousseau had done their work. France was ripe for the Great Revolution, whose purpose, if it had a purpose at all, "was not the reform of the ancient régime, but its destruction. A blind, irresistible force, it acted with all the power of a furious element let loose, and it overthrew society from top to bottom, uprooting everything after the manner of a cyclone, leaving the ground strewn with ruins wherever it had passed" (Kurth).

It is only with one aspect of the gigantic catastrophe that we are concerned here—with the change it wrought in the condition of the Church.

The Fate of the Church in France.—On the eve of the Revolution there was no real hatred towards the Church among the lower classes, the *tiers état,* as they were called, in France. It is true, the higher clergy were not popular; they all belonged to the nobility, were attached to the court, mostly absent from their bishoprics and monasteries, worldly-minded, and completely out of touch with the common people. The inferior clergy, on the other hand, enjoyed the respect and confidence of the people, whose economic difficulties they not only felt, but fully shared. When the States-General, that is, the assembly of the three orders of the kingdom, the Clergy, the Nobility, and the Commonalty (tiers état), met at Versailles on May 5, 1789—the first time since 1614—the lower clergy made common cause with the Third Estate and formed with them the controlling factor in the Constituent Assembly, whose purpose it was to frame a new constitution. During the famous night-session on August the 4th the clergy and nobility generously sacrificed their ancient privileges for the welfare of the whole nation. The Church was thus placed at the mercy of the National Assembly—and it proved no very tender mercy.

In order to alleviate the financial distress of the State the National Assembly, in November, 1789, decreed the confiscation of all the immovable property of the Church, assuming in return the obligation of maintaining the Church and her ministers from the public funds. The clergy had thus become at one stroke the paid servants of the State. Nor did the Assembly stop there. In the following year the monasteries, convents, and other religious houses were suppressed, and all Church property was placed under the control of the State.

In July, 1790, Gallicanism celebrated its greatest triumph. The "Civil Constitution of the Clergy" was passed by the Assembly. Fifty-one of the 154 bishoprics were suppressed, leaving one bishopric for each of the 83 Departments into which France had been divided. All French citizens, including Protestants and Jews, were given the right to choose the bishops and the pastors. Every ecclesiastical office not directly connected with the care of souls was abolished. Every priest and bishop was obliged to take an oath on the new Constitution. Only four of the bishops, among them Talleyrand, Bishop of Autun, and about half of the clergy took the oath. Those who refused were deprived of their offices. When Pope Pius VI condemned the Constitution, suspended the priests and bishops who had taken the oath, and declared the elections to ecclesiastical offices invalid, many priests retracted their oath. Thus a disastrous schism arose in France. The Legislative Assembly banished all the priests who refused to take the oath. Three hundred and eighty were deported to French Guiana in South America, where few survived the murderous climate. Thousands emigrated to England and Germany, and some found a refuge in the United States. Louis XVI accepted the Civil Constitution of the Clergy, but refused to sanction the oath necessary to enforce it. His firmness on this point sealed his fate. The monarchy fell on August 10, 1792. September witnessed the Reign of Terror. A number of bishops and 215 priests were guillotined. The Christian religion was proscribed. The Gregorian Calendar was replaced by a revolutionary one, the new era beginning September 22, 1792, a week of ten days was introduced, the "décadi" (tenth day) taking the place of Sunday, Republican holidays—Feast of Labor, Feast of Genius, Feast of Good Deeds—the place of the Holydays of the Church. The orgy of blasphemy was crowned by placing a girl of ill repute on the altar of Notre Dame of Paris and worshiping her as the Goddess of Reason (November 10, 1793). After a few months this horror came to an end. Robespierre, one of the bloodthirstiest of the Revolutionaries, was a Deist, and on his motion, the Convention decreed that the future religion of France should be Deism, with belief in a Supreme Being and in the immortality of the soul as its fundamental tenets. On June 8, 1794, Robespierre solemnly celebrated the "Feast of the Supreme Being." A month later he was overthrown and guillotined.

The Holy See and the French Republic.—Under the "Directory" (1795-1799) the Church was separated from the State, and freedom of worship was proclaimed. But in 1797 persecution began anew. Again hundreds of priests were exiled to Guiana, and because Pope Pius VI had sided with the Allies in their war against the French Republic, General Bonaparte invaded the States of the Church. Pius was forced to sign the Treaty of Tolentino, by which he surrendered large portions of his territory to the French, as well as many valuable manuscripts and priceless works of art. The murder of a Frenchman in Rome in 1798 gave the French an excuse for occupying the Eternal City and putting an end to the Papal temporal power. The aged Pontiff himself was carried off into exile to Valence, where he died in 1799. The enemies of the Church rejoiced. The last Pope, they declared, had reigned. They were, as usual, mistaken. Under the protection of the German Emperor Francis II the Cardinals met in conclave on the island of San Giorgio near Venice and elected Pius VII (1800-1823).

Napoleon Bonaparte and the Church.—Louis XVI, as we have seen, had refused to accept that part of the revolutionary constitution which put the Church under the State, and this refusal had cost him his throne and his life. The Church had also refused this degrading slavery, and though hunted down and persecuted, had remained in hiding in the villages and towns, even when her bishops had fled oversea. The Catholic faith was still enshrined in the hearts of the people. Napoleon realized this and resolved to make peace with the Church. In 1801 he opened negotiations for a *Concordat* with the Pope.

The most important provisions of this famous agreement were the following: the free exercise of the Catholic Religion, as the religion of the majority of the French people, is guaranteed; the teaching of religion is to be free from State interference. The Pope grants the right of nominating bishops to the State, but reserves to himself the right of canonical institution. All the Church property confiscated during the Revolution is to remain in the hands of the State or of the private individuals who had acquired it; by way of compensation the State engages to give the bishops and pastors suitable salaries. The bishops and the clergy must take the oath of allegiance.

Napoleon set up the French Empire in 1804 and secured the presence of Pope Pius VII in Paris for his coronation. Five years later, when Pius refused to declare war on all the enemies of France, Napoleon seized Rome, arrested the Pope, and imprisoned him, first at Savona on the Riviera, and then at Fontainebleau, where he remained till the advance of the Allies brought about his liberation (1814).

Fate of the Church in the Rest of Europe.—The Revolution had not been confined to France. The Netherlands, the lands west of the Rhine, Switzerland, and Italy had all been revolutionized. Suppression of religious houses, redistribution of bishoprics, and secularization of Church property were everywhere enforced. While Napoleon labored to restore Catholicity in France by the Concordat of 1801, he was eagerly engaged in destroying the stately fabric of the Church in Germany. He confiscated all the possessions of the Church in the Rhineland and Westphalia. The three ecclesiastical Electorates of Mainz, Trier, and Cologne were abolished. Lands and buildings belonging to abbeys and convents were seized and sold to the highest bidders. Bishoprics were left vacant, parishes were without priests, and the government interfered constantly in the spiritual administration of the Church. On the left bank of the Rhine the German princes followed the example of Napoleon, secularized all the possessions of the Church and suppressed hundreds of religious houses.

Such wholesale robbery as that committed against the Church during the era of the French Revolution and the Empire of Napoleon had never been heard of since the days of Diocletian. In the Protestant countries all her possessions had been turned over to the secular rulers or been appropriated by them; in the Catholic countries the Revolution and the insatiable greed of the princes had completely despoiled her. After the downfall of Napoleon the Church stood before the world stripped of every vestige of her temporal splendor. She was once more the poor Bride of Christ.

Additions Made by Napoleon to the French Catechism

After his coronation as emperor of the French (1804) and his victories over Russia and Austria, which brought about the enforced abdication of Francis as emperor of Germany, Napoleon's ambition grew beyond all bounds. It was at this time that he made the additions to the French Catholic Catechism which declared that it was the sacred duty of every subject of the Emperor to take part in his wars, and that opposition to his wishes was a sin deserving eternal damnation:

Q. What are the duties of all Christians toward the Emperor?

A. Christians owe to the princes who govern them, and we owe in a special manner to our Emperor Napoleon I love, reverence, obedience, loyalty, military service, and the taxes imposed for the preservation of his empire and of his throne.

Q. Why are we obliged to perform our duties to our Emperor?

A. Because God, who raises up empires and distributes them as He wills, by heaping favors upon our Emperor in peace and in war, has set him up as our sovereign and has made him the minister of His power and His image on earth. To honor and serve our Emperor is, therefore, to honor and serve God Himself.

Q. How should we regard those who fail to perform their duty to our Emperor?

A. According to the Apostle St. Paul, they resist the order established by God and deserve eternal damnation.

Q. Will the duties which we owe to our Emperor be also binding with regard to his lawful successors?

A. Yes, without any doubt; because we read in the Sacred Scriptures that God, the Lord of Heaven and earth, by an order of His supreme will and by His Providence, gives empires not only to one person in particular, but also to his family.

> —*Catéchisme à l'usage de toutes les églises de l'Empire Français.* Paris, 1806.

Hints for Study

1. On the fortunes of the Church during the French Revolution and under Napoleon see MacCaffrey, *The Church in the XIX Century*, Vol. I.
2. A good novel dealing with the Revolution is Canon Sheehan, *The Queen's Fillet.*
3. Summarize the events related in this chapter in the form of a chronological table.
4. Explain briefly: *Civil Constitution of the Clergy, Secularization, Conclave, Concordat, Revolutionary Calendar, Ecclesiastical Electorates.*

CHAPTER II

FROM PIUS VII TO PIUS IX

When Pius VII excommunicated Napoleon in 1809, that despot scornfully remarked: "Does the Pope think that the weapons will fall from the hands of my soldiers because of his excommunication?" A few years later an army report from the icy plains of Russia read: "The weapons are falling from the hands of our soldiers."

Napoleon was forced to a disgraceful retreat from Moscow in 1812; in 1813 and 1814 he was completely beaten by the allied armies. In the same castle of Fontainebleau in which he had kept the Pope a prisoner, the Emperor of the French had to sign his own abdication. Pius VII had in the meantime returned to Rome amidst the rejoicings of the Roman people.

1. *Pius VII and the Catholic Revival*

The Holy Alliance.—After the fall of Napoleon the Emperor Francis I of Austria, King Frederick William III of Prussia, and Alexander I of Russia formed the "Holy Alliance." The treaty was distinctly religious in character and stated that the sovereigns bound themselves to administer the affairs of Europe in a Christian spirit. Most of the kings of Europe joined the Holy Alliance, which revived the conception of a centralized Europe and a common European responsibility, and recognized the truth so loudly proclaimed by the Church at all times: that the principles of Christianity should be applied to politics. It was only a short-lived experiment, however, and was afterwards replaced by purely political alliances.

Restoration of the States of the Church.—At the Congress of Vienna (1814-1815), through the efforts of the famous Papal Secretary of State, Cardinal Ercole Consalvi, the States of the Church were restored almost in their entirety, but the property of the Church which had been confiscated in 1803, was not re-

527

turned. During the following years Pius VII entered into agreements with the various European States, by which the States guaranteed to contribute annual sums towards the support of the Church, and received in return rather far-reaching rights in regard to the nomination of bishops and pastors.

One of Pius' first official acts after his return to Rome was to restore the Society of Jesus (1814), as well as the Propaganda, and the national colleges at Rome. Gradually, one by one, the hundreds of vacant sees throughout Christendom were filled with worthy incumbents. Everywhere there was a marked re-awakening of Catholic life.

The Restoration in France.—Pius VII attempted to negotiate a new concordat with France after the restoration of the Bourbons. But the Bourbons, who had "learned nothing and forgotten nothing," were still wedded to Gallicanism, and the attempt ended in failure. Some redress, however, was granted to the Church. The number of bishoprics was increased, a sum of money was voted for the support of the Church, and the right of the Church to own property was recognized.

In the meantime a great Catholic revival, moral and intellectual, was in progress throughout France, promoted by a notable band of talented and zealous laymen. The standard-bearer of this movement was Count Chateaubriand, who in 1802 had published his epoch-making *Genie du Christianisme* ("Genius of Christianity"), in which he showed that of all religions Christianity was "the most poetical, the most human, the most favorable to freedom, art, and letters." If that is so, argued the younger generation of Frenchmen, then no one need be ashamed to profess it; and the best of them began to gravitate back to the Church. Lamartine gave poetic expression to the movement, and Joseph de Maistre, in his celebrated work "On the Pope," attacked Gallicanism with uncompromising logic and held up the Roman Pontiff as "the one great champion of Christianity against all its enemies."

Among the visitors to Rome during the Pontificate of Pius VII was Madame Letitia Bonaparte. The Pope welcomed the mother of his old persecutor and supported her and her family for the rest of their days. Napoleon himself died in exile on the island of St. Helena in 1821. Pius VII had successfully pleaded with the British Government that he should be more mildly treated, and had sent a priest to attend him on his deathbed and to give him the Apostolic Benediction.

2. Pontificate of Leo XII

Pius VII, who died in 1823 in his eighty-fourth year, was succeeded by Leo XII (1823-1829). Leo's health was so poor that he was at death's door before he had been Pope a year. The saintly Passionist, Msgr. Strambi, offered his life for him and predicted his recovery. Leo XII was an exceedingly austere man, both in his own private life and in his rule, which was on that account disliked by the free and easy living Roman populace. The revolutionary ideas planted in the minds of the Italian people by the French invaders manifested themselves during his reign in the secret societies that sprang up everywhere, and especially in the party of the Carbonari, founded expressly for the overthrow of the Papal power and the unification of Italy.

Leo XII displayed his love for science and art by his elaborate reformation of ecclesiastical and secular education in Rome, by removing from the Index the books of Galileo and other scientists, by restoring the Vatican printing-press, and enriching the Vatican Library.

3. Catholic Emancipation in the British Isles

The short Pontificate of Pius VIII (1829-1830) saw the passing of the Catholic Emancipation Act in the British Isles, the July Revolution in France, and the establishment of the Catholic kingdom of Belgium.

The fear that the Irish Catholics would ally themselves with the enemies of England on the Continent, the desire to secure recruits for the army and the navy, the spread of religious indifference and, in consequence, of religious toleration, but, above all, the fearless espousal of the Catholic claims by such men as Edmund Burke and Henry Grattan, brought about the first relaxation of the Penal Code in Great Britain. In 1771 the Catholics were permitted, under certain conditions, to lease bogland in Ireland, and in 1778 they were empowered to hold leases for 999 years. In 1782 the laws against the bishops and the regular clergy were abolished, and Catholic schoolmasters were allowed to teach with the permission of the Protestant bishop of the district. In 1792 a great Catholic convention met in Dublin, which frightened the Protestant Irish Parliament into making some political concessions. Catholics obtained the right to vote for members of the Irish Parliament, to serve on juries, to become members of the town corporations, and to hold certain civil and military offices, but they remained excluded from the British House of Commons and the House of Lords, as well as from most of the higher offices of state in the British Empire.

The Irish insurrection of 1798, which was crushed with little difficulty, was followed by the dissolution of the Irish Parliament, and the legislative union between England and Ireland. Pitt had

DANIEL O'CONNELL

promised the Irish Catholics complete emancipation as soon as the union should have been effected. But he forgot his promises, and, from now on the Catholics determined to rely entirely on themselves. Nothing was accomplished until, in 1810, Daniel O'Connell was chosen to lead the fight for emancipation. Mainly through his exertions the Catholic Association was formed in 1823. By his fiery eloquence O'Connell revived the spirits of the discouraged Catholics, who only now became conscious of their united strength. They passed a resolution to oppose all parliamentary candidates who refused to pledge themselves for emancipation. O'Connell stood for Parliament and was returned amidst the acclamations of the people (1828). When he presented himself in the House of Commons he refused to take the oath which denounced Transubstantiation, the Mass, and the Invocation of Saints as idolatrous. Four million Irishmen stood behind him. The Duke of Wellington, who had just been made Prime Minister, alarmed at the danger of civil war, forced George IV to give his consent to the introduction of an Emancipation Bill, which was passed in March, and received the royal signature in April, 1829. The pressure of centuries of persecution was thus lifted from the Catholics of England, Ireland, Scotland, Wales, and the British colonies.

Even after emancipation the Catholics of Ireland were still obliged to pay tithes and to contribute to the support of the Protestant churches. It was not until 1869 that this crying injustice was removed by the disestablishment of the Protestant Church. For eighteen years O'Connell strove in vain to win political independence for Ireland. But the luster of his fame is not dimmed by this failure: he taught two generations of Irishmen, heirs of misery and slavery, to stand up and fight as freemen. His lessons bore full fruit only in our own day.

4. Belgium Becomes a Kingdom

The union between Belgium and Holland effected at the Congress of Vienna was very unfortunate and led to constant disputes between the Belgians, who were Catholics, and the Dutch, who were overwhelmingly Protestants. A revolution broke out at Brussels in 1830, which ended in the establishment of an independent Belgian kingdom and the adoption of a constitution favorable to the Catholic Church. Still, the anti-Catholic spirit engendered especially in the French-speaking parts of the country by the French Revolution, was by no means dead, and gradually led to the formation of two political parties on religious lines, the Catholic party and the anti-clerical, or Liberal, party. The Belgian hierarchy reopened the famous University at Louvain which became the center of Catholic intellectual life and in time made its influence felt far beyond the limits of the kingdom.

5. Gregory XVI and the Scholastic Revival

The result of the conclave which met a fortnight after the death of Pius VIII and lasted seven weeks, was the election of Gregory XVI (1831-1846), a member of the Camaldolese Order. The new Pope was throughout his life the uncompromising opponent of secret societies and of rebellion. The old Carbonari had lost their hold on the people—they had been too anarchical in their tendencies—but their place was taken by the Young Italy Party, who wished to unite all the Italian States into one Italian kingdom. Several uprisings took place in the Papal States, and it was only with the aid of Austrian and French troops that peace could be restored and maintained.

Gregory XVI was one of the most learned of the Popes. He was instrumental in bringing about a revival in the study of philosophy and theology, known as Neo-Scholasticism. The men who headed this movement—Liberatore, Palma, Patrizi, and Perrone—began the task of adapting the work of Aristotle and the great Scholastics of the Middle Ages to modern conditions and hence deserve the gratitude of all lovers of true Catholic science. Matteo Liberatore was a remarkable man. At twenty-six he was a professor of philosophy at the Jesuit College at Naples. In 1840 he published the first modern textbook of Thomistic Philosophy, which has maintained its popularity to this day. With two other learned Jesuits, Sanseverino and Taparelli, he founded the first Italian scientific journal, *La Scienza et la Fede* ("Science and Faith") and in 1850, in Rome, the *Civiltà Cattolica*, which is still one of the leading Catholic periodicals of the world.

Under Gregory XVI the College of Cardinals could boast of men of extraordinary genius: Cardinal Angelo Mai, who revolutionized textual criticism by his discovery and deciphering of *palimpsests*, that is, parchments over whose all but effaced first writing a later hand had written; and Cardinal Mezzofanti, who spoke with fluency some fifty or sixty languages of the most widely separated families, besides having a less perfect acquaintance with many others.

In France a great disappointment was in store for Gregory XVI. As a protest against the enslavement of the Church in that country by the Gallican Government, Lamennais, Lacordaire and Montalembert founded the newspaper *L'Avenir* ("The Future") and attempted the formation of a Catholic party that would bring about a union of the Church and democracy. Their zeal carried these men too far, and Gregory saw himself obliged to condemn the writings of Lamennais (1832). Lamennais ended his career, which had begun with such splendid Christian promise, in revolt against the Church and in despair. Lacordaire and Montalembert submitted to the judgment of the Holy See and remained throughout their lives, as powerful writers and orators, fearless and successful champions of the liberty of the Church in France. Famous are the words of Montalembert before the French Parliament: "We are the successors of the martyrs and tremble not before the successors of Julian the Apostate; we are the sons of the Crusaders and will not retreat before the sons of Voltaire."

6. The Catholic Awakening in Germany

The reaction against Rationalism and Josephinism in Germany started with the great literary and artistic revival known as the Romantic Movement, which began "with the worship of medieval art and literature and ended with the worship of medieval religion." The centers of the Catholic revival were Münster in Westphalia, Landshut in Bavaria, Mainz, Munich, and Vienna. Here the men and women whose names are dear to every Catholic heart gathered in friendly circles, discussed the needs of the Church, wrote works of enduring value, and were in their own daily lives illustrious examples of the living, transforming power of Christianity.

In Vienna St. Clement Hofbauer, the second founder of the Redemptorists, attracted the best minds of the capital around him and was such a mighty power for good that he has been styled the Apostle of Vienna. Among those who felt his influence most were the philosopher and historian Frederick von Schlegel and his wife Dorothea, the poet Eichendorff, the dramatist and pulpit orator Zacharias Werner, the political economist Adam Müller, and the painter Philip Veit. In Münster we meet the pioneers of modern pedagogy, Franz von Fürstenberg and Bernard Overberg, the poet and Church historian Leopold von Stolberg, the noble and talented Princess Amalia von Gallitzin, the mother of the renowned American missionary Prince Demetrius Gallitzin, and those uncompromising champions of the liberty of the Church August and Max von Droste-Vischering. In Landshut John Michael Sailer, later bishop of Ratisbon, trained the candidates for the priesthood in the true Catholic spirit, and by his numerous writings and the charm of his saintly personality profoundly influenced thousands of his contemporaries and brought many Protestants back to the Catholic fold. In Munich Joseph von Görres and his friends carried Catholic principles into the State University and laid the foundations of German Catholic scholarship which was to mean so much to the Catholic cause throughout the world. In Mainz Bruno Liebermann founded the Catholic monthly *Der Katholik* (1821), which, with the *Historisch-Politische Blaetter* of

Goerres, became the chief exponent of Catholic ideas in Germany and enjoyed a European reputation. In Tübingen John Adam Möhler (1796-1838) founded the Catholic historical school, and wrote his famous *Symbolik* ("Symbolism," Symbol meaning Creed), which was perhaps the heaviest blow, as an English Protestant writer says, ever dealt to the Reformation.

During the reign of Gregory XVI the first trial of strength between the reawakened German Catholics and the Protestant Prussian State took place. The struggle centered around the question of Mixed Marriages, the conditions for which Prussia

insisted on laying down. In 1830 Pope Pius VIII published a Brief which forbade the clergy to assist at mixed marriages unless they had obtained a written promise for the Catholic bringing-up of the offspring of such marriages. The Prussian Government declared that in such cases the boys should follow the religion of the father, the girls that of the mother. Clemens August von Droste-Vischering, Archbishop of Cologne, stood up for the rights of the Church and defied the Government. He was arrested and thrown into prison (1837). All Germany was aroused and took sides.

BISHOP VON KETTELER

Joseph von Görres published his *Athanasius* (1838), which marks the climax in the Catholic revival. It was a sharp indictment of the Prussian Government and its intolerance. The book went through four large editions in a few months. No one had ever dared to speak in such plain language to a secular ruler since the great Ages of the Faith. The Archbishop's heroism and Görres' pen won the victory for the Catholic cause—the first of a long series of victories. Incidentally the *Kölner Wirren* (Cologne Conflict) caused the young Westphalian nobleman, Wilhelm Emanuel von Ketteler, to exchange the service of the State for the service of the Church. As Bishop of Mainz, Ketteler became the pioneer of Christian Social Reform and carried on the traditions of his master, Görres, in championing the liberty of the Church against State encroachment. Leo XIII called him his "great precursor" in social reform work.

7. *The Oxford Movement*

The progress of Catholicity in England between 1829, when the Emancipation Bill was signed, and 1850, when the hierarchy was reëstablished, was nothing short of marvelous. This progress was due partly to immigration from Ireland, and partly to the very great number of converts who came to the Church as a result of the Oxford Movement. State control had paralyzed the spiritual energies of the Anglican Church for years, and the progress of numerous dissenting bodies had threatened its very existence. This crisis aroused many of its ablest defenders to action. Some, such as Whately and Arnold, thought that the storm could be best weathered by throwing open the doors of Anglicanism to all who professed the fundamental dogmas of Christianity; while others, mostly Oxford men,

CARDINAL NEWMAN

such as Pusey, Keble, Hurrell Froude, and Newman, believed that salvation lay in a return to the ancient Church by bringing the Anglican practices and beliefs into closer touch with the practices and beliefs of the Church of the first five centuries. The former were known as the Broad Church Party, the latter as the High Church Party. Because the Oxford men set forth their aims in a series of doctrinal and practical papers entitled "Tracts for the Times," they were also called Tractarians.

John Henry Newman, one of the greatest religious geniuses of modern times, soon became the leader of the Oxford Movement. His attempt, in "Tract 90," to give a Catholic interpretation to the Thirty-nine Articles precipitated a storm in the English Church. Before it blew over, Newman had entered the Catholic Church (1845). His example was followed by hundreds of his friends and disciples. Newman was ordained a priest in Rome, and on his return to England he founded an English Congregation of the Oratory of St. Philip Neri at London and Birmingham. After more than thirty years of writing and speaking upon a vast array of religious subjects his genius and nobility of character were recognized by Pope Leo XIII, who raised him to the cardinalate in 1879. When he died in 1890, in his ninetieth year, he chose for his epitaph the words, *Ex umbris et imaginibus in veritatem*—"Out of shadows and symbols unto truth." Newman is universally considered one of the great masters of English prose. His *Apologia pro Vita Sua* is a religious autobiography of unsurpassed interest, and in his *Dream of Gerontius* he "ranks next to Dante in expressing the Catholic penetration of eternity."

The Catholic Church in England at the Beginning of the Nineteenth Century

"Three centuries ago, and the Catholic Church, that great creation of God's power, stood in this land in pride of place. It had the honors of nearly a thousand years upon it; it was enthroned in some twenty sees up and down the broad country; it was based in the will of a faithful people; it energized through ten thousand instruments of power and influence; and it was ennobled by a host of Saints and Martyrs. . . .

"But it was the high decree of heaven, that the majesty of that presence should be blotted out. . . . No longer, the Catholic Church in the country; nay, no longer I may say, a Catholic community;—but a few adherents of the Old Religion, moving silently and sorrowfully about, as memorials of what had been. 'The Roman Catholics';—not a sect, not even an interest, as men conceived of it—not a body, however small, representative of the Great Communion abroad—but a mere handful of individuals, who might be counted like the pebbles and *detritus* of the great deluge, and who, forsooth, merely happened to retain a creed which, in its day indeed, was the profession of a Church. Here a set of poor Irishmen, coming and going at harvest time, or a colony of them lodged in a miserable quarter of the vast metropolis. There, perhaps, an elderly person, seen walking in the streets, grave and solitary, and strange, though noble in bearing, and said to be of good family, and a 'Roman Catholic.' An old-fashioned house of gloomy appearance, closed in with high walls, with an iron gate, and yews, and the report attaching to it that 'Roman Catholics' lived there; but who they were or what they did, or what was meant by calling them Roman Catholics, no one could tell;—though it had an unpleasant sound, and told of form and superstition. And then, perhaps, as we went to and fro, looking with a boy's curious eyes through the great city, we might come to-day upon some Moravian chapel, or Quakers' meeting-house, and to-morrow on a chapel of the 'Roman Catholics'; but nothing was to be gathered from it, except that there were lights burning there, and some boys in white, swinging censers; and what it all meant could only be learned from books, from Protestant Histories and Sermons; and they did not report well of the 'Roman Catholics' but, on the contrary, deposed that they had once had power and had abused it. And then, again, we might, on one occasion, hear it pointedly put out by some literary man, as a result of his careful investigation, and as a recondite point of information, which few knew, that there was this difference between the Roman Catholics of England and the Roman Catholics of Ireland, that the latter had bishops, and the former were governed by four officials, called Vicars-Apostolic. . . .

Such were the Catholics of England, found in corners, and alleys, and cellars, and the housetops, or in the recesses of the country; cut off from the populous world around them, and dimly seen, as if through a mist or in twilight, as ghosts flitting to and fro, by the high Protestants, the lords of the earth."

—From John Henry Newman's Sermon, *The Second Spring*, preached in St. Mary's College, Oscott, at the First Provincial Synod of Westminster, July 13, 1852.

Hints for Study

1. On the Popes treated in this chapter see Cardinal Wiseman, *Recollections of the Last Four Popes* (among the collected works of Wiseman).

2. Catholic Emancipation is well treated in *Catholic Emancipation; 1829-1929. Essays by Various Writers* (London, 1929).

3. Newman's conversion is told by himself in his *Apologia pro Vita Sua,* with which every educated Catholic should be familiar. There is a new life of Newman by Lewis May.

4. Write a brief paragraph on each of the following: *Holy Alliance, Consalvi, National Colleges at Rome, The Genius of Christianity, Young Italy, Catholic Emancipation, Neo-Scholasticism, Romantic Movement, Oxford Movement, Palimpsests, Apostle of Vienna.*

5. For the beginnings of the Christian Social Reform Movement, see Metlake, *Ketteler and the Christian Social Reform Movement.*

6. Who said: "My heart to Rome, my body to Ireland, my soul to God"?

7. Write a chronological summary of the events related in this chapter.

CHAPTER III

PIUS IX AND THE VATICAN COUNCIL

1. *Internal Troubles*

Gregory XVI died just as a new rebellion was about to break out in the Papal States, leaving to his successor Pius IX (1846-1878) a task too difficult even for such a man to cope with successfully.

Immediately after his accession Pius IX proceeded to meet the

POPE PIUS IX

wishes of the people. A general amnesty was proclaimed; Rome received a civil municipal government; a Council of State was appointed to which laymen were admitted, and in 1848 a very liberal constitution was granted to the Papal States. The Pontiff was seriously planning a confederation of all the Italian States under his presidency, when a violent Revolution broke out in Rome. Count Rossi, the Papal Minister, was stabbed to death in broad daylight; Msgr. Palma, the Pope's private secretary, was shot, and the Pope himself was besieged in the Quirinal Palace. On November 24, 1848, Pius fled in disguise to Gaeta. In answer to his appeal to the Catholic Powers, French and Spanish troops landed in Italy and took Rome. In the summer of 1849 Pius returned to his capital, and a few French regiments were quartered in the city to maintain order. During the long period from 1849 to 1870 Pius governed Rome in comparative security, in spite of occasional revolutionary outbreaks, and "in kindness if not always in wisdom."

Murillo

THE IMMACULATE CONCEPTION

2. *Restoration of the English Hierarchy*

During this period Pius IX restored the English hierarchy (1850). Dr. Nicholas Wiseman, who as a scholar, a writer, an orator, and a churchman had few equals in the nineteenth century, was appointed Archbishop of Westminster and created Cardinal, while England was divided into a number of dioceses. This step aroused the latent bigotry of the English masses. Cries of "Papal aggression," "No Popery," "Down with the Romish tyrants" were heard on all sides. Wiseman did much with his preaching and writing to quell the tempest. It soon passed, and everyone forgot about it. The agitation had one good result: it brought Dr. Henry Edward Manning, the friend of Gladstone and future Cardinal, into the Church. Since the restoration of the hierarchy the position of the Church in England has been gradually strengthened. Pius X divided England and Wales into the three ecclesiastical provinces of Westminster, Birmingham, and Liverpool; under Benedict XV a fourth province, Cardiff, was added. The Catholic Relief Act of 1927 removed the tax on charitable bequests and endowments formerly exacted from Catholics. The only position that a Catholic cannot hold in England today is that of King of Great Britain and Ireland and Emperor of India.

3. *Spiritual Triumphs. The Vatican Council*

On the 8th of December, 1854, to the joy of the entire Catholic world, Pope Pius IX proclaimed the Immaculate Conception of the Blessed Virgin a dogma of the Church—"a unique affirmation of *supernatural Holiness*, not of mere holiness of morals, or of natural perfection, but of that Holiness of the Lord which flows from Grace" (Rickaby).

In 1858 (we might almost say in confirmation of the Papal definition) the Blessed Virgin appeared many times to the young peasant girl Bernadette Soubirous in the grotto of Massabielle, near Lourdes, France. "I am the Immaculate Conception," were the words of the vision. A miraculous spring suddenly came into existence. More than half a million pilgrims annually visit the shrine of Our Lady of Lourdes from all parts of the world, and many well-attested cures have been wrought there by bathing in the water or by merely visiting the shrine, but especially by the Benediction of the Blessed Sacrament. Bernadette was canonized on Dec. 8, 1933.

In 1864 Pius IX published the famous *Syllabus*, a collection of eighty propositions which reiterated the condemnation of pantheism, naturalism, socialism, communism, freemasonry and other forms of religious liberalism, some of which were then finding support outside and inside the Church. "The sense of the propositions must be gathered from the various allocutions, encyclicals, and letters of the Pontiff in which the context will give their full condemned meaning," because the condemned propositions are nothing but excerpts from these documents.

The greatest spiritual triumph of Pius IX was the Vatican Council, the first General Council held since Trent. When he

THE VATICAN COUNCIL IN SESSION

convened it by the Bull *Aeterni Patris* (June 29, 1868), the times were so troubled that few believed it could ever meet. But on December 8, 1869, 719 representatives of the Church, amongst whom were almost three fourths of the entire episcopate, assembled at the Vatican. In the first sessions the fundamental truths of Christianity: God's existence, nature, and providence; the possibility and fact of revelation; the harmony between reason and revelation were defined, and the principal errors of the day: atheism, materialism, rationalism, and pantheism, were condemned.

In the fourth session the question of Papal Infallibility occupied the attention of the Council. The members were divided into

two parties. The great majority favored a definition of the doctrine as the best bulwark against the inroads of Rationalism. A
considerable minority, consisting chiefly of bishops from countries
of mixed religious population—France, Germany, Austria, Hungary, North America—were opposed to a formal definition, not
because they were opposed to the doctrine itself, but because they
feared "that such a definition, at such a time, would have the
effect of driving away many who were in sympathy with Catholicism and might also lead to a new schism in the Church." When
the final vote was taken on July 18, 1870, only two bishops—one
from Naples and one from the United States—voted against the
definition.

In most parts of the Church the definition of Papal Infallibility was
received with enthusiasm. In Germany, however, a number of priests and
university professors, notably the celebrated scholar and historian Döllinger
of Munich, continued to oppose it and were excommunicated. They formed
a new sect known as the Old Catholics, which gained many adherents not
only in Germany, but also in Austria and Switzerland. When the Governments of these countries ceased to protect them, the Old Catholics steadily
lost ground. At present they number less than a hundred thousand.

4. End of the Temporal Sovereignty of the Pope

The spiritual triumph of Pius IX in the Vatican Council was
followed two months later by a temporal disaster which marks
an epoch in the history of the Papacy.

When King Victor Emanuel II of Piedmont, backed by France
and England, attacked the Austrian provinces in North Italy
(1859), an insurrection promptly broke out in the Papal States.
The Romagna was annexed to Piedmont, or rather to the newly
proclaimed kingdom of Italy. In the following year the Piedmontese, without any declaration of war, seized Umbria and the
March of Ancona. The little Papal Army of six thousand men
was crushed at Castelfidardo. Only Rome and its immediate en-
virons remained to the Pope. When France withdrew its garri-
son from Rome at the outbreak of the Franco-Prussian War
(1870) and the Empire of Napoleon III crumbled to pieces after
the battle of Sedan, the Piedmontese troops entered Rome by the
Porta Pia on the 20th of September, 1870. The Italian King
took up his quarters in the Papal Palace of the Quirinal, and

graciously permitted the Pope to retain possession of the Vatican and the Lateran Palaces and Castel Gandolfo on the Alban Lake.

The Italian "Law of Guarantees" (1871) declared the person of the Pontiff inviolable, granted him the privileges of a sovereign, and offered him a yearly sum of three and a quarter million *lire* (*lira* = 20 cts.). Pius IX refused the proffered annual allowance, protested vigorously against the flagrant injustice committed against the Holy See, and remained a voluntary prisoner in the Vatican, depending for his support mainly on the contributions of his children all over the world.

5. The "Kulturkampf" in Germany

The Austrian Government made the decrees of the Vatican Council on Papal Infallibility an excuse for an attempted abrogation of the Concordat, while Germany found in them a pretext for the inauguration of an era of persecution against the Catholics, which the scientist Rudolph Virchow called a *Kulturkampf*, a conflict of civilizations.

The conflict began in 1871 when the Prussian Government supported some teachers in the public schools whom the bishops wished to dismiss because of their opposition to Papal Infallibility. In 1873 the infamous May Laws were passed, which sought to bring the education, appointment, and discipline of the clergy completely under State control, and to regulate the use of spiritual penalties such as suspension, deposition, and excommunication. When the bishops refused to obey, the Prussian Minister of Worship, Falk, resorted to force. The Jesuits and allied teaching Orders of men and women were banished from the German Empire and most of the other Orders from Prussia. The Archbishops of Cologne and Gnesen-Posen, the Bishops of Trier, Muenster, Paderborn, Limburg, and Breslau, and many minor dignitaries were imprisoned or exiled. Civil marriage was made obligatory, and divorce was introduced. In 1874 the so-called *Brotkorbgesetz*, "Bread-basket Law," was passed to force the clergy to submission by suspending the salaries of the recalcitrant. "The result of these severities was exactly the opposite of what Falk and his master Bismarck intended. They had meant only to lop off a few 'Ultramontane extremists'; they succeeded in sending Catholics of every shade and color pell-mell into the arms of Rome."

The Center, or Catholic, Party in the Reichstag and in the Prussian Landtag, under the leadership of such splendid Catholic laymen as Mallinckrodt, Reichensperger, Windthorst, Schorlemer and Franckenstein, became a powerful force in German politics, whose aid Bismarck sorely needed in his struggle with his enemies, especially the Social-Democrats. Negotiations with Rome were begun. They were long and difficult. Concessions were made on both sides, which led to a gradual abrogation of the May Laws.

Pius IX did not live to see peace and liberty restored to the Church in Germany. He died February 6, 1878. "His remains were carried through a rioting mob, screaming that his ashes should be thrown into the Tiber, to the ancient basilica of San Lorenzo: and there, in a chapel, to whose decoration the whole Catholic world contributed, he sleeps with the calm face of the Good Shepherd bent towards him."

The Vatican Council Defines Papal Infallibility

"Faithfully adhering to the tradition received from the beginning of the Christian faith, for the glory of God our Savior, the exaltation of the Catholic religion, and the salvation of the Christian people, the Sacred Council approving, we *teach and define* that it is a dogma divinely revealed: that the Roman Pontiff, when he speaks *ex cathedra,*—that is, when in the discharge of the office of pastor and teacher of all Christians, by virtue of his supreme Apostolic authority, he defines a doctrine regarding faith or morals to be held by the Universal Church,—is, by the divine assistance promised him in Blessed Peter, possessed of that infallibility with which the Divine Redeemer willed that His Church should be endowed for defining doctrine regarding faith or morals; and that, therefore, such definitions of the Roman Pontiff are irreformable of themselves, and not from the consent of the Church."

—Denzinger, *Enchiridion Symbolorum*, N. 1839 (ed. 1928, p. 489).

Hints for Study

1. For a detailed account of Pius IX see Maguire, *Pius IX and His Times,* or Shea, *Life and Pontificate of Pius IX.*
2. Summarize the events narrated in this chapter in the form of a chronological table.
3. Write a brief paragraph on each of the following: *Restoration of the English Hierarchy, Syllabus, Lourdes, Law of Guarantees, Kulturkampf, Windthorst, Center Party, May Laws.*
4. For a clear treatment of the Definition of Papal Infallibility see *The Papacy,* ed. by Rev. C. Lattey, S. J. (Herder 1924) pp. 181-202: "The Vatican Council and Papal Infallibility."

CHAPTER IV

PROGRESS OF THE CHURCH IN THE UNITED STATES

Among the eminent ecclesiastics raised to the purple by Pius IX after the Vatican Council was John McCloskey, Archbishop of New York. He was the first American Cardinal, and his elevation naturally focused the attention of the world on the Church in the great Republic of the West. It was really but of yesterday, and yet how marvelous had been its growth!

Space does not permit us to write a detailed account of the history of the Church in the United States; we must be content to touch on a few outstanding incidents in its development.

1. *The Age of Discovery and Colonization*

The First Parish in the United States.—The oldest Catholic community in the territory now comprised within the limits of the United States dates from 1565, when the Spanish colony of St. Augustine, Florida, was founded by Pedro Menendez. Franciscan and Dominican missionaries had visited Florida before, and in 1549 Father Luis Cancer de Barbastro, O.P., had perished in an attempt to found a mission near Tampa Bay. The parish of St. Augustine—the first in the United States—was established as a part of the diocese of Santiago de Cuba, with Father Mendoza as pastor. The Jesuit missionaries, sent to Florida by St. Francis Borgia in 1566 and 1568, extended their labors as far north as the Rappahannock, where several of them died at the hands of the Indians. The Jesuits were succeeded by the Franciscans, whose missionary labors, begun in 1573, were crowned with remarkable success. The work of the missionaries was stopped by Governor Moore's invasion from Carolina in 1704. When Florida was ceded to England in 1763, the Spanish population withdrew, and Catholicity practically disappeared. Later a number of families from the island of Minorca emigrated to the colony and settled with their clergy at St. Augustine.

Catholicity in New Mexico and California.—Missionaries accompanied Coronado on his exploring expedition in 1540 and preached among the Indians of New Mexico; but they soon perished. The first attempt to found a permanent mission was made in 1581 by three Franciscans, who gave the region the name of New Mexico. All met death at the hands of the Indians. A more successful beginning was made in 1598 by the noted military leader, Don Juan de Oñate. He was accompanied by ten Franciscans, who established the first mission at San Juan de Caballeros, about thirty miles north of Santa Fé. Santa Fé itself was founded about 1609, and provided with a parish church in 1622. The conversion of the Indians progressed rapidly. In 1639 there were fifty Franciscan Friars and about sixty thousand Catholic Indians in ninety pueblos around Santa Fé. During the Indian revolts which began in 1680, twenty-one missionaries were killed, the churches destroyed, and all traces of Christianity obliterated. Reestablished in 1696, the missions failed to prosper, and in 1800 the Christian Indians had diminished to less than a thousand. Real missionary activity was not resumed until the cession of New Mexico to the United States in 1848 and the appointment of the saintly and zealous apostle, John Baptist Lamy, as Vicar-Apostolic of the territory.

The first mission in what is now the State of California was founded at San Diego, July 16, 1769, by the Franciscan Friar Junipero Serra. Father Serra was one of the most remarkable of the host of apostles sent by the Old World to the New. Born on the island of Majorca in 1713, his comely exterior, his unbounded energy and extraordinary eloquence marked him out at an early age for preferment in Church or State in his native land. But he spurned the offer of a position at the Spanish Court, and sought admission into the ranks of the Franciscans. In 1749 he joined the missionary college of San Fernando, Mexico, and won his spurs as a knight of the cross in the wild and inhospitable region of the Sierra Gorda. It was during his stay here that he suffered an injury which rendered him lame for life.

When Charles III of Spain banished the Jesuits from all his domains in 1768, Father Serra was sent by his superiors with fifteen companions to take over the Jesuit missions in Lower California. But he was not destined to remain long in the peninsula. At this time Russian trappers began to make their way from

Alaska southward. Spain became suspicious, and immediately took measures to secure the possessions which she claimed along the Pacific coast in *Alta California*, the present State of California. An expedition was fitted out whose primary object was to occupy the harbors of San Diego and Monterey, which had been discovered as early as 1602. Father Junipero Serra with a band of well-trained missionaries was ordered to accompany the expedition.

FATHER SERRA'S MONUMENT AT MONTEREY

On July 1, 1769, we find him on the shore of San Diego Bay. A fortnight later the Mission of San Diego was founded. Other missions arose in rapid succession, some on the seashore, others farther inland, but all within easy reach of the sea-border: San Carlos de Monterey, near Carmel-by-the-Sea, San Antonio de Padua, San Gabriel near Los Angeles in 1771; San Francisco (or Dolores) in the present city of San Francisco, and San Juan Capistrano in 1776; Santa Clara in 1777; San Buenaventura in 1782. All these were founded and in active operation during Father Serra's lifetime. Fifteen more were established after his death, the last, San Francisco Solano (or Sonoma), in 1820.

"Wherever the mission walls threw their shadows upon sand or sward, wherever the sound of the mission bells floated upon the pure air of California with welcoming notes, the Indian gradually left the darkness of savagery and superstition and stepped into the clearer light of a higher civilization and a living faith" (*Catholic Builders of the Nation*, Vol. I, p. 151).

Father Junipero Serra breathed his last on August 28, 1784, at the Mission of San Carlos, where he lies buried. His work was carried on with great zeal, but amidst ever increasing opposition from the Government, especially after Mexico, with which California was united, had severed herself from Spain. In 1833 the Mexican Government confiscated the mission property, and in 1842 seized the "Pious Fund," an endowment for mission work which originated in voluntary contributions for the propagation of the Faith in California. The result was the total ruin of the missions, and their ruin spelt disaster for the whole of California. "The country was deprived of its religious establishments," says Wilkes in his *Exploring Expedition*, "upon which its society and good order were founded. Anarchy and confusion began to reign. Some of the Missions were deserted, their property was dissipated, and the Indians turned out to seek their native wilds. The property became a prey of the governor, the administrators and their needy officers."

The "Holy Man of Santa Clara."—Before their disruption, the Missions of California gave a saint to the New World—Magin Catalá, the "Holy Man of Santa Clara." Father Catalá was born in 1761 in the province of Catalonia, Spain. At the age of sixteen he entered the Order of Friars Minor in Barcelona, and after making his vows and receiving ordination, came to California, where he labored for thirty-six years, from 1794 till his death in 1830. During all that time the Santa Clara Indian Mission was his only field of work.

"He was constant in his solicitude for the spiritual and temporal welfare of the Indians, preaching to them, instructing them and ministering to them. His life was one continual round of prayer, labor and sacrifice. To the regular fasts and austerities of his Order he added severer ones of his own. He spent long hours in prayer and in watching before the Blessed Sacrament, so that while preaching or teaching he often appeared so weak and feeble that he drew tears of sympathy from his listeners. Throughout practically his whole life he was afflicted with rheumatic pains. and during the last two years could neither stand nor walk without the aid of another Nevertheless he continued his daily ministrations, preaching and speaking with those who came to him, while seated at the communion rail. When news of the saintly man's death was spread abroad, people came from all parts of the country to venerate his holy body, so great and widespread was his reputation for sanctity. 'The saint has left us' was the cry that went out from all who knew him" (*Official Catholic Year Book*, p. 16).—Father Catalá was renowned for his miraculous powers and his gift of prophecy. The figure of a crucifix in the church of Santa Clara is said to have leaned forward to commend him when preaching. The cause of his beatification was introduced in 1884 and is at present being examined in the ecclesiastical courts at Rome.

The Church in the English Colonies.—The New England colonies, Virginia, the Carolinas and Georgia were all settled by Protestants—Puritans or Anglicans—and no Catholics, except in the rarest cases, entered these territories. Catholics were also excluded from the Dutch colonies on the Hudson and the Swedish settlements on the Delaware. "Suffer no papists," William Crashaw warned the Virginia Company; "let them not nestle there; nay, let the name of pope or popery never be heard in Virginia."

Some Jesuit Fathers resided in New York during the term of office of the Catholic governor, Thomas Dongan, who had been appointed by James II in 1683; but in 1700 "it was by law enacted that every popish priest caught within the province should be imprisoned for life; and if he escaped and was recaptured, he could be hung." The few Catholics living in New York at the time of the War of Independence had to go to Philadelphia to receive the sacraments.

Maryland, planned by the Catholic George Calvert, First Lord Baltimore, and founded, in 1634, by his son Cecil Calvert, Second Lord Baltimore, became the home of most of the Catholic immigrants to the English colonies. The first settlers, many of whom were Catholics, were accompanied by Jesuit Fathers, who ministered not only to their co-religionists at St. Mary's, but also labored zealously for the conversion of the Pascatoway Indians. Religious toleration was from the first the law of Maryland; but in later years, when the Protestants got the upper hand, the Catholics were restricted and even disfranchised, and these disabilities were not completely removed until after the War with England.

Pennsylvania, founded in 1681 by William Penn, can be justly proud of its record for religious toleration, a record marred only by a few attempts at persecution during the reign of William and Mary and during the French and Indian War. Mass was probably said in Philadelphia as early as 1686; but the beginnings of Catholicity date from 1730, when Father Joseph Greaton, S.J., was sent to the city as the first resident missionary. Three years later St. Joseph's church was built. The congregation consisted of only thirty-seven families. Irish and German immigrants swelled this number considerably, and St. Joseph's soon became too small. In 1763 St. Mary's church was built; and in 1768 the German Catholics began the erection of Holy Trinity. Outside of Philadelphia there were mission stations at Goshenhoppen, Conewago and Lancaster. The needs of the widely-scattered Catholics were served by such sturdy pioneer priests as Theodore Schneider,

Courtesy of Maryland Historical Society
THE TREATY PRECEDING THE FIRST MASS IN MARYLAND

Henry Neale, Ferdinand Farmer and Robert Harding. Father Farmer's intellectual attainments gained for him membership in the Philosophical Society and a place on the Board of Trustees of the University of Pennsylvania.

According to the report made in 1756 by Bishop Challoner, Vicar-Apostolic of London, and ecclesiastical superior of the Church in the American colonies, the total population of Catholic colonists was about seven thousand. At that time there were no Catholic missions outside of Maryland and Pennsylvania.

Beginnings of Catholicity in Louisiana.—Two French Franciscans accompanied La Salle when he sailed down the Mississippi

River to its mouth in 1682. They offered the first Masses said in Louisiana. The first church was built near Spanish Lake in 1717 for the Indian Mission of San Miguel de Linares. The Capuchins had a church and resident priest at the French trading-post of Natchitoches in 1728. New Orleans was founded by Bienville in 1718. The first chapel, built by the Capuchins in 1721, was destroyed by a hurricane and replaced by a brick church on the site of the present cathedral. The Capuchins opened a school for boys, with Father Cecilius as first teacher.

The Coming of the Ursulines.—New Orleans is the proud possessor of the oldest educational institution for women in the United States. The story of this achievement, though well known, deserves to be told again.

In 1726 Father Nicholas Beaubois, S.J., was appointed vicar-general for all the Indian missions of the Lower Mississippi district. After looking over the ground, he returned to France to obtain more help. He wanted not only men, but women also to aid in the work. His appeal to the Ursulines of Rouen was answered with alacrity. A royal patent authorizing the daughters of St. Angela to found a convent in Louisiana was issued September 26, 1726, and in January of the following year Mother Mary Tranchepain, with seven professed nuns and one novice, set sail for the New World. They reached New Orleans on the 6th of August and immediately opened the first convent for women within the present limits of the United States. Their activities included a school for girls, a hospital, and an orphan asylum. The building which the Ursulines occupied in 1734 still stands, the oldest religious house in the United States, and the oldest building within the vast territory known as the Louisiana Purchase. The work of teaching begun by the Ursulines on that August day in 1727 has gone on without interruption to the present day. Their 1930 commencement bore the proud caption: "202nd Commencement."

The Illinois Country. Kaskaskia.—We have already recorded the establishment of the Mission of the Immaculate Conception at the original village of Kaskaskia by Father Marquette in 1675. In 1700 the mission was removed by Father Gravier to the present Kaskaskia, near the junction of the Kaskaskia River with the Mississippi. For twenty years Father Gravier labored to convert and civilize the Illinois Indians. In the end he suffered martyrdom at the hands of a cruel savage whose vices he had rebuked. From the Indian wigwams at New Kaskaskia "grew up the first permanent settlement in Mid-America, a village, town, city, that became the seat of government for the French until 1763, and of the English Government until the close of the Revolutionary War; then the Capital of the Territory and State of Illinois until 1821" (Thompson, *Pioneer Catholics of the Illinois Country*). The records of the Church of the Immaculate Conception in Kaskaskia are still preserved, the first entry bearing the date June 17, 1719. In 1721 a Jesuit College was established at Kaskaskia which was maintained under a charter of the French Government down to the date of the banishment of the Jesuits from France and the French dependencies in 1765. When the English obtained possession of the French colonies in North America, the old college building, or Jesuit Foundation, as it was called, was converted into a fort, which was taken by George Rogers Clark on July 4, 1778. The college then became the seat of government of the Illinois territory, and later the first capitol of the State of Illinois.

The "Patriot Priest of the West."—After the expulsion of the Jesuits, Father Pierre Gibault of the Quebec Seminary came to Kaskaskia. The life-story of this devoted and persevering champion of Christianity and unswerving advocate of the cause of American independence should be familiar to every American school-boy. His missionary circuit was vast and his activity astounding. "With headquarters at Kaskaskia he mounted his horse and rode thence to Vincennes, which had been founded in 1742 by Father Sebastian Meurin; from Vincennes to the Indian settlements and villages up to the Great Lakes; thence he traveled by water to Mackinac and Detroit, returning by way of Peoria, Cahokia and the other missions. For years he literally spent himself in these missions, but he became the most powerful individual in all the territory included in his jurisdiction" (Thompson). It was through the influence of Father Gibault that Kaskaskia, Prairie du Rocher, Cahokia, and Vincennes were won to the side of George Rogers Clark in the contest between the British and the Americans for the possession of these pivotal posts of the Great Northwest, thus securing for the United States the vast empire included in the States of Ohio, Indiana, Illinois, Michigan, and Wisconsin.

Painting in State House at Springfield

GEORGE ROGERS CLARK AND FATHER GIBAULT TREATING WITH THE INDIANS

2. After the War of Independence. The Organization of the Church in the United States

The Catholics of the colonies, almost to a man, ranged themselves on the side of the colonists in the War of Independence. Three Catholics—Thomas Fitzsimmons, Daniel Carroll, and Charles Carroll of Carrollton—were among the signers of the Declaration of Independence, the Articles of Confederation, or the Constitution, while another Catholic, Thomas Sim Lee, was war-governor of Maryland.   Catholics joined the Continental Army and the Navy in goodly numbers, and a regiment of Catholic Indians was recruited from Maine.   The alliance with France brought numerous Catholic officers from Europe to the service of the American Republic.

The Establishment of the Hierarchy.—The Revolutionary War brought liberty of worship into the colonies, although discrimination against Catholics was practiced in some of the new States till far into the 19th century. During the discussions preceding the adoption of the Constitution, the Reverend John Carroll, a native of Maryland, who had been appointed by the Holy See Prefect-Apostolic for the Catholics of the former English colonies, presented a memorial to the delegates assembled at Philadelphia in

BISHOP CARROLL

which he championed the rights of his fellow-Catholics. This memorial was undoubtedly instrumental in bringing about the adoption of the sixth article of the Constitution, which abolishes all religious tests for any office or public trust.

In 1789 Father Carroll was made Bishop of Baltimore, and given charge of all Catholic interests in the United States. Besides those scattered throughout the Northwest Territory, whose number could not be determined, there were then about 25,000 Catholics in the land: 15,000 in Maryland, 7,000 in Pennsylvania, 1,500 in

New York, and 200 in Virginia. By 1807 they had grown to 150,000, with 70 parishes and 80 churches. In the following year Baltimore found itself the first Metropolitan See of the United States, with New York, Philadelphia, Boston, and Bardstown (Kentucky) as suffragans. As a result of the annexation of Louisiana, the diocese of New Orleans, which had been established in 1793, was added to the province of Baltimore.

Rapid Growth of the Catholic Population.—During the 19th century the Catholic population advanced by leaps and bounds. John Gilmary Shea, the noted historian of the Church in the United States, calculated its growth by decades from 1820 to 1890 as follows:

1820..............244,500	1860.............3,000,000
1830..............361,000	1870.............4,685,000
1840............1,000,000	1880.............7,067,000
1850............1,726,000	1890............10,627,000

In 1906 the number was 12,079,142, and 20,268,403 (including 211,437 Negroes and 84,995 Indians) in 1933. The main source of growth has been immigration. Irish and Germans furnished the greater quota for many years. Later the French-Canadians, Poles, Italians, Mexicans and the various Southern Slavs added notably to the number. Natural increase, especially among the first Catholic immigrants, was a contributory source. Conversions from Protestantism add about twenty-five or thirty thousand annually to the Catholic population.

"Trusteeism."—For many years the peace of the young American Church was disturbed by what is known as the Trustee System, or "Trusteeism." This system originated in New York City. In 1785, shortly after the appointment of Father Carroll as Prefect-Apostolic, the board of "Trustees of the Roman Catholic Church in the City of New York" was incorporated, and purchased a site for a church. The trustees, all of them laymen, were not content with holding the property, but maintained that the congregation represented by them had the right not only to choose its pastor but to dismiss him at pleasure, and that no ecclesiastical superior, Bishop or Prefect, had any right to interfere. Such a situation, as Father Carroll wrote to the New York Trustees, was bound to result in the formation of distinct churches and independent societies in nearly the same manner as the congregational Presbyterians. As a matter of fact, several churches for a time firmly resisted the authority of the Bishops (*Official Cath. Year Book*, p. 112). Pope Pius VII condemned the Trustee System, but nearly half a century elapsed before Trusteeism was finally abolished and the present system of holding church property was adopted. The disappearance of the pernicious and thoroughly un-Catholic system was mainly due to the uncompromising stand taken by Bishop Francis Patrick Kenrick of Philadelphia, and Bishop John Hughes of New York.

Rise of the Great Seminaries and Colleges.—When the diocese of Baltimore was formed, there were practically no opportunities for the Catholic education of the young in all the United States. Provision had above all to be made for the training of a native clergy in place of the older missionaries, mostly Jesuits, who were fast passing away. The immediate need was met in a measure by the coming of four priests of the Sulpician Congregation, which had been disrupted by the French Revolution. They founded a seminary in Baltimore in 1791, the five students who had accompanied them from France constituting the first seminarians. In 1796 the number had grown to ten. A roadhouse on the outskirts of the city, called "The One Mile Tavern," was the first seminary. Progress was so slow, and the obstacles to be overcome were so numerous that the Sulpicians determined to return to France, where better days had dawned since the advent of Napoleon. The Holy Father Pius VII saved the situation by his message to Father Emery, the Superior-General of the Society: "My son, let that seminary stand; it will bear fruit in its own time." And it did, as the glorious history of St. Mary's Seminary amply testifies. From 1850 till the outbreak of the Civil War in 1861 twenty-six dioceses were furnished with 112 priests. In recent years the annual enrollment has reached the total of more than 300 students.

One of the first students of St. Mary's and the second priest to be ordained in the United States was *Demetrius Augustine Gallitzin*, a Russian Prince, who had come to America in 1792 for purposes of travel and scientific study. Warmly welcomed by Bishop Carroll, the Prince gave up the idea of journeying through the States and entered St. Mary's Seminary, where he edified his fellow-students by his zeal for study and his exemplary conduct.

After his ordination in 1795, Father Gallitzin labored in Baltimore and various places in Maryland under the name of Augustine Schmet, an abbreviation of his mother's maiden name, Von Schmettau. In 1799, accompanied by several poor families from Maryland, he went to McGuire's Settlement at the summit of the Alleghany Mountains. Here he erected two small log cabins, one to serve as a church, the other as a rectory. On Christmas eve he offered up the first Mass in the vast wilderness of Western Pennsylvania. A large part of his own land he laid out for a town, which he called Loretto, in honor of the Queen of Heaven. For forty-one years this truly humble, learned and apostolic man labored indefatigably in the mountain country, receiving no salary and spending all he received of his inheritance to develop the growing colony both spiritually and industrially. Father Gallitzin was made Vicar General of Western Pennsylvania in 1827. He twice refused to have his name proposed to the Holy See for a bishopric. He passed to his reward May 6, 1840. The name Gallitzin has since been given to a thriving village in the Alleghanies. A bronze statue, the gift of the steel magnate Charles M. Schwab, a native of Gallitzin, has been erected over the rough stone monument which so appropriately marks the great missionary's last resting-place.

Once the ground was broken, the work of higher education steadily advanced. Mt. St. Mary's, Emmitsburg, Maryland, was founded by the Sulpicians in 1806 as a seminary, but it was later changed into a college open to all students, clerical and lay. Georgetown College on the Potomac, established by Bishop Carroll in 1789, was taken over by the Jesuits in 1806, and raised to the rank of a University in 1815. When Bishop Flaget went to Bardstown, Kentucky, in 1811 to take possession of his vast diocese, the first beyond the Alleghanies, Father John David, of St. Mary's Seminary, Baltimore, offered him his services to found a theological Seminary. St. Thomas' Seminary was the result of their combined efforts. Bishop Spalding, one of the first students, thus describes the life in the institution:

We set out accompanied by a subdeacon and two young laymen and were soon joined by a Canadian priest. The boat on which we descended the Ohio became the cradle of our seminary and the Church of Kentucky. The bishop lived in a log cabin which had but one room and was called the 'Episcopal Palace.' And the seminarians lodged in another cabin. In 1817 there were at St. Thomas' fifteen seminarians, of whom five were studying theology and of whom but two were able to pay annually the sum of fifty dollars. The young seminarians united labor with study. They made the bricks, prepared the mortar and cut the wood to build the church of St. Thomas, the seminary and the convent. Every day they devoted three hours to labor in the garden, the fields or the woods. Nothing could be more frugal than their table, which was also that of the bishop, and in which water was their ordinary drink. Nothing at the same time could be more simple than their dress . . . (*Catholic Builders of the Nation*, V, p. 194).

The first institution of learning west of the Mississippi, St. Mary's of the Barrens, Perry County, Missouri, was the creation of the saintly Felix de Andreis, founder of the Congregation of the Mission (Lazarists) in the United States. The original buildings consisted of two log cabins. "The larger of them contained in one corner the theological department, in another the school of philosophy, in a third the tailor shop, and in the fourth a shoemaker." Another log cabin housed the secular college. Such were the humble beginnings of what eventually became the magnificent Kenrick Theological Seminary of St. Louis.

The Athenaeum, the precursor of the present Mount St. Mary's Seminary of the West, Cincinnati, Ohio, was opened by Bishop Fenwick in May, 1829, on the site where later arose St. Francis Xavier College. Perhaps no institution of learning, of which there is record, was subjected to so many vicissitudes and underwent so many migrations as Bishop Fenwick's foundation, the training school of the future priests of the States of Ohio, Illinois, Michigan, Kentucky, and Tennessee.

The first building of the College of Notre Dame du Lac, now the far-famed Notre Dame University, South Bend, Indiana, was erected in 1843 by Father Sorin and six Brothers of the Congregation of the Holy Cross. In 1854 an epidemic of cholera ravaged the ranks of the Congregation and threatened its total extinction. But such a dire visitation could not cast down a man of Father Sorin's heroic mold. The new college building erected in 1865 was reduced to ashes by a disastrous fire in 1879. Before the ashes of the old buildings were cold the work of constructing a new and larger group of edifices was begun.

With the growth of the Catholic population the number of colleges and seminaries increased. The greatest share in this development falls to the Religious Orders, Augustinians, Benedictines, Dominicans, Franciscans, Jesuits, Marists, Capuchins, Sulpicians, and a score of others. The debt which the Church in America owes to the Religious Orders as pioneers in the work of education has been often publicly acknowledged by the American Hierarchy and the Supreme Head of the Church.

The Teaching Sisterhoods.—We have already mentioned the coming of the Ursulines to Quebec and New Orleans. In the English colonies those who sought a Catholic education for their daughters sent them abroad, to the English convents and schools in France and Flanders. Sometimes the girls entered the religious communities in which they had received their education. It was one of these voluntary exiles, Mother Bernardine of St. Joseph, superior of the Carmelites in Hoogstraet, Flanders, that founded the first religious house for women in the Thirteen Colonies on a farm at Port Tobacco, Md., in 1790. Bishop Carroll wished them to undertake teaching, but the Sisters were unwilling to give up their contemplative life, and the project had to be abandoned.

In 1792 some Poor Clares from France opened a monastery at Frederick, Md., and in 1801 an academy at Georgetown. Their venture in the field of education met with no success, and they returned to their native land in 1805. Their place was taken by the "Pious Ladies," an association of teaching Sisters founded by Mother Teresa Lalor in 1799 and later affiliated with the Visitation Order (1816). A new academy—the historic George·town Academy—was built by the Sisters in 1823.

Mother Teresa was born in Ireland; the foundress of the Sisters of Charity of St. Vincent de Paul in the United States was a native American, Elizabeth Ann Seton (n. Bayley). She was born of non-Catholic parents in New York City, August 28, 1774. Her piety and her unceasing ministrations to the poor obtained for her the title of "The Protestant Sister of Charity." She married in 1794, and was left a widow with five children in 1803. A visit to Italy opened her eyes to the truth and beauty of the Catholic Faith. On her return to New York she was received into the Church with her five children. In 1808 she went to Baltimore and at the suggestion of Father Dubourg, of St. Mary's Seminary, opened a school for girls. She was joined by three pious and zealous young women of good family, and with the approval of Archbishop Carroll the four formed the first community of Sisters of Charity in the United States. A Virginia convert gave them a tract of land at Emmitsburg, Md., and here the motherhouse of the new Order was permanently established. The Sisters adopted the Rule of St. Vincent de Paul with some modifications to suit American conditions. Much against her will Mrs. Seton was elected first superior. She died in 1821 in the odor of sanctity. The cause of her beatification was opened in 1907 by Cardinal Gibbons (J. B. Code, *Mother Seton*).

The year 1812 witnessed the founding of two more distinctively

American Sisterhoods. When Father David opened the Bards. town Seminary in Kentucky, he realized the necessity of Christian training for the children of the Catholic settlers in the vicinity. A group of young girls, Teresa Carrico at their head, declared their readiness to co-operate with him. He formed them into a religious community under the Rule of St. Vincent de Paul, a copy of which was sent to him by Mother Seton. Catherine Spalding. daughter of one of the oldest Catholic families of Kentucky, became the first superior. Their convent, a log cabin, was called Nazareth, and the new congregation has been known ever since as the Sisters of Charity of Nazareth. It has no connection with the French Sisters of Charity nor with any other American congregation of this name. The Sisters were admitted to the vows in 1816 and opened an academy which soon made a reputation for high scholarship and sound Christian training. Like most of the Congregations of Charity, the Sisters of Nazareth combine charitable with educational work.

Two sterling pioneer priests of Kentucky, Fathers Charles Nerinckx and Stephen Badin were the founders of another purely American community, the Sisters of Loretto at the Foot of the Cross. Mary Rhodes, who had been educated at Baltimore, opened a school in Father Nerinckx' mission district in 1812. She was soon joined by other devout young women. Father Nerinckx formed them into a religious community with headquarters at Loretto, Kentucky.

The Religious Orders of women grew with giant strides once they had taken root in American soil. At the present writing nearly two hundred different congregations of nuns, most of them of French or German origin, are engaged in benevolent and educational work throughout the length and breadth of the land.

The Work of the Catholic Brotherhoods.—The teaching Sisterhoods were followed in time by the teaching Brotherhoods. They came from France and Germany, Ireland, Holland, Belgium, and Italy, and the Catholics of America owe a deep debt of gratitude to them for their unselfish labors in the fields of education and literature, science and benevolence. The Alexian Brothers conduct hospitals and asylums for male patients, and a training school for male nurses. The principal teaching Brotherhoods are the Brothers of the Christian Schools, the Christian Brothers of

Ireland, the Brothers of Mary (Marianists), the Marists, the Xaverian Brothers, the Brothers of Christian Instruction (Lamennais), and the Brothers of the Holy Cross.

The first teaching Brotherhood in the United States was the Congregation of the Holy Cross (Priests and Brothers), in 1841. It was founded at Le Mans, France, in 1839 by Rev. Basile Moreau, but the Mother House is now at Notre Dame, Ind., and it has labored in almost every section of the country.

We have already recorded the founding of the Brothers of the Christian Schools by St. John Baptist de la Salle. Since 1846 they have been teaching in practically all the larger cities of the United States.

The Brothers of Mary, consisting of Priests and Brothers, were established at Bordeaux, France, in 1817 by Canon William Joseph Chaminade. They came to Cincinnati in 1849 and now have schools in many large cities.

Theodore J. Ryken, of Bruges, Belgium, established the Xaverian Brothers in 1839. Since 1854, they have taught in the United States, with schools in Baltimore, Louisville and other important centers.

The Marist Brothers, founded in 1817 in France by Ven. Benedict M. Champagnat, entered this country in 1885. They have schools in Boston, New York, Manchester and Savannah.

The Brothers of Christian Instruction were founded in 1817 at Saint-Brieuc, France, by Jean Marie de la Mennais. They were established in Canada in 1886 and came to the United States shortly afterwards, where they have foundations in New York, Ogdensburg, Fall River, and Portland, Me.

The Christian Brothers of Ireland were founded in 1802 at Waterford by Edmund Ignatius Rice. They entered the United States in 1906 and conduct schools in New York, Chicago, Helena and Seattle.

The Catholic Educational System.—The self-sacrifice of the teaching Orders, coupled with the generosity of the Catholic people, made possible the splendid parochial school system, which is one of the greatest glories of the Church in America.

As the elementary school system developed in the United States in the early decades of the 19th century, it was under the complete control of the various Protestant denominations, who introduced the reading of the Protestant version of the Bible into the schools. The Catholics naturally objected to such conditions. The result was that public education was separated entirely from the control of any religious body. But education without religion being unthinkable to the Catholics, they initiated and developed, at enormous material sacrifices, the parochial school system, which is distinctive to America. How difficult it is to build up and maintain such a net-work of Catholic primary schools is evidenced by the fact that today, in spite of truly herculean efforts on the part of the hierarchy, the clergy, the laity, and the teaching Orders, only about half of the Catholic children are receiving a Catholic education. In 1928 over two million pupils attended more than seven thousand Catholic elementary schools. In the same year there were 117 distinct Religious Communities, with a combined membership of over 70,000, engaged in primary educational work.

Most of the Catholic high schools, normal schools, colleges, seminaries, and universities are also conducted by the Religious Orders. Their efforts have been supplemented in recent years by central high schools under diocesan supervision and maintained by diocesan funds, or by assessments levied on the parishes located in the districts they serve; but the burden of supplying the teaching staffs still rests, in great measure, on the Religious Communities.

The Catholic University of America.—The whole Catholic educational system is crowned by the Catholic University of

© *Fairchild Aerial Surveys, Inc.*
PARTIAL VIEW OF THE CATHOLIC UNIVERSITY, WASHINGTON, D. C.

America at Washington, D. C., established by Pope Leo XIII and the American Hierarchy in 1889, and endowed with all the privileges of the old pontifical universities of Europe.

The Pope had expressed the wish that the Religious Orders should become sharers, as far as their means permitted, in all the advantages of the Catholic University. This wish was met from the very beginning. The Sulpicians took over the administration of Divinity Hall. The Paulists were the next to respond. Then the Marists and the Holy Cross Fathers settled in the neighborhood. In more recent times eleven other Religious Communities have erected Houses of Study on lands adjoining the site of the University: the Franciscans and Dominicans, the Brothers of Mary, the Oblates, the Capuchins, Black Franciscans, or Minor Conventuals, Christian Brothers, and Carmelites. In 1897 Trinity College for Catholic Women was founded and placed in charge of the Sisters of Notre Dame de Namur. At no small labor and expense a Catholic Sisters' College was established in 1914 for the better formation of teaching Sisters under the guidance of the University. Several communities of Sisters have already built convents within easy reach of the College, and others are preparing to follow their example. In 1921 the National Catholic School of Social Service was founded by the National Council of Catholic Women and affiliated with the Catholic University.

Anti-Catholic Movements.—One of the first amendments to the Constitution declares that "Congress shall make no law respecting an establishment of religion or prohibiting the free exercise thereof." Being thus under the protection of the Constitution, and enjoying the advantages of the common law, the Church has never met with official opposition from the United States Government. There have been occasional outbreaks of fanaticism followed by rioting and destruction of property—at Charleston and Boston in 1834; in Philadelphia in 1844; in various cities, especially in Cincinnati and Louisville, from 1852 to 1855 in consequence of the "Know-Nothing" movement, and from 1891 to 1896 in the Northern States as a result of the anti-Catholic agitation of the American Protective Association. But all these eruptions of bigotry and intolerance were temporary and local, and did not represent the true feelings of the vast body of American citizens. An attempt made in recent years to legislate the Parochial School out of existence in Oregon was thwarted by a decision of the Supreme Court of the United States.

"The fundamental theory of liberty," says this important decision, "upon which all governments in this Union repose excludes any general power of the State to standardize its children by forcing them to accept instruction from public teachers only. The child is not the mere creature of the State; those who nurture him and direct his destiny have the right, coupled with the high duty, to recognize, and prepare him for additional duties" (*U. S. Supreme Court Decision in the Oregon School Case, June 1, 1925*).

Provincial and Plenary Councils.—An important feature in the organization of the Church is the system of ecclesiastical councils, or assemblies of church dignitaries to discuss and regulate doctrinal and disciplinary matters. There are general or ecumenical, plenary or national, and provincial councils. A provincial council includes the bishops within the territory of an archbishop; a plenary or national council is an assembly of all the bishops of a country. There is also the diocesan synod, which is an assembly of the priests of a diocese.

Courtesy of St. John's Seminary Brooklyn, N. Y.

THIRD PLENARY COUNCIL OF BALTIMORE, AT ST. MARY'S SEMINARY

The first diocesan synod in the United States was held in Bishop Carroll's house in Baltimore in 1791. Its purpose was to regulate the distribution of the voluntary offerings of the faithful for religious needs. The first Provincial Council was summoned by Archbishop James Whitfield in 1829. It met in the new Cathedral of the Assumption, which had been completed in 1821. Six other Provincial Councils were held between the years 1837 and 1849, at all of which very important measures for the welfare of the Church in the United States were discussed and enacted. When St. Louis was made an archbishopric in 1847, the last Provincial Council of Baltimore petitioned Pope Pius IX to erect a number of new ecclesiastical provinces and to give his permission for the holding of a Plenary or National Council. Both petitions were granted. The First Plenary Council convened at Baltimore in 1852. It was attended by six archbishops and twenty-six bishops. Archbishop Francis Patrick Kenrick of Baltimore presided as Apostolic Delegate. The assembled bishops "declared enactments of the seven Provincial Councils obligatory for all dioceses of the country, prescribed the Roman Ritual and the Baltimore Ceremonial, and adopted various measures for parochial and diocesan government."

The Third Plenary Council (1884) under the presidency of Archbishop James Gibbons will ever be memorable for its enactments on the education of the clergy, the establishment of parochial schools, and the founding of the Catholic University of America. It decreed six holy days of obligation for the country, appointed a commission to prepare a Catechism for general use ("Baltimore Catechism") and signed the petition for the introduction of the cause of beatification of the Martyrs Isaac Jogues and René Goupil, and of the Indian virgin Catherine Tekakwitha.

CARDINAL GIBBONS

Some Prominent Churchmen.—Two years after the Third Plenary Council Archbishop Gibbons was promoted to the Cardinalate by Pope Leo XIII, and occupied, until his death in 1921, a conspicuous place in American public life as a man of great piety and prudence, an ardent patriot, an eloquent preacher and writer, and an unswerving champion of the rights of labor. His book *The Faith of Our Fathers,* a simple exposition of Catholic doctrine and practice, has been the means of bringing thousands of truth-seekers into the Church. A letter which he wrote to the Prefect of the Propaganda in favor of the Knights of Labor in 1887 created a sensation throughout the world.

A powerful organization of workingmen, known as the Knights of Labor, came into existence during the fierce struggle between Capital and Labor which developed in the seventies of the last century. The Knights of Labor adopted for a time a policy which gave them the appearance of being a secret society. They were accused of revolutionary and socialistic tendencies, of working for the overthrow of Church and State. That they were not crushed by the strong opposition aroused against them was due to the Catholic members guided by their priests and bishops. The policy of secrecy was abandoned. Still the agitation against the Knights continued. They were condemned by the ecclesiastical authorities of Canada as a forbidden society, and Rome was urged to uphold this condemnation. Under the leadership of Cardinal Gibbons, the bishops of the United States made a thorough investigation of the character and aims of the organization. The result was the report of Cardinal Gibbons to the Prefect of the Propaganda mentioned above. "This report not only saved the Knights of Labor from condemnation at Rome, but it became the classical exposition of the attitude of the Church on the subject of Trade-Unionism in this country. It was so temperate and yet so constructive in its policy that the conservatives who had organized to fight the Knights and who feared that Cardinal Gibbons and his colleagues had gone over to the radicals were forced to admit the justice of its statements and demands" (Patrick J. Healy, in *Catholic Builders of the Nation,* III, p. 103). Pope Leo's Encyclical on the Labor Question, which followed a few years later, showed that the American Cardinal had won every point for which he contended.

Cardinal Gibbons was only one of the many great churchmen with whom the Church in the United States was blessed during the 19th century. A brief notice of three or four of them must suffice. We have already recorded the achievements of Archbishop John Carroll. One of the first bishops consecrated by him was Louis de Cheverus, who had been named bishop of Boston in 1808. All New England was comprised in the new Bishop's jurisdiction, and to his saintly character, and his eminence as a preacher and controversialist were due the influence, growth, and stability which the Diocese of Boston attained in a short time. He was so highly esteemed by his non-Catholic fellow-citizens that they publicly protested against his retirement in 1823. William Ellery Channing said of him: "How can we shut our hearts against this proof of the Catholic religion to form good and great men!" Recovering his health in his native France, Bishop Cheverus was made Archbishop of Bordeaux in 1826 and created Cardinal shortly before his death in 1836.

A brief sketch cannot do justice to John Hughes, Archbishop of New York. Born in Ireland in 1797, John Hughes arrived with his father in America in 1817. Two years later he entered St. Mary's College, Emmitsburg, Md., working his way as gardener and then as teacher. After his ordination in 1826 he was assigned to St. Joseph's Church, Philadelphia. Here he came in contact with "Trusteeism" and all the evils it entailed. He determined to crush it entirely. When pastor of St. Mary's he defeated his rebellious trustees, and as coadjutor of Bishop Dubois of New York he induced the congregation of St. Patrick's to elect trustees who supported his views on Church government. He succeeded Bishop Dubois in 1842. By his eloquence and his fearless championing of the rights of Catholic citizens to defend their property by force, he prevented an outbreak of the fanatical Native American riots in New York in 1844 and of Know-Nothingism in 1854. He was named Archbishop of New York in 1851. During the Civil War he visited Napoleon III and helped to secure French loyalty to the Federal Government. In 1858 he laid the cornerstone of St. Patrick's Cathedral, one of the finest ecclesiastical structures in the United States. His last public speech was made in an attempt to stop the Draft Riots in 1863. Few churchmen did more than Archbishop Hughes to diffuse general popular respect for Catholics and the Catholic Church in America. The great Bishop's body, buried first in old St. Patrick's was removed to the crypt of the present cathedral in 1883.

A year after John Hughes was made Archbishop of New York, John Nepomucene Neumann was elevated to the see of Philadelphia, succeeding Bishop Kenrick. Neumann was born at Prachatitz, Bohemia, of a Bavarian father and a Czech mother. He entered the seminary of Budweis in his native land, but came to America before his ordination. He was raised to the priesthood by Bishop Dubois of New York in 1836 and devoted the next four years to missionary work in Western New York. In 1840 he joined the Redemptorists. Compelled under obedience by Pius IX to accept the Bishopric of Philadelphia, he governed his large diocese with wisdom and skill, erecting many educational institutions within its boundaries. A profound theologian, he was prominent at the First Plenary Council of Baltimore, and was one of the American bishops invited to Rome by Pius IX for the definition of the dogma of the Immaculate Conception. Devotion to the Blessed Sacrament was an outstanding characteristic of his life and he did all in his power to promote this devotion among the faithful. He was the first American bishop to establish the Forty Hours' Devotion in his diocese. He is the author of several works, among them a Catechism of Christian Doctrine which was approved by the First Plenary Council of Baltimore. Bishop Neumann died in 1860. His tomb, in St. Peter's Church, Philadelphia, became almost immediately a place of pilgrimage for the

VEN. JOHN NEPOMUCENE NEUMANN

diseased and afflicted. He received the title of "Venerable" on December 15, 1896, and the process of his beatification is in progress in Rome.

When Pope Pius IX, in 1853, erected the northern peninsula of Michigan, with the adjacent islands, into a Vicariate-Apostolic, he confided it to the noted missionary, Frederick Baraga, who had already won the title of "Apostle to the Indians." The new Vicar-Apostolic was consecrated in the Cathedral of Cincinnati by Archbishop Purcell, assisted by the pioneer Bishops Henni of Milwaukee and Lefebre of Detroit.

Bishop Baraga was born June 29, 1797, at the Castle of Treffen in Austria. He was a brilliant student, mastering with ease, under private tutors, not only all the intricacies of his mother tongue, German, but also Latin, Greek, French, Italian and Slovenian. He began the study of theology only after finishing a course of law at the University of Vienna. After seven years of the priesthood in his native land he resolved to devote the rest of his life to mission work among the North American Indians. He landed in New York in 1830 and as soon as possible made his way to northern Michigan. Within a short time he acquired a complete command of several Indian dialects. During the first eight years of his apostolate he made seven hundred converts, whom he settled in villages. When appointed Vicar-Apostolic he had labored among the Indians uninterruptedly for twenty-two years: five among the Ottawas, and the rest on Lake Superior. His first Pastoral Letter appeared in English and in the Chippewa language.

In 1856 the Vicariate was converted into a diocese, with the see first at Sault Ste. Marie and since 1865 at Marquette. All recognized the Bishop's zeal, learning and piety. A Protestant paper proclaimed him "one of the truest, most useful friends of the Indian race upon the continent," and the Government of the United States recognized the great services rendered by him and his devoted clergy and teachers in Christianizing and elevating the remnant of the Indian tribes in Upper Michigan. Bishop Baraga ranks among the foremost writers in American Indian Literature. He is the author of a Chippewa Grammar and Dictionary, the only ones in existence; of Prayer Books in Ottawa and Chippewa, and of a Life of Christ and several devotional works in Chippewa. (Cf. John Gilmary Shea, *History of the Catholic Church in the United States,* Vol. IV, pp. 589-593.)

The National Catholic Welfare Conference.—The most important Catholic event in recent years was the organization of the "National Catholic Welfare Conference," with its nationwide activities. The Conference grew out of a wartime patriotic work as Cardinal Hayes said, into a peacetime agency.

In the spring of 1917 the United States became involved in the World War. Immediately the problem arose of caring for the moral and spiritual welfare of the hundreds of thousands of Catholics enlisted in the army and navy, at home and abroad. Under the patronage of Cardinal Farley the Chaplains' Aid Association was formed in New York. Bishop, now Cardinal, Hayes was appointed by the Holy Father as Chaplain Bishop of the United States forces. Under his jurisdiction over one thousand Catholic chaplains served the American troops during the War.

On August 11, 1917, representatives of the Catholic clergy and laity and of all the Catholic organizations met at the Catholic University in answer to a call issued by the American Cardinals. The result of this meeting was the organization of the "National Catholic War Council." The Council consisted of the fourteen

Archbishops of the United States, and functioned through an Administrative Committee of four Bishops. Two subordinate bodies, the Knights of Columbus Committee and the Committee on Special War Activities, served under the Administrative Committee. The war service of the Knights of Columbus and the general work of the National Catholic War Council were of such magnitude that several volumes were required to record them.

After the war a committee of Bishops was appointed to survey the post-war situation and to report on the question of a permanent organization to succeed the National Catholic War Council. On the 24th of September, 1919, the Bishops met at the Catholic University to discuss this report. The results of the discussions were made public in a joint Pastoral Letter on the Religious Situation in the United States, called "The Bishops' Program of Social Reconstruction," in which the Bishops gave their reasons for perpetuating the work of the National Catholic War Council, to be known in future as the National Catholic Welfare Council (later changed to Conference):

"In view of the results obtained through the merging of our activities for the time and purpose of war, we determined to maintain, for the ends of peace, the spirit of union and the co-ordination of our forces. We have accordingly grouped together under the National Catholic Welfare Council the various agencies by which the interests of religion are furthered. Each of these continuing its own special work in its chosen field will now derive additional support through general co-operation and all will be brought into closer contact with the Hierarchy, which bears the burden alike of authority and of responsibility for the interests of the Catholic Church."

The National Catholic Welfare Conference (N.C.W.C.), thus created, includes six departments, with a Bishop at the head of each: the Executive Department, the Department of Education, the Press Department, the Social Action Department, the Legal Department, and the Department of Lay Organization, composed of two co-ordinate branches—the National Council of Catholic Men and the National Council of Catholic Women. Eight different bureaus operate under the Executive Department. Through its News Service the Press Department supplies most of the Catholic newspapers in the United States and abroad each week with a vast array of varied Catholic current news and feature articles from all parts of the world.

During the sixteen years of its existence the National Catholic

© F. B. Conlin

His Eminence
WILLIAM CARDINAL O'CONNELL
Archbishop of Boston

© The Phillips Studio

His Eminence
DENNIS CARDINAL DOUGHERTY
Archbishop of Philadelphia

© Underwood & Underwood
His Eminence
GEORGE CARDINAL MUNDELEIN
Archbishop of Chicago

Photo from Brown Brothers
His Eminence
PATRICK CARDINAL HAYES
Archbishop of New York

Welfare Conference has measured up to the objects and ideals set for it by the Bishops when founding it, and fully deserves the words of praise bestowed upon it by Pope Pius XI:

"It appears with abundant evidence how timely and useful was the organization of the National Catholic Welfare Conference which you lately established, with its departments, the News Service, and the Bureau of Immigration. This organization is not only useful, but also necessary for you. Cease not, therefore, to labor in this spirit of unity for the welfare of our holy religion, in that great Republic where the Church, under God's providence, enjoys such wide freedom and such a high degree of prosperity" (*Official Catholic Year Book*, p. 603).

Catholic Charitable and Social Work.—When the need for organized Christian charity increased enormously with the vast economic transformation which America has been going through during the last fifty years, the response on the part of the hierarchy, the clergy, the Religious Orders and the laity has been nothing short of marvelous. "From birth to death, Catholic charities follow the individual through the mazes of modern life, ever ready to protect him from mishap." Maternity hospitals have been established, and Catholic day nurseries to relieve mothers forced to work away from home, and asylums to shelter infants who have no homes. Catholic charity endeavors to grapple with that thorny problem—juvenile delinquency and its prevention. Hence the Catholic Big Brothers and Big Sisters, and the Catholic Protective Society; the Boy Scouts and Girl Scouts, the Catholic Boys' Brigade, and the summer camps for city children. Wayward girls are given shelter, encouragement and help in the Houses of the Good Shepherd. When sickness comes coupled with destitution, there are scores of Catholic hospitals which give treatment free of charge or for a nominal payment. The battle against poverty and sickness in the home is waged by the members of the St. Vincent de Paul Conferences, who yearly rescue thousands upon thousands of families from disaster. When there is no son or daughter to care for the aged, the Little Sisters of the Poor welcome them to their Homes. The deaf, the dumb, the blind, the crippled, the mentally deficient, the emigrant from foreign lands, the working girl alone in the great city, the young man exposed to the loss of faith and morals in the whirlpool of modern industrial life—there is some Catholic agency, some institution, some club, to care for them all.

Until quite recently Catholic charitable and social work had suffered, as Father Kerby says, from certain forms of particularism. There was too little co-operation, too little interchange of ideas. In order to correct this defect, Cardinal Gibbons, in 1910, founded the National Conference of Catholic Charities, at whose annual sessions the social worker gains "a new breadth of vision, a new inspiration." The far-reaching effects of these annual meetings attended by hundreds, or rather thousands, of delegates from every State in the Union was well brought out by the Rt. Reverend Rector of the Catholic University at the session held in Washington in 1916:

"The National Conference of Catholic Charities has definitely closed the old parochial epoch of isolation and has opened an era governed by our new national outlook and the inspirations that come from it. It has tended greatly to correct extremes of conservatism and radicalism by setting forth clearly and temperately the Catholic spirit and traditions of relief work, and by endeavoring to absorb all that is wholesome and approved in modern philanthropy. It has provided a place where the charity of Christ may meet scholarship and experience, and it traces the pathway along which all three may walk hand in hand toward the better day for which we hope."

Keeping the Faith Pure.—The Catholic Church in the United States has been free from any noteworthy schisms or heresies. Towards the close of the 19th century certain opinions were propagated that are not in accordance with Catholic principles. In a letter to the Hierarchy of the United States Leo XIII warned against them. The "Polish National Catholic Church," formed in 1904, is the only schismatic movement that has had any permanency. In 1925 the schismatics counted 71 churches and 84,000 communicants. They reject the doctrine of the infallibility of the Pope and hold that all men have the right to interpret the Word of God according to the dictates of their conscience.

The unity of doctrine, discipline, and moral ideals is preserved among the Catholics of America by an intimate union with the See of Peter. The immediate representative of the Pope, since 1893, is the Apostolic Delegate, who resides at Washington, D. C. It is his special duty to settle the difficulties that must of necessity arise from time to time in an organization of such magnitude as that of the Catholic Church in the United States.

The future of the Catholic Church in the United States is assured. Every American Catholic feels, with the late Bishop

O'Gorman, "that the Catholic Church is in accord with Christ's revelation, with American liberty, and is the strongest power for the preservation of the Republic from the new social dangers that threaten the United States as well as the whole civilized world. She has not grown, she cannot grow, so weak and old that she may not maintain what she has produced—Christian civilization" (*A History of the Catholic Church in the United States*, p. 506).

The following graphic chart shows the growth of the Church in comparison with the non-Catholic denominations between 1790 and 1920 while the table of religious bodies shows their comparative strength as of 1926.

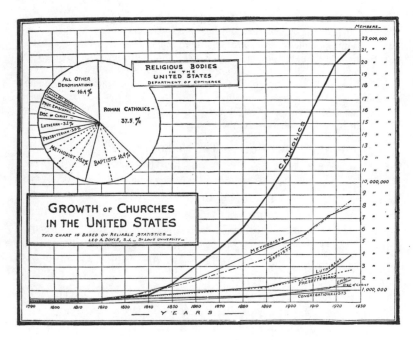

Denomination	Total number of members	Per cent of total
All denominations............	54,576,346	100.0
1. Roman Catholic*............	18,605,003	34.1
2. Jewish	4,081,242	7.5
3. Methodist Episcopal**......	4,080,777	7.5
4. Southern Baptist	3,524,378	6.5
5. Negro Baptists	3,196,623	5.9
6. M. E. South..............	2,487,694	4.6
7. Presbyterian, U. S. A......	1,894,030	3.5
8. Protestant Episcopal	1,859,086	3.4
9. Disciples of Christ........	1,377,595	2.5
10. Northern Baptist	1,289,966	2.4
11. United Lutheran	1,214,340	2.2
12. Lutheran Mo. Synod........	1,040,275	1.9
13. Congregational	881,696	1.6
14. African M. E.............	545,814	1.0
15. Latter-Day Saints	542,194	1.0
16. Norw. Lutheran	496,707	0.9
17. A. M. E. Zion...........	456,813	0.8
18. Presb. U. S.............	451,043	0.8
19. Churches of Christ........	433,714	0.8
All other	6,117,356	11.2

* The figures on the chart, though higher than the Government figures, seem to give a more accurate picture of the growth of the Catholic Church. They are based, for the years 1790-1920, on the scholarly work of Gerald Shaughnessy *"Has the Immigrant Kept the Faith?"* the most reliable book published on this subject.

** On the chart the non-Catholic bodies are treated as "families"—that is, the 19 denominations of Methodists are united to form one "family" of Methodists; the 18 denominations of Baptists form one "family"; the 12 denominations of Lutherans form one "family"; etc.

The figures for these bodies were taken from the reports of the Bureau of Census of Religious Bodies, Department of Commerce, of 1890, 1906, 1916 and 1926. The figures are estimated backwards prior to 1890.

The inserted circle diagram in the chart is for the year 1916. The percentages refer to the total population of religious bodies, which is in turn somewhat less than half the total population of the United States.

Religious Toleration Proclaimed in Maryland

Before the *Ark* and the *Dove*, which carried the first English Catholic colonists to the New World, left England in November, 1633, Cecilius Calvert, the Proprietor of Maryland, instructed the colonists not to make any distinction between Catholics and Protestants. It was his wish that the privileges of the colony of Maryland should be extended regardless of religious affiliation.

The expedition landed in Maryland on March 25, 1634. Two days later the foundations of St. Mary's were laid, and "religious liberty obtained a home, *its only home in the wide world*" (Bancroft). In 1636 the Government prescribed an oath for officials, a part of which reads:

"I will not, by myself or any other, directly or indirectly, trouble, molest, or discountenance any person, professing to believe in Jesus Christ, for, or in respect of, religion; but merely as they shall be found faithful and well-deserving; my aim shall be public unity, and if any person or officer shall molest any person, professing to believe in Jesus Christ, on account of his religion, I will protect the person molested and punish the offender."

In 1649 the Assembly of Maryland, urged by Lord Baltimore, passed the famous *Toleration Act*, the main provisions of which are the following:

"And whereas the enforcing of the conscience in matters of religion hath frequently fallen out to be of dangerous consequence in those commonwealths where it hath been practiced, and for the more quiet and peaceable government of the province and the better to preserve mutual love and amity amongst the inhabitants thereof: Be it enacted that no person or persons whatsoever within this province, professing to believe in Jesus Christ, shall henceforth be in any ways troubled, molested or discountenanced for or in respect of his or her religion or in the free exercise thereof within this province, nor in anything compelled to the belief or exercise of any other religion against his or her consent."

The Third Plenary Council of Baltimore (1884) Orders the Establishment of Parochial Schools

"Near each church, where it does not yet exist, a parish school is to be erected within two years from the promulgation of this Council and is to be maintained *in perpetuum* unless the bishop, on account of a grave difficulty, judge that a postponement be allowed. . . . All Catholic parents are obliged to send their children to the parish schools, unless either at home or in other Catholic schools they may sufficiently provide for the Christian education of their children, or unless it be lawful to send them to other schools on account of a sufficient cause, approved by the bishop and with opportune cautions and remedies. . . .

"Let the laity provide a sufficient and generous support for the schools. For this end they will unite their forces so as to be enabled to meet at all times the expenses of the parish and of the parochial school. Let the faithful be admonished, either by pastoral letters or by sermons or private talks, that they gravely neglect their duty if they do not provide, according to their means and power, for the Catholic schools. Especially ought those to be made to realize this obligation who rank above others in wealth and influence."

—Acta et Decreta Concilii Baltimorensis III, nn. 199, 202.

Hints for Study

1. The following works are indispensable for the study of the progress of the Church in the United States:
   John Gilmary Shea, *The Church in the United States*, 4 vols.
   Bishop O'Gorman, *The Church in the United States.*
   Catholic Builders of the Nation, 5 vols.
2. For the Missionary work of the Franciscans in California see Engelhardt, *Franciscans in California* and *Missions and Missionaries of California*, 4 vols.
3. For the Indian Missions in the Far West see De Smet, *Oregon Missions and Travels over the Rocky Mountains*, and *Western Missions and Missionaries.*
4. The Missions in the Michigan and Wisconsin districts are well treated by Chr. Verwyst, *Life and Labors of Frederick Baraga.*
5. For the Catholic Educational System see J. A. Burns, C.S.C., *The Catholic School System in the United States.*
6. The *Official Catholic Year Book* for 1928 and Henry J. Spalding, S.J., *Social Problems and Agencies* (pp. 287-413) furnish excellent data on the Charitable and Social work of the Church in the United States.
7. Dr. Peter Guilday has written splendid lives of two of the most famous churchmen of the United States, *John Carroll* and *John England.*
8. For a fine picture of early mission life in New Mexico, Arizona and Colorado read Willa Cather, *Death Comes for the Archbishop.*
9. In the *Catholic Encyclopedia* you will find articles on all the men and women, and on all the events and movements mentioned in this chapter. There you will also find a wealth of bibliographical data.
10. As statistics are quickly out of date, very few have been given in this chapter. The *Official Catholic Directory* furnishes the latest from year to year.
11. Write a brief sketch of the Church (a) in your State, (b) in your diocese, (c) in your city and parish.
12. Supplement the Chronological Table at the end of this Church History by noting down important happenings from year to year.

CHAPTER V

FROM LEO XIII to BENEDICT XV

1. *Pontificate of Leo XIII*

The pontificate of Leo XIII (1878-1903) belongs to the most brilliant in the history of the Church. After the loss of the purely temporal power during the reign of Pius IX the spiritual power of the Papacy rose to its zenith under his successor. Nor was the Catholic world alone in its homage to its Supreme Shepherd; non-Catholics did not fail, when occasion offered, to pay him the tribute of their highest admiration.

Leo XIII was a born ruler of men. Though sixty-eight years old at his election, and doomed to a speedy death, so people said, his indomitable vitality carried him through a quarter of a century of struggle and triumph, till his name and his fame, his learning and prudence, were known to the ends of the earth. By his conciliatory nature and his diplomatic skill he succeeded in improving the condition of the Church in many lands. He brought the *Kulturkampf* in Germany to a successful issue, made peace with Austria, pacified Belgium and Switzerland, which had been waging a Kulturkampf on a small scale, opened up negotiations with Russia, which had been persecuting its Catholic subjects, and, for a while at least, held in check the anti-clericalism of France. About 1886, and again in 1900, hopes even ran high that he was on the eve of a reconciliation with King Humbert of Italy. These hopes were vain. The time was not yet ripe for the settlement of the "Roman Question." Death spared him from seeing the failure of his policy of reconciliation with the French Republic.

With clear vision Leo XIII saw the needs of the time. To meet them was the aim of his truly classical Encyclicals. In them he treated all the great questions of the day—Faith and

Science, Church and State, the dangers of Socialism, the sanctity
of marriage, liberty and authority, the rights of labor. A glance
at his "social encyclicals," beginning with the one on Socialism
in 1878 and ending with that on Christian Democracy in 1901,
reveals a gigantic constructive undertaking, for what he gives is
"no mere picture and appraisement of facts, but a complete,
though flexible, theory for all future social action." (Rickaby.)

POPE LEO XIII BORNE ON THE SEDIA GESTATORIA THROUGH
THE SIXTINE CHAPEL

Himself a profound theologian, Leo XIII was a zealous promoter of ecclesisatical studies. He recommended above all the
study of the works of St. Thomas Aquinas, and by his celebrated
encyclical *Providentissimus Deus* (1893) stimulated in a marvelous way the scientific study and popular use of the Scriptures.
Early in his reign he threw open the Vatican Archives to the students of the world with a liberality that put all the other governments of the world to shame.

Personally Leo XIII was a polished scholar of the old-fashioned

type and a fine Latinist, who wrote and spoke the language of
Cicero with classical elegance. He loved the Latin poets and in
his leisure hours wrote poems—stately hymns as well as fugitive
verses—in the Horatian meters.

2. Pius X, the Pope of the Holy Eucharist

Pius X (1903-1914) ascended from the humblest of stations to
the Throne of Peter. Having been a parish priest for many

POPE PIUS X

years in a country town, he retained much of the parish priest as
Supreme Pontiff. In his first Encyclical (Oct. 4, 1903) he out-
lined in a few words the program of his reign: "God's interests
shall be Our interests, and to promote them We are ready to
give Our strength and Our life itself. If asked what is Our
motto, it is this: *To restore all things in Christ.*" That he remained true to his motto, all his acts testify. By the decree of
the 20th of December, 1905 a great change was wrought in the

administration of the Holy Eucharist. All the faithful are bidden to come often, even daily, to the chief channel of grace. The Blessed Sacrament, they are told, is not merely a reward for the good, but above all a medicine for the spiritually ill. The little children are also invited to come; for as soon as they are able to sin, they have a right to the strongest antidote against temptation and sin. In the same year Pius directed a reorganization of the teaching of Christian Doctrine in all the Church, and ordered a reform of Church Music. In 1909 he founded in Rome the Biblical Institute, a school for biblical studies, leading to the doctorate in Sacred Scripture, and entrusted the Benedictine Order with the task of preparing an improved text of the Vulgate.

At the very beginning of his pontificate Pius X undertook the delicate and difficult task of redrafting the laws of the Church (Canon Law). With the assistance of a commission of cardinals and with that of the episcopacy of the whole world and of learned consultors versed in these matters, the task was carried out rapidly. The result was the new *Codex Juris Canonici* (Code of Canon Law), completed in 1916, officially promulgated on Pentecost Sunday, 1917, and declared operative for the whole Latin Church on May 19, 1918. The Code contains 2,414 canons. Commenting on the codification of Canon Law and the reorganization of the Roman Congregations, the *London Times* declared that Pope Pius X would go down to posterity as the greatest legislator of modern times.

Pius X showed admirable insight in detecting and condemning the errors of "Modernism." Modernism is an attempt to remodel Christianity on the lines of Rationalistic philosophy, especially that of Kant, and of false mysticism. In his famous Encyclical *Pascendi Dominici Gregis* (Sept. 8, 1907), by which he crushed it once for all, the Pope calls Modernism the "synthesis of all heresies." It contains three fundamental errors: (a) the existence of God, the immortality of the soul, the existence of revelation, in fact, all that is not matter of personal experience, cannot be known with certainty by our reason—*Agnosticism*; (b) Holy Scripture and tradition do not contain revelations from God to men, but merely feelings and experiences of highly-gifted religious persons—*Immanence* or *Immanentism*; (c) Christ did not found a Church with a divine constitution and unchangeable dogmas and moral standards, but these are the result of a gradual evolution and must continue to develop and give place to others as times change—*Evolutionism*.

In his encouragement of learning, Pius X followed in the footsteps of his predecessor. On receiving a copy of Dr. Ludwig Pastor's *History of the Popes*, he renewed Pope Leo's assurance that the Vatican Archives would always be open to all. "It is a mistake," he added, "to withold from investigators, no matter what their religion, any documents that belong to history. Truth must go her own way, and it is belittling to be afraid of her."

Pius X also closely followed Leo XIII in his social action. "In addition to the food of truth," he used to say, "the workingman must be given the material wage indispensable for him." Even before he became Pope, and before the appearance of Pope Leo's Encyclical "On the Condition of Workmen," he declared at the first Italian Congress of Social Associations that met at Piacenza in 1890, that "the two great foundations of the future solution of the labor question are: the principle of co-operation, and the admission of workers to a share of the profits."

Trials and disappointments were not wanting in the life of Pius X. The French war on religion was at its height when he became Pope. For five years after the fall of Louis Napoleon and the establishment of the Third Republic the Church in France was at peace. In 1876 a sharp reaction set in. The Catholic monarchists, passionately supported by the clergy, were defeated, and the anti-clerical party came into power. From 1879 to 1889 a series of anti-religious measures were passed: the right to confer degrees was taken from the Catholic universities, Sunday labor was authorized, lay (i.e., non-religious, or rather anti-religious) primary education was made obligatory, military chaplaincies were suppressed, divorce was legalized, military service was imposed on the clergy.

In spite of this orgy of anti-clericalism Leo XIII, in 1891, proclaimed the duty, for Catholics, of rallying to the Republic. There was an interval of peace. The war was resumed in 1901 by the passage of the "Associations Law," which ordered all religious associations to solicit special authorization. Only a few were granted. Then in 1902 all petitions of "teaching and preaching" Congregations were rejected in advance. In June, 1902, 2,920 schools were closed, and in the following year 3,000 more. A year later Premier Combes boasted that he had destroyed 13,904 Catholic schools. Thousands of nuns were flung penniless and companionless on the world. "Christ, for whom they had given up all, asked them to follow Him to Calvary." The suppression of the Congregations was followed in 1905 by the rupture of the Concordat and the separation of Church and State. Pius X condemned the separation law and rejected the proffered *Associations of Worship* which were to take over the administration of the property of the Church. Thereupon all ecclesiastical buildings were put at the disposal of the civil communities, bishops were expelled from their residences, and seminarists from their seminaries (1907). The material losses of the Church in France were immense; but these are counterbalanced by undoubted spiritual gain.

"Since the rupture, the Church is become free. Her bishops are chosen by herself, unhampered in action, and far superior to the Concordataire generation. The priest is forced into far closer communication with his flock, and often must work with his hands for the food of which the State has twice robbed him; the faithful themselves have to take a far more personal attitude to their religion. Naïve optimism has yielded to an energetic work of reconstruction; and spiritually, the *tone* of France has risen high" (Rickaby, *The Modern Papacy*, p. 23).

During the pontificate of Pius X the foreign missionary work of the Church flourished as never before. The missionary societies of men and women, which had been founded in the course of the nineteenth century—the White Fathers of Cardinal Lavigerie, the Fathers of the Holy Ghost, the Society of the Divine Word, the Missionaries of the Sacred Heart, the Congregation of Scheut, the Pallotines, the Oblate Fathers, the Salesians—all showed a marked increase in membership, and new mission fields were thrown open from year to year in every quarter of the globe. In 1911 the Catholic Church in the United States began to take an active part in the evangelization of the Far East by the founding of the Catholic Foreign Mission Society of America at Maryknoll, N. Y. The "Maryknoll Fathers" have three missions in China, one in Korea, and one in Manchuria. In 1929 the Society numbered 100 priests (71 in the Far East); 88 seminarians at Maryknoll; 82 aspirants in preparatory schools, and 51 auxiliary Brothers.

3. Benedict XV, the Pope of the World War

Pius X died in the odor of sanctity on the 20th of August, 1914, a little more than a fortnight after the outbreak of the World War. He was succeeded by Benedict XV (1914-1922). With far-seeing eye and rare energy Benedict XV ruled the Church for eight years. He observed the strictest neutrality both before and after Italy had entered the war against her former

allies. He was at all times conscious of his sublime duties as
shepherd of the nations. Three times during the first year of his
pontificate—September 8, November 1, and December 24, 1914—
he addressed himself with apostolic fearlessness to the rulers of
the warring nations, conjuring them in the name of Christianity
and humanity, to put an end to the dreadful carnage. As often
as an opportunity offered during the following years, he repeated
his admonitions. He denounced the violation of Belgian neutrality, and the cutting off of food supplies from the starving peoples
of central Europe, gave freely to the victims of the war, the

POPE BENEDICT XV IN HIS STUDY

wounded, the widow, and the orphan, and established for prisoners
of war a bureau of communication with their relatives. Even the
bitterest enemies of the Papacy had to admit the truly magnani-
mous peace policy of the Pope. When the war came to an end at
last, but the flame of hatred burned on, and misery, poverty,
famine rose higher and higher, the Vicar of Christ sent out his
celebrated Peace Encyclical (Pentecost, 1920), which did more
than all other agencies combined to break down the huge barrier
of hate that divided the nations.

During the reign of Benedict XV the prestige of the Papacy

grew from year to year. Even non-Catholic and hitherto anti-Catholic Governments entered into relations with the Holy See. England and Holland, for the first time since the Reformation, sent representatives to the Vatican. The Prince of Wales, the English Prime Minister, and the President of the United States visited the Pope. Turkey established an embassy, and France and Portugal resumed diplomatic relations, which had been interrupted for many years. The German Imperial Government abrogated the Anti-Jesuit Law in 1917. The friendly relations between the German Republic and the Holy See have never been seriously disturbed. A German embassy has replaced the former Prussian embassy in Rome, and an Apostolic Nunciature has been established in Berlin.

Benedict XV was as zealous as his predecessor for the purity of Catholic doctrine and the healthy development of Catholic life. Perhaps his most significant act, which marks a new departure in the foreign mission work of the Church, was his letter to all the superiors of the Missionary Societies, stressing the international character of the missions and warning the missionaries against every activity not in harmony with this character.

The Resurrection of Poland.—The independent Republic of Poland was proclaimed in 1918, one hundred and twenty-three years after the ancient kingdom of Poland had been partitioned for the third and last time amongst its powerful neighbors, Russia, Austria, and Prussia (1795). Russia had received the lion's share of the spoils, and all the world knows how heroically the Catholics of Poland defended their faith against the religious tyranny of the Czars. All the world knows, too, how they stood shoulder to shoulder with the Catholics of Germany in the hundred years' war with Prussian Protestant aggression. Every friend of liberty rejoiced when the great Catholic nation's long week of martyrdom was over, and it arose again out of that Red Sea of Blood which was the World War.

For nearly three years (1918-1921) Pope Pius XI, then Msgr. Achille Ratti, Prefect of the Vatican Library, labored with remarkable success as Apostolic Visitor and Nuncio to the new Republic. He prepared the way for the Concordat which was concluded in 1925 to regulate the relations of Church and State. Provision was made for maintaining a Papal Nuncio at Warsaw and a Polish Ambassador at the Vatican. The churches of the Latin

Rite were organized into five Metropolitan Sees, with fifteen suffragans. The Greek Ruthenian Rite, which counts nearly three million adherents, has an Archbishop in Lwow (Lemberg), with three suffragans. Since Lwow has also a Latin and an Armenian Archbishop, it is the only city in the world that can boast of being the residence of three Metropolitan Archbishops.

The Catholics of all Rites form about three quarters of the entire population of thirty millions. About three millions of the remainder belong to the Orthodox Church, which was formerly known as the Russian Orthodox Church, but is now autonomous. The Polish Constitution grants equal rights and freedom of worship to all denominations. Since 1918 many religious orders have been reestablished in the country. They are especially active in charitable and educational work.

Leo XIII on the Workingman's Right to a Living Wage

"Wages, we are told, are fixed by free consent; and, therefore, the employer, when he pays what was agreed upon, has done his part, and is not called upon for anything further. The only way, it is said, in which injustice could happen, would be if the master refused to pay the whole of the wages, or the workman would not complete the work undertaken; when this happens the State should intervene, to see that each obtains his own, but not under any other circumstances. . . .

"Now, if we were to consider labor merely so far as it is *personal*, doubtless it would be within the workman's right to accept any rate of wages whatever; for in the same way as he is free to work or not, so he is free to accept a small remuneration or even none at all. But this is a mere abstract supposition; the labor of the workingman is not only his personal attribute, but it is *necessary*; and this makes all the difference. The preservation of life is the bounden duty of each and all, and to fail therein is a crime. It follows that each one has a right to procure what is required in order to live; and the poor can procure it in no other way than by work and wages.

"Let it be granted, then, that, as a rule, workman and employer should make free agreements, and in particular should freely agree as to wages; nevertheless, *there is a dictate of nature more imperious and more ancient than any bargain between man and man, that the remuneration must be enough to support the wage-earner in reasonable and frugal comfort.* If, through necessity or fear of worse evil, the workman accepts harder conditions because an employer or contractor will give him no better, he is the victim of force and injustice. . . .

"If a workman's wages be sufficient to enable him to maintain himself, his wife, and his children in reasonable comfort, he will not find it difficult, if he is a sensible man, to study economy; and he will not fail, by cutting down expenses, to put by a little property: nature and reason would urge him to do this."

—Leo XIII, *Encyclical Letter on the Condition of Labor.*

Hints for Study

1. *The Great Encyclicals of Leo XIII* (edited by Father Wynne, S.J., 1902) should be in every High School library. There is also another collection of them entitled *The Pope and the People* (C. T. S.).

2. For a detailed account of Pius X see Bazin, *Life of Pius X* (London 1929).

3. Show how Pius X carried out his motto: "To restore all things in Christ."

4. What solution of the Labor Question did Pius X propose?

5. Why was the persecution of the Church in France a benefit in disguise?

6. What did Benedict XV do to promote the Foreign Mission work of the Church?

7. In regard to the new *Code of Canon Law* one point is of special interest to the historian: the Code says expressly that all penalties not mentioned in it are *abrogated;* consequently, torture and the death penalty against heretics will not only not be resorted to in the Church, as they were in former times, but they are abolished.

8. In one of his first public pronouncements Pope Benedict XV answers the question, What is meant by a "Christian"? as follows: "The nature and character of the Catholic faith is such that nothing can be added to it or taken from it; either the whole is accepted or the whole repudiated. . . . There is no need, then, for qualifying words wherewith to signify one's profession of the Catholic faith; it is quite sufficient for a person to say: 'Christian is my name, Catholic my surname': a man has only to strive to be in reality what these names signify" (*Acta Apostolicæ Sedis,* VI, 577). Comment on these words.

CHAPTER VI

PONTIFICATE OF PIUS XI

Benedict XV was succeeded by Pius XI on February 6, 1922. Born in 1857 at Desio in the Archdiocese of Milan, the new Pontiff had been ordained at the age of 22, after a brilliant course of studies at Milan and Rome. After teaching in the Milan Seminary for five years, he occupied various important posts for which his great learning well fitted him. He was known throughout the world as a linguist, an historical scholar, a patron of learning, and an expert mountain climber. In 1912 he was summoned to Rome, where Pius X associated him with Cardinal Ehrle in the administration of the Vatican Library. He became the intimate friend of Benedict XV, who admired his great erudition, but also learned to appreciate his gifts as diplomat and administrator. His successful mission to the newly-constituted Polish State in 1918 led to his appointment as Nuncio at Warsaw. In 1921 he was named Archbishop of Milan and created Cardinal. Before a year had elapsed, he had to exchange the government of the Church of St. Ambrose for that of the universal Church of God. From the crowded story of the first eight years of his pontificate we can excerpt only a few outstanding events.

Pius XI and the Foreign Missions.—The foreign missions had suffered much during the World War. Hundreds of French and Italian missionaries had been called home to serve in the army, and many had been banished from the German colonies and had not been permitted to return after the war. Pius XI encouraged the efforts made to fill the gaps, opened new fields of labor for the German missionaries, and in a famous letter declared that henceforth all missions which are capable of it should be provided with a native clergy. To give emphasis to this policy he had six Chinese bishops consecrated in Rome at one time, and insisted on the founding of seminaries for the training of native priests in the mission countries themselves. In order to make it clear to all the world that missionary work is international in the full sense of the word, he had the head offices of the Association of the Propagation of the Faith, which had been in France up to that time, transferred to Rome. During the Jubilee (Holy) Year (1925), when over a million pilgrims visited Rome, a Missionary Exhibition was a prominent feature in the celebrations. Its purpose was "to give the pilgrims an object lesson in what is being done, and a silent exhortation as to what they should do, to promote the preaching of the Gospel to the heathen."

POPE PIUS XI BREAKING OPEN THE HOLY DOOR FOR THE JUBILEE

According to the latest official world survey of the foreign missions of the Church published by the Sacred Congregation of the Propaganda and printed by the Vatican Polyglot Press (1930), the missionary personnel in June, 1927, totaled 46,174, including 12,952 secular and religious priests (8,038 foreign born, 4,305 native born, 609 origin not listed); 5,110 Brothers (3,222 foreign born, 1,314 native born, 574 origin not listed); and 28,112 Sisters (13,929 foreign born, 11,399 native born, 2,784 origin not listed).

These workers were distributed in 374 ecclesiastical divisions in 81 countries, and hailed from 51 different nations.

There were 281 bishops and 91 prefects-apostolic in the mission lands. Of the lay workers, 51,507 were catechists, 38,679 teachers, and 25,684 so-called baptizers. Of the medical workers, 226 were doctors and 855 trained nurses. The grand total of workers in the mission field was 163,615.

The total Catholic population of the mission lands was 13,345,373, distributed as follows:

Europe	1,041,399	Japanese Empire	206,754
India and Burma	2,172,340	Africa	3,202,993
Indo-China	1,237,339	Malaysia and Oceania	596,534
China	2,373,677	Americas	2,280,541

From June, 1926, to June, 1927, there was an increase in Catholics of 479,-955. There were 45,826 churches and chapels, but only 13 per cent of these, or 6,100, could accommodate 500 or more persons.

In the mission world there were 103 major seminaries with 2,495 seminarians, and 206 minor seminaries with 7,476 students; 156 normal schools with 8,032 pupils; 638 training schools for catechists with 14,896 candidates. Schools of every class, from elementary to college and university, totaled 31,418 with 1,521,710 pupils.

Hospitals of every class totaled 961; dispensaries 1,848; orphan asylums 1,525 with 81,240 orphans; homes for the aged 299 with 11,332 inmates; leper asylums 81 with 14,060 lepers; other charitable institutions 134 with 9,966 inmates.

The Mexican Persecution.—The independence of Mexico from Spain was proclaimed in 1810 by the Mexican priest Miguel Hidalgo. The government of the new Republic soon passed into the hands of an anti-Catholic party. The Constitution of 1857 was frankly anti-Catholic, decreeing separation of Church and State and placing severe restrictions on the Church. For long periods these laws were not strictly enforced, but they were eventually revived. The Constitution of 1917, unfortunately approved by President Woodrow Wilson, contained measures against the Church as drastic as those passed during the French Revolution. Federal and State authorities were given powers to regulate religious worship, to limit the number of priests and the extent of their activities, and even to specify the hours for religious services. Priests were debarred from voting and were obliged to register as required by the Government; no foreign priests or religious were tolerated; no religious bodies were permitted to own or administer property; places of public worship were declared the property of the State; no trial by jury was to be granted for infraction of these measures. In 1927 President Calles put these laws in force. Catholic priests and laymen, women especially, were subjected to barbarous persecution. Exile and death were common penalties. Pope Pius XI, supported by the protests of the American hierarchy, of the Knights of Columbus, and of Catholic bodies all over the world, condemned the cruelty and injustice of the Mexican Government.

In July, 1929, the persecution came to an end. An agreement was reached between the successor of Calles, Emilio Portes Gil, and the Apostolic Delegate, "allowing the bishops to designate the priests who were to register, permitting religious instruction in the churches, and acknowledging the right of the Mexican hierarchy to apply for modifications of the Constitution of 1917." The storm of persecution had the good effect of stirring up the faith and courage of the great body of the Mexican people.

The Lateran Treaty.—The pontificate of Pius XI will ever be memorable for the settlement of the vexed Roman Question. On many occasions the Pope gave proof of his good will and friendship for Italy and its Government; but he refused to give up the ancient rights of the Holy See. The freedom of the Papacy requires that the Pope be subject to no temporal power. The freedom of the Church is guaranteed only by a free Papacy in a free territory. In the Italian Premier and Fascist leader Benito Mussolini the Pope found a man broad-minded enough to agree with him in this contention, and powerful enough to carry it to its logical conclusion. On February 11, 1929, Italy entered into a Concordat and a Treaty with the Church. By the Treaty the conflicting claims to the temporal sovereignty of the Papal States were settled. The Vatican State was established. It embraces little more than the grounds used by the Popes since 1870 —about 160 acres in all. The Vatican State was restricted to this small area at the express wish of the Pope, "in order to manifest to the world that the object in acquiring territory was to safeguard the independence of the Holy See, and not the attainment of political power and kingly splendor." In this territory the Holy See possesses full property rights, and exercises exclusive and absolute power and sovereign jurisdiction. The subjects of the Pope, numbering about 300 and consisting for the most part of employees of the Vatican and their families, are voluntary subjects, free to depart at any time. Internationally the Vatican State is neutral and inviolable territory. By the Concordat a detailed understanding was reached in regard to all matters· in which both Church and State are interested; legalization of religious marriages, the permanent institution of religious teaching in Italian public schools, the removal of all ecclesiastics from the jurisdiction of the civil courts and from civil restrictions.

SIGNING OF THE LATERAN TREATY

Premier Mussolini reading the terms of the Treaty to Cardinal Gasparri, Papal Secretary of State

Pius XI and the Christian Education of Youth.—The Lateran Treaty and Concordat had hardly been signed, when Mussolini gave public expression to certain views on education which ran counter both to the letter and the spirit of the agreement. He claimed for the State rights in education which the Church could never allow. The Pope replied in dignified and unmistakable terms, first in a letter to the Cardinal Secretary of State, and then in various public addresses and inspired articles in the *Osservatore Romano*. To this controversy we owe one of the most important pronouncements on Christian education that has ever issued from the highest teaching authority in the Church—the *Encyclical Letter on the Christian Education of Youth*, of December 31, 1929.

The Holy Father wishes the Encyclical to be the record of his Sacerdotal Jubilee. He dedicates it to his "beloved youth," and commends it to all those whose office and duty is the work of education. It deserves indeed the careful perusal of every educator and every Christian parent; for it is nothing less than an epitome of the Philosophy of Education. Nowhere before has there been set forth a clearer and more definite idea of Christian education in its essential aspects.

Speaking of the school, our Holy Father pays a fine tribute to the Catholics who, as is the case in the United States, "under the guidance of their Bishops and with the indefatigable co-operation of the clergy, secular and regular, support Catholic schools for their children entirely at their own expense, with a generosity and constancy worthy of all praise; who are firmly determined to make adequate provision for what they openly profess as their motto: 'Catholic education in Catholic schools for all the Catholic youth.'" In a few trenchant sentences he repels the oft-repeated charge that Catholics are meddling in politics when they agitate for Catholic schools:

"Let it be loudly proclaimed and well understood and recognized by all, that Catholics, no matter what their nationality, in agitating for Catholic schools for their children, are not mixing in party politics, but are engaged in a religious enterprise demanded by conscience. They do not intend to separate their children either from the body of the nation or its spirit, but to educate them in a perfect manner, most conducive to the prosperity of the nation. Indeed a good Catholic, precisely because of his Catholic principles, makes the better citizen, attached to his country, and loyally submissive to constituted civil authority in every legitimate form of government."

A Spiritual Crusade.—On the 19th of March, 1930, St. Peter's in Rome was the scene of a most impressive celebration—not a celebration of joy and thanksgiving, but of mourning and reparation and earnest petition. No *Te Deum* was sung; the vast dome re-echoed instead the solemn strains of the *De Profundis* and the petitions of the *Litany of the Saints*.

The Holy Father had informed the whole Christian world that, on the Feast of St. Joseph, the Protector of the Universal Church, he would celebrate the Sacred Mysteries in St. Peter's in reparation for the continued blasphemous insults offered to the Divine Majesty in Russia, and for the victims of the cruel persecution raging in that unhappy country; and he had asked all Christians to join their acts of reparation and petition to his. The Pontiff's call to this "Spiritual Crusade" found an eager response in every Christian heart. In St. Peter's itself a vast multitude of men and women of every nation and creed assisted at the Papal Mass, and in every church and chapel throughout the world devotions of reparation were held.

What had happened in Russia to cause the Holy Father to launch this crusade of prayer? On January 21, 1918, the Socialist Soviet Republic of Russia, as the old empire of the Czars styles itself since the Communistic Revolution of 1917, decreed the separation of Church and State and declared the free profession of all religions. But this was only a meaningless gesture; for the radical Bolshevistic atheists who rule the land with an iron hand immediately forbade all public divine services, banished religious instruction from all public and private schools, and murdered in cold blood twenty bishops and eight hundred priests and condemned hundreds of others to exile or imprisonment. In March, 1922, they confiscated all the property of the churches and monasteries, and deliberately committed themselves to a campaign against all religion as such, not simply against the Russian Orthodox Church, but against all belief in God—the first persecution of this kind in the history of the world.

The Communistic dictators and their henchmen are trying to make the Russians believe that Religion and prosperity are incompatible; they try to stimulate by every means in their power the thirst for material goods; "to kill off all sense of any values in life except the use and enjoyment of such goods; to uproot all moral restraints." To attain their purpose they flood the whole country with pamphlets and newspapers containing the most virulent attacks on Religion and the most indecent and blasphemous illustrations and caricatures. From 1923, when it began to appear, till 1930, twenty million copies of the atheistic magazine *Bezboshnik* (The Godless) were distributed broadcast throughout Russia. Thousands of churches of all denominations, among them very famous and precious works of art, have been wantonly destroyed. In 1929 nearly fifteen hundred churches were closed to divine worship and converted into club houses for the infamous "Club of the Godless," into power houses, fire stations, granaries, public dining halls, moving picture halls, gymnasiums, and other "institutions of culture and enlightenment," as the Soviet fanatics term them. But the most diabolical thrust of all to religion is the ban on the teaching of the youth. There may be no schools for the teaching of any religious doctrine whatsoever to children under eighteen, and no teacher may be privately hired to teach more than three children at a time.

Is Religion doomed in Russia? The question is often asked

today. This is the answer of the Holy Father: "We are certain that Divine Providence is preparing the necessary means to restore in His own good time the moral and material devastation of that immense land, which constitutes one-sixth of the earth's surface. In the meantime We shall, with all the devotion of Our soul, persevere in prayer, in making reparation, in imploring for the Russian people the mercy of God."

A Notable Event in the History of the Church in India.— Conversions to the Church go on uninterruptedly from day to day throughout the world. Occasionally the conversion of whole groups of men and women is recorded. In 1909 the Franciscan Friars of the Atonement, founded in 1899 at Graymoor, N. Y., by Paul James Francis, an Episcopalian clergyman, were received into the Church. Before their conversion the "friars" had originated the "Church Unity Octave" extending annually from the Feast of the Chair of St. Peter at Rome, January 18th, to the Feast of the Conversion of St. Paul, January 25th. Pope Benedict XV extended the observance of the Octave to the Universal Church.

Four years after the conversions at Graymoor a community of Anglican "Benedictines," who had settled on Caldey Island, entered the Church in a body. In the following year they were canonically erected as a Benedictine monastery. At the same time as the monks of Caldey, the Anglican Benedictine Nuns of Milford Haven, South Wales, made their submission to the Holy See. Both of these communities had faithfully observed the Church Unity Octave introduced from Graymoor, and their conversion was no doubt due in a considerable measure to this fact.

The next group conversion takes us to far-off Southwest India. On September 20, 1930, Mar (Bishop, Lord) Ivanios, the Metropolitan of the Bethany Congregation of Jacobite monks, his suffragan Mar Theophilos, Jacobite Bishop of Tiruvella, and nearly their whole community, were received into the Church by the Right Rev. Aloys Benziger, Bishop of Quilon. After a careful examination into their ordination and episcopal consecration, the Holy See granted the converts the use of their ancient rite, the so-called Syrian Liturgy of St. James, the oldest rite in Christendom, and confirmed them in their respective sees.

THE PATH TO ROME

Archbishop Ivanios and Bishop Theophilos, who were received into the Catholic Church on September 20, 1930. In the center is the Most Rev. Mar Augustine Kandathill, Archbishop of Ernakulam and Metropolitan of the Syro-Malabar Catholic Church of India.

This event drew the eyes of the Christian world to a corner of the vast Indian Empire, the home of the *St. Thomas Christians.* Christianity is said to have been brought to Malabar, as the southwest coast of India is called, by the Apostle St. Thomas in the year 52. There seems to be some historical foundation for the legend, because the Christians of Malabar have claimed from time immemorial to be descended from the Brahmans converted by St. Thomas. There may have been Syrian colonists amongst the first Christians of Malabar, and this would explain the relations which have subsisted from an early date between Malabar and the Syrian Church, as well as the use of Syro-Chaldaic as the liturgical language. A Syro-Chaldaic bishop "of India and Persia" was present at the great Council of Nicaea in 325.

According to some accounts the St. Thomas Christians adopted Nestorianism in the eighth century; but this is seriously contested by others. There was a famous shrine of St. Thomas in India which was visited occasionally even by pilgrims from Western Europe. St. Gregory of Tours (6th cent.) was acquainted with such a pilgrim, and in 883 King Alfred of England sent Sighelm, Bishop of Sherborne, on a pilgrimage to "the Church of the Apostles Bartholomew and Thomas in India" in fulfillment of a vow.

The Christians of Malabar were brought into contact with the Western Church through the discoveries and conquests of the Portuguese at the end of the fifteenth century. In 1502 Vasco da Gama estimated their number to be about 200,000. In 1599 Alexius Menezes, the Portuguese Archbishop of Goa, summoned a Council of all the St. Thomas Christians. A general reunion with Rome was decreed, the Patriarchal See was transferred from Anga-mala to Cranganore, the Latin rite was introduced, and a Portuguese bishop installed. Discontent with this arrangement, and especially the unreasonable zeal of Bishop Garcia to replace native customs and usages by Latin ones, led to a deplorable schism in 1653. Italian Carmelites succeeded in bringing back 84 of the 116 parishes. The other 32 parishes, after remaining without a bishop for some years, appealed to the Jacobite (i.e., Monophysite) Patri-arch of Jerusalem to consecrate their Archdeacon. Henceforth they were known as the *Jacobite Church of Malabar*. They number some 375,000, and have their own hierarchy. It was to this schismatic body that Mar Ivanios, Mar Theophilos, and their monastic community belonged. The Catholics of India are very optimistic about the future of this "latest rite in the Catholic Church." Forty-one schismatic priests have already made their submission to the Pope.

An Epoch-making Document.—No Papal utterance in mod-ern times, not even the *Syllabus* of Pius IX or the condemnation of Modernism by Pius X, aroused such universal interest as Pope Pius XI's *Encyclical on Christian Marriage*. The entire text of sixteen thousand words was printed in all the leading news-papers of the world, and the amount of editorial comment devoted to it was unprecedented. Within two months of its appearance on January 8, 1930, a copy of the Encyclical could be found in nearly every Catholic family in the United States.

The eminent opportuneness of the Papal pronouncement was the chief reason for the unexampled response which it awakened. The whole world seemed to have been waiting for just such a re-statement of the doctrine on Christian Marriage, and just such a severe condemnation of unnatural practices that have, in recent years, become a menace to civilization.

The Holy Father addresses himself not only to the faithful in every land, but to the whole human race. "In Our office as Christ's Vicar upon earth," he says, "and as Supreme Shepherd and Teacher, We consider it Our duty to raise Our voice to keep the flock committed to Our care from poisoned pastures and, as far as in Us lies, to preserve it from harm. We have decided there-fore to speak to you, Venerable Brethren, and through you to the whole Church of Christ and indeed the *whole human race*."

The Encyclical is arranged in three parts. The *first* deals with the Sacrament of Marriage, its divine nature and purposes; the *second* points out and condemns the insidious "modern vices and errors" which are tending to undermine the sanctity of marriage and destroy the family, the State and society; the *third* discusses the remedies for securing to the individual and to society the blessings that flow from the inviolable character of matrimony.

There are a number of passages in the Encyclical of such clearness and force that they are indelibly imprinted in the mind of the reader. Take the words in which the Divine Authorship of marriage is described:

"Let it be repeated as an immutable and inviolable fundamental doctrine that matrimony was not instituted or restored by man but by God; not by man were the laws made to strengthen and confirm and elevate it, but by God, the Author of Nature, and by Christ our Lord by whom nature was redeemed; and hence these laws cannot be subject to any human decrees or to any contrary pact even of the spouses themselves. This is the doctrine of Holy Scripture; this is the constant tradition of the Universal Church; this is the solemn definition of the sacred Council of Trent, which declares and establishes, from the words of Holy Writ itself, that God is the Author of the perpetual stability of the marriage bond, its unity and its firmness."

Seldom, if ever, have such wise and beautiful words been penned as those with which the Holy Father explains the true meaning of the words of St. Paul: "Let women be subject to their husbands as to the Lord, because the husband is the head of the wife, as Christ is the head of the Church":

"This subjection does not deny or take away the liberty which fully belongs to the woman both in view of her dignity as a human person, and in view of her most noble office as wife and mother and companion; nor does it bid her obey her husband's every request even if not in harmony with right reason or with the dignity due to wife . . . but it forbids that exaggerated license which cares not for the good of the family; it forbids that in this body which is the family, *the heart be separated from the head to the great detriment of the whole body and the proximate danger of ruin. For if the man is the head, the woman is the heart, and as he occupies the chief place in ruling, so she may and ought to claim for herself the chief place in love."*

In language that is authoritative and uncompromising, Pius XI condemns the far-reaching and deplorable evils of divorce, companionate marriage (which he calls a "hateful abomination"), sterilization, murder of the unborn child, birth control by unnatural methods, and all those distorted views propagated under the general name of "emancipation." The climax of the Encyclical is reached in the solemn *non licet* (words of condemnation) pronounced against birth control:

"Since, therefore, openly departing from the uninterrupted Christian tradition, some recently have judged it possible solemnly to declare another doctrine regarding this question [The Holy Father alludes to a resolution passed by the Lambeth Conference of Anglican bishops in 1930], the Catholic Church, to whom God has entrusted the defense of the integrity and purity of morals, standing erect in the midst of the moral ruin which surrounds her, in order that she may preserve the chastity of the nuptial union from being defiled by this foul stain, raises her voice in token of divine ambassadorship and through Our mouth proclaims anew: Any use whatsoever of matrimony exercised in such a way that the act is deliberately frustrated in its natural power to generate life is an offense against the law of God and of nature, and those who indulge in such are branded with the guilt of a grave sin."

The Encyclical closes with an eloquent plea for harmonious relations between the Church and the State in procuring the greatest blessings for the individual and for society: "We earnestly exhort in the Lord all those who hold the reins of power that they establish and maintain firmly harmony and friendship with this Church of Christ, in order that, through the united activity and energy of both powers, the tremendous evils may be checked which menace civil society as well as the Church, fruits of those wanton liberties which assail both marriage and the family."

The Holy Father's Radio Message to the World.—On the 12th of February, 1931, the ninth anniversary of his coronation, Pope Pius XI inaugurated the Vatican City Radio Station HVJ, (Holy See-Vatican-Jesus), and on this occasion delivered an address which was relayed, it is said, by the greatest number of stations all over the world ever assembled for a single event. The Holy Father spoke in Latin for fifteen minutes. He addressed himself first to all God's creation.

"Having in God's mysterious designs [he began] become the successor of the Prince of the Apostles, those Apostles whose doctrine and preaching were by divine command destined for all nations and for every creature, and being the first Pope to make use of this truly wonderful invention of Marconi, We, in the first place, turn to all things and to all men and We say to them in the very words of Scripture: '*Hear, O ye heavens, the things I speak; let the earth give ear to the words of my mouth; hear these things, all ye nations!*' Let our first word be: '*Glory to God in the highest and on earth peace to men of good will.*' Glory to God, who in our days hath given such power to men that their words should reach, in very truth, to the ends of the earth."

Turning to men, the Holy Father spoke words of praise and encouragement to all faithful Catholics, to the Hierarchy, to Religious of both sexes, to the Missionaries in every land. Those outside the Fold he assured of a daily remembrance in his prayers and at the holy Altar; the Rulers he reminded of their duty to "govern in justice and in charity"; Subjects were to be obedient, not as to men, but as to God; the Rich should consider themselves as "ministers of God's Providence, trustees and stewards of His gifts"; the Poor should think of the poverty of Jesus Christ, of His example and His promises, and not neglect the acquisition of spiritual wealth, whilst they are endeavoring, as is lawful, to better their temporal condition; Laborers and Employers must put aside hostile rivalry, unite in brotherly accord, seek what is just and give what is just. To the Afflicted, who are first in his thoughts and the affection of his heart, he promised his prayers and as far as possible his help, and recommended them to the charity of all. In conclusion he imparted the Apostolic Blessing upon the whole world.

Quadragesimo Anno.—In the middle of May, 1931, thousands of workers from many lands gathered in Rome to commemorate the fortieth anniversary of Pope Leo's famous Encyclical *Rerum Novarum*. An open-air address by Pope Pius XI to the pilgrims assembled in the courtyard of San Damaso formed the climax in the celebrations. The Holy Father spoke by turns in three languages—Italian, French, and German. His words were broadcast by the Vatican Radio Station to all parts of the world. The purpose of his address was to welcome the pilgrims and to give them an outline of his forthcoming Encyclical *Quadragesimo Anno*, on Capital and Labor.

In this Encyclical, which was published on the 23rd of May, the Pope reaffirms the principles of social and economic reform laid down by Leo XIII forty years ago, and adapts them to present-day conditions. It is a challenging appeal to men and women of all stations to work in harmony for social justice. Prayer, action, sacrifice —these three words sum up the Holy Father's program for constructive remedy of the grave evils with which the social order is afflicted.

The greatest dangers await our industrial civilization, he says, and it is "absolutely necessary to reconstruct the whole economic system by bringing it back to the requirements of social justice, so as to insure a more equitable distribution of the united proceeds of capital and labor." Socialism, which had boasted that it alone could heal the ills of society, proved to have a remedy worse than the disease. Since the days of Leo XIII it has split into two divisions. The first, which is known as Communism, is "unbelievably cruel and inhuman, as is evidenced by the ghastly destruction of Eastern Europe and Asia. Its teaching can in no wise be reconciled with the teachings of the Church." The other division, which is still called Socialism, has frequently and notably mitigated its program. Although, like all error, it contains a certain element of truth, "it is nevertheless founded upon a doctrine of human society which is opposed to true Christianity. No one can be at the same time a sincere Catholic and a true Socialist."

Even more severely than Socialism and Communism the Holy Father censures those who encourage the great concentration of wealth among the few, which, he says, prepares the way for Communism. This concentration of wealth and economic power, leading inevitably to economic dictatorship, must be curbed, if we are to avert the destruction of the richest values of our civilization.

The Spanish Republic Turns Against the Church.—The municipal elections held in Spain on April 12, 1931, resulted in a large Republican majority. This meant the death-knell of the Spanish monarchy. Alphonso XII left the country. The Republic was proclaimed immediately.

A month later, a waive of incendiary riots directed against the Church and Religious Orders started in Madrid and swept across the country. Two hundred churches and religious institutions were attacked, plundered and burned by bands of anti-clericals with the manifest connivance of the civil authorities.

In the elections to the Constitutional Cortes held in July, the Socialists and Freemasons won the largest number of seats. The new Republican Constitution was adopted on December 9. Complete separation of Church and State is decreed, but the religious paragraphs prove conclusively that by separation the anti-Catholic politicians of Spain mean complete domination of the Church by the State. The most radical anti-religious provisions are the following: the dissolution of marriage by mutual consent; State monopoly of education; abolition of the Concordat with the Holy See; suppression of all State subsidies to Catholic worship; dissolution of the Society of Jesus and confiscation of all its property; subjection of all Religious Orders to an arbitrary régime.

Following the advice of the Holy Father, the Bishops of Spain accepted the Republic, reserving their right to work for the revision of the unjust provisions of the new Constitution.

In 1936 the Leftists abetted by the Communists formed a new government called "The Popular United Front." A reign of terror ensued during which bishops, priests, nuns, and laity became the victims of extreme persecution. All church property was confiscated. On July 17, 1936, the murder of a deputy who had denounced the government for these atrocities precipitated a crisis. The army, led by General Franco and supported by the conservative political parties who had meanwhile united and later became known as the "Nationalists," moved against the Popular Front government. A civil war had begun. It lasted almost three years, ending on March 28, 1939, with the victorious entry into Madrid by General Franco's Army. The conduct of the war by the Popular Front government was marked by an excess of anti-religious fury. Countless churches and Religious institutions had been profaned or destroyed. Nine bishops and thousands of priests and nuns were slain. Great massacres of the faithful laity took place. On the day of victory, Pope Pius XII sent this message to General Franco: "Raising our hearts to God, we thank Him and your excellency for the desired victory of Catholic Spain and pray that this beloved country, having found peace, may renew with vigor her ancient Christian traditions which made her so great. With these sentiments we send your excellency and the whole Spanish people our Apostolic blessing."

A Plea for the Reunion of Christendom.—On Christmas Day, 1931, Pope Pius XI issued an Encyclical bearing the title *Lux Veritatis,* "The Light of Truth." It marked the closing of the fifteenth centenary of the great Council of Ephesus. As a memorial of this celebration the Holy Father authorized a new Mass and Office for the Feast of the Maternity of Mary. In his Letter the Pope treats fully the hypostatic union of the divine and human natures in the one Person, Jesus Christ, the Divine Motherhood of the Blessed Virgin Mary, the unity of the Church, and the divine right of the Roman Pontiff to teach the whole Church of Christ in matters of faith and morals with supreme and infallible authority.

In the course of the Encyclical—after discussing the necessity of union between all who profess belief in Christ—the Holy Father addresses a paternal invitation to those separated from the Catholic Church by heresy or schism to return to the one Fold and the one Shepherd. He makes a special appeal to the schismatic Churches of the East, which have always been conspicuous for their devotion to the Blessed Virgin Mary, to return to their "ancient common Father," who, in the person of Pope Celestine fifteen hundred years ago at the Council of Ephesus, joined them in proclaiming the Blessed Virgin to be the Mother of God. The Pope's appeal aroused widespread comment in non-Catholic circles throughout the world, especially in England and the United States. Much of this comment was appreciative and hopeful, but much also openly hostile. The Greek Orthodox Church replied to the Pope's invitation that with regard to the two natures and one Person in Christ, and the doctrine of the Divine Motherhood of Mary the two Churches were in perfect accord, but not with regard to the primacy of the Roman Pontiff.

An Important Decree on Mixed Marriages.—On February 5, 1932, the Sacred Congregation of the Holy Office issued a decree approved by the Holy Father, requiring stricter guarantees from those applying for permission to contract mixed marriages. In future the promises made by contracting parties, especially the one regarding the Catholic education of the children, must be drawn up in such a manner that neither the parties themselves nor any other person will be able effectively to hinder their actual carrying out. If the civil laws of any State do prevent the fulfillment of the promises, or it is foreseen that they will, the dispensation will be null and void, and the marriage resulting from it will be *illegal*, if it was contracted between two baptized persons, or *invalid*, if one of the contracting parties was unbaptized. The penalty of non-fulfillment in the case of a valid marriage will be to refuse the sacraments to the Catholic party.

Pius XI and the Economic Crisis of 1932.—On October 2, 1931, Pius XI invited "all men of good will to unite in a holy crusade of love and succor, in order to alleviate the terrible consequences of the economic crisis" under which the human race was struggling. The answer to his appeal was most gratifying. But the world-wide distress increased by leaps and bounds during the early months of the year 1932. On May 18, 1932, the Holy Father issued a second appeal to the world. The present distress, he declared, was unparalleled in the history of the world, because never before were the races and nations so closely bound together. He then proceeds to analyze the causes of the cataclysm: The first is *greed* from which "arises mutual distrust, that casts a blight on all human dealings; hateful envy, which makes a man consider the advantages of another as losses to himself; narrow individualism which orders and subordinates everything to its own advantage, without taking account of others, on the contrary, cruelly trampling under foot all rights of others."

The second cause is *exaggerated nationalism,* which "insinuates itself into the relations between people and people" and is a fruitful source of injustice. The third, "The most dreadful evil of all times," is *militant and organized atheism,* led by "the enemies of all social order, be they called Communists, or any other name. . . . In this conflict there is really question of the fundamental problem of the universe and of the most important decision proposed to man's free will. For God or against God, this once more is the alternative that shall decide the destinies of all mankind. . . .

Against the first two evils, the Pope says, he had already spoken in his Encyclical *Quadragesimo Anno,* and advocated certain remedies; but in the face of the satanic hatred of religion mere human means and expedients were not enough. Prayer and penance alone could stay the onrush of the powers of darkness. Accordingly he ordained that on June 3, the Feast of the Sacred Heart, there be made "in all churches throughout the world" a public act of reparation for all the offenses which wound that Divine Heart. He expressed the wish that the Feast would be "for all the Church one of holy rivalry of reparation and supplication."

The Papal Encyclical attracted world-wide attention, as well it might. Even the secular press looked upon it as "an extraordinary event, intended to meet an extraordinary situation." The Senate of the United States gave unanimous consent to have it printed in full in the *Congressional Record* (May 19, 1932, pp. 11080-11083).

Pax Christi in Regno Christi.—"The Peace of Christ in the Kingdom of Christ." This is the motto of Pius XI. To give it, as it were, outward and permanent expression, he proclaimed, at the close of the Great Jubilee (1925), the new Festival of the Kingship of Christ. The purpose of the feast is "to bring home to all mankind the fact that Christ is King not merely over individuals, but over families and societies, over states and nations, over rulers and tribunals as well. The duty of Catholics is to hasten the return of the world to His authority by their prayers, their influence, and their actions. They are reminded that they must courageously fight under His royal banner, with the weapons of the spirit, for the rights of God and of His Church."

CHRIST THE KING

Van Eyck

Eucharistic Congresses.—Of all the peace agencies at work in the world to-day to promote the peace program of the Holy See, "the peace of Christ in the kingdom of Christ," the most effective are undoubtedly the biennial *International Eucharistic Congresses.* The idea of these congresses originated in France, where the first was held at Lille in 1881. They grew in scope and importance from year to year, until they attained truly gigantic proportions during the first decades of the twentieth century. North America has twice been host to the myriads of lovers of the Eucharistic King of Peace, at Montreal in 1910 and at Chicago in 1926.

The Thirty-First Eucharistic Congress, which met at Dublin, the capital of the Irish Free State, in the summer of 1932, was of more than ordinary significance. It formed a fitting climax of the centennial celebrations commemorating the coming of St. Patrick to Ireland, and at the same time reminded the world that the Irish people, after fifteen centuries, both professed and lived in public and private life the faith which their glorious Apostle had brought to their shores.

Ireland and the Church.—We saw how the Irish Catholics won religious liberty in 1829, though they continued handicapped in many ways, especially by their political disabilities. The Irish revolution of 1916-1921 resulted in the establishment of the Irish Free State, consisting of all Ireland except six counties in the Northeast. The Irish Free State, though more than ninety-two percent of the population is Catholic and nearly all the members of the government are practical Catholics, cannot in the technical sense be called a Catholic State. Its constitution guarantees equality in matters of conscience and religious practice for all its citizens. Article 8 expressly provides that "no law may be made either directly or indirectly to endow any religion or restrict the free exercise thereof or give any preference or impose any disability on account of religious belief." Protestants, who used to fear that under any form of self-government in Ireland they would be treated unfairly, have acknowledged that they receive fair play. They even admit that in public life they play a larger and more influential part than their numbers account for.

But in a population which is so predominantly Catholic it is natural to expect that the Catholic religion must be regarded as the law by which the nation should live the Catholic life. In fields in which religion and politics overlap, Catholic ideas are given preference. Thus, in Ireland both the censorship of motion pictures and the censorship of publications are applied more rigorously than in other countries; and divorce, as distinguished from separation, cannot be granted by the courts. Governmental control of education has been increased, but the local management for Catholic schools is still in the hands of the parish priest. University education is in theory non-confessional, but is Catholic in control, personnel and atmosphere.

In the early Middle Ages Ireland was known as the "Island of Saints and Scholars"; it bids fair in our own day to regain this glorious title. "There is a change in the things that the priest has loved; the modern world is pressing more and more into the green fields of Ireland; a great revolution has shaken the country morally as well as materially to its foundations. God in His own good time has seen fit to give to some of the Irish people some of the secular blessings they have prayed for during seven hundred years. To our blurred vision it would seem that He is likewise reviving old or raising new forces to meet changed needs" (James F. Kenny, *The Catholic Church in Contemporary Ireland*).

Extraordinary Holy Year.—On December 24, 1932, Pius XI proclaimed an extraordinary Holy Year of Jubilee to mark the nineteenth centenary of the death of Christ. The announcement of the Jubilee, which came as a surprise to the whole world, formed part of the annual Christmas message broadcast personally by the Holy Father over the Vatican City radio station. "We dispose that the celebration itself take place during an entire year," he said, "in order that it may gain the greatest possible value in prayer, expiation, propitiation, holy indulgences, and reform of life. . . . It will be no slight benefit that the world should no longer hear or talk of conflicts, antagonisms, lack of confidence, armaments and disarmaments, damages and reparations, debts and payments, economic and financial interests, individual miseries and social miseries: that it should not hear these notes but, instead, those of a high spirituality, and of a strong recall to the life and interests of souls; of the dignity and value of these souls, redeemed by the blood and grace of Christ; of the brotherhood of all men, divinely united in the same Blood; of the saving mission of the Church; of all other holy thoughts and aspirations which cannot be dissociated from the Divine deeds which will be the object of this centenary, however little attention the spirit of the day pays them."—From the opening of the Holy Year on April 2, 1933, an uninterrupted stream of pilgrims poured into the Eternal City from every land under heaven. The closing celebrations, which extended over a fortnight, were especially impressive. They were devoted exclusively to the commemoration of the institution of the Holy Eucharist and the Priesthood. On Thursday, March 15, the Holy Father took part with all the clergy of Rome in a Holy Hour of Adoration before the Blessed Sacrament exposed in St. Peter's Basilica. On the following Thursday he conducted another Holy Hour, this time with the laity of Rome. On Passion Sunday a Holy Hour was observed in all the Catholic churches throughout the world. On Holy Thursday, at the invitation of the Sovereign Pontiff, millions of the faithful in every land received Holy Communion in thanksgiving to Our Lord for the gift of the Holy Eucharist, and in reparation for the coldness and indifference of so many men towards the Sacrament of Divine Love.

Catholic Action.—The Holy Year of the Redemption was marked by an encouraging increase of conversions to the Catholic Church throughout the world—60,322 in the United States alone —and by the continued expansion and consolidation of *Catholic Action,* a movement so dear to the heart of Pius XI and a distinctive feature of modern Catholic life.

Catholic Action in the wider sense of lay apostolate is as old as the Church itself. Its Scriptural basis is St. Peter's teaching on the "royal priesthood" of all the faithful (1 Pet. 2, 5 ff.) in virtue of which they are to offer "spiritual sacrifices" and to "proclaim the perfections of Him who hath called them out of darkness into His wondrous light." As we know it today, Catholic Action is comparatively new, dating from the program laid down by Pius XI in the encyclical *Ubi arcano* of Dec. 23, 1922. The Pope defines Catholic Action as "the participation of the laity in the apostolate of the hierarchy," and, more specifically, as the "union of the organized Catholic forces for the affirmation, diffusion, actuation, and defence of Catholic principles in individual, family, and social life." He desires the lines of the new structure to be national in scale, having one central committee, with organization throughout the country on the basis of diocesan and parish committees; in this way the lay apostles would work in close association with the hierarchy and the clergy.

Towards the close of the Holy Year Pius XI admirably summarized the aims of Catholic Action in a letter to the Cardinal-Patriarch of Lisbon. The reader will be glad to have at least the most characteristic portions of this pronouncement.

"The apostolate," the Holy Father wrote, "is one of the duties inherent to Christian life. If one considers well,'it will be seen that the very Sacraments of Baptism and Confirmation impose—among other obligations—this *apostolate of Catholic Action,* which is spiritual help to our neighbor. Through Confirmation we become soldiers of Christ. The soldier should labor and fight not so much for himself as for others. Baptism, in a manner less evident to profane eyes, imposes the duty of apostolate since through it we become members of the Church, or of the mystic body of Christ; and among the members of this body—as of any organism—there must be solidarity of interests and reciprocal communication of life. One member must therefore help the other; no one may remain inactive and as each receives he also must give.

"Now, as every Christian receives the supernatural life which circulates in the veins of the mystic body of Christ—that abundant life that Christ Himself said He came to bring on earth—so he must transfuse it into others who either do not possess it, or who possess it too meagrely and only in appearance.

"When the fundamental truths of the Faith are well considered by the faithful, We do not doubt that a new spirit of apostolate will take possession of their hearts and germinate into intense activity; since real life cannot be conceived without activity, for it is not only a manifestation, but also a necessary coefficient and measure of life. And, please God, may this Holy Year of the Redemption—as it is Our desire and hope—bring everywhere a renewal of Christian life. For this purpose We trust greatly to the contribution of Catholic Action, which, to Our great consolation, is being extended to and is becoming more fervent in every part of the Catholic world, including the countries of the missions, with evident benefits not only for the Church, but also for civil society.

"It is well understood that Catholic Action, like the Church whose direct collaborator it is, has not a *material* end but a *spiritual* one. Therefore it is in its very nature that, like the Church, it keeps itself aloof and outside any political party, being no longer directed to safeguard special interests of groups, but to procure the real salvation of souls diffusing as much as possible the Kingdom of Our Lord Jesus Christ in individuals, in families, in society and to unite under its banners of peace, in perfect and disciplined harmony, all those faithful who intend to bring their contribution to so holy and so vast a work of apostolate.

"However this does not prevent each Catholic from taking part in organizations of a political character when they, in program and activity, give the necessary guarantees for safeguarding the rights of God and of their conscience. Nay, it must be added that participating in the political life responds to a duty of social charity, for the fact that each citizen must, according to his opportunities, contribute to the welfare of his own nation. And when this participation is inspired by the principles of Christianity much good is derived from it not only for the social life, but also the religious.

"Therefore Catholic Action shall, though not taking part in politics in the strict sense of the word, prepare its soldiers to participate in political affairs, inspired with all the principles of Christianity, the only ones that may bring prosperity and peace to peoples. This must be, for it is not right that men who profess themselves Catholic should have one conscience in their private life and another in public.

"There are many other activities, to which Catholic Action must dedicate itself; we shall say, rather, that *no activity, which is possible and useful to Christian life, must be excluded from its program.*

"Among all these activities, however, there are some particularly urgent, because they respond to the greatest and most felt needs. Among which we enumerate, today, the assistance to the working classes; and We wish to say assistance not only spiritual—which must always occupy the first place—but also material, through those institutions that have the specific aim of actuating the principles of *social justice and of evangelic charity.*

"Catholic Action will then take care to promote these institutions, although it must leave to them a distinct responsibility and autonomy in things purely technical and economic. Its principal task will be always to see that they derive inspiration from the principles openly Catholic and the teaching of this Apostolic See. . . .

"In order to achieve such a noble object it is also necessary that there should be presented to the masses—whose ignorance too often renders them an easy prey to wicked agitators—the *light of Christian truth,* which consoles every grief, disperses every doubt, opens to every well-disposed mind the calm paths of Christian virtues and truths. Therefore, among the first and foremost tasks of Catholic Action is that of closely uniting the workers around their own pastors to assist in the work of evangelization, in the teaching of Christian Doctrine so that children may be given that fundamental instruction which should be their sure guide throughout all their lives; so that youth may be given knowledge of the Doctrine of Christ; so that adults may be shown that in the study and meditation of the truths taught by Our Lord Jesus Christ they will find, in every contingency of life the light, the comfort and the strength of which they stand in need. Thus this generous *catechist apostolate* will be a very vast field open to the activity of good people, a most efficacious means to lead souls to Our Lord Jesus Christ.

"Another activity to which Catholic Action must attend with special care, is that of procuring and circulating a *good press.* When We speak of a good press We mean one that not only contains nothing injurious to the principles of faith, but is a proclaimer of its principles. Nor is it necessary to demonstrate what and how much is the educative efficacy of such a press, since daily experience demonstrates it well: as it demonstrates on the other hand, the imminent evil being sown especially among young people, by a bad press, which is often more widely circulated than the good."

A New Kulturkampf in Germany? How providential the Papal call to Catholic Action was, is felt nowhere more keenly than in Germany. "The Catholic Church is in greater peril today in Germany," says one well-informed Catholic observer, "than it ever was in German history." This statement may be exaggerated, but there is no doubt whatever that the Church in Germany is undergoing a severe trial since the advent of Adolf Hitler and his National Social Democratic Labor Party to power in 1933. A brief chronological retrospect will help the reader to understand the present critical situation.

1918. Following the armistice which brought the World War to a close, revolution breaks out in Germany; all the rulers are forced to abdicate; a Republic is set up with the Socialists in power.

1919. Constitution adopted at Weimar. Separation of Church and State decreed. The Church free to regulate her own affairs. Denomina tional School System saved through efforts of the Catholic Center Party.

1919. German Labor Party founded in Munich; *Adolf Hitler* (b. 1889 at Braunau, Upper Austria; draftsman and painter by trade; volunteer in German army during World War) is seventh charter member.

1920. First mass meeting of the German Labor Party in Munich.

1921. Papal Nunciature erected in Berlin. Hitler First Chairman of the Labor Party. Alfred Rosenberg, an aggressive neo-pagan, editor of the Party organ, the *Voelkische Beobachter* (Munich). The Storm Troop organized.

1922. Goebbels joins Hitler.

1923. First convention of the Labor Party in Munich. Hitler, aided by General Ludendorff, attempts to seize the government in Munich and plans march on Berlin. The "putsch" fails; Hitler condemned to five years' imprisonment.

1924. Hitler pardoned after eleven months. Bavaria concludes Concordat with Holy See.

1925. Hitler reorganizes the Labor Party, which is now known as the *National Social German Labor Party* (abbr. "Nazi."). Publishes his book "My Battle."

1926. Second convention of the National Socialists. The Party Program drawn up, unanimously adopted, and declared to be "unchangeable." It consists of 25 paragraphs. Paragraphs 4 and 5 are directed against the Jews: they are denied the right of citizenship, and are to be treated as aliens. Paragraph 21 calls for regulation by state law of athletic sports, in which all young people *must* take part. Paragraph 24 declares war on the "Jewish materialistic mentality." The party declares itself to be "fundamentally Christian," but grants freedom of worship to all religious denominations "in so far as they do not jeopardize the existence of the State or violate the moral sense of the German race."

1927. The Nazis send seven members to the Reichstag.

1928. Fourth convention of the Nazis at Nuernberg. Hitler invades Berlin.

1929. Prussia concludes Concordat with Holy See.

1930. Overwhelming victory of Hitler at the Reichstag elections; gains 107 seats. The German Bishops forbid Catholics to join the National Socialist Party, because it "sets up race and nationality as the highest life values, and because many of its spokesmen deny all value to Christian faith and practice." Concordat between the Holy See and Baden. Rosenberg, now high in the councils of National Socialism, publishes his violently anti-Christian, anti-Semitic *Myth of the Twentieth Century*.

1931. Opening of the "Brown House," headquarters of the National Socialists, in Munich.

1932. Hitler candidate for the Reichspresidency; defeated by Hindenburg. Victory of Hitler at the Reichstag election in November (33 per cent of all the votes cast).

1933 (Jan. 30). Hitler appointed Chancellor of the Reich by Hindenburg. *Dissolution of the Center Party* and the other political parties. Dictatorship of Hitler and the National Socialists established. The *Swastica*, the Hitlerite banner, flies besides the black-white-red flag of the German Reich. All opposition to the new regime is beaten down by force. Thousands of communists and their sympathisers interned in concentration camps. The formation of any political parties beside the National Socialists forbidden by law. Strict censorship of the press decreed. Jews are deprived of all offices in the Reich.

The victory of National Socialism was in a large measure the result of the maltreatment of the German nation by the Allies; opposition to the Treaty of Versailles gave much of its driving power to Hitler's movement.

In a speech before the Reichstag, March 28, 1933, Hitler recognized the Christian denominations as "most important factors for the preservation of the German nation" and solemnly guaranteed the rights of the Churches. Thereupon the German Bishops lifted the ban against membership in the National Socialist Party, trusting the word of the "Leader" that difficulties which might arise would be settled by direct negotiations with the ecclesiastical authorities. On the tenth of July, 1933 a Concordat, known as the *Reichskonkordat*, because it was to apply to the whole of Germany, was concluded between the Apostolic See and the German Government.

Article 1 guarantees freedom of profession and public exercise of the Catholic religion. The Reich recognizes the independence of the Catholic Church "within the limits of the existing laws," as well as the right of the Church to make laws binding on her subjects. According to Article 4 the Holy See enjoys full liberty of communication with the German bishops; the bishops enjoy the same right in regard to the faithful "in all matters pertaining to their pastoral office." Articles 5-10 treat of the rights and duties of priests and religious in the exercise of their spiritual functions. In the execution of their official duties they are to enjoy the same protection as the State officials. The existing Catholic public schools are to be retained and new ones to be erected whenever required (Art. 23). Religious Orders are granted the right to establish private Catholic schools subject to the general educational laws (Art. 25). Article 31 concerns Catholic organizations: "Catholic organizations whose purpose is exclusively religious, cultural or charitable, and which are as such under ecclesiastical authority, shall be protected in their activity." Catholic organizations which serve other than purely religious ends, shall enjoy the same protection, "provided their activity is exercised independently of every political party." Catholic members of athletic or other youth organizations sponsored by the State shall be given ample opportunity to perform their religious duties on Sundays and Holydays; they shall not be induced to do anything conflicting with their religious convictions and duties. In Article 32 the Holy See engages to issue instructions "forbidding priests and religious to become members of any political parties or to act in any way in the interests of such parties." It is expressly added, however, that this does not mean that the priests and religious are to be restricted and hampered in their explanation of the dogmatic and moral teachings and principles of the Catholic Church.

We have cited only the most important provisions of the Concordat, because it is around these that the coming conflict between the Catholics and the leaders of the National Socialist Government will be waged. The Concordat was hardly ratified (Nov. 10, 1933), when the leaders of National Socialism began to act counter to its fundamental stipulations. The neo-pagan element in the party led the attack. A few extracts from the Pastoral Letter issued by the German Bishops assembled at Fulda in August, 1934, will give some idea of this phase of the persecution to which the Catholics were and still are subjected:

"In their rebellion against Christ, the Savior of the world, the neo-pagans are promoting another church, a 'German National Church,' with an alleged 'racial dogma and morality,' and are introducing 'racial requirements' in the place of the holy liturgy of the Universal Church. They claim that blood and race are the basis and the determining forces of faith and religion in the nation, and claim for the State complete mastery of all human relations so that every right of individual personality, every right of the family and all human society would be subjected incessantly to its domination. . . In newspapers, magazines and pamphlets, by word and by picture, the Church and her ministers are publicly assailed and ridiculed; Jesus Christ, our Redeemer, is mocked; God's infinite majesty offended. An extremely radical book (Rosenberg's *Myth of the Twentieth Century*), which seeks to undermine faith in God, and the Christian religion and respect for the authority of Christ and the Church, is spread freely in the schools, among the teaching personnel, in the 'courses for leaders' and in the employment camps. . . Not only individuals but even officials are found among the supporters and propagators of neo-pagan ideas, and they have at their disposal vast influence and great powers.

"And now we pass to another picture. While paganism is spreading its poisonous propaganda, our Catholic press no longer enjoys the freedom to discuss the great problems of these times in the light of Catholic doctrine on faith and morals, or to parry assaults upon Christianity and the Church. Sunday, the day of God and of the family, has become so filled with routine celebrations and excursions ordained by organizations recognized by the State, that no time is left for devotional participation in divine services and for the fostering of Christian family life. Narrow regulations hamper the work of our Catholic societies. In many localities Catholic youths are being persecuted for nothing more than giving public evidence of their faith in Christ and loyalty to the Church societies, protection for which was solemnly assured by the State. . ."

The protest of the German bishops went unheeded; in fact it appeared to be the signal for intensified persecution. Systematic attempts were made to do away with Catholic public schools; it was made a crime to speak against the infamous sterilization law; Catholic newspapers were in many instances suppressed entirely; it was practically made obligatory on all Catholic young men and women to join the Hitlerjugend, i.e., Nazi youth organizations, which are submitted to a constant deluge of anti-religious propaganda, and which abet unethical practices. All civil employees were ordered to cancel their memberships in Church organizations, and many industrialists, following the lead of the Government, would employ only young people who belonged to State-sponsored associations. Reichsbishop Mueller, head of the Protestant church in Germany and a tool in the hands of the Nazi extremists, declared in a communication to the press of the world: "What we want is a German church, independent of Rome. One State, one People, one Church." A new Kulturkampf appears inevitable in Germany. It will find the Catholics politically defenseless, but not hopeless; for, as the German Bishops assured them in their joint Pastoral Letter of 1935: "The spirit of Christ achieves victory by other weapons than those of the spirit of this world."

The forcible annexation on March 11, 1938 of Austria by Germany was followed in October of the same year by the taking over of the Sudeten area of Czechoslovakia. Austria almost entirely Catholic and Sudetenland predominantly so, Catholics in the German Reich now numbered close to 29,000,000, almost 40% of the entire German population. But the Government continued its anti-Catholic attitude. The same intolerance and persecution that has marked its course in the dechristianization of Germany is not only now also exercised in the new territories but is even more general and intense. A very large number of Catholic Parochial Schools have been secularized, the Religious expelled from them as also debarred from Catholic Hospitals and other institutions. False charges have been brought against the Catholic clergy and many have been incarcerated. The Bishop of Rottenburg was evicted from his See. On March 14, 1937 Pope Pius XI addressed an Encyclical to German Catholics on the condition of the Church in Germany in which he exhorted bishops, priests and the laity each in their particular sphere of duty to be faithful to God and the Church. Our Holy Father also reminds those who have strayed away to reflect on the teachings of Christ and return to the fold.

The Close of the Pontificate of Pope Pius XI. In the last few years of his reign the Pope was faced with a continuance of the weighty problems caused by the ever-increasing social unrest of the world. Though his health was failing, he did not spare himself in the exercise of his supreme mission to teach, guide and govern the souls of men as the visible head of Christ's Church. His death occurred on February 10, 1939. In that period he furthered the progress of the cultural sciences, restored the temporal heritage of the Church, proclaimed himself the defender of the workingman's rights. He confirmed the divine law for the reconstruction of the Social Order and vigorously attacked atheistic communism and all foes of Religion. He stoutly vindicated the sanctity of marriage and the home and preached the principles underlying true Christian education. He safeguarded the priesthood and worked indefatigably for the spread of Christ's Kingdom everywhere, especially propagating the Missions. He was ever zealous in his efforts to bring back to the Church's fold the Schismatic Eastern Church and to restore the peace of Christ to a harassed world.

Some Articles of the Treaty Between the Holy See and Italy

ART. I

Italy recognizes and reaffirms the principle set forth in Art. 1 of the Constitution of the Kingdom of Italy of March 4, 1848, whereby the Roman Catholic and Apostolic Religion is the sole religion of the State.

ART. 2

Italy recognizes the sovereignty of the Holy See in the field of international relations as an attribute that pertains to the very nature of the Holy See, in conformity with its traditions and with the demands of its mission in the world.

ART. 3

Italy recognizes full possession and absolute power and sovereign jurisdiction of the Holy See over the Vatican, as at present constituted, with all its endowments and appurtenances.

ART. 4

The sovereignty and exclusive jurisdiction which Italy recognizes on the part of the Holy See with regard to the State of the Vatican implies that there can be no interference on the part of the Italian Government therein, nor any other authority than that of the Holy See.

ART. 5

Italy, considering the person of the Sovereign Pontiff as sacred and inviolable, declares any and every attempt against him, as well as any incitement to commit such, to be punishable by the same penalties as attempts against the person of the King or incitement to commit the same.

Public offenses or insults committed in Italian territory against the person of the Sovereign Pontiff, whether by deed or by spoken or written word, are punishable by the same penalties as similar offenses and injuries against the person of the King.

ART. 26

The Holy See maintains that with the agreements signed today adequate assurance is guaranteed, as far as is necessary, for the said Holy See to provide, with due liberty and independence, for the pastoral régime of the Diocese of Rome and of the Church of Italy and in the world. The Holy See declares the "Roman Question" definitively and irrevocably settled and, therefore, eliminated; and recognizes the Kingdom of Italy under the dynasty of the House of Savoy with Rome as the Capital of the Italian State.

—From *Treaty and Concordat between the Holy See and Italy.*
Official Documents. N.C.W.C. Washington, D. C.

Hints for Study

1. Since Sept. 29, 1908, the official journal of the Holy See is the *Acta Apostolicae Sedis*, published monthly in Rome. A decree or a decision published in it is thereby officially promulgated. The Encyclicals of the Popes are usually printed in the more important modern languages.
2. In what way can you help the Home and Foreign Missions? Write a paragraph on the following: *Society for the Propagation of the Faith, Holy Childhood Association, Students' Mission Crusade, Catholic Church Extension Society, Marquette League, Negro and Indian Mission Bureau.*
3. Which are the principal public devotions practiced in the Church today?
4. What is the aim of the "Liturgical Movement"?
5. Draw up a list (with dates) of the Oecumenical or General Councils of the Church.
6. From the bibliographical notes scattered throughout this Church History select twenty books that you have read or would like to read.
7. For a good account of Pope Pius XI see Fontenelle and Brown, *His Holiness, Pope Pius XI, the Pope of the Lateran Treaty* (Benziger).
8. On *Catholic Action* see Burton Confrey, *Social Studies* (Benziger, 1934) and the monthly issues of the magazine "Catholic Action," published in Washington by the N. C. W. C.

Scan the Book Review columns of our Catholic Magazines and note down the important works dealing with any phase of Church History, especially with the history of the Church in America. Insert the titles in their proper places in your Church History, giving full name of the author, title of book, year and place of publication, name of publisher, and price (if known). E.g., Guilday, Dr. Peter, *History of the Councils of Baltimore,* 1932, N. Y. Macmillan.

CHAPTER VII

POPE PIUS XII

The Successor to Pius XI in Peter's Chair. "I bring you tidings of great joy. We have a Pope, the Most Eminent and the Most Reverend Eugenio Pacelli who has given to himself the name Pius XII." With these words Cardinal Caccia Dominioni announced from the balcony of St. Peters, Vatican City, on March 2, 1939, the election of the new Pope, the 262nd Successor to St. Peter. The Cardinals, 62 in number, had entered the Conclave on the evening of March 1st. Within 24 hours, the shortest time in 316 years, a selection had been made.

The new Pope was born in Rome, on March 2, 1876, of a family which had very close relationship to the Holy See. His grandfather, Marcantonio was undersecretary of the interior for the Papal States from 1851 to 1870, under Pius IX, and his father Filippo, was at one time dean of the College of Consistorial Advocates. He was ordained priest in March, 1899, after which, having completed his studies at the *Academia del Nobili,* he became a member of the Congregation for Extraordinary Ecclesiastical Affairs, of which he eventually became Prefect. His work in this connection made it necessary for him to acquire an expert knowledge of international and Roman law; and even at that early date he specialized in all matters connected with the relations of the Vatican with Germany.

In 1912 he was also made Consultor, or adviser, to the Holy Office.

Consecrated Bishop by Benedict XV in 1917, Msgr. Pacelli was sent immediately afterwards to Germany on a diplomatic mission connected with Pope Benedict's efforts to secure an armistice. After the War, in June, 1920, Msgr. Pacelli was sent to Berlin as Nuncio, and during the nine years which he spent there he did a great amount of work to improve relations between the Vatican and the German Republic. It is necessary only to recall the Con-

POPE PIUS XII

cordats that were, through him, separately concluded with Bavaria and Saxony, and that which was made with Switzerland. The Concordat of 1933 between the Vatican and the Third Reich was also really the work of Msgr. Pacelli. The late Holy Father speaks of the Concordat in his encyclical as having been "in scriptis" since 1922—that is, as resting on foundations that were laid during the nunciature of Msgr. Pacelli.

At the Consistory of December, 1929, Msgr. Pacelli was made a Cardinal, and some months later Pope Pius XI appointed him Secretary of State in succession to Cardinal Gasparri, an office which he filled with conspicuous distinction until his election to the Throne of St. Peter. In 1935, Cardinal Pacelli was elected Cardinal Camerlengo, and on several occasions he represented Pope Pius XI as Legate, notably at Lourdes, Lisieux, Buenos Aires and in 1938 at the Budapest Eucharistic Congress. In 1936 the Cardinal Secretary of State visited the United States. It was the first time that an Ecclesiastic of such eminent position ever came to this country.

The first paternal message of the new Pope, Pius XII, was addressed to the whole world from the Sistine Chapel, over the Vatican City Radio, on March 3rd, the day after his election. Greeting his "venerable brothers of the Episcopate," he blessed the "priests, religious and nuns" and "all his children scattered everywhere throughout the world, especially those who suffer in poverty or pain." He also addressed "all those outside the Church" and for whom he "raises to God his best and greatest prayer and wishes for every good." He invited all to work and pray for peace between nations and said that he would pray God that those who lead the nations may guide "their people in ways of prosperity and progress."

These expressions as well as the Pope's motto *"Opus Justitiae Pax"* (The work of justice is peace) may be taken as an indication of the tasks Pope Pius XII has set for himself outside of the spiritual realm to bring to a successful conclusion those tremendous problems which confronted his predecessor in regard to the right ordering of the fundamentals of those natural institutions—social, economic, cultural, political—of which the Church is most solicitous as the Mother of all peoples.

The Holy Father had appointed the month of May, 1939, as a period of prayer to the Blessed Virgin Mary in behalf of peace.

Germany.—The Bishops issued a joint pastoral on the Sacrament of Matrimony. They re-asserted the teachings of the Church, stating that in the supernatural order Marriage is subject to the jurisdiction of the Church and that a simple civil marriage was not a legitimate union. They also condemned sterilization. Almost immediately after the Pope had issued his first encyclical *"Summi Pontificatus,"* the government increased its measures for the persecution of the Church. During 1939, 687 monasteries and convents were closed. In the Tyrol priests were incarcerated, others were forbidden to teach religion in schools. Over 50 Catholic schools were suppressed. Restrictions were placed on the Catholic Press and only five Catholic papers are now permitted to be published in a country having thirty million Catholics.

Poland Loses Its Religious and Political Liberty.—The dispute between Germany and Poland over the former's demand that she be given control of Danzig and a passage through the Polish Corridor which had been going on for some time, had reached a stage which foreboded the outbreak of hostilities. On August 24, 1939 the Holy Father made a plea for peace over the radio. He said that he was "armed only with the words of truth and standing above all public disputes and passions . . . Empires which are not founded on justice are not blessed by God . . . Nothing is lost with peace; all may be lost by war." But his words fell on deaf ears. On September 1, the German armies invaded Poland, conquering this nation in a month, notwithstanding the heroic defense put up by the Polish soldiers. At the same time Soviet Russia, with whom Germany had made an agreement to partition Poland, entered from the east and occupied that part of the country. By this division, millions of Catholics were deprived of their religious rights. Religious instruction cannot be given, not even privately, and although a few churches are permitted to remain open, even these will eventually close because of social and economic pressure.

The First Encyclical.—About this time, Pope Pius XII issued his first encyclical *"Summi Pontificatus."* In it he deplores the evils of today and attributes them to a weakening of the faith. He opposes the assumption of unrestricted powers by the leaders of the peoples and gives expression to his horror of war and its accompanying terrors. He exhorts all to pray and work for a return of the world to peace and order, which he maintains must be founded on God's law.

The Persecution of Catholic Poland.—The Holy Father had requested the German government not to extend the religious persecution now obtaining in Germany to Poland. Reports having reached the Ecclesiastical Authorities in Rome that excessive cruelties were being enacted on the helpless Poles, the Vatican radio station broadcasted three denunciations of the atrocities committed by the Germans and the Russians. The Poles were being dispossessed of their lands and subjected to deportation. The clergy were arrested and sent to concentration camps and even massacred. The news that Archbishop Andreas Szeptycki of Lwow had been killed by the Russians was confirmed. Religion was generally suppressed. Persecution is so general according to a report made to the Vatican by Cardinal Hlond, the Primate of Poland, that if there is no cessation soon, there will be a vast territory completely de-Christianized.

The Spread of the War.—The invasion of Poland caused Great Britain and France to declare war on Germany on September 3, 1939. While in Great Britain, the clergy and men studying for the priesthood were exempted from military service, great numbers of the French clergy, in addition to the regular Army Chaplains, because the military laws required it, enlisted in the ranks of the armies of France. On November 3, 1939, Russia made war on Finland. The Holy Father in his address to the Sacred College of Cardinals on Christmas Eve assailed "premeditated aggressions against a small, industrious, and peaceful people," meaning the Finns. The Finns defended their country valiantly, but, their man-power exhausted, they were forced to yield and on March 13, 1940 made peace with Russia. The next nation which was to fall a victim to the war was Denmark, which submitted to the German government on April 9, 1940. Almost at the same time, the Germany army disembarked in Norwegian ports and took possession of Norway. The king called upon his people to defend their country and the people bravely supported him. The British and French sent aid. Then on May 10, 1940 the German armies invaded Holland, Belgium, and Luxembourg. Again Pope Pius speaking from a pulpit outside the Vatican prayed that Christ "may disperse the whirlwind of death which is crushing humanity." The Pope also sent a message to Leopold, the King of Belgium: "In a moment when for the second time against its will and right the Belgian people sees its territory exposed to the cruelties of war, we, being profoundly moved send to Your Majesty and to the entire nation so beloved by us, our Apostolic blessing." The Holy Father also said that he prayed "to the All-Powerful God that this stern trial may end with the restoration of her liberty and independence." Somewhat similar messages were sent to the rulers of the other invaded countries.

Portugal's New Concordat with the Church.—A bright spot in the dark picture of war-torn Europe is the signing of a concordat between Portugal and the Vatican in which that country recognizes the juridical status of the Church and its societies, restores religious instruction to the schools and admits the Divine right of the Church to found and maintain educational institutions. The Canon Law of the Church on marriage and her teachings on divorce assume legal status. The regulation of the activities of missionaries as they affect the State in Portugese colonies also form part of the agreement. Thus, through the just attitude of Portugal's ardent Premier, Dr. Oliveira Salazar, there has happily been brought to a close the long period during which anti-Christian forces ruled the country with serious injury to the people's religious liberty.

New Saints and Blessed for the Church's Altars.—Alike heartening and spiritually encouraging were the events at which four holy women were made saints and blessed. Blessed Gemma Galgani, called the "Flower of the Passion" who died at the age of 25 on April 11, 1903, and Blessed Mary Euphrasia Pelletier, foundress of the Sisters of the Good Shepherd, who died on April 24, 1868, were canonized on May 2, 1940. The venerable Rose Philippine Duchesne, a member of the Society of the Sacred Heart and foundress of that order in the United States, who died November 18, 1852, at the age of 83, was beatified on May 12, 1940 and venerable Joaquina de Mas, foundress of the Spanish Carmelite Sisters of Charity born April 16, 1783, and who died August 28, 1854, was beatified on May 19, 1940.

Pope Pius XII, Unequivocal Apostle of World Peace.—Again for 1940 the Holy Father, in his anxiety for a permanent peace among nations, turned to the Mediatrix of all Graces, our Blessed Lady. He appointed the month of May a continuous period of invocational prayer, that through Mary's intercession God might turn the hearts of men toward peace the world over. While seeking this help from Heaven he has not stood still. In thirty-four different addresses he made appeals for peace, set forth the fundamentals necessary for a permanent peace, or gave dirctions for finding the way to peace. He has been fearless in voicing his principles. Thus on Easter day he said: "Only Christ and His law can return just relationships, restrain the lust for conquest, temper cold justice with the breath of charity" and again in unmistaken terms, so that all concerned could not misinterpret their reference, he said "that not a few people have lost peace because their prophets or rulers have turned away from God and His Christ." And so the Holy Father, the Father of Christendom will continue in his campaign of prayer until he has wrung from Heaven the much coveted prize of peace.

The United States.—On the occasion of the 150th anniversary of the appointment of the first Bishop in the United States—John Carroll, Pope Pius XII sent an encyclical dated November 1, 1939, to the American hierarchy. He expressed his esteem for the American people and praised the growth and work of the Church in our country. He emphasized, however, that this commendation be salutary and pointed out certain deplorable conditions. He complained "that in so many schools of your land Christ is often despised or ignored, the explanation of the universe and mankind is forced within the narrow limits of materialism or of rationalism, and new educational systems are sought after which cannot but produce a sorrowful harvest in the intellectual and moral life of the nation." He referred to the accumulation of ills resulting from the plague of divorce and stated that mixed marriages were usually a grave loss to the Catholic faith. He expressed fatherly affection for the Negro people dwelling among us and besought us that we give them special care in the field of religion and education. He approved Labor Unions and asserted that every worker should have employment and that the earnings of such must be sufficient for the maintenance of their families. He invited the cooperation of "them, too, whom the Church laments as separated brethren."

Catholic Refugees from Europe.—The work of the Episcopal Committee, of which Most Reverend Joseph Francis Rummel, D.D., Archbishop of New Orleans is the chairman, in charge of the settling of Catholic refugees from Germany has been seriously interrupted and rendered most difficult by the European War. But up to the close of 1939 over 4,000 cases had been taken care of, a very noteworthy achievement.

President Roosevelt and Pope Pius XII.—In view of the European War and to further his efforts for peace between nations, Franklin Delano Roosevelt, President of the United States wrote a letter to Pope Pius XII on December 23, 1939, in which he said: "I am therefore suggesting to Your Holiness that it would give me great satisfaction to send to You my personal representative in order that our parallel endeavors for peace and the alleviation of suffering may be assisted. When the time shall come for the re-establishment of world peace, it is of utmost importance to humanity and religion that common ideals shall have united expression." . . . In reply the Holy Father expressed through the Most Reverend Amleto Giovanni Cicognani, D.D., the Apostolic Delegate to the United States, his profound gratitude to the President. Welcoming the President's cooperation, the Pope in his letter, while admitting that there was now slight probability of immediate success declares that he is continuing to dedicate his efforts and solicitude to the purpose of reestablishing peace. At the same time President Roosevelt announced that he would send Myron C. Taylor, retired Chairman of the United States Steel Corporation, and Vice-Chairman of the Intergovernmental Committee on Political Refugees, as his personal representative with the standing, but not the title of Ambassador. There having been some protests against the appointment, the President conferred with the leaders of certain Protestant denominations and assured them that no one church would receive greater recognition than another. On February 27, 1940, Mr. Taylor, the personal ambassador of the President presented himself to the Pope. President Roosevelt said in his letter: "I shall be very happy to feel that he (Mr. Taylor) may be the channel for the communication of any views you and I may wish to exchange in the interest of concord among the peoples of the world."

New Saints for the United States.—Two spiritual events of particular interest and importance to Catholics in our Country were the elevation to the altars of the Church of two holy women, who had made notable contributions to the cause of Catholic education. On May 12, 1940, the beatification of the Venerable Philippine Duchesne took place. Born in France on August 29, 1769, she made her profession in the Society of the Sacred Heart on November 21, 1805. Delegated by the foundress of that Community, Saint Madeleine Sophie Barat to found a convent in the United States, she arrived with five companions in St. Louis on August 22, 1818, and going to St. Charles, Mo., there established the first Academy of the Sacred Heart. Gradually new foundations were made and the successful spread of the Society and its cultural work for girls are the results of that beginning. Her death occurred November 18, 1852, aged eighty-three years.

The Missionary Sisters of the Sacred Heart were founded by Frances Xaxier Cabrini at Lodi, Italy, in 1880. The Community grew quickly. On March 31, 1889, she came to the United States and made numerous foundations, the work of the sisters being both educational and charitable. She died in Chicago on December 22, 1907, at the age of sixty-seven years. Pope Pius XII declared her a Saint in 1946. Her relics are preserved in the Chapel of the Cabrini High School, New York.

Spain.—General Franco completed his work of reorganization by announcing himself as the "Supreme Chieftain responsible only before God and History." In October, 1939, General Franco condemned atheism connected with the Bolshevik invasion of Poland, and for this was commended by the Holy Father. Somewhat later the Spanish government decreed restoration of clergy salaries by the state and also took measures to repair the damage done by the "Reds" to the Church property. It also returned to the Jesuit Order the properties which had been confiscated by the Republic. Another measure taken was that of suppression of Masonry. Early in 1940 General Franco stated in regard to the European war that "Spain has united her voice to that of the Catholic Church" and to those states who desire to bring about peace.

Mexico.—While there is comparative quiet, the anti-Christian forces are steadily at work to undermine and destroy religion. In January, 1940, the Mexican Chamber of Deputies passed legislation excluding all religious instruction from schools and providing for socialist education. The Bishops urged all Catholics to aid in all peaceful efforts leading to a modification of this new Mexican atheistic educational law. The government also denied permission to build two Catholic Churches in Monterey, suggesting that the funds be spent for "Social utility."

CONCLUSION

LOOKING BACKWARD

Looking back upon the history of the Church, the "right glorious City of God," the truth of Cardinal Newman's words comes home to us: "The Church is ever militant; sometimes she gains, sometimes she loses; and more often she is at once gaining and losing in different parts of her territory. What is ecclesiastical history but a record of the ever-doubtful fortune of the battle, though its issue is not doubtful? Scarcely are we singing *Te Deum*, when we have to turn to our *Misereres*: scarcely are we in peace, when we are in persecution: scarcely have we gained a triumph, when we are visited by a scandal. Nay, we make progress by means of reverses; our griefs are our consolations; we lose Stephen to gain Paul, and Matthias replaces the traitor Judas. . . ."

We need have no fear as to the fate of Holy Church. She has lost nothing of her fecundity and her immortal youth. Fifteen hundred years ago St. Augustine said of her: "Her enemies look upon her and say, 'She is about to die; soon her very name will disappear; there will be no more Christians; they have had their day.' Whilst they are thus speaking, I see these very men die themselves, day by day, but the Church lives on, and preaches the power of God to every succeeding generation."

And how could she fail or prove unfaithful to her trust? Did not her Divine Founder build her upon an impregnable Rock, and did He not give her the promise: "Behold I am with you all days, even to the consummation of the world"?

To all the enemies of the Church, her enemies of to-day and to-morrow, we say with Gamaliel, the teacher of St. Paul:
> *"If this work be of men, it will come to nought;*
> *but if it be of God, you cannot overthrow it."*

SUMMARY

Turning Points in the History of the Church in Modern Times

A.D.

1517 to 1555 In the 16th century the Church is assailed by a most formidable religious revolution. *Protestantism* appears. Wittenberg, Geneva, and London are its starting points; Luther, Calvin, and Henry VIII, its leaders. Destruction of all religious authority is its aim. Calumny, mob violence, penal laws are its weapons. The Bible alone, privately interpreted, is its platform. The absolute corruption of man and the enslavement of his will by Original Sin, justification by faith alone, predestination, State supremacy in religion, are its dogmas. Protestantism reaches the zenith of its power on the Continent in 1555 at the *Peace of Augsburg*. Of the northern nations Ireland alone resists the religious innovators.

1555 to 1648 The Catholic reaction sets in. Protestantism is checked in its onward march by the arms of the princes who had remained faithful to the Church. The *Council of Trent* (1542-1563) saves Catholicism. Animated, equipped, and organized for the struggle, and led on by holy and energetic Popes, bishops, priests, monks, and nuns, lay men and women, the Church advances against the forces of rebellion. The ascendancy of Catholicism is re-established in the greater part of Europe. Its losses in the Old World are compensated for by conquests in the newly discovered continents.

1648 to 1789 The *Treaty of Westphalia,* guaranteed by Protestant Sweden and Catholic France, secures to Protestantism permanent possessions on the Continent. The Western Church is definitely rent in twain. *Cuius regio, eius religio.* Royal absolutism, Jansenism, Gallicanism Rationalism, Unbelief prepare the stage for the tragedy of the Frencl Revolution. It is the saddest and most depressing period of Churcl history.

1789 to 1815 The *French Revolution* sweeps over Europe leaving ruin in it. wake. The Church suffers most. She is despoiled of all her pos¬ sessions, her treasures of art are pillaged, her sacred vessels stolen, her institutions of charity and learning suppressed. The fall of Napoleon sees the Church poor, dependent on the State and the generosity of the faithful for her subsistence.

1815 to 1870 The poor Bride of Christ slowly but steadily wins back her empire over the souls of men. In France, in Germany, and then throughout Europe a great *Catholic revival* takes place, which, though interrupted at times, never ceases to grow. A veritable "second spring" bursts upon the Church in the British Isles after *Emancipation* has been won, while in the New World, under the fostering sun of free-dom, she grows from a small and tender plant into a mighty tree spreading its branches from coast to coast.

1870 to 1929 Deprived of her temporal sovereignty, of political influence, of her ancient wealth, the Church stands before the world as the **greatest** of *moral powers*, resting on the consciences and the hearts **of her** children.

1929 The *Lateran Treaty* transforms the Vatican into a sovereign **State.** The new State is the smallest, but at the same time the **greatest of** European States. The Pope is temporal Sovereign over a **few hun-** dred subjects, but spiritual ruler of two hundred million **Europeans—** of the hearts of two thirds of the inhabitants of Europe, and **of more** than a hundred million in the rest of the world.

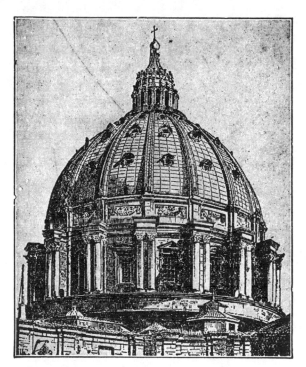

"The Most Beautiful Cupola in the World"

APPENDIX

A.D.

1492 Christopher Columbus discovers America.

1493 Fr. Juan Perez, friend and counselor of Columbus, says the first Mass in the New World at Point Conception, Haiti, in a chapel built of boughs and thatched with straw.—Pope Alexander VI draws line of demarcation to divide the Portuguese field of exploration on the East from the Spanish field on the West.

1510 Ordination of Fr. Bartolomé de Las Casas, the first in America.

1513 Diocese of Porto Rico created.

1521 Ponce de Leon, accompanied by missionaries, explores Florida.

1526 First Mass in Virginia said in a log chapel at San Miguel, near the present Jamestown, by a Dominican Friar.

1527 Bartolomé de Las Casas defends the Indians against oppression.

1537 Pope Paul III vindicates the liberty of the Indians, maintaining that they are heirs to the natural rights of man.—First consecration of a bishop in America (Francisco Morroquin, bishop-elect of Guatemala, consecrated by Bishop Zumarraga of Mexico).

1542 Spain promulgates the "New Laws" for the Indies in which the rights of the Indians are safeguarded.

1549 Fr. Luis Cancer de Barbastro, O.P., proto-martyr of Florida.

1565 First parish in the United States founded at St. Augustine, Fla.

1569 The Jesuit Fr. John Rogel erects a chapel for the Indians at Orista, near St. Helena, on Port Royal Sound, South Carolina.

1597 First church in New Mexico is built at San Juan by Fr. Martinez.

1604 First Mass in New England is said by Fr. Aubry on Ste. Croix Island, Maine.

1606 Santa Fé, New Mexico, founded.

1626-1640 A line of missions stretching across the present State of New York established by the Jesuits.

1629 Spanish Franciscans begin evangelization of Moki Indians in the present State of Arizona.

1630 The Propaganda establishes the Prefecture of New England and entrusts it to the Capuchins; the Prefect is the famous Père Joseph de Tremblay, the right arm of Cardinal Richelieu.

1633 Capuchins establish missions on the Penobscot, Me.

1634 The Catholic colony of Maryland founded by Leonard Calvert. Freedom of worship is granted to all Christians.

1642 St. Isaac Jogues preaches to the Chippewas near Sault Ste. Marie.

1646 St. Isaac Jogues martyred by the Mohawks near Auriesville, N. Y. Jesuits establish missions on the Kennebec, Me.

1648 Law passed in Connecticut expelling Jesuits and threatening them with hanging if they returned.

1649 Toleration Act passed by the Assembly of Maryland.

1650 At the request of Queen Henrietta Mary, the Propaganda establishes a mission in Virginia for the Catholic Cavaliers who fled there to escape the persecution of Cromwell. The mission is placed in charge of the Capuchins.

1666 First Mass in Vermont said in chapel at Ft. Anne. Fr. Claude Allouez, S. J., builds first chapel in Wisconsin on Madeleine Island

1670 Quebec made a bishopric, with Laval as first bishop.—Green Bay, Wisconsin, founded.

1671 Fr. Jacques Marquette, S. J., establishes Mission of St. Ignace, Michigan.

1673 The Franciscan Fr. Louis Hennepin visits Niagara and writes first description of the cataract.—Joliet and Marquette explore the Mississippi.

1*

1674   Marquette winters on the present site of Chicago.
1675   Marquette establishes Mission of the Immaculate Conception at Old Kaskaskia, two months before his death.
1680   Indian revolts destroy the flourishing missions in New Mexico.
1683   Thomas Dongan, Catholic Governor of New York, enacts first law establishing religious liberty passed in New York. The first Catholic chapel in New York City is erected at Ft. James.
1685   The New York Latin School, the first Catholic educational institution in New York, is founded by the Jesuits Harvey, Harrison and Gage.—The Catholics in the English colonies are placed under the jurisdiction of the Vicar-Apostolic of London.
1692   Restoration of the missions in New Mexico.—Anglicanism established as the religion of Maryland. Mass is tolerated in private houses.
1696   Mission of the Guardian Angel established on the site of Chicago.
1698   First Mission in Mississippi founded by priests from Quebec Seminary.
1699   Sieur d'Iberville makes a settlement at Old Biloxi, Miss. He is accompanied by two missionaries.
1700   Fr. Eusebius Kino, S. J., establishes Mission of San Xavier del Bac just south of Tucson, Arizona.—Fr. Gravier transfers mission of Old Kaskaskia to Kaskaskia, Ill.
1701   Fort Pontchartrain, with chapel of St. Anne, built on the site of Detroit.
1704   The parish church of Old Mobile, Alabama, is founded, with Fr. de la Vente, of the Paris Foreign Missions, as pastor.
1709   Jesuit Missions in New York abandoned.
1718   New Orleans founded by Bienville.—Franciscans establish a mission at San Pedro Springs, Texas.
1724   Jesuit Missions in Maine destroyed; Fr. Sebastian Râle martyred.
1727   Capuchins establish school for boys in New Orleans. Ursulines come to New Orleans and open an academy.
1733   St. Joseph's Church, Philadelphia, the first Catholic church in Pennsylvania, erected by Fr. Joseph Greaton, S.J.
1741   German Jesuits (Wappeler, Schneider, Steinmeyer) enter American mission field, laboring among German Catholic immigrants in Pennsylvania and New Jersey.
1744   The Alamo, that is, the Franciscan church, hospital and convent with a walled enclosure, erected in San Antonio, Texas.
1745   Jesuits establish a classical Academy at Bohemia Manor, Md.
1749   Fr. Sebastian Meurin, S.J., founds the Church of St. Francis Xavier at Vincennes, Indiana.
1750   The first parish in Missouri founded at St. Genevieve.
1755   The Acadians deported; many dispersed through English colonies.
1768   German Catholics build Holy Trinity Church, Philadelphia.
1769   Mission of San Diego, Cal., founded by Junipero Serra; 21 other missions founded till 1823.
1770   First church in St. Louis, Mo., on the site of the present Cathedral, blessed by Fr. Pierre Gibault of Kaskaskia.
1773   Suppression of the Society of Jesus. Jesuits in colonies continue to labor as secular priests.
1775   About 25 Catholic families from Maryland settle in Kentucky, south of Louisville.
1776-1783 War of the Revolution. Catholics rally to the support of the cause of independence. The War brings religious liberty into the United States.
1776   Religious freedom enacted by law in Virginia and Maryland.—Constitution of North Carolina keeps from office "those who deny the truth of the Protestant religion."
1776   Fr. John Carroll (1735-1815), of Maryland, goes with Franklin, Chase and Charles Carroll to Canada, in vain attempt to win back the sympathy of the Canadians alienated by the protest of John Jay

and other anti-Catholic bigots against the Quebec Act which gave justice to the Catholics of Canada.

1778 The Northwest Territory won for the United States mainly through the efforts of Fr. Pierre Gibault.

1783 The fine Byzantine Church of San Xavier, on the outskirts of Tucson, Arizona, erected.

1784 Fr. John Carroll appointed by the Pope Superior of the Missions of the United States.

1786 St. Peter's Church, New York City, erected; "Trustee System" inaugurated.

1788 First Catholic church erected in Boston, Mass.

1789 Fr. Carroll named Bishop of Baltimore, his diocese reaching from Georgia to Maine and westward to the Mississippi. It contained less than 30,000 Catholics.

1790 First church in Kentucky erected at Holy Cross. Sulpicians (David, Badin, Flaget, Nerinckx) become apostles of Catholicity in Kentucky.

1791 Bishop Carroll calls first Synod of Baltimore, attended by 22 priests. Opening of Georgetown College and St. Mary's Seminary and College, Baltimore. Bishop Carroll visits Boston; Gov. John Hancock attends Mass in his honor.

1791-1799 The storm of the French Revolution drives a score of French priests to the United States, among them Marechal, Cheverus, Bruté, Flaget and Dubois, who all became bishops.

1793 Several thousand Catholics, among them a number of Negroes, come to the United States from San Domingo and other West India islands to escape the effects of the French Revolution and the Negro insurrections. In the same year Bishop Carroll conferred Holy Orders, for the first time in the United States, on Rev. Stephen Badin.

1793 Rt. Rev. Luis Cardenas consecrated first Bishop of the newly created see of New Orleans. He inaugurates a program of strict reform, and holds a synod.

1799 Prince Demetrius Augustine Gallitzin, ordained priest by Bishop Carroll in 1795, goes to McGuire's Settlement in the Alleghanies, erects a small log church where Loretto, Pa., now stands, and remains at his post 41 years. He is one of the first in the United States to defend the Church by writing. He is known as "the Apostle of the Alleghanies."

1800 Bishop Carroll consecrates his coadjutor, Rt. Rev. Leonard Neale.

1803 The Louisiana Purchase increases the number of Catholics in the United States by nearly thirty thousand.—German Catholics build the first church in New Jersey at Echo Lake.

1805 Revival of the Society of Jesus in the United States by Bishop Carroll, under the direction of Fr. Robert Molyneux.

1806 First establishment of Dominicans founded in Washington County, Ky., by Fr. Edward Fenwick, O.P.

1808 The Dioceses of New York, Philadelphia, Boston and Bardstown (now Louisville) are erected as suffragans of Baltimore. Bishop Carroll received the pallium.—Frances Allen, daughter of the patriot Ethan Allen, converted. She becomes a nun in Montreal.

1809 Sisters of Charity organized at Emmitsburg, Md., by Mother Seton.

1812 Sisters of Charity of Nazareth and Sisters of Loretto founded in Kentucky. St. Thomas' Seminary opened at Bardstown, Ky.

1815 First Church in present diocese of Covington founded at White Sulphur, near Frankfort, Ky.

1817 St. Mary's Seminary of the Barrens opened by Lazarists in Perry Co., Mo.

1818 Bishop Dubourg of New Orleans transfers his residence to St. Louis, Mo. He founds the Latin Academy which develops into the present St. Louis University.—The new Connecticut Constitution establishes religious freedon —The first church in Ohio, St. Joseph's, near Somerset, is blessed by Fr. Fenwick.

1819   The first church in Cincinnati, Ohio, a rude plank structure at Vine and Liberty Streets, blessed by Fr. Nicholas Young.

1820   Rt. Rev. John England, staunch champion of Catholic Emancipation in Ireland and friend of Daniel O'Connell, is made first Bishop of Charleston, S. C. His diocese embraces the States of North Carolina, South Carolina and Georgia.—Trusteeism creates much trouble especially in New York, Baltimore and Philadeipiia.

1821   Richmond, Va., and Cincinnati, Ohio, become dioceses. The Cincinnati Diocese includes Ohio, Michigan and the Northwest Territory. Fr. Edward Fenwick is consecrated Bishop (1822).

1822   Fr. Barber, a convert from Episcopalianism, erects the first church and school in New Hampshire at Claremont.

1823   Bishop John England founds the *United States Miscellany*, the first Catholic newspaper in the United States.—The first church in North Carolina is built at Washington.

1824   A school for Indian boys is opened by the Jesuits at Florissant, Mo.; Ven. Philippine Duchesne, foundress of Religious of the S. Heart in America (St. Charles, Mo., 1818), opens a school for Indian girls.

1826   The Diocese of St. Louis erected. The first Catholic chapel in Arkansas built at Arkansas Post.

1827   Father Gallitzin made Vicar General of Western Pennsylvania.

1829   Mobile, Ala., made a diocese. The Sisters of Charity of Mother Seton establish their first house in Cincinnati.—First Provincial Council of Baltimore. Its thirty-three decrees on Church discipline approved by Rome.

1829   The Leopoldine Association, named after Leopoldina, Empress of Brazil and daughter of Francis I of Austria, is founded in Austria to help the missions in America with men and money.

1833   Second Provincial Council of Baltimore makes arrangements to care for Indian missions. Lazarists are placed in charge of missions on the Mississippi; Jesuits of those on the Missouri. A regular mode of nominating bishops to vacant sees is adopted. The erection of the sees of Detroit and Vincennes recommended.

1833   Rev. John Martin Henni, Vicar General of the Cincinnati Diocese and later first Bishop and first Archbishop of Milwaukee, founds the first German Catholic weekly, *Der Wahrheitsfreund*.

1834   The beginning of the ruin of the California Missions.

1835   Article in the North Carolina Constitution disqualifying Catholics from holding office repealed through efforts of the eminent Jurist William Gaston, first graduate of Georgetown University.

1837   Third Provincial Council of Baltimore solemnly protests against the fanatical spirit of persecution aroused in the country by the rapid growth of the Church. Anti-Catholic calumnies are refuted. The erection of the following dioceses is recommended: Dubuque for the Territories of Iowa and Minnesota; Nashville for Tennessee; Natchez for Mississippi. Bishop Loras of Dubuque attracts tide of Catholic immigration to his territory.

1840   Fourth Provincial Council of Baltimore. See of Bardstown is transferred to Louisville. Jesuits take charge of St. Xavier's College, Cincinnati. Fr. Peter John De Smet, S.J. (1801-1873) visits the Flatheads west of the Rocky Mountains and establishes flourishing missions amongst them, and later amongst the Blackfeet and the Sioux. His writings contain valuable information concerning Indian life.

1841   Fr. Sorin introduces the Congregation of the Fathers and Brothers of the Holy Cross and founds Notre Dame, Indiana.

1841   Bishop John Hughes is instrumental in founding the Irish Emigrant Society and the Emigrant Industrial Savings Bank.

1842   Rt. Rev. John Hughes succeeds Bishop Dubois in New York. He is the great figure in the constructive period of New York. He abolishes Trusteeism, defeats the Native American and Know Nothing Movements, overthrows the Public School Society which is subversive of Catholic interests, and inaugurates a successful Parochial School System.—Bishop Blanc of New Orleans founds the Sisters of the Holy Family for the care of colored orphans and aged poor, the second colored Sisterhood in the United States.

1843   Fifth Provincial Council of Baltimore. Erection of following sees recommended: Little Rock, Ark., comprising the State of Arkansas and the Choctaw and Cherokee nations in the Indian Territory; Chicago; Hartford for Connecticut and Rhode Island; Pittsburgh for Western Pennsylvania, and Milwaukee. William Tyler of the Barber family of New Hampshire made first bishop of Hartford. Oregon, which has become a fertile field for missionary labor, is erected into a Vicariate-Apostolic.

1843   The first community of Sisters of Mercy (from Carlow, Ireland) is established in Pittsburgh, Pa.

1844   St. Michael's Church, Philadelphia, burnt in anti-Catholic riot.

1844   *Brownson's Review*, published quarterly, exhibits the great ability and religious loyalty of its editor, the eminent convert Orestes A. Brownson (1803-1876).

1845   Rev. Boniface Wimmer, O.S.B., establishes the first Benedictine house in the United States at St. Vincent's, Beatty, Pa.

1845-1850   Famine in Ireland and political upheavals in Germany bring about a great increase of Catholic immigrants from those countries.

1846   Sixth Provincial Council of Baltimore. Twenty-three bishops are present. They choose the Blessed Virgin Mary, conceived without sin, as the patroness of the Church in the United States. The sees of Buffalo, Albany and Cleveland are erected. John Timon, C.M., an eminent missionary in Missouri and Texas, is appointed first Bishop of Buffalo.

1847   The learned Peter Richard Kenrick becomes first Archbishop of St. Louis. Galveston, Texas, is made an episcopal see.

1849   Seventh Provincial Council of Baltimore. The Bishops express the wish that the Immaculate Conception of the B.V.M. might be proclaimed a dogma of faith. The following new sees are erected: Wheeling, W. Va., Savannah, Ga., St. Paul, Minn.

1850   New York, Cincinnati, New Orleans and Oregon City are raised to Archbishoprics. Rev. John B. Lamy of Ohio is appointed Vicar-Apostolic of the Territory of New Mexico. The Indian Territory is made a Vicariate-Apostolic. The Sisters of Loretto and the Sisters of the Sacred Heart open schools among the Pottawatomies and Osages in the Indian Territory.

1851   What was probably the first organized mission in the United States with English as the language used by the preachers is opened in old St. Joseph's, New York City, on Passion Sunday (April 6) by Father Bernard, C.SS.R. From 1851-1858 the American Redemptorist Fathers conduct 86 organized missions in 22 dioceses "with immeasurable fruit to souls." The good work is also taken up by devoted bands of Lazarists, Jesuits, Passionists, Dominicans, etc.

1852   First Plenary Council of Baltimore. Six archbishops and 26 bishops are present. Ven. John Nepomucene Neumann, who had just succeeded Bishop Kenrick in the see of Philadelphia, and the coadjutor-bishop of Louisville, Martin J. Spalding, take a prominent part in the deliberations. The Fathers direct their attention especially to the subject of the establishment of parochial schools. "We exhort the Bishops, and, considering the very serious evils which commonly follow from defective training of youth, we beseech them, through

the bowels of divine mercy, to see that schools be established in each of the churches in their dioceses."
The erection of the following dioceses is recommended: Erie, Pa., Covington, Ky., Burlington, Vt., Portland, Me., Newark, N. J., Brooklyn, N. Y., Quincy, Ill., Natchitoches (now Alexandria), La., Monterey, Cal., Santa Fé, N. M.

1853   San Francisco, which had been part of the diocese of both Californias erected in 1840, becomes an archiepiscopal see. Upper Michigan is formed into a vicariate, with the renowned missionary Frederick Baraga, author of the first Chippewa Grammar and Dictionary, as Vicar-Apostolic. His first residence at Sault Ste. Marie is later transferred to Marquette.
Archbishop Bedini, Papal Nuncio at the Court of Brazil, visits the United States. His visit of inspection gives occasion to scandalous outbreaks of anti-Catholic bigotry. An attempt is made on his life at Cincinnati. He is courteously received by President Pierce at Washington. The Know-Nothing movement gathers strength. Catholic churches are burned, Catholic citizens killed and other outrages are committed in various States between the years 1851 and 1855.
Bishop Neumann introduces the Forty Hours' Devotion into the United States. The Passionists are brought to America by Bishop O'Connor of Pittsburgh.

1855   The Catholic Central Verein of America for Catholics of German birth or descent is formed at Baltimore.

1857   The American College, Louvain, founded. It gave many bishops and more than a thousand priests to the United States.—The dioceses of Marquette and Fort Wayne and the vicariates of Florida and Nebraska are formed.

1858   By Papal Decree of July 25, the primary rank in the American hierarchy is granted to the incumbent of the metropolitan see of Baltimore.—The Congregation of St. Paul the Apostle (Paulists) is founded in New York City by Fr. Isaac T. Hecker.

1859   The North American College is founded at Rome.

1861-1865   During the Civil War Catholic priests and members of various Sisterhoods find ample opportunity to manifest the spirit of Christian charity in self-sacrificing care of the sick and wounded in the hospitals and on the battlefields.

1865   *The Catholic World* is founded by the Paulists and the *Ave Maria* by Fr. Sorin of Notre Dame, Ind.

1866   Second Plenary Council of Baltimore is attended by 7 Archbishops, 38 Bishops, 3 Mitred Abbots, 14 superiors of Religious Orders, and upward of 100 theologians. Rt. Rev. Martin J. Spalding presides as Papal Legate.

1868   The following new dioceses are erected: Wilmington, Del., Scranton and Harrisburg, Pa., Green Bay and La Crosse, Wis., St. Joseph, Mo., Columbus, Ohio, Grass Valley, Cal., Rochester, N. Y., and the Vicariates of North Carolina, Idaho, Montana, and Colorado.

1869   The Vicariates of Arizona and the Dioceses of St. Augustine, Fla. and Springfield, Mass., are erected.

1870   Many American Bishops attend the Vatican Council.

1872-1874   The sees of Ogdensburg, N. Y., Providence, R. I., San Antonio, Tex., and the Vicariates of Brownsville, Tex., and St. Cloud, Minn., are formed. Philadelphia, Boston, Milwaukee, and Santa Fé are raised to metropolitan rank.

1873-1878   The "Kulturkampf" in Germany drives many zealous priests and religious to our shores. A number of religious congregations of men and women are established.

1874   A Catholic Bureau is established at Washington to look after the interests of the Catholic Indians.

1875   Archbishop McCloskey of New York is raised to the Cardinalate.

1876 An Apostolic Prefecture is assigned to the Indian Territory. Alleghany, Pa., is made a diocese. The *American Catholic Quarterly Review* is founded at Philadelphia.

1877 Political disabilities of Catholics are removed in New Hampshire. Peoria is made a bishopric. The see of Alleghany is reunited to the see of Pittsburgh.

1879 President Grant inaugurates an Indian policy unfavorable to Catholic Indians. The Vicariate of Dakota is established.

1880 Marked increase of Catholic immigration from Germany, Italy and the various Slavic countries.—Kansas City, Davenport, Grand Rapids, and Trenton become episcopal cities. Chicago is raised to the rank of an Archbishopric.

1882 The Knights of Columbus, a fraternal benefit society for Catholic men, founded at New Haven, Conn.

1883 Dignity of a Pontifical Institution conferred on the North American College at Rome.

1884 Third Plenary Council of Baltimore meets in compliance with a call from Leo XIII. Archbishop James Gibbons presides as Papal Legate. —Helena, Mont. and Manchester, N. H., become bishoprics.—There are in this year in the country 12 ecclesiastical provinces, 54 bishoprics, 7 vicariates, 1 prefecture, 7,043 priests, 6,626 churches, 907 chapels, 1,895 stations, 9 Benedictine abbeys, 2 Trappist abbeys. The number of Religious Orders of men is about 30, that of women, nearly 50.

1889 The Catholic University is opened at Washington, D. C. Mother Catherine Drexel founds the Sisters of the Blessed Sacrament at Philadelphia for missionary labor among the Negroes and Indians of the United States.

1889 The Leo House is founded for German emigrants to supplement the work of the Society of St. Raphael (established in Germany in 1871, and in New York in 1883) which ministers to the spiritual and temporal needs of German Catholic emigrants.

1892 St. Joseph's Society for Negro Missions (Josephite Fathers) is established at Baltimore.

1893 The Apostolic Delegation established at Washington, with Msgr. Satolli as first Apostolic Delegate.

1894 The anti-Catholic activity of the American Protective Association (A.P.A.) reaches its height.

1899 In a Letter to Cardinal Gibbons Pope Leo XIII condemns the tendencies at variance with Catholic doctrine and practice known as "Americanism."

1901 American Federation of Catholic Societies organized in Cincinnati.

1902 The Apostolic Mission House, a Catholic Missionary Union, affiliated with the Catholic University, under the management of the Paulists is founded. Its object is to prepare priests for giving missions to Catholics and non-Catholics in city and rural parishes.

1904 The Catholic Educational Association is organized at St. Louis to advance the general interests of Catholic education.

1905 Catholic Church Extension Society founded in Chicago by Father (now Bishop) Kelley to develop missionary spirit among Catholics and to build and support churches in poor localities. Its organ is *Extension Magazine*.
Work is begun on the *Catholic Encyclopedia*, the standard Catholic reference work in English; it was completed in 1914.

1907 Modernism, which never gained much ground in this country, condemned by Pius X.
Pius X sends a Ruthenian Bishop, Stephen Ortynsky, to take charge of the Ruthenian Catholics in the United States.
A Catholic Board is organized at Washington to promote the spiritual and temporal welfare of the Catholic Negroes, of whom there are about 150,000 in the United States.

1908 The Central Verein establishes the Central Bureau in St. Louis, as the headquarters of its religious and sociological activity, and begins the publication of the sociological monthly, the *Centralblatt and Social Justice*, in German and English.

1909 The National Headquarters of the Holy Name Society, with which nearly two million men are affiliated, established in New York City.

1909 *America*, a national Catholic weekly review, is founded by the Jesuits.

1910 The diocese of Toledo is established. The Metropolitan of Cincinnati now has more suffragan bishops than any other archbishop in the United States, ten in all; Baltimore, New York and St. Paul have eight each.

1911 The Catholic Foreign Mission Society of America (Maryknoll) is founded with the sanction of Pius X by Fr. Thomas Price and Fr. James Walsh.

1912 *Our Sunday Visitor*, a Catholic weekly, is founded by Fr. (now Bishop) John F. Noll, at Huntington, Ind.
The American Center of the Society for the Propagation of the Faith leads all others in contributions to the Foreign Missions.

1916 Alaska is made a Vicariate. Its 10,000 Catholics are in charge of 20 Jesuits, 3 secular priests, and 49 nuns.

1916 The present mode of nominating bishops to the vacant sees is regulated by a Decree of the Congregation of the Consistory. The bishops of the various ecclesiastical provinces are requested to send in to their metropolitan the names of a few priests whom they deem worthy of the episcopal office. Each year after Easter, the bishops and the metropolitan meet and discuss the merits of those whose names have been proposed. The result of the discussion is forwarded to the Apostolic Delegate, who in turn forwards the list to the Congregation of the Consistory. This carefully selected list serves as a guide to the Holy Father in the selection of our future bishops.

1917 National Catholic War Council organized to promote the moral and spiritual welfare of Catholic soldiers during the World War.

1918 The Catholic Students' Mission Crusade is organized at St. Mary's Mission House, Techny, Ill., to enlist and maintain the participation of the youth of the country in the cause of the Catholic missions.

1919 The Hierarchy of the United States issue a joint Pastoral Letter on the Religious Situation after the War. The National Catholic Welfare Conference is inaugurated.
The Chinese Mission Society of St. Columban (founded in Ireland in 1916) is established at St. Columban's, Nebraska.

1924 *The Commonweal*, a Catholic weekly, is founded by a body of laymen known as the Calvert Associates.

1926 The Twenty-eighth International Eucharistic Congress at Chicago surpasses all its predecessors as a public demonstration of faith.
San Antonio, Texas, becomes an Archdiocese.

1926 The Bishops of the United States issue an important Pastoral Letter on the religious situation in Mexico (Dec. 12).—The American Catholic Philosophical Association is founded at the Catholic University.

1927 The Catholics of Mexico are subjected to a barbarous persecution. The American Hierarchy solemnly protest and generously aid the the victims: bishops, priests, and nuns.

1928 The Laymen's Retreat Movement of the United States, a national association of the Lay Retreat Leagues of the country, is organized in Philadelphia.

1929 Mainly through the efforts of Archbishop Fumasoni-Biondi, the Apostolic Delegate to the United States, and Dwight Morrow, the U. S. Ambassador to Mexico, the persecution in Mexico is ended.

1930 Pope Pius XI, on June 29, canonizes the Jesuit Martyrs of North America.

1930 Sept. 23-25, Sixth National Eucharistic Congress of the United States held at Omaha, Nebr. Delegates and visitors from every State in the Union were present. Twenty-five thousand men, women, and children took part in the closing ceremonies, at which His Excellency the Apostolic Delegate Msgr. Fumasoni-Biondi presided. These Congresses have grown steadily since the first was held at Washington, D. C., in 1895.

Oct. 18, the statue of the famous Franciscan missionary explorer Fr. Hennepin was unveiled in Minneapolis, Minn. The statue stands on the city's main arterial highway, Hennepin Ave.

Nov. 14, the Sacred Congregation of Rites examined the cult of the Venerable Felix de Andreis, first Superior of the Lazarists in the United States (d. 1820). The process of his canonization was begun in Aug., 1902.

1931 *The Catholic Telegraph,* the oldest Catholic weekly in the United States celebrates its hundredth anniversary. The State of California erects the statue of Fr. Junipero Serra in Statuary Hall in the United States Capitol at Washington.

March. His Eminence Patrick Cardinal Hayes, Archbishop of New York, attends the brilliant functions held at San Antonio, Texas, to mark the bi-centennial of the founding of that city and the Franciscan Missions of Concepcion, San Juan Capistrano and San Francisco. He also addresses the State Senate at Austin.

The International Federation of Catholic Alumnae organizes a nation-wide movement for the canonization of *Mother Elizabeth Seton.*

March 26. Brother Joseph Dutton, who had devoted more than half of the 88 years of his life to the victims of leprosy in the Leper Colony of Molokai Island, died at Honolulu. Born in Vermont in 1843, Ira Barnes Dutton joined the Union Army in 1861, served throughout the war and rose to the rank of first lieutenant. He was received into the Church at Memphis, Tenn., in 1883. Reading of the heroic work of Father Damien, the Leper Apostle of Molokai, he decided to join him and entered the Order of the Sacred Hearts of Jesus and Mary as a lay Brother. On the death of Father Damien, April 15, 1888, Brother Dutton carried on his work. He never contracted the dread disease, although he lived forty-four years in daily contact with its victims. Speaking, some time before his death, of his approaching ninetieth birthday, he said that the graph of his life represented "forty-five years down, and forty-five years up."

April 29. The Holy See established the Diocese of Reno, comprising the whole state of Nevada. The Rev. Thomas K. Gorman was named the first Bishop. Every State of the Union now has at least one diocese within its limits.

June 10. The memory of the heroic Jesuit missionary, *Claude Allouez,* who labored in the Northwest from 1665 till his death in 1689, was signally honored by the citizens of Green Bay, Wisc. A statue entitled "The Spirit of the Northwest" was dedicated to the memory of the pioneers of the State. It comprises three figures: an Indian, standing

1931 for the aborigines of the Northwest, Nicolas Perrot, symbolizing its earliest industrial efforts, and Father Claude Allouez, representing the labors of the missionaries.—August. The seat of the Diocese of Lead, S.D., is transferred to Rapid City, S.D.—Dec. 8. The fifteenth centenary of the *Council of Ephesus* is celebrated with fitting ceremonies throughout the U. S.—The *Liturgical Arts Society* founded in New York for the betterment of Catholic Art and Architecture. Publication of the organ of the Society, *Liturgical Arts*, begun.—The nine thousand and more *Sisters of Mercy* in the United States celebrate the centenary of the founding of their institute by the saintly Mother *Catherine McAuley,* in Dublin, Dec. 12, 1831.

1932 Feb. 7. Cardinal Hayes of New York officiates at the installation of the Rt. Rev. Bernard Kevenhoerster, O.S.B., as first Prefect Apostolic of the Bahama Islands. Heretofore the islands had been a spiritual dependency of New York.

March 9. Bishop Thomas J. Shahan died at Washington, D. C. He was associated for forty years with the Catholic University as professor and as Rector. For almost half a century he was a leader in every progressive movement in Catholic education from the elementary school to the University.

March 29. The Knights of Columbus celebrate the 50th anniversary of the order.

August 14. Statue of Cardinal Gibbons unveiled in Washington, D. C.

1933 The cause of the beatification of the *Venerable Antonio Margil de Jesus, O.S.F.,* actively promoted by Francisco Orozco y Jimenez, Archbishop of Guadalajara, Mexico, an exile from his native land. Antonio Margil, born in Valencia, Spain, 1657, spent nearly half a century in the Indian missions of Central and North America, including about five years in Texas. He baptized no less than 80,000 aborigines. Three noted colleges in Mexico owe their origin to him. He came to East Texas in 1716. In 1720 he founded San José. He died in 1726.

April 2. Under the auspices of Cardinal Hayes, leaders of "all faiths" joined in a public celebration to inaugurate the opening of the Holy Year in Rome. The celebration was held in Radio City Music Hall. It was designated as "both a patriotic and a religious act of consecration to God and nation."

The Catholic school system, in the school year 1932-33, comprises 10,578 institutions, staffed by 90,000 teachers and attended by 2,680,000 students; about 2.268,000 pupils in 7,920 elementary schools, 266,000 students in 2,254 high schools, 10,000 in 47 normal schools, 116,000 in 169 colleges and universities, and 20,000 in 188 major and minor seminaries.

The total circulation of the Catholic press put at 7,308,456 by the new Directory of the Catholic Press.

Dec. 22. At Chicago, closing of the formal inquiry into the heroic virtues and authentic miracles attributed to the intercession of *Mother Francis Xavier Cabrini,* Foundress of the Missionary Sisters of the Sacred Heart, who died at Columbus Hospital, Chicago, Dec. 22, 1917. Mother Cabrini's remains were transferred, Oct., 1933, to the Chapel of Cabrini High School, Ft. Washington Ave., New York.

The *National Conference of Catholic Charities* meets in New York to commemorate the centenary of the founding of the St. Vincent de Paul Society. President Roosevelt addresses the meeting. During 1933 the St. Vincent de Paul Society collects and spends $6,000,000 in relief, finds 13,000 jobs for the unemployed, validates 3,000 marriages, reclaims 7,000 lapsed Catholics, and assists 144,000 needy families.

The *Study Club* movement spreads far and wide. Thousands of new clubs are organized—400 in the Diocese of Great Falls alone. Favorite subjects of study are the Sacrifice of the Mass and the Papal Social Encyclicals.

The *Catholic Evidence Guilds* extend their activities. Laymen and laywomen, trained in the art of public speaking and in Catholic doctrine and apologetics, organize seven guilds in eastern, mid-western and southwestern states. Their audiences are, for the most part, composed of non-Catholics. They lecture in the city parks and other public places with gratifying results.

1934   May 5. The old Vincennes, Indiana, Cathedral, restored by a general committee of citizens, was the scene of the centennial celebrations commemorating the founding of the diocese of Vincennes, the seat of which was later transferred to Indianapolis.

May 30. A solemn pontifical military field Mass in the Baltimore Stadium marked the tercentennial celebration of the founding of Maryland by the Calverts. More than 75,000 persons were present. Seven thousand children sang the Mass. In a message to Archbishop Curley President Roosevelt referred to "the great fight that Lord Baltimore made three centuries ago for religious freedom in America." The tabernacle used is said to be the one used by Father Andrew White, S.J., when he said the first Mass in Maryland, March 25, 1634.

August 12-15. Commemorating the 19th centenary of the Redemption and the 7th centenary of the founding of the Order of Servants of Mary, a national Marian Congress—the first in the United States—was held at Portland, Oregon. Cardinal Lepicier, a distinguished member of the Servites, presided as Papal Legate.

1935   September 23-26. Seventh National Eucharistic Congress is held in Cleveland, Ohio; 150,000 present at the closing services in the great Municipal Stadium; Pope Pius XI addresses the worshippers by radio.

Oct. 27. The Catholic Students' Mission Crusade and their friends of the Diocese of Richmond erect a memorial to the eight Spanish Jesuits, priests, Brothers and Scholastics, who suffered martyrdom at the hands of the Indians near Aquia, Va., February 4-9, 1571.

1936   April 14. Bishop James A. Walsh, Superior General and co-founder with Father Thomas F. Price of the Maryknoll Foreign Mission Society, dies. Bishop Walsh was "the greatest missionary that America has given to the Church" *Archbishop John T. McNicholas*

1936   September 22. Constitution of a new Ecclesiastical Province of Los Angeles and the erection of the Diocese of San Diego. The new Province includes, besides the Archdiocese of Los Angeles, the Dioceses of Monterey-Fresno, Tucson and San Diego as suffragan sees. Most Rev. John J. Cantwell named Archbishop of Los Angeles. The Diocese of San Diego is made up of San Diego, Imperial Riverside and San Bernardino counties in California.

October. Cardinal Pacelli, Papal Secretary of State visits the United States. Addresses student bodies at eight Catholic colleges and universities.

1937   February 3-7. Thirty-third International Eucharistic Congress meets at Manila, Philipine Islands. Dennis Cardinal Dougherty, Archbishop of Philadelphia, presided as Papal Legate.

1937   The number of ecclesiastical provinces was increased to nineteen in 1937 through the creation of the archdioceses of Detroit, Newark and Louisville. The number of dioceses was raised to ninety-three, including the Ukrainian Greek Catholic diocese and the diocese of Pittsburgh (Greek Rite), besides the two vicariates apostolic of Alaska and Hawaii. Four new sees were erected in 1937—Lansing, in Michigan; Paterson and Camden in New Jersey and Owensboro in Kentucky.

The number of dioceses was raised to ninety-three, including the Ukrainian Greek Catholic diocese and the diocese of Pittsburgh (Greek Rite), besides the two vicariates apostolic of Alaska and Hawaii.

Catholics throughout the United States joined wholeheartedly in the observance of the 150th anniversary of the signing of the Constitution of the United States. Cardinals, Archbishops, Bishops, priests and the laity took part in the various observances, and Catholic colleges, schools, lay organizations and institutions of various kinds conducted programs.

The Third National Catechetical Congress, held at St. Louis, which the Most Rev. John J. Glennon, Archbishop of St. Louis, described as being "like unto a great university," was enormously successful.

The Catholic population of the United States, including Alaska and the Hawaiian Islands, is placed at 21,406,507 in the Official Catholic Directory. The total number of priests is given as 33,540, and the number of churches as 18,757, an increase of 139.

Some 360 aspirants for the priesthood came from Mexico in September to enter the Montezuma Seminary, established by the hierarchy of the United States near Las Vegas, New Mexico.

1938   The diocese of Saginaw, Mich., is created, bringing the total of Sees in Continental United States up to 112.

Sept. 3. Patrick Cardinal Hayes, Archbishop of New York, dies. He is universally extolled as a "valiant leader and truly great patriot."

Oct. 12. Beginning of the Golden Jubilee of the Catholic University of America. At the request of the Holy Father steps are taken to establish special schools of Civics, Sociology and Economics at the University as a bulwark against anti-Christian teachings in these important branches.

Oct. 18. The 8th National Eucharistic Congress opened in New Orleans, La., under the auspices of Archbishop Rummal. Cardinal Mundelein, Archbishop of Chicago, was the Apostolic Delegate. President Roosevelt sent a letter of greeting in which he said "I trust that the deliberations of the Congress will quicken the spiritual life of all who participate and inspire them with new zeal for the work of the Master whom we all serve." The Holy Father broadcast a message and his blessing.

Nov. 13. Beatification of Mother Francis Xavier Cabrini marks the first time an American citizen has been so honored by the Church. Cardinal Mundelein officiated at the ceremonies in St. Peter's at Rome. The Apostolic Delegate Archbishop Cicognani celebrated Mass at the new Beata's tomb in the Chapel of Mother Cabrini High School, New York.

The number of radio stations carrying the "Catholic Hour" conducted by the National Conference of Catholic Men increased to seventy-five.

1939   Feb. 10. The death of our Holy Father, Pope Pius XI occurred. He had reigned since Feb. 6, 1922. The tributes to the deceased pontiff were worldwide. Untold Masses and prayers were offered on our Altars and in our Churches. The Congress of the United States adjourned and State Legislatures passed resolutions of regret. Flags were at half-mast on many public buildings.

1939 April 15. His Excellency, the Most Rev. Francis J. Spellman, D.D., Auxiliary Bishop of Boston is appointed Archbishop of New York. The diocese of Belleville celebrates the golden jubilee of its establishment.

Dedication of a monument to Fra Marcos de Nica in Arizona, Franciscan missionary and explorer 1539.

The 20th anniversary of the issuance of the "Bishops' Social Reconstruction" was notable for the fact that of eleven proposals all except one are now the law of the Land.

The Catholic World, a magazine established by Father Isaac Hecker, founder of the Paulists celebrates its 75th anniversary.

May 29. The Sesquicentennial of the founding in 1789 of Georgetown College is commemorated.

May 31. The first time a Solemn Mass was ever celebrated in the Amphitheater of Arlington National Cemetery.

Little Sisters of the Poor celebrate the centenary of their foundation.

June 29. In recognition of his outstanding merits and on the eve of his sacerdotal golden jubilee, His Excellency, the Most Rev. Joseph Schrembs, D.D., Bishop of Cleveland, was elevated to the rank of Archbishop.

At the centennial observance of the death of Bishop Bruté, the first Bishop of the diocese of Vincennes, which later became the diocese of Indianapolis, the present Bishop, the Most Rev. Joseph E. Ritter, D.D., said in his sermon that Bishop Simon Gabriel Bruté de Remur deserved a place among the founders of the Church in the United States.

August. A monument erected to the memory of Bishop Marty, the first Bishop of Sioux Falls, S. Dak., who as a missionary among the Indians risked his life during an Indian rising in 1877 to persuade the Sioux tribe to return to their reservation.

A monument to St. Isaac Jogues is dedicated on the shores of Lake George by the State of New York.

September. A cross is erected near Cape Vincent, N. Y., on the eastern shore of Lake Ontario to the memory of Father Charles Dablon, a Jesuit missionary among the Iroquois, who journeyed there in 1655.

The diocese of Fargo, N. D., celebrates the golden jubilee year.

The hundredth anniversary of the saving of the first Mass in Montana is commemorated by the diocese of Helena.

October 2. The death of George Cardinal Mundelein, Archbishop of Chicago and notable for his achievements and wide influence occurs. Washington, D. C., is created an Archdiocese of equal rank with Baltimore under the jurisdiction of the Archbishop of Baltimore.

November. The observance of the 150th anniversary of the establishment of the Hierarchy in the United States took place in the National Shrine of the Immaculate Conception, Washington, D. C., in the presence of Cardinal Dougherty and 72 Archbishops and Bishops.

December 23. President Roosevelt announced that he would send Mr. Myron C. Taylor, retired chairman of the United States Steel Corporation as his personal representative to Pope Pius XII. Mr. Taylor has the standing, but not the title of an ambassador.

December 23. The new diocese of Gallup, New Mexico is established.

1940 January 3. The Most Rev. Samuel A. Stritch, D.D., Archbishop of Milwaukee, is appointed Archbishop of Chicago.

January 4. The Most Rev. Moses E. Kiley, D.D., Bishop of Trenton, N. J., is appointed Archbishop of Milwaukee.

February. The Right Rev. Msgr. Joseph M. Corrigan, S.T.D., LL.D.,

1940 Litt.D., Rector of the Catholic University, Washington, D. C., is elevated to the Episcopacy.

The action of the German Government in seizing Austria and Czecho-Slovakia, followed by the invasion soon after of Poland, by the German armies provoked a declaration of war against Germany and Italy by Great Britain and France in the Fall of 1939. The second World War had begun. Persecution of the Church by the Nazi Government was extended to the occupied countries, increasing the difficulties of the Catholic Bishops and people.

Regular radio broadcasts from the Vatican to the Americas were initiated.

Pope Pius XII in a letter to President Roosevelt praises the President's action in sending Myron C. Taylor as his personal representative to the Vatican to collaborate with officials there to restore world peace.

Very Rev. John F. O'Hara, C.S.C., consecrated Titular Bishop of Mylassa and Auxiliary Bishop of the Military Diocese.

The Most Rev. Joseph M. Corrigan, Rector of the Catholic University, consecrated Titular Bishop of Bilta.

The Catholic World, widely known monthly published by the Paulist Fathers celebrates 75th year of publication.

Canonization of St. Euphrasia Pelletier, foundress of the Sisters of the Good Shepherd; canonization of St. Gemma Galgani, Passionist Tertiary.

April. The New York State Legislature passed a bill permitting public-school children to be excused from classes at certain times for religious training.

May 12. Bl. Philippine Rose Duchesne, foundress of the Religious of the Sacred Heart in the United States, was solemnly beatified in St. Peter's Basilica.

A vice-postulator was appointed for the cause for beatification of the Ven. Bishop Neumann, C.SS.R., of Philadelphia.

May 28. Public honor and recognition was paid to Dennis Cardinal Dougherty, Archbishop of Philadelphia on the occasion of the Golden Jubilee of his Ordination to the Priesthood.

May. The Catholic Directory for 1940 shows the Catholic population of the United States, Alaska and the Hawaiian Islands to be 21,403,136. During 1939 there were 73,677 converts, the largest number ever recorded.

June. Celebration of the 150th anniversary of the establishment of the Catholic Hierarchy in the United States is commemorated in the Cathedral of the Archdiocese of Baltimore.

In Cincinnati a group of secular priests inaugurates campaign of street preaching on Friday nights during the summer.

July. The Most Rev. William A. Griffin, D.D., formerly Auxiliary Bishop of Newark is installed as Bishop of Trenton. The Most Rev. Thomas A. Boland, D.D., consecrated Auxiliary Bishop of Newark.

The Most Rev. Bernard T. Espelage O.F.M., D.D., named first Bishop of the newly created diocese of Gallup.

The Bishops' Committee on Youth takes steps to co-ordinate Catholic Youth activities in the United States.

Sisters of St. Francis of the Immaculate Conception celebrate their diamond jubilee.

September. Jesuits throughout the United States celebrated the 400th anniversary of the approbation of the Society of Jesus by Pope Paul II. The 375th anniversary of the founding of St. Augustine, Fla., is celebrated in the Cathedral of that city.

1940 The Most Rev. Joseph P. Hurley, D.D., consecrated Bishop of St Augustine, Fla.

October. The first National Liturgical Congress is held in Chicago. The Sisters of Providence of St. Marys of the Woods, Indiana, celebrate the centenary of their foundation in the United States.

The people of Michigan dedicated a statue to the memory of Fr. Gabriel Richard, founder of the first newspaper in Michigan, and the only priest ever to serve in the Congress of the United States.

Monument to our Lord Jesus Christ, King, placed atop Mount Christo Rey of the El Paso Range.

1941 January. The Most Rev. J. Francis A. McIntyre, D.D., is consecrated Auxiliary Bishop of New York.

The Most Rev. Robert E. Lucey, D.D., Bishop of Amarillo is named Archbishop of San Antonio.

March. The Most Rev. Joseph C. Plagens is installed as fifth Bishop of Grand Rapids.

The Most Rev. Francis J. Magner is consecrated Bishop of Marquette.

The Most Rev. Joseph T. McGucken, D.D., is consecrated Auxiliary Bishop of Los Angeles.

April. The revised text of the Baltimore Catechism is approved by the Pontifical Commission and by the Sacred Congregation of the Council.

The Bishops of the Administrative Board of the National Catholic Welfare Conference, Washington, D. C., issue a statement emphasizing Pope Pius XII's five points for a just peace.

The Committee under the Chairmanship of Bishop Gannon of Erie, working toward the canonization of early American Martyrs sends to the Cardinal Prefect an abstract dealing with the life of each martyr.

The Sulpician Fathers, Baltimore, celebrate the 150th anniversary of their arrival in that city.

Archbishop Lucey of San Antonio addresses the joint session of the Senate and the House of Representatives of Texas, on the subject of "Religion and Government."

May. Monsignor William R. Arnold, Chief of the Chaplains of the United States Army, breaks ground at Arlington Cantonment, near Washington, D. C., for the first of 555 chapels for the Nation's Army Camps.

The 50th anniversary of the issuance by Pope Leo XIII of his encyclical "Rerum Novarum" and the 10th of Pope Pius XI encyclical "Quadragesimo Anno" is commemorated throughout the United States.

The completion of the American revision of the Challoner-Rheims New Testament, popularly called the Douay Version, under the supervision of the Confraternity of Christian Doctrine is observed on May 18th as Biblical Sunday.

Monsignor James Joseph Sweeney of the Archdiocese of San Francisco is named first Bishop of Honolulu, a See newly erected in 1941.

June. Fordham University, New York, celebrates the 100th anniversary of its foundation.

The ninth National Eucharistic Congress is held in the Twin Cities of St. Paul and Minneapolis. Archbishop Murray addresses a welcome to Cardinal Dougherty of Philadelphia, who had been named Papal Legate for the occasion.

The first Eucharistic Congress of Eastern Rites is held in Chicago under the Most Rev. Constantine Bohachevsky, Bishop of the Ukranian Greek Rite.

1941   July. The 400th anniversary of the martyrdom of Fra Juan de
       Padilla is commemorated at Lyons, Kansas, with a Solemn Pon-
       tifical Mass.
       On July 6th began the celebration of the Golden Jubilee of the Cath-
       olic Summer School of America at Cliff Haven, N. Y.
       The cause for the beatification of Mother Elizabeth Seton, foundress
       of the Sisters of Charity in the United States is discussed by the
       Sacred Congregation of Rites.
       The tercentennial of the arrival of the Jesuit Missionary, St. Isaac
       Jogues at Sault Ste Marie is celebrated with a Solemn Pontifical
       Mass in that city.
       August. The cornerstone of the new building of the National Catholic
       Welfare Conference is laid, Aug. 18.
       The official celebration of the centenary of Catholicism in Montana
       began with a Solemn Pontifical Mass, Aug. 24.
       September. Myron C. Taylor, President Roosevelt's envoy to the
       Vatican makes his second official visit to Vatican City and is received
       in audience by Pope Pius XII on September 10.
       October. Cardinal Dougherty lays cornerstone, Oct. 5, of Holy Re-
       deemer Church and School, for exclusive use of Chinese Catholics.
       Diocese of Salt Lake City celebrates its Golden Jubilee, Oct. 12.
       The Most Rev. Laurence J. FitzSimon, consecrated Bishop of Am-
       arillo, Texas.
       Rev. John T. Gillard, S.S.J., in his book "Negroes in the United
       States," estimates the number of colored Catholics at 296,988 for
       this country.
       November. The Administrative Board of the National Catholic Wel-
       fare Conference, Washington, D. C., on Nov. 16 issues statement
       condemning "Nazism and Communism" as subversive forces, both
       in control of powerful governments, both aiming at world dominance
       and neither understanding nor permitting freedom in its true Chris-
       tian sense.
       The Diocese of Denver elevated to a Metropolitan See, the present
       Bishop, The Most Rev. Urban J. Vehr, becoming its first Archbishop.
       The City of Pueblo, Colo., is created a Diocese.
1942   January. Pope Pius XII approves Constitutions of the Congregation
       of Xaverian Brothers.
       President Roosevelt acknowledges pledge of co-operation of the
       Bishops of the United States as giving him "strength and courage."
       February. United States Navy selects Notre Dame University as
       indoctrination center for Naval Reserve Midshipmen.
       Secretary of the Treasury Henry C. Morgenthau names the Most Rev.
       Bernard J. Sheil, Auxiliary Bishop of Chicago, as his consultant.
       The Most Rev. Joseph C. Willging, consecrated first Bishop of the
       newly created Diocese of Pueblo, Colo.
       Dr. James J. Walsh, noted scholar and author dies at age of 76.
       March. Most Rev. William P. O'Connor, consecrated fifth Bishop of
       Superior.
       The fourth annual Conference on Oriental Rites and Liturgies held at
       Fordham University.
       April. Resurrectionist Fathers in Chicago, celebrate their first
       centenary.
       The Bishops' Relief Committee provides $100,000 for Polish Relief,
       the money to be spent for goods to be shipped to Polish refugees
       in Russia. This is later supplemented by a second allotment of
       $130,000.

1942 Missionary Oblates of Mary Immaculate, at Lowell, Mass., accept missions in Haiti at request of Pope Pius XII to take over the spiritual needs of the inhabitants, formerly ministered to by French clergy.

May. Archbishop Spellman delivers baccalaureate address to Catholic members of graduating class at U. S. Military Academy at West Point.

June. Decree of the Sacred Congregation of the Sacraments permits celebration of afternoon and evening Mass for the armed forces of the United States when unable to attend morning Mass.

August. The Most Rev. Aloysius M. Benziger, O.C.D., retired Bishop of Quilon, India, dies at age of 78.

September. The First American made edition of "Missale Romanum" completed and published by Benziger Brothers, New York.

Ralph Adam Cram, internationally distinguished architect dies at age of 78.

October. Golden Jubilee of Dominican Sisters Congregation of the Most Holy Rosary celebrated at Motherhouse, Adrian, Mich.

Canada mobilization regulations exempt priests and seminarians.

November. Vatican radio announces that 86 German Franciscans had died for their country or were reported missing in action; 221 Franciscans had been decorated for their war services by the government.

The Most Rev. Francis J. Monaghan, D.D., Bishop of Ogdensburg, dies at age of 52.

General George C. Marshall, Chief of Staff, reports spiritual guidance of United States Army best in the world.

Sisters of the Holy Family celebrate 100th anniversary in their Motherhouse at New Orleans.

At the 37th annual meeting of the Catholic Church Extension Society in Chicago, attended by more than 20 members of the Hierarchy, announcement is made that Most Rev. William D. O'Brien, Auxiliary Bishop of Chicago has been appointed by the Holy See to serve a fourth term as the Society's President.

1943 January. The Most Rev. Leo Binz, D.D., is installed as Coadjutor Bishop of Winona.

The University of Notre Dame issues a history of the institution on occasion of its centenary.

January 17. The 75th anniversary of the founding of the oldest colored parish in Charleston, N. C., is celebrated by the Most Rev. Emmett Michael Walsh, D.D., Bishop of Charleston.

January 21. The Most Rev. Edward Francis Hoban, D.D., formerly Bishop of Rockford, is installed as Coadjutor Bishop of Cleveland.

The Most Rev. William T. McCarty, C.SS.R., D.D., recently named Military Delegate, is consecrated Titular Bishop of Anea in St. Patrick's Cathedral, New York.

January 27. The Most Rev. Martin J. O'Connor, D.D., is consecrated Titular Bishop of Thespiae and Auxiliary Bishop of Scranton.

February. Pope Pius XII approves the introduction of the cause of beatification of Father Arnold Janssen, founder of the Society of the Divine Word.

February 17. The Most Rev. John J. Boylan, D.D., is consecrated third Bishop of Rockford.

The Most Rev. Thomas E. Molloy, S.T.D., Bishop of Brooklyn, issues a pastoral letter exhorting parents to send their children to Catholic schools to prepare them for life in a democracy.

1943 The principle of religious freedom is upheld by the U. S. Supreme Court, reversing the conviction of "Jehovah's Witnesses" for distributing handbills and literature of this sect contrary to Texan municipal ordinances.

The Bishops War Emergency and Relief Committee of the United States announces that $1,322,493.00 has been distributed to victims of the war during 1942.

The use of public school buses is denied to private and parochial school pupils in the State of Washington by a decision of the State Supreme Court.

The Diocese of Little Rock commemorates its centennial.

Catholic Colleges in the U. S. for the academic year 1943-1944 offer 151 scholarships to Latin-American students.

The Eudist Fathers (The Congregation of Jesus and Mary), so named after their founder, St. John Eudes, begin on March 25 the commemoration of their tercentenary.

April. The New Hampshire House of Representatives kills a bill to permit public school children to take an hour off each week for religious education.

The Most Rev. Joseph Aloysius Burke, D.D., is named Titular Bishop of Vita and Auxiliary Bishop of Buffalo.

May. Pope Pius XII appoints the Rt. Rev. Monsignor Patrick J. McCormick Rector of the Catholic University of America.

President Roosevelt in a letter on the occasion of the observance of "National Family Week" states that no more important task faces the American community today "than that of maintaining the home."

The Sacred Congregation of Rites discusses the miracles proposed in the cause of the canonization of Blessed Frances Cabrini, foundress of the Missionary Sisters of the Sacred Heart.

The 150th anniversary of the founding of the Diocese of New Orleans opens on May 11.

The protest of the German Bishops against Nazi persecution of the Catholic Church in invaded countries is printed in the "Congressional Record."

The Administrative Board of the National Catholic Welfare Conference opposes the Senate bill providing for the appropriation of federal funds to assist in financing systems of public education during emergencies as interfering with local control of education and because Catholic schools are excluded from its benefits.

June. The new Diocese of Youngstown, Ohio, is created by Pope Pius XII, and the Most Rev. James A. McFadden, D.D., Auxiliary Bishop of Cleveland, is named the first Bishop.

The Right Rev. Monsignor Bryan Joseph McEntegart is named Bishop of Ogdensburg.

The Most Rev. Edwin B. Byrne, D.D., Bishop of San Juan, P. R., is elevated to the Archbishopric of Santa Fe.

July. The Most Rev. James P. Davis, D.D., of the Diocese of Bisbee, is named Bishop of San Juan, P. R.

The Most Rev. Johannes Gunnarsson, D.D., is consecrated Titular Bishop of Holar and Vicar Apostolic of Iceland in St. Patrick's Church, Washington, D. C., by the Apostolic Delegate, the Most Rev. Amleto Giovanni Cicognani, D.D. Thus, Iceland receives its first native Bishop in four centuries.

1943   In a broadcast from Portuguese East Africa, where he is on a visitation as Military Vicar, the Most Rev. Francis J. Spellman, D.D., Archbishop of New York, says: "My admiration for the valor and value of my countrymen whom I meet everywhere grows almost daily. . . . These soldiers of the flag and soldiers of the cross are offering their lives for the highest and greatest ideals in human expression."

The Archdiocese of New Orleans observes the 150th anniversary of its founding.

During "Polish Week," in observance of the fourth anniversary of the German invasion of Poland, President Roosevelt repeats his assurance of "justice and liberation" for the Poles, and Archbishop Mooney, of Detroit declares, "In the face of certain martyrdom Poland kept her soul, and to remember Poland surely will help us to keep our soul."

The first number of the official bulletin of the Holy See entitled "Acta Apostolicæ Sedis" is published by the National Catholic Welfare Conference, to whom this privilege has been accorded for the duration of the war.

The Most Rev. Francis J. Haas, D.D., is named Bishop of Grand Rapids.

The Society of St. Joseph of the Sacred Heart, consisting of priests who minister to the colored people, celebrates its Golden Jubilee on October 10 in Baltimore.

The Diocese of Pittsburgh on October 25 celebrates its centennial with a solemn Pontifical Mass by the Most Rev. Hugh C. Boyle, D.D.

November. At the annual general meeting of the Archbishops and Bishops of the United States a statement is issued calling for a just and good peace and warning that there must be social reconstruction in our own country.

The observance of the 100th anniversary of the founding of the Archdiocese of Chicago is marked by the celebration of a solemn Pontifical Mass by the Most Rev. Samuel A. Stritch, D.D., Archbishop of Chicago.

The new official English translation of "The Raccolta," the book which contains the complete collection of indulgenced prayers and pious acts, is published for the first time in the United States. The publishers, Benziger Brothers, Inc., New York, receive special authorization from the Holy See for its issuance.

At the annual meeting of the Archbishops and Bishops of the United States, November 10-13, a statement is issued insisting that the coming peace must avoid every compromise with evil and that lasting world peace requires a recognition of the sovereignty of God and of the moral law.

The Archdiocese of Milwaukee celebrates its centennial.

1944   April. His Eminence William Cardinal O'Connell, Archbishop of Boston, dies on April 22, at the age of 84.

May. Report shows that at present 4,200 priests are serving as Chaplains in the U. S. Army and Navy.

June. Our Holy Father, Pope Pius XII, expresses his appreciation to the Hierarchy and the laity of the United States in answer to their message of hope for the safety of Rome against invasion.

Later when Rome is liberated by American troops, they are received by Pope Pius XII.

1944 July. The Most Rev. Henry P. Rohlman, D.D., presently Bishop of
Davenport, is appointed Coadjutor Bishop of Dubuque.
September. The Most Rev. Richard J. Cushing, D.D., LL.D., Auxil-
iary Bishop of Boston, is named Archbishop of that Archdiocese by
Pope Pius XII.
October. The entire nation mourns the death of Alfred E. Smith,
fervent Catholic, able statesman, loyal and faithful citizen.
November. Pope Pius XII elevates the Most Rev. Joseph E. Ritter,
D.D., to the Archiepiscopacy, creating Indianapolis an Archdiocese.
The Holy Father also names five new Bishops: the Most Rev. Michael
J. Ready, D.D., formerly General Secretary of the National Catholic
Welfare Conference, Bishop of Columbus; the Most Rev. John
G. Bennett, D.D., Bishop of the newly created Diocese of Lafayette
(Ind.); the Most Rev. Henry J. Grimmelsman, D.D., Bishop of the
newly created diocese of Evansville (Ind.); the Most Rev. William T.
Mulloy, D.D., Bishop of Covington; and the Most Rev. Edward F.
Ryan, D.D., Bishop of Burlington. The Holy Father appoints the
Most Rev. Eugene J. McGuiness, D.D., Bishop of Raleigh, to be
Coadjutor Bishop of Oklahoma City and Tulsa, and the Most Rev.
Stanislaus V. Bona, D.D., Bishop of Grand Island to be Coadjutor
Bishop of Green Bay.
In his Christmas message the Holy Father deals with underlying
realities and basic principles on which only a constructive world order
can be established. Secular newspapers throughout the United States
extol it as one of the great documents of our time.

LIST OF SUPREME PONTIFFS

According to the "Annuario Pontificio" 1939

The chronological list of popes given herewith corresponds to that printed in the latest (1939) edition of the *Annuario Pontificio*, an official publication of the Holy See. This "official" list in turn, as stated in the same *Annuario*, is taken from the catalog of popes depicted during the V century, or at the time of Pope St. Leo, the Great (440-461), on the south side of the original and ancient Basilica of St. Paul's beyond the Walls of Rome. Pope Benedict XIV (1740-58) ordered the remaining popes down to this time to be added. Pope Pius VIII in 1829 had the list further revised to include the popes up to his pontificate (1829-30). When at the beginning of the XIX century the venerable old basilica was totally destroyed through the ravages of a fire, the present sublime edifice was constructed and eventually consecrated in 1854 by the then reigning Pope Pius IX (1846-78). In the course of construction, i.e., during the second quarter of the XIX century, the original portraits of the popes were redone in mosaics and now adorn the frieze in the transept and on both sides of the Pauline basilica. The list has thus the direct approval of Popes Benedict XIV and Pius IX, and all succeeding popes down to our day who have permitted their portraits to be added.

1. St. Peter, native of Bethsaida in Galilee, Prince of the Apostles, who received from Our Lord and Saviour Jesus Christ the Supreme Pontificate, to be transmitted to his successors; and, having resided for a time at Antioch, established his See at Rome, where he suffered martyrdom on the 29th of June, 67.

		Elected	Died
2.	St. Linus, Volterra, M..	67	78
3.	St. Cletus, Roman, M...	78	90
4.	St. Clement I, Roman, M.	90	100
5.	St. Anacletus, Athens, M.	100	112
6.	St. Evaristus, Bethlehem, M.	112	121
7.	St. Alexander I, Roman, M.	121	132
8.	St. Sixtus I, Roman, M.	132	142
9.	St. Telesphorus, Greece, M.	142	154
10.	St. Hyginus, Greek, M..	154	158
11.	St. Pius I, Aquileia, M..	158	167
12.	St. Anicetus, Syria, M..	?	175
13.	St. Soter, Campania, M.	?	182
14.	St. Eleutherius, Epirus, M.	?	193
15.	St. Victor I, African, M.	193	203
16.	St. Zephyrinus, Roman, M.	203	221
17.	St. Calixtus I, Roman, M.	221	227
18.	St. Urban I, Roman, M.	227	233
19.	St. Pontian, Roman, M..	233	238
20.	St. Anterus, Greece, M..	238	239
21.	St. Fabian, Roman, M..	239	253
22.	St. Cornelius, Roman, M..	253	255
23.	St. Lucius I, Roman, M.	255	257
24.	St. Stephen I, Roman M.	257	260
25.	St. Sixtus II, Greek, M.	260	261
26.	St. Dionysius, Greek....	261	272
27.	St. Felix I, Roman, M..	272	275
28.	St. Eutychian, Luni, M..	275	283
29.	St. Caius, Dalmatia, M..	283	296
30.	St. Marcellinus, Roman, M.	296	304
31.	St. Marcellus I, Roman, M.	304	309
32.	St. Eusebius, Greek.....	309	311
33.	St. Melchiades, African.	311	313
34.	St. Sylvester I, Roman..	314	337

		Elected	Died
35.	St. Marcus, Roman.....	337	340
36.	St. Julius I, Roman.....	341	352
37.	St. Liberius, Roman....	352	366
38.	St. Felix II, Roman....	363	365
39.	St. Damasus I, Spaniard	367	384
40.	St. Siricius, Roman.....	384	398
41.	St. Anastasius I, Roman	399	402
42.	St. Innocent I, Albano..	402	417
43.	St. Zozimus, Greek.....	417	418
44.	St. Boniface I, Roman..	418	423
45.	St. Celestine I, Roman..	423	432
46.	St. Sixtus III, Roman..	432	440
47.	St. Leo I (*the Great*), Tuscany	440	461
48.	St. Hilary, Cagliari.....	461	468
49.	St. Simplicius, Tivoli...	468	483
50.	St. Felix III, Roman...	483	492
51.	St. Gelasius I, African..	492	496
52.	St. Anastasius II, Roman	496	498
53.	St. Symmachus, Sardinian	498	514
54.	St. Hormisdas, Frosinone	514	523
55.	St. John I, Tuscan, M..	533	526
56.	St. Felix IV, Sannio....	526	530
57.	Boniface II, Roman.....	530	532
58.	John II, Roman........	532	535
59.	St. Agapitus, Roman....	535	536
60.	St. Silverius, Campania, M.	536	538
61.	Vigilius, Roman	538	555
62.	Pelagius I, Roman......	555	560
63.	John III, Roman........	560	573
64.	Benedict I, Roman.....	574	578
65.	Pelagius II, Roman.....	578	590
66.	St. Gregory I (*the Great*) Roman	590	604
67.	Sabinianus, Bieda	604	606
68.	Boniface III, Roman...	607	607
69.	St. Boniface IV, Marsi..	608	615
70.	St. Adeodatus I (Deusdedit), Roman	615	619
71.	Boniface V, Naples.....	619	625
72.	Honorius I, Campania..	625	638
73.	Severinus, Roman	640	640
74.	John IV, Dalmatia.....	640	642
75.	Theodorus I, Greek.....	642	649
76.	St. Martin I, Todi, M...	649	655
77.	St. Eugenius I, Roman..	655	657
78.	St. Vitalian, Segni......	657	672
79.	Adeodatus II, Roman...	672	676
80.	Donus I, Roman........	676	678

	Elected	Died
81. St. Agatho, Palermo....	678	682
82. St. Leo II, Sicilian.....	682	683
83. St. Benedict II, Roman.	684	685
84. John V, Antiochian.....	685	686
85. Conon, Thracia	686	687
86. St. Sergius I, Palermo..	687	701
87. John VI, Greek........	701	705
88. John VII, Rossano......	705	707
89. Sisinnius, Syrian	708	708
90. Constantine, Syrian	708	715
91. St. Gregory II, Roman..	715	731
92. St. Gregory III, Syrian.	731	741
93. St. Zacharias, Greek....	741	752
94. Stephen II, Roman.....	752	752
95. Stephen III, Roman.....	752	757
96. St. Paul I, Roman......	757	767
97. Stephen IV, Sicilian....	768	771
98. Hadrian I (Adrian), Roman	771	795
99. St. Leo III, Roman.....	795	816
100. Stephen V, Roman......	816	817
101. St. Paschal I, Roman....	817	824
102. Eugenius II, Roman....	824	827
103. Valentine, Roman	827	827
104. Gregory IV, Roman.....	827	844
105. Sergius II, Roman.....	844	847
106. St. Leo IV, Roman.....	847	855
107. Benedict III, Roman....	855	858
108. St. Nicholas I (the Great), Roman	858	867
109. Hadrian II (Adrian), Roman	867	872
110. John VIII, Roman......	872	882
111. Marinus I (Martin II), Gallese	882	884
112. Hadrian III (Adrian), Roman	884	885
113. Stephen VI, Roman.....	885	891
114. Formosus, Ostia	891	896
115. Stephen VII, Roman...	896	897
116. Romanus, Gallese	897	898
117. Theodorus II, Roman...	898	898
118. John IX, Tivoli........	898	900
119. Benedict IV, Roman....	900	903
120. Leo V, Ardea..........	903	903
121. Christopher. Roman	903	904
122. Sergius III, Roman.....	904	911
123. Anastasius III, Roman..	911	913
124. Landone or Landus, Sabinian	913	914
125. John X, Ravenna.......	915	928
126. Leo VI, Roman........	928	929
127. Stephen VIII, Roman...	929	931
128. John XI, Roman.......	931	936
129. Leo VII, Roman........	936	939
130. Stephen IX, German...	939	942
131. Marinus II (Martin III), Roman	942	946
132. Agapitus II, Roman.....	946	956
133. John XII. Roman.......	956	964
134. Benedict V, Roman.....	964	965
135. John XIII, Roman......	965	972
136. Benedict VI, Roman....	972	973
137. Donus II, Roman......	973	973
138. Benedict VII, Roman...	975	984
139. John XIV, Pavia.......	984	985
140. John XV, Roman......	985	996
141. Gregory V, Saxon......	996	999
142. Sylvester II, French....	999	1003
143. John XVI (or XVII), Roman	1003	1003
144. John XVII (or XVIII), Roman	1003	1009
145. Sergius IV, Roman.....	1009	1012
146. Benedict VIII, Roman..	1012	1024
147. John XVIII (or XIX or XX), Roman	1024	1033

	Elected	Died
148. Benedict IX, Roman....	1033	*1044
149. Gregory VI, Roman.....	1044	*1046
150. Clement II, Saxon......	1046	1047
151. Damasus II, German...	1048	1048
152. St. Leo IX, German....	1049	1054
153. Victor II, Bavarian.....	1055	1057
154. Stephen X, German.....	1057	1058
155. Nicholas II, Burgundian	1059	1061
156. Alexander II, Milanese.	1061	1073
157. St. Gregory VII, Sovana	1073	1085
158. B. Victor III, Benevento	1087	1087
159. B. Urban II, Rheims...	1088	1099
160. Paschal II, Bleda......	1099	1118
161. Gelasius II, Gaeta......	1118	1119
162. Calixtus II, Burgundy..	1119	1124
163. Honorius II, Bolognese.	1124	1130
164. Innocent II, Roman.....	1130	1143
165. Celestine II, Citta di Castello	1143	1144
166. Lucius II, Bolognese....	1144	1145
167. B. Eugenius III, Pisan.	1145	1153
168. Anastasius IV, Roman..	1153	1154
169. Hadrian IV (Adrian, Breakspear), English..	1154	1159
170. Alexander III, Sienese..	1159	1181
171. Lucius III, Lucca......	1181	1185
172. Urban III, Milanese....	1185	1187
173. Gregory VIII, Benevento	1187	1187
174. Clement III, Roman....	1187	1191
175. Celestine III, Roman...	1191	1198
176. Innocent III, Anagni...	1198	1216
177. Honorius III, Roman...	1216	1227
178. Gregory IX, Anagni....	1227	1241
179. Celestine IV, Milanese..	1241	1241
180. Innocent IV, Genoese...	1243	1254
181. Alexander IV, Anagni..	1254	1261
182. Urban IV, Troyes......	1261	1264
183. Clement IV, Sainte-Gilles	1265	1268
184. B. Gregory X, Piacenza.	1271	1276
185. B. Innocent V, Tarantasia	1276	1276
186. Hadrian V. (Adrian), Genoa	1276	1276
187. John XIX (or XX or XXI), Lisbon	1276	1277
188. Nicholas III, Roman....	1277	1280
189. Martin IV (or II), de Brie	1281	1285
190. Honorius IV, Roman...	1285	1287
191. Nicholas IV, Ascoli.....	1288	1292
192. St. Celestine V, d'Isernia	1294	*1294
193. Boniface VIII, Anagni.	1294	1303
194. B. Benedict X (or XI), Treviso	1303	1304
195. Clement V, Gascony....	1305	1314
196. John XX (or XXI or XXII), Cahors.......	1316	1334
197. Benedict XI (or XII), Toulouse	1334	1342
198. Clement VI, Limoges...	1342	1352
199. Innocent VI, Limoges...	1352	1362
200. B. Urban V, Mende....	1362	1370
201. Gregory XI, Limoges...	1370	1378
202. Urban VI, Neapolitan..	1378	1389
203. Boniface IX, Neapolitan	1389	1404
204. Innocent VII, Sulmona.	1404	1406
205. Gregory XII, Venetian..	1406	*1409
206. Alexander V, Candia...	1409	1410
207. John XXII (or XXIII or XXIV), Neapolitan	1410	*1415
208. Martin V (or III), Roman	1417	1431
209. Eugenius IV, Venetian..	1431	1447
210. Nicholas V, Sarzana....	1447	1455
211. Calixtus III, Valencia..	1455	1458

*Resigned.

LIST OF SUPREME PONTIFFS

	Elected	Died
212. Pius II, Sienese.......	1458	1464
213. Paul II, Venetian......	1464	1471
214. Sixtus IV, Savona.....	1471	1484
215. Innocent VIII, Genoese.	1484	1492
216. Alexander VI, Valencia.	1492	1503
217. Pius III, Sienese.......	1503	1503
218. Julius II, Savona.......	1503	1513
219. Leo X. Florentine......	1513	1521
220. Hadrian VI (Adrian), Utrecht	1522	1523
221. Clement VII, Florentine	1523	1534
222. Paul III, Roman.......	1534	1549
223. Julius III, Monte San Savino	1550	1555
224. Marcellus II, Montepulciano	1555	1555
225. Paul IV, Neapolitan....	1555	1559
226. Pius IV, Milanese......	1559	1565
227. St. Pius V, Bosco......	1566	1572
228. Gregory XIII, Bolognese	1572	1585
229. Sixtus V, Grottammare.	1585	1590
230. Urban VII. Roman.....	1590	1590
231. Gregory XIV, Milanese, originally from Cremona	1590	1591
232. Innocent IX, Bolognese.	1591	1591
233. Clement VIII, Florentine	1592	1605
234. Leo XI, Florentine.....	1605	1605
235. Paul V, Roman........	1605	1621

	Elected	Died
236. Gregory XV, Bolognese.	1621	1623
237. Urban VIII, Florentine.	1623	1644
238. Innocent X, Roman.....	1644	1655
239. Alexander VII, Sienese.	1655	1667
240. Clement IX, Pistoia....	1667	1669
241. Clement X, Roman.....	1670	1676
242. Innocent XI, Como.....	1676	1689
243. Alexander VIII, Venetian	1689	1691
244. Innocent XII, Neapolitan	1691	1700
245. Clement XI, Urbino....	1700	1721
246. Innocent XIII, Roman..	1721	1724
247. Benedict XIII, Neapolitan	1724	1730
248. Clement XII, Florentine	1730	1740
249. Benedict XIV, Bolognese	1740	1758
250. Clement XIII, Venetian	1758	1769
251. Clement XIV, S. Arcangelo, Diocese of Urbino	1769	1774
252. Pius VI, Cesena........	1775	1799
253. Pius VII, Cesena.......	1800	1823
254. Leo VII, Spoleto.......	1823	1829
255. Pius VIII, Cingoli......	1829	1830
256. Gregory XVI, Belluno..	1831	1846
257. Pius IX, Sinigaglia.....	1846	1878
258. Leo XIII, Carpineto....	1878	1903
259. Pius X, Riese..........	1903	1914
260. Benedict XV, Genoese...	1914	1922
261. Pius XI, Desio.........	1922	1939
262. Pius XII, Roman.......	1939	....

THE GENERAL, OR ECUMENICAL, COUNCILS

1. Nicaea (I), 325
2. Constantinople (I), 381
3. Ephesus, 431
4. Chalcedon, 451
5. Constantinople (II), 553
6. Constantinople (III), 680
7. Nicaea (II), 787
8. Constantinople (IV), 869-870
9. Lateran (I), 1123
10. Lateran (II), 1139
11. Lateran (III), 1179
12. Lateran (IV), 1215
13. Lyons (I), 1245
14. Lyons (II), 1274
15. Vienne, 1311-1312
16. Constance, 1414-1418
17. Basel-Florence, 1431-1439
18. Lateran (V), 1512-1517
19. Trent, 1545-1563
20. Vatican, 1869-1870

DOCTORS OF THE CHURCH
(Date is that of death)
a. The Great Greek and Latin Doctors

1. St. Athanasius, 373
2. St. Basil, 379
3. St. Gregory Nazianzen, 389
4. St. John Chrysostom, 407
5. St. Ambrose, 397
6. St. Jerome, 420
7. St. Augustine, 430
8. St. Gregory the Great, 604

b. Those Declared Doctors by the Popes since 1568

1. St. Hilary of Poitiers. 368
2. St. Ephrem the Syrian, 373
3. St. Cyril of Jerusalem, 386
4. St. Cyril of Alexandria, 444
5. St. Peter Chrysologus, 450
6. St. Leo the Great, 461
7. St. Isidore of Seville, 636
8. St. Bede the Venerable, 735
9. St. John Damascene, 780
10. St. Peter Damian, 1072
11. St. Anselm, 1109
12. St. Bernard, 1153
13. St. Thomas Aquinas, 1274
14. St. Bonaventure, 1274
15. St. Albertus Magnus, 1280
16. St. Peter Canisius, 1597
17. St. John of the Cross, 1605
18. St. Robert Bellarmine, 1621
19. St. Francis de Sales, 1622
20. St. Alphonsus Liguori, 1787

21. St. Anthony of Padua, 1231

INDEX

[An asterisk * indicates an illustration of the subject.]

If you have enjoyed this book, consider making your next selection from among the following . . .

At your Bookdealer or direct from the Publisher.

Prices guaranteed through December 31, 1993.